Liverpool John Moores Ui
An Introduction to Penol
5022LAWCJ

Featuring extracts from
Probation: Working with Offenders, by Rob Canton
Handbook on Prisons, Second Edition, edited by Yvonne Jewkes, Ben Crewe and Jamie Bennett
The Penal Landscape, edited by Anita Dockley and Ian Loader
The Prison Officer, Second Edition, by Alison Liebling, David Price and Guy Shefer
Rehabilitation Work, by Hannah Graham
Working within the Forensic Paradigm, by Rosemary Sheehan and James Ogloff
Delivering Rehabilitation, by Lol Burke and Steve Collett
Community Punishment: European Perspectives, edited by Gwen Robinson and Fergus McNeill
Probation Practice and the New Penology, by John Deering
Doing Probation Work, by Rob C. Mawby and Anne Worrall
Handbook of Probation, edited by Loraine Gelsthorpe and Rod Morgan
Prisoner Resettlement: Policy and Practice, edited by Anthea Hucklesby and Lystra Hagley-Dickinson

Routledge
Taylor & Francis Group

LONDON AND NEW YORK

First published in 2018

by Routledge
2 Park Square, Milton Park, Abingdon, Oxon OX14 4RN

Routledge is an imprint of the Taylor & Francis Group, an informa business

© 2018 Routledge

Previously published as 978-1-843-92373-2 Probation: Working with Offenders
(Chapters 5 and 12) (2012); 978-0-415-74566-6 Handbook on Prisons, Second
Edition (Chapters 1, 3, 5, 7, 33 and 34) (2016); 978-0-415-82329-6 The Penal
Landscape (Chapter 2) (2013); 978-1-843-92269-8 The Prison Officer, Second Edition
(Chapter 3) (2011); 978-1-138-88872-2 Rehabilitation Work (Chapter 6) (2016); 978-
1-138-28844-7 Working within the Forensic Paradigm (Chapter 18) (2014); 978-0-
415-54038-4 Delivering Rehabilitation (Chapter 2) (2014); 978-1-138-78378-2
Community Punishment: European Perspectives (Chapter 3) (2016); 978-1-409-
40140-7 Probation Practice and the New Penology (Chapters 3 and 4) (2011); 978-0-
415-54028-5 Doing Probation Work (Chapter 1) (2013); 978-1-843-92189-9
Handbook of Probation (Chapter 16) (2007); and 978-1-843-92253-7 Prisoner
Resettlement (Chapter 2) (2008) by Routledge.

British Library Cataloguing in Publication Data
A catalogue record for this book is available from the British Library

ISBN: 978-1-138-55098-8

Printed and bound in Great Britain by Ashford Colour Press Ltd.

Contents

Delivering interventions in custodial settings

Theorising community sanctions and measures

Organisation and structure of community sanctions and measures

Probation cultures

Delivering interventions in the community

Resettlement and through-the-gate provision

Welcome to *An Introduction to Penology*

On the 8th February 2017, the then Justice Secretary Liz Truss announced a major re-structure of the Ministry of Justice (MoJ). A major component of this re-structure was the introduction of 'Her Majesty's Prison and Probation Service (HMPPS)', a new service that is responsible for reducing reoffending and protecting the public. HMPPS has full operational responsibility for the policy and practice in and around two of the main criminal justice institutions: prison and probation services. The fundamental purpose of HMPPS is the safe and secure management of lawbreakers in both custodial and community settings. Working alongside lawbreakers, whether it be in custody or the community, occupies a central position in the delivery of 'justice'. Indeed, it is a task that has remained the subject of intense debate and controversy throughout history.

Throughout this module, students will be encouraged to critically engage with both longstanding and emerging penological debates, taking into consideration the theory, policy and practice which surrounds both custodial and community interventions. When designing this module, we felt that a custom publication (which consists of a series of essential chapters and/or articles that have been taken from the existing literature to complement each taught session) would help to focus and direct your independent study, wider reading and assessment preparation. In addition to the recommended reading outlined in the module guide, this custom publication is designed to help you prepare for each taught lecture and it is essential that you read the relevant contributions beforehand. Please remember that this is not a stand-alone, end of story text. We still expect you to read widely around this vast subject area.

We hope that you enjoy reading it as much as we have enjoyed putting it together!

Drs Lol Burke and Helena Gosling

12   Probation and prison

The prison casts its long and sombre shadow over many aspects of probation's history, its policies, practices and organisation. Dismay at the sheer pointlessness of sentence after sentence of imprisonment was a stimulus to the development of probation originally. At times, probation has declared the provision of alternatives to imprisonment as its principal purpose and Secretaries of State have often spoken as if the main worth of probation lies in its potential contribution to reducing the prison population – although, as we saw in Chapter 5, any such potential has seldom been realised. In a quest for 'credibility', probation has sometimes attempted to present itself as prison-like in its capacity to punish and to protect the public.

Some probation officers work full-time in prison while, where the offender manager model is in operation, community-based offender managers oversee sentence plans for serving prisoners. Probation has long worked with prisoners during sentence and, for even longer, has offered help and supervision to them after release. (For part of its history the service's name was the Probation and After-Care Service.) Probation staff may be instrumental in the recall to prison of offenders whose release is conditional and indeed the prospect of imprisonment is sometimes among the incentives to comply with a community sentence. The aspiration that prison and probation should work better together has led to radical organisational change. In all these respects, probation's work is moulded by the realities of the prison and by beliefs about what prison could or should be.

In this chapter, then, we shall consider probation and prison. After a brief account of the characteristics of the prison population, not forgetting prisoners held awaiting trial, probation's work with serving prisoners will be discussed, including the work of probation staff inside the prison. Most of the rest of the chapter is about resettlement – the preferred term nowadays for work with people after they have left prison, when many are not yet released from the statutory requirements of their sentence and can be recalled.

The prison

It was suggested in earlier chapters that prison is often the first thing that people think about when they hear the term *punishment*. While offenders should in law only be sent to prison when no other sentence is suitable, while many more convicted offenders are dealt with in other ways and for all its manifest failures to reform, prison remains an icon of the state's response to crime and the standard against which 'alternatives to custody' must prove themselves.

Remand

> On remand, a prisoner is theoretically not yet proven guilty, but in effect he is a prisoner and treated as guilty; his warders have no training in how to deal with him otherwise . . . Innocent or not, he learns the culture of criminals. As one prisoner said, 'I'll never get rid of it, the stink of jail. It's in me, in my skin, in my hair, in my gear. Anyone I meet will know it and smell it. I'll never get shot of it.'
>
> (Smith 1989: 42)

People accused of offences have a legal right to bail unless certain circumstances can be shown to obtain: bail may be refused if offending seems likely, for instance, or if there are substantial concerns that the defendant may fail to attend court as required, or might interfere with the process of justice; and in these cases, defendants are sent to prison to await trial.

On 31 July 2010, 83,962 people were in prison (79,630 men; 4,332 women) in England and Wales. Of these 13,291 were remand prisoners, of whom 8,903 were untried and 4,388 were convicted and awaiting sentence. Thus just over 10 per cent of those in prison are unconvicted. Some will be acquitted, with prospects of compensation remote and no formal support from probation, and perhaps as many as half will eventually receive non-custodial sentences (Haines and Morgan 2007). Proportions of 'pre-trial detainees' are much higher in some other countries (Walmsley 2009).

Remand prisoners are often overlooked in discussions of imprisonment but plainly the usual justifications of punishment cannot apply to those who must be presumed to be innocent. Yet they often experience the worst of conditions, with serious over-crowding and fewer opportunities for meaningful out-of-cell activities than other prisoners (Coyle 2005). Custodial remand can jeopardise employment and accommodation and its negative impact on stabilising factors that might otherwise have been adduced in mitigation may be part of the explanation why those held in prison awaiting trial are more likely to receive a custodial sentence in the end (Haines and Morgan 2007).

Probation has been variably but significantly involved in helping to prevent avoidable remands in custody, by providing information to the court (or perhaps to the Crown Prosecution Service to assure them that bail need not be opposed) or providing services that directly address the grounds for refusing bail (bail support or accommodation). Much of this work is now undertaken by private or independent organisations rather than by probation: probation-run approved premises are primarily now a resettlement facility, with bail accommodation managed in the independent sector. As Octigan (2007: 264) suggests, probation's potential here is insufficiently realised: 'remand services continue to be vulnerable to changes in policy and other priorities have sometimes deflected attention away from their development'. Haines and Morgan (2007) deprecate probation's forced retreat from pre-trial services, insisting that the presumption of innocence, the principle of prison as a last resort and the human and emotional cost of custodial remand all require this to be a much greater priority.

People in prison

> I used to cut myself to try and get attention, and they've had me in straitjackets for that in Holloway. Sometimes I've tried to kill myself, like when I did this scar on my arm. I had a hundred stitches – it goes all the way up, and it was infected as well. I never cut myself on the outside, only in prison. I set my cell on fire because I hate being locked in . . . I couldn't have been trying to kill myself, because as soon as I set it on fire, I rang the bell. But as I was always getting put in my room and ringing the bell they probably thought, 'Oh, she's messing around again.' When they did come, I could have been dead, because all the smoke had got to me . . .
>
> (Joanne in Padel and Stevenson (1988): 156)

Notoriously, numbers of people in prison have been increasing and this is especially marked for women – an increase of 60 per cent over the past decade, compared to 28 per cent for men (Prison Reform Trust 2009). The reasons for this are far from clear. It cannot be explained by increases in the seriousness of their offending: women offend less often and less seriously than men (Gelsthorpe and Morris 2002). The vulnerability and distress experienced by many women in prison has been highlighted by the Corston Report (2007), which also emphasises the need to take account of their troubled lives and experiences of abuse.

Corston too drew attention to the consequences for children of their mothers' imprisonment. The court's first responsibility in taking decisions that affect children is to have regard to their welfare, but this principle has so far insufficiently influenced the sentencing of parents, whose incarceration inevitably has immeasurable consequences for the children (see http://www.familiesoutside.org.uk/).

In June 2008, 27 per cent of people in prison were from a minority ethnic group (compared with about 9 per cent in the general population), just over half of whom are black. The over-representation of black and minority ethnic groups in prison is quite well known; less well known, perhaps is the number of non-national offenders (Bhui 2008 and references there cited). In the last ten years or so, there has been an increase of 144 per cent in the number of foreign nationals in prison and as many as one in five women in prison are from other countries, more than half of them serving (often very long) sentences for drug offences. Other countries too are having the same experiences:

> One day last week I had to sentence a peasant woman from West Africa to 46 months in a drug case. The result for her young children will undoubtedly be, as she suggested, devastating . . . confirming my sense of depression about much of the cruelty I have been party to in connection with the 'war on drugs'

> . . . At the moment . . . I simply cannot sentence another impoverished person whose destruction has no discernible effect on the drug trade . . . I am just a tired old judge who has temporarily filled his quota of remorselessness.
>
> (US judge, quoted in Doob 1995: 229)

Foreign nationals often have an uncertain right of residence, complicated by their status as offenders. In popular debate, the matter becomes entangled with the politically volatile topics of immigration and deportation. While there has been agitation about the dangers of offenders released who 'should have' been deported, in truth this is an exceptionally vulnerable group of people, whose needs and risks cannot always be reliably managed at the interface between NOMS and the UK Border Agency. Some central probation concepts – reintegration, community, social capital – have a quite different significance for people who may be sent back to countries who may not want them and to which they may have no wish to return. Probation practice in this area is complex and still developing (Hammond 2007).

As noted in Chapter 3, it is often in the overlaps among groups (which figures sometimes fail to capture) that the most extreme disadvantages occur. For example, the chances for mothers to make adequate arrangements for their children are much worse for foreign nationals.

By any criteria, the prison population is a hugely disadvantaged group. The incidence of socio-economic marginalisation, lack of opportunities, inadequate access to services and ill-health is by now well known (Social Exclusion Unit 2002; Prison Reform Trust 2009). Prisoners are several times more likely to be mentally ill and the combination of vulnerabilities, stresses of incarceration and poor conditions lead to a high incidence of self-harm and suicide. Less well known perhaps are the difficulties associated with a 'young but ageing' prison population (Morgan and Liebling 2007) and an emerging recognition that the incidence of learning disability may be much higher than had been realised (Talbot 2008).

The extent to which disadvantage is associated with offending is disputed, although it is hard to think that troubled lives and deprivation are not part of the explanation of some offending careers and it is certain that social disadvantage is an obstacle to desistance. Punitive strategies, however, prefer to withhold the compassion they feel for some victims of some crimes from the many deprived and abused offenders who are serving sentences. As we shall see in Chapter 13, these can turn out to be the same people.

In prison

Figure 12.1 shows the steep increases in the prison population in recent years. An immediate consequence has been severe overcrowding, with pressure on all resources: demand exceeds supply for all facilities – cell space, out-of-cell activities, staff time with prisoners and training/rehabilitative programmes. Prisoners may be moved around the prison estate to ease pressure on the most overcrowded establishments. All of this subverts sentence planning and reduces opportunities for staff to provide purposeful regimes or sometimes even safe and

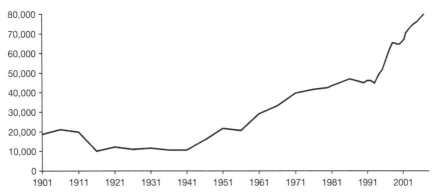

Prison population, England and Wales, 1901–2003

Figure 12.1 Prison population, England and Wales, 1901–2008

decent conditions (Bhui 2007). As was seen in Chapter 5, the greater the size of the population, the larger the number of prisoners likely to be reconvicted after release (Hedderman 2008).

While overcrowding and resource pressures have put the prison estate under enormous strain, Cavadino and Dignan (2007) argue that at the heart of the problem is a *crisis of legitimacy*. The penal system – perhaps prison in particular – is 'morally indefensible' (*ibid*.: 31) and courts, the public, offenders, victims and its own staff are not persuaded of its worth, its effectiveness and the justice of its practices. Prison's difficulties, then, arise from more than a crisis of resources: attempts to reorganise typically fail because these are not problems that are amenable to managerial solutions, but deeply based in moral and political uncertainties about punishment itself and in contradictory ideas of what punishment could and should achieve. (This is an example of how the theoretical models set out in Chapter 1 contribute to our understanding: questions of the moral significance of punishment are illuminated by the expressive model, while questions of social justice can scarcely be discussed without reference to the power model.)

This idea of legitimacy consciously echoes one of the main findings of Lord Woolf's (1991) inquiry into the riots that had taken place in a number of prisons in April 1990. Woolf argued that one of the main reasons for the disturbances was that prisons had been unable to persuade numbers of prisoners that they were being dealt with fairly. He urged prisons to found themselves on three principles: security, discipline (which Morgan later suggested might better be referred to as *good order*) and justice. These principles are inter-related: a just prison will be better ordered than one that is not just; a well-ordered prison will be more secure; the manner in which security and good order are accomplished affects staff and prisoner perceptions of fairness. The quality of relationships between prisoners and prison officers also makes a decisive difference to the legitimacy of the regime and the behaviour of the prisoners (Liebling 2004).

Although there have been changes in the language in which these matters are discussed, there is a clear thread – from the justice that Woolf affirmed, through the idea of legitimacy and the 'decency agenda' (Cavadino and Dignan 2007) to an awareness of the importance of prison's *moral performance* (Liebling 2004) – which recognises the meaning and significance of prison, not just its material characteristics. Again, these debates demonstrate the *expressive* character of criminal justice (Chapter 1) and the limitations of trying to understand prison simply in instrumental terms.

Rehabilitation in prison

One aspect of prisons' legitimacy is that people should go out from prison, if not reformed, at least not 'in an embittered and disaffected state' (Woolf 1991, quoted in Morgan and Liebling 2007: 1112) or posing an even greater risk of reoffending than before. Can prisons, in the nature of the case, achieve their contemporary statement of purpose to 'help [prisoners] lead law-abiding and useful lives in custody and after release' (HM Prison Service n.d.)?

Historically, attempts to effect reform in prison have been through work, schooling, moral influence and discipline (Mathiesen 1990). Yet reformative aspirations have commonly been frustrated: through the process of what Carlen (2002) has termed 'carceral clawback', prison by its very nature militates against constructive rehabilitative work, subordinating other objectives to the imperatives of security and control. Foucault's seminal analysis (1977) too suggests that prison generates power relationships of its own, imposing priorities of security and control that transcend any 'purposes' that may be set for it.

This is by no means to deny the value of much that takes place in prison. Accredited programmes run in prison, for example, have constituted an influential part of the evidence base for effectiveness (Raynor 2004a). While programmes in the community have been found to have better results (see Chapters 6 and 8), effectiveness is also known to be associated with programme completion – something that prisons might, at least in principle, be better placed to ensure. Yet prison is an artificial setting, providing few opportunities to apply and test out learning from programmes in the real world.

> For me, prison was a positive experience. I know – I'm thoroughly convinced – that if I hadn't gone to jail at that time there would have been some sort of disaster waiting for me. Because I was up to my eyeballs in gear, I was taking sulphate, everything to try and blot out my father's death, my job loss, my daughter going, everything. And I didn't care – I became reckless because of it. The crime thing didn't matter to me, it was something that gave me a buzz, this getting involved in crime.
>
> (Milos 'Mish' Biberovic in Devlin and Turney 1999: 117)

There may be times when imprisonment is unavoidable for public protection or to mark the seriousness of a grave offence. There are also times when people's behaviour is so offensive and self-destructive that, at least for a while, there is benefit from the constraint that prison can bring. None of this should be allowed to conceal the destructive effects of prison, not least its capacity to undermine or to destroy almost all the factors known to be associated with desistance. If we consider the 'pathways' (Chapter 8), it is hard to think of one that is not obstructed by a term of imprisonment.

An intrinsic problem is that a total institution effectively precludes inmates' taking responsibility for themselves or for others. There are, however, approaches to imprisonment that try to envisage how this could be different. The European Prison Rules (Council of Europe 2006a) include a principle of *normalisation* – a prisoner's life should be as much like life in the community as possible. Pryor (2001) explores how regimes might change to maximise opportunities to accept responsibility. These include not only personal responsibilities and duties towards dependants, but also the duties of citizenship that members of a community have towards one another (Faulkner 2002).

> Parts of me had changed and for the first time in my life I was thinking not as a victim but as a person who had been responsible for doing things that I shouldn't have. I qualify this by pointing out that whenever I was sentenced in the past for something and came into prison, the humiliation and degradation I met with there made me think of myself as the victim. I hadn't given a shit for the person or deed I was in for, or had any sympathy, as I had been too concerned with my own miseries and misfortunes . . . this unit was allowing me to function responsibly and in order to achieve this one had to think responsibly.
>
> (Boyle 1977: 251)

Jimmy Boyle strikingly contrasts earlier experiences of imprisonment with his time in the Barlinnie Special Unit, but such regimes could not be said to be typical. The tragic irony is that offenders, often denounced by courts for being irresponsible, are put in a position where, typically, they are insulated from all the responsibilities that they need to learn to accept.

It is has been argued that the legitimacy of imprisonment rests at least partly on its capacity to release people who are less likely to reoffend than when they went in. There are ways of developing prison regimes to enable and encourage prisoners to take more responsibility (Pryor 2001) and a number of valuable initiatives that seek to enhance the personal skills offenders will need in order to cope on release. Even so, there are tensions in the very idea of imprisonment – especially the denial of responsibility in a total institution – that militate against these initiatives.

The role of probation

The offender management model envisages a key role for community-based probation staff who, as offender managers, should assess and plan, influencing the individual's experience of prison. This involves close liaison with staff in prison

7

who are in regular contact with the offender. While much of this communication takes place directly with prison officers, the role of seconded probation officers is central. These are probation staff who work in prison, accountable to the governor but also to their employing Trust, who represent probation to the prison and, especially in local prisons, may often act as the link with outside services involved in the resettlement and rehabilitation of short-term prisoners, thus representing the prison to the community.

Probation staff in prison undertake different tasks in different prisons, depending partly on the type of establishment, but also on the governor's conception of their role (Williams 2008). They are typically involved in assessment and planning and contribute to decisions on temporary release, parole and release subject to home detention curfew. They are often part of a larger team who deliver accredited programmes. The days when probation staff were regarded as affable but naive 'welfare' officers, both by prisoners and by staff, have largely gone and there is greater understanding between probation and prison staff and integration in their work. Senior probation officers have often become a key part of the prison management team, even though they continue to work on secondment, assigned roles like 'head of resettlement', in which they may supervise prison staff (Hancock 2007e). Hancock anticipates that the implementation of OMM will increasingly shape the character of the probation prison team, as prisons move to establish offender management units, but this has been an uneven process and many prisoners in effect remain outside of the model.

Resettlement

> Prison culture, it dominates you, it's all around you. Some guys in prison, they climb up on chairs and tables in the cells and look out through the bars at what they can see of the outside world. And they talk of it, and talk of it, but it's never anything else but fantasies and dreams. 'When I get out, when I get out . . .'
>
> ('Andy Reid' in Parker 1991: 110)

In the 1980s and 1990s, the emphasis on community sentences arguably displaced work with former prisoners as a priority for probation. Yet in the past ten years this has changed markedly and resettlement work has attracted initiatives in policy, practice and in research. A joint thematic inspection (HMI Probation /HMI Prisons 2001) urged both agencies to assert the central importance of this work and to collaborate in its implementation. The Social Exclusion Unit Report (2002) was signally influential, drawing attention to the large volume of crime committed by ex-prisoners and linking this with their multiple needs and social exclusion, stimulating an inter-agency, cross-departmental approach to resettlement. And indeed the Carter Report, deploring the 'silos' of prison and probation, found this to be a principal reason to create a National Offender Management Service (see Chapter 14).

The Halliday report spoke of implementing prison and post-release interventions 'seamlessly' and the seamless sentence has become a guiding idea. Yet it is hard to think of a sharper facture in an individual's life – being in prison on one day and in the community the next. All the parameters of behaviour that were considered in Chapter 9 – normative, instrumental, constraint-based and habitual – are all completely different. Routines and constraints have obviously changed; just as plainly, the reasons to behave in particular ways – the costs and benefits of certain courses of action, normative considerations, even the possibility of taking independent action – are entirely altered.

The aspiration is to provide a seamless continuity of service, but can services be abstracted from the context of their provision? Resource shortages and the logistics of managing an overcrowded estate conspire against seamlessness. The term *throughcare* had well expressed this idea of integration, but practice had deteriorated over time (Maguire and Raynor 2006) and the recent political re-emphasis may not be assumed to have been matched by an enhancement in practice. Prisoners report that they value working with the same person during and after the sentence (Raynor and Maguire 2006; Maguire 2007), but role specialisation and costs are making prison visits ever harder to undertake, undermining the relationships that are believed to be so important in the process of desistance (Chapter 9). Again, there are circumstances in which community providers come to pre-release groups and present a market-place of services (Maguire 2007), but many prisoners are some distance from the areas where they will live on release. Continuity of role and of the type of service provided may be the best that can be hoped for, but even this is variably achieved and it is doubtful anyway that this is enough. It seems to be a continuity of personal relationship that matters most (Raynor and Maguire 2006).

This hoped for continuity has a long history – and perhaps a history of disappointment.

> Borstal training falls into two parts. In the first part a lad is trained in custody at an Institution: in the second part he enjoys the comparative freedom of licence or supervision, and is under the training of the Borstal Association. The functions of the two bodies dovetail closely into one another. The one sort of training will fail if the other is badly done.
>
> (Prison Commission 1932: 31)

While this Borstal vision deploys the (better) metaphor of woodwork (*dovetail*) rather than needlecraft (*seam*), the idea is much the same.

Among the most important changes in post-release work has been the change of emphasis from voluntary support to statutory compulsion. Until the Criminal Justice Act 1991, while many serious offenders were supervised compulsorily on parole or life licence, most adult offenders left prison without further obligation and after-care was voluntary. (It was voluntary in the sense that ex-prisoners could choose whether or not to avail themselves of this offered support, though the Probation Rules required services to provide it.) But subsequently all those serving sentences of more than 12 months became subject to a period of formal super-vision and a further period during which the possibility of recall remained. These are people who did not choose probation involvement and may not be assumed to be suitable for community supervision (Maguire 2007).

The political imperatives that have shaped these developments have been public protection and the management of risk posed by former prisoners, but also the need to deploy early release mechanisms to manage the prison population while trying to avoid any sense that this is a premature ending of the deserved punish-ment. Contemporary resettlement often emphasises that the period of licence following release is *a continuation of the sentence, only in the community*. Here we have an inversion of the principle of normalisation: instead of prison regimes aspiring to be like life in the community, the conditions of post-release supervision strive to be prison-like.

> MAPPA and other arrangements (Chapter 10) are often deployed to manage the risks posed by people released from prison. Approved premises (Dunkley 2007) constitute one important component of an overall strategy. Formerly known as hostels, and often in the past accommodating people on bail to avoid custodial remand, premises (approved under Offender Management Act 2007 s. 13) are increasingly filled by prisoners believed to pose a high risk of serious harm. This provision is especially necessary for people who have nowhere else to live. Perhaps because they may not return to a former residence, premises often accommodate sex offenders – a change in the resident profile that can cause concerns among communities and alters the character of the establishment. Approved premises are staffed 24 hours a day, require residents to be in by a certain time and seek to provide a coherent programme of activities. But they are (emphatically) not prisons.

This conception of post-release work leads to an approach to resettlement characterised by compulsion, tight enforcement and a focus on risk and crimino-genic need. One consequence has been the substantial increase in the incidence of recall to prison: not only reoffending or an assessed increased risk, but also non-compliance in itself are grounds for recall – with significant inflationary impact on the prison population (Padfield and Maruna 2006).

The move away from voluntary after-care has entailed the effective withdrawal of service from short-term prisoners who have high(er) reconviction rates and high(er) social needs (Maguire 2007). These prisoners had fewer rehabilitative opportunities in prison, inadequate preparation for release and help with release plans, and in the community experience exclusion, for example, discrimination in employment markets and perhaps in finding accommodation. Some medium-term prisoners too have very short periods of supervision and inadequate support on release. Resettlement work then concentrates on longer-term prisoners, many of whom do not need it, while the short-termers are denied service (Hough *et al.* 2006).

There is widespread scepticism about the value of short sentences. There is little or no chance to offer prisoners useful rehabilitative interventions. Any respite for the public from their offending is brief – postponement more than prevention. High 'turnover' is resource-intensive, making it difficult for prison to focus on the work of rehabilitation of more serious offenders. Most of the efforts of post-release work are spent on trying to put right problems that have been caused or aggravated by prison itself – for example, loss of accommodation or employment and disruption to personal relationships. Courts, however, continue to impose short sentences. People serving six months or less made up half of all prison receptions in 2007 – more than 90,000 people. The many attempts to change this, most recently through the idea of custody plus (not implemented) (J. Roberts 2007), have all foundered. Changes in law and policy here seem likely.

While approaches to resettlement have typically been evaluated for their effects on reconviction, a more rounded approach recognises the importance of other criteria besides (Lewis *et al.* 2007). After pointing out that the term *resettlement* evokes an often entirely misleading idea of resuming a settled life that was enjoyed before, Maguire (2007) considers several models. A desistance paradigm, for example, might emphasise the strengths and potential of former prisoners, in the belief that through agency and generativity offenders may achieve and sustain desistance (Burnett and Maruna 2006; also Chapter 9). A community model importantly recognises that reintegration calls not only for a reformed ex-offender, but a responsive and receptive community, implying a responsibility to provide accessible services and opportunities to enable offenders to desist.

While punitive strategies may emphasise continuing the sentence in the community, there is a moral basis for resettlement. Robinson and Raynor (2006: 339) urge a conception of rehabilitation that is conceptually distinct from punishment and may even be an 'antidote to punishment's harmful effects', while Lewis (2005) reaffirms a *right to rehabilitation*. Since imprisonment has effectively blocked so many legitimate 'pathways' and closed off so many opportunities, since the state has confined prisoners to the total institution and assumed responsibility for their lives, it incurs weighty corresponding responsibilities towards them (Canton 2010b).

The lexicon of the Council of Europe (see the Glossary in Council of Europe 2010) includes *after-care* which is distinguished from resettlement by its voluntary character, but affirmed as a duty of the state towards those of its members who have completed their sentence and have a right to meaningful opportunities of reintegration.

> I do feel prison's where I belong. There are good days and bad days, but even on the good days that feeling doesn't change . . . if the truth's to be said, I'm beyond the pale of ordinary society and couldn't ever get back inside it again. I don't think I'm properly living in society and never could because I'm not

a fit member of it, I only belong to it in theory, I'd like to put it like that. I'm outside humanity, both in humanity's eyes and mine.

('Philip Derbyshire' in Parker 1991: 167)

As Maguire (2007) notes, different models of resettlement are rarely found in a pure form and typically represent an accommodation among competing conceptions of what is due to people after release. As we have seen, political strategies have reframed this question and replaced it with (legitimate) concerns about public protection, but the extent to which the state and the community has responsibilities to reintegrate, as well as rights against offenders, is insufficiently part of the political debate.

What does this mean for probation? It suggests that the current understanding of practice should be complemented by a perspective that recognises the value of the personal relationship in facilitating change, appreciating that the change process is appropriately led by the ex-prisoner rather than the practitioner, acknowledging that reoffending must be understood as among the vicissitudes of desistance, and developing new skills – especially those of advocacy, representing to the community the ex-prisoner's needs and legitimate aspirations and calling upon their responsibilities (McNeill *et al.* 2005).

The National Action Plan (Home Office 2004b) represents a clear recognition of the social preconditions of effective reintegration. Maguire (2007: 416), however, summarises some of the difficulties, including:

- the sheer scale of the problem – the numbers of ex-prisoners and the extent of their needs;
- questions about how services are to be paid for, especially after a licence period ends;
- resources are likely to be matched to OMM tier (Chapter 7), but many, denied the services they need, will go on to pose an increasing risk;
- can hard-pressed public services give priority to offenders? Priority usually is (arguably should be) given to those in most need and while some offenders are among the neediest, there are many others whose need is quite as great.

Summary

We must not forget that when every material improvement has been effected in prisons, when the temperature has been adjusted, when the proper food to maintain health and strength has been given, when the doctors, chaplains, and prison visitors have come and gone, the convict stands deprived of everything that a free man calls life. We must not forget that all these improvements, which are sometimes salves to our consciences, do not change that position.

(Winston Churchill, Speech to Home Office Supply, July 1910)

Newspapers occasionally incite warm and righteous indignation among their readers with stories of the luxuries of imprisonment. Yet a moment's reflection reveals the truth of Churchill's words: practically everything that is valued in a worthwhile life is lost or jeopardised through imprisonment. In Chapter 9 we saw that it is in the context of a meaningful life that desistance is achieved and sustained: imprisonment is to this extent inherently obstructive of desistance.

In this chapter, we have seen probation's relationship with prison, looked at some of the characteristics of prison and prisoners and considered resettlement. It has been suggested that a different focus – attending to rights to rehabilitation no less than to risks of reoffending – would represent a sounder ethical base for probation's work here. Since this would serve to enhance probation's legitimacy, it would tend to strengthen compliance and may turn out to be more effective even by the criteria of reconviction.

Questions for discussion

- A Home Secretary famously once claimed 'Prison works'. Do you agree?
- Who ought to be in prison?
- What kind of arrangements should be made to support foreign nationals in prison and to prepare for their release?

Further reading

Jewkes (2007) is a valuable collection of papers on many aspects of imprisonment. Coyle (2005) is very useful. Morgan and Liebling (2007) is a brief but authoritative overview. Statistics about prison and prisoners are well compiled in the Prison Reform Trust (2009). On resettlement, Raynor (2004), Maguire and Raynor (2006), Raynor and Maguire (2006) and Maguire (2007) are strongly recommended. Hucklesby and Hagley-Dickinson (2007) includes many important contributions about resettlement.

Chapter 1

Prisons in context

Andrew Coyle

Introduction

This chapter provides a personal overview of some features of imprisonment over the last 40 years. In the early 1970s the world was quite different in many relevant respects. The colonial empires of European countries were being dismantled to be replaced by newly independent countries, and the Cold War was a major part of our political lives. Prisons and labour colonies throughout the Soviet Union and neighbouring countries held well over 1 million men and women in virtual slavery, and the very existence of many of these places of detention was a state secret. In the United Kingdom the world of prisons was also largely hidden from public view and a number of prisons were places of brutality and inhumanity. Within a few years the first cracks began to appear in that closed world. In 1975 the European Court of Human Rights reached its first decision in a case concerning a prisoner in the United Kingdom (Golder v United Kingdom [1975] 1 EHRR 524). In this case the Court concluded that the refusal of the UK authorities to allow a prisoner access to a solicitor constituted a violation of European Convention on Human Rights Article 6 (right to a fair and public hearing within a reasonable time by an independent and impartial tribunal) and Article 8 (right to respect for private and family life, home and correspondence). The Council of Europe Committee for the Prevention of Torture and Inhuman or Degrading Treatment or Punishment (CPT) began its work in 1990 when it visited Denmark, Turkey, the United Kingdom, Malta and Austria. In respect of the United Kingdom the CPT reached a damning conclusion about conditions in Brixton, Leeds and Wandsworth Prisons:

> The CPT's delegation found that the conditions of detention in the three male local prisons visited were very poor. In each of the three prisons there was a pernicious combination of overcrowding, inadequate regime activities, lack of integral sanitation and poor hygiene. In short, the overall environment in which the prisoners had to lead their lives amounted, in the CPT's opinion, to inhuman and degrading treatment.
>
> (Council of Europe 1991)

This report was published shortly after I became governor of Brixton Prison. The Optional Protocol to the United Nations Convention against Torture and Other Cruel, Inhuman or Degrading Treatment or Punishment entered into force in 2006 and led to the establishment of an international inspection system for places of detention in countries that have ratified the Protocol. All of these developments are discussed in greater detail elsewhere in this volume.

There are now over 10.2 million men, women and children in prison in the world (Walmsley 2013) – a number which would have been beyond belief 40 years ago – and in many countries the conditions and environment within prisons have changed dramatically. The overview in this chapter is intended to provide a context for the succeeding contributions which deal with specific issues relating to imprisonment. It invites the reader to consider the nature of imprisonment in the first two decades of the 21st century and whether the prison as now constituted is fit for its purpose.

As it was then

I entered the world of prisons in 1973 when I was appointed as one of the first assistant governors in Edinburgh Prison (Coyle 1994). Until that point the management structure in prisons in Scotland, as in the rest of the United Kingdom, had been very simple, with a single governor, assisted in larger prisons by a deputy governor. The vast majority of staff were 'discipline officers' of various grades, led by a chief officer. Other groups of uniformed officers with varying or no specialized training were responsible for the prison 'hospital', the industrial and working units, maintenance, catering and administration.

The prisoners' day was structured and predictable. It began with cell doors being unlocked around 7.00am, leading to the infamous 'slopping out' parade with a procession of prisoners rushing to the 'arches' or 'recesses', each carrying a brimming chamber pot which was emptied into or around the toilets and slop basins. Each prisoner also had a bottle or jug which he filled with water from the same sink before heading back to his cell. The lucky or experienced prisoners made use of the toilets in the vicinity. The stench pervaded the whole prison and was no respecter of persons. As a new assistant governor and one of the few people who wore civilian clothes, I quickly learned that the suits which I wore to work had to be kept separate from all my other clothes at home and be cleaned regularly to minimize the prison smell that saturated them.

Prisoners were then locked in their cells for a short period while they shaved and washed the best they could with the water that they had brought back, after which they went to one of four dining rooms for breakfast. They then went directly to their work parties. Some of the work was relatively sophisticated and required a degree of skill: printing, bookbinding, carpentry. At the other end of the spectrum there was work that was basically monotonous and unskilled. In those days prisons still had contracts with what was then the Post Office to make and repair hemp mailbags. The most unpopular work was in the salvage party, stripping out redundant copper and other wiring. The prisoners allocated to this work were generally those who had no skills and little ability to learn, by and large men on the merry-go-round of short sentences for repetitive low-level offences. A small number of prisoners were employed on general maintenance in the prison, working alongside prison officer tradesmen, in the prison kitchen or on general cleaning duties. At the end of the morning the men returned to their cells for a numbers count before going on to the dining rooms for lunch, after which there was a one-hour period of exercise in the open air, although in reality there was not much exercise and most prisoners spent the time walking around the yard in small groups. It was then back to the work parties until it was time for the evening meal, usually served around 4.00pm. Following a short period locked in cells while numbers were checked, there was evening recreation, spent in the accommodation halls, playing table games, watching the communal television or cleaning their cells. By 9.00pm all prisoners were locked in their cells until the following morning.

Prisoners on remand or unsentenced were held in an accommodation hall separate from sentenced prisoners and were not required to work. This meant that they spent most of each day locked in their cells, apart from meal and exercise times. They were also entitled to a short daily visit from family or close friends and to see lawyers or other persons in connection with their cases.

In the early 1970s there were no full-time teachers, social workers or other specialists in the prison. Criminal justice social workers (who were the Scottish equivalent of probation officers) visited to prepare reports on remand prisoners when requested to do so by the court, as did psychiatrists and psychologists, and also to report, if required, on prisoners who were being considered for early release. There was a welfare officer who was employed by the prison and who acted as a conduit between prisoners and their families when asked to do so, and who might liaise on behalf of a prisoner with authorities, for example, in respect of housing tenancies. The prison chaplain was a key figure in terms of prisoners' access to external support. If a prisoner wished for educational support he applied to the chaplain who would decide whether the man would have access to the small number of ad hoc people who came into the prison to provide this. The chaplain also coordinated volunteer visitors who befriended individual prisoners. In 1974 a qualified full-time education officer was appointed in Edinburgh Prison, the first such appointment in any Scottish prison.

The primary task of the new group of assistant governors that I joined in 1973 was to organize and oversee the writing of reports on prisoners who were to be considered for early release under the new parole arrangements which had recently been introduced following the Murder (Abolition of the Death Penalty) Act 1965 and the consequent legislation in the Criminal Justice Act 1967. In those days a prisoner serving a sentence of more than 18 months became eligible for early release after serving 12 months or one third of the sentence, whichever was longer. Most prisoners who were serving life sentences became eligible for release after they had completed about nine years in prison, and the preparation of reports and documentation had to begin some 18 months before that date. Prisoners serving indeterminate and other long sentences now serve much longer periods before being considered for early release.

One undoubtedly positive change in the last 40 years has been the increase in transparency in prisons. Prisons used to be described as the last great secretive institutions in modern society because of the shortage of information about what happened within them. Given the reach of modern communications it is no longer possible to prevent much of what happens in prisons from coming into the public domain. The publication of regular reports from HM Inspectorate of Prisons and the work of Independent Monitoring Boards (IMBs) in each prison has also brought much of what goes on inside prisons in England and Wales into the public spotlight. A changed public climate as to what is and is not acceptable behaviour on the part of public servants has resulted in significant changes in the behaviour of many staff. For example, it is hard to imagine that today there might be such a sequence of events as surrounded the death of Barry Prosser in Birmingham Prison in 1980. These were summarized in a statement by the Home Office minister of state to the House of Commons on 1 July 1982:

Mr. Prosser was found dead in his cell in the hospital wing of Birmingham prison in the early morning of 19 August 1980. The post mortem which was held that afternoon revealed the full and horrifying extent of Mr. Prosser's injuries. The pathologist's report was that Mr. Prosser had extensive bruising all over his body. His stomach, his oesophagus and one of his lungs had been ruptured, and the pathologist thought that the cause of death was a blow, probably by a heavy weight. The inquest into Mr. Prosser's death was held in April 1981. It lasted for seven days and heard the evidence of nearly 50 witnesses ... At the end of the proceedings, the jury returned a verdict that Mr. Prosser had been unlawfully killed.

The minister then moved on to deal with some of the recommendations that the coroner had made. His comment on the last of these recommendations is a reminder of how weak management of staff was in those days:

> The coroner's final recommendation was that hospital officers should submit a report if they had to use force on a prisoner ... We recognise that when, in the proper execution of his duties, an officer has to use physical force, there is always the possibility that there will later be a complaint by a prisoner or an inquiry into the incident. Thus, we issued instructions last year reminding staff that, as a safeguard, each prison officer, including any hospital officer or nurse involved in such an incident, should write a brief factual report to the governor in addition to making any other record. Some concern was expressed by the Prison Officers Association about this instruction and it advised its branches not to comply with it.
>
> (HC Deb 1982: 1130–1132)

The final sentence of the minister's statement includes a damning indictment of the mores of the time within the Prison Service. A mentally ill prisoner had been 'unlawfully killed' in a punishment cell. A coroner made what today would be considered a straightforward and entirely proper recommendation that prison staff should in future submit a report whenever force had to be used on a prisoner. The Home Office issued an instruction that this should be done. The Prison Officers Association took issue with this and instructed their members not to comply with the instruction. The minister appeared to accept this as an end to the matter. There is little doubt that the behaviour and reaction of the successors of all those involved – staff, management, trade unions and ministers – would be quite different today.

As it is now

Conditions

Physical conditions in prisons have improved significantly in a number of respects. The daily degradation of hundreds of prisoners carrying foetid chamber pots along landings to stinking slop sinks is thankfully long gone. In his seminal 1991 report following riots at Strangeways and other prisons, the then Lord Justice Woolf described this practice as an uncivilized and degrading process, which destroyed the morale of prisoners and staff (Woolf 1991: 24). Woolf had recommended that ministers should set a timetable to provide access to sanitation for all prisoners not later than February 1996. In April of that year, Prisons Minister Ann Widdecombe travelled to Leeds Prison to witness, in the words of *The Independent* newspaper (13 April 1996), the last plastic pot being discarded as slopping out came to an end in prisons in England and Wales.

It soon became clear that the much-heralded end to slopping out was not all that it might seem. In 2004 the chief inspector of prisons found that there was still slopping out in a women's prison (Lewis 2006) and in 2010 the National Council for Independent Monitoring Boards published a report on the difficulties that some prisoners had in getting regular access to toilet facilities. The haste to abolish collective slopping out had meant that what had been implemented in many cases fell far below what would be considered decent. In his introduction to the IMB report, its president described the arrangements in the following terms:

> Like many who will read this report I had assumed that following the acceptance of Lord Woolf's recommendations slopping out was a thing of the past. Only when the annual reports of IMBs became part of my staple reading diet did I realise that it had been replaced by a situation in which – as IMBs constantly report – two men will be living, eating and spending most of the day in what is in effect their shared lavatory.
>
> (National Council for Independent Monitoring Boards 2010: 2)

This comment indirectly draws attention to another feature of prison life that has become increasingly prevalent: the fact that many prisoners now spend the bulk of each day locked in their cells with little or nothing to do. This has been the situation in England and Wales for many years as far as the 20% of prisoners who are not sentenced are concerned, but shortage of work, training or educational opportunities now means that many convicted prisoners are left in their cells each day. Independent commentators, including successive HM chief inspectors of prisons and local IMBs, have regularly raised concerns about these matters over the years. Speaking to the BBC in July 2014, Chief Inspector Nick Hardwick issued a warning in unusually stark terms:

> We are seeing a lot more prisons that are not meeting acceptable standards ... There is a danger of the politicians over-analysing the figures and miss[ing] what is under their noses on the wings ... people being held in deplorable conditions who are suicidal, they don't have anything to do and they don't have anyone to talk to.
>
> (BBC *Newsnight* 2014)

Speaking on the same programme, the chief executive officer of the National Offender Management Service (NOMS) acknowledged that there had been 'some deterioration' in standards in prisons, with additional pressures arising over the previous six months, including an increase in prisoner numbers (among them, more remand prisoners and sex offenders, who present particular challenges, than anticipated) and fewer staff than were needed. Some 23% of prisoners were sharing cells designed for one prisoner. He went on to confirm that there had been a 25% reduction in spending over 'the spending review period' and that in order to eliminate overcrowding he would require an increase in budget of £900 million which was not going to materialize.

There have been many other improvements in prisons since the early 1970s. Prisons are undoubtedly managed in a much more efficient manner now, although as the quotations above demonstrate, that does not of itself imply an improvement in decency and humanity. Increased efficiency can sometimes lead to an excessive emphasis on how things are done rather than on what is being done, which results in an attention to detail that misses the reality, as noted by the chief inspector.

Violence

The gratuitous violence that went unremarked in some prisons in the United Kingdom 30 or so years ago would not be tolerated today. This is not the case in some other countries. Prisons in Latin America are marked by unbelievable levels of violence. I have visited prisons in Brazil where staff will only enter the areas where prisoners live if they have a heavily armed escort. In Venezuela some years ago I was accompanied on a visit to the main prison in Caracas by the deputy director of the national prison service. He reluctantly took me into an accommodation block. The gate to each unit was manned by a prisoner throughout each 24-hour cycle. His task was to ensure that no prisoner from another gang was able to enter the unit. If he was found asleep at his post he would face instant death at the hands of his own gang members. The toilet areas were the dirtiest I had ever seen, with detritus lying almost a metre deep. The deputy director told me that prisoners kept the area in this state so that guns and other weapons could be hidden there, and he pointed out wires sticking out at various points, explaining that these were attached to the weapons which could be recovered when needed. He also pointed out loose bricks in the walls and told me that weapons and cell phones were being kept there. Numbers of prisoners followed us everywhere and the director spoke quite openly about all of this in front of them.

This scenario is a far cry from anything that might be seen in the United Kingdom yet there is little room for complacency. Following an inspection of Feltham Young Offenders' Institution in March 2013, the chief inspector of prisons reported that:

> Levels of violence at Feltham were too high, resulting in high levels of adjudications and use of force. Some of the incidents were serious and sometimes involved gangs attacking single prisoners. Many prisoners had felt unsafe at some time and/or victimised. The unprecedented and illegitimate use of batons at Feltham B was emblematic of this problem and the broader weakness of effective relationships between staff and prisoners.
>
> (HM Inspectorate of Prisons 2013b: 16)

In January 2013 the chief inspector had inspected the part of Feltham that held children and young people between the ages of 15 and 17 years. He was every bit as concerned about what he discovered there:

> We had serious concerns about the safety of young people held at Feltham A. Many told us they were frightened at the time of the inspection, and that they had little confidence in staff to keep them safe. Gang-related graffiti was endemic. There was an average of almost two fights or assaults every day. Some of these were very serious and involved groups of young people in very violent, pre-meditated attacks on a single individual with a risk of very serious injury resulting.
>
> (HM Inspectorate of Prisons 2013a)

In an interview with *The Independent* newspaper he commented further: 'It was a very disturbing place. If you were a parent with a child in Feltham you would be right to be terrified. It would be very hard not to join a gang in Feltham.' Responding to the chief inspector's report, the chief executive of NOMS acknowledged the depth of the problem: 'All the gangs in London meet in Feltham. There are fewer young people in prisons but the ones who are there are troubled, difficult and challenging' (Peachey 2013).

These problems are not peculiar to Feltham; they are also to be found in adult prisons. In Oakwood Prison in the West Midlands, 'a huge and structurally impressive facility capable of holding more than 1,600 category C prisoners' which opened in April 2010, the chief inspector found that:

> Too many prisoners felt unsafe and indicators of levels of violence were high, although we had no confidence in the quality of recorded data or in the structures and arrangements to reduce violence. Even the designated units meant to protect those declared vulnerable were not working effectively and too many prisoners on these units also felt unsafe. Levels of self-harm, some linked to day-to-day frustrations as well as perceived victimisation, were high but again processes to support those in crisis were not good enough.
>
> (HM Inspectorate of Prisons 2013c)

Number of prisoners

One of the most outstanding changes over the last 40 years has been the growth in the number of people being held in prison. In 1973 the average number of people in prison in Scotland was just over 4,600, of whom 180 were women (Scottish Executive 2006). I well remember the concern that was expressed in 1986 when the figure broke through the 5,000 mark, a level of imprisonment that had never before been experienced in Scotland. There was less public discussion when it broke through the 6,000 mark in 2003. In mid-2014 there were 8,200 people in Scottish prisons, of whom 420 were women. The story in England and Wales has been a similar one. In 1973 there were 35,700 people in prison (Home Office 1984), and a few years later Home Secretary Roy Jenkins expressed great concern at the prospect that the prison population might eventually reach 45,000 (HL Deb 2009). In mid-2014 there were 85,500 people in prison in England and Wales, of whom almost 4,000 were women (Ministry of Justice 2014b).

The growth in the number of prisoners has been influenced in the main not by any increase in the number of offences and crimes, nor by increased detection rates but, as observed by a recent report from the British Academy (2014), by changes in penal policy. The British Academy report notes that courts are now much more likely than they were in the past to sentence offenders to prison, that prison sentences have been getting longer and that there has also been a steady increase in the number of prisoners serving life or indeterminate sentences. One might add to this the fact that the proportion of prisoners being granted conditional early release has reduced, as has the period of the early release.

The United Kingdom does not stand alone in this matter. I first visited federal prisons in the USA in 1984, when they held a total of 45,000 prisoners. In mid-2014 they held 216,000. Commenting on the massive rise in the number of incarcerated Americans in the late 20th century, Timothy Lynch, director of The Cato Institute's project on criminal justice, observed:

America's criminal justice system is going to make history this month as the number of incarcerated people surpasses 2 million for the first time. To appreciate why this is such an extraordinary moment, one needs to put the 2-million-prisoner factoid into context. It took more than 200 years for America to hold 1 million prisoners all at once. And yet we have managed to incarcerate the second million in only the past 10 years.

(Lynch 2000)

By any measure these are extraordinary increases in respect of an institution that involves a significant degree of human suffering as well as a massive input of public resources. There are now signs that this trend is being reversed. The prison population in the USA has shown a consistent reduction since 2010 (US Department of Justice 2013), with the greatest reduction occurring in some of the largest state prison systems. California has accounted for over half of the decrease in the entire state prison population.

During an extended period in which prison populations in the UK have risen consistently, a number of other European countries have shown quite different patterns. The Netherlands provides an example of how changes in government policies can push rates of imprisonment higher or lower. In 1992 the country had one of the lowest rates, with a prison population of 7,397. By 1995 this had increased to 11,886 and it continued to increase annually until it peaked in 2004 at 20,075, almost three times higher than it had been 12 years previously. Since then the number of prisoners has fallen year-on-year, and in 2013 it stood at 12,638 (World Prison Brief 2014c). Throughout this period, near-neighbour Denmark retained a remarkably stable and relatively small prison population, moving from 3,597 in 1992 to 4,091 in 2013 (World Prison Brief 2014a). In Germany there were 57,448 prisoners in 1992; the figure rose to 81,166 in 2004 but in 2013 it had fallen back to 62,632 (World Prison Brief 2014b) – this for a country of over 80 million inhabitants, compared with 85,582 prisoners in England and Wales with a population of just over 57 million.

There is very little evidence from any country that crime levels are affected for better or for worse by variations in levels of imprisonment. Instead, social scientists have gathered evidence which demonstrates that rates of imprisonment are influenced by socio-economic structures and levels of social trust. Where these are strong and there is a consensual rather than a confrontational approach among politicians on these matters, the use of imprisonment tends to be lower. Where the opposite is the case, the use of imprisonment is more likely to be high and increasing.[1]

The prisoners

Other chapters in this volume deal in detail with issues relating to specific groups of prisoners. The underlying message from these contributions is that prisoners are not a homogeneous group, identified solely by the fact of their imprisonment. In this contextual chapter two groups are worthy of mention.

In many countries a significant proportion of those in prison are awaiting trial or other court process. In India, for example, two thirds of all prisoners fall into this category. In Scotland almost one fifth of prisoners are on some type of remand, while in England and Wales 10% of prisoners have not been convicted. Despite this fact, they are held in the care of the NOMS, where their treatment gives only limited recognition to the fact that they are legally innocent. In many cases their treatment is even more restricted because of reduced access to a variety of facilities in the prison, including education and work.

The second group that is of particular importance in England and Wales includes all of those who are serving indeterminate sentences. Almost 15% of all prisoners are serving life imprisonment or an Extended Determinate Sentence (Ministry of Justice 2014a). The history of this latter group demonstrates the unforeseen consequences of legislation. The Criminal Justice Act of 2003 introduced imprisonment for public protection (IPP), a new sentence designed to be used for serious sexual and violent offenders. The government indicated that it expected the prison population to increase by around 900 as a result of this provision. In fact there were 6,000 such prisoners in 2012 when the government abolished IPP and replaced it with the Extended Determinate Sentence. Some 5,500 prisoners are still in prison under the IPP legislation (Prison Reform Trust 2014). Speaking to the BBC in March 2014, former Home Secretary David Blunkett, who had introduced the IPP legislation, acknowledged that '[t]he consequence of bringing that Act in has led, in some cases, to an injustice and I regret that' (Conway 2014). That injustice is still being suffered by the prisoners involved.

Learning from our past

Before attempting any prediction of what the future might hold for prisons in the UK, it is worth considering what we might learn from past experience. In my travels to the prisons of the world I am frequently struck by the consistent lack of institutional memory; many prison systems appear to be institutionally incapable of learning from past successes or failures. They will frequently fail to develop existing examples of effective practice, either because they do not register them for what they are, or they are unaware of them, or because the examples do not conform to mainstream thinking. In England and Wales an example of unwillingness to learn from success is Grendon Prison, which has consistently performed well in terms of what are considered sound operational indicators: the positive management of men who have been difficult if not unmanageable in other secure settings and rates of successful resettlement of men who are released. Yet after more than 50 years of existence, Grendon continues to be regarded as experimental and unique because it simply does not fit in with the public rhetoric about how a prison should operate.

In the same jurisdiction the treatment of young offenders provides an example of the inability to learn from the past. In the early 20th century the English Prison Commission introduced a new type of institution for young offenders which was based on the public school system. Accommodation units were described as 'houses'; the persons in charge of the units were known as 'housemasters' and often recruited from a public school background; each unit had a mature female prison officer who was known as 'matron'. Sir Alexander Paterson described the institutions in the following way:

> A Borstal Institution is a training school for adolescent offenders, based on educational principles, pursuing educational methods. To be sent there is a punishment, for the training involves a very considerable loss of liberty, but to stay there is to have a chance to learn the right way of life, and to develop the good there is in each.
> (Paterson 1934: 13)

The borstal system lasted for 75 years. This is not the place to embark on an assessment of its merits or demerits but the system came to an end because it had outlasted its time. Fast forward to 2014 and the Ministry of Justice announced its intention to build a 'secure college', led by a 'head teacher or principal' and housing up to 320 young men aged between 12 and 17.

> The Government is introducing a new model of youth custody, the Secure College, which will improve outcomes and reduce cost. Education will be firmly at the heart of the Secure College, with other services designed around and intended to support innovative and intensive education delivery.
>
> (Ministry of Justice 2014c: 2)

In 1934 Alexander Paterson had pleaded for an alternative name for borstals, given to the first such institution after the Kent village in which it was located. Eighty years later his plea was heard; they are to be recreated as secure colleges.

These two examples are from England and Wales, but one could identify similar examples from many other countries. It could be argued that this demonstrates a systemic failure to update a concept of imprisonment that is rooted in the 18th and 19th centuries. This concept is founded in the very buildings that go to make up the prison. Architecture is very important for communicating a sense of purpose to any institution, a subject dealt with in this volume (Chapter 7) and by Jewkes (2013). It has been said that if Charles Dickens were to return to Pentonville Prison in London today he would immediately recognize its wings and landings. The same might be said if Tolstoy were to return to Butyrka Prison in Moscow, or Victor Hugo to La Santé in Paris. In the 1960s and early 1970s in the UK there was an attempt to alter the structure of prisons by building accommodation blocks with hotel-like corridors, but in recent decades there has been a return to what is basically the older panopticon style which fits best with the surveillance model of imprisonment. In other words the mindset of what prisons should be and even what they should look like has changed little in the last 200 years.

Learning from others

I have had the privilege of visiting prison systems all over the world, usually at the invitation of national governments or of international bodies such as the United Nations (UN) or regional bodies such as the Council of Europe, the Organization of American States or the African Commission on Human and Peoples' Rights. My involvement has often coincided with periods of traumatic political upheaval or radical legislative change which have led to fundamental changes within prison systems on an unprecedented scale. A common thread that ran through events in many of these countries was that after the collapse of a totalitarian system or after a democratic change of government, one of the priorities was general reform of the justice system and specifically reform of the prison system which had frequently been the epitome of the worst excesses of the former regime. This was the case in Russia, which I first visited in 1992, at a time when the democratic future of the country was not at all clear. Despite the continuing struggle for the political soul of the country, the authorities were determined to begin the process of reform of the infamous Gulag system. I continued to visit Russian prisons regularly for over ten years, sometimes assisting the Ministry of the Interior and later the Ministry of

Justice in their reform efforts, at other times with intergovernmental bodies such as the Council of Europe and the Organization for Security and Co-operation in Europe. In 1998 and 1999 I was an expert member of the first two missions of the CPT to the Russian Federation, when we inspected infamous prisons including Butyrka in Moscow and Kresty in St Petersburg and travelled beyond the Urals to Chelyabinsk, which had been a transport hub in Soviet times for prisoners being exiled to the Siberian Gulag. In 1998 the number of prisoners in Russia was estimated at over 1 million. In mid-2014 it stood at 670,000, a significant reduction but still one of the highest rates in the world (World Prison Brief 2014d).

At the beginning of 1995 I worked with the UN Centre for Human Rights in providing advice to the new government that had replaced the Khmer Rouge in Cambodia. The prison in Siem Reap, a few kilometres from the monastery of Angkor Wat, remained much as it had been in French colonial times and the new administration had little idea as to how it should be managed. At that time there were 2,600 prisoners in the country and I still have a copy of my report in which I cautioned about the danger that the introduction of a Western model of imprisonment which took no account of local traditions might lead to a vastly inflated prison population. In mid-2014 the number of prisoners had indeed increased almost six-fold to 14,500, while the population of the country had risen by 75%.

Also in 1995, in the company of the reforming commissioner of prisons for Uganda, I was invited to visit prisons and to speak to prison staff in South Africa. Our main discussions were held in the staff training school in Kroonstad in the Orange Free State. The school was still known as the John Vorster Training Centre; his bust was in the main foyer and his photograph hung in the senior staff mess. We were met by General Sitole, the first black provincial commissioner, who had previously been a schoolmaster in Soweto. The commissioner of the Department of Corrections told us that he was determined to correct the racial imbalance at senior level and expected that within five years 70% of the senior staff would be black. Reality moved rather more quickly than the commissioner had anticipated. Within a very short period he had retired and the whole cadre of senior staff had been replaced.

All of these experiences and others have helped me to identify two key issues that require attention if prisons are to deliver their stated aims. They apply in all countries, including the UK.

Political will

The first is political will. Prisons are not as a matter of course a high priority for most governments. They do not interest the public in the way that health, education or the economy do. Imprisonment is something that happens to 'other people' and those other people are generally regarded as undeserving of sympathy. Experience in many countries demonstrates that if there is no government will for prison reform then it will be unlikely to make any headway. I recollect hearing a commissioner of prisons at a regional conference in Eastern Africa a decade ago encouraging politicians to take an interest in ensuring that there were decent and humane conditions inside prisons and quoting the example of a vice-president of one country who had refused to allow prisoners to have mattresses and later was subject to his own rule when he was sent to prison for corruption. That was a case of using whatever argument would best win the day in a particular situation. It is probably not one that could be advanced in many countries.

The Dominican Republic provides an interesting example, which I have observed at first-hand over several years, of how determined political will can lead to dramatic change in a manner appropriate to the local situation. In common with many countries in the region, the history of prisons in the Dominican Republic has been one of gross overcrowding, chronic shortage of resources for basic human needs, and lack of proper budgetary arrangements. There was no proper prison administration, with half of the prisons being under military control and the remainder in the charge of the police. In 2003 a new attorney-general who had the president's political support decided to take action. Having taken advice, he decided that rather than continue nugatory attempts to reform the existing prison system he should set about creating a new one to replace it. The key to any decent prison system is the quality of the staff, particularly those who interact directly with prisoners, and the attorney-general decided to base the reforms on that premise. His first and most crucial action was to find the right person to develop and lead the New Model, as it came to be called. Roberto Santana, a nationally distinguished educator and former rector of the University of Santo Domingo, took up the challenge. Santana, who had in the past been a prisoner under the dictatorship, appointed a former director of the capital's largest prison as his deputy. One of his first moves was to establish a National Penitentiary School. He recruited several of his previous colleagues in the world of education, administration and professional development as tutors in the school, alongside some carefully chosen men and women with previous experience of working in prisons. He then set about selecting a completely new cadre of students to be trained for work in prisons, all of whom were young and highly motivated. One requirement was that they should have no previous experience in either the police or the military. They were trained for a full academic year and on graduation in 2004 they went as a group to staff the first of the New Model prisons. The same practice has continued over the past decade, with new prisons being opened as each new cohort of staff matriculated. Roberto Santana has brought all his skills as an educator to bear in the New Model system which provides decent living conditions for prisoners and humane treatment by staff. Education has a high priority and the target is that by the time they are released, all prisoners will be literate. Official sources claim that only 5% of persons from the new prisons have been convicted of further crimes within three years of release. Because of shortage of resources the government has continued to develop the new system on a gradual basis, and in 2014 over half of the country's prisons were part of the New Model.

The 'Nuevo Modelo' has attracted regional and international attention. The director of the United National Latin American Institute commented: 'What's remarkable about the Dominican Republic's example is that it has taken place in a country that has the same socio-economic conditions as other Latin American countries. Before when I would go to a government and say, "Look at what they're doing in Switzerland" they'd say, "That's a different world". But now I can say, "Look at the Dominican Republic"' (Fieser 2014).

Not all problems have been solved. In the ten years since the New Model was launched the number of prisoners in the country has risen from 13,500 to 25,500, largely as a result of harsher sentencing practices. This confirms the fact that it is very difficult to effect reform of a prison system in isolation from wider developments in criminal justice. Despite this, the message from the Dominican Republic is clear. A determined senior government minister rose above the political pressures of the day and adopted a radical strategy for change. He identified a person who was capable of achieving the desired change, agreed with him a plan of action and then gave him operational authority to deliver that change with full political support and no operational interference. Successive governments of different political persuasions have maintained that position and the benefits of this are now becoming clear. There are examples of similar positive reforms stemming from a political consensus in a number of other countries. Finland is an obvious example within Europe as it determined to move away from the historical influence of the former Soviet Union to align itself with its Scandinavian neighbours in respect of the restricted contribution that prisons have to play in contributing to their countries' safety and security.

Leadership

The second key issue is leadership. I saw the importance of this in Poland, which I visited several times in the 1990s. After the collapse of communism in 1989 the new democratic government invited Pavel Moczydlowski, professor of sociology in Warsaw University, to lead the Polish prison administration. For several years thereafter Moczydlowski led a radical reform of the former system (Moczydlowski and Rzeplinski 1990; Moczydlowski 1992). His leadership had a number of essential elements. In the first case he and his senior staff had a clear vision of what they wanted to achieve, which was to introduce a culture in which prisoners were treated decently and humanely by staff and in which they were to be given the opportunity to maintain and develop links with family and friends. The new leadership was confident that they could implement this without placing public security in danger and without sacrificing good order in prisons. They replaced the bureaucratic centralized structure with a lean regional structure. In the early years they spent a great deal of time visiting prisons and explaining their vision to both staff and prisoners. Moczydlowski told me that by his estimation, one in five members of staff never quite shook off the old mentality. He adopted a pragmatic and sympathetic response to them by making clear that dissent was not an option while making great efforts to support them through the transition process. For the small number who found this impossible he arranged early retirement. He also spent considerable time ensuring that the prisoners were aware that along with the new rights to which they were entitled came a responsibility to behave positively.

Throughout this period of change the senior prison administrators made sure that they retained the confidence of their new government ministers. They asked for and received operational autonomy but regularly explained to the politicians what they were attempting to achieve and how they could contribute to public stability. Finally, they explained the changes to the media and to local community groups and were given their support. As the changes took hold, the prison system then became more open to the press and to the public. Non-governmental organizations, church and other groups began to come into the prisons regularly.

For a few years during the last decade of the 20th century the Polish prison system shone as a beacon. As a model of how a decent and humane prison system might operate it was an example not only to other countries in Central and Eastern Europe, but also for those in the West. As both the prison system and the country were drawn into the orbit of Western Europe and its regional structures, the new vision for prisons became submerged in the complicated target-driven cultures so favoured in the West and models of centralized management all but obliterated the regional partnerships that had been introduced in the early 1990s (Coyle 2002).

An important function of leadership in the prison environment is to set the requisite ethical standards and to ensure that they are observed by all staff. Without a strong ethical context the circumstances in which one group of people has considerable power over another can easily degenerate into an abuse of that power. The world was shocked a few years ago when it saw the photographs of abuse of prisoners by American soldiers in Abu Ghraib prison in Iraq. What was particularly disturbing was that several of those involved were part-time soldiers and had been employed in civilian life as prison officers in the USA. They knew that what they were doing was wrong but they had lost their moral compass and had ceased to see the prisoners for whom they were responsible as human beings. The story of what went wrong in Abu Ghraib in 2003 is recounted from the perspective of some of the staff involved in Morris and Gourevitch (2009). The title of their book is a reference to the standard operating procedures (SOP) that are part and parcel of the daily life of prison staff in the USA – procedures that specify every detail of what staff must do in every conceivable situation. Prison staff in Abu Ghraib did not have any such procedures, a fact which was not lost on at least one of them:

> An orthodox SOP leaves nothing to the imagination, and as Ambuhl settled into her job, it occurred to her that the absence of a code was the code at Abu Ghraib. 'They couldn't say that we broke the rules because there were no rules', she said. 'Our mission was to help Military Intelligence, and nobody ever said, "This is your SOP". But that was in a sense what it became, because our job was to stress out the detainees, and help facilitate information to the interrogators, and save the lives of other soldiers out there.'
>
> (Morris and Gourevitch 2009: 92)

One lesson to be drawn from the terrible pictures from Abu Ghraib is that those who work in prisons or are responsible for prisons must repeatedly ask themselves the question, 'Is what we are doing the right thing to do?' This ethos must pervade the whole management process from the top down. It must also go beyond the prison administration to politicians and government officials who have ultimate responsibility for prison systems.

In the early 1970s junior assistant governors in the UK would from time to time ruminate on the profession that they had entered and the demands it made of them. One way of formulating the discussion was to consider at what point one might have to decide that what one was being asked to do was personally unacceptable. In those days, relatively soon after the abolition of the death penalty, there was a consensus that if ever hanging were to be reintroduced, the requirement on a governor to supervise an execution would be the Rubicon that could not be crossed and which would lead to resignation. One wonders what might trigger the Rubicon moment of today.

Conclusion

So 40 years after I first entered prison, what am I to conclude? I have always recognized that for the foreseeable future there will be no alternative other than imprisonment for some offenders. When I was governor of Peterhead Prison in the late 1980s, the prison held a cohort of young men who had all been involved in serious criminal acts both in their communities and while serving their sentences. There was no doubt that prison was the proper location for them at that point. My task and that of all staff was to hold them in custody as decently and humanely as possible – a task which was relatively simple in theory but extremely complex in practice. Throughout the early and mid-1990s I was governor of Brixton Prison. During my early years Brixton held a small number of prisoners who required very high security but the majority of the prisoners in my charge did not come into that category. Brixton at that time could better have been described, as could many prisons today, as a place of asylum in the proper sense of that word, a place of safety for the mentally ill, for the drug and alcohol addicted and for the wide spectrum of men who for one reason or another find it difficult to secure the accommodation, employment and support that would enable them to live a full life in society. These men often operate under the radar of the institutions of society that deal with health, with accommodation, with employment and similar matters. They only come above the institutional radar when they commit or are accused of committing an offence, and the part of the radar that picks them up is the criminal justice system. Prisons provide singularly inappropriate environments for dealing with these persons other than in exceptional circumstances.

As this chapter has demonstrated, there have undoubtedly been significant changes in prisons in a number of countries over the last 40 years. At the same time the nature of imprisonment itself has become increasingly restrictive, with large numbers of prisoners being held in conditions of maximum security, often with little or no justification. This situation has grown steadily over the last 30 years as Derek Jeffreys describes in his chapter, and has accelerated since 2001 as countries respond to perceived threats of terrorism. The justification for this has been, as Prime Minister Tony Blair said in 2005 when talking about those who 'meddle with extremism', 'Let no one be in any doubt. The rules of the game have changed' (Jeffery 2005). The reality is somewhat different. The events in Abu Ghraib prison in Iraq in 2003 and the continuing events in Guantanamo are not evidence that the principles on which good prison management should operate are no longer applicable. Instead, they are evidence that little has been learned from experiences such as those of the UK with republican and loyalist prisoners in Northern Ireland in the 1970s and 1980s, and those of Turkey more recently with PKK (Kurdistan Workers' Party) and other prisoners.

The increased use of imprisonment is also a reflection of new insecurities in a changing world order. As inequality increases between nations and within nations, governments are making greater use of criminal justice systems to deal with social and economic problems. In the decade from 1997 there were over 50 new major pieces of Home Office legislation with criminal justice implications (Faulkner 2010), and more than 1,000 new offences for which a person could be given a prison sentence were created (Johnston 2009). The increased use of imprisonment has been a direct consequence of this expanded reach of criminal justice. This in turn has placed an intolerable burden on prisons as they struggle to provide minimally decent living conditions for men and women who have myriad personal, social and health problems that cannot be resolved within the high walls and fences of a prison.

Successive governments have concluded that the answer to the failure of prisons to rehabilitate those who are sent there is to send more people to prison and to send them there for longer periods, while at the same time berating those who work in prisons for not doing more to ensure that those who leave prison do not break the law again after they return to the community. That is rather like blaming the surgeon who mends a skier's broken leg for the fact that the person later returns to the slopes and breaks his or her leg again. In recent years prison systems throughout Europe have become much more efficient in their processes, but being more efficient is of little moment if what is being done is itself the wrong thing. The result is merely that one ends up doing the wrong thing better, but it remains wrong. The prison services of the UK generally do what they do well; they do what they are asked to do. Yet the question remains, are they being asked to do the right thing?

A recent report from the British Academy (2014: 17) recognized the sterility of merely rehearsing arguments about costs and benefits in respect of the use of imprisonment. Instead it pointed to the need:

> to develop a different kind of argument, one that appeals not to empirical evidence about the effects of imprisonment but to a set of fundamental social and political values – liberty, autonomy, solidarity, dignity, inclusion and security – that penal policy should support and uphold rather than undermine. Such values should guide our treatment of all citizens, including those convicted of criminal offences: we should behave towards offenders not as outsiders who have no stake in society and its values but as citizens whose treatment must reflect the fundamental values of our society.

The report concluded that it is 'very hard to see how our current use of imprisonment could be said to reflect these social values'.

This is a challenge that merits a response.

Note

1   See for example, Lappi-Seppälä 2008.

Bibliography

BBC Newsnight (2014) 9 July.

British Academy (2014) *A presumption against imprisonment: Social order and social values*, London: British Academy.

Conway, Z. (2014) 'David Blunkett "regrets injustices" of indeterminate sentences', *BBC News* website, 13 March.

Council of Europe (1991) *Report to the United Kingdom government on the visit to the United Kingdom carried out by the European Committee for the Prevention of Torture and Inhuman or Degrading Treatment or Punishment from 29 July 1990 to 10 August 1990*, Strasbourg: Council of Europe.

Coyle, A. (1994) *The prisons we deserve*, London: Harper Collins.

Coyle, A. (2002) *Managing prisons in a time of change*, London: International Centre for Prison Studies.

Faulkner, D. (2010) *Criminal justice and government at a time of austerity*, London: Criminal Justice Alliance.

Fieser, E. (2014) 'Dominican Republic's more humane prison model', *Reuters* website, 22 May.

HC Deb (1982) 01 July, vol. 26, cc1130–1136.

HL Deb (2009) 27 April, vol. 710, col. 32.

HM Inspectorate of Prisons (2013a) *Report on an unannounced inspection of HMP/YOI Feltham (Feltham A – children and young people) 21–25 January 2013*, London: HMIP.

HM Inspectorate of Prisons (2013b) *Report on an unannounced full follow-up inspection of HMP/YOI Feltham (Feltham B – young adults) 18–22 March 2013*, London: HMIP.

HM Inspectorate of Prisons (2013c) *Report on an unannounced inspection of HMP Oakwood 10–21 June 2013*, London: HMIP.

Home Office (1984) *Prison statistics England and Wales 1983*, London: HMSO.

Jeffery, S. (2005) 'The rules of the game are changing', *The Guardian* website, 5 August.

Jewkes, Y. (2013) 'Penal aesthetics and the pains of imprisonment', in J. Simon, N. Temple and R. Tobe (eds) *Architecture and justice: Judicial meanings in the public realm*, Farnham: Ashgate.

Johnston, P. (2009) 'Why is Labour so keen to imprison us?', *Telegraph* website, 4 January.

Lappi-Seppälä, T. (2008) 'Trust, welfare and political culture: Explaining differences in national penal policies', *Crime and Justice* 37(1).

Lewis, P. (2006) 'End "degrading" slopping out, says prison watchdog', *The Guardian*, 1 June.

Lynch, T. (2000) 'All locked up', *The Washington Post*, 20 February.

Ministry of Justice (2014a) *Offender management statistics: Quarterly Bulletin October to December 2013*, London: MoJ.

Ministry of Justice (2014b) *Prison population bulletin: Weekly 27 June 2014*, London: MoJ.

Ministry of Justice (2014c) *Criminal Justice and Courts Bill. Fact sheet: Secure colleges*, London: MoJ.

Moczydlowski, P. (1992) *The hidden life of Polish prisons*, Indianapolis: Indiana University Press.

Moczydlowski, P. and Rzeplinski, A. (1990) *Collective protests in penal institutions*, Oslo: University of Oslo.

Morris, E. and Gourevitch, P. (2009) *Standard operating procedure: A war story*, Basingstoke: Picador.

National Council for Independent Monitoring Boards (2010) *Slopping out? A report on the lack of in-cell sanitation in Her Majesty's Prisons in England and Wales*, London: National Council for Independent Monitoring Boards.

Paterson, A. (1934) 'Introduction', in S. Barman, *The English Borstal system*, London: P.S. King & Son Ltd.

Peachey, P. (2013) 'Gang violence "out of control" in Feltham prison', *The Independent*, 10 July.

Prison Reform Trust (2014) *Prison: The facts – Bromley Briefings Summer 2014*, London: PRT.

Scottish Executive (2006) *High level summary of equality statistics: Key trends for Scotland 2006*, Edinburgh: Scottish Government.

US Department of Justice (2013) *Prisoners in 2012 – Advance counts*, Washington, DC: USDOJ.

Walmsley, R. (2013) *World prison population list*, tenth edn, London: International Centre for Prison Studies.

Woolf, L.J. (1991) *Prison Disturbances April 1990: Report of an Inquiry by the Rt Hon. Lord Justice Woolf (Parts I and II) and His Honour Stephen Tumim (Part II)* (The Woolf Report), London: HMSO.

World Prison Brief (2014a) *Country page: Denmark*, www.prisonstudies.org/country/denmark (accessed 28 July 2014).

World Prison Brief (2014b) *Country page: Germany*, www.prisonstudies.org/country/germany (accessed 28 July 2014).

World Prison Brief (2014c) *Country page: Netherlands*, www.prisonstudies.org/country/netherlands (accessed 28 July 2014).

World Prison Brief (2014d) *Country page: Russian Federation*, www.prisonstudies.org/country/russia n-federation (accessed 28 July 2014).

Chapter 5

The sociology of imprisonment

Ben Crewe

Introduction

It is because of the prison's social role and function that studies of its interior life always hold more than abstract or intrinsic interest. At the same time, the prison's distinctive qualities – pain, deprivation, inequalities of power, social compression – are such that its inner world provides particularly striking illustrations of a range of social phenomena. There are few other environments in which the relationship between constraint and agency can be so clearly observed, in which the consequences of power and powerlessness are so vividly manifested, and in which groups with divergent values and interests are put into such close proximity. Few other social contexts expose so barely the terms of friendship, conflict, loyalty and alienation, make questions of order and stability so germane, or bring into such sharp relief the qualities and capacities of humanity and inhumanity. Such issues will be returned to throughout this chapter, following a detailed exposition of Sykes's *The Society of Captives*, which will provide the basis for discussion of a range of debates, concepts and concerns. The chapter's main focus will be the inner world of the prison rather than its broader social and political functions.[1] However, in elaborating the debate about how prison culture is best explained, the chapter will explore the relationship between the prison and its external environment as well as its interior features.

The 'society of captives'

Although Sykes was by no means the first person to provide an academic account of the prison, *The Society of Captives* (1958) is commonly cited as the field's seminal text (Sparks et al. 1996; see Reisig 2001). Sykes regarded the prison as emblematic of systems of domination, such as concentration camps and labour colonies, and saw its study as a means of exploring the nature, consequences and potential limits of totalitarian control. With the US prison system having seen a spate of disturbances in the period preceding the study, including two riots in the maximum security facility in New Jersey where Sykes undertook his fieldwork, questions about penal order and disorder were particularly salient. He also recognized the intrinsic value of understanding prison life, at a time when changes in the aims and means of incarceration had been introduced with little understanding of how ambitions to control and rehabilitate prisoners might be hindered or supported by what went on, day to day, between prisoners: their everyday social life and culture.

The Society of Captives carries two, connected arguments, the first of which relates to power and institutional order. Sykes argued that the total dominance over prisoners that the prison ostensibly possessed was, on closer inspection, something of a fiction. The number of violations of the prison's regulations indicated how often institutional dominance was compromised, and illustrated the incessant nature of the struggle to maintain control. Sykes provided a number of reasons why order was far from guaranteed. Prisoners had no 'internal sense of duty' to comply: even if, at one level, they recognized the legitimacy of their confinement, in their daily behaviour they lacked intrinsic – i.e. moral or 'normative' – motivation to conform to the prison's demands. In theory, the prison could simply coerce prisoners into obedience through force. However, as Sykes pointed out, this was an inefficient and dangerous way to get things done: prisoners outnumbered officers, and violence could easily spiral out of control. Rewards and punishments were, likewise, much less effective than might be expected. Given the prison's conditions – Sykes argued – the latter could do little to worsen the prisoners' circumstances, whilst the former were not powerful enough to motivate prisoners positively.

There were also reasons why prison officers struggled to maintain formal boundaries and apply rules. First, it was difficult to remain aloof from prisoners when one worked with them all day and might identify with them, or even grudgingly admire them. Second, officers were surprisingly dependent on those they guarded. Prisoners carried out everyday functions and minor chores (delivering mail, checking cells, cooking and washing clothing), and if they withheld their services, this not only interfered with the smooth running of the wing, but was also taken to reflect the competence of the staff responsible. Officers were also aware that if riots did occur, their personal safety might depend on how they had used their apparently limitless power.

Sykes considered these defects in the prison's supremacy – 'cracks in the monolith' (Sykes 1958: 53) – to be virtually intrinsic to prison organizations, and to lead to a number of compromises between the prison officials and prisoners. 'In effect, the guard buys compliance or obedience in certain areas at the cost of tolerating disobedience elsewhere' (ibid.: 57); that is, officers ignored minor infractions in order to keep the peace and successfully undertake their daily tasks. As well as turning a blind eye to some activity, they also induced compliance through the provision of unofficial rewards and information to inmate leaders (e.g. extra food or coffee, warnings about upcoming searches, good jobs or cells), who in turn distributed these privileges within the inmate population. This informal arrangement was crucial for the maintenance of order. First, it directly relieved some of the tensions and deficits of imprisonment. Second, by sweetening them into compliance, it kept in check those prisoners who might otherwise 'cause trouble'. Third, it reinforced the power and status of inmate leaders – men who had a stake in institutional calm and were committed to inmate solidarity (see below). For Sykes, disorder was likely to occur if this relationship of negotiation and compromise was broken – if the rules were too strictly enforced, or the informal power of dominant prisoners were to be eroded, leading to a disintegration of the normal bonds and hierarchies between prisoners. To summarize at this point, then – and we will return shortly – order was *negotiated*, and it functioned *through* the inmate hierarchy, via those men at the apex of the prisoner community.

It is through the figure of the inmate leader that Sykes links his theory of order to his other primary argument, which is about the role and function of the 'inmate code': the set of norms and values that prisoners publicly espoused as a guide to behaviour. Sykes outlined five chief tenets of this code, crudely summarized as follows: 'don't interfere with other inmates' interests, or 'never rat [grass] on a con'; don't lose your calm, or 'play it cool and do your own time' (Sykes and Messinger 1960: 8); don't exploit or steal from other prisoners; don't be weak, or 'be tough; be a man'; and don't ever side with or show respect for the institution and its staff. This normative system had been described before (see particularly Clemmer 1958 [1940]). However, Sykes sought to explain both its origins and its functions. Noting that this was a 'strikingly pervasive value system', which could be found among apparently diverse prison populations and regimes (Sykes and Messinger 1960: 5), he reasoned that the roots of the code lay in the fundamental properties of imprisonment.

These properties were identified as the 'pains of imprisonment': those deprivations beyond the loss of liberty that defined the experience of incarceration and had a profound effect on the prisoner's self-image. These included various forms of moral condemnation, and the deprivations of goods and services, heterosexual relations, autonomy and personal security. Sykes and Messinger argued that the inmate code could be explained as a mechanism for alleviating these pains. If prisoners developed a positive shared identity, if they were loyal and respectful towards each other, if they shared their goods, caused no unnecessary frictions, kept their promises, showed courage and fortitude, and remained in staunch opposition to the prison administration, they could collectively deflect the moral censure of lawful society and mitigate many of the practical and psychological problems of incarceration.

Sykes (1995: 82) was explicit in stating that this code was 'an ideal rather than a description of how inmates behaved'. It was a set of norms to which prisoners pledged allegiance, but which most did not actually follow. In response to the pains and deprivations that they encountered, the majority of prisoners acted in ways that were 'alienative' rather than cooperative. Indeed, Sykes claimed that the various labels ('argot roles') used within the prisoner community were organized around different kinds of deviation from the central value system. There were terms for prisoners who profited from others ('merchants') or threatened them with force ('gorillas'), informed on their peers ('rats'), were insufficiently masculine ('punks' and 'fags'), or caused unnecessary friction with officers ('ballbusters'). All prisoners had good reason to espouse the code and demand that others conform to it – for there was no benefit in encouraging others to be exploitative or disloyal, even if one was oneself – but only one prisoner type embodied its doctrine. In doing so, this prisoner – the 'real man' – generated admiration among the inmate body, for he personified its collective ideals.

Real men could act as intermediaries between prisoners and officers because they stood up for the former and derided the latter without needlessly provoking incidents or pushing officers too far. They walked 'the delicate line between rejection of the officials and cooperation' (Sykes 1958: 126). Crucially, too, their commitment to the inmate code meant that they served to assist the prison officials. Although they exemplified a value system that appeared 'anti-institutional', by encouraging other prisoners to curb hostilities against each other and to protest against the prison only if really necessary, they were central figures in ensuring institutional stability. As Clemmer had noted, the code contained admonitions to 'do one's own time' – to limit social bonds and activity – which were 'the exact counterparts of the official admonitions' (Clemmer 1958: ix). Through both material and cultural means – the distribution of favours, and the dissemination of a value system that discouraged in-group antagonism and helped relieve the deprivations of imprisonment – real men prevented the prisoner community from exploding into unrest *and* from disintegrating into a state of rampant exploitation. In short, then, it had a double function: as a collective coping mechanism for prisoners, and a vital source of institutional order.

Sykes's work merits this lengthy elaboration because it covers and connects a number of key issues in prison sociology: the relationship between the prison and the outside world; the everyday culture of prison life; the pains of imprisonment; adaptation, hierarchy and social relationships; and questions of power, order and resistance. The sociology of imprisonment is by no means limited to these concerns, but it is to these areas that we now turn.

The prison, inmate culture and the outside world

The clearest theoretical contribution of *The Society of Captives* was its assertion that inmate culture was determined by the inherent deprivations of prison life. Sykes made some comments about the influence of personality factors on inmate adaptation, and some references to the influence of outside society on the prison's inner world, but these were tentative and tokenistic. It is tempting to speculate that Sykes deliberately underplayed the relevance of external factors in order to shore up the theoretical simplicity of his case. It is also important to note that at the time of his writing, prisons were more socially isolated, more 'total' institutions than they are today: without the same avenues to the outside world that telephones and televisions now provide. Still, Sykes clearly conceptualized prison culture as something determined by the inherent deficits of incarceration, consistent across spatial boundaries (i.e. regardless of a prison's location), and distinctive to the penal environment. Each of these claims has been developed and challenged in subsequent work.

In his classic (1961) text, *Asylums*, Goffman drew upon Sykes to make the case that the prison was just one of a range of 'total institutions' which shared certain functions and characteristics. Goffman defined a total institution as 'a place of residence and work where a large number of like-situated individuals, cut off from the wider society for an appreciable period of time, together lead an enclosed, formally administered round of life' (Goffman 1961: 11), a definition which therefore included mental hospitals, monasteries, boarding schools and navy ships. Like Sykes, Goffman presented the prison – and all other total institutions – as a social system that was largely autonomous from the outside world. Indeed, this autonomy was critical to its ambition to reconstruct and rehabilitate the inmate. Goffman listed practices such as the removal of personal possessions, the assignment of numbers or uniforms, the shaving of hair and the banning of normal contact with the outside world as ways of stripping inmates of their prior identities, and creating a ritual break with their past. Total institutions sought to rebuild the identities of their inhabitants by limiting their physical and psychological autonomy (regulating basic tasks such as washing and spending money; placing curbs on personal movement; withholding information), at the same time as providing a new set of rules, relationships and rewards around which identity could be reconstituted. Issues that were minor and taken for granted in the outside world – a jar of coffee, the right to smoke – became levers around which behaviour could be refocused.

Just as Sykes highlighted how imprisonment engendered a profound attack on the inmate's self-identity, Goffman's concern was the struggle of the individual to maintain self-integrity in the face of persistent attack from social rituals and institutions. Despite being socially and physically sequestered from the outside world, inmates were rarely obliterated or overwhelmed by institutional imperatives. Invariably, they sought some control over the environment, and retained some kind of independent self-concept, resulting in a range of 'secondary adaptations' to the prison's restricted social environment (see below). The resulting culture was one in which institutional and individual objectives existed in tension, and it was coloured appropriately by a preoccupation with the self. This was manifested in a generalized sadness about the inmate's lowly status or in a narrative about his (or her) social demise; and by a tendency for inmates to immerse themselves in 'removal activities' (education, exercise, card playing, fantasy) that created a space between themselves and the institution.

Although Goffman's focus was individual rather than collective adaptation, like Sykes he located the resources for adjustment as lying inside the institution. He conceived of the inmate as an individual cut off from wider social ties and stripped of pre-prison characteristics, and gave no meaningful description of how personality factors or cultural orientations influenced prison conduct. It is for this reason that Goffman is generally identified with Sykes as a proponent of 'deprivation' or 'indigenous' theory, which focuses on prison-specific variables in explaining inmate culture and behaviour. The opposing view is normally ascribed to Irwin and Cressey, who resurrected Clemmer's (1958: xv) earlier observation that the 'penitentiary is not a closed culture'. Although they acknowledged that inmate society was a 'response to problems of imprisonment', they questioned 'the emphasis given to the notion that solutions to these problems are found within the prison' (Irwin and Cressey 1962: 145). Rather, they argued, prisoners 'imported' into the prison characteristics and orientations from the external community, and adapted in ways that *maintained* or were consistent with these pre-existing selves. The inmate code was by no means distinctive to the prison, but was a version of criminal cultures existing beyond the prison.

More specifically, Irwin and Cressey regarded inmate culture as the outcome of three distinctive subcultures imported into the penal institution. The first was a 'thief culture', carried by professional and serious criminals, emphasizing reliability, loyalty, coolness in the face of provocation and 'moral courage'. Thieves were oriented to criminal life rather than the prison world itself, and aimed to serve their sentences as smoothly as possible, seeking out occasional luxuries to make life easier. The second was a 'convict subculture', carried by prisoners whom Irwin (1970) subsequently labelled 'state-raised youth'. These were men with long records of confinement in juvenile institutions, who were socialized within these individualistic, exploitative and manipulative cultures. Convicts actively sought status and influence within the prison – this being the world they knew – and were likely to be involved in the prison's illicit activities as a means to these ends. The third, more marginal, subculture was the 'legitimate' value system held by 'straight' prisoners, with anti-criminal attitudes, who generally conformed to institutional goals and acted in accordance with conventional, lawful principles. Prison culture as a whole was 'an adjustment or accommodation of these three systems within the official administrative system of deprivation and control' (Irwin and Cressey 1962: 153).

The importation-deprivation debate has continued to provide the primary framework for discussions of prison social life and culture, but has advanced in a number of directions. The notion that there was any such thing as 'The Prison', with stable properties and consistent characteristics, was challenged by a number of studies which showed how much variety existed between different regimes, populations and even a prison's physical design (see Chapter 7, this volume). As was broadly consistent with Sykes's model, custody-oriented establishments generated more oppositional cultures than treatment-based facilities. Studies of women's prisons found very different inmate social systems from those described in men's establishments, raising further questions about whether prisons could be said to have 'intrinsic' features at all (Ward and Kassebaum 1965; Giallombardo 1966). Meanwhile, Mathiesen's (1965) account of a Norwegian treatment-oriented establishment described a prisoner community with little cohesive behaviour, little faith in the effectiveness of norms promoting solidarity, a flat inmate hierarchy, no apparent ban on contact with prison staff, and no 'honourable' inmate identity (the latter features apparently reflecting Norway's relatively undeveloped criminal culture). Lacking peer solidarity or a positive collective identity, prisoners developed alternative means of coping from those identified by Sykes, primarily oriented around accusations that power holders were deviating from their own established norms or those rooted in broader notions of justice. Thus, a value system emphasizing opposition to the institution and solidarity to one's peers did not appear to be the only functional responses to the pains of imprisonment.

The picture of prison life in Jacobs's (1977) *Stateville* bore even less resemblance to Sykes's account, and its analysis represented an advanced challenge to indigenous theories of prison culture. Instead of a single normative code, Jacobs found a prisoner community that was fragmented into mutually antagonistic, ethnically defined gangs, with codes of loyalty that stretched little beyond in-group members. Significantly, these gangs had emerged on the streets of Chicago, from where their values and leadership structures had in effect been *transplanted* into the prison. Jacobs (1974: 399) contrasted Goffman's description of the 'role-stripping' of new prisoners with what he observed as a 'home-coming ceremony', whereby new entrants were greeted and looked after by affiliates from the streets. Here, then, external identities defined and were reinforced by the prison's social structure. Moreover, it was the gang system, rather than informal negotiation with prison officials, that buffered many prisoners from the pains of prison life by providing a sense of collective identity as well as social and economic support.

Stateville was significant not only in capturing the transformation of the prison's social organization, but in explicitly identifying the macro-mechanisms that rendered it historically mutable. While Irwin and Cressey had illustrated the permeability of the prison to external cultures and dispositions, Jacobs showed how its social life and administration were moulded by wider social, political and legal conditions. Prisoner expectations had been raised by expanded notions of rights and 'citizenship', and these expectations were validated by court interventions that secured for them a growing range of entitlements. Meanwhile, the politicization of ethnic-minority prisoners reflected political cultures outside the institution. For Jacobs, such changes represented 'the movement of the prison's place in society from the periphery towards the center' (Jacobs 1977: 6). The prison could no longer insulate itself from the trends and values of the outside world, and from demands for its inhabitants to be treated as normal citizens.

This description of the prison's rationale and societal location has not been without criticism. Although long-term patterns suggest that prisons have been subject to certain kinds of 'civilizing' processes, the coercive turn within prison management (as embodied by the 'supermax' prison in the USA), the contracting out of imprisonment to the private sector, and the potency of law-and-order politics in both the USA and Western

Europe indicate a more complex configuration of the prison–society relationship. First, then, while the prison – and crime control more generally – has become central to political discourse (Simon 2007), it has done so in a way that reassures the 'respectable' classes of their difference from the 'criminal class', and has little compunction about treating the latter in ways that are highly punitive (Christie 1981). Some scholars have characterized the 'extra-penological' role of the prison as the primary means of managing and neutralizing the American underclass, with money drained from welfare into penal services in the interests of neo-liberalism (Wacquant 2001). Clearly, the prison has multiple functions beyond its technical ends (Garland 2001) – indeed, judged by its primary aims, it is an astonishing failure. Symbolically, it serves to represent state authority and reinforce moral boundaries and sentiments (Durkheim 1933); at the level of political economy, it acts as an instrument of class domination and a means of maintaining social order (Rusche and Kirchheimer 1939). As feminist scholars have also highlighted (Carlen 1983; Howe 1994), often drawing on the work of Foucault (1977), the prison may be emblematic of a web of social control strategies that regulate and discipline women throughout society: within the family, relationships, by the state and in terms of general definitions of femininity. Here then, the conceptual distinction between the prison and the outside world begins to crumble.

Second, privatization could be seen as a de-coupling of the prison from the state, especially in the USA, where regulation practices are less stringent than in the UK. Further, private companies form part of the bloc of interest groups whose political lobbying reinforces the momentum for mass incarceration: thus, the penal body now feeds into political life, as well as vice versa. Third, imprisonment rates in the USA (and, to a more limited extent, in Western Europe) are such that the prison and its culture can no longer be seen as mere reflections of or appendages to a separate, external world. Imprisonment has become a 'shaping institution for whole sectors of the population' (Garland 2001: 2), stripping some communities of young men, disenfranchising them from the political process, and creating generational spirals of criminality. In some areas of the USA (and other countries, to a lesser degree), incarceration is not just a normal social expectation and experience, but a source and requirement for status. For Loic Wacquant (2000, 2001), the prison and the ghetto are now barely distinguishable. The ghetto has been swamped by criminal justice agencies, and deserted by non-state, civic agencies. Meanwhile, the 'warehouse' prison has little purpose beyond containment and control. Like the ghetto, it merely quarantines its inhabitants from the rest of the social body. Both prison and ghetto are characterized by racial cleavages, enforced idleness, and by cultures of suspicion, distrust and violence. Wacquant argues that street culture is no longer simply imported into the prison – as Jacobs described – but has itself been deeply imprinted by norms and values from the prison that have been re-exported and integrated over many years.[2] In such respects, the separation of these cultural domains may be fatuous, and the importation-deprivation debate appears somewhat obsolete.

It is important to maintain some distinction between theories of prison culture and empirical accounts of its terms and influences. A multitude of quantitative studies have shown that the relationship between pre-prison variables and in-prison behaviour is complex and variable, and that activities such as drug taking and homosexuality have both imported and indigenous components (Zamble and Porporino 1988). The prison's inner world is best seen as a *distorted* and *adapted* version of social life and culture outside. However, for reasons discussed below, studies that would more sharply illuminate the complex interplay between imported factors and the imperatives generated by the prison remain uncommon. At the structural level, few scholars now seek to explain the role or function of the prison through a single theoretical lens (be it derived from Marx, Durkheim, Talcott Parsons or Foucault). Rather, it is generally accepted that the values and sensibilities that shape the broad purposes and practices of imprisonment derive from multiple sources, and are realized in practice in complex and messy ways.

David Garland (2001) has provided the most recognized account of this kind, arguing that on both sides of the Atlantic, penal welfarism has been replaced by a 'culture of control', one element of which is the emergence of more coercive and punitive penal sanctions, and the reinvention of the prison. Such broad characterizations tend to be over-schematic. As Liebling (with Arnold 2004) has shown, Garland's narrative cannot explain some of the countervailing tendencies in UK imprisonment, such as the re-emergence of rehabilitative ambitions, and the advancement of a 'decency agenda'. Such discourses are promoted and undermined by powerful individuals (e.g. ministers, Prison Service heads) and unanticipated events (e.g. riots, escapes, high-profile crimes), significantly altering the general climate of incarceration, in ways that have a demonstrable impact on the degree to which prisons feel decent or distressing. Since some prisons are evidently more respectful or safe than others, it is also clear that management styles, staff cultures and institutional histories mediate the ways that penal values and sensibilities are translated into material practices (see also Kruttschnitt and Gartner 2005). Thus, through the messages that prison staff receive and instantiate about the moral status of prisoners and the boundaries of acceptable behaviour, the prison experience is sensitive to both the macro- and micro-politics of imprisonment.

Prison adaptation and socialization

Sykes noted that the roles taken up by prisoners were not static, and that many prisoners moved between different roles over the course of their sentence. However, he provided no account of how or why this might happen and did little to develop the concept of 'prisonization', a term that captures the *dynamic* process of prisoner socialization. Clemmer had defined prisonization as the 'taking on in greater or lesser degree of the folkways, mores, customs and general culture of the penitentiary' (Clemmer 1958: 299). He argued that the degree to which a prisoner became assimilated into prison culture depended on a range of factors, including personality, demographic characteristics, and relationships within and outside the prison. The implications for rehabilitation were gloomy. Prisoners who became socialized into prison culture had 'no chance of being salvaged' (ibid.: 313). If rehabilitation occurred, it did so *in spite* of the influence of prison culture, and it happened to those prisoners who were the least oriented to criminal subcultures in the first place. However, such conclusions relied on the assumption that socialization into the norms of imprisonment simply deepened over time. By exploring prisoner attitudes at different sentence stages, Wheeler (1961) showed this supposition to be faulty. Prisonization took the shape of a 'U-curve': it was in the middle stage of a sentence that prisoner values most closely conformed to the inmate code. As prisoners anticipated release back into the community, these values shifted back to the more 'conventional' norms with which they initially entered the prison community.

To some degree, Wheeler's findings supported Sykes's theorization of the inmate code as a problem-solving mechanism (and Goffman's belief that inmates were able to readjust to non-institutional life relatively quickly). It was when prisoners were furthest from the outside community, i.e. when the pains of imprisonment were most acute, that they were most dependent on the prisoner society and the code was most potent. Subsequent work has confirmed that there are particular stages of a sentence at which prisoners feel most isolated and distressed, albeit generally earlier than Wheeler suggested (Liebling 1999), and that sentence length has a considerable impact on adaptation (Sapsford 1983). Prison behaviour of various kinds can be plotted against time served, and certainly many prisoners report that they deliberately curb illicit activities as they approach release and have more to lose from such exploits (Crewe 2009).

However, as Sykes's work illustrated, there is no single pattern of adjustment to prison life. A comprehensive – though static – typology of adaptations can be provided by combining the frameworks presented by Merton (1938) and Goffman (1961). First, then, some prisoners 'withdraw', 'retreat' or 'regress', focusing on little beyond immediate events around themselves. Often these prisoners are former drug addicts, whose mission is simply to get themselves 'back on track' (Crewe 2009). Retreatism might also include what would be considered maladaptations, such as self-isolation and repeated self-mutilation (Liebling 1992), but could also incorporate the obsessive bodybuilding that some prisoners take up, or the deep absorption into art or education that allows others some mental escape from institutional life (Cohen and Taylor 1972; Boyle 1984).

Second, some prisoners rebel against the prison, attempting escapes, engaging in concerted physical resistance, or 'campaigning' against prison practices and conditions. In the UK, such activities tend to be concentrated within higher-security establishments, where long sentences generate profound frustration, and where prisoners themselves may be more anti-authoritarian, or sufficiently resourceful to orchestrate effective campaigns against the system. As some scholars have suggested, however, resistance is not limited to these prisoners, or to its more spectacular and confrontational manifestations. Power is not simply held by the powerful, to be directly confronted and seized. It flows throughout the social body, through surveillance, petty rules and assumptions about 'appropriate behaviour' (Foucault 1977). Resistance therefore occurs through everyday, minor acts of subversion (backstage jokes, the use of in-group language, stealing from prison supplies) and through assertions of identity ('as a mother ...'; 'as a black woman ...') that contest and recast the meanings, directives and restrictions imposed by the institution. Ugelvik (2014) highlights a set of creative practices, including forms of improvised cooking and the transformation of cells into private spaces, which enable prisoners to reclaim some sense of masculinity, individuality and moral status. These forms of micro-resistance – which make use of the body as a tool of violence, a site of representation (e.g. through modes of dress or make-up), or an object of desecration and destruction (e.g. dirty protests; self-harm) – may be particularly common when prisoners have little collective organization.

A third kind of adaptation is represented by 'conformity' (Merton 1938), 'colonization' or 'conversion' (Goffman 1961), where prisoners appear relatively satisfied with their existence in prison, where they internalize official views of themselves, and where they comply with sincerity and enthusiasm to the demands of the system. This category includes the 'centre-men' and 'straights' described in the early ethnographies – men who identified with conventional values prior to imprisonment. It also incorporates those 'gleaners' whom Irwin (1970) described as seeking change and self-improvement through official programmes and structures. Some researchers have implied that this adaptation is uncommon or superficial, because it means prisoners discarding anti-social values or accepting their inferior moral status (Morris and Morris 1963; Carrabine 2005). In fact, there are an increasing number of drug addicts entering prison who compare it favourably to life on the streets on drugs, and whose shame and self-loathing lead them to act as model inmates, desperate to prove their moral reformation (Crewe 2005b, 2009).

Fourth, there are prisoners who fit into the category of 'innovators' that Merton described as accepting official objectives but rejecting the institutional means of attaining them. Mathiesen (1965) identified this 'censoriousness' as the primary response among prisoners in his study of a Norwegian prison: criticism of those in power for not conforming to their own stated rules and standards, or for acting in ways that would be considered unjust within a broader moral framework. These strategies – which can be seen as a form of resistance – are significant because, rather than representing a stance of normative opposition (as Sykes described), they accept the norms of the officials. Mathiesen argued that, in this respect, they derive from a position of weakness and social atomization: a lack of other, more collective means of challenging the regime. At the same time, they may be highly effective ways of contesting the terms of one's incarceration, and blurring the moral divide between prisoners and their state custodians.

The majority of prisoners find ways of coping with imprisonment that do not involve either extreme resistance or complete acquiescence, and which combine the strategies and adjustments described above. Whether described as 'playing it cool', 'ritualism' or 'doing time', this involves supporting other prisoners, albeit within limits, showing little enthusiasm for the regime, and seeking to make the prison experience as comfortable as possible, while trying to avoid trouble. Some prisoners – perhaps a sixth category – will also seek to *manipulate* the system (Morris and Morris 1963; King and Elliott 1977; Crewe 2009), using their prison experience to exploit rules, work 'angles' and perform desired behaviour to prison officials whilst flouting it elsewhere. Most prisoners want to 'do their time and get out' (Carrabine 2004), but how they choose to do so – whether they get involved in trade, or the accumulation of status – depends on peer obligations, criminal and institutional careers, family loyalties, economic and psychological needs within prison, and future hopes whose inter-relationships remain under-researched. Certainly though, prisoners do not just 'undergo' imprisonment as passive agents of prisonization and socialization, as much of the early literature seems to imply. Rather, as Cohen and Taylor (1972) emphasized, they are often highly conscious of their social predicament and are strategic in the choices they make about how to address it.

It is also clear that imprisonment is considerably more painful for some prisoners than for others (Liebling 1992), and that prisoner *sub-groups* experience and adapt to the prison environment in different ways. In part, as the next section illustrates, this relates to aspects of social organization within and outside the prison. However, it also indicates the different psychological preoccupations that prisoners import into the environment, and the ways in which institutions address their populations. Evidence from the USA has suggested that the concerns of black prisoners are focused on issues of freedom, autonomy, disrespect and discrimination, while white prisoners are more likely to fear for their physical safety and experience prison as a loss to self-esteem (Toch 1977). In the UK, black prisoners feel lower levels of respect, humanity and fairness than other prisoners (Cheliotis and Liebling 2006), while the prison system has been described as 'institutionally thoughtless' about the needs of the old and disabled, to whom it is not primarily oriented (Crawley 2005; Chapter 29, this volume).

Research consistently reports that for female prisoners, the rupturing of ties to children and intimate others, and the possibility of being in prison during one's fertile years, are particularly painful dimensions of imprisonment (Walker and Worrall 2000). Female prisoners also express greater concern than male prisoners about privacy, intimate intrusions, personal health and autonomy, and those dynamics of penal power that can evoke memories of abuse (Carlen 1998; Zaitzow and Thomas 2003). Such concerns reflect, and are exacerbated by, the nature of women's imprisonment. Female prisoners are often incarcerated at great distance from their homes, while the regimes to which they are subjected are generally more petty and infantilizing (as well as domesticated and medicated) than those in men's prisons (Carlen 1998). These higher expectations about the personal behaviour of female prisoners are emblematic of the discourses of 'normal femininity' that are embedded in the practices and philosophies of women's incarceration (Bosworth 1999; Carlen 1983, 1988), and which amplify the gendered dimensions of collective adaptation that are described within the section that follows.

Social relations and everyday culture

Sykes did not claim that the prisoner world was defined by inmate cohesion or actual solidarity. However, by describing a society with a single normative framework, and by providing only passing reference to social and ethnic cleavages within this community, he portrayed prisoners as unified by some kind of common purpose. This may have reflected the nature of the 'Big House' prison, in which prisoners were subjected to a stupefying regime, rigid timetabling and highly authoritarian staffing, and yet were allowed to develop a relatively self-contained world, which they managed with little interference from the authorities (Irwin and Austin 1997; Irwin 2005). In such a context – and given Sykes's interest in systemic order and equilibrium – communal objectives and collective functions may well have appeared more significant than social divisions and interpersonal relationships.

Other accounts of the prison, both during the Big House era and in later periods, have explored the nature of social relations *within* the prisoner community. Generally, they have emphasized conflict, 'disorganization' and sub-group rivalry as much as collective organization. Clemmer (1958) described a tiered hierarchy of elite, middle-class and lower-status prisoners. The latter – around 40% of prisoners – tended to be solitary, being civil to others but not close or cooperative. Higher-status prisoners were more sociable, mixing within their class either in 'semi-primary' groups, sharing luxuries and information, or in smaller cliques, where resources were shared and members thought collectively. Subsequent accounts of prison life have depicted similar patterns of loosely structured, interlocking social groups, with little formal organization or leadership, based upon locality, religion, age, lifestyle and criminal identity (Irwin 2005; Crewe 2005a, 2009). Such groups offer forms of material and social support, and physical backing if required, while also providing networks for trade and avenues for settling disputes. As Clemmer noted, though, loyalties are generally limited and groups rarely display genuine cohesion (Mathiesen 1965; though see McEvoy 2000). Prisoners tend to differentiate between acquaintances, with whom relationships are transient, instrumental and defensive (often based on self-interest and fear of exploitation rather than affection and admiration), and a very small number of trusted friends, often known prior to the sentence. For most prisoners, then, the prisoner community is 'an atomized world', characterized more by 'trickery and dishonesty' than by 'sympathy and cooperation' (Clemmer 1958: 297).

Whether race was a significant factor in the Big House era is difficult to know. Jacobs (1983) suggests that, given the discriminatory values of white prisoners and officials, black prisoners were probably excluded from certain roles within the prison and were unlikely to be as committed to the inmate code as whites.[3] In any case, over the two decades that followed the publication of Sykes's work, any notion of a single solidarity culture among prisoners in the USA was obliterated as racial and ethnic conflict became the dominant feature of American prisons. By the 1950s, black Muslims had begun to preach their racial superiority, rejecting the notion of inmate equality (Jacobs 1983). In the years that followed, as prisons became more open to the outside world, and as the percentage of non-white inmates began to rise, racial and ethnic differences were amplified. Prisoners started to organize themselves into ethnically homogeneous cliques, with separate informal economies. Ethnic co-mingling became more limited. When there was enthusiasm for a more rehabilitative regime (Irwin 2005), and while the numerical dominance of white prisoners counterbalanced the greater solidarity of black prisoners, peace and tolerance prevailed. By the 1970s, the changes described in *Stateville* had eroded this social accord. Informal segregation had hardened into factional conflict, both between and within ethnic groups, and violent gangs from the streets began to dominate the prisoner social world. The norms of these gangs stressed intense in-group allegiance while encouraging the exploitation of non-members (Jacobs 1977; Irwin 1980). Unaffiliated prisoners either had to 'prove themselves' worthy of membership, usually through violence, or withdraw from the prison's public culture. As gang members and state-raised youth took over the prison social world, random violence, robbery and sexual predation became everyday facts of life, turning the prison into 'an unstable and violent social jungle' (Johnson 1987: 74).

Recent work suggests that although race remains the primary axis of social life in American prisons, and informal segregation persists, 'the intensity and importance of racial identities and gang affiliations has diminished somewhat' (Irwin 2005: 86). To a large degree, this social 'détente' (Irwin 2005) is explained by the emergence of the supermax prison, which has allowed for the segregation of violent and gang-affiliated prisoners, and which stands as a potent threat to those who want to remain in more humane conditions. Here then, prison culture has been moulded by a particular form of administrative control. Most European societies have had neither the gang culture nor the racial cleavages whose importation into prison have led to so many problems in the USA (Morgan 2002). In UK prisons, despite fairly widespread prejudice and frequent verbal skirmishes, race relations have historically tended to be relatively harmonious (Genders and Player 1989). Black and Muslim prisoners are more cohesive than whites – and this can generate envy and hostility from white prisoners, who consider themselves somewhat marginalized – but their solidarity functions primarily in defensive, self-supporting ways rather than as a means of achieving collective power. Prisoners are loosely self-segregating, but such groupings reflect shared cultural backgrounds rather than racial hostility or political assertions of ethnic difference. In most establishments, prisoners mix across ethnic lines, espouse 'a desire to see themselves and others simply as human beings, not defined by their race or ethnicity' (Phillips 2012: 86), and publicly express norms of multicultural liberalism.

One reason for this culture of 'multicultural conviviality' (Phillips 2012: 124) is that many prisoners are raised in diverse inner-city areas, and socialize naturally in ethnically heterogeneous groups both inside and outside prison. Indeed, in most UK establishments, locality is at least as important as ethnicity in defining prisoners' loyalties. Alliances and networks are normally founded on hometown contacts, such that groups from large urban centres tend to be dominant in a prison's informal economy – without normally seeking wider control of the prison's public spaces. Occasionally such groups come into conflict with each other over trade and collective reputation; more often, disputes stem from relatively minor disagreements between individuals. On the whole though – as in the USA, prior to racial Balkanization (Irwin 2005) – the social world is balanced by a multitude of cliques and social clusters which are relatively fluid and interconnected (see also Sparks et al. 1996).

In England and Wales, the starkest exception to this picture can be found in some high security establishments, where the social world is much more sharply defined by the increasing collective power of Muslim prisoners. Liebling et al. (2012) describe considerable tension between the growing Muslim population and other prisoner groups (see also Liebling and Arnold 2012). Importantly, they argue that the appeal of Islam is to some degree institutionally determined: in a culture of violent insecurity and lengthening sentences, Islam – like other faith systems – offers valuable forms of fraternity, safety, hope and meaning. Muslim prisoners, who in previous decades were considered highly compliant (Genders and Player 1989), have become the most challenging and oppositional members of the prisoner community, in part because of suspicion and cultural distance between them and prison staff.

In all penal jurisdictions, certain criminal offences appear to generate status and stigma (Winfree et al. 2002). Thus, sex offenders are widely reviled by other prisoners, while armed robbers, terrorists, high-level drug dealers and organized, professional criminals are given a certain amount of kudos.[4] As Morgan (2002) notes, though, such labels are problematic: drug addicts committing small-scale post office robberies to fund their habits have little social standing; spouse murderers and contract killers generate very different levels of fear and status among other prisoners; and while terrorists and 'faces' (prisoners with reputations) are given 'respect', this tends to be based upon fear as much as admiration. Many petty criminals are as morally judgemental about serious, violent offenders and the activities of drug dealers as these more powerful prisoners are socially judgemental about them (Crewe 2009).

Meanwhile, although certain offences almost categorically lead to stigma, few in themselves 'carry an automatic bonus of prestige' (Morris and Morris 1963: 226). Status and power are also associated with certain kinds of acts and attributes (Clemmer 1958; King and Elliott 1977). Low status tends to be assigned to prisoners who are unintelligent, provincial, cowardly, mentally unstable, poor copers, criminally naïve, or who inform on others. Prisoners who are unpredictably violent or uncompromisingly hostile are given little credibility, but their aggression allows them to carve out a certain degree of social space and autonomy. Those who are intelligent, charismatic, strong, and criminally mature, who are faithful to inmate values and who do not subordinate themselves to officials, tend to generate respect (Clemmer 1958; Sykes 1958; Irwin 2005).

These terms appear to have changed little since the early ethnographies, yet the precise nature of the prisoner hierarchy is related to the prison's institutional properties and to changes in the external world. Many UK prisoners report a decline in the currency of violence since prisons introduced anti-bullying strategies and challenged cultures of staff brutality. In the current system of England and Wales, it is significant that status and stigma are so closely bound up with the drugs economy. Since its widespread presence in the prison system from the late 1980s, heroin's economic potency, and the desire it generates, has made it a major source of power in the prisoner world, albeit in a form that is somewhat ephemeral and is different from respect (Crewe 2005b). In contrast, heroin users are stigmatized and disrespected. Their consumption indicates weakness and dependency, and is associated with a range of behaviours – such as stealing and manipulation – that constitute serious breaches of the prisoner value system. It remains to be seen how the recent influx of legal highs into the prison system, particularly synthetic cannabinoids, might reshape these kinds of hierarchies and social relations.

The nature of power is also defined by an establishment's security status. In medium security conditions, where prisoners are in sight of release, few seek to impose their power upon others for fear of what they might lose. Although a distinction between 'lads' and 'idiots' is apparent, on the whole, interpersonal power is granted rather than actively sought out, and has implications rather than ends: it means being safe from violence, receiving a certain amount of recognition, and having the capacity to intervene in wing issues and disputes, but it is rarely imposed upon others directly or for its own sake (also see Sparks et al. 1996: 177–178).

Like the prisoner hierarchy, the inmate code is more complex than basic maxims suggest, and while showing continuity with early formulations, has been responsive to changes in the nature of prison life. First, then, there is no simple consensus on its terms. Prisoners may agree that informing is generally wrong, but many believe that it is justified in extreme circumstances, for example if a prisoner or staff member is going to be seriously assaulted. Likewise, while some prisoners consider charging others for small favours or demanding interest on loans to be shrewd, others regard it as exploitative. Second, there is considerable variance between its form, not only across the prison estate, but also within individual establishments (Sparks et al. 1996). The therapeutic prison, HMP Grendon, exhibits a culture without conventional norms about not informing on or disclosing to others, distrusting staff and publicly denigrating sex offenders (Genders and Player 1989; Stevens 2013). In Young Offender Institutes, the ritual humiliation of vulnerable prisoners is legitimated by norms that revile weakness. Violence and victimization are rife (Edgar et al. 2003; HMCIP 2001). By contrast, in adult prisons, although weakness is disdained, its exploitation is not celebrated.

Additionally, the code is subject to change, both in its content and its primary functions. Early theorists recognized that there was considerable disparity between the solidarity that prisoners verbally demanded, and the individualistic behaviour that many of them actually exhibited. Clemmer suggested that code violations were most likely to occur among prisoners with loyalties to people both within and outside the institution. In Sykes's formulation, verbal allegiance to the code was virtually unanimous, but was based on markedly different motivations. 'True believers' (Sykes and Messinger 1960: 18) were normatively committed to its values; other prisoners were more pragmatic, supporting it to stop themselves being exploited ('believers without passion'), or asserting it disingenuously to protect their violations from being reported. Nevertheless, writers agreed that the code was universally acknowledged, and that without it, the prisoner world would be all the more conflictual and unpredictable. It provided a common source of identity and self-respect, promoted mutual aid, and reduced the degree to which less respected prisoners were exploited. By the 1970s, as the prisoner community factionalized, normative consensus likewise splintered (Jacobs 1977; Irwin 2005).

Skarbek (2014) argues that as prison populations expanded, more first-time prisoners entered the system and prisons become more crowded, the system of norms (a reputation-based system) was no longer able to govern prisoner behaviour effectively. Gang culture emerged because it was a more effective mechanism for protecting property, enforcing informal agreements and arbitrating disputes. Soon, though, the ideals of toughness and machismo that had formerly served as a collective mechanism for coping with the prison experience became sources of exploitation; aggression supplanted fortitude as the basis of admiration. Meanwhile, the informal economy functioned less to cushion prisoners against the prison's daily deprivations than as a wellspring of profit, power and exploitation. White-collar criminals and white prisoners who refused to join neo-Nazi counter-gangs developed a code that illustrated the new, defensive terms of prison survival: 'Don't gamble, don't mess with drugs, don't mess with homosexuals, don't steal, don't borrow or lend' (Hassine 1999: 42).

Notwithstanding the variations and complexities sketched out above, a number of commentators have remarked that the cultures of men's prisons appear deeply inscribed by discourses of masculinity, the celebration of violence and toughness, the stigmatization of weakness and femininity, and fraternal codes of in-group loyalty (e.g. Sim 1994; Carrabine and Longhurst 1998; Sabo et al. 2001). Sykes's (1958) description of the manner in which, in the absence of normal gender relations, male prisoners seek to demonstrate their masculinity through the 'secondary proof of manhood', remains an elegant summary of what has now become prevailing wisdom about the culture of men's prisons. As Newton (1994) argues, the prison breeds hyper-masculinity by taking men who already lack conventional means of establishing masculine status, besieging them with further threats to their gender identities, and thus encouraging them to shore up anxieties about weakness and dependency through the hardening of stereotypically male traits, in particular those that demonstrate power over the self and others. Prison rape has been taken as the ultimate symbol of this dynamic (Scacco 1975). Although sexual coercion is relatively uncommon in UK prisons (O'Donnell 2004), in some jurisdictions it appears endemic, and is saturated with gendered (and racial) meanings, creating a surrogate gender hierarchy. Typically, the man who rapes another man is not considered homosexual. Rather, his actions are taken to indicate dominance and masculine power, while the victim is irrevocably stigmatized and emasculated – often expected to carry out 'female' duties, such as housekeeping, on behalf of the aggressor. Those men who choose to take up a homosexual role within the prison's sexual subculture are less reviled than those who have the passive, 'feminine' role forced upon them. Correspondingly, within the prisoner hierarchy, respect seems to correlate with crimes and behaviours that entail the imposition of will and self-definition upon others: armed robbery, terrorism and the willingness to 'go all the way', regardless of risk. Discourses of masculinity – mutual interest in sports, shared notions of 'giving your word' – may also serve to lubricate relationships between male prisoners and staff (Carrabine and Longhurst 1998).

However, these mechanisms are complex and, in the UK at least, prisons do not exhibit a homogeneous culture of ruthless and uncompromising machismo, nor are their emotional cultures uniform (Crewe et al. 2014). In relating to female officers, male prisoners are just as liable to use discourses of charm, chivalry and the 'good son' as those of sexism to confirm their masculine identities. There is a danger that by focusing on the 'hyper-masculinity' of men's prisons, we portray the prisoner world as a lawless jungle, without moral baselines. Such representations ignore the banal kindness that characterizes prison life alongside all its depredations. These everyday details of the prison have tended to be documented within the margins of other studies. They have highlighted: the importance to prisoners of clothing and body maintenance; the performative nature of public discourse in prison, based around embellished tales of past behaviour and the street, cynical pronouncements about criminal justice and 'the man', and often grandiose plans for the future (Irwin 1985); the private stories of personal demise and shame (Goffman 1961); the surprising punitiveness of many prisoners (Winfree et al. 2002); the 'mind games' played out on the landings between prisoners and staff (McDermott and King 1988); the combination of wariness, opportunism and improvisation that characterizes the 'rabble mentality' (Irwin 1985); the raw, 'pungent argot [language] of the dis-possessed' (Sykes and Messinger 1960: 11); and the wit of prison humour, with its wry appreciation of the surreal (Morris and Morris 1963). Highlighting such dimensions is important in humanizing a world that is often portrayed to be completely alien and inhumane.

Formulations that equate prison culture with masculinity are also troubled by findings that reveal the presence of coercion, violence and sexual exploitation in women's prisons. In general, however, the cultures of women's prisons have differed from men's estab-lishments: being less tense and predatory (Zaitzow and Thomas 2003), harbouring higher rates of distress and self-harm (Liebling 1992; see Chapter 31, this volume), and lacking such strong norms of general solidarity. At the level of social structure, in women's prisons in the USA, race operates as a subtext in daily life rather than as its defining axis (Owen 1998). Many of the roles identified in the early ethnographies of men's facilities, such as the 'politician', 'tough' and 'merchant', have not been found in women's prisons. Rather, their social worlds have been organized through same-sex relationships and pseudo-family units, which seem to provide important forms of intimacy and the kinds of emotional roles that imprisonment threatens (Ward and Kassebaum 1965; Giallom-bardo 1966). Relative to men's prisons, then, collective adaptations function to provide emotional as much as social and economic support, while sex serves as a basis for comfort rather than power.

At the same time, it is important not to overstate the uniqueness of women's prison adaptations. 'Homegirl' networks of friendships and acquaintances from outside the prison are similar to the kinds of social lattices that shape the affiliations of male prisoners (Owen 1998). Furthermore, it is clear that the nature of social life in women's prisons is influenced by the degree to which the regime is itself gendered. In their comparison of adaptations in two women's prisons in California, Kruttschnitt and Gartner (2005) found little evidence of racial tension, and intimate relationships between women were common, indicating some continuities with older studies that emphasized the distinctive social lives of men's and women's prisons. However, women in the more restricted, gender-neutral prison were more likely to be distrustful of other prisoners and staff, to self-isolate and to report emotional distress than those in the prison that had retained more traditional assumptions about femininity and women's criminality. Research of this kind alerts us to the danger of ascribing all aspects of prison culture to the imported gender identities of prisoners without paying sufficient attention to the role of the insti-tution itself in reproducing certain kinds of gendered roles and behaviours. In relation to men, this means attributing cultures of violence and aggression to aspects of the administration – harsh regimes, hostile staff cultures, etc. – as well as to the characters of prisoners themselves.

Power, order and resistance

Some comments have already been offered on individual forms of resistance, but power is also exercised by prisoners at a collective level, most obviously in the form of riots, but also in everyday attempts to push back against the imposition of institutional power. As Sykes (1958) suggested, one basis of collective power is a shared set of values generated by common predicament – what might be referred to as structural solidarity – and the bargaining power that this provides. Collective power might also stem from values imported from networks and organizations located outside the prison (Jacobs 1977). Most notably, political convictions appear to be among the only adhesives that can bind prisoners into organized and purposeful collective action, particularly when reinforced through support in a wider social or ideological community. McEvoy (2000) describes how shared commitments to political ends among paramilitary prisoners in Northern Ireland provided both the will and solidarity that enabled them to sustain long-term hunger strikes and dirty protests. Meanwhile, the power of these prisoners was bolstered by the strength of the paramilitary organizations within Northern Irish society, and their ability to intimidate prison staff. Polite but persistent requests over relatively small matters were underwritten by threats to the safety of staff members' families, allowing para-military factions to establish control incrementally not only over prisoners' cells and landings, but other public spaces within the institution. The ability of individual prisoners to instigate legal interventions that apply collectively to prisoners is another potent source of collective power, one that can be engaged in with complete moral legitimacy. Like-wise, the appeal to collective, moral norms can be a powerful means of holding the authorities to account (Mathiesen 1965).

The ways that prisoners assert and resist power are defined to a significant degree by the ways it is imposed upon them. Imprisonment restricts normal means of coping (alcohol, drugs, friendship), and provides alternative means of exercising agency. In Foucault's terms, 'where there is power, there is resistance, and yet, or rather consequently, this resistance is never in a position of exteriority in relation to power' (Foucault 1978: 95). Equally, prison institutions deploy power with forms of resistance in mind – primarily, that is, to achieve *order*. Order in prison is an issue of particular interest given the obsta-cles to its accomplishment that seem inherent in the penal situation. For Sykes, then, the pragmatic trade-off between rulers and rules was a *necessary* accommodation. Subsequent writers continued to explore how order was achieved through the values and hierarchy of the inmate community, stressing the combination of solidarity ('don't exploit others') and anomie ('but do your own time …') that made the code such an effective source of stability, and the conservatism of prisoner leaders keen to maintain the status quo. However, by the time of *Stateville*, with gangs less inclined towards negotiation, and less in need of its benefits, powerful prisoners were undermining rather than contributing to institutional stability. Liebling and colleagues' recent (2012) research in the UK suggests that similar processes may be occurring in high security prisons, with Muslim prisoners less inclined than the 'old-school' gangsters of the past to negotiate with the authorities.

Of course, order had never been achieved through informal accommodation alone. It is also clear that Sykes's theory rested on a number of flawed assumptions. One tenet of his argument was that the rewards and punishments offered by prison officials had little persuasive influence. Yet there is plentiful evidence that the opposite is the case, and that prisoners can be motivated a great deal not only by the prospect of freedom (early release, home leave), but also by 'details' whose significance is amplified in the spartan context of the prison (extra spending money, in-cell televisions). In the UK, the introduction of the incentives and earned privileges (IEP) scheme in 1995 was explicitly guided by the assumption that prisoners were more likely to comply when good behaviour brought material benefits (Liebling et al. 1997). Such rational choice models of prisoner behaviour are flawed: many prisoners are not 'rational choice' thinkers, and resent being addressed by a 'carrot and stick' approach to behaviour modification, especially if it is implemented unfairly. Nonetheless, by easing the material deficits of imprisonment through formal channels (rather than leaving them to be filled by informal arrangements between prisoners), prison officials have reduced both the need for peer solidarity and the basis of collective identification. Prisoners do not share the same predicament, and focus on individual rather than collective concerns. Prospects and living standards can be more easily enhanced through compliance rather than collective action, while the material improvements on offer directly reduce the feelings of deprivation that can inflame group unrest.

Second, it is not the case that prisoners will inevitably lack any 'inner moral compulsion to obey' (Sykes 1958: 48). Few prisoners dispute the right of the state to imprison them and some 'enthusiasts' place themselves on the same moral plane as the institution, expressing shame about their previous behaviour and identifying themselves as fundamentally non-criminal people (Crewe 2009). More importantly, the degree to which prisoners submit to a regime depends partly on *how* their imprisonment is delivered, and whether it conforms to broad principles of justice. Prisoners recognize the difference between treatment that is fair, humane and respectful, or brutal, inconsistent and dehumanizing (Sparks et al. 1996; Liebling, with Arnold 2004). These differentials are critical, for even when prisoners dislike the outcomes of institutional practices, they are more likely to comply with them and accept the prison's authority if decisions and treatment can be justified in terms of the values, beliefs and expectations that prisoners hold. Here, then, the interface between officers and prisoners is critical. Prisoners will make normative judgements about an establishment according to its material provisions – decent cells, access to telephones – and whether its systems deliver fair procedures and consistent outcomes. However, as frontline representatives of the prison, it is officers whose everyday behaviour comes to embody the perceived legitimacy of the institution. It is at the level of staff–prisoner relations that the prison's everyday moral climate is determined, and its pains cushioned and crystallized.

Third, although, as Sykes suggested, physical force remains a dangerous and inefficient way of running a prison with complex institutional tasks, it is by no means impossible to generate order through highly coercive and controlled regimes. In the USA, supermax prisons do this by separating prisoners from each other, minimizing contact between prisoners and staff, and employing stringent measures of restraint (e.g. handcuffs, leg irons) whenever dealing with prisoners. These organizations are a world away from the Big House, in which prisoners mixed relatively freely and were integrated into the daily maintenance of the establishment. In the UK, although very few prisoners exist in supermax-style conditions, situational control measures introduced since the widespread disturbances of 1990 – smaller wings, fewer communal areas, more surveillance – have placed greater limits upon movement, association and potential disorder. As Foucault (1977) highlighted, the use of timetabling and spatial organization is a key means by which prisons – and other state institutions such as schools and hospitals – regulate and discipline their members.

The achievement of control via architecture and restraint contributes to a fourth source of order: fatalistic resignation or 'dull compulsion'. For many prisoners, the sheer power imbalance within the prison, the stultifying routine, and the constant symbolic reminders of powerlessness (security cameras, barbed wire, etc.) lead to a feeling that nothing much can be done about one's current predicament. This distinction between power that is accepted as legitimate and power that is taken for granted is crucial. Not least, it would be a mistake to interpret the absence of open resistance as an indication of normative consent. As analysis of the Strangeways riot implies (Carrabine 2004), if the only thing preventing insurrection is acquiescence to the apparent inevitability of the situation, once this impression is shattered, a disturbance might very rapidly spread.

There is a great deal of variation in the degree to which prisons achieve order, and the means by which they do so. Supermax prisons come close to embodying a control–coercion model of order, while democratic–therapeutic prisons such as Barlinnie and Grendon have achieved high levels of legitimacy, even when dealing with difficult prisoners (see Boyle 1984; Sparks et al. 1996; Stevens 2013). On the whole, though, most establishments rely on a combination of techniques to achieve stability, and cannot be characterized according to a simple model of coercion or consent. In the UK, in recent years, situational control measures and the IEP scheme have co-existed alongside efforts to boost legitimacy through improved physical conditions, and attempts to humanely recondition staff cultures. Meanwhile, prisoners are increasingly encouraged to self-govern and assume responsibility for the terms of their own incarceration, in a way that represents neither direct coercion nor autonomous consent (Garland 1997; Liebling, with Arnold 2004; Crewe 2009). They participate in defining their own sentence plans, but have no option to refuse one; they are motivated to address their offending behaviour, with the knowledge that there are implications in not doing so for their release date; and they are aware that to gain 'enhanced' status, passive obedience is insufficient. Through a discourse of threats and opportunities, then, they are channelled and stimulated into producing institutionally desirable behaviour.

Different ways of accomplishing order have different effects. Sparks et al. (1996) have demonstrated how an apparently more 'liberal' and legitimate prison might harbour more backstage violence than one that appears more authoritarian. However, everyday violence differs significantly from the breakdown of order, which is more likely to occur in less legitimate regimes, where prisoners feel a profound 'lack of justice' (Woolf 1991: para. 9.24).[5] While riots have multifaceted roots, recent theories suggest that they tend to occur when widespread prisoner grievances exist alongside administrative confusion and disorganization (Useem and Kimball 1989). However, if these were the only conditions necessary to provoke major disturbances, they would happen far more frequently than they do. To understand why riots occur in particular times and places, we need to theorize the pleasures and triggers of disruptive activity, and explore the mechanisms by which disorder spreads.

Sykes's claim that unrest occurred when the informal power of inmate leaders was undermined was simplistic, but there remains much of value in his analysis of the role of the prisoner community in securing order. First, the prisoner hierarchy is influenced by the deficits of prison life. By shaping these deficits, institutions can mould the adaptations that prisoners are required to make and the currency within the prisoner community of violence, trade and manipulation. Second, where overseen judiciously, the capacity of prisoners to self-govern can be harnessed to positive effect. Prisoners themselves can reduce levels of alienation and can benefit from being placed in roles that allow them to take responsibility and mentor their peers. In turn, prison officials may not want *too much* solidarity among prisoners, but nor do they want the prisoner community to fragment into clusters of mutually hostile, untrusting individuals. The shape of the inmate body – the nature of leadership, the balance of different prisoner groups, levels of trust and friendship – can contribute positively or negatively to order. Finally, even if negotiation no longer seems the most effective means of securing order, prisons *are* systems of cooperation, where staff and prisoners have many common interests and values, and where these values contribute in significant ways to legitimacy, well-being and order. In the USA, DiIulio (1987) has argued, with great influence, that the informal accommodation approved by Sykes was a disastrous surrender of authority whose resulting lawlessness was inevitable. However, a prison that relies on rules and restrictions, at the cost of relationships and consensus, might produce stability at the price of pain and social resentment.

Conclusion

The sociology of prison life covers a vast landscape, but has been mapped selectively and sporadically. Meaningful comparisons between the inner social world of prisons in different jurisdictions are made difficult by the scarcity of comparative ethnographic studies. One reason why, in the USA, studies of the prisoner society have become less common is that the relationship between policymakers and the penological community has changed. At the time of Sykes's study, social science was regarded as having a key role in forging a more ordered and successful penal system (see Chapter 37, this volume). Now, such optimism about the state's ability to manage society through informed governance of its social institutions has receded, and there is less interest in prison social life as an object of study and intervention. In the era of the 'warehouse prison' and the supermax, prisoners are to be stored, contained and processed: their values, adaptations and social relationships are somewhat irrelevant to prison managers. There are more risks than gains in allowing researchers to document this world and, at a time when the prison population is exploding, prison ethnography is 'not merely an endangered species but a virtually extinct one' (Wacquant 2002: 385).

In the UK and some other European countries – notably, Belgium and Norway – prison research seems to be undergoing something of a revival, and the links between policymakers and academics remain relatively strong. There are dangers that research findings become simplistically co-opted into managerial agendas, and that attempts to reform the prison serve to legitimate its use as a substitute for broader social policy and welfare provision, but the dangers of leaving the prison's culture and social dynamics uncharted are surely greater. This is not only to document what prisons are like and how they are experienced, but to help address questions about their social roles and consequences – what they should and should not be for, and what claims can be made for them. Likewise, prisons are more than just abstract systems, and their study should continue to illustrate not only the humanity of prisoners, but the more universal aspects of humanity – distress, endurance, adaptation and social organization – that the prison's special conditions make visible.

Notes

1 Since discussions of prison staff can be found elsewhere in this volume, although the chapter will highlight how institutional factors influence the prison's inner world, it will not dwell on issues such as staff practices or the effects of the prison on its workers.
2 Beyond the ghetto, prison culture has penetrated the mainstream through rap music, clothing (e.g. baggy, belt-less trousers), tattoos, slang, and a range of body gestures that register the perverse kudos of incarceration among those people least likely to experience it.
3 Sykes (1956) noted that 38% of his sample were black, but said little else about race. Writing some years later (Sykes 1995), he explained that researchers at the time assumed that the experiences of white and black prisoners were the same, and that being white also made it more difficult to undertake research among black prisoners.
4 In most UK prisons, sex offenders are housed separately from other prisoners, but continue to function in the moral hierarchy of mainstream prisoners as examples of what they distinguish themselves from.
5 There is insufficient space here to explore the causes of interpersonal violence, but see Edgar et al. (2003) for a symbolic interactionist analysis, and Gambetta (2005) and Kaminski (2004) for innovative discussions based upon behavioural and game theory.

Bibliography

Bosworth, M. (1999) *Engendering Resistance: Agency and Power in Women's Prisons*, Aldershot: Dartmouth.
Boyle, J. (1984) *The Pain of Confinement*, Edinburgh: Canongate.
Bukstel, L. and Kilman, P. (1980) 'Psychological Effects of Imprisonment on Confined Individuals', *Psychological Bulletin* 88: 469–493.
Carlen, P. (1983) *Women's Imprisonment: A Study in Social Control*, London: Routledge & Kegan Paul.
Carlen, P. (1998) *Sledgehammer: Women's Imprisonment at the Millennium*, Basingstoke: Macmillan.
Carrabine, E. (2004) *Power, Discourse and Resistance: A Genealogy of the Strangeways Prison Riot*, Dartmouth: Ashgate.
Carrabine, E. (2005) 'Prison Riots, Social Order and the Problem of Legitimacy', *British Journal of Criminology* 45: 896–913.
Carrabine, E. and Longhurst, B. (1998) 'Gender and Prison Organisation: Some Comments on Masculinities and Prison Management', *The Howard Journal* 37(2): 161–176.
Cheliotis, L. and Liebling, A. (2006) 'Race Matters in British Prisons', *British Journal of Criminology* 46(2): 286–317.
Christie, N. (1981) *Limits to Pain*, Oxford: Martin Robertson.
Clemmer, D. (1958 [1940]) *The Prison Community*, second edn, New York: Holt, Rinehart and Winston.
Cohen, S. and Taylor, L. (1972) *Psychological Survival: The Experience of Long-Term Imprisonment*, Harmondsworth: Penguin.
Crawley, E. (2005) 'Institutional Thoughtlessness in Prisons and its Impacts on the Day-to-Day Prison', *Journal of Contemporary Criminal Justice* 21: 350–363.
Crewe, B. (2005a) 'Codes and Conventions: The Terms and Conditions of Contemporary Inmate Values', in A. Liebling and S. Maruna (eds) *The Effects of Imprisonment*, Cullompton: Willan, 177–208.
Crewe, B. (2005b) 'The Prisoner Society in the Era of Hard Drugs', *Punishment and Society* 7(4): 457–481.

Crewe, B. (2009) *The Prisoner Society: Power, Adaptation and Social Life in an English Prison*, Oxford: Oxford University Press, Clarendon.

Crewe, B., Bennett, P., Smith, A. and Warr, J. (2014) 'The Emotional Geography of Prison Life', *Theoretical Criminology* 18(1): 56–74.

DiIulio, J. (1987) *Governing Prisons: A Comparative Study of Correctional Management*, New York: The Free Press.

Durkheim, E. (1933) *The Division of Labour in Society*, New York: The Free Press.

Edgar, K., O'Donnell, I. and Martin, C. (2003) *Prison Violence: The Dynamics of Conflict, Fear and Power*, Cullompton: Willan.

Foucault, M. (1977) *Discipline and Punish: The Birth of the Prison*, Harmondsworth: Penguin.

Foucault, M. (1978) *The History of Sexuality*, Vol. I, trans. Robert Hurley, New York: Pantheon.

Foucault, M. (1991) 'Governmentality', in G. Burchell, C. Gordon and P. Miller (eds) *The Foucault Effect*, Hemel Hempstead: Harvester Wheatsheaf, 87–104.

Gambetta, D. (2005) 'Why Prisoners Fight', in *Crimes and Signs: Cracking the Codes of the Underworld*, Princeton, NJ: Princeton University Press.

Garland, D. (1997) '"Governmentality" and the Problem of Crime: Foucault, Sociology, Criminology', *Theoretical Criminology* 1: 173–214.

Garland, D. (2001) *The Culture of Control: Crime and Social Order in Contemporary Society*, Oxford: Oxford University Press.

Genders, E. and Player, E. (1989) *Race Relations in Prisons*, Oxford: Oxford University Press.

Giallombardo, R. (1966) *Society of Women: A Study of a Women's Prison*, New York: John Wiley.

Goffman, E. (1961) *Asylums: Essays on the Social Situation of Mental Patients and Other Inmates*, Harmondsworth: Penguin.

Hassine, V. (1999) *Life Without Parole: Living in Prison Today*, Los Angeles, CA: Roxbury Publishing Company.

HMCIP (HM Chief Inspector of Prisons) (2001) *HM YOI and Remand Centre Feltham*, London: Home Office.

Howe, A. (1994) *Punish and Critique: Towards a Feminist Analysis of Penality*, London and New York: Routledge.

Irwin, J. (1970) *The Felon*, Englewood Cliffs, NJ: Prentice Hall.

Irwin, J. (1980) *Prisons in Turmoil*, Chicago, IL: Little, Brown.

Irwin, J. (1985) *The Jail*, Oakland, CA: University of California Press.

Irwin, J. (2005) *The Warehouse Prison: Disposal of the New Dangerous Classes*, Los Angeles, CA: Roxbury.

Irwin, J. and Austin, J. (1997) *It's About Time: American's Imprisonment Binge*, second edn, Belmont, CA: Wadsworth.

Irwin, J. and Cressey, D.R. (1962) 'Thieves, Convicts and the Inmate Culture', *Social Problems* 10: 142–155.

Jacobs, J. (1974) 'Street Gangs Behind Bars', *Social Problems* 21(3): 395–409.

Jacobs, J. (1977) *Stateville: The Penitentiary in Mass Society*, Chicago, IL: University of Chicago Press.

Jacobs, J. (1983) *New Perspectives on Prisons and Imprisonment*, Ithaca, NY: Cornell University Press.

Johnson, R. (1987) *Hard Time: Understanding and Reforming the Prison*, Pacific Grove, CA: Brooks/ Cole Publishing.

Kaminski, C. (2004) *Games Prisoners Play: The Tragicomic Worlds of Polish Prison*, Princeton, NJ: Princeton University Press.

King, R. and Elliott, K. (1977) *Albany: Birth of a Prison – End of an Era*, London: Routledge & Kegan Paul.

Kruttschnitt, C. and Gartner, R. (2005) *Marking Time in the Golden State: Women's Imprisonment in California*, Cambridge: Cambridge University Press.

Liebling, A. (1992) *Suicides in Prison*, London: Routledge Press.

Liebling, A. (1999) 'Prison Suicide and Prisoner Coping', in M. Tonry and J. Petersilia (eds) *Crime and Justice: A Review of Research*, Vol. 26, Chicago, IL: University of Chicago Press, 283–360.

Liebling, A., with Arnold, H. (2004) *Prisons and their Moral Performance: A Study of Values, Quality, and Prison Life*, Oxford: Clarendon Press.

Liebling, A. and Arnold, H. (2012) 'Social Relationships between Prisoners in a Maximum Security Prison: Violence, Faith, and the Declining Nature of Trust', *Journal of Criminal Justice* 40: 413–424.

Liebling, A., Arnold, H. and Straub, C. (2012) *An Exploration of Staff-Prisoner Relationships at HMP Whitemoor: Twelve Years On*, London: Ministry of Justice.

Liebling, A., Muir, G., Rose, G. and Bottoms, A.E. (1997) 'An Evaluation of Incentives and Earned Privileges: Final Report to the Prison Service', unpublished report to the Home Office, London.

McDermott, K. and King, R. (1988) 'Mind Games: Where the Action is in Prisons', *British Journal of Criminology* 28(3): 357–377.

McEvoy, K. (2000) *Paramilitary Imprisonment in Northern Ireland*, Oxford: Clarendon Press.

Mathiesen, T. (1965) *The Defences of the Weak: A Sociological Study of a Norwegian Correctional Institution*, London: Tavistock.

Merton, R. (1938) 'Social Structure and Anomie', *American Sociological Review* 3: 672–682.

Morgan, R. (2002) 'Imprisonment: A Brief History, the Contemporary Scene, and Likely Prospects', in M. Maguire, R. Morgan and R. Reiner (eds) *The Oxford Handbook of Criminology*, Oxford: Oxford University Press.

Morris, P. and Morris, T. (1963) *Pentonville: A Sociological Study of an English Prison*, London: Routledge & Kegan Paul.

Newton, C. (1994) 'Gender Theory and Prison Sociology: Using Theories of Masculinities to Interpret the Sociology of Prisons for Men', *The Howard Journal* 33(3): 193–202.

O'Donnell, I. (2004) 'Prison Rape in Context', *British Journal of Criminology* 44: 241–255.

Owen, B. (1998) *In the Mix: Struggle and Survival in a Women's Prison*, Albany: State University of New York Press.

Phillips, C. (2012) *The Multicultural Prison: Ethnicity, Masculinity, and Social Relations*, Oxford: Oxford University Press.

Reisig, M.D. (2001) 'The Champion, Contender, and Challenger: Top Ranked Books in Prison Studies', *The Prison Journal* 81(3): 389–407.

Rusche, G. and Kirchheimer, O. (1939) *Punishment and Social Structure*, New York: Russell and Russell.

Sabo, D., Kupers, T. and London, W. (eds) (2001) *Prison Masculinities*, Philadelphia, PA: Temple University Press.

Sapsford, R.J. (1983) *Life-sentence Prisoners: Reaction, Response and Change*, Milton Keynes: Open University Press.

Scacco, A. (1975) *Rape in Prison*, Springfield, IL: Charles C. Thomas.

Sim, J. (1994) 'Tougher than the Rest? Men in Prison', in T. Newburn and E. Stanko (eds) *Just Boys Doing Business*, London: Routledge.

Simon, J. (2007) *Governing Through Crime: How the War on Crime Transformed American Democracy and Created a Culture of Fear*, Oxford: Oxford University Press.

Skarbek, D. (2014) *The Social Order of the Underworld: How Prison Gangs Govern the American Penal System*, Oxford: Oxford University Press.

Sparks, R., Bottoms, A. and Hay, W. (1996) *Prisons and the Problem of Order*, Oxford: Clarendon Press.

Stevens, A. (2013) *Offender Rehabilitation and Therapeutic Communities: Enabling Change the TC Way*, Abingdon: Routledge.

Sykes, G. (1956) 'Men, Merchants and Toughs: A Study of Reactions to Imprisonment', *Social Problems*: 130–138.

Sykes, G. (1958) *The Society of Captives: A Study of a Maximum-Security Prison*, Princeton, NJ: Princeton University Press.

Sykes, G. (1995) 'The Structural-functional Perspective on Imprisonment', in T. Blomberg and S. Cohen (eds) *Punishment and Social Control: Essays in Honor of Sheldon L. Messinger*, New York: Aldine de Gruyter.

Sykes, G. and Messinger, S. (1960) 'The Inmate Social System', in R.A. Cloward et al. (eds) *Theoretical Studies in the Social Organization of the Prison*, New York: Social Science Research Council, 5–19.

Toch, H. (1977) *Living in Prison: The Ecology of Survival*, New York: The Free Press.

Ugelvik, T. (2014) *Power and Resistance in Prison: Doing Time, Doing Freedom*, Basingstoke: Palgrave Macmillan.

Useem, B. and Kimball, P. (1989) *States of Siege: US Prison Riots, 1971–1986*, Oxford: Oxford University Press.

Wacquant, L. (2000) 'The New "Peculiar Institution": On the Prison as Surrogate Ghetto', *Theoretical Criminology* 4(3): 377–389.

Wacquant, L. (2001) 'Deadly Symbiosis: Where Ghetto and Prison Meet and Merge', *Punishment and Society* 3(1): 95–133.

Wacquant, L. (2002) 'The Curious Eclipse of Prison Ethnography in the Age of Mass Incarceration', *Ethnography* 3(4): 371–398.

Walker, S. and Worrall, A. (2000) 'Life as a Woman: The Gendered Pains of Indeterminate Imprisonment', *Prison Service Journal* 132: 27–37.

Ward, D.A. and Kassebaum, G. (1965) *Women's Prison: Sex and Social Structure*, Chicago, IL: Aldine.

Wheeler, S. (1961) 'Socialization in Correctional Communities', *American Sociological Review* 26: 697–712.

Winfree, T., Newbold, G. and Tubb III, H. (2002) 'Prisoner Perspectives on Inmate Culture in New Mexico and New Zealand: A Descriptive Case Study', *The Prison Journal* 82(2): 213–233.

Woolf, L.J. (1991) *Prison Disturbances April 1990: Report of an Inquiry by the Rt Hon. Lord Justice Woolf (Parts I and II) and His Honour Stephen Tumim (Part II)* (The Woolf Report), London: HMSO.

Zaitzow, B. and Thomas, T. (eds) (2003) *Women in Prison: Gender and Social Control*, Boulder, CO: Lynne Rienner Publishers.

Zamble, E. and Porporino, F.J. (1988) *Coping, Behaviour and Adaptation in Prisons Inmates*, Secaucus, NJ: Springer-Verlag.

The aims of imprisonment

Ian O'Donnell

Introduction

The stated aims of imprisonment became markedly less ambitious when the confidence that characterized the 19th-century reform movement was displaced by a realization that places of confinement – no matter how well designed or humanely intentioned – could never 'grind rogues honest and idle men industrious'. Today the emphasis is on risk reduction and performance management; lofty aspirations have been trumped by narrow measures of target delivery. In an attempt to find principled common ground upon which to advance the debate, a new formulation is offered in this chapter, namely: the aim of imprisonment is to reconstitute the prisoner's spatiotemporal world without causing avoidable collateral damage. It is argued that this minimalist statement provides a foundation upon which to build prison regimes that are oriented towards the future and acknowledge that all prisoners, no matter what they have done, possess the capacity to redirect their lives. Devoid of hope, imprisonment is pointless pain:

> II. [T]he supreme aim of prison discipline is the reformation of criminals, not the infliction of vindictive suffering ...

> XIV. The prisoner's self-respect should be cultivated to the utmost ... There is no greater mistake in the whole compass of penal discipline, than its studied imposition of degradation as part of punishment. Such imposition destroys every better impulse and aspiration. It crushes the weak, irritates the strong, and indisposes all to submission and reform. It is trampling where we ought to raise ...

> XXII. The state has not discharged its whole duty to the criminal when it has punished him, nor even when it has reformed him. Having raised him up, it has the further duty to aid in holding him up.
> (Principles promulgated by the congress of the National Prison Association held in Cincinnati, Ohio, in October 1870, cited in Wines 1871: 541–7)

Antecedents

Two hundred years ago the aims of imprisonment were clear, namely: (i) to contain debtors until what was owed was paid; (ii) to detain accused persons pending trial; (iii) to hold convicted persons pending the execution of the sentence of the court (e.g. corporal or capital punishment, or transportation); (iv) to punish offenders for periods so brief that ascribing to them a purpose other than incapacitation seems somewhat grandiose – little can really be expected of prison terms that are completed in a matter of days or weeks; (v) to profit gaolers.

The focus of the debate about the aims of imprisonment was sharpened by the stuttering emergence, across Europe and the USA, of a penal philosophy that stressed the importance of reflective solitude as an engine for reform. This coincided with, and was given impetus by, the discovery of architectural solutions to the problem of unauthorized prisoner communication which meant that prisons could be designed to enforce silent separation, something that had not previously been possible. For a time in the early 19th century there was a close alignment between broadly agreed aims (i.e. reformation underpinned by deterrence), the technologies required to deliver them (e.g. timetables, surveillance, diet, cellular accommodation), the associated regimes (whether congregate and silent – the Auburn system, or separate – the Pennsylvania system), and administrative imperatives (e.g. uniformity, hierarchy, security, micro-regulation). This cohesion is evident in the adoption of the Pennsylvania system of prison discipline across much of Europe. Prison chaplains enthusiastically propounded the merits of this approach and their assertive writings, assured tone and assumed universality of appeal have few parallels today. The rival Auburn system, which thrived in the USA, was characterized by a lower level of confidence in the individual prisoner's capacity to reform and the maintenance of silence required the frequent use of the whip (for a review and reappraisal of these competing paradigms, see O'Donnell 2014: Chapters 1, 2; see also Chapter 2 of this volume).

Adding urgency to the debate in the UK was the shift in temporal parameters that accompanied the ending of transportation. If men and women were to be incarcerated for years, some thought had to be given to why, as well as to how and where. The Penal Servitude Acts of 1853 and 1857 played an important, but often overlooked, role in this regard. Prior to their enactment the primary aim of the prison was to hold convicts for a fixed period of time in order to ready them for a new life in the colonies (minor offenders, debtors and those on remand continued to be sent to local gaols for brief periods). When the option of transportation was withdrawn, men and women faced the prospect of spending years behind bars on home soil, something that had not previously been contemplated. This stretching of time horizons forced a reappraisal of penal purposes at a juncture when the optimism that had breathed life into the separate system was waning. Consequently the emphasis shifted away from the prison cell as a crucible for personal transformation and it became, for a time, a place of unyielding discipline, of hard labour, hard fare and a hard bed. While the clarity of purpose may have dulled somewhat, the technologies, regimes and administrative imperatives remained largely unchanged. Rupturing the link between what was desired and how this was to be delivered had lasting ramifications. Subsequent waves of hope and despair occurred within a built environment that was slow to change, and against a background where discipline was pursued as an end in itself, untethered from a reformative ethic.

The confidence of the early reformers evaporated when it became apparent that new prison designs, and the muscular Christianity espoused by their advocates, were insufficient to the task of inspiring wholesale cognitive, spiritual and behavioural change. A truncated version of the 37 principles espoused by the National Prison Association in the USA in 1870 – three of which were quoted at the start of this chapter – was adopted by the International Penitentiary Congress in London two years later (Wines 1873: 177–8).

Despite initial enthusiasm, these eloquently phrased and ebulliently expressed aspirations soon came to be seen as disconnected from the realities of imprisonment, however noble the sentiments they embodied.

Thinking about aims requires consideration of how they have changed over time. The disappearance of benevolent intent meant that imprisonment felt different to those forced to endure its strictures. Despite the harshness of the silent and separate systems, and concern about the adverse mental health implications of regimes that required the termination of meaningful human relationships, their champions wished to force change upon the prisoner so that when he or she re-entered society it was on mutually beneficial terms. Bentham (1843: 226) described the panopticon prison as 'a mill for grinding rogues honest and idle men industrious', a description that might equally be applied to prisons of the late 19th century when the hope that penal treatment could bring the prisoner closer to God, and into harmony with his law-abiding fellows, proved to be misplaced. However grim Bentham's philosophy might appear, it is a world away from grinding without purpose.

Contrast the use of solitary confinement in Eastern State Penitentiary in Philadelphia, or Pentonville prison in London, or any of their numerous imitators in the 1800s, with the 20th-century manifestation of penal solitude in the supermax (see Chapter 10). There are two important distinctions for present purposes. The first is the absence of any pretence that prolonged isolation is for the good of the prisoner. The second is that for a significant cohort of those so detained, there is no prospect of eventual release, no 'fold' to return to. Supermax custody defines prisoners by their criminal conduct, is pessimistic (at worst) or disinterested (at best) about the possibility of personal change, and its advocates have no compunction about administering a kind of treatment that would be adjudged harsh and degrading by anything but the most elastic of standards. Modern technology allows a studied indifference to be paid to prisoners; they command less personal attention than did their 19th-century predecessors and this reinforces their status not only as morally repugnant but also as socially redundant.

I do not wish to suggest that the past was an unproblematically better place, but simply to advert to the fact that there was a singularity of purpose (especially among the proponents of the Pennsylvania system), and an irrepressible confidence that the stated aims could be delivered that, to a great extent, has disappeared from the discourse. When the first wave of penal optimism receded it was replaced by a lurch to harsh – and hopeless – discipline. In Priestley's (1999: 119) words, 'the darkness closed in around the Victorian prisoner'. However, confidence returned eventually, a rehabilitative ethic came to dominate, and there was renewed emphasis on the individual prisoner's capacity to change in a pro-social direction. The disappointing results of empirical studies and the hasty and erroneous conclusion that nothing worked when it came to prisoner rehabilitation caused a fresh reappraisal of the aims of imprisonment. The wheel of penal change completed another revolution. The emergence in recent decades of cognitive behavioural programmes, along with more sophisticated approaches to programme design and better measurement of effects, has renewed confidence in the potential for imprisonment to catalyse meaningful personal change and to improve community safety. As expectations and the associated aims have risen and fallen, the distance between the opposite ends of the spectrum of penal treatment has reduced considerably. When cognitive behaviourism is supplanted by a new approach, it is likely that the impact on prison regimes will be modest.

Official formulations

So what are the expressed aims of imprisonment today? Box 3.1 presents a selection of official declarations of purpose. This is by no means a representative sample, being biased towards (but not limited to) Anglophone jurisdictions. Nonetheless, the selected mission statements give a flavour of contemporary priorities and indicate the range of public messages that prison systems strive to convey. There are noteworthy omissions. Imprisonment in some parts of the world has been designed to serve the interests of the ruling class, unapologetically and unambiguously, through the suppression of political dissent or the control of prisoners' minds. While forced re-education through labour was abolished in 2013, the aims of imprisonment in China are said to still include political indoctrination (laogai.org, accessed 20 May 2014). The prison systems of many African countries are severely overcrowded, poorly resourced, and controlled by their inmate populations (e.g. Jefferson and Martin 2014; see also Chapter 24). In these circumstances to aim for much more than perimeter security, the avoidance of malnutrition, the containment of infectious diseases and the preservation of bodily integrity, may be to aim unfeasibly high.

Accepting the inevitably limited generalizability of the analysis, it is suggested that examining a range of countries avoids the pitfall of adopting an unreflectively ethnocentric approach and proceeding on the basis that an examination of, for instance, the situation in England and Wales, is necessarily of cross-national significance (the Council of Europe and the United Nations have published detailed sets of prison rules that address the purposes of imprisonment but constraints of space preclude analysis of their contents and how they have been revised over time). With these caveats in mind, what can be learned from the official pronouncements of a cross-section of prison services in developed countries?

Box 3.1 A miscellany of aims

Ireland

'Providing safe and secure custody, dignity of care and rehabilitation to prisoners for safer communities' (www.irishprisons.ie/index.php/about-us/mission-statement).

Scotland

'We will be recognised as a leader in offender management services for prisoners, that help reduce re-offending and offer value for money for the taxpayer. We will maintain secure custody and good order; and we will care for offenders with humanity and provide them with appropriate opportunities' (www.sps.gov.uk/AboutUs/aims-of-the-sps.aspx).

England and Wales

'Her Majesty's Prison Service serves the public by keeping in custody those committed by the courts. Our duty is to look after them with humanity and help them lead law-abiding and useful lives in custody and after release' (www.justice.gov.uk/about/hmps).

Finland

'The goals of the Criminal Sanctions Agency are to contribute to the security in society by maintaining a lawful and safe system of enforcement of sanctions and reduce recidivism and endeavour to break social exclusion that also reproduces crime' (www.rikosseuraamus.fi/en/index/criminalsanctionsagency/goalsvaluesandprinciples.html).

Sweden

'Our vision is that spending time in the prison and probation system will bring about change, not simply provide secure custody. We want to encourage our clients to live a better life after serving their sentence' (www.kriminalvarden.se/sv/Other-languages/).

Canada

'The Correctional Service of Canada, as part of the criminal justice system and respecting the rule of law, contributes to public safety by actively encouraging and assisting offenders to become law-abiding citizens, while exercising reasonable, safe, secure and humane control' (www.csc-scc.gc.ca/hist/mission-eng.shtml).

New Zealand

'The Department of Corrections works to make New Zealand a better, safer place by protecting the public from those who can cause harm and reducing re-offending' (www.corrections.govt.nz/about_us.html).

USA (Federal Bureau of Prisons)

'It is the mission of the Federal Bureau of Prisons to protect society by confining offenders in the controlled environments of prisons and community-based facilities that are safe, humane, cost-efficient, and appropriately secure, and that provide work and other self-improvement opportunities to assist offenders in becoming law-abiding citizens' (www.bop.gov/about/agency/agency_pillars.jsp).

(All website addresses correct as of 20 May 2014)

Most official statements mention post-release behaviour or public protection. It is a high expectation to have of any institution that it would continue to be influential even when no longer part of an individual's life, but an enduring impact is commonly demanded of the prison. Mission statements tend to be silent on the needs of particular prisoner groupings, such as persons on remand, women, juveniles, foreign nationals and those sentenced to die behind bars (whether having received the death penalty, a sentence of life without parole or a determinate sentence that exceeds their life expectancy). These groups may pose particular challenges and require bespoke aims.

Official formulas tend not to mention staff or victims, although both of these con-
stituencies are name-checked in the mission statements of several US states, such as
Oklahoma ('Our mission is to protect the public, to protect the employee, to protect the
offender'; www.ok.gov/doc/About_Us/Agency_Mission/index.html, accessed 20 May
2014) and Texas ('The mission of the Texas Department of Criminal Justice is to provide
public safety, promote positive change in offender behavior, reintegrate offenders into
society, and assist victims of crime'; www.tdcj.state.tx.us/index.html, accessed 20 May
2014). Some mention value for money (e.g. Scotland, US Federal Bureau of Prisons).
Others stress dignity (e.g. Ireland). Finland refers to tackling social exclusion in order to
reduce the likelihood of future crime. Sweden connects prison and probation treatment.
Canada draws attention to the rule of law. None mentions the saving of prisoners' souls,
which was a pressing concern for those who defined the aims of imprisonment in previous eras. While a religious dimension is largely absent from the official discourse, it
continues to resonate among prisoners, who have long found comfort, and a higher
purpose, in the tenets of Christianity and, more recently and in increasing numbers, in
Islam (Pew Forum on Religion and Public Life 2012). In this way their individual and
collective aims are facilitated by prison systems that will not always share them.

Mission statements are accompanied by targets, the achievement of which is considered to indicate progress towards realizing the mission. These targets and the associated
tasks are specified with varying degrees of precision. If they are to be of value they must
be amenable to reliable measurement, but if they are too narrowly defined they lose
contact with the worlds they are supposed to shape and become empty signifiers.

Thinking in terms of aims inclines us towards the adoption of an instrumental
approach which emphasizes what works (and at what cost) as opposed to what is right
(and for whom). It frames problems so that they are susceptible to technical solutions and
thereby closes off potentially fruitful lines of enquiry. It risks prioritizing means over
ends. Such a focus has a seductive appeal in that it offers the possibility of demonstrable
progress, however faltering it may prove to be. It privileges calculating and comparing.
However, it deflects attention from the ethics of imprisonment and the place of prison in
society. As Garland (1991: 117) expressed it:

> [P]enal measures and institutions have social determinants that have little to do with
> the need for law and order, social effects that go well beyond the business of crime
> control, and a symbolic significance that routinely engages a wide population,
> making it inappropriate to think of them in purely instrumental terms.

An instrumental view of the prison might examine its impact in terms of reducing crime
and incapacitating offenders. This in turn lends itself to questions regarding efficiency and
economy, the design of attainable targets, and performance monitoring; it is the dominant perspective in corrections today. It could be argued that there has been a further
shift away from the objective of crime control – the results of recidivism studies have
dented confidence that it is achievable – and towards the management of prison populations, almost regardless of any post-release effects. The emphasis has narrowed from
having an impact on the world outside to ensuring the smooth running of the prisoner
society. There is an associated shift from outcomes to outputs. For example, rather than
aiming to reduce reoffending, the target becomes the completion rate for offending
behaviour programmes.

While managerial approaches are fraught with difficulty in complex human environments such as prisons, especially when management imperatives become disconnected from a broader sense of purpose, it would be incorrect to suggest that precise measurements and ulterior motives are incompatible. The 18th- and 19th-century prison reformers were great counters and calibrators. They did not deviate from the timetable. They devised dietary scales that ensured prisoners' appetites were never sated while starvation was kept at bay (just). They tallied the number of times the crank had been turned and the treadwheel spun and adjusted the resistance so that these pointless exercises brought prisoners to the brink of exhaustion but did not render them unfit for the next day's exertions. However, all of this counting and checking and rule enforcement was aligned with clear aims, at least in the early years – namely, the prevention of contagion (whether of physical diseases or criminal beliefs), the assertion of a principle of less eligibility, and the promotion of deterrence and reformation as two sides of the same providential coin. This overarching purpose and the accompanying belief that time apart would prompt self-examination ensured a firmness of resolve even when fears surfaced regarding the deleterious consequences of the new arrangements. When full-throttled confidence was supplanted by uncertainty, then scepticism, and finally pessimism, the counting continued but to no apparent end.

Attempting a new definition

Are there any grounds for consensus when it comes to formulating the aims of imprisonment? One aim around which it is likely that wide agreement could be secured is that prisons should have a null effect. In other words, strenuous efforts should be made to ensure that their occupants are no worse off at the end of their sentences than at the beginning. After all, they have been sent there *as* punishment not *for* punishment. If we define 'worse off' in terms of harm endured as well as risk posed, the corollary is that prisoners must be safe, that their bodily integrity must not be compromised. There will always be some observers who are careless as to the consequences of incarceration for the prisoner society, who would not be concerned if prisoners wreaked havoc on each other, but even those espousing such a view would desire that staff were not caught in the cross-fire and that communities were not endangered when prisoners were released. Imprisonment is associated with a range of unavoidable harms such as the rupturing of community and family ties and the diminution of career prospects. The goal for the prison system must be to anticipate these harms and soften their impact while not adding to them.

Another aim around which it would be possible to generate consensus is that imprisonment should involve the deprivation of liberty. This is vitiated when prisoners escape. Even at open prisons, where perimeter security is largely non-existent, the retention of prisoners is a sine qua non. While prisoners can often influence the duration and conditions of their confinement through their behaviour, they cannot administer their sentences according to personal priorities and proclivities.

Imprisonment necessitates the loss of time. Courts award punishments measured in units of time and the point of any prison system is to ensure that they are served. The removal of sovereignty over time is an aim of imprisonment the effects of which cannot be dodged. The prisoner must march to a new disciplinary cadence and while liberty can at least be restored, lost time cannot be. This is something of which prisoners are acutely aware and against which they marshal whatever resources are at their disposal (O'Donnell 2014: Chapter 10). This allows us to posit the following definition. Stripped to its undeniable essentials, the aim of imprisonment is to reconstitute the prisoner's spatio-temporal world without causing avoidable collateral damage. A statement of intent along these lines would seem appropriate to prison systems everywhere and it is difficult to imagine that it would meet with principled resistance. Although minimalist, it acts as a foundation upon which to layer additional, and always subsidiary, aims. It has the twin virtues of clarity and parsimony.

The Irish political prisoner Michael Davitt (1885: 180) described hope as the 'all-sustaining prison virtue'. Devoid of hope, imprisonment is pointless pain. This is degrading for all concerned. If the carceral experience can be imbued with the possibility of something better this will redound to our collective advantage. By definition, hope is slippery, elusive and difficult to operationalize. It cannot be weighed or measured. Nonetheless, there is a need to orientate prison treatment towards the future so that prisoners' capacity to change their lives for the better is acknowledged. There is something to be said for striving towards a worthwhile goal even if it remains somewhat inchoate. There is something to be said, also, for accepting that prisoners are not entirely defined by their pasts. Like all of us, their life stories can be re-narrated and later chapters can be very different in style and substance from earlier ones. Hope is the state of remaining open to this possibility.

There are clear parallels here with the debate about 'humane containment' versus 'positive custody' that took place in England and Wales in the late 1970s and early 1980s. There was a concern that to allow the former concept to act as an organizing principle for prison regimes was to require staff to work in a moral vacuum and to expect too little of prisoners (see Bottoms 1990). Such an approach, it was believed, would be damaging because it would strip the prison experience of a wider sense of purpose. Undergirding my cautiously expressed aim is the firm belief that improved behaviour is a welcome bonus and should always be hoped for and worked towards.

Accepting the desire for a null effect as a starting place, what does this mean? The first implication is that prisoners must be at least as safe as an equivalent group in the community. The evidence suggests that when it comes to lethal violence they are (Mumola 2005; Sattar 2001); when it comes to sexual victimization they may not be, especially in the USA (O'Donnell 2004); and when it comes to routine victimization not enough is known. It cannot be gainsaid that assault, theft and robbery are common in prisons (Edgar et al. 2012), but whether they are significantly more hazardous environments than the areas of urban deprivation from which many prisoners are drawn, and the domestic environments in which they dwell, we cannot be certain. Without doubt, prisoners should be safe from the predations of staff. Regrettably, they are not (Kaiser and Stannow 2013). This is an important difference from community life, where it does not appear that offenders face the threat of being sexually violated by authority figures to whom they report.

The second dimension of the null effect relates to post-release behaviour. Does imprisonment place society at elevated risk? There are three possible answers to this question. First, that risk is unchanged but put in abeyance. Such an outcome may disappoint but it is consistent with the achievement of a null effect. Second, that risk is reduced and the community to which the prisoner returns is safer as a result. This may be a consequence of deterrence, rehabilitation, ageing, the removal of suitable targets, or some other process, and it is an improvement on a null effect. Third, that risk is elevated and the prison has failed to meet its most basic aim.

As Box 3.1 shows, prison systems everywhere strive to exceed the modest baseline of neutral spatio-temporal reorientation. Key personnel desire that prisons are secure, safe and humane places for both inmates and staff. They are alive to the potential for prisons to entrench disadvantage. They seek an extramural impact in terms of community protection and, while reluctant to take responsibility for changing the lives of those in their charge, wish to equip prisoners with the tools necessary for self-improvement should they be motivated to learn how to use them. How aims are implemented is influenced by the values and beliefs held by those who are required to give effect to them (e.g. Rutherford 1994) and, significantly, by the relationships between staff and prisoners (Liebling, with Arnold 2004).

A constriction of ambition

It could be argued that there has been shrinkage over time in the breadth of ambition associated with the expressed aims of imprisonment. There has been a shift from the articulation of nebulous aspirations to the specification of tasks that can be measured and targets that are associated with the successful completion of these tasks. Partly this constriction of ambition was brought about by the disappointing results of penal practice; prisoners all too rarely repaid the brimming confidence of the reformers with good behaviour after release. Partly it reflects the encroachment of new ideas about performance management and a sense that the prison should not be immune from the chastening effects of the 'three Es' of economy, efficiency and effectiveness. Partly it is a logical extension of the squeezing out of the person that accompanies advanced bureaucratization when the rule book comes to dictate the terms of engagement (O'Donnell 2011).

It is entirely reasonable, of course, to adopt aims that can be operationalized, but it is important not to lose sight of the fact that what is measured is never more than a proxy for what is important. Performance measures and targets should flow from aims, and regularly be reconciled with them. If the measurement fails, this does not imply that the aim should be jettisoned. Aims that are narrowly focused, uniformly applicable, unfreighted by ideology or complex sentiment, and amenable to quantification appeal to the managerial mind (it is a bonus if they are disconnected from the world outside the prison walls). They have the undoubted advantage of precision, however poorly they grip the complexities of prison life. However, like the metrics that accompany them, they are guilty of offering false hope regarding the potential of ever more precise measurement to capture – or to catalyse – meaningful change. The instrumental approach can efface its alternatives, with aims collapsing into metrics and measurement becoming an end in itself. In this way a sense of purpose can become detached from the day-to-day organization of prison life. The many things that prisons aim to do, and the resources that are devoted to ensure that they are done – quantifiably – eclipse the overarching sense of purpose that might otherwise attend the enterprise. Seeing the completion rate of an offending behaviour course as indicative of anything else is fraught with difficulty.

Modern mission statements, like those included in Box 3.1, are characterized by the qualified nature of their claims. They aid to encourage and to provide opportunities rather than to reform and to cultivate self-respect. Such caution is understandable given the limited positive effects of imprisonment and the reluctance to make claims that will not be supported, but it is more difficult to generate enthusiasm around a mission statement that is descriptive and unambitious than one which suggests the possibility of personal transformation or institutional triumph against the odds. The flipside of extravagant aims is the pessimism that follows when they are not realized (or when the realization dawns that they never will be). The aims embedded within, and emanating from, modern mission statements are predominantly intramural ones: to provide safety, security and order; to ensure compliance with disciplinary codes; to monitor participation in appropriate programmes; and to remain within budget.

Aims have been progressively narrowed, management techniques have become increasingly sophisticated, and the attempt to connect these manifold measures to something that unites and elaborates them is missing. It could be said that today's 'aims' reflect imperatives that relate to the smooth running of the institution rather than the transformation of the prisoner (and, as a corollary, the improvement of society), but what happens when aims conflict and there is no larger sense of purpose that might help to resolve such conflicts? The difficulty with a piecemeal approach is that it reflects a particular view of the prisoner, who is seen in a disaggregated way, rather than as a whole person, whose needs and drives, strengths and weaknesses, history, character and potential, require attention. My minimalist definition of aims does not overcome these difficulties but it remains open to the manifold possibilities associated with human development and maturation.

The prison in society

The aims of prisons cannot be divorced from the characteristics of the societies in which they take root. Local legislative and policy contexts, together with societal values and community sentiment, play a critical role.

Mathiesen (1974: 76–78) argued that imprisonment remained dominant in advanced capitalist countries such as those in Box 3.1 because it served several social functions. The first of these was *expurgatory*: the prison acted as a repository for unproductive members of society who threatened social order. The second was a *power-draining* function: the capacity to resist is reduced through incarceration and oppositional voices become muffled behind prison walls. The third was a *diverting* function: the use of imprisonment, largely targeted at petty offenders, distracts attention from the really damaging crimes of the powerful. The fourth was a *symbolic* function: by turning prisoners into scapegoats, other citizens are reassured of their moral rectitude. Some years later he added a fifth, which he described as an *action* function: by building prisons and legislating for longer sentences the state conveys an impression that something is being done, that decisive action is being taken (Mathiesen 1990: 138).

It would be going too far to equate Mathiesen's social functions with the aims of imprisonment. The value of his critique is that it alerts us to some of the ancillary impacts of imprisonment and the need to place the prison in its national environment to understand what it does and what it might be expected to do. More recently, there have been several attempts to relate cross-national imprisonment rates to varieties of welfare state regime. The earliest of these was probably Kilcommins et al. (2004: 278), who found that 'countries with well-developed, universalistic, generous welfare regimes tend to have lower prison populations than those with low levels of welfare provision'. Box 3.1

comprises a mixture of social democratic (Finland and Sweden) and liberal (USA, Canada, New Zealand, Scotland, Ireland, England and Wales) countries, and it is not surprising that the aims of imprisonment differ according to welfare arrangements. As might be expected, the social democratic mission statements are outward looking and inclusive (e.g. Finland), while the liberal countries prioritize values of cost effectiveness (e.g. USA) and public protection (e.g. New Zealand). The fact that a cursory glance at prison service mission statements raises issues around national political and social priorities demonstrates the importance of viewing prisons in context.

Even if the social functions of imprisonment are seldom spelled out by the architects, administrators and subjects of the system, they remain important. Examining the role of prison in society allows for the possibility that the institution may 'succeed' in some respects just as it 'fails' in others. Indeed, a failure for one observer may be a success for another as the same outcome can lend itself to a variety of interpretations. The prison might 'fail' when it comes to reducing recidivism but 'succeed' in expressing popular revulsion at certain forms of misconduct. Some effects may be welcomed even if they are not aimed for.

The delivery of aims requires the allocation of resources. When Ireland's economy was booming, a commitment was made to expand the prison system with little thought given to the necessity or the wider ramifications; this is an instance of Mathiesen's 'action function' at work. A deep recession caused a change of direction (O'Donnell 2011). Prosaically, then, economic imperatives can have implications for the aims of imprisonment and the role of the prison vis-à-vis other sanctions and measures. This phenomenon is not confined to Ireland. Webster and Doob (2014) have argued that reductions in the prison population in Alberta in the mid-1990s were driven by budget cuts, but given added traction by core Canadian values rooted in the belief that imprisonment plays a minor role in crime control and should be used sparingly.

Garland (1991: 115) suggested that the sociology of punishment offered an analytical framework that was superior to 'the punishment-as-crime-control' or 'punishment-as-moral-problem' approaches of penological studies. This shift of focus downplays concerns about the rationales and effects of punishment and promotes thinking about the social functions that punishment discharges and the relationships between prisons and other institutions. This is a necessary element of any analysis of the prison, which can then be considered from a variety of perspectives, each of which speaks to its possible functions. For example, a Durkheimian might look at imprisonment as enhancing social solidarity and reinforcing social boundaries; a Marxist might prioritize issues of class domination and the need to siphon off surplus labour or to exploit captive populations; a Foucauldian might locate the prison within a broader carceral archipelago, as an instance of a more general disciplinary strategy with surveillance as a route to docility; an Eliasian might emphasize the prison's role in pushing punishment behind the scenes as characterizing a civilizing process. As Garland (1991) noted, and as many chapters in this volume attest, the penal system is not only instrumental in purpose, but also has a cultural style and an historical tradition, which shape the ways in which objectives are pursued.

The value of situating the prison, historically, as but one of a range of sites of social control has largely disappeared from contemporary debate. However, when reinserted, the implications for understanding are profound. As O'Sullivan and O'Donnell (2012: 1–41) have shown, the prison's move to centre stage has occurred against a background where aggregate levels of what these authors term 'coercive confinement' have dropped steeply.

The beneficiaries of this waning culture of control have been numerous women and children whose lives are no longer interrupted by involuntary detention in custodial settings such as psychiatric hospitals, reformatory and industrial schools, mother and baby homes, and Magdalen asylums, places that were experienced as punitive, whatever their expressed rationales. Understanding the aims of imprisonment, therefore, requires consideration of the rise and fall of other modes of incarceration and how these trajectories relate to shifts in family structures, economic opportunities, political priorities and moral imperatives (O'Sullivan and O'Donnell 2012: 250–294). Thinking in terms of coercive confinement allows us to see the prison with fresh eyes. It leads us away from approaches that are rooted in singular interpretations and makes it impossible to consider the prison outside the historical and cultural context that it has shaped and been shaped by. It allows us to draw on the richness of a variety of theoretical traditions and to explore points of convergence and divergence.

What I am attempting to do in this chapter is to keep in sight the social dimensions of punishment as manifest in the prison and to shake off the constraints of an approach that is equated with an examination of instrumental utility. To consider the aims of imprisonment requires loosening the prison-crime nexus and exploring where the prison fits more generally, and why. Absent such contextualization, any attempt at explanation falls short. As this chapter is limited to the aims of 'imprisonment' in particular rather than addressing the aims of 'coercive confinement' more generally, I am relieved of this explanatory burden, but it must be acknowledged that without this wider view, the full picture cannot be painted.

Fragmentation

When it comes to formulating the aims of imprisonment it is necessary to consider who has standing in the debate. Who can speak and who is heard? When multiple voices are raised are they cacophonous or in harmony?

It seems reasonable to suggest that the debate about the prison's role attracts a greater variety of contributors than heretofore. No longer is it restricted to a stratum of legislators and policymakers who had much in common including gender, race, age, social class background and level of educational attainment, and for whom arriving at a consensus was often relatively unproblematic, especially in a context where a high level of public trust could be assumed and crime was not a pressing concern. The situation today is far more fragmented, with numerous actors clamouring to express a view. It is possible that this multiplicity of viewpoints has contributed to a narrowing of ambition and a retrenchment of official aims in order to find a position that excites, at worst, manageable opposition.

The views of legislators may collide with those of judges and prison administrators. Policies and laws may conflict. Communities may wish to have a say, either through the politicians they elect or more directly, on particular issues. Victim organizations have grown in significance, sometimes representing a particular class of victims, sometimes standing for victims (or survivors) in general. Specific victims can act as lightning rods for concerted action. They are often young, vulnerable and horribly violated and may lend their names to legislative initiatives. Prisoners may wish to contribute to the debate and they are sometimes given a voice through organizations like KRUM (in Sweden), KROM (in Norway), KRIM (in Denmark), Preservation of the Rights of Prisoners (in the UK), and the Prisoners' Rights Organisation (in Ireland). Such bodies seldom endure. Even among prisoner organizations there can be dissent and division with little tolerance for certain categories of offender, such as those who commit sex crimes against children (while never mainstream, paedophile support groups had a higher profile in the past; O'Donnell and Milner 2007: 9–15).

Sometimes ex-prisoners can play an important role in creating fresh thinking about the role of imprisonment. Winston Churchill was held captive briefly in a Boer prison and Nelson Mandela spent more than a quarter of a century in custody. While their African experiences were dramatically different, each offered an informed and compassionate voice to the debate about penal reform. Academic commentators, often drawn from the swelling ranks of professional criminologists, sometimes contribute their perspectives in various public forums.

Penal reform bodies also have something to contribute to the debate about aims. The preamble to the 1787 constitution of the Philadelphia Society for Alleviating the Miseries of Public Prisons, which remains in existence as the Pennsylvania Prison Society, set out a number of underlying principles (Anonymous 1987: 1–2), which when read from a distance of almost 230 years, are seen to have lost little of their cogency, even if they have faded from view in many policy contexts. They stress the common humanity of those who find themselves on either side of the law. They express a deep scepticism about the effects of harsh punishment and offer an optimistic view of the human capacity to change direction. They are strongly echoed in the 1870 principles that open this chapter, and are heard more faintly today. These principles are:

- Prisons are 'public' institutions and the public should be concerned about their objectives and their effectiveness.
- Criminals are human beings and not made less so by the commission of crimes.
- It is legitimate to punish those who commit crimes.
- Harsh and degrading treatment tends to increase crime.
- Ways of turning law breakers into law-abiding citizens can be found.
- Society benefits from a system that 'reforms' criminals.

In addition to prisoners, policymakers, victims and reformers of various hues, there is another group that seeks to play a role in determining the aims of imprisonment. This comprises the shareholders in companies that build and manage prisons. In some jurisdictions they are becoming influential.

Where prison privatization exists (largely, it must be said, in the common law world), this brings in its wake an additional – and novel – aim of imprisonment, namely, the creation of shareholder value out of human suffering. Under such funding arrangements, profitability is an essential goal of imprisonment. The wheel has completed another revolution here as the entrepreneurial (and exploitative) gaoler was a much-maligned feature of the pre-reform prison. Today prison managers do not benefit to the immediate financial detriment of prisoners, but the companies that employ them, and their shareholders, have a vested interest in keeping the stock price high. The imperatives of the market also play a role when it comes to selecting appropriate locations for building new prisons, as the construction and operation of these facilities are believed to provide a vital economic stimulus to economically depressed rural communities (a belief that would appear to be exaggerated, according to King et al. 2003).

Oscar Wilde (1891: 301, emphasis in original) lamented in his essay, 'The Soul of Man under Socialism', published several years before his imprisonment, that the sickening lesson of history is not 'the crimes that the wicked have committed, but ... the punishments that the good have inflicted; *and a community is infinitely more brutalised by the habitual employment of punishment, than it is by the occasional occurrence of crime*'. While there is no end to human ingenuity when it comes to inflicting pain, what is novel about today's arrangements is that investors can benefit from its infliction. In the past gaolers made a comfortable living through the extraction of fees from those in their 'care', but they lived in close proximity to the degradation that generated their livelihoods. Recent developments have led to the disturbing scenario whereby shareholders may never set foot in prisons but can grow rich from their existence. The financial imperative has returned with a twist: those who receive the dividends are distanced from the pain that turns their profit.

A final area characterized by novel challenges relates to prisoners serving sentences of life without parole (LWOP) or determinate sentences that exceed their life expectancy. For these prisoners the issues are starkly drawn. When release is no longer a possibility, thinking of the aims of imprisonment in terms of potential societal benefits is highly problematic. What can be expected of a prison system where, for some, the prospects of eventual community return have been obliterated? Looking at LWOP prisoners specifically, there were more of them in Angola prison in Louisiana in the early 21st century – 3,660 according to Ridgeway (2011: 48) – than there were across the entirety of the USA at the end of the 19th century (2,766 in 1890 out of 70,295 prisoners who had been sentenced and for whom further particulars were available; Department of the Interior, Census Office 1896: 199). This prison now has a hospice as well as a more traditional death row. In the former, death is certain and comes soon after arrival there. In the latter, execution is far from inevitable and the wait for it, in maximum-security conditions, is long and fraught. The aim in both places is bleak: to prevent premature death.

Conclusion

There are obvious challenges associated with attempting to define the aims of imprisonment in a way that will take account of the prison's relationship to other carceral institutions, its historical trajectory, the need to accommodate a variety of stakeholder perspectives, and pragmatic considerations around the specification of targets and tasks that are derived from the aims but can still be meaningfully related to them. One way forward is to adopt a minimalist statement of aims such as that set out in this chapter – to reconstitute the prisoner's spatio-temperal world without causing avoidable collateral damage – and to insist that its articulation occurs in a context that is optimistic about the individual's capacity to seize control of, and redirect, his or her life. The degree to which such insistence will be effective will vary by time and place, but it chimes with the mission statements of modern prison services such as those summarized in Box 3.1. What an attitude of hope means for the practical operation of prison regimes is similarly variable but the point is that keeping it firmly in view means that the debate about aims will be regularly resuscitated. It would be regrettable if the search for aims that can be easily and reliably translated into practice was at the expense of necessarily imprecise sentiments about dignity, the cultivation of self-respect and the releasing of human potential.

Bibliography

Anonymous (1987) 'Introduction', *The Prison Journal* 67: 1–37.

Bentham, J. (1843) *The Works of Jeremy Bentham published under the Superintendence of his Executor, John Bowring, Vol. X (Memoirs Part I and Correspondence)*, Edinburgh: William Tait.

Bottoms, A.E. (1990) 'The aims of imprisonment', in D. Garland (ed.) *Justice, Guilt and Forgiveness in the Penal System, Occasional Paper No. 18*, Edinburgh: University of Edinburgh Centre for Theology and Public Issues, 3–36.

Davitt, M. (1885) *Leaves from a Prison Diary, or Lectures to a Solitary Audience*, Vol. 1, London: Chapman and Hall.

Department of the Interior, Census Office (1896) *Report on Crime, Pauperism, and Benevolence in the United States at the Eleventh Census: 1890, Part I Analysis*, Washington, DC: Government Printing Office.

Edgar, K., O'Donnell, I. and Martin, C. (2012 [2003]) *Prison Violence: The Dynamics of Conflict, Fear and Power*, London: Routledge.

Garland, D. (1991) 'Sociological perspectives on punishment', in M. Tonry (ed.) *Crime and Justice: A Review of Research*, Vol. 14, Chicago, IL: University of Chicago Press, 115–165.

Jefferson, A.M. and Martin, T.M. (eds) (2014) 'Everyday prison governance in Africa', *Prison Service Journal* (Special Edition) 212 (March).

Kaiser, D. and Stannow, L. (2013) 'The shame of our prisons: New evidence', *New York Review of Books* 60(16) (24 October).

Kilcommins, S., O'Donnell, I., O'Sullivan, E. and Vaughan, B. (2004) *Crime, Punishment and the Search for Order in Ireland*, Dublin: Institute of Public Administration.

King, R.S., Mauer, M. and Huling, T. (2003) *Big Prisons, Small Towns: Prison Economics in Rural America*, Washington, DC: The Sentencing Project.

Liebling, A., with Arnold, H. (2004) *Prisons and their Moral Performance: A Study of Values, Quality, and Prison Life*, Oxford: Oxford University Press.

Mathiesen, T. (1974) *The Politics of Abolition*, Scandinavian Studies in Criminology No. 4, London: Martin Robertson.

Mathiesen, T. (1990) *Prison on Trial: A Critical Assessment*, London: Sage.

Mumola, C.J. (2005) *Suicide and Homicide in State Prisons and Local Jails, Bureau of Justice Statistics Special Report*, Washington, DC: US Department of Justice.

O'Donnell, I. (2004) 'Prison rape in context', *British Journal of Criminology* 44: 241–255.

O'Donnell, I. (2011) 'Criminology, bureaucracy and unfinished business', in M. Bosworth and C. Hoyle (eds) *What is Criminology?* Oxford: Oxford University Press, 488–501.

O'Donnell, I. (2014) *Prisoners, Solitude, and Time*, Oxford: Oxford University Press.

O'Donnell, I. and Milner, C. (2007) *Child Pornography: Crime, Computers and Society*, Cullompton: Willan.

O'Sullivan, E. and O'Donnell, I. (eds) (2012) *Coercive Confinement in Ireland: Patients, Prisoners and Penitents*, Manchester: Manchester University Press.

Pew Forum on Religion and Public Life (2012) *Religion in Prisons: A 50-State Survey of Prison Chaplains*, Washington, DC: Pew Research Center.

Priestley, P. (1999 [1985]) *Victorian Prison Lives: English Prison Biography 1830–1914*, London: Pimlico.

Ridgeway, J. (2011) 'God's own warden', *Mother Jones*, July/August: 44–51.

Rutherford, A. (1994) *Criminal Justice and the Pursuit of Decency*, Winchester: Waterside Press.

Sattar, G. (2001) *Rates and Causes of Death among Prisoners and Offenders under Community Supervision*, Home Office Research Study 231, London: Home Office Research, Development and Statistics Directorate.

Webster, C.M. and Doob, A.N. (2014) 'Penal reform "Canadian style": Fiscal responsibility and decarceration in Alberta, Canada', *Punishment and Society* 16: 3–31.

Wilde, O. (1891) 'The soul of man under socialism', *Fortnightly Review* XLIX: 292–319.

Wines, E.C. (ed.) (1871) Transactions of the National Congress on Penitentiary and Reformatory Discipline, held at Cincinnati, Ohio, 12–18 October 1870, Albany, NY: The Argus Company.

Wines, E.C. (1873) *Report on the International Penitentiary Congress of London, held 3–13 July 1872,* Washington, DC: Government Printing Office.

Chapter 7

Prison design and carceral space

Dominique Moran, Yvonne Jewkes and Jennifer Turner

Introduction

Prison design is crucial to the relationship between the 'carceral' and the state, in that it is the process which determines, in large part, how the goals of a criminal justice system are materially expressed (Moran 2015). With this in mind, this chapter takes forward the notion of prison buildings as coded, scripted entities, exploring the design of prisons and the intentions behind their operation in terms of the imperatives of states and their criminal justice systems. It pursues the notion that the design of carceral space has a significant role to play in understanding the extent to which the aims of a carceral system are translated into experiences of imprisonment.

Drawing on scholarship at the intersection between criminology and carceral geography (Moran 2015), the chapter begins by briefly tracing the history and significance of prison design, with a focus on the UK. It suggests that prison buildings can be read, and are experienced, as symbolic of the relationship between the 'carceral' and a punitive state – in terms of who prisoners 'are' and what they represent in the minds of those involved in producing the buildings in which to incarcerate them. Outlining the policy context for current UK prison building, the chapter then sketches out the processes involved in the construction of new-build prisons and the imperatives that shape their design; it briefly draws out contrasts between the UK and other penal regimes; and it suggests that both the intentions behind their design and the lived experience of the resulting prisons are worthy of further interrogation.

Prison design

> [J]ails and prisons represent more than just warehouses of bed space for arrested or convicted men and women. They are more complicated environments than just good or bad, comfortable or not. The design of a jail or prison is critically related to the philosophy of the institution, or maybe even of the entire criminal justice system. It is the physical manifestation of a society's goals and approaches for dealing with arrested and/or convicted men and women, and it is a stage for acting out plans and programs for their addressing their future.
>
> (Wener 2012: 7)

As this quote suggests, prison design is about more than accommodating and securing populations from whom society needs to be protected – although these two functions are themselves challenging and complex. The design of a prison reflects the penal

71

philosophy of the prevailing social system; its ideas about what prison is 'for' and what it is considered to 'do'; and the messages about the purpose of imprisonment that it wants to communicate to prisoners, potential offenders and to society at large. As comparative criminology points out, offending behaviour is sanctioned in different ways in different places. Punishment and crime are argued to have very little to do with one another, with imprisonment rates 'to a great degree a function of criminal justice and social policies that either encourage or discourage the use of incarceration' (Aebi and Kuhn 2000: 66, cited in Von Hofer 2003: 23; see also Tonry 2004; and Chapters 4 and 6, this volume), rather than a function of the number of crimes that are committed. Imprisonment is not inevitable, therefore; rather it is a conscious choice about the appropriate response to offending behaviour, and the purpose of that response – in terms of the prevailing understanding of what it is that prison is intended to achieve – both for society as a whole, and for offenders themselves (Moran 2015).

The following statement, made to *The Guardian* newspaper by the then UK Home Secretary Theresa May, neatly sums up the intentions of imprisonment in the UK, as expressed by politicians to the electorate:

> Prison works but it must be made to work better. The key for members of the public is that they want criminals to be punished. They want them to be taken off the streets. They also want criminals who come out of prison to go straight. What our system is failing to do at the moment is to deliver that for the public. And that's what we want to do.
>
> (*The Guardian*, 14 December 2010; see Travis 2010: n.p.)

The notion that 'prison works' is of course highly contentious, as numerous contributions to this volume attest, but in her statement the home secretary communicated three 'aims' of imprisonment: to remove ('taking them off the streets'); to punish; and to rehabilitate ('going straight'). These aims characterize most prison systems, albeit the extent to which prison can achieve all, or indeed any, of these ends is highly debatable; and the balance *between* them – both as stated in public discourse, and as manifest and experienced in the criminal justice system itself – can vary widely (see Chapter 3). Just as prison design has yet to be foregrounded in academic literature, it also seems strangely largely disconnected from public discourses of imprisonment, despite being an integral part of prison commissioning and the expansion of the carceral estate.[1]

Whereas the USA and Western Europe are highly incarcerative (or perhaps hypercarcerative), other countries are by contrast *decarcerative* – actively deploying different techniques and sanctions to decrease their prison populations. This divergence reflects a different underlying principle of imprisonment. For example, a 'less eligibility' principle informs much prison policy in the USA and Western Europe, based on an understanding that prisoners should 'suffer' in prison, not only through the loss of freedom but also by virtue of prison conditions, which should be of a worse standard than those available to the poorest free workers. In other contexts, such as in Finland, prison conditions are intended to correspond as closely as possible to general living conditions in society (Ministry of Justice of Finland 1975). Penalties for offences are implemented in such a way that they do not unduly interfere with prisoners' participation in society, but as far as possible, promote it. The intention here is neither to oversimplify nor to romanticize the 'penal exceptionalism' of the Nordic countries (Pratt and Eriksson 2012; Ugelvik and

Dullum 2012; Shammas 2014), but rather to point out that both the different philoso-phies of imprisonment, and the different relative prison populations that these deliver, require and enable different intentions to be translated into the built form of prisons.

With regard to Anglophone penal 'excess' rather than Nordic 'exceptionalism', as Theresa May's comments suggested, prisons must not only deliver a punished offender, but must do so in a way that satisfies the 'assumed punitiveness' of the public (Frost 2010; Garland 2001; Greer and Jewkes 2005; Hancock 2004; Young 2003) – those whose apparent desire is for 'prisoners to be punished'. To these ends, prisons are subject to a new government-imposed 'public acceptability test' which, although devised to provide a check on educational and constructive activities that prisoners are permitted to undertake while serving their sentences (following negative media coverage of a comedy course at HMP Whitemoor), also impacts on ideas around what prisons should look like and feel like. UK prisons today must both punish and *be seen* to punish, as well as removing offenders from society in order to deliver some form of rehabilitation that reduces their future likelihood of reoffending. Although as UK prison architecture has evolved, there has been no transparent, linear translation of 'punishment' into prison design, the interplay between philosophies of punishment and theories of prison design has resulted in preferred types of building thought capable of accomplishing the prevailing goals of imprisonment – which themselves have changed over time as penal philosophies have ebbed and flowed (Johnston 2000; Jewkes and Johnston 2007).

A comprehensive survey of the history of UK prison design and the interrelationships between the various influences that have affected it (considered in detail by Brodie et al. 1999, 2002; and Fairweather and McConville 2000) was discussed in depth by Jewkes and Johnston in the first edition of this *Handbook* (2007), and is beyond the scope of this chapter. However, considering prison buildings as scripted expressions of political–eco-nomic imperatives allows the aesthetics of prison buildings to be viewed as imbued with cultural symbolism (Moran and Jewkes 2015). Although when focusing on the UK carceral estate there is no 'typical' prison, for the majority, exterior architectural features render them instantly recognizable, within that cultural context, as places of detention and punishment. Mid-19th-century prisons, for example, were built to resemble fortified castles (e.g. HMP Leeds 1847), or gothic monasteries (e.g. Strangeways, 1868), and exterior facades communicated the perils of offending and the retributive power of the state. The 20th century gradually saw a more utilitarian style reject the decorative aes-thetic, communicating an ideal of modern, 'rational' justice and authority (Hancock and Jewkes 2011). In the 1960s and 1970s, new prisons such as Gartree and Long Lartin, whilst still communicating authority and efficiency, echoed the austere, functional styles of high, progressive modernism (ibid.). By the end of the 20th century, UK prison architecture demanded higher walls, tighter perimeters and heightened surveillance in response to earlier escapes, riots and security breaches,[2] and in parallel with the rise of 'new punitiveness' in wider criminal justice policy. The evolution of prison architecture has at various points been intended to communicate a message about the nature of the imprisoning state and the legitimacy of its power to imprison, with the 'audience' for the various messages of this architecture being the inmate who receives the punishment handed down by the state, and society at large to whom imprisonment as punishment must be legitimated (Moran and Jewkes 2015).

Research into prison design

As early as the 1930s, architectural researchers pointed out the importance of prison design in shaping the experience of incarceration. In 1931, Robert Davison, former director of research for the *Architectural Record*, published a caustic article that castigated both US prison commissioners – for lack of knowledge about what they wanted new prisons to achieve – and penologists – for being 'surprisingly insensitive to the enormous importance of the building in the treatment of the prisoner' (Davison 1931: 39). Recognizing that the design of prisons seemed to be a blind spot for the criminal justice system, he advocated that it was the job of the architect, even though they could 'scarcely be expected to be a penal expert', to indicate the 'necessity for a prolonged and careful study of this problem', and for 'thorough research in [prison] building' (ibid.).

Despite the subsequent expansion of the penal estate and the immense investment in prison building in the UK and elsewhere, prison design has received remarkably little academic attention, and Davison's 'prolonged and careful study' is still to materialize. In the early 1960s, interest in new prison architecture and design reached its peak when a special issue of *British Journal of Criminology* was devoted to the topic. In subsequent decades, however, criminological interest in this subject seems to have waned; academic commentary on prison design has been sparse and its focus has been largely historical rather than contemporary, tracing the 18th- and 19th-century 'birth of the prison' (e.g. Johnston 2000). The dearth of scholarship on this topic is remarkable since the voices of prisoners, reflecting their experiences of incarceration in media such as autobiographies and poetry, speak vividly of prison design and its effects on the lived experience of incarceration (e.g. Boyle 1977, 1984; Hassine 2010; McWatters 2013). However, whilst criminological prison research has long been dominated by Sykes's (1958) notion of the 'pains of imprisonment', recent work has started to consider new and different ways of understanding the experience of incarceration, which lend themselves more readily to dialogue with the notions of carceral space and prison design. Encompassing discourses of legitimacy and non-legitimacy (Sparks et al. 1996); security (Drake 2012); therapy (Stevens 2012); compliance and neo-paternalism (Liebling, with Arnold 2004; Crewe 2009); quality of life and healthy prisons (Liebling 2002; Liebling, with Arnold 2004); normalization (Jewkes 2002); the depth, weight and tightness of imprisonment (Crewe 2009); the resurgence of the doctrine of less eligibility (White 2008); and public acceptability (Liebling, with Arnold 2004), these studies hint at, if not fully articulate, a relationship between these notions and aspects of prison design.

The late 1980s saw a fleeting interest in prison design and prisoner well-being emerge within environmental psychology, with research identifying a link between physical environment and social climate (Houston et al. 1988), and finding that prison architecture that creates overcrowded conditions causes significant stress to inmates (Schaeffer et al. 1988). Although Canter (1987: 227) argued that a 'systematic, scientific evaluation of the successes and failures' of prison design was urgently required in order to explore this relationship further, no such evaluation has taken place. What is more, in the intervening period, research in environmental psychology has tended to focus its attention chiefly on negative prisoner behaviours and the risk factors that are perceived to contribute towards them; for example, focusing on 'hard' prevention techniques for prison suicide, such as developing cell designs with no ligature points from which prisoners can hang themselves. In other words, focus has shifted away from a concern for social climate, towards the designing-out of risk of physical harm from prisoners' destructive behaviour through environmental modification, and by maximizing control on the part of the prison authorities (Tartaro 2003; Krames and Flett 2002). Recent attempts have been made to establish a broad-brush link between different architectural types and elements of prisoner behaviour – for example, in the USA between prison layouts (as determined by satellite imagery) and 'misconduct' on the part of inmates (Morris and Worrall 2010), and in the Netherlands between prison design and prisoner perceptions of interactions with prison staff (Beijersbergen et al. 2014). These are tantalizing studies, although their quantitative methodologies preclude further explication of the means by which any such linkages take form.

Despite, then, guarded transdisciplinary recognition that the design of carceral spaces has a direct effect on prisoner behaviour and control (Foucault 1979; Alford 2000), the lived environment of prisons, including its potential for positive experience, has been relatively overlooked. Moreover, the dominance of psychological methodologies in extant research on the prison environment has delivered rather a narrow range of largely quantitative studies, based on, for example: urine tests to determine stress responses (Schaeffer et al. 1988); the deployment of suicide or misconduct statistics as a proxy for stress, towards which the physical environment might (or might not) be a contributory factor (Tartaro 2003; Morris and Worrall 2010); and true/false questionnaire responses as part of the Correctional Institution Environment Scale (CIES), which lacks an explicit environmental dimension, simply being used to measure 'well-being' in different institutions (Houston et al. 1988). At the other end of the methodological spectrum, in his work with prisoner poetry, McWatters adds to understandings of how prison space is actually experienced by those for whom 'it is an ordinary space of daily life' (McWatters 2013: 199), describing carceral space as 'more plastic, fluid and manifold than totalizing notions permit' (ibid.: 200), and arguing in support of efforts to expand the imaginary of lived spaces of incarceration.

Having recognized that the carceral environment 'matters' to prisoners' experiences, and having demonstrated it to some degree using a variety of methodologies, without exception, these studies call for a more nuanced investigation of the impact of design on those using and occupying prison spaces.

The policy context of prison design

Globally, the imprisonment of offenders takes place within a framework of primary international covenants and conventions, such as the Convention Against Torture and Other Cruel, Inhuman or Degrading Treatment or Punishment, which is intended to guarantee proper treatment for those in detention under all circumstances. Driven by a concern for the humane treatment of those detained, these conventions do not extend to prescriptions about the exact nature of prison buildings, in terms either of their outward appearance and architectural style, or internal configuration.

Contemporary UK penal architecture reflects government reports commissioned within this policy context, which have transformed prison security and with it prisoners' quality of life (Liebling 2002; Liebling et al. 2011; Drake 2012; see also Chapter 13, this volume). A preoccupation with 'hardening' the prison environment to design-out risk through environmental modification coincided with the UK Prison Service becoming an executive agency in 1993, and with the early 1990s enabling of private contracts for the design, construction, management and finance of penal institutions. An approach to prison control based on a balance between situational and social control has arguably swung towards an understanding of the situational dependence of behaviour, 'creating safe situations rather than creating safe individuals' (Wortley 2002: 4).

In recent years, UK prison new-builds have been driven by logics of cost, efficiency and security. However, there is also a need to comply with HM Prison Service Orders about the specification of prison accommodation, which lay out 'measurable standards' that can be 'applied consistently across the estate' in order to enable the prison service to provide 'decent living conditions for all prisoners' (HMPS 2001: 1). In this context, prison exteriors have tended to adopt a bland, presumably cheap, unassuming and uniform style with vast expanses of brick, few, small windows and no unnecessary decoration (Jewkes 2013). Internally, the imperative in spending the Ministry of Justice's approximate £300 million annual capital budget is to deploy indestructible materials to create custodial environments with no ligature points so that prisoners cannot physically harm themselves or others (RICS 2012). For example, one of the most recent UK prison new-builds, constructed as a part of the 'custodial architecture' portfolios of a specialist building contractor, was described as 'very operationally efficient' with 'a modern custodial aesthetic'.[3] Advertising their 'Custodial and Emergency Services' project capabilities, the contractor, whilst conceding the need for a prison building to 'have a positive impact' and to be 'safe, non-threatening, secure and aesthetically pleasing', highlighted the imperative for 'value for money [to] be carefully balanced against the need for robustness and security'. Their experience and expertise in this area was described as bringing 'efficiencies at the design stage' including the kind of modified environments that create safe situations (Wortley 2002), such as 'designing ligature free environments by incorporating junctions and fixing details within structural walls and floors' (Pick Everard n.d.: n.p.).

Nineteenth-century prison buildings still in service are usually considered the least desirable environments within the UK penal estate, but while these Victorian 'houses of correction' ensured inmates' restricted economy of space, light and colour, imprisoning psychologically as well as physically, it has yet to be established empirically whether 'old' always means 'bad' or whether the kind of 'contemporary' prison described above necessarily equates to 'progressive' or 'humanitarian' (Hancock and Jewkes 2011; Moran and Jewkes 2015). For example, within a year of reopening in 1983, the 'new' Holloway Prison was criticized by the UK Prisons Inspectorate as engendering a form of torture that could result in acute mental illness. Levels of self-harm, suicide and distress were high, and vandalism, barricading of cells, floods, arson and violence against other prisoners and staff were common (Medlicott 2008). Among interior layouts recently advocated to manage problems like these is the 'new generation' campus-style arrangement of discrete housing units connected by outdoor space and flexible planning and design. Such prisons have experienced different levels of success. Although prison architecture may reflect underlying penal philosophies, the ways in which it is experienced depend heavily on local contingencies and on the human subjectivity of the habitation of buildings. For example, Feltham and Lancaster Farms Young Offenders' Institutions have been perceived differently on issues such as bullying, self-harm and suicide. Lancaster Farms has been held up as a shining example of commitment and care, whilst Feltham's reputation is coloured by years of damning reports and a high-profile murder (Jewkes and Johnston 2007).

The 'new punitiveness', discussed earlier with regard to the relationship between the carceral and the state, comes clearly into view when considering the prison estate. Latterly, it has expanded to accommodate those imprisoned under circumstances of increasing (and, increasingly, indeterminate) prison sentences, more punitive prison sanctions, and more austere and spartan prison conditions, operating to a greater or lesser extent in various contexts (Pratt et al. 2011; Hallsworth and Lea 2011; Lynch 2011; Snacken 2010). This hardening of penal sensibilities is coupled in the UK and elsewhere with more severe sentencing policies (Criminal Justice Act 2003); the fetishizing of risk and security within and outside the penal estate; and a rising prison population (which, in England and Wales, has grown by 30% since 2001 and stood at 85,414 in June 2014). All of this makes questions of prison design and the lived experience of carceral space particularly pertinent. Although chronic overcrowding, high rates of drug use, mental illness, self-harm and suicide and recidivism and its associated financial and social costs, mar the UK system, abscondments from closed prisons have fallen dramatically, due in part to prison design: prison walls are higher, prison space is sequestered through zoning, and CCTV cameras and other technologies proliferate.

In the USA, perceived public endorsement for rigorous and unpleasant conditions has also resulted in new prisons being built with 'a level of security above "high security"' and internal routines not seen for 150 years (Johnston 2000: 4). Morin (2013: 381) has argued that the 'latest punitive phase' in the USA neither simply *eliminates*, as in the premodern spectacle, nor *creates* the docile, rehabilitated bodies of the modern panopticon. Rather, she argued that the late-modern prison 'produces only fear, terror, violence, and death' (see Chapter 3 of this volume). In support of this view, Victor Hassine, a 'lifer' who committed suicide after serving 28 years in various correctional facilities in the USA, comments on the 'fear-suffused environments' he endured, and writes:

> To fully understand the prison experience requires a personal awareness of how bricks, mortar, steel, and the endless enforcement of rules and regulations animate a prison into a living, breathing entity designed to manipulate its inhabitants ... Prison designers and managers have developed a precise and universal alphabet of fear that is carefully assembled and arranged – bricks, steel, uniforms, colors, odors, shapes, and management style – to effectively control the conduct of whole prison populations.
>
> (Hassine 2010: 7)

Carceral geography and prison design

Recent work within carceral geography has addressed the significance of carceral space (Moran et al. 2013; Moran 2015), recognizing space as more than the surface where social practices take place (Gregory and Urry 1985; Lefebvre 1991; Massey 1994). Although geographers understand that space can affect the ways people act within it and are increasingly applying this perspective to carceral spaces, Siserman (2012) points out that studies of prisons as buildings and environments where the behaviour of inmates can be dramatically changed, and which investigate how this might happen, remain scarce. Commentaries within architectural geographies and cultural geographies have argued for the importance of considering buildings in a number of connected ways (e.g. Kraftl 2010; Jacobs and Merriman 2011; Rose et al. 2010; Jacobs 2006; Kraftl and Adey 2008):

as everyday spaces in which people spend a significant proportion of their lives; as expressions of political–economic imperatives that code them with 'signs, symbols and referents for dominant socio-cultural discourses or moralities' (Kraftl 2010: 402); and in terms of perspectives that emphasize materiality and affect.

A representationalist focus on prison buildings as sites of meaning, symbolic of intentions and imperatives is itself arguably underdeveloped in prison scholarship. However, there is the potential to go beyond the symbolic meaning of prison buildings to consider the 'inhabitation' (Jacobs and Merriman 2011: 213) in terms of the dynamic encounters between these buildings and their constituent elements and spaces, design, planners, inhabitants, workers, visitors, and so on. Like any other buildings, prisons are sites in which myriad users and things come into contact with one another in numerous complex, planned, spontaneous and unexpected ways, and where the encounters are both embodied and multi-sensory, and resonant of the power structures that exist both within and beyond the prison building, and which shape its inhabitation.

Recent developments in both prison architecture and design (albeit outwith the context of the 'new punitiveness') and criminological research into prison aesthetics and 'anaesthetics' (Jewkes 2013) echo Kraftl and Adey's suggestion that one function of buildings can be an attempt to stabilize affect, 'to generate the possibility of pre-circumscribed situations, and to engender certain forms of practice, through the design and planning of buildings, including aspects such as form and atmosphere' (Kraftl and Adey 2008: 228). In their work, they found that certain generic expressions of affect evoked certain kinds of inhabitation, materialized via buildings in their 'potential capacities to affect their inhabitants in certain ways' (ibid.). In other parts of the world – in which the 'new punitiveness' of the USA, UK and elsewhere has not taken hold – prison designers have focused on the rehabilitative function of imprisonment, and have experimented with progressive and highly stylized forms of penal architecture. There, internal prison spaces exhibit soft furnishings, colour zoning, maximum exploitation of natural light, displays of art and sculpture, and views of nature through vista windows without bars.

For example, in designing a planned women's prison in Iceland, the project team from OOIIO Architecture intended:

> to design a prison that doesn't look like a prison, forgetting about dark spaces, small cells, and ugly grey concrete walls … we based the building design on natural light, open spaces, and natural green materials like peat, grass and flowers.
>
> (OOIIO Architecture 2012: n.p.)

Instead of designing one large building (like a 'typical repressive old prison'), they decided to break it into several 'human-scale, connected' pavilions, which must be efficient and functional to enable the spatial separation of prisoners, but must also have 'natural light and exterior views, to increase the feeling of freedom'. The architects also had an eye to the speed and ease of construction, and to the eco standards of the building, planning to draw upon Icelandic vernacular architecture to insulate the building. With a facade constructed from peat-filled cages planted with local flowers and grasses, they intended to deliver a building 'that changes with the seasons', making prison life 'less monotonous and more human and natural related' (OOIIO Architecture 2012: n.p.).

This kind of design of new prisons in Norway, Iceland and Denmark arguably plays up and enhances certain generic expressions of affect connected to openness, flexibility and 'humane' treatment. It evokes certain kinds of inhabitation that encourage personal and intellectual creativity, and even a lightness and vividness of experience (Hancock and Jewkes 2011). Away from this Nordic context, however, what drives the building of new prisons in the UK, and how much do we know about it?

Building new prisons in the UK

Kraftl and Adey (2008: 228) called for further research into the ways in which architectural forms try to manipulate and create possibilities, and into how those affects are experienced and negotiated in practice, via the notion of inhabitation. Attending to the processes of architectural design and construction reveals the multiple political, affective and material ways in which prison buildings are designed and constituted. These in turn play a part in constructing the affectual potentialities of prison buildings that are negotiated in and through practices of inhabitation.

The design process is, as Wener noted, 'the wedge that forces the system to think through its approach and review, restate, or redevelop its philosophy of criminal justice' (Wener 2012: 7). Embedded within this process is the conscious and intentional design of carceral spaces, in response to contingent policy imperatives and in the context of local budgetary constraints. In the UK, the contemporary process of designing and building new prisons now rests upon a complex and varied framework with an intricate network of individuals, companies and capital, and is driven primarily by concerns for security, cost and efficiency – concerns which materially shape the buildings themselves.

Since the recommendation of the 1987 Select Committee on Home Affairs report that the Home Office should enable private companies to tender for the management of prisons, the landscape of UK prison construction has shifted considerably. The 1990 Criminal Justice Bill provided enabling legislation for prison privatization, and Section 84 of the Criminal Justice Act 1991 allowed for the private running of new prisons. These 'Manage & Maintain' (M&M) contracts involved the then Ministry of Prisons leasing prisons to private operators contracted to run them, and maintain their buildings and infrastructure, for 15 years. The Conservative government's introduction in 1992 of the Private Finance Initiative (PFI) enabled 'public–private partnerships' (PPPs) to fund public infrastructure projects with private capital, and the 1994 Criminal Justice and Public Order Act allowed for the private *provision* as well as the operation and maintenance of prisons. Following a tendering process in which the public sector was barred from participating, Group 4 (now G4S) was awarded a contract to manage HMP Wolds, a newly built remand prison that opened in April 1992. What started as an 'experiment', however, soon became routine policy (Panchamia 2012) and, in 1997, the incoming New Labour government adopted PFI. HMP Altcourse in Liverpool, and HMP Parc at Bridgend in Wales, became the first PFI builds under Labour in England and Wales, respectively.

Now known as Design, Construct, Manage and Finance (DCMF) contracts, PFI builds involve private sector finance for the construction of new prisons, as well as providing their custodial services. A consortium of financiers, constructors and a facilities operator form a special purpose vehicle (SPV) or special operating vehicle (SOV), which, in a PFI, carries the profit or loss from the venture. The secretary of state contracts with the SPV which, in turn, subcontracts the immediate construction to a Design and Build Contractor (D&B), and the long-term operation of the prison to a Buildings and Facilities Management company (BFM), typically for 25 years. In some cases in the UK, prisons are still built and run using public funds, whereas others may be publicly financed, but operated by private companies under M&M contracts. Recent examples of these generic types of construction in the UK include HMP Oakwood (opened 2012 – M&M) in Staffordshire, HMP Thameside (2012 – DCMF) in London, and HMP Grampian (2014 – public funds and publicly run) in northern Scotland.

In terms of the build process itself, contractors that have had previous success delivering prisons on time and within budget tend to be commissioned for subsequent projects. At HMP Thameside, for example:

> Skanska brought together its in-house expertise in construction, piling, structural and civil design, and the installation of mechanical and electrical services to deliver the project. It also built on its experience from similar projects, such as the HMP Dovegate project in Staffordshire.
>
> (Skanska 2012: 1)

Experience is important, therefore, but so is cost. In the case of the planned prison HMP North Wales, four main contractors were in competition: Carillion, Interserve, Lend Lease and Kier. Lend Lease's award of the contract in May 2014 perhaps rewarded a projected build cost of £212 million, 15% below the government's original planned budget of £250 million, as well as a commitment to spend £50 million with small and medium-sized enterprises, and £30 million with local businesses. For a government eager to stimulate local economic activity and development, Lend Lease's plan to recruit 50% of the site workforce from the local area, including around 100 apprenticeships (Morby 2014) may also have increased the attractiveness of their bid. The cost of operation is also critical. HMP Oakwood, for example, accommodates up to 2,000 prisoners relatively cheaply (at £13,200 per inmate per year, compared with the England and Wales average of £21,600 per year for Category C prisoners and £31,300 for all prisoners). The G4S-run facility has been lauded as a 'model' prison by the secretary of state for justice.

In terms of the built form of new prisons, cost concerns – in relation to both building materials and build duration – heavily influence the fabric of the resulting facility. In order to reduce both the build time and the on-site workforce, off-site pre-fabrication is preferred. HMP Oakwood, for example, consists of 12 precast buildings, including four, four-storey house blocks, and entry and facilities buildings. These buildings were quickly assembled on site from precast concrete panels with window grilles, sanitary provisions and drainage pre-installed. At HMP Thameside, Skanska coordinated a similar process of the delivery of off-site precast concrete components, the use of which facilitated swift construction on the small and confined site, allowing some buildings to be handed over 14 weeks early (Skanska 2012: 1). In prison building, time is money. Whilst HMP Grampian was under construction, prisoners from closed prisons at Aberdeen and Peterhead had to be held elsewhere (Premier Construction 2014). Finishing on time and on budget meant that they could be rehoused quickly, with minimal additional cost, security worries or disruption to their sentence planning.

The pre-eminence of financial considerations shapes a government procurement process that is arguably engineered towards the most cost-effective solution. In a prevailing climate of cuts to justice spending, contractors who have delivered previous projects on time and on budget are well placed to win subsequent tenders. This has two implications. First, breaking into the marketplace as a new SPV/D&B company is difficult, as newcomers face considerable disadvantages. Second, and connectedly, alternative or experimental prison designs that deviate from a 'tried and tested' template amenable to precast construction and on-site assembly may simply be priced out of the market. This often, and perhaps understandably, results in contractors sticking to designs whose construction costs and build times they can confidently predict, in order to bid competitively for new contracts. What this effectively means is that new prisons tend to be virtually identical to other recently built prisons (Jewkes and Moran 2014), with architectural aesthetics taking a back seat, and innovation limited to efficiency of build, rather than creativity of design.

Discussion

In addition to the conscious and intentional meanings attached to carceral spaces (relating to cost, reliability, security and so on) that are embedded in the procurement and contracting processes outlined above, research on emotional geographies of prisons (Crewe et al. 2013) highlights the more subtle ways in which architecture and design communicate the aims and techniques of penal authority. We have argued elsewhere that the large, bland prison warehouses that are now built in the contemporary UK may communicate a particular message about society's attitudes to prisoners (Jewkes and Moran 2014; Jewkes 2015; Jewkes, Moran and Slee 2016). The nondescript external appearance of new-build prisons could be regarded as a visual metaphor for the loss of public empathy for the excluded offender, where 'municipal' architecture enables us to turn a blind eye to the plight of the confined. Although such a benign facade might suggest a benevolent regime, it has recently been argued that concerns for security within many countries' penal systems have risen to such a level of prominence that they eclipse almost every other consideration, including what it means to be human (Drake 2012). In this context, the benign exterior can mask a sterile, 'mean-spirited', assembly line quality (Hassine 2010: 125).

The penal philosophies and imperatives underpinning the design of newly commissioned and newly built facilities thus shape the relationship between space, meaning and power, and have an undeniable impact on the experience of imprisonment and on the behaviour of those who occupy and move through carceral spaces. The 'dynamic encounters' (Jacobs and Merriman 2011: 213) that occur between the inhabitants of prison buildings, the technologies operational within them, and the buildings themselves, are critical to understanding their inhabitation. Criminologists recognize that prisoners constantly 'manage' issues of self and identity and adapt socially under intense and inescapable duress; and the kinds of encounters between prisoners and prison staff that are encouraged by, or which are even possible within, differently designed prison buildings are worthy of investigation. 'Dynamic security', in which prison staff are encouraged to develop good relationships with prisoners through direct contact and conversation, is no longer possible in many new-build prisons where staff are physically separated from prisoners.

Where surveillance technologies enhance the observation of carceral space, some prisoners may value CCTV as a means of protecting their personal safety and for its capacity to provide evidence of bullying and assaults. However, these technologies also reinforce the absence of privacy and create additional stresses for both prisoners and staff (Liebling et al. 2011). The utilization of surveillance and monitoring technologies in prisons as workplaces has inevitably brought prison employees under closer scrutiny from their managers (Townsend and Bennett 2003; Ball 2010), and it is argued that the notion of trust, once regarded as essential to prison management-staff relationships, has been undermined by surveillance systems that ensure that 'correct' organizational procedures are followed. Increasingly, prisons routinely monitor everyone passing through them via an interface of technology and corporeality, encouraging flexibility of movement while retaining high levels of security. For example, cameras wirelessly transmit digital images, which are then screened for unusual objects and atypical movements; biometric and electronic monitoring of prisoners and visitors allow the tracking of bodies within in the prison; listening devices monitor the spectral content of sound to spot illicit use of mobile phones or early signs of aggressive behaviour; and prison officers' Blackberry-style devices enable immediate reports to be relayed to Security (OIS 2008; cited in Hancock and Jewkes 2011).

Whereas Morin's (2013) work suggested that like the UK, the USA is experiencing a trend towards increasingly severe and restrictive prison designs, elsewhere, prison buildings are being designed with different intentions in terms of the manipulation and creation of possibilities. In north-west Europe, decarcerative policies deliver smaller numbers of prisoners, and for these smaller prison populations the use of surveillance technologies facilitates 'humane', open-plan, 'progressive' prisons with a greater degree of movement among and between inmates and staff, and a wider range of possible encounters. Here, new-build prisons are not only the result of experimentation with progressive and highly stylized forms of penal architecture, but they also have internal prison spaces that explore more open, flexible and normalized spatial planning than is the norm in the UK. Among the design features to be found in these new prisons are: soft furnishings replacing hard fixtures and fittings; zoning different parts of the prison through colour coding and use of psychologically effective colour schemes; attention to the maximum exploitation of natural light and/or artificial light that mimics daylight; greater access to outdoor spaces with trees, planting and water features; the incorporation of differing levels, horizons and building materials to ward off boredom and monotony; and displays of art and sculpture (Hancock and Jewkes 2011; Moran and Jewkes 2015). This kind of strategic application of architectural and aesthetic principles to the design of new prisons in, for example, Norway, Iceland and Denmark, has been found to encourage personal and intellectual creativity, and even a lightness and vividness of experience (Hancock and Jewkes 2011), in contrast to the depth, weight and tightness commonly associated with imprisonment (Crewe 2011) and its material darkness, even hellishness (Wacquant 2002; Jewkes 2014, 2015).

Even in the Nordic countries, however, prison design may not be straightforwardly humane and positive – or may at least have perverse consequences. For example, although the appearance of these prison buildings – in terms of their natural materials, large windows and natural light – conveys a sense of ease and relaxation, it arguably replicates and perhaps enhances some of the issues of privacy, identity management and presentation of self-identity in more obviously 'restrictive' settings. Meanwhile, Shammas (2014: 104) has called for attention to be paid to the 'pains of freedom' inherent in Norway's more 'humane' prisons. There is some evidence that technology-assisted, decentralized, podular designs approximate 'normality' by providing safer and more comfortable living environments, and removing security gates, bars and grilles, enabling prison officers to be more than 'turn-keys' (Spens 1994), but as Hancock and Jewkes (2011) have argued, there has been scant official or scholarly discussion of other potential uses of technology, such as the identification of abuse or aggressive behaviour by prison officers (either to prisoners or their colleagues), the surveillance of staff smuggling contraband into the prison or behaving in ways disapproved of by prison authorities. Similarly, there is little debate about the moral and ethical implications of near-constant surveillance of prisoners and officers, or the difficulties in establishing trust when basic standards of privacy are compromised. The use of technologies could exacerbate complex horizontal and vertical relationships between prison inmates, officers, managers and ministers. Everyone who moves within and through these 'hyper-organizational spaces' (Zhang et al. 2008) is not only enmeshed in a surveillance assemblage that forces them to manage their own presentation of self within the regulative framework of the institution, but is further encouraged to watch while knowingly being watched. Although lack of privacy has long been recognized as a 'pain of imprisonment' for inmates, for prison staff the new panopticism is a novel form of control (Hancock and Jewkes 2011).

Conclusion

With Wener's (2012: 7) proposition that 'the design of a jail or prison is critically related to the philosophy of the institution, or maybe even of the entire criminal justice system', a better understanding of prison design could in turn enable a better understanding of the lived experience of carceral spaces – a central theme of recent research in carceral geography. Geographers have made valuable contributions to understanding how, even within the most restrictive conditions of confinement, prisoners employ effective spatial tactics within surveilled space, create individual and collective means of resistance to carceral regimes, and succeed in appropriating and personalizing carceral spaces (Moran and Jewkes 2015). Yet, the majority of research to date has tended to focus on inmate responses to, and adaptations of, the physical spaces of incarceration, rather than drawing attention to the processes that led those spaces to *be* as they are, and what this means for the ends prison buildings serve for the state that creates them. Missing from this work is a consideration of the ways in which punitive philosophies are manifest in prison commissioning and construction, and subsequently in prison buildings themselves.

The challenge, therefore, is to start to address *why* those spaces are as they are, and to interrogate the intentions behind their design. Returning to Davison's (1931) condemnation of US prison design, research needs to illuminate further the commissioning process, to uncover what it is that architects are asked to draw, contractors to build and facilities managers to maintain, and how those demands are articulated and addressed. Davison argued that prison authorities would 'never get the most out of their architects until specifications are presented not in terms of definite plans and materials, but in terms of performance' (ibid.: 33). He called for commissioners not to request cell blocks, but sleeping places; not to demand mechanical ventilation, but instead to require good air for every prisoner. Then, he concluded, 'let the solution be worked out. In many instances the result will be astonishing. It will not resemble the present jail at all' (ibid.: 34). Designing a prison based on the requirements of the building, rather than simply accepting and replicating what has been built before, was for him the key to delivering 'better' prisons.

Pursuing these questions could enable us not only to better understand the experience of incarceration, but also to open the design process itself to scrutiny and reflection (Moran and Jewkes 2015; Jewkes and Moran 2014).[4] Wener (2012: 7) argued that prison environments represent both an 'overt' agenda that provides measurable quantities of space for accommodation, training, therapy, education and so on, and also a 'covert' agenda that reflects what or who inmates 'are' in the minds of planners, designers, and those who commission them to design and build prisons. Opening a space for the articulation of this 'covert' agenda could contribute positively to the ongoing debate over the expansion of the penal estate.

Notes

1 In the UK, a former home secretary recalled that he was never asked to adjudicate on matters of prison design, rating 'the prison designs of much of the post-war period' as 'shoddy, expensive and just a little inhuman' (Hurd 2000: xiii–xiv).
2 1990s security breaches included prisoner rooftop protests at Strangeways in 1990 and escapes from Whitemoor and Parkhurst prisons in 1994.
3 David Nisbet, partner at Pick Everard (see Pick Everard 2012: n.p.).
4 To these ends, the authors are currently conducting a three-year research study. Taking a lead from Victor Hassine's biographical writings on his experience as a prisoner in the US system, the project is entitled 'Fear-suffused environments or potential to rehabilitate? Prison architecture, design and technology and the lived experience of carceral spaces' (ESRC Standard Grant ES/K011081/1).

Bibliography

Adey, P. (2008) 'Airports, mobility and the affective architecture of affective control', *Geoforum* 39: 438–451.
Aebi, M.F. and Kuhn, A. (2000) 'Influences on the prisoner rate: Number of entries into prison, length of sentences and crime rate', *European Journal on Criminal Policy and Research* 8(1): 65–75.
Alford, C.F. (2000) 'What would it matter if everything Foucault said about prison were wrong? Discipline and Punish after twenty years', *Theory and Society* 29(1): 125–146.
Allen, J. (2006) 'Ambient power: Berlin's Potsdamer Platz and the seductive logic of public spaces', *Urban Studies* 43: 441–455.
Ball, K.S. (2010) 'Workplace surveillance: An overview', *Labor History* 51(1): 87–106.
Beijersbergen, K.A., Dirkzwager, A.J.E., Van der Laan, P.H. and Nieuwbeerta, P. (2014) 'A social building? Prison architecture and staff-prisoner relationships', *Crime & Delinquency*, DOI: 10.1177/0011128714530657.
Boyle, J. (1977) *A Sense of Freedom*, London: Pan.
Boyle, J. (1984) *The Pain of Confinement*, Edinburgh: Canongate.
Brodie, A., Croom, J. and Davies, J.O. (1999) *Behind Bars: The Hidden Architecture of England's Prisons*, London: English Heritage.
Brodie, A., Croom, J. and Davies, J.O. (2002) *English Prisons: An Architectural History*, London: English Heritage.
Canter, D. (1987) 'Implications for "new generation" prisons of existing psychological research into prison design and use', in A.E. Bottoms and R. Light (eds) *Problems of Long-term Imprisonment*, Aldershot: Gower.
Crewe, B. (2009) *The Prisoner Society: Power, Adaption, and Social Life in an English Prison*, Oxford: Oxford University Press.
Crewe, B. (2011) 'Depth, weight, tightness: Revisiting the pains of imprisonment', *Punishment and Society* 13(5): 509–529.
Crewe, B., Warr, J., Bennett, P. and Smith, A. (2013) 'The emotional geography of prison life', *Theoretical Criminology*, DOI: 1362480613497778.
Davison, R.L. (1931) 'Prison architecture', *Annals of the American Academy of Political and Social Science* 157: 33–39.
Drake, D. (2012) *Prisons, Punishment and the Pursuit of Security*, London: Palgrave Macmillan.

Fairweather, L. and McConville, S. (eds) (2000) *Prison Architecture: Policy, Design, and Experience*, Oxford: Elsevier.

Foucault, M. (1979) *Discipline and Punish: The Birth of the Prison*, New York: Vintage.

Frost, N.A. (2010) 'Beyond public opinion polls: Punitive public sentiment and criminal justice policy', *Sociology Compass* 4(3): 156–168.

Garland, D. (2001) *The Culture of Control*, Oxford: Oxford University Press.

Great Britain (1991) *Criminal Justice Act 1991*, London: The Stationery Office, www.legislation.gov.uk/ukpga/1991/53/contents (accessed 4 July 2014).

Great Britain (1994) *Criminal Justice and Public Order Act 1994*, London: The Stationery Office, www.legislation.gov.uk/ukpga/1994/33/contents (accessed 4 July 2014).

Great Britain (2003) *Criminal Justice Act 2003*, London: The Stationery Office, www.legislation.gov.uk/ukpga/2003/44/contents (accessed 4 July 2014).

Greer, C. and Jewkes, Y. (2005) 'Extremes of otherness: media images of social exclusion', *Social Justice* 32(1): 20–31.

Gregory, D. and Urry, J. (eds) (1985) *Social Relations and Spatial Structures*, London: Macmillan.

Hallsworth, S. and Lea, J. (2011) 'Reconstructing Leviathan: Emerging contours of the security state', *Theoretical Criminology* 15(2): 141–157.

Hancock, L. (2004) 'Criminal justice, public opinion, fear and popular politics', in J. Muncie and D. Wilson (eds) *The Cavendish Student Handbook of Criminal Justice and Criminology*, London: Cavendish.

Hancock, P. and Jewkes, Y. (2011) 'Architectures of incarceration: The spatial pains of imprisonment', *Punishment and Society* 13(5): 611–629.

Hassine, V. (2010) *Life Without Parole: Living and Dying in Prison Today*, New York: Oxford University Press.

HMPS (HM Prison Service) (2001) *Prison Service Order 1900: Certified Prisoner Accommodation*, London: HMPS.

Houston, J.G., Gibbons, D.C. and Jones, J.F. (1988) 'Physical environment and jail social climate', *Crime & Delinquency* 34(4): 449–466.

Hurd, D. (2000) *Memoirs*, London: Little, Brown.

Jacobs, J.M. (2006) 'A geography of big things', *Cultural Geographies* 13(1): 1–27.

Jacobs, J.M. and Merriman, P. (2011) 'Practising architectures', *Social & Cultural Geography* 12(3): 211–222.

Jewkes, Y. (2002) *Captive Audience: Media, Masculinity and Power in Prisons*, London: Routledge.

Jewkes, Y. (2013) 'On carceral space and agency', in D. Moran, N. Gill and D. Conlon (eds) *Carceral Spaces: Mobility and Agency in Imprisonment and Migrant Detention*, Farnham: Ashgate.

Jewkes, Y. (2015) 'Fear-suffused hell-holes: The architecture of extreme punishment', in K. Reiter and A. Koenig (eds) *Extraordinary Punishment: An Empirical Look at Administrative Black Holes in the United States, the United Kingdom, and Canada*, London: Palgrave.

Jewkes, Y. and Johnston, H. (2007) 'The evolution of prison architecture', in Y. Jewkes (ed.) *Handbook on Prisons*, London: Routledge.

Jewkes, Y. and Moran, D. (2014) 'Should prison architecture be brutal, bland or beautiful?', *Scottish Justice Matters* 2(1): 8–11.

Jewkes, Y., Moran, D. and Slee, E. (2016) 'The visual retreat of the prison: non-places for non-people', in M. Brown and E. Carrabine (eds) *The Routledge Handbook of Visual Criminology*, London: Routledge.

Johnston, N. (2000) *Forms of Constraint: A History of Prison Architecture*, Urbana, IL: University of Illinois Press.

Kraftl, P. (2010) 'Geographies of architecture: The multiple lives of buildings', *Geography Compass* 4(5): 402–415.

Kraftl, P. and Adey, P. (2008) 'Architecture/affect/inhabitation: Geographies of being-in buildings', *Annals of the Association of American Geographers* 98(1): 213–231.

Krames, L. and Flett, G.L. (2002) *The Perceived Characteristics of Holding Cell Environments: Report of a Pilot Study*, Regina: Canadian Police Research Centre.

Leech, M. (2005) *The Prisons Handbook*, Manchester: MLA Press.

Lefèbvre, H. (1991) *The Production of Space*, Oxford: Blackwell.

Liebling, A. (2002) *Suicides in Prison*, London: Routledge.

Liebling, A., with Arnold, H. (2004) *Prisons and their Moral Performance: A Study of Values, Quality, and Prison Life*, Oxford: Oxford University Press.

Liebling, A., Arnold, H. and Straub, C. (2011) *An Exploration of Staff-Prisoner Relationships at HMP Whitemoor: Twelve Years On*, London: MoJ.

Lynch, M. (2011) 'Mass incarceration, legal change, and locale', *Criminology & Public Policy* 10(3): 673–698.

McWatters, M. (2013) 'Poetic testimonies of incarceration: Towards a vision of prison as manifold space', in D. Moran, N. Gill and D. Conlon (eds) *Carceral Spaces: Mobility and Agency in Imprisonment and Migrant Detention*, Farnham: Ashgate.

Massey, D. (1994) *Space, Place and Gender*, Cambridge: Polity Press.

Medlicott, D. (2008) 'Women in prison', in Y. Jewkes and J. Bennett (eds) *Dictionary of Prisons and Punishment*, London: Routledge.

Ministry of Justice of Finland (1975) *Statute on Prison Administration*, Helsinki: Ministry of Justice.

Moran, D. (2015) *Carceral Geography: Spaces and Practices of Incarceration*, Farnham: Ashgate.

Moran, D., Gill, N. and Conlon, D. (eds) (2013) *Carceral Spaces: Mobility and Agency in Imprisonment and Migrant Detention*, Farnham: Ashgate.

Moran, D. and Jewkes, Y. (2015) 'Linking the carceral and the punitive state: Researching prison architecture, design, technology and the lived experience of carceral space', *Annales de la Geographie*.

Morby, A. (2014) 'Lend Lease wins £212m Wrexham super prison', *Construction Enquirer*, www.constructionenquirer.com/2014/05/30/lend-lease-wins-212m-wrexham-super-prison/ (accessed 19 June 2014).

Morin, K.M. (2013) '"Security here is not safe": Violence, punishment, and space in the contemporary US penitentiary', *Environment and Planning D: Society and Space* 31(3): 381–399.

Morris, R.G. and Worrall, J.L. (2010) 'Prison architecture and inmate misconduct: A multilevel assessment', *Crime & Delinquency*, DOI: 10.1177/0011128710386204.

OIS (Offender Information Services) (2008) *Prison Technology Strategy, Version 0.8*, London: NOMS.

OOIIO Architecture (2012) 'Female prison in Iceland', *OOIIO Architecture* website, plusmood.com/2012/06/female-prison-in-iceland-ooiio-architecture/ (accessed 2 February 2014).

Panchamia, N. (2012) *Competition in Prisons*, London: Institute for Government, www.instituteforgovernment.org.uk/sites/default/files/publications/Prisons%20briefing%20final.pdf (accessed 22 July 2014).

Pick Everard (2012) 'Pick Everard completes UK's largest public funded prison project', *Pick Everard* website, www.pickeverard.co.uk/news/2012/Pick-Everard-completes-UKs-largest-public-funded-prison-project.html (accessed 4 February 2014).

Pick Everard (n.d.) 'Custodial and emergency services', *Pick Everard* website, www.pickeverard.co.uk/custodial-emergency-services/index.html (accessed 3 February 2014).

Pratt, J., Brown, D., Brown, M., Hallsworth, S. and Morrison, W. (eds) (2011) *The New Punitiveness: Trends, Theories, Perspectives*, Oxford: Routledge.

Pratt, J. and Eriksson, A. (2012) *Contrasts in Punishment: An Explanation of Anglophone Excess and Nordic Exceptionalism*, London: Routledge.

Premier Construction (2014) 'Unveiling HMP and YOI Grampian', *Premier Construction* website, premierconstructionnews.com/2014/02/25/unveiling-hmp-and-yoi-grampian/ (accessed 19 June 2014).

RICS (Royal Institute of Chartered Surveyors) (2012) *Modus: The Security Issue* 22(11).

Rose, G., Degen, M. and Basdas, B. (2010) 'More on "big things": Building events and feelings', *Transactions of the Institute of British Geographers* 35: 334–349.

Schaeffer, M.A., Baum, A., Paulus, P.B. and Gaes, G.G. (1988) 'Architecturally mediated effects of social density in prison', *Environment and Behavior* 20(1): 3–20.

Shammas, V.L. (2014) 'The pains of freedom: Assessing the ambiguity of Scandinavian penal exceptionalism on Norway's Prison Island', *Punishment & Society* 16(1): 104–123.

Siserman, C. (2012) *Reconsidering the Environmental Space of Prisons: A Step Further towards Criminal Reform*, Santa Cruz, CA: GRIN Verlag.

Skanska (2012) 'Case study 98 HMP Thameside', *Skanska* website, skanska-sustainability-case-studies.com/HMP-Thameside-UK (accessed 16 June 2014).

Snacken, S. (2010) 'Resisting punitiveness in Europe?', *Theoretical Criminology* 14(3): 273–292.

Sparks, R., Bottoms, A. and Hay, W. (1996) *Prisons and the Problem of Order*, Oxford: Clarendon Press.

Spens, I. (ed.) (1994) *Architecture of Incarceration*, London: Academy Editions.

Stevens, A. (2012) *Offender Rehabilitation and Therapeutic Communities: Enabling Change the TC Way*, London: Routledge.

Sykes, G.M. (1958) *The Society of Captives: A Study of a Maximum Security Prison*, Princeton, NJ: Princeton University Press.

Tartaro, C. (2003) 'Suicide and the jail environment: An evaluation of three types of institutions', *Environment and Behavior* 35(5): 605–620.

Tonry, M. (2004) *Thinking about Crime: Sense and Sensibility in American Penal Culture*, Oxford: Oxford University Press.

Townsend, A.M. and Bennett, J.T. (2003) 'Privacy, technology and conflict: Emerging issues and action in workplace privacy', *Journal of Labor Research* 24(2): 195–205.

Travis, A. (2010) 'Prison works, says Theresa May', *The Guardian* online, www.theguardian.com/politics/2010/dec/14/prison-works-says-theresa-may (accessed 3 July 2014).

Ugelvik, T. and Dullum, J. (eds) (2012) *Penal Exceptionalism? Nordic Prison Policy and Practice*, London: Routledge.

Von Hofer, H. (2003) 'Prison populations as political constructs: The case of Finland, Holland and Sweden', *Journal of Scandinavian Studies in Criminology and Crime Prevention* 4(1): 21–38.

Wacquant, L. (2002) 'The curious eclipse of prison ethnography in the age of mass incarceration', *Ethnography* 3(4): 371–397.

Wener, R.E. (2012) *The Environmental Psychology of Prisons and Jails: Creating Humane Spaces in Secure Settings*, Cambridge: Cambridge University Press.

White, A.A. (2008) 'Concept of less eligibility and the social function of prison violence in class societies', *The Buffalo Law Review* 56: 737.

Wortley, R. (2002) *Situational Prison Control: Crime Prevention in Correctional Institutions*, Cambridge: Cambridge University Press.

Young, J. (2003) 'Searching for a new criminology of everyday life: A review of the "culture of control"', *British Journal of Criminology* 43(1): 228–243.

Zhang, Z., Spicer, A. and Hancock, P. (2008) 'Hyper-organizational space in the work of JG Ballard', *Organization* 15(6): 889–910.

2

PRISONS AND PRIVATISATION

POLICY, PRACTICE AND EVALUATION

ELAINE GENDERS

INTRODUCTION

Private prisons are on the rise. The UK government praises their benefits – others question the vaunted success of these institutions. Thus evaluating the engagement of the private sector in the provision, management and administration of prisons becomes a key question in contemporary prison policy. However, adequate evaluation must adopt a binary approach: one that takes on board normative debates about whether it is legitimate to delegate the task of punishment to private organisations and an empirical investigation into its efficacy. Participants in these double-sided debates need to scrutinise the various evaluative criteria of incarceration, which include how well the routines of daily prison life are managed and whether policy objectives are met. Responses to any of these questions have also to take into account the structures and processes through which accountability and legality are negotiated.

This chapter takes the view that prisons aim to protect the public by segregating those who have committed grave offences and pose a serious risk to the safety of the community. Yet, it also recognises the negative impact that prison can have on the lives of those who are incarcerated. It follows that the use of imprisonment should be kept to an irreducible minimum. The inclusion of private sector providers and the embracing of competitive practices in the delivery of prison services reflect an ideological shift in conceptions of the role of the public sector. However, they have also been hailed as a means of easing the financial burden of providing the required prison places whilst driving up standards of service and performance. The fear is that whether or not it meets these objectives, the input of the private sector will lend pragmatic legitimacy to the practice of imprisonment and thereby endorse its maintenance as a dominant criminal justice intervention.

This chapter outlines the historical foundations of private entrepreneurship in the criminal justice system and describes the current arrangements of the penal economy. It examines the main arguments for and against prison privatisation, identifying key issues in the debate about the boundaries of legitimate and effective public–private collaboration. The chapter goes on to discuss important questions raised by the continued strategic development of a mixed penal economy and the increasing commercialisation of criminal justice with specific reference to the government's Green Paper *Breaking the Cycle: Effective Punishment, Rehabilitation and Sentencing of Offenders* (Ministry of Justice 2010). This leads to the ultimate question to be explored: whether an arrangement which is founded on system interests can serve the needs of social as well as criminal justice. The chapter concludes by identifying key questions to be addressed in order to evaluate the case for the privatisation of prisons.

BRIEF HISTORY OF PRIVATISATION IN THE CRIMINAL JUSTICE SYSTEM

Within much of the academic literature there is a widespread assumption that the punishment of criminals is, at root, a public function and, as such, an exercise of governmental power. Yet a brief consideration of penal history shows us that this has not always been the case (Lichtenstein 2001). Although criminal law was separated from the private law of torts and made an offence against the crown in the middle ages, most features of the administration of criminal justice remained in private hands until well into the eighteenth century.

Feeley (2002) argues that historical developments in the criminal just-ice system must be viewed in the context of commercial and industrial developments in society generally. His work examines the shift from feudalism to capitalism, charting the development of the criminal just-ice system from the inept and capricious arrangements overseen by the aristocracy and landed gentry, to the modern and more efficient system familiar today. He describes how the interests of the new commercial classes played an important role in this process, claiming that as the rising new business elite demanded more efficient and more effective criminal justice administration, private entrepreneurs stepped in. A key example of this is the development of transportation in the seventeenth century. Pioneered by merchant shippers, those who had committed offences were taken to the United States at low cost in exchange for the right to auction them off into limited-term slavery to the cotton and tobacco plantations. It was not until the Transportation Act 1718 that this system became institutionalised as a punishment and was controlled by means of Home Office contracts. Indeed, the private sector contin-ued its involvement in the administration of punishment even when the modern government-operated prisons such as Milbank (built in 1816) and Pentonville (built in 1844) took over from transportation as the major institution of punishment in the late nineteenth century.

Bentham's vision of the panopticon, where maximum surveillance is made possible at minimum cost, is a familiar concept. However, for 20 years Bentham also tried to obtain a contract from the government of the day to build and operate a self-financing 'prison factory' that would yield huge profits from the productive labour of the convicts. Bentham's business venture never came to fruition but his efforts did lend legitim-acy to the idea that prisoners could be put to profitable work to produce income for the government. Similar ideas gathered support in the United States where it was common in the nineteenth century for states to build prisons and then turn them over to private contractors to operate as a business, in the expectation that the state would share in any surpluses.

THE NEW WAVE OF PRISON PRIVATISATION

A new wave of state-led private sector involvement in the criminal jus-tice system has proliferated in the twentieth and twenty-first centuries.

In the UK, this has been largely restricted to prisons, court escort services, police detention, IT provision and other administrative and support services. This new trend should be understood as part of a much wider ideological shift that has recently taken place in several leading western democracies. There has been a rolling back of the state in many spheres of public life and a redesignation of the government's responsibilities to the regulation rather than provision of certain services. It started in the UK in the 1980s with the flotation on the Stock Exchange of a number of public utilities (gas, then electricity, then water). Since then there has been a continuing political commitment by successive British governments to privatisation as a means of reducing public spending.

The inclusion of prisons in the privatisation programme, as a result of the Private Finance Initiative (PFI) in 1992, was partly driven by the increasing remand population, which grew by a massive 76 per cent between 1979 and 1988. Since then, the prison population (both sentenced and remand) has continued to grow apace, and prisons have become an expensive business. The first modern privately run prison, the Wolds, opened in 1992 to house remand prisoners. Today, the UK has 14 privately run prisons, housing remand and sentenced prisoners, both adults and young people.

The first four privately run prisons were contracted out on a management-only basis, on agreements lasting five years. However, since 1995 most contracts have been issued for new build privately run prisons under the design, construct, manage and finance scheme (DCMF). DCMF means that the private contractor undertakes the whole range of activities that go into turning an empty site into an operational prison; from architectural planning and building through to staffing and running the prison. Legally, ownership of the land on which the prison stands remains with the government and the contractor receives a lease of the plot which has typically been set at 25 years. For this term the government pays the contractor a monthly fee to cover both set-up and running costs.

It is significant that the growth of private sector involvement in prisons closely followed the return to a 'just deserts' penal policy, evidenced in the Criminal Justice Act 1991. It also coincided with an expansionist prisons policy fuelled by the unprecedented public announcement by the Conservative government's Home Secretary,

Michael Howard, in 1993, that 'prison works'. The 'prison works' rhetoric underpinned the Conservative administration's Crime (Sentences) Act 1997 and led to a substantial increase in spending on prisons. Informed by principles of deterrence and incapacitation, the Act extended the use of mandatory life sentences and introduced compulsory minimum custodial terms.

The 'prison works' philosophy marked a radical departure in official thinking about penal policy, which up until then had emphasised the need to reserve imprisonment for only the most intractable cases. Despite two changes of government, there appears to be no significant change of direction. In 2008 the Labour Home Secretary, Jack Straw, endorsed Lord Carter's support for continued, albeit reined in, expansion of the prison estate. Whilst Kenneth Clarke, the Coalition government's former Minister of Justice, announced a planned reduction of 3,000 prisoners by 2014 (Hansard, 1 November 2010), after a forced U-turn on reduced sentences for guilty pleas in 2011, it is not clear how that will be achieved.

From a financial perspective, prisons are expensive capital items with high running costs. Thus, there is considerable attraction for government in any policy designed to reduce those costs. The proportion of the UK prison population held in private prisons is approximately 15 per cent (Prison Reform Trust 2012). This figure is set to rise with eight public sector prisons (Lindholm, Moorland, Hatfield, Acklington, Castington, Durham, Onley and Coldingley) being put up to competition. Currently, private prison contracts are shared between just three companies; Sodexo Justice Services operates three, Serco operates five and G4S operates six.

WHAT ARE THE ATTRACTIONS OF PRIVATE SECTOR PROVISION?

The purported benefits of private sector provision extend beyond a simple consideration of fiscal cost. Advocates of privatisation argue that private contractors are more efficient, more effective and represent better value for money than state providers. However, whether they are more cost-effective and whether they do deliver a better service is currently unclear. These issues are more complex than might be imagined and are discussed further below.

Better service

One quantitative measure to determine whether private prisons deliver a better service might be the official prison performance ratings. The National Audit Commission report (2003) found that privately contracted prisons were, on the whole, performing better than public prisons in areas related to the Prison Service decency agenda (for example, time out of cell, respect, etc.) but that, generally, they performed less well in areas such as safety and security. However, there have been problems of comparability related to the different ways in which data is collected for public and private sector prisons, and it is only in the past few years that a fairly reliable common measurement tool, the Prison Performance Assessment Tool (PPAT), has been developed.

Prison performance data is published quarterly and, according to this measure, the privately contracted estate has not fared well. Although there has been some variation over time, at the end of 2010 the average score for privately contracted prisons was lower (2.64) than for public prisons (2.90). Privately contracted prisons ranked about the same as public sector prisons on excellence: a similar proportion in each sector received the top rating. However, privately contracted prisons were over-represented amongst those requiring development or giving rise to serious concern, and this has been a consistent pattern until the last reported year of 2011–12.

Looking behind these figures, an inquiry under the Freedom of Information Act 2000 by More4 News revealed that in 2008–9, almost double the number of prisoner complaints were upheld in private prisons as in state-run institutions (5.8 per cent against 3.1 per cent). In addition, private prisons have held a higher percentage of their prisoners in overcrowded accommodation than public sector prisons every year for the last 14 years. In 2011–12 the private prisons average was 30.2 per cent, compared to an average of 23.3 per cent in the public sector (Ministry of Justice 2012a). Further evidence of poor performance by the private sector has been provided on an international scale with the revelation of riots, wrongful detention and high levels of self-harm in privately contracted detention centres in the United States, UK and Australia (*Observer* 2011).

Numbers of deaths in custody or instances of self-harm might constitute more specific measures to determine whether private prisons deliver a better service than public prisons. Between 2007 and 2009 there were 206 self-inflicted deaths in prison investigated and concluded by the Prison and Probation Ombudsman (PPO). Fewer than 5 per cent of these occurred in privately contracted prisons. Such institutions, at that time holding 11 per cent of the total prison population, were therefore under-represented in the PPO caseload (Prisons and Probation Ombudsman for England and Wales 2011). However, this type of measure can be misleading as some populations, such as remand prisoners and young people, have tended to produce higher rates of suicide and self-harm than others. Such simple statistical data also reveal nothing of the circumstances surrounding these deaths. Subsequent inquests are more enlightening: the second inquest in January 2011 into the death of 14-year-old Adam Rickwood in 2004 at Hassockfield Secure Training Centre found serious shortcomings in both the conduct of Serco and the exercise of the Youth Justice Board's responsibility, which, it was stated, reflected a failure of accountability and the structure of governance.

An alternative tactic might be to look at the reports of Her Majesty's Chief Inspector of Prisons (HMCIP) and at individual cases. For example, the Inspectorate's report on Rye Hill (a privately run prison) in June 2007 contained accounts of assaults, deaths, hostage taking and indiscipline as well as criticism of the high availability of drugs, drink and mobile telephones for prisoners. At Rye Hill alone, there were three deaths in the year 2005–6: two were self-inflicted and the third was caused by a stabbing by another prisoner. As a result of this report (and a subsequent investigation by *Panorama*), a Rectification Notice was served on GSL (the prison contractor) in August 2007. The Notice directed that GSL produce written proposals to be agreed by the authority and take remedial action on six key measures identified in an operational review.

This type of approach to evaluating the relative merits or demerits of different types of prison management is prone to the criticism of proof by selective instances. A number of HMCIP reports have been highly critical of private sector institutions, especially from a safety angle, but there are also problems at public sector prisons and immigration detention centres. Any study of such reports would need to be comprehensive and control for the type of establishment concerned.

More methodologically rigorous empirical research has been carried out on service delivery, physical conditions and the quality of life in privately and publicly managed prisons in the UK, Australia, New Zealand and the United States (Cooper and Taylor 2005; Harding 2001; Hatry *et al.* 1993; James *et al.* 1997; Moyle 1995; Logan 1992; Rynne *et al.* 2008). Most of the studies concur, highlighting the better facilities and more positive attitudes of staff on issues concerning fairness, respect and humanity in privately run rather than publicly managed prisons. Improved attitudes are attributed to the practice of private contractors recruiting staff with no prior experience of prison work. Hence staff in the privately managed prisons will not have been exposed to the negative influences of staff culture found within many prisons in the public sector. Yet, the research cautions that the relative inexperience of staff in privately contracted prisons can lead to negative consequences in the form of safety, well-being and institutional order.

A recent study in the UK examined the quality of life in two public and two private sector prisons, focusing on institutional cultures, interpersonal relationships and the respective experiences of prisoners and staff. The researchers found that the two public sector prisons scored higher than their private sector comparators on a number of measures and below them on none (Liebling and Crewe 2011). Yet in their evaluation of three further privately contracted prisons, they found that prisoner quality of life was higher in two of these than in the public sector prisons (ESRC 2011). Whilst these results are inconclusive, they highlight the importance of social relations in prisons. This is significant since custodial officers have the power to influence the quality of prisoners' lives on a daily basis, controlling their access to well-being, health and opportunities for risk reduction and release through the provision of structured programmes and routine interaction. As the researchers noted: 'where relationships have the right balance of control and respect almost all aspects of the prisoner experience are enhanced' (ESRC 2011). The research highlights the importance of experience and competence, as well as attitudes in determining how authority is exercised and experienced within public and private sector prisons (Crewe *et al.* 2011).

Cost-effectiveness

Many consider privately contracted prisons to be more cost-effective than their public sector counterparts. However, it has been suggested that whilst the strategy results in short-term gain it leads to long-term costs; and that the government could borrow money at better rates to build and run prisons themselves. It is further argued that the refinancing practices in which some of the contractors have engaged incur a potential long-term cost to the public sector because they expose the government to greater risk of the venture failing.

According to a parliamentary written answer, the costs of private prisons per place are higher than public sector prisons in most categories (Hansard, 9 January 2007). However, a real problem exists in comparing the price of public and private sector prisons in that the full public sector costs of PFI are difficult to evaluate. The task is compounded by the private sector's resort to claims of commercial confidentiality over matters relating to their competitive interests. Various studies have attempted to assess the relative costs of public and private prisons but their findings fail to provide conclusive evidence of financial efficacy (see, for example, Abt. Associates 1998; Park 2000; Pratt and Maahs 1999; Perrone and Pratt 2003).

A further fiscal issue is raised by the current drive for efficiency savings across prison services. In response to a question relating to budgetary cuts in 2009, Lord Bach stated that 'services provided by prisons run by private sector operators are stipulated and priced within a contract and therefore cannot be varied in the same way as public sector prisons, without agreement between the authority and the contractor' (Hansard, 14 December 2009). Yet, it has also been claimed that the private prison sector is not immune from the government's spending constraints and is being hit by a similar programme of efficiency savings. There is need for an independent and comprehensive research programme to look into the question of relative cost. This programme should include consideration of a wide range of social, economic and environmental factors and should examine how the privately contracted sector is affected by the financial cuts that are being imposed on the public sector.

Driving up standards in the public sector

It has been proposed that the introduction of privately run prisons has encouraged innovation and driven up standards in the public sector.

In July 2011 the Ministry of Justice stated that decisions about 'which prisons were selected for competition or closure [were] based on a wide range of criteria, including the potential for efficiency improvements, service reform and innovation' (Ministry of Justice 2011a). The ordering of the criteria is noteworthy. The importation of competitive practices to the public sector (e.g. performance management through target setting and the market testing of prisons) is said to have reduced the costs of public sector prisons largely by breaking down the power of prison officer unions and enabling more flexible staffing structures to be used (Carter 2007). There may well be something in this argument, as two of the originally privately managed prisons (Blakenhurst and Buckley Hall) have now returned to Prison Service management after retendering; the implication being that the public sector outperformed the private consortia in their bids. Yet, the Ministry of Justice's (2011a) own assessment tool (PPAT) shows no evidence of overall improvement in performance amongst public sector prisons. Indeed, returns have indicated a drop in performance by both public and private sector establishments.

ARGUMENTS AGAINST PRIVATISATION

Traditionally, those who argue against private prisons have done so on grounds other than cost-effectiveness. Some of the concerns relate to the effects of privatisation on the nature and form of imprisonment whilst others relate to issues of legitimacy and accountability. These are discussed in more detail below.

Effects on the nature and form of imprisonment

It seems reasonable to assume that the growth of privatised prisons will lead to an even greater expansion in the use of imprisonment as predicted by Lilly and Knepper's (1992) corrections-commercial complex thesis. This holds that because the privatisation of prisons satisfies both public and private sector interests, there will be an inevitable increase in the prisons estate and in the number of people held in them. England and Wales has one of the highest prison populations in the European Union at 153 per 100,000 (International Centre for Prison Studies). The need to contain the growth of the prison population has been acknowledged by the recent Carter report (Carter 2007) and by the government's Green Paper (Ministry of Justice 2010).

The danger of a commercially propelled upward drive in prison numbers should not be underestimated. Vivien Stern's disturbing study of imprisonment throughout the world uses the United States as a key example of potential trouble. In the United States, prisons are becoming big business. Small towns are 'queuing up' to get one built in their neighbourhood and advertising brochures describe the profits to be made from crime, urging investment managers to 'get in on the ground floor of this booming industry' (Stern 1998). In the UK there are also profits to be made from criminal justice investment. In evidence to the House of Commons Public Accounts Committee (2011), Dexter Whitfield reported that two sectors had higher than average profits from equity sales: health and criminal justice.

A further argument is that privatisation promotes an increased concern with security and militates against the rehabilitation of prisoners. Private companies have been involved in the development of community treatment programmes and the first purpose-built therapeutic community prison, Dovegate, is run by a private contractor (Serco). In theory, there is a tension between a penal policy aimed at rehabilitation and an operational policy that allows the private sector to formulate and run prison regimes. This is because the underlying force of rehabilitation is reductionist, the logical deduction of which would be that the profit motive would disappear in a shrinking market. By providing rehabilitative regimes, prisons would appear to be in the business of putting themselves out of business. In practice, the effects of a rehabilitative policy would be unlikely to have any great impact on the overall crime and imprisonment rate because it is only those who are caught and treated or trained who can be rehabilitated. However, privately operated institutions which have the declared aim of rehabilitation are left in the theoretical position where they have conflicting goals depending on whether success is defined in terms of penal policy values or commercial market interests.

There is, though, more than a simple theoretical issue here. Mona Lynch (2002) has argued that the involvement of the private sector in the penal market has coincided with an ideology of risk management and the commoditisation of security. Hence, prison is no longer designed to discipline the individual but has become a site of segregation and risk control, or as she puts it, prisons have become human warehouses for marginalised segments of the population. Lynch argues that the expansion of the penal commodities market is in keeping with a broader trend, involving the successful mass commoditisation of security throughout society over the past few decades, as seen in the increased reliance on hardware such as gates, barriers and alarms to promote safety in the home. To support her argument, Lynch analysed the advertisement columns of the US trade periodical *Corrections Today* between 1949 and 1999. She tracked how over this 50-year period advertisements by those in the corrections products and services industry showed less concern with the prisoner as an individual to be rescued or rehabilitated and more concern with institutional operations.

The relationship between supply and demand is complex and it is impossible to identify which came first: supply in the form of commercial innovation or demand, stemming from a new need based on a shifting ideology of risk and security. Nevertheless, Lynch's conclusion is that those in the corrections products and services industry appear to play at least a contributory role in the growing acceptance of the security-oriented 'warehouse' prison that has ascended in the United States over the past 20 years.

Accountability

Accountability in relation to prison privatisation needs to be assessed in two forms: (1) democratic accountability (sometimes linked to legitimacy); and (2) operational accountability.

Democratic accountability concerns the legitimate authority of the state and how much that authority can be delegated to private companies. Some argue that punishment, as a form of coercive force, is the quintessential function of government and should not under normal circumstances be delegated to private contractors. To do so, they warn, impoverishes the public sphere and weakens the moral bond between citizen and state (DiIulio 1990). Others argue that an important distinction can be made between the allocation of punishment (one of the core powers of government under social contract theory) and the administration of that punishment (which is not a core power and can therefore be delegated). The key questions are:

- How exactly does one distinguish between the allocation and administration of punishment?
- Does the allocation of punishment begin and end in the court?
- Are prisons only concerned with the administration of punishment?

The answers are not straightforward; for example, what about prison discipline, parole reports, sentence planning and classification? All of these processes affect the prisoner's experience of imprisonment and may be seen as part of the allocation and not simply the administration of punishment. In the UK, every privately operated prison has a controller, who is a crown servant. Under section 85(3) of the Criminal Justice Act 1991, the controller was charged with the duty to investigate and report on any allegations against custody officers in relation to the performance of their custodial obligations and with the task of inquiring into and adjudicating on all disciplinary charges brought against inmates. However, section 19 of the Offender Management Act 2007 repealed previous legislation and introduced measures to transfer to directors of privately contracted prisons the power to adjudicate, segregate and authorise the use of force against prisoners. Whilst they were in effect, the restrictions on the powers of directors went some way towards assuaging disquiet about both the formal and informal disciplinary procedures within prisons. But they did not address concerns relating, for instance, to the consequences of sentence planning or parole reports. The major objection here pertains to the chain of accountability within private sector prisons: beginning with custodial officers and ending with shareholders.

This can be explored further by examining the issue of operational accountability. All prisons, whether publicly or privately managed, are subject to performance testing by means of certain output orientated key performance indicators and targets. In the case of private prisons there is a supplementary method of accountability through the contract. Under the contract, the private company undertakes to provide a specified level of service in return for a monthly fee. The ultimate sanction for breach of contract is termination, but most common is the withholding of some portion of the monthly fee. This provides a powerful incentive to the contractor to meet the agreed performance standards. The knowledge that one can lose major profits creates a powerful pressure on the private sector to which the public sector has never been subject. There are two dangers in this. First, the threat of financial damage provides a strong incentive for the contractor to purport to have achieved specified targets when in reality they have failed to do so. This is made possible by the concern of key performance tools with ends rather than means. For example, should performance in a therapeutic community prison be measured by reconviction rates or time in therapy? If the measure is reconviction rates then this may lead to the selection of 'easy bets'. If the measure is time in therapy this may result in the prison retaining in therapy those who are unsuitable to continue (Genders 2003). Second, the overriding accountability of private contractors to their shareholders might result in the failing contractor making a commercial calculation to sustain the financial penalties imposed by the state rather than significantly increase investment to meet its performance targets. In both scenarios, the contractors could hardly be expected to behave otherwise: they have acted in accordance with the system set up to structure their operations and have behaved predictably in seeking to carry out their commercial obligations in ways which best accord with their own priorities and standards (Genders 2002). Such behaviour may result in the derailment of official policy objectives (Genders and Player 2007).

Although there is a need to explore new or additional methods by which private contractors might be held accountable for their behaviour, the prospect of the public authority being able to keep ahead of the game is bleak. At a structural level, the government operates as a nation state, whereas contractors operate at a global level. They are financed by international capital and engage in a diversified market. For example, it has been reported that Serco's $10 billion portfolio includes many businesses in addition to the prisons and immigration detention centres it operates in Australia, the United States and UK, from air traffic control and visa processing, to nuclear weapons maintenance, video surveillance and welfare to work programmes (*Observer* 2011).

CURRENT GOVERNMENT POLICY: THE STRATEGIC DEVELOPMENT OF A MIXED PENAL ECONOMY AND THE INCREASING COMMERCIALISATION OF CRIMINAL JUSTICE

Three features characterise the Coalition government's current strategy in respect of prison provision over the present spending period: (1) an increased commitment to competition and greater contestability; (2) the targeting of better outcomes in the form of a reduction in reoffending; (3) the introduction of an ideology of payment by results. As Secretary of State for Justice, Kenneth Clarke described how the use of contracting models where providers are paid by results would drive innovation, improve outcomes and ensure better value for money (Ministry of Justice 2011b). The current provisions apply to custodial services but will be developed and extended to non-custodial services. Hence, whilst the previous Labour government's policy appeared to favour a mixed economy of public and private provision (where competition was used as a means to select providers for new services or to address poor public sector performance), the new Coalition administration has pledged that competition will apply to all services not bound to the public sector by statute (Ministry of Justice 2011b).

This strategy marks a shift in the scale of contestability and the way in which competition is used in custodial and community services. At the same time, structural changes to the delivery of services have resulted in certain changes to the lines of accountability. Privately contracted prisons are no longer accountable to the Prison Service Agency (PSA) but to the Director General of the National Offender Management Service (NOMS), who is, in turn, accountable to the Ministry of Justice. Whilst the PSA continues to exist, it has essentially been subsumed within NOMS. Therefore, NOMS is now responsible for ensuring contestability in the provision of custodial and community based services, and for attracting new providers from the commercial and third sectors to the market through a planned programme of market testing. This new structure radically changes the role of the PSA, which now operates as a delivery arm of NOMS, placing it, at least theoretically, on a level playing field with private providers. One question that seems to arise from the new structural arrangements concerns the role of commercial confidentiality and the extent to which the ability of private sector organisations to withhold commercially sensitive information may place public sector providers at a disadvantage in bidding processes since public providers must, presumably, continue to submit to the process of transparency.

Michael Spurr, as Chief Executive Officer of NOMS, stated that the shift in the scale and way in which competition is to be used would enable the delivery of better outcomes for the taxpayer for less money, as contestability will be used to drive quality of service, value for money, innovation and market development (Ministry of Justice 2011b). The Ministry of Justice business plan additionally commits the department to creating an effective market in the provision of offender management and rehabilitation by ensuring that services are provided by whoever can most effectively and efficiently meet public demand. The application of payment by results (PbR) principles is designed to stimulate providers to focus on outcomes, giving them the freedom to offer new approaches to service delivery (Ministry of Justice 2011b).

The Green Paper *Breaking the Cycle: Effective Punishment, Rehabilitation and Sentencing of Offenders* (Ministry of Justice 2010) sets out plans for reducing reoffending without reducing punishment. It proposes the development of working prisons and drug rehabilitation programmes, with providers from all sectors (public, private and voluntary) to be paid by results. The Legal Aid, Sentencing and Punishment of Offenders Act 2012 incorporates provisions to give effect to the Green Paper's proposals that require primary legislation. A Ministry of Justice business plan details the strategies to be employed for the 'rehabilitation revolution', including paying private and voluntary organisations by results; working with the Department of Health to pilot and roll out drug recovery wings in prisons; and increasing the numbers of prisoners doing meaningful work for real wages. Eight publicly managed prisons were put up for competition in 2012; already, the first payment by results pilot scheme is under way at Serco-run Doncaster prison, with at least six further projects planned before 2015 (Ministry of Justice 2011b). The NOMS subsequently announced that a further nine prisons would be put out to competitive tender during 2012–13 (Ministry of Justice 2012b).

In its competition strategy document, the Ministry of Justice explicitly states:

- competition will be based on the required outcomes and the demand for services;
- competition activity should be focused on achieving mid- to long-term savings, not finding the cheapest solution at the expense of quality;
- competition should be used to deliver public sector reforms, ensuring providers are more effectively held to account for the outcomes they deliver;

- competitions should be run and regulated fairly;
- providers should work with each other to deliver the best outcomes for communities.

(Ministry of Justice 2011b)

These mandates raise a number of issues of interpretation and application, relating to the factors to be employed in evaluating 'the best outcomes for communities' and the indices to be used to calibrate performance and gauge success. Reconviction rates are the usual yardstick but are a poor choice as they count only offences for which the person has been caught and convicted. Softer measures such as getting a job or attending education might be attractive since they reflect current criminological understanding that desistance from crime is a gradual and multifaceted business built on integration into the community, employment and other social institutions. However, this type of approach may be criticised as reflecting more of a payments for 'process' than payments for 'results' scheme. More problematic is the issue of attribution. For example, since desistance may be influenced by numerous divergent factors and a variety of independent interventions, how might payment be fairly distributed amongst the different agencies involved? A collaborative scheme might provide the most equitable means but how would this synchronise with the competitive ethos of the private market?

Further questions should be asked of the strategy document, informed by what is already known about the involvement of private contractors in prison service provision. These should bear in mind contractors' access to global capital and business expertise; their commitment to the profit incentive; and the many issues associated with accountability, such as commercial confidentiality, lack of transparency and the inherent duty of private enterprise to its shareholders.

CONCLUSION

The most difficult question surrounding prison privatisation is how far structural arrangements rooted in system interests can serve the needs of criminal and social justice. The drivers of change propelling the increased commercialisation of criminal justice are informed less by concerns for the interests of justice or security and more by a commitment to a particular political ideology (evident in the transformation of the role of the state from service provider to service commissioner) and the exigencies of economic expediency (manifest in the pursuit of efficiency and cost-effectiveness). The dilemma is whether a mixed penal economy can meet the requirements of social and criminal justice whilst adhering to the dictates of market forces. For instance, the recognition that detainees are profitable not just for their labour, but also for their ability to generate payment by their very incarceration, generates disquiet about the nature of the investment by entrepreneurs in the production and commoditisation of prisoners. Particular concern might be raised when the structural relationships that designate prisoners amongst the most socially, economically and politically disempowered segments of society are acknowledged (see Mathiessen 2006; Bennett 2008; Wacquant 2005; Marchetti 2002). The influence of lobbying groups with a vested interest in the prison industry continues to be most evident in the United States (Leighton and Reiman 2010). Yet in the UK too, for example, private contractors raised objections, on grounds of cost, to the inclusion of prisons within the Corporate Homicide and Corporate Manslaughter Act (*Guardian* 2011), elevating considerations of profit over concern for human safety. This begs the question of how the government will manage the ostensibly competing objectives generated by market imperatives and the dictates of justice.

Finally, it must be questioned whether the current drive towards increasing commercialisation of prison management and the provision of a mixed economy of working prisons is likely to lead to a proliferation of the penal estate. The government's commitment to meting out tough criminal sanctions and its reductivist policy of driving down crime by delivering prisons that offer rehabilitation through hard work might accede to the demands of penal populism, but they raise an inherent contradiction. The policy of payment by results is designed to encourage service providers to deliver programmes that lead to desistance from crime. This appears to be a laudable aim since it aspires to reduce the risk of victimisation in the community whilst rebalancing social justice by providing enhanced opportunities for education, employment and social inclusion. Yet, from a reintegrative perspective, such efforts might be more effectively delivered through community schemes. From an economic perspective, too, community provision would be more cost-efficient.

Increasing private sector involvement in the provision of penal regimes is an attractive option for the government, enabling the realisation of its vision of encouraging desistance from crime whilst maintaining a tough stance on those who commit offences. The question is whether the meeting of these aspirations will succeed in providing rehabilitative opportunities to a reduced prison population comprising those who have committed the most serious offences; or trigger a net widening effect, whereby more people are drawn into the prison system for less serious offences, thus militating against the attainment of a reductionist prison agenda.

FURTHER RESEARCH

Analysis of these issues has identified a number of questions and directions for research, which, if pursued, could extend existing knowledge around prison privatisation. These include:

1. An extension of existing research on prisoner–staff relationships in publicly and privately managed institutions, incorporating:
   - an examination of staff attitudes and behaviours, and how these might influence prisoner outcomes;
   - an evaluation of management styles and practices, and how they shape the boundaries of staff action.

   To be comprehensive, it is imperative that such research take account of the issue of staff retention, in particular the ways in which retention rates contribute to the evolution of particular institutional cultures and how these may change over time.
2. An independent and comprehensive comparison of the relative costs of public and private sector prisons. This should include consultancy fees, the bidding process, borrowing arrangements, staff engaged in the competition process as well as risk transfer, since the cost of failure must ultimately be borne by the public purse. This type of analysis could be broadened out to incorporate social, economic, employment and environmental factors as well as community well-being. For example, questions could address the cost-effectiveness of operating privately contracted prisons with fewer and less experienced staff than in public sector prisons. In particular, research should examine:
   - how existing privately contracted prisons are affected by the financial cuts that are hitting the public sector;

- to what extent and in what ways they might be protected from fiscal clawback by the contractual arrangements that are already in place.
3. An investigation to identify innovations that have arisen from private sector management or PFI projects: whether these have been adopted by the public sector and to what effect. A prior question might be in what ways PFI contracts enable creativity and innovation and in what ways they constrain them.
4. An analysis of some of the concepts used in the Ministry of Justice's current strategy for competition, including the factors to be used in evaluating 'the best outcomes for communities'. At a more empirical level, the Ministry of Justice's payment by results projects will require ongoing critical and independent assessment, not least, a consideration of the indices that might be employed to calibrate performance and gauge success. Further questions include whether:
   - the level of risk entailed in the system of payment by results will deter smaller players or the voluntary sector from competing or might lead providers to mitigate potential loss by negotiating higher fees for their services;
   - the focus on payment by results might encourage contractors to manipulate outcomes or to play it safe by focusing their resources on easy targets;
   - the competitive ethos so intrinsic to the market model of service provision will lead to fragmentation and militate against the collaborative working practices required of a rehabilitative system.
5. A frank inquiry as to how the government will ensure that penal policy is not derailed by the fiscal imperatives of private contractors and that it is not outmanoeuvred as it has been before.

References

Abt. Associates (1998) *Private Prisons in the US: An Assessment of Current Practice*. Cambridge, MA: Abt. Associates.

Bennett, J. (2008) *The Social Costs of Dangerousness: Prison and the Dangerous Classes*. London: Centre for Crime and Justice Studies.

Carter, P. (2007) *Securing the Future: Proposals for the Efficient and Sustainable Use of Custody in England and Wales*. London: Cabinet Office.

Cooper, C. and Taylor, P. (2005) 'Independently verified reductionism: prison privatisation in Scotland'. *Human Relations* 58(4) pp. 497–522.

Crewe, B., Liebling, A. and Hulley, S. (2011) 'Staff culture, use of authority and prisoner quality of life in public and private sector prisons'. *Australian and New Zealand Journal of Criminology* 44(1) pp. 94–115.

Dilulio, J. (1990) 'The duty to govern: a critical perspective on the private management of prisons and jails' in McDonald, D. (ed.) *Private Prisons and the Public Interest*. New Brunswick: Rutgers University Press, pp. 155–78.

ESRC (2011) *Staff-Prisoner Relationships are Key to Prison Quality* – Press Release 17. Available at: www.esrc.ac.uk/news-and-events/press-releases/15594/staff-prisoner-relationships-are-key-to-prison-quality.aspx [accessed August 2012].

Feeley, M. (2002) 'Entrepreneurs of punishment'. *Punishment and Society* 4(3) pp. 321–43.

Genders, E. (2002) 'Legitimacy, accountability and private prisons'. *Punishment and Society* 4(3) pp. 285–303.

Genders, E. (2003) 'Privatisation and innovation – rhetoric and reality: the development of a therapeutic community prison'. *Howard Journal* 42(2) pp. 137–57.

Genders, E. and Player, E. (2007) 'The commercial context of criminal justice: prison privatisation and the perversion of purpose'. *Criminal Law Review*, pp. 513–29.

Guardian (2011) 'Privatisation will not rehabilitate our prisons'. Available at: www.guardian.co.uk/commentisfree/2011/apr/01/privatisation-prisons/print [accessed 6 May 2012].

Hansard HC, 9 January 2007, c546W.

Hansard HC, 14 December 2009, cWA179.

Hansard HC, 1 November 2010, C514W.

Harding, J. and Wortley, R. (2008) 'Market testing and prison riots: how public sector commercialisation contributed to a prison riot'. *Criminology and Public Policy* 7(1) pp. 117–42.

Harding, R. (2001) 'Private prisons'. *Crime and Justice* 28 pp. 265–346.

Hatry, H., Brounstein, P. and Levinson, R. (1993) 'Comparisons of privately and publicly operated corrections facilities in Kentucky and Massachusetts' in G. Bowman, S. Hakim and P. Seidenstat (eds) *Privatizing Correctional Institutions*. New Brunswick: Transaction Publishers, pp. 193–212.

House of Commons Public Accounts Committee (2011). Written evidence presented by Dexter Whitfield. Available at www.publications.parliament.uk/pa/cm201012/cmselect/cmpubacc/1201/1201we03.htm [accessed 25 January 2013].

International Centre for Prison Studies (2012) World Prison Brief. Available at: www.prisonstudies.org/info/worldbrief [accessed January 2013].

James, A., Bottomley, K., Liebling, A. and Clare, E. (1997) *Privatizing Prisons: Rhetoric and Reality*. London: Sage.

Leighton, P. and Reiman, J. (2010) *The Rich get Richer and the Poor get Prison*. Boston: Allyn and Bacon.

Lichtenstein, A. (2001) 'The private and public in penal history'. *Punishment and Society* 3(1) pp. 189–96.

Liebling, A. and Crewe, B. (2011) *Values, Practices and Outcomes in Public and Private Sector*. Available at: www.esrc.ac.uk/my-esrc/grants/RES-062–23–0212/outputs/Read/3e0fdcb7–238d-44e8-a54a-2d8cc7571c8c [accessed June 2012].

Lilly, J.R. and Knepper, P. (1992) 'An international perspective on the privatisation of corrections'. *Howard Journal* 31(3) pp. 174–91.

Logan, C.H. (1992) 'Well-kept: comparing quality of confinement in private and public prisons'. *Journal of Criminal Law and Criminology* 83(3) pp. 577–613.

Lynch, M. (2002) 'Selling securityware'. *Punishment and Society* 4(3) pp. 305–19.

Marchetti, A. (2002) 'Carceral impoverishment: class inequality in the French penitentiary'. *Ethnography* 3 pp. 416–34.

Mathiessen, T. (2006) *Prison on Trial*. Winchester: Waterside Press.

Ministry of Justice (2010) *Breaking the Cycle: Effective Punishment, Rehabilitation and Sentencing of Offenders*. Available at: www.justice.gov. uk/consultations/docs/breaking-the-cycle.pdf [accessed June 2012].

Ministry of Justice (2011a) *National Offender Management Service Annual Report 2009/10*. London: Ministry of Justice.

Ministry of Justice (2011b) *Competition Strategy for Offender Services*. Available at: www.justice.gov.uk/downloads/publications/moj/2011/ competition-strategy-offender-services.pdf [accessed June 2012].

Ministry of Justice (2012a) *National Offender Management Service: Annual Report 2011/12*. London: Ministry of Justice.

Ministry of Justice (2012b) *National Offender Management Service: Business Plan 2012–13*. Available at: www.justice.gov.uk/downloads/publications/ corporate-reports/noms/2012/noms-business-plan-2012–2013.pdf [accessed 20 December 2012].

Moyle, P. (2001) 'Separating the allocation of punishment from its administration'. *British Journal of Criminology* 41 pp. 77–100.

National Audit Commission (2003) *The Operational Performance of PFI Prisons Report by the Comptroller and Auditor General*. London: The Stationery Office.

Observer (2011) New York Times Supplement, Sunday 16 October.

Park, I. (2000) *Review of Comparative Costs and Performance of Privately and Publicly Operated Prisons, 1998–9*. Home Office Statistical Bulletin 6/00, London: Home Office.

Perrone, D. and Pratt, T. (2003) 'Comparing the quality of confinement and cost effectiveness of public v private prisons: what we know, why we do not know more and where to go from here'. *The Prison Journal* 83(3) pp. 301–22.

Pratt, T.C. and Maahs, J. (1999) 'Are private prisons more cost-effective than public prisons? A meta-analysis of evaluation research studies'. *Crime and Delinquency* 45(3) pp. 358–71.

Prison Reform Trust (2012) *Bromley Briefings Prison Fact File June 2012.* Available at: www.prisonreformtrust.org.uk/Portals/0/Documents/Fact%20 File%20June%202011%20web.pdf [accessed January 2013].

Prisons and Probation Ombudsman for England and Wales (2011) *Learning from PPO Investigations: Self-Inflicted Deaths in Prison Custody 2007–2009.* Available at: www.ppo.gov.uk/docs/self-inflicted-deaths-in-prison.pdf [accessed June 2012].

Rynne, J., Harding, R. and Wortley, R. (2008) 'Market testing and prison riots: how public-sector commercialization contributed to a prison riot'. *Criminology and Public Policy* 7(1) pp. 17–142.

Stern, V. (1998) *A Sin against the Future: Imprisonment in the World.* London: Penguin.

Wacquant, L. (2005) 'The great penal leap backward: incarceration in America from Nixon to Clinton' in J. Pratt, D. Brown, M. Brown, S. Hallsworth and W. Morrison (eds) *The New Punitiveness; Trends, Theories, Perspectives.* Cullompton: Willan, pp. 3–26.

Understanding prison officers and their role

Staff were gatekeepers, agents of criminal justice, peacemakers, instruments of change and deliverers and interpreters of policy. (Liebling and Price 1999: 86)

I think the straightforward answer to what the prison officer does on the wing ... is that he operates the routine and the regime as decided by the governor ... So you get the core prison officers who are the ones who can do the routine. They unlock, they lock-up, they can do the routines. That's the absolute base level that prison officers can do to get the money. But that's not sufficient. It's about the other bits – it's about interacting with prisoners, having the proper relationship with them, it's helping them with their problems, dealing with their short-term needs and wants and their long-term needs and wants. (Senior manager)

What is the role of the modern prison officer? Arguably the primary role of a prison officer is the maintenance of safe custody (Thomas 1972). But there is clearly more to the officer's role than this. A good place to start is with the official definition of the prison officer's job – Figure 3.1 shows the information available on the Prison Service website for applicants interested in joining the Prison Service. This is a concise summary of the tasks facing a prison officer.

It is clear from the job description that prison work can be complex and challenging. Some of the broad objectives are apparently contradictory, prisoners are often found in highly charged emotional

42

Prison officers work in different types of prisons – open (low security), female, high security, juveniles, young offenders and remand centres. They help ensure the security and safety of prisoners.

What prison officers do

- help offenders deal with being in prison and help them to address their offending behaviour

- supervise prisoners' activities

- aid in rehabilitating and training offenders, giving prisoners advice, support and counselling via a Personal Officer scheme

- deal with any disruptions to the regime, maintaining control and order and helping to create a safe and secure environment

- receive and process new prisoners into prisons, assessing their needs and identifying possible self-harm issues

- search prisoners, accommodation blocks, vehicles, grounds and visitors into prisons.

Key skills for prison officers

- interest in dealing with social problems

- ability to react quickly and effectively under pressure, i.e. in incidents, acts of disorder

- sensitivity to others' problems and issues

- good communication skills

- an ability to get on with people from different social backgrounds

- initiative, good leadership and people management skills

- an ability to defuse conflict in a professional and sensitive manner.

Source: Prison Service website.

Figure 3.1 Prison officer job description

states and a single 'ill-considered word or action' can sometimes precipitate violence or tragedy. It is plain enough that the prison is a 'strange and demanding environment' (see the Prison Service website for further details).

Despite the apparently simple daily tasks of a prison officer ('you will unlock prisoners, deal with any requests they may have, make sure

43

they are where they should be and doing what they should be doing') it is the relationships an officer establishes with prisoners that hold the key to being a successful prison officer. These should be 'honest', but officers also need to know how to cajole, negotiate, persuade – 'you will require good listening, assertive, influencing, negotiating and verbal communication skills'. Further, these relationships have to be seen within other dimensions of this complex job: maintaining security, providing care, performing routines efficiently, balancing sometimes contradictory goals, and so on.

There is little in this formal definition about the rewards of the job of prison officer, other than the implicit suggestion that making a positive contribution to the care of those in custody might be rewarding in itself. We get an idea of the kind of personality that might be involved: someone that has 'strength of character, a balanced and mature approach to life, plenty of patience, understanding and common sense' – here, it is already possible to see why many prison officers compare their role to that of a parent.

However, the outline does not say much about how a prison officer might be expected to go about these many difficult tasks, nor does it provide any basic detail about the structure of a typical prison day, the working environment or their colleagues, for example.

Much sociological literature suffers from the same deficit – a lack of attention to the work and responsibilities of the prison officer. Some empirical studies have been carried out, many of these in the US (for example, Jacobs 1977, 1978; Johnson 1977; Johnson and Price 1981; Lombardo 1981; Toch and Klofas 1982; Klofas 1986; Marquart 1986), some in Australia (for example Williams 1983; Williams and Soutar 1984) and some in the UK (Morris and Morris 1963; Emery 1970). Many of these studies are now dated, in particular in their depiction of the nature of prison work, although there are useful insights which remain of interest (such as the finding that officers share a liberal socio-political perspective on the causes of crime and may have a 'greater commitment to rehabilitation than the academic penologists and prison administrators' (Jacobs 1978: 193). Some significant recent work conducted in the UK (Biggam and Power 1997; Liebling and Price 1999; Arnold 2008; Shefer and Liebling 2008), Australia (Rynne, personal communication) and the US (Gilbert 1997) suggest that officers may define their role differently, some preferring a mainly custodial interpretation, others having a 'treatment' orientation. These basic orientations are linked to staff perceptions of prisoners, their attitudes towards non-custodial staff and the type of rewards they seek in their work (Williams 1983). The need for clarity may

44

encourage officers to adhere to a disciplinary or rule orientation, to treat all prisoners alike and to develop individual and collective psychological defences in the form of negative stereotypes over time (Williams 1983: 53–4). Officers in the modern prison deliver (and help to deliver) professional treatment and development programmes for sex offenders, violent offenders, drug users and others, and arguably have developed a strengthened 'treatment intervention' role over recent years. Research has shown that officers who have a favourable or human services orientation towards prisoners have a more satisfying occupational experience (Whitehead *et al.* 1987).

Despite the research mentioned above, we would argue that prison staff have been generally neglected in the academic literature. Writing in 1991, Hay and Sparks (1991: 1) wondered whether 'the role of the prison officer [had] become so poorly defined, or alternatively so contradictory, as to make it unusually hard for anyone to occupy it satisfactorily'. Hay and Sparks felt that policy documents and official pronouncements on the role of the prison officer – like the job description above – said little about what officers should do on a daily working basis. Prison officers 'have not been well served by those above them whose job it is ... to provide them with a clear and consistent sense of identity and purpose' (Hay and Sparks 1991: 3). Within what guiding principles should officers work? How should they describe what they do?

The role of the prison officer is a difficult one to explain accurately. Most of the work is 'low visibility' and staff work to overall goals that may be in conflict with each other. How individual prison officers reconcile these problems in individual situations encountered during a typical working day is one of the main subjects of this book (see especially Chapter 6 on the use of discretion).

First, this chapter provides a basic description of prison officer work. We illustrate a typical day for a prison officer, using research we conducted as a template. There are over 140 public and private sector prison establishments in England and Wales, and each one operates slightly differently. As a result, the routine outlined below is a composite picture; it contains some of what we have seen of how officers might spend their time and a sense of the different roles that can be assumed by an officer. The chapter then goes on to define the role of the prison officer from the ground, using research that explored with prison officers and prisoners what qualities were considered important in being a 'role model' prison officer (Liebling and Price 1999; see also Arnold 2008).

45

A typical day for a prison officer

We focus here on the landing officer: arguably the key role in any prison. What might a day look like to an observer?

The amount and type of physical interaction between an officer and a prisoner varies depending on the designated role of the officer and the individual prisoner.[1] Landing officers unlock a landing in the morning and, generally, remain on the wing or spur while breakfast is served, controlling the flow of prisoners collecting their meals. Interaction might occur about the order in which the spurs are to receive breakfast, or a question or comment about some other aspect of the prison routine might come from a prisoner.[2] When most prisoners are off the spur at work (with officers sometimes needed to chivvy one or two along or to check why a prisoner is not going to work that day), landing officers are normally placed on the required daily task of checking locks, bolts and bars (LBBs) or another spur-based task (searching, for example). Teamed up with another officer, they move round a spur one landing at a time checking each cell and all communal areas. Within the wing, this is usually the quietest period of the unlocked day – both prisoners and officers are working at set tasks. Officers on LBBs speak to prisoners, perhaps asking them to step out of their cells if they are 'banged up' (not at work) – this is often a quick and relatively formal interaction, although some officers might banter and talk with prisoners (particularly those they get on with well) more than others. The prisoner might request to fetch some hot water or to hand in an application (written request) before he is locked up again. LBBs are often carried on during the afternoon work period. Thus the role of the landing officer is one of maintaining security and control, and in carrying out both relating effectively to prisoners.

The afternoon activity (work, training or education) period is more relaxed – much of the set work of the day is done both by prisoners and officers. On occasions, officers and prisoners might be observed leaning over the railings together chatting, often about prison issues but more general conversation might develop: the progress someone is making on education, a family issue, a crime, the news, a football match. When prisoners return from their activities – in the morning or the afternoon – the wing becomes much busier, and interaction between officers and prisoners is more varied and frequent. Longer and deeper conversations are normally reserved for an office or a quieter period of the day. The progression of prisoners to get their lunch or dinner often produces rapid bursts of talk – good humoured

46

insults are traded – but prisoners are usually too anxious to get their meal and start eating to talk for longer than a few minutes.

Evening association tends to be seen as 'prisoner time'. Some officers play pool or table tennis with prisoners or chat, but other officers are either busy and unable to talk or prefer to leave prisoners alone unless they wish to approach an officer. This does not stop the occasional casual remark or round of banter, however. Prisoners approach officers – particularly officers they know well – at any time, often to talk about any (prison-related) issue: a problem with a visit, a request for an application form, a query over private cash or a part of a procedure or the regime. Conversations are generally cooperative and civil. All-out arguments are rare – raised voices and emotions are more common among prisoners, with officers more frequently taking on the 'peacemaking' role.

There are occasions where there is a more formal opportunity for officers and prisoners to talk to each other about subjects other than prison – in sentence planning or personal officer interviews, for example – but general conversation about subjects other than prison is relatively rare. In part, this may be due to staff fears about 'conditioning' and 'boundaries' but it also reflects each side's knowledge of the reason for any relationship in the first place – often an instrumental one ('they need us, and we need their cooperation').

Staff shifts are an important factor in the physical structuring of their relationships with prisoners. Prison officers are contracted to work an average 39-hour week (meal breaks not included) and most work every other weekend. Because prisons operate 24 hours a day, a complex pattern of shifts determines the deployment of staff. This inevitably means that in the course of several weeks prisoners see a number of different officers. With time used for training, holidays and sickness (which can be high among officers), officers work on average 31.2 'effective' hours each week, scheduled in shifts covering the 24-hour period. The structural constraint of this lack of continuity is an important factor in the development and endurance of relationships. Events constantly 'happen' that affect a wing's operation (e.g. tensions between prisoners, staffing and management changes or disagreements, and general 'events' – a fire, an alarm, a successful parole result, a fight, a cell change, or even – as we once witnessed – a bird flying on to the wing where a staff member who was afraid of birds worked). Each event can bond, sever, strain, generate laughter or lead to a different atmosphere on the wing. Officers who come back on duty having been off for a week sometimes find it difficult

47

to catch up on all the small and subtle but important changes that have occurred. Similarly, prisoners often express frustration that they have not been able to see their personal officer for an extended period because of shift patterns and leave. In local prisons where the turnover of prisoners is particularly high, a change in the mix of prisoners can have a profound effect on the wing.

In one day, an officer can be a supervisor, custodian, disciplinarian, peacekeeper, administrator, observer, manager, facilitator, mentor, provider, classifier and diplomat. Different situations require slightly different blends, and different types of establishments or populations may demand a slightly different mix. Versatility and flexibility are key requirements.

Role model prison officers

The above sketch gives a brief idea of the many tasks in which officers are engaged during a typical day, from turning down a request, to giving unwelcome news, to assisting a prisoner with their sentence plan, to rub down searching or strip searching.[3] It illustrates the centrality of relationships to prison life. At every point of the day, the relationships an officer has established with prisoners are called upon: to unlock prisoners successfully without rancour, to cajole stragglers along to work, to make sure that the visits policy is explained clearly to dispel anxiety in a prisoner who is missing his or her family. Even in seemingly 'technical' matters – for example, censoring letters (an officer can draw upon their knowledge of a wing and the prisoner in reading letters) or in completing the locks, bolts and bars (checking around a prisoner's cell – their home – in a way that does not disturb or upset them) – relationships matter.

These relationships are mediated through the officer's own personality. What kinds of personal skills are required to be a successful prison officer? Is it possible to identify a 'role model' officer? A study in Denmark (Kriminalforsorgens Uddannelsescenter, 1994) addressed those questions. The team of researchers asked prison officers and their managers to identify the qualities that the ideal prison officer might have. They asked staff to nominate an individual who they thought operated effectively, handled conflict situations well and set a good example for other staff. The researchers then interviewed these nominated officers about their working styles, attributes and thoughts about their work. They were then able to produce a long profile of the skills that an ideal prison officer should possess. A selection of these qualities is listed in Table 3.1.

48

Table 3.1 Role model characteristics of prison officers

---

1 Physical characteristics
- good physical condition
- satisfactory strength to respond to hard working conditions
- ability to act with reasonable self-confidence and personal authority
- verbal skills

2 Mental capacity
- ability to think
- able to hold many things in mind at the same time

3 You should have the ability to:
(i) Learn:
- have the ability and need to learn new things
- be receptive to new ideas and alternative solutions
- understand consequences and connections in what oneself and others do
- come up with ideas and proposals and be able to see them through
- view and assess complex situations and deal with them

(ii) Watch:
- be alert and aware of yourself through observations and information
- be able to see, understand, evaluate and account for a situation without distortion
- be able to overview several activities at the same time without confusion
- be able to 'control' own attitudes and prejudices when people act in ways that disturb or annoy you, and to keep these people in order

(iii) Make decisions:
- use new information, understand it, form your own opinions and make your decision
- be loyal to decisions already made
- be flexible and able to change opinion when the circumstances change

(iv) Solve problems:
- be able to mentally prepare information to solve problems
- try to reach solutions which will be understood and accepted
- relate to others in a way that brings opinions from them
- be satisfied with half-solutions when the perfect solution is impossible

(v) Do administrative tasks:
- handle 'paperwork' exactly and quickly
- be organised
- understand and accept the necessity of routine work

Table 3.1 continues over

49

Table 3.1 continued

---

4 You should be able to:
- interact with others
- bear difficult emotions
- seek to understand other people's thoughts and emotions
- be sensitive in personal interaction
- be interested in one's environment as much as in oneself
- stand out as trustworthy
- live with the fact that from time to time it is hard to see the overall context
- live with the negative societal picture of the prison officer and imprisonment
- have a sense of humour
- lead others and create respect around oneself without becoming aggressive
- have self-confidence and self-esteem
- handle conflict situations
- communicate ideas clearly and easily and influence others
- express oneself in a clear and obvious way that is right for the person and the situation
- give clear signals that cannot be misinterpreted by the other person, and make sure that the receiver understands the signals
- acquire verbal and non-verbal signals from different individuals and groups with varied cultural characteristics
- build trust by one's actions
- possess self-confidence
- acquire positive energy outside the institution
- be professional enough to act 'sensibly' under pressure from colleagues and prisoners
- live with and strengthen relationships with others
- stand alone without support when the situation demands
- say 'no' when the situation demands
- be reliable, trustworthy and responsible for the tasks given to you
- be flexible enough to handle more than one duty and long irregular working hours
- understand different people's attitudes and behaviour and be able to express the reasons for their attitude and behaviour
- keep going, even if there is no pressure on you to do so.

Source: Kriminalforsorgens Uddannelsescenter (1994).

What is evident from this profile is that many of the attributes required to be a 'role model' prison officer are in tension. If we look at the section titled 'Make decisions', for example, two attributes follow one another: be loyal to decisions already made; and be flexible and

50

able to change opinion when the circumstances change. 'Solutions' requires the officer to be satisfied (and, implicitly, be able to recognise this point) with 'half-solutions' to problems but other attributes require the right solution to be sought. The profile is an aspirational one – no one person can be all of these things. If these are the attributes of the 'perfect' prison officer, can such an officer exist?

Role model officers at Whitemoor prison

We were intrigued by the Danish study and used it in our study of staff–prisoner relationships at Whitemoor. We asked prison officers, their managers and prisoners which prison officers they admired most and why. One general conclusion was that a mix of officers was necessary:

> You need the friendly and the fair; you need the very strict; you need the very easy. You need all of them. *Porridge* is the closest that outside people understand. You need your McKays and your Barracloughs, as well as everybody in-between. If we were all exactly the same, the job wouldn't tick, would it? (Officer)

> You need professional skills – leadership, decision-making, problem-solving skills, good communications skills; and the correct personal qualities – integrity, energy, enthusiasm, taking personal responsibility … but you need a blend. You don't want too many people with the same quality in one area. I don't think that there is a perfect officer. It's all about how you get individuals generally using common sense working with other people, being reasonable to their colleagues as many people of one type. (Senior manager)

Importantly, we found that slightly different 'role model' officers, and reasons for the choices of these officers, were given for different locations within the prison and by different groups. For example, managers were more likely to cite factors such as reliable attendance, enthusiasm and smartness; officers looked for reliability and willingness to do jobs when asked, the ability to 'keep a calm head' and the ability to resolve conflict. Prisoners preferred officers who were 'down to earth' and not 'petty'. However, throughout these different areas and the many different viewpoints, there was a common 'core' of desirable characteristics that were relevant in all locations and that were identified by senior managers, prison officer

51

colleagues and prisoners alike (see Table 3.2). Good officers had verbal skills of persuasion, could use authority appropriately, had human relations skills and leadership abilities and could use straight talk or honesty. They had the ability to maintain boundaries – all boundaries – with different departments, between management and staff, and with prisoners. They had personal strength or 'moral courage' and a sense of purpose. They needed patience, empathy, courage and a professional orientation.

Table 3.2 Factors common to 'role model' prison officers

- Having known and consistent boundaries. It did not matter so much precisely where these boundaries were, provided they were effectively communicated to prisoners and consistently policed.
- A quality for which we were unable to find a better term than 'moral fibre' – confidence, integrity, honesty, strength or conviction, good judgement (flexibility).
- An awareness of the effects of their own power.
- An understanding of the painfulness of prison.
- A 'professional orientation'.
- An optimistic – but realistic – outlook: the capacity to maintain hope in difficult circumstances.

The 'professional orientation' is usefully described by Gilbert, who uses work descriptors or typologies first used by Muir in relation to the police (Gilbert 1997; Muir 1977). Gilbert argues that studies of prison officers have not typically recognised the 'rich diversity of work behaviours' displayed by staff, and he supports our view that those characterisations which do exist tend to consist mainly of negative stereotypes (Gilbert 1997; see also Liebling *et al.* 1999). He developed a typology which characterises prison officers' working styles as 'professionals',[4] 'reciprocators', 'enforcers' and 'avoiders'. These working styles – into which we could place many officers we have encountered during fieldwork – provide a useful conceptual scheme for understanding the professional role described to us by prisoners and staff.[5] The nature and the extent of discretionary power used by prison officers differs, Gilbert argues, in these four broad ways:

- *The professional* – is open and non-defensive, makes exceptions when warranted, prefers to gain cooperation and compliance through communication, but is willing to use coercive power or force as a last resort.

52

- *The reciprocator* – wants to help people, assists them in resolving their problems, prefers clinical or social work strategies, may be inconsistent when making exceptions, prefers to 'go along to get along' and tends not to use coercive authority or physical force even when it is justifiable.

- *The enforcer* – practises rigid, 'by the book' aggressive enforcement, actively seeks out violations, rarely makes exceptions, has little empathy for others, takes unreasonable risks to personal safety, sees most things as either good or bad, and is quick to use threats, verbal coercion and physical force.

- *The avoider* – minimises offender contact, often does not 'see' an offence, avoids confrontation and coercion, views interpersonal aspects of the job as not part of the job, often backs down from confrontation and blames others.

What is interesting about Gilbert's typology is its usefulness in linking the variations we have witnessed with 'what should be' in most of our respondents' views. We would not always agree with Gilbert's normative judgements and his work is based on US examples. But this account is intended to provide empirical descriptions and some of the conceptual tools required to think about the work of prison officers. We hope to assist in this way with the more difficult normative task. What should officers be like? There is overlap between some of the categories – for example, some of the 'role model' staff identified at Whitemoor could be described as a combination of the 'professional' and 'enforcer' types. This version of the 'professional' officer may be the desired type in this sort of setting. Gilbert provides a detailed list of what he calls (after Muir 1977) 'work style descriptors' (see Table 3.3).

The best officers we saw were discerning, committed and unafraid to use force. They were neither over-eager to resort to force, nor reluctant. They were confident, physically fit (usually) and had a fairly clear sense of their broader purpose. They did not bear grudges (see Wilson 2000) and were enthusiastic, despite setbacks.

According to each particular wing of the prison, these role model characteristics changed a little, to adapt to the different circumstances and 'working way' of each area. Whitemoor (a high security or dispersal prison[6]) had four wings. At the time of our original research, A and B wings housed vulnerable prisoners (VPs); C and D wings were mainstream dispersal wings. There were subtle but important differences within each 'pair' of wings. In addition to the common

53

Table 3.3 Gilbert's 'work style descriptors'

The professional
- Develops the housing unit (wing)
- Takes educated risks
- Provides prisoners advice on rules and regulations
- Increases pressure over time to change behaviour
- Uses the 'write-up' (adjudication) as a last resort
- Tries to preserve the dignity of prisoners through the use of non-demeaning behaviours and attitudes
- Views offenders as not much different from self
- Empathises with the human condition of prisoners
- Allows for exceptions in own and others' behaviour
- Uses coercion and force judiciously
- Calm and easy-going
- Articulate and open
- Focuses on ensuring due process and decency in security and control tasks
- Views most other officers as being enforcer-oriented

The reciprocator
- Allows prisoner leaders to keep the wing quiet – a mutual accommodation
- Uses clinical/social work strategies to help prisoners 'worthy' of assistance
- Rationalises situations
- Attempts to educate, cure or solve the prisoner's problems
- Low tolerance for rejection of offered assistance
- Easily frustrated
- Often does not use coercion when it should be used
- Inconsistent job performance
- Irrational behaviour by prisoners stymies the officer
- Often displays a superior attitude towards others
- Highly articulate

The enforcer
- Aggressive rule enforcement
- Issues many 'tickets' (places many on report)
- Actively seeks violations
- Frequently uses force or excessive force
- Tends to view treatment functions as what 'others' do with/for prisoners
- Strict security and control orientation, limits service delivery duties
- Little or no empathy for the human condition of prisoners
- Prisoners often submit grievances over this officer's behaviour

54

- Rigid, rule-bound, makes few exceptions even when appropriate
- Maintains a dualistic view of human nature (good/bad, officer/prisoner, strong/weak)
- Dislikes management
- Postures for effect – Crazy/brave 'John Wayne' behaviours, takes unnecessary risks
- Views other officers as 'soft'/'weak' if not like him/her
- Views officers like him/her as being the majority of officers

The avoider
- Often leaves situations as quickly as possible
- Tends to view human communications with prisoners as not being part of security and control
- Uses the mechanical aspects of security and control to reduce contact with prisoners
- Often among the last to arrive at an emergency scene
- Likely to select isolated/prisoner-free positions
- Plays the 'phoney' tough and frequently backs down
- Tends to blame others for avoidance behaviours or inadequacies
- Structures the work to avoid observing infractions and use of coercion
- Avoids confrontations and interactions with prisoners

Source: Gilbert (1997).

'role model' characteristics above, prisoners and staff in the different wings put emphasis on different characteristics of their most admired officers. While the function of many of these and the specialist wings at Whitemoor has changed, as is so often the case in prisons, we draw on this account to illustrate a typical range of wing functions and styles.[7]

On *A Wing*, a vulnerable prisoner wing which housed the Sex Offender Treatment Programme (SOTP: an intensive offending behaviour programme), role model officers were often those engaged in SOTP work. These officers 'stood out' and were perceived by prisoners as caring and working hard for them. A Wing role models were patient with prisoners, knew their prisoners and were not afraid of interacting with them; they were comfortable in close relationships with prisoners, but were aware of their boundaries and unafraid to enforce the rules where necessary. Officers had a paternalistic-therapeutic orientation towards prisoners – they recognised their problems and were willing to help. They had a sense of humour with prisoners and colleagues, although this was generally not the quick-fire banter often found on C and D Wings, the main dispersal wings.

55

For *B Wing*, a VP wing without the explicit focus on the SOTP, role model officers were also listeners; they too could recognise that some of their prisoners had problems and difficulties – although such problems were less likely to be as explicitly offence-oriented as on A Wing. It was important that officers did not judge prisoners or cast moral aspersions on their offences. Good staff were aware of their power and of the difficulties of exercising it properly on a VP wing.[8] Role model staff appreciated respectful treatment from prisoners, but were prepared to forgive transgressions, up to a point. Rather than the 'close' and often personal relationships found on A Wing, officers on B Wing had 'working' relationships, which at their best were 'understanding' and 'helpful'.

Role model officers on *C Wing*, a dispersal wing, were efficient and competent. They expected to work hard, but they also expected some cooperation from prisoners. They would permit the expression of some of the frustrations of prison life, but had clear boundaries that were effectively communicated to prisoners. Their 'line' was a stricter one than on D Wing (see below). They would use their discretion, but within clear parameters. They were also individually (and, to some extent, as a team) consistent over time. They worked well with other staff and with some common sense of purpose, linked to maintaining 'a tight ship' and clear boundaries on the wing. There were fairly formal relationships with prisoners, but this was informed by a close knowledge of individuals on the wing. One area of the wing, known as 'blue spur', was the 'incentive spur', where prisoners on the enhanced level of the IEP scheme could apply to be placed as a reward for their good behaviour. On this spur, the general C Wing formality was broken and the relationship became one of 'shared' investment in a small community.

On *D Wing*, the other traditional dispersal wing, role model staff were confident but had a more relaxed and interactive style than their colleagues on C Wing. They were prepared to respect the agency (individuality) of prisoners (perhaps a little too much in the eyes of some of their colleagues and managers) and to joke and banter with them, but could be absolutely firm when this was needed. They were willing to take on extra duties when requested by colleagues and would tackle tasks without prompting. There was less commonality of working styles between officers on the wing compared to C Wing, but there was good teamwork and a strong sense of attachment to the wing. Relationships between staff and prisoners were very good humoured and traded on mutual insults – but there was clearly respect on both sides for the abilities and ways of the other. The 'peace' was

56

kept on D Wing, paradoxically, through a lot of noise and a lot of talk. D Wing had a lot of ex-SSU staff[9] who were also keen gym attendees. There was no doubt that strong, articulate, challenging prisoners respected strong, street-wise and confident staff.[10]

This is not to say that every good officer on each wing matched their role model characteristics; indeed, it could have been the case that no officer was a perfect representation of the desired role model. A broad mix of officer styles, skills and attributes was considered vital to the efficient running of a wing.

We observed that in general, officers from A and B Wings (the VP wings) were nominated less often, or less quickly, as role models than officers from the ordinary dispersal wings. In particular, senior managers mentioned officers from C and D Wings and we sometimes had to prompt them specifically about the VP wings to elicit mention of officers from that part of the prison. Once asked, officers came easily to mind. This 'invisibility' seemed linked to a common perception that somehow work on VP wings was 'easier' than the 'real prison work' found on ordinary dispersal wings. This was not our experience, as both halves of the prison seemed to us to bring special difficulties and to require special skills. C and D Wings were more visible and seemed to require and receive more senior management attention, with prisoners arriving and departing more frequently, often to the segregation unit.

Wing differences and adjudications

All adjudications at Whitemoor over an eight-month period were analysed in order to explore possible differences between the wings empirically.[11] Adjudications are not a simple measure of either prisoner behaviour or officer style, but they are an interesting starting point for exploring possible differences in both. Wings which accommodate prisoners who are part of an intensive offending behaviour programme (like SOTP) are less likely to contravene the rules because of the sort of prisoners they are as well as because the relationships they are required to establish with staff are different. The nature of offending behaviour courses may encourage a more 'consultative' or 'conciliatory' approach by prisoners. Other factors, such as the number of formal complaints, formal applications, the length of time prisoners have served and the overarching vulnerability sex offender prisoners may feel could further qualify statistical adjudication differences. However, knowing all this (and, to some extent, controlling for some of these

57

variables), the results of our study showed clear differences which seemed to be related to some of the observations made above. The number of proven adjudications were low on A Wing (a VP wing), but much higher on D Wing (a dispersal wing), and highest of all within the segregation unit, as Table 3.4 shows. An incident leading to an adjudication occurred approximately every ten days on A Wing, but every two and a half days on D Wing. They were almost daily occurrences in the segregation unit. Although the segregation unit had a population of around 25 prisoners – compared to well over 100 on the wings – it contributed well over a third of all adjudications at the prison.[12]

Table 3.4 Proven adjudications at Whitemoor by location of incident (July 1997 to February 1998)

A Wing	B Wing	C Wing	D Wing	Seg.	Other*	Total
24 5.1%	58 12.3%	72 15.3%	99 21.0%	178 37.7%	41 8.7%	472 100%

*'Other' comprises all areas of the prison other than the wings and the segregation unit, for example healthcare, visits and the workshops.

The total number of adjudications on C Wing (a mainstream dispersal wing, but the less lively of the two) was influenced by the fact that one spur held 'enhanced' prisoners only: of all adjudications from C Wing that were traceable back to a specific location, only one occurred on this spur, with 15 each occurring on the other two spurs over this period. There were also differences between the wings on the types of offences (or rather, those for which prisoners were most commonly placed on report). Four offences arose most often:

- *paragraph 9(a)* – possession of an unauthorised item (17 per cent);
- *paragraph 17* – threatening, abusive or insulting words or behaviour (17 per cent);
- *paragraph 19* – disobeying a lawful order (26 per cent);
- *paragraph 20* – failing to comply with any rule or regulation (16 per cent).[13]

Together, offences against these paragraphs made up over three-quarters of all disciplinary offences at the prison. Paragraph 1 – used if a prisoner committed any assault – contributed a small but significant proportion to the total number of adjudications (6.8 per cent).

Figure 3.2 shows offences against these four main paragraphs according to the amount they contributed to the total number of proven adjudications on each wing. Paragraph 17 (threatening, abusive or insulting words or behaviour) made up 33 per cent of A Wing's total adjudications (though this was only eight offences of a total of 24). Paragraph 9(a) (possession of an unauthorised item) contributed almost the same amount to D Wing's total (though this amounted to over 30 separate incidents). Two interesting trends can be seen in Figure 3.2.

• The contribution offences against paragraph 17 (using threatening, abusive or insulting words or behaviour) made to each wing's total declines from A Wing to D Wing.

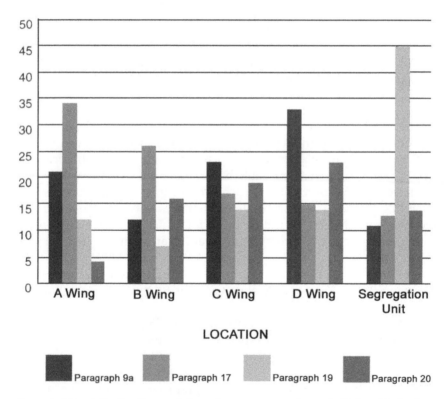

Figure 3.2 Adjudication arising from paragraphs of Rule 47 broken (percentage) (HMP Whitemoor, July 1997–February 1998)

59

- Conversely, the total contribution of offences against paragraph 20 (failing to conform with any rule or regulation) went up from A Wing to D Wing.

Both prisoner behaviour and officer responses to prisoner behaviour differed according to location and population. Our observations (and the rest of the data) led us to conclude that officers on the VP wings were more inclined to sanction small resistances (see also Sparks *et al.* 1996), and that prisoners on vulnerable prisoner units tended to confine their misbehaviour to verbal complaints. Prisoners on D Wing were 'allowed' a certain amount of 'resistant language', but were sanctioned instead for more serious breaches of the rules, including trade.

Incidents that led to proven adjudications also differed according to the day of the week, with incidents rising in number from a low on Sunday to a high on Wednesday and then declining again towards the end of the week. Again, this pattern could be linked to routine features of prison life, such as pay day, and an arguably more relaxed atmosphere at the weekend (see also Sparks *et al.* 1996).

Conclusion

This outline of different role model staff in just one prison and the extent of variation between wings illustrate the wide range of roles that prison officers can adopt, but tries to demonstrate the common 'core' characteristics of the best staff as identified by prisoners and their officer colleagues. We found that many officers gravitated to a particular wing or section of the prison whose working style suited their own personality. This point demonstrates the need for officers to 'be themselves' as far as possible – to invest the role of the prison officer with their own personality and characteristics. The prison may be a highly artificial environment, but values of truth, honesty and integrity were vital. Officers were certain that you could not be effective if you were not yourself. There was an important need to be 'professional', but this professional orientation was best achieved through working with the grain of your own personality.

One of the most significant themes to arise from our own research was the question of role and whether this was clear. What was 'being a prison officer' at Whitemoor about? Did the prison have a clear purpose and direction? The answer differed slightly from officer to officer. All were convinced of the need to maintain security, and

60

the need to keep order on the wing (a version of Dunbar's term 'dynamic security', Dunbar 1985). The emphasis given to helping prisoners tackle their offending behaviour was greater for some officers than for others. Some officers, for example, were keen to stress the importance of helping prisoners to maintain family contacts. What this meant was that each officer had their own 'bigger picture' consisting of a view about the role of imprisonment, the role of their own prison, the role of their particular wing and, therefore, their own role as a prison officer. This individualisation of some of the most important questions in a prison was in some ways unfortunate and detracted from the otherwise impressive work being carried out. We look at role diversity in the next chapter. Some diversity of role is inevitable and desirable, particularly given the diverse nature of the prison population and the need to have a wide range of officers bringing different strengths to the job. There are limits to this need for diversity when it comes to overall purpose. One of the main conclusions of our research at Whitemoor – and we have heard this plea from prison staff elsewhere – was that it might have been an outstanding establishment if its own best work had been channelled in a more consistent and recognised direction. This is a point we return to in Chapter 6.

Notes

1   For example, a censor usually saw a large number of prisoners for very short, relatively formal periods at his (or her) office door during the morning. (Censors are allowed to open both the incoming and outgoing mail of any prisoner, except for legal correspondence. All correspondence to and from prisoners held in units housing any Category A prisoners, and to and from any prisoners on the E list, must be read 'as a matter of routine' (Security Manual, 36.14). All letters to and from prisoners in closed prisons must also be examined for illicit enclosures.) A cleaning officer had more sustained contact with a smaller number of prisoners throughout the day, from morning and afternoon labour to the serving of breakfast, lunch and dinner. The 'default' job of the prison officer – the landing officer – brought with it numerous occasions on which he or she might interact with a prisoner, adding up to at least ten or fifteen minutes of conversation with certain prisoners each day.

2   With breakfast served, the landing officer gravitated towards the 2's gate (the gate onto the second landing) and the centre officer to check prisoners' names off as they moved to work or education. Again, comments and interaction were generally limited at such a time – a

61

'morning' or equivalent as the prisoners passed through. There was much more interaction between prisoners – particularly on some wings – than between prisoners and officers.

3   The searching of a prisoner's body and clothing for unauthorised articles including concealed drugs or weapons.

4   Gilbert uses the term 'professional' here as a categorisation. As employees, he refers to prison staff as 'paraprofessionals', that is they are not professionals in the 'classic' sense of the term but they do apply a 'specific body of knowledge and skill' in their work (see Gilbert 1997: 50).

5   Other similar 'prototypes' appear in the literature, for example Ben-David and Silfen's 'punitive', 'custodial', 'patronage', 'therapist' and 'integrative' (see Ben-David and Silfen 1994).

6   Dispersal prisons contain a high proportion of category A (maximum security) prisoners.

7   For a more recent account of wing differences and characteristics at Whitemoor, see Drake (2008).

8   Sparks et al. (1996) found that some prison officers in the Vulnerable Prisoner Unit (VPU) at Albany were unaware of their own power and used it carelessly, often offending prisoners who felt that they in turn were powerless to say anything in their defence.

9   Special Security Unit – a unit within Whitemoor which housed exceptional risk category A prisoners, those deemed most dangerous to the public and most at risk of escape. Following the escape of six prisoners from the Unit in 1994, the regime followed was very strict, with a minimal use of discretion among officers. The Unit also encouraged officers to work closely as a team and appeared to inspire a great deal of confidence in the officers who worked there. The management of the Unit at the time of our research is discussed further in Chapter 5.

10   The role of D Wing is now very different. See later.

11   An adjudication is a formal hearing following a charge of misbehaviour or rule breaking by prisoners.

12   A substantial number of these adjudications were straightforward – one prisoner was placed on report 17 times over the period (a far greater individual total than any other prisoner over this period) simply for refusing to return to normal location.

13   These reference numbers refer to the pre-1999 Prison Rule 47 paragraph numbering.

62

Chapter 33

The prisoner
Inside and out

Jason Warr

The Prisoner looks to liberty as an immediate return to all his ancient energy, quick-
ened into more vital forces by long disuse. When he goes out, he finds he still has to
suffer. His punishment, as far as its effects go, lasts intellectually and physically, just as it
lasts socially. He still has to pay. One gets no receipt for the past when one walks out into
the beautiful air.

(Oscar Wilde – *Letter to Frank Harris*, in Conrad 2006: 174)

There is a peculiarity to prisons in England and Wales. They occupy a space in the collective conscience of politicians, the public and academics to varying degrees, yet this is
an abstract space, a space with little or no corporeal content. Without first-hand experience the information that people have about prison, its practices and effects, is filtered
through agenda-shaped and value-laden media representations and political rhetoric
which rarely, if ever, correspond to the reality of prisoners' lived experience (Warr
2012). This chapter aims to redress this dissonance, focusing upon classic penological
themes and utilizing a mix of first-hand experiences and academic literature. What follows is a discussion of how imprisonment can affect the individual psychologically,
emotionally and physically throughout their carceral life and beyond. Starting at the
point of arrest and initial imprisonment and tracing through to release and reintegration,
I will explore how an individual's sense of self and placement is teleologically altered by
the 'institution'.

   The purpose of this chapter is to move the discussion on the pains of imprisonment beyond the focal point of the prison, and to explore how these pains may be
generated before entrance to the institution, as well as how they may pertain beyond the
physical boundaries of the walls. As the quote above from Oscar Wilde notes, the 'suffering' of the prisoner does not cease at the point of release. These 'pains' can, and do,
pursue the prisoner into their outside life and can be as burdensome there as they are
whilst the prisoner is inside. Any exploration of the prisoner and the pains we, as a society,
subject them to must take note of this reality and elucidate what the consequences of this
may be.

   This chapter is informed by both my own history as an academic and as a former
prisoner as well as work conducted on behalf of a third sector organization during a
number of projects based in various prisons and with former prisoners in the community.
With regard to the prison-based projects, my function was as an objective Prison Council
facilitator employed to engage, formally and informally, both staff and prisoners and to
collate their collective experiences of the prison and report them to the prison's

management in a structured and solution-focused manner. In addition, though not there primarily to conduct academic research, I was to both observe and report on the prison, via written monthly and annual reports, to the governor/director regarding issues and problems noted within their establishments. These reports combined the experiences of myself and colleagues, quantitative data collected on issues raised/actioned, and experiences and accounts of prisoners and staff gathered during our interactions. Informed consent was sought for any and all quotes, case studies or instances reported.

The pains of imprisonment: genesis

Goffman (1961) speaks of 'mortifications' and Sykes (1958) refers to 'deprivations' and the 'pains of imprisonment'. These descriptives convey the process by which the individual is shaped by the prison or total institution. These are the traditional discourses utilized to examine how a person becomes a prisoner, a process inherent to the institution in which a person is incarcerated. The process of becoming a prisoner is presumed to commence, and be exemplified by, the reception process, where the first assaults on the person take place and 'entry shock' is initially experienced (Zamble and Porporino 1988). However, the process of mortification and the first psychological assault on the individual, their sense of self, their identity and their subjective narrative occurs not in the prison but at the point of arrest. It is here that examination of the inner and outer worlds of the prisoner shall begin.

> I was sat in the front, I saw a blur then SMASH the window came in … glass everywhere, in my face, in my ear. I could hear shouting but couldn't make it out coz all I was aware of was this fucking barrel about an inch from my eye. At first I thought we were getting merc'ed, innit, but nah the police. 'GET OUT, GET OUT' they shouted. I had my seatbelt on so couldn't … fuck sure wasn't reaching down to undo the seatbelt! My brethren vanished as he was dragged out the motor. I looked at the copper and said I'm undoing the seatbelt … I showed him as I moved in slowmo. BLAM, cunt bucked me upside my head! Next thing I know I'm between pavement and car, hands cuffed behind me, boot on my neck, and someone saying 'Who's the big man now?'[1]

> I remember them knocking on the door … as soon as I got the latch off they were through the door and rushing through the hallway. I was knocked out the way. A police woman, who was very kind to me, said I had to go with her. She was very gentle … I didn't really know what was going on. Obviously I knew my boyfriend dealt drugs but I never thought, I never … They bundled him away in a van then one of them came out with the bags. There was loads … that's when the nice police woman handcuffed me and arrested me for possession with intent to supply too.

For many, the point of arrest is shocking and, even if anticipated, discombobulating. The point of arrest represents both a drastic change in circumstance and a stark shift in the power relationship between state and individual. While the first example's extremity – the experience of one young offender convicted of armed robbery – contrasts with the second account, the elements of intrusion (into what were considered safe spaces), the display of power by state representatives and the forced acknowledgement of the self as a powerless individual are concomitant in both. Goffman (1961: 24) notes that upon entrance to a closed institution the individual begins a process of moral shift and 'disculturation' (movement away from the moral identity embodied in society) which is catalysed by a series of 'abasements, degradations, humiliations and profanations'. The individual is 'systematically' (if, perhaps, unintentionally) 'mortified', which ultimately results in 'civil death'. These practices have two purposes: reinforcement of the institution's power and authority, and the erosion of the public self. If one considers the process of arrest – cuffing, searching, forced transportation, finger printing, strip searching, removal of belts and laces, interrogation, placement in a cell, dictated regime, food, surveillance, etc. – the course of abasements and mortifications of the 'prisoner' acquire a continuous aspect. A process that begins at the point of arrest is reinforced in the police station, again in the reception of the prison, and at multiple points thereafter.

Prison reception rituals have been represented in numerous films and programmes and may be familiar to many. The stripping of the novel prisoner, the scrubbing, the delousing, the cavity search, the parade, the issuing of a bed pack, are all components that relate to the USA and media representations. They do not reflect the experience of the many in England and Wales. The rituals of abasement and moral decortication, the stripping of one's previous moral identity (and narrative) and the processes of prisonization (socialization into prison norms; Clemmer 1940; Thomas 1973) to which the prisoner in the UK is subject are no less destructive to the self. This is one of the most pernicious aspects of the modern prison experience and can result in a profound normative conflict and an entrenched ontological insecurity.

New, and intentionally punitory, policies introduced in 2013 have seen this aspect of the induction ritual become even more profound for new receptions. The new, and punitively weighted, incentive and earned privilege (IEP) system has been reconstructed in order to make induction into a prison more intensely impactful. The new initiate is no longer able to access the same privileges as longer-serving peers, undermining a decade or more of effective 'first night' practice. Instead they are to be placed on the new 'reception' level which limits access to their own clothing, the prison regime, time out of cell, funds necessary to maintain family contact and other materials and goods that would ease the transition to prison life. It is too early to say whether or not this new approach will constitute a new mortification in and of itself, but it will inevitably lead to a more painful and – given identification as a 'newbie' to the wider population – problematic entrance, exacerbating the pains associated with entering the closed world of the prison.[2]

The traditional pains of imprisonment

Sykes (1958) identified five core deprivations which he argued marked carceral life: the deprivations of liberty, security, autonomy, goods and services, and heterosexual relationships. These have formed the basis of much prison research but are worth revisiting in order to understand their nature and impact on the lived experience of prisoners. For the purposes of this chapter, the focus will be on the first three of these deprivations: liberty, security and autonomy. The popular media have long evoked the image of the prison as a place of ease and luxury as opposed to the places of stress, psychological turmoil and trauma that they are (Mason 2006). As a consequence, the deprivation of liberty, the loss of freedom, is no longer understood as a pain. The hegemonic ideology infecting criminal justice discourse reverses the age-old notion that prison is the punishment, not a place where punishment is enacted (Tonry 2004). This reflects a wider shift in the notion of freedoms which can be seen in the prosperous (and predominantly neo-liberal) West where participation in consumerism is, erroneously, regarded as synonymous with personal freedom (Perez and Esposito 2010). Freedom has a much more pressing and immediate meaning for prisoners who no longer have sovereignty over their own bodies (Gunn 2010), who cannot walk where they want, when they want, cannot eat when they want, speak to whom they want, read what they want, watch they want, buy what they want, wear what they want, sleep where they want, wash when they want and even, in certain circumstances, go to the toilet when they want. It is the constraint of these acts (and countless others) that reinforces in a most invasive manner both what freedom means and how devastating to the self is its loss. As one former prisoner noted:

> It's the first time you try to do something mundane that is forbidden that the 'prison' hits you in the nuts. Its like that, that … what's gone, your freedom, when you notice it its like being hit in the nuts … constantly.

For the prisoner, it is the micro intrusions into their quotidian reality, more than the situational control measures (locks, gates, bars, walls, cameras), that reinforce the carceral reality to which they are subject. Another prisoner noted that he could 'get used to the walls' but could not become accustomed to not being able 'to do' the things he used to and not being able to 'go outside when you want'. For this prisoner, who described himself as an 'outdoorsy' person, the real pain of the loss of liberty was not being able to be outside. He noted that he would normally have spent most of his time outside – he worked out of doors and would even camp out at least once a week, but now he only got to be outside when he 'walked between the wing and the workshop, or to visits or healthcare'. He explained that he had not been outside after dark for four years and that he was struggling to 'get his head round that'. This reflected the experience of another interviewee, who described that after 11 years he had moved to open conditions and was able to sit outside with a friend of an evening. He related:

> that first day I sat out the back of the main housing unit, at 8 p.m., there was a local power cut so the lights in the area were all out, no light pollution, and stared into a cloudless night sky. There were stars. For the first time in over a decade, in fact since I was 17, I could see the stars. Right there, right then I felt the weight of those years as a prisoner … like, right in your guts … but could also begin to feel what getting out may be like.

Many describe the loss of freedom as a 'hollow' feeling or, more poetically, 'a cancer of the soul', something that hits at 'the core of you', and these emotive descriptions give weight to the sense that the deprivation of freedom is a profoundly experienced assault on the self.

Every minute of being is managed by the prison, the more evident this control of liberty, the 'deeper' one can be said to be within the prison (King and McDermott 1995) and the 'tighter' the range of burdens experienced (Crewe 2011). Being constrained, or even 'smothered' as one prisoner phrased it, by the institution, its routines and the manner in which the experience of time is mediated impacts the prisoner in a profound way. These very real pains impact on every aspect of self, identity, internal and emotional personhood, and social and performed character (Jewkes 2002). These 'pains' are not experienced in any linear or conjunctive fashion; they are a perpetual aspect of prison life. They do not affect certain aspects of a prisoner's self or identity in isolation but as a whole and all the time.

It is argued here that it is the micro-interactions between prisoner and prison that exemplify the pains felt by the deprivation of liberty. There may also be a sense in which the situational aspects of imprisonment intrude into the consciousness of the prisoner, reinforcing the relationship between themselves and the institution in a way that transcends their mere physicality. Herrity (2014) notes that although frequently included in prisoner accounts (for example, see Hassine 1996), there is a distinct lacuna of academic understanding with regard to the manner in which the acoustic elements of these measures, and their addition to the overwhelming sound ecology of a prison, reinforce and impose the institution onto prisoners' psychological reality.

The deprivation of security is often recognized as the most obvious of the 'pains' of imprisonment because prisons are perceived as 'dangerous'. Sykes (1958) argues that one of the most acute pains is an enforced proximity to fellow prisoners who pose, by their very circumstance, a danger. It has been argued elsewhere (Crewe et al. 2014; Warr 2014) that traditional understanding of the brutality of the prison environment has been somewhat misread. Although the episodic outbreaks of violence or disorder that mark the prison environment can pose a physical threat to the individual, it is the state of *diffidence*, constant and 'consumptive wariness', that can be a profound pain to the individual. Every interaction, conversation, bodily movement, glance, laugh, smile and even yawn must be monitored by the individual to ensure it is not causing offence, being taken out of context or rendering the prisoner vulnerable in the eyes of peers:

> Big Man t'ing [seriously] Fam[3] … mans have to watch everyone and everything, innit? If next man is gassing [winding] up someone on the landing and calling him a pussy hole you gotta watch that he don't see you as a pussy hole he can come tax [rob]. Coz if he does then he's gonna come test innit? Like that 24/7. Man's gotta come strong, innit fam?

> I just found it … wearing. Having to be on the lookout all the time, careful what you say and to whom. It was exhausting … exhausting.

It is in this sense that Bentham's panopticon, with the intent that the 'persons to be inspected should always feel themselves as if under inspection' (Bentham 1791: 24), has gained some reality. What marks the modern prison are these varying levels of interspection and intraspection by those occupying the spaces within the confines of the walls. Prisons are places where everything you do is watched by others (as you watch them in turn), but that censorious gaze is also focused inwards, at the self. This leads to adaptive behaviours that, in terms of the prison at least, can be seen as anti-social (or maladaptive). Due to these deprivations in security, prisoners, to borrow Goffman's (1959) dramaturgical language, learn to manage their 'front stage' behaviours in ways that may obfuscate their 'back stage' realities from their peers as well as the authorities. Crewe

(2009) highlighted one aspect of this when discussing the 'soft power' of the institution, the means by which people can be 'killed off' on file, and prisoner responses to that. He noted that prisoners, especially those serving indeterminate or parole-governed sentences, would attempt to manage/control how they were perceived and what was officially recorded about them. This may become more widespread given that the new IEP scheme, implemented in November 2013, limits the opportunities to gain privileged statuses, thus making perception management necessary for a greater portion of the population.

How prisoners cope with the episodic but high levels of violence (physical, emotional, psychological and indeed sexual) that they experience or witness within prison[4] is another aspect of these behaviours. For myself, and other former prisoners, one of the mechanisms was the divorcing of empathy from sympathy (Warr 2012). When in a highly hostile and frequently violent environment, the invocation of sympathy towards others can become wearying and a 'deep' pain. When your own well-being becomes paramount, the misery of others must be 'managed' so as not to cause you further injury. As these prisoners noted:

> You may see some yout' getting banged in his face every day. You may feel sorry for him ... to begin with. But when 'bang' it happens again and 'bang' it happens again ... you can't keep feeling sorry for him, or some next br'er [brother]. You gotta ignore that shit, innit? Learn to deal with yours and fuck them ...

> You would hear [some of the women] screaming of a night time. I couldn't deal with their pain on top of my own ... and I had a lot of my own ... so you learn to ... I don't know ... not feel. You just block it out ... otherwise you won't survive.

Here, the interviewees' references are to the need to manage empathetic feelings to such a degree that they no longer result in vicarious trauma. They 'learn' to separate the evocation of sympathy from their empathetic response to witnessing someone's suffering. This emotional work, or labour, is designed to protect them, a defensive means of guarding against the emotional vicissitudes of the environment. However, these behaviours, though understandable adaptations, can be interpreted by authorities in negative ways. They can be seen as evidence of both callousness/'shallow affect' and, when occurring alongside self-censoring and front-stage management, of an overly controlled personality.

There is also a wider sense in which the deprivation of security goes beyond the mere physical or psychosocial threat thus far discussed. The security of ontology and sense of place, which in many carceral settings and for many prisoners is also an aspect where pain is experienced, must too be noted. I shall discuss later the newer pains of indeterminacy and the deprivations of certainty faced by specific populations, but there are also issues with regard to the bureaucracy of prisons and how the retreat of front line power has evinced new pains that relate to the navigation of a prison sentence and a subsequent loss of ontological security.

Giddens (1991) notes there is a distinction between the security felt when in structured and predictable (i.e. navigable) circumstances and the insecurity that is evoked when those boundaries are eroded or absent. Placed in environments, such as prisons, where the rules and regulations that govern and control an individual's existence are assured, there can be ontological security – the individual can be confident in the nature of their reality. Where those rules are opaque or transgressed without recourse, and their trustworthiness and reliability are shadowed in doubt, people become ontologically insecure – they no longer have confidence in their reality. Both Warr (2007) and Crewe (2009) have argued that the primary power that was once held by the uniformed staff body has now retreated away from the wing to senior managers who are located away from the centrality of prison life. This has resulted in levels of bureaucracy which can stymie effective decision-making processes – all the more so given the deleterious effect that benchmarking, budget cuts and staff reductions have had on the operations of many prisons.

This situation has resulted in many prisons becoming less navigable than would once have been true. As one prisoner stated, '[you] used to know where you stood, but now? Don't even know if we getting unlocked, let out for work or if there be association, nothing …' Whilst another noted that in their prison it was no good submitting applications, as you would not hear anything back, and when they chased a 'Guv' about it, they were told to 'put in another fucking application'. This position was supported by a uniformed staff member of long standing who noted that they now could not do much 'for the lads' as they had to 'pass everything on'. As a consequence, in many circumstances, the bureaucratic legitimacy or administrative organization (Carrabine 2005) of the prison has been eroded. If a prisoner's attempts to access some element of the regime are denied, either through the disempowerment of the uniformed body or the inefficiencies of the bureaucratic system, then trust in the system begins to wane. If this situation begins to affect a large percentage of the prisoner population, then not only are trust and faith in the system diminished, but so too is the sense of personal placement and ontological security. The more difficult the prison is to navigate or abide within, then the more difficult it is to feel safe and secure within the environment, and this can exacerbate the other pains that the prison inflicts upon the prisoner.

This was evident in one of the prisons in which I operated that had undergone a number of major shifts of both management and remit over a period of 30 months. It had been subject to a budget reduction of £3 million, which resulted in significant loss of front line staff. The prisoner population had drastically altered, and there had been three core-day regime changes and two alterations to staff shift patterns. The impact of the rapid programme of changes introduced by the Ministry of Justice (MoJ) as well as policy implications introduced by the 'hubs and spokes' agreement between the National Offender Management Service (NOMS) and the UK Border Agency (UKBA) (MoJ and UKBA 2009; Kaufman 2013) added to these operational challenges. Accumulatively, this had a disastrous effect on the running of the prison. Core deliverables were not being met, there were systemic failures in communication, increases in instances of self-harm and interpersonal violence, and a number of deaths in custody. All contributed to high levels of distress amongst prisoners. The bureaucracy of the prison had become the 'institutional black hole into which problems could be cast' (Crewe 2009: 112), and was grindingly slow and impersonal (often with blanket responses being issued). Prisoners' activities, IEP statuses and risk levels were changed or altered with little or no information being supplied. Finally, nearly all aspects of the prison had adopted a default 'no' response to most prisoner requests. This resulted in a significant proportion of the population feeling alienated, in despair and with no hope that they could either navigate or securely exist within the prison. As one prisoner noted:

> Nothing, they give nothing. You ask for what PSO [Prison Service Orders] say you should have, they say 'You right, PSO say that, put in application' so you put in application … Nothing. You put in next application. Nothing. Put in next … then they say no. No longer you trust them to keep to rules. No longer can we trust prison. No trust … no hope. There is no hope here.

Legitimacy (see Sparks 1996; Loader and Sparks 2013) was falling, the prison had become difficult to navigate and exist within (Liebling et al. 2005), and trust was non-existent. Unsurprisingly, a bout of concerted disorder followed.

Trust is an essential element of the prison emotional landscape, but is little understood. Minimal trust is afforded to prisoners as they are seen as a wilfully untrustworthy group (Melvin et al. 1985). This attitude of the powerful allows them to deny, in the sense that Cohen (2001) explicates as a form of interpretive denial, the impact that their practice has on the prisoner. However. trust necessarily flows in both directions: the prison and its staff must also be trusted by the prisoners in their care. This relationship is a delicate matter, something often forgotten by ministers and Ministry of Justice officials. This 'relationship' is really earmarked by the manner in which trust, and its role in interactions and relationships within the prison, either flows or is constrained. However, the question of trust goes beyond that of the authorities and manifestly impacts on every interaction and relationship within the prison; its absence can form a particular and acute pain for a prisoner related to the deprivation of security.

The deprivation of autonomy is potentially the most destructive of the pains of imprisonment as it confers a direct assault on one's sense of self and erodes any positive notion of the self. Haney (2001) notes that imprisonment, with its attendant impositions of identity (de)valuing, strips the notion of 'adult' from the prisoner and can be infantilizing. Whilst the prisoner is expected to take 'responsibility' for their past, present and future actions (in order to reduce perceived risk), they have little or no power to do so. Prisoners are forced constantly to confront their lack of power, their lack of ability to affect decision-making parameters via their reliance on official others. Whilst Haney notes that this is an acute pain in and of itself, especially for those who never manage to adjust to this loss, he further argues that there are a number of consequences to this infantilization which represent additional pains: first, the destruction of a sense of self-value which can result in a prisoner accepting or believing that any ill directed towards them is deserved because of their (offender) stigmata; second, robbing the prisoner of decision-making faculties which can result in a passivity towards authority. These factors result in what I shall refer to as a reduced penological imagination – the ability to discern the structure of a prison, the manner in which its power is manifest, the dominating operational mechanics and how these affect wing life and the complexities of the prison's social landscape. This imagination loss also leads to an inability to 'imagine' efficacious forms of resistance, which may result in resistant behaviours that are ill conceived or reactive in nature and which do little more than reaffirm the power and control of the prison authorities.

Deprivation of autonomy is evident in even the minor interactions between the adjunct (the prison and its agents) and the subaltern (the prisoner). However, it is when events occur outside the institution that the prisoner is really confronted by their powerlessness, and the deprivation of autonomy truly becomes a 'pain'. The Irish poet Joseph Campbell equates the state of being imprisoned as like being chess pieces 'taken, Swept from the chessboard' ('Chesspieces' by Campbell 1923, cited in Crotty 2010: 611), which captures the powerlessness of prisoners as they are unable to affect any outcome in the world outside whilst they are 'taken'. They must await a new game (release) before they can become actors again. It is this aspect that can cause a great deal of pain for the prisoner, as one elderly prisoner related:

> it was when my wife died. I know she wanted to be sent off in a particular church, where her mum was buried, but there was no one to organise it. I was in here. What could I do? I ain't got no money or nothing. The prison were good … but … that's when it hit home you know? I could do fuck all. Never forgive myself for that …

For me, the lack of autonomy was brought home by what happened to a very close friend. K had started out as a pen pal, introduced to me through a fellow prisoner. After a number of years, she began to visit on a regular basis. She met my family. We grew close. One day I sat on the wing waiting for my visit to be called. At first my fellow cons were bantering that she had 'blown me out', for they knew she was always never more than a few minutes late. The wing staff made repeated calls to visits as they too knew she would have contacted the prison if she could not make it. Nothing. I tried to call her from the prison phones. No answer. I phoned my mum to see if she had heard from K. Nothing. The banter stopped. One of the most painful aspects of prison life is when a visitor fails to materialize. The inability to locate them, establish reason or to gain any reassurance is a terrible stress for the prisoner. Your imagination runs to the worst possible scenarios – car crashes, death, rejection. Here the deprivation of autonomy (as well as liberty) becomes keen, is felt most profoundly. You cannot do anything.

After nearly a month of no contact I was notified that K had booked a visit. I knew something was wrong, but the relief I felt was intoxicating, until I saw her. K was always smartly dressed in expensive clothing with immaculate hair and make-up. This day, K was in baggy jeans and jumper. Hair tied back. No make-up. I barely recognized her. When I went to give her a hug she flinched away from me so hard she nearly fell. I knew. We sat down and she said nothing for 20 minutes. Eventually she told me. She told me that she had been raped – raped by a friend of a friend after he had drugged her on a night out and left her dazed, abused and naked in a house full of strangers. She told me she only remembered flashes, snippets, impressions. She told me that she had not told anyone else; had not reported it to the police. She said the only reason she had told me was because I was safe to tell – I could not do anything, I was in prison. She told me because she could completely control what I heard and what response she had from me. If I gave her anything but the cold analysis and the comfort she gained from talking about it without emotion, she could walk away.

When you enter a prison, you enter a pseudo-static state, a state of 'abeyance' (Mathiesen 1990). Those you love and care for, whom you need and rely upon, do not. As Fishman (1990) points out, the lives of partners and families continue: they have trials and tribulations, successes and traumas. However, the prisoner feels as if they only play a minimal role in those events. They are not actors in those events, nor can they be. In terms of the events of the outside world, the prisoner experience is that of a voyeur peeking over the walls at the lives that play out on the other side. They can only impact on those people's lives from afar and at a time removed. In one sense, this is how pernicious the deprivation of liberty and autonomy is – for the prisoner, the outside world retreats to an abstract, only to be perceived, barely, via memory and secondary sources (letters, media, film, music). This becomes, with every example, with every reinforcement, with every realization an acute and inescapable pain for the prisoner.

In terms of the deprivation of autonomy the prisoner suffers a decortication of their moral identity and self. Herein lies an emotional, or even psychological, danger – if the outside world is so retreated or abstracted how do you engage with it emotionally or in any pro-social and healthy way? I was in Wormwood Scrubs when 9/11 occurred. My abiding memory was the laughter of the prisoners and the horror of the staff. For the prisoners, many of whom were long termers or lifers, it did not feel real, there was no emotion attached to it, it was an amusement much like anything else on TV. For the staff, the reaction of the prisoners was a source of horror and evidence of their deviance.

A further problem of the outside world having become an abstracted entity is in the planning for release. As noted, the responsibilization agenda is contraindicated with the deprivation of autonomy. This results in the 'side-effect' of putting prisoners in a position whereby they must take responsibility for their actions and their rehabilitation but have no means of doing so; and are then punished for this 'irresponsibility' by the various disciplinary discourses to which they are subject. Nowhere is this Catch-22 more evident than when it comes to lifers and their need to make plans for a future beyond the prison. During the long expanse of time that a lifer can spend in prison, the outside world can change dramatically. However, having no substantive interaction with the world at large when in closed conditions, this 'planning' can be problematic and result in unrealistic or fantastical plans and objectives. To believe that the prison aids the prisoner in truly preparing for the outside world is to believe a myth or an 'imagined' penal reality (Carlen 2008). When conjoined with other consequences or adaptive behaviours, this can pose a significant problem for the lifer or long-term prisoner.

The new pains of imprisonment

The prison is a mutable entity that is subject to the vicissitudes of time, political influence and shifts in penal discourse. With every shift comes the potential for new deprivations and pains. Developments in penal policy and wider society have brought a number of pains of imprisonment into sharper focus. Increased technologies of surveillance, expanded economies of scale (40% of the population are now housed in prisons that hold 1,000+ prisoners; PRT 2014), creeping self-governance or self-punishment (see Crewe 2011), the lack of access to newer technologies and information sources, and the pains related to separation and censure suffered by new mothers (see Rowe 2012), are amongst those concerns informing contemporary penology. However, this section will focus on the deprivation of certainty.

For certain populations, the problem of navigability is an inherent aspect of their sentence. Those serving indeterminate sentences and the expanding number of foreign national prisoners experience an additional 'pain': the deprivation of certainty. Mason (1990) argues that the indeterminate sentence, once seen as the 'backbone' of therapeutic sentences, actually became, in the USA, a new and unusually cruel form of punishment.

141

Others (e.g. Jewkes 2005; Crewe 2011; Addicott 2011; Rose 2012) have argued that indeterminate sentences, especially the indeterminate sentence for public protection (IPP), and life sentences in the context of England and Wales, can be viewed through the same lens. There are currently around 12,500 people (19% of the prison population) serving indeterminate sentences in England and Wales (PRT 2014).

Indeterminate sentences in England and Wales are in effect 99 years long but will entail a minimum punitive aspect (tariff). A prisoner must complete this tariff before being considered for release by the Parole Board. The key consideration for the indeterminately sentenced prisoner is that the amount of time they will eventually serve in prison is unknown. As noted, prisoners are transformed into risk subjects whose risk must be 'managed', but this is especially so for indeterminately sentenced prisoners. Release is difficult to achieve and time in custody often exceeds their minimum tariff (at the end of March 2014, 69% of IPP prisoners were post-tariff) (see PRT 2014). Addicott (2011) identifies a number of acute pains that characterize the deprivation of certainty for indeterminately sentenced prisoners, including: feelings of being lost within the system; unknown (and potentially unknowable) barriers to release; not being able to settle into the sentence and feeling constantly on 'remand'; an absence of accurate and usable information regarding the sentence and securing release; and the interminability of the sentence – not being able to see or predict an end. Although Addicott was researching IPP prisoners, the same factors pertain to all indeterminate- and life-sentenced prisoners. One 'lifer', having started as a juvenile, had served eight years of his 18-year tariff, and described his situation as follows:

> It's like you're supposed to be making progress all the time … and the prison makes you do that, jump through all those hoops … but 1. You don't know if you're making progress cause the goal posts keep on shifting and 2. When you think about it you ain't actually going anywhere. Its not real progress. Its illusionary progress. Do this, do that … and for what? I still got another 10–15 years to do. Don't matter what I do now … I'm still in prison. There ain't no fucking progress, just running to stand still. Drives you fucking mad …

This sense of being on a Penrose staircase (Penrose and Penrose 1958; also Escher 1960), of going round and round but not getting anywhere, is a common theme even amongst those early in their indeterminate 'career'. In a Young Offender Institution, where 40% of the population were serving indeterminate sentences, a number of aggravating factors were identified. These issues related to knowledge of sentence, the perceived legitimacy of their sentence and the erosion of the lifer officer scheme. It became evident that amongst the group I was working with were a number of IPP prisoners who were not aware of the indeterminate nature of their sentence. In one instance we had to inform the prisoner a matter of weeks before his first parole hearing (which he had thought was his release date) of the likelihood of a parole 'knockback'. This resulted in a form of 'shock', similar to that experienced on first entry to the prison, as they struggled to readjust and come to terms with the actual nature of their sentence.

In terms of legitimacy there were two issues: first, many IPP prisoners felt that receiving what is in effect a life sentence, for relatively minor but repeat offences, was overly harsh and unwarranted. Second, many of those convicted of Joint Enterprise little understood their conviction, and as such questioned the legitimacy of their sentence.

Under the common law principle of Joint Enterprise (JE) individuals can be 'parasitically' guilty if their presence at, or in the precursory events leading to, an offence is seen as adding either assistance or encouragement to the primary actor or if they were able to 'foresee' the likelihood of the offence resulting from some agreed criminal action (Krebs 2010). For these 'lifers', convicted of homicide under the JE principle, not only did the sentence feel unjust but so too the mechanisms by which they were risk assessed. They were counted as murderers though they had often not physically taken anyone's life. Both IPP prisoners and those convicted under the principle of JE often found it difficult to reconcile their offending behaviours with the sentences that they subsequently received. This disjunction undermined both their sense of self as social actors and their ontological security, thus entrenching further this sense of deprived certainty. A consequence of this could be, as the prisoner attempts to maintain some stability in their perceived reality, for IPP prisoners to deny the seriousness of their offending and for JE convicted prisoners to deny the offence for which they were convicted. This could pose problems in terms of progression through the system as well as in terms of the new IEP scheme, where their 'denial' could prevent them gaining privileges and work. As one young prisoner stated:

> it's peak [rubbish] fam ... me nah do nothing, me nah bore [stabbed] the brae [brother] but me were there when da t'ing kick off innit. Me, was on way to [bed], but buck up on [meet] da mans [friends] them on da bus. We all get off on the ends [home area] ... BAM it's off. Next thing man's got blood on him and splitting ... didn't even see what, who, where nothing ... them wrap [arrest] us all up fam ... we all get guilty. I tell these pussyhole guvs that I was just there, that it was nah me who bore the yout' but them just say 'in denial' and BAM ... they nah give me nothing, nah enhanced, nah good job, nothing. Can't get nothing.

The last issue related to the erosion of the lifer officer scheme. Once, every lifer was assigned a trained personal 'lifer' officer who would understand the administration of the sentence, the means of navigating the parole process and the specific needs of their wards. There was also a wider support network of lifer governors and clerks who would maintain the institutional knowledge base of lifer issues and developments. The system was not perfect but it worked, after a fashion; however, in the mid-2000s, after the explosion in numbers of indeterminate prisoners it was felt that the system was too burdened and specialist, and was thus scrapped. Consequently, the ever growing numbers of indeterminately sentenced prisoners have largely lost specialized support. There has been an institutional loss of knowledge, and the rapid changes in legislation and parole protocols, whilst disseminated, are rarely explained. This has led to a situation where such sentences are barely navigable and many indeterminate-sentenced prisoners feel abandoned in a system that denies them certainty. This boundless form of incarceration, with its nebulous progressions and unknowable parameters, is experienced as a deep and pervasive pain.

However, it is not just lifers/IPPs who now have to cope with the deprivation of certainty; foreign nationals who have to prove or resolve their immigration status now face similar issues. Simon (1998) argued that the political shift occurring in the USA in the 1980s would result in the targeting and imprisoning of refugees as a tool of political utility. Bosworth and Kaufman (2011) argue that although 'prescient' in many ways, it is not the refugee who has become the focus of this US and UK politico-carceral shift but instead 'alien others': the 'undocumented worker' and the designated 'non-citizen'. Since the UK Borders Act of 2007 came into effect, every non-European Economic Area prisoner with a sentence of more than 12 months and every European Economic Area prisoner with a sentence of 24 months or more is designated as a non-citizen and is, as a matter of Home Office priority, earmarked for expulsion. There are somewhere in the region of 10,700 prisoners who are classified as foreign nationals (PRT 2014). The above authors argue that these specialized populations are subject to new matrices of political, carceral and ethical practices that both place them beyond the gaze of much contemporary criminological inquiry and render them especially vulnerable. To quote one such prisoner:

> No longer am I prisoner. My sentence finish. But still these UKBA bastards keep me here. I can not go home. Can not go to family. They say they send me to [country of origin]. What I do there? Where I go, live? I been here 17 years. I work. I pay tax. Now I get into trouble. Now they want to send me back. I have children here. Life is here. They issue IS91[5] so I am fighting but I am stuck here. I not know for how long. I not know what happen. My family not know what happen. I am not prisoner, this no longer prison. This internment!

This sense of being 'interred' was common and was iterated by many of those consulted; they felt as if they were in a liminal stage, not quite in prison but not quite in immigration detention either. This resulted in a number of frustrations. As with the indeterminate prisoners, there was a lack of information, the prison had become unnavigable, many felt lost, there was little or no chance of progression and there was no predictability with regard to their carceral future. However, as the above quote indicates, there were unique factors that relate to foreign national prisoners specifically: remaining in prison past the end of the sentence and not knowing how long that period would be; the prospect of removal from the country if appeals were unsuccessful; the potential loss of family life; and an uncertain ability to resettle beyond the prison. The problem faced by these prisoners is that, as Bosworth (2011) notes, the UKBA and prison authorities expect the foreign national prisoner to be simply and easily 'removed', either at the end of the sentence or under Repatriation Agreements, or through mechanisms like the Facilitated/Early Returns Scheme, without any fuss or bother. Yet many will 'not go quietly'. They are often people who have built a life here and who wish to remain. As another prisoner stated:

> I was to go home but then two days before they give IS91. Now … I am staying. I thought this was sorted. I spoke to my children last night and they ask me why I not home. What can I say to them? I try bail but court decline … say no because not all papers done. I give them but they say they not got. I feel hopeless now. No one cares. No one cares that my children … about my wife … No one care that I am depressed now. They make you not to want to live … never during sentence I feel like this but now …?

There is no succour for these prisoners, as this trauma is neither expected nor catered for. The process 'imagined' by the UKBA and the prison does not match the reality, but there is little accounting for this dissonance. This can result in an extreme assault on the prisoner's ability to cope – especially if, as with the person here, they had completed their sentence and were expecting to be released. To have that snatched away at the last minute can result in a profound pain and a degree of psychological trauma.

Thus far, this chapter has concentrated on the incarcerated prisoner, but of course most prisoners will be released back into the communities from where they were drawn. Although the prisoner may long once again to be an active chess piece, the reality is that getting 'out' can often be just as painful as being 'in'. In terms of practicality, there are the issues of securing housing, finances and re-establishing relationships/networks and mechanisms of support. All can pose real and lasting problems for the prisoner which can hamper successful reintegration. However, what must also be overcome are the pernicious effects of incarceration. In order to reintegrate successfully those adaptations, those learned behaviours, that enabled the prisoner to survive the prison environment, must be shed. As noted elsewhere (Warr 2012), the first challenge is to recognize the damage and harms that prison has caused and to then learn ways to overcome them.

For some this process begins in open conditions and will involve release on temporary licence (ROTL). Working outside the prison, having visits in the community, being able to attend family functions, spending time 'on the out' all aid this process of identifying the harms caused by being inside and allow the prisoner to work on them prior to release. This can include re-establishing relationships, overcoming the deprivation of hetero-social skills, learning to cope with new technologies, once again moving beyond the parasitic lifestyle that prisoners are forced into, and beginning to utilize the goods and services that they have previously been denied. It may even involve something mundane like learning to smile in response to people again. Time out of the prison can be fundamental to this process. Yet the incumbent justice secretary has ordered this tool to be granted to fewer individuals in the future. Of course, not every prisoner has the opportunity to go to open conditions and get used to the outside world via ROTL; for many, release comes with little preparation. For these individuals, released with £48 in their pocket, if they do not have the benefit of a family or support network, then the outside world can be a place of chaos and turmoil.

If going to prison represents a 'civil death' (Goffman 1961), then release should represent a 'civil rebirth', but unfortunately it does not. As Mathiesen (1990) notes, societies are 'absolved of responsibility' in this regard and thus do not fund or resource, or even truly support, this 'return'. Instead, he argues that all the resources are channelled into the 'pomp and circumstance' of the procedures that strip the prisoner of their moral worth and rehabilitation (whatever its form) is, to a certain degree, starved or 'neutralized'. Proponents of probation will no doubt argue that its function is to aid and support this 'return', escape from moral abeyance, but unfortunately this has long ceased to be its function. Probation has moved well beyond a remit of 'befriend, advise and assist' (Mair and Burke 2012), to one of public protection, risk supervision and management. In this context, and in the manner noted by Hannah-Moffatt (2005), the needs of the probationer are, once more, translated into risks that are to be managed, not necessarily resolved. As this lifer explained:

> When the parole board ordered my release I thought 'that's it, it's over'. But it wasn't, not by a long shot. I've had to put up with probation ever since. I'm still on weekly reporting and it's … well it's pointless. They don't do nothing. I needed

help with housing and benefits and they started talking about me not coping and that being a risk. Well okay that may be a risk … but then fucking help me with that shit, you know? What did they do? They gave me a number to call, a fucking number! Not for housing association or nothing, a charity that gives advice. That's it. That's all the help I got from them, all they could do.

Another former prisoner noted a similar issue:

all good if you're a smack head [heroin addict], then they got time for ya. Bend over for ya then. Get you support and help and what have ya. But if you're stuck and can't get work and that, then what? Nothing. Fuck all. Nada. Useless mate, know what I mean? I couldn't get a job for love nor money mate, tried everything and everywhere. Ain't proud. Can't afford to be at my age but … couldn't even get an interview. Me … felt like a proper leper, know what I mean? So I asked my probation officer for help … all she could say was 'we could get you on a fork lift truck driving course'. I laughed right in her face, I did that course 15 odd years ago. There weren't any fork lift driving jobs around then and there's even fucking less now!

This brings me to the final issue that faces the prisoner once out in the community: the problem of getting a job, having to declare the criminal offence and stigma. Stigma can take many forms and can result in a number of harms for differing people. There can be cultural 'shames' associated with having been in prison – for instance one Bangladeshi woman explained that, after being released from a fraud conviction, her family had refused to house her, give her access to her children or give her any aid at all. She was also shunned by others in what she had once considered a close-knit community. In the end she had to move away and try to start a life over again in a new town, away from a Bangladeshi community, where she and her past were not known. For others, stigma can relate to forming relationships. Echoing the findings of Lebel (2012a, 2012b), one former prisoner who had been convicted of kidnap, torture and robbery and had spent 13 years in prison explained that when meeting people for the first time, the fear of them rejecting him due to his 'past' resulted in him avoiding many interactions and from starting any conversation. This individual's perception of the type of stigma that their past conferred on them, and the subsequent discrimination they felt they would be subject to, did not allow them to construct any form of 'redemptive script' (Maruna 2001) which paralyzed them in terms of social reintegration. As such, he was now lonely and disengaged from those around him and felt that he had no future.

There are particular areas, however, where the impact of prison stigmata is all-pervasive – one such is employment. In virtually all circumstances in official and bureaucratic life, there is now a requirement to declare an offence (insurance, bank loans, mortgages, etc.). Nowhere is this more evident than when it comes to applying for jobs. This poses some real problems for the former prisoner, as it is a factor that can deter the employer from even considering the application – but to decline to declare it can also have negative consequences. That is even if the application makes it to the employer for consideration. In some instances, online job application software will, as a default setting, automatically side-line applications if the criminal convictions box has been ticked. HR departments and employers may not even be aware that this is happening unless they have had cause to check the default settings. As Loeffler (2013) explains, post-release unemployment is a substantive problem where interaction with the criminal justice system can radically impact on a person's life course and narrow their opportunities for employment.

A further barrier to employment can be the Disclosure and Barring procedures which have been established to protect vulnerable populations from those who may predate them in some way. The contemporary practice of criminal conviction checks came into effect with the Police Act of 1997 and then later with the creation of the Criminal Records Bureau (CRB) in 2002 (Mustafa et al. 2013). The CRB was later merged with the Independent Safeguarding Authority to become the Disclosure and Barring Service (DBS) (MoJ 2014). Whilst few would argue against organizations working with vulnerable populations having the right to vet potential staff, or that some individuals should not be allowed to work with vulnerable groups, sometimes the protocols can act as a needless barrier. Two recent examples are people barred from holding Police and Crime Commissioners positions due to juvenile convictions dating back many decades (Travis 2012). A further example is a lifer with an Enhanced DBS working for a third sector organization within criminal justice who, when accepted for a new job, was made to wait for more than four months, without recourse, for the police to complete their checks.

Attempting to make a new life after prison is hard, but these examples show that in some regards a former prisoner cannot move beyond their conviction. McNeill et al. (2014) note this as a particular issue and one which needs to be addressed if we are to move towards a more effective criminal justice system. However, currently the shedding of the 'offender' or 'prisoner' label is difficult as they are particularly adhesive. Even if employers do not access the DBS, there is still the problem of Google and information held on the Internet. There are sites dedicated to naming people with convictions and any Internet search holds the potential to reveal a former prisoner's past. Their tarnished moral identity is forever and is inescapable – a point made in the film *The Dark Knight Rises* (Nolan 2012) by the character Selina Kyle:

> There's no fresh start in today's world. Any twelve-year-old with a cell phone could find out what you did. Everything we do is collated and quantified. Everything sticks.

Conclusion

I have in this chapter tried to explicate some of the pains that are associated with contemporary imprisonment and those issues that can haunt the prisoner once beyond the wall. Whether it is having to learn how to adjust to the loss of liberty and the constraint of mundane activity, surviving the decortication of your moral and social self, having the institution, and its ever present oculus, intrude into every aspect of your being, having to hide your trauma from front stage performances, having to suppress emotional and sympathetic responses to the brutality that you witness, being forced into a parasitic lifestyle and relying on the graces of family, friends and official others, having to invent stimulation to hold back the crushing boredom, being consumptively wary, or surviving any of the other flagitious impositions, the prison is harmful and that harm continues far beyond the ending of the period of incarceration. All are assaults on the self and impact on the manner in which an individual perceives themselves and their place in the world.

Notes

1 All quoted material is taken from field notes and permission to utilize it was sought and agreed at the time. No identifiers are included in order to maintain anonymity. Where prisoners have been quoted, permission was sought and obtained from the establishments at the time the projects were running for use in reports and academic publications.
2 It is worth noting that a report released by the Prison and Probation Ombudsman in April 2014 noted that there has been an increase in self-inflicted deaths in custody in the period since these changes were introduced, but no direct correlation has been drawn.
3 'Fam' is an informal mode of address utilized by young urban men which denotes friendship or association. In use it is similar to the term 'mate'.
4 See for instance the video sent out of HMP Elmley that was reported in the *Daily Mirror*, www. mirror.co.uk/news/uk-news/video-brutality-uk-prisons-exposed-3603883.
5 The IS91 is an authorization to detain a prisoner under Immigration powers and will be issued by the Home Office.

Bibliography

Addicott, P. (2011) *An Exploratory Study of Frustrations, Compliance and Resistance Among Prisoners Serving Indeterminate Sentences*, MSt dissertation, Institute of Criminology, University of Cambridge.
Bentham, J. (1791) *Panopticon, or The Inspection House*, London: T. Payne, Mews Gate.
Bosworth, M. (2011) 'Deportation, Detention and Foreign National Prisoners in England and Wales', *Citizenship Studies* 15(5): 583–595.
Bosworth, M. and Kaufman, E. (2011) 'Foreigners in a Carceral Age: Immigration and Imprisonment in the United States', *Stanford Law & Policy Review* 22(2): 429–454.
Campbell, J. (1923) '*As I was Among Captives': Joseph Campbell's prison diary* (ed. Eilean Ni Chuilleanain 2001), Cork: Cork University Press.
Carlen, P. (2008) 'Imaginary penalities and risk crazed governance', in P. Carlen (ed.) *Imaginary Penalities*, Cullompton: Willan.
Carrabine, E. (2005) 'Prison Riots, Social Order and the Problem of Legitimacy', *British Journal of Criminology* 45: 896–913.
Clemmer, D. (1940) *The Prison Community*, Hanover, MA: Christopher Publishing House.
Cohen, S. (2001) *States of Denial: Knowing about atrocities and suffering*, Cambridge: Polity Press.
Cohen, S. and Taylor, L. (2006) 'Time and deterioration' in Y. Jewkes and H. Johnston (eds) *Prison Readings: A critical introduction to prisons and imprisonment*, Cullompton: Willan.
Conrad, T. (2006) *Oscar Wilde in Quotation: 3,100 Insults, Anecdotes and Aphorisms, Topically Arranged with Attributions*, Jefferson, NC: McFarland & Co. Inc.
Crewe, B. (2009) *The Prisoner Society: Power, adaptation and social life in an English prison*, Clarendon Studies in Criminology, Oxford: Oxford University Press.
Crewe, B. (2011) 'Depth, weight, tightness: revisiting the pains of imprisonment', *Punishment & Society* 13(5): 509–529.
Crewe, B., Warr, J., Bennett, P. and Smith, A. (2014) 'The Emotional Geography of Prison Life', *Theoretical Criminology* 18(1): 56–74.
Crotty, P. (ed.) (2010) *The Penguin Book of Irish Poetry*, London: Penguin Books.
Escher, M.C. (1960) 'Ascending and Descending', www.mcescher.com/gallery/lithograph/ascending-and-descending/.

Fishman, L.T. (1990) *Women at the Wall: A study of prisoners' wives doing time on the outside*, Albany: State University of New York Press.

Giddens, A. (1991) *Modernity and Self Identity: Self and society in the late modern age*, London: Polity.

Goffman, E. (1959) *The Presentation of Self in Everyday Life*, London: Penguin.

Goffman, E. (1961) *Asylums: Essays on the social situation of mental patients and other inmates*, London: Penguin Books Ltd.

Gunn, B. (2010) 'Ben's prison blog – lifer on the loose: my body isn't mine', blog entry, Friday 5 November 2010, prisonerben.blogspot.co.uk/2010/11/my-body-isnt-mine.html (accessed 15 May 2014).

Haney, C. (2001) 'The psychological impact of incarceration: implications for post-prison adjustment', in *National Policy Conference – From Prison to Home: The effect of incarceration and re-entry on children, families and communities*, 30–31 January 2002, Washington, DCUS Department of Health and Human Services, The Urban Institute.

Hannah-Moffatt, K. (2005) 'Criminogenic needs and the transformative risk subject: Hybridizations of Risk/Need in Penality', *Punishment & Society* 7(1): 29–51.

Hassine, V. (1996) *Life without Parole: Living in prison today*, Los Angeles, CA: Roxbury Publishing.

Herrity, K.Z. (2014) *The Significance of Music to the Prison Experience*, BSc, Royal Holloway, University of London.

Jewkes, Y. (2002) *Captive Audience: Media, masculinity and power in prisons*, Cullompton: Willan.

Jewkes, Y. (2005) 'Loss, liminality and the life sentence: managing identity through a disrupted lifecourse', in A. Liebling and S. Maruna (eds) *The Effects of Imprisonment*, Cullompton: Willan, 366–388.

Kaufman, E. (2013) 'Hubs and spokes: the transformation of the British prison', in K.F. Aas and M. Bosworth (eds) *The Borders of Punishment: Migration, citizenship and social exclusion*, Oxford: Oxford University Press.

King, R. and McDermott, K. (1995) *The State of our Prisons*, Oxford: Clarendon Press.

Krebs, B. (2010) 'Joint criminal enterprise', *The Modern Law Review* 73(4): 578–604.

Lebel, T. (2012a) 'Invisible stripes? Formerly incarcerated persons' perceptions of stigma', *Deviant Behavior* 33(2): 89–107.

Lebel, T. (2012b) '"If one doesn't get you another will": formerly incarcerated persons' perceptions of discrimination', *The Prison Journal* 92(1): 63–87.

Liebling, A. and Arnold, H. (2004) *Prisons and their Moral Performance: A study of values, quality and prison life*, Clarendon Studies in Criminology, Oxford: Oxford University Press.

Liebling, A., Durie, L., Stiles, A. and Tait, S. (2005) 'Revisiting prison suicide: the role of fairness and distress', in A. Liebling and S. Maruna (eds) *The Effects of Imprisonment*, Cullompton: Willan.

Loader, I. and Sparks, R. (2013) 'Unfinished business: legitimacy, crime control and democratic politics', in J. Tankebe and A. Liebling (eds) *Legitimacy and Criminal Justice: An international exploration*, Oxford: Oxford University Press.

Loeffler, C.E. (2013) 'Does imprisonment slter the life course? Evidence on crime and employment from a natural experiment', *Criminology* 51(1): 137–166.

McNeill, F., Farrall, S., Ligthowler, C. and Maruna, S. (2014) 'Desistance and supervision', in G. Bruinsma and D. Weisburd (eds) *Encyclopaedia of Criminology and Criminal Justice*, New York: Springer, 958–967.

Mair, G. and Burke, L. (2012) *Redemption, Rehabilitation and Risk Management: A history of probation*, London: Routledge.

Maruna, S. (2001) *Making Good: How ex-convicts reform and rebuild their lives*, Washington, DC: The American Psychological Society.

Mason, G.L. (1990) 'Indeterminate sentencing: cruel and unusual punishment, or just plain cruel?' *New England Journal on Criminal and Civil Confinement* 16(1): 89–120.

Mason, P. (2006) 'Lies, distortion and what doesn't work: monitoring prison stories in the British media', *Crime Media Culture* 2(3): 251–267.

Mathiesen, T. (1990) *Prison on Trial*, London: Sage Publications Ltd.

Melvin, K.B., Gramling, L.K. and Gardner, W.M. (1985) 'A scale to measure attitudes towards prisoners', *Criminal Justice and Behaviour* 12(2): 241–253.

MoJ (Ministry of Justice) (2013) *Criminal Justice Statistics: Quarterly Update to March 2013*, London: Ministry of Justice.

MoJ (Ministry of Justice) (2014) 'Disclosure and barring service: overview', www.gov.uk/dis closure-barring-service-check/overview (accessed 20 June 2014).

MoJ (Ministry of Justice) and UKBA (UK Border Agency) (2009) *Service Level Agreement to Support the Effective and Speedy Removal of Foreign National Prisoners*, 1 May, London: Ministry of Justice.

Morris, J.A. and Feldman, D.C. (1996) 'The dimensions, antecedents and consequences of emotional labour', *Academy of Management Review* 21(4): 986–1010.

Mustafa, N., Kingston, P. and Beeston, D. (2013) 'An exploration of the historical background of criminal record checking in the United Kingdom: from the eighteenth to the twenty-first century', *European Journal on Criminal Policy and Research* 19(1): 15–30.

Nolan, C. (dir) (2012) *The Dark Knight Rises*, film, Warner Bros. Legendary Pictures.

Penrose, L.S. and Penrose, R. (1958) 'Impossible objects: a special type of visual illusion', *British Journal of Psychology* 49(1): 31–33.

Perez, F. and Esposito, L. (2010) 'The global addiction and human rights: insatiable consumerism, neoliberalism and harm reduction', *Perspectives on Global Development and Technology* 9(1): 84–100.

PRT (Prison Reform Trust) (2014) 'Prison: the facts – Bromley Briefings summer 2014', www. prisonreformtrust.org.uk/Portals/0/Documents/Prison%20the%20facts%20May%202014.pdf (accessed 5 June 2014).

Rose, C. (2012) 'RIP the IPP: a look back at the sentence of imprisonment for public protection', *Journal of Criminal Law* 76(4): 303–313.

Rowe, A. (2012) 'Women prisoners', in B. Crewe and J. Bennett (eds) *The Prisoner*, Abingdon: Routledge.

Simon, J. (1998) 'Refugees in a carceral age: the rebirth of immigration prisons in the United States', *Public Culture* 10(3): 577–607.

Sparks, R., Bottoms, A.E. and Hay, W. (1996), *Prisons and the Problem of Order*, Oxford: Oxford University Press.

Sykes, G.M. (1958) *The Society of Captives – A Study of a Maximum Security Prison*, Princeton, NJ: Princeton University Press.

Thomas, C.W. (1973), 'Prisonization or resocialization? A study of external factors associated with the impact of imprisonment', *Journal of Research in Crime and Delinquency* 10(1): 13–21.

Tonry, M. (2004) *Punishment and Politics: Evidence and emulation in the making of English crime control policy*, Cullompton: Willan.

Travis, A. (2012) 'Second police commissioner candidate withdraws over juvenile conviction', *The Guardian*, www.theguardian.com/uk/2012/aug/10/police-commissioner-candidate-withdra w-conviction (accessed 20 June 2014).

Walker, S. and Worrall, A. (2006) 'Life as a woman: the gendered pains of indeterminate imprisonment', in Y. Jewkes and H. Johnston (eds) *Prison Readings: A critical introduction to prisons and imprisonment*, Cullompton: Willan.

Warr, J. (2007) 'Personal reflections on prison staff', in J. Bennett, B. Crewe and A. Wahidin (eds) *Understanding Prison Staff*, Cullompton: Willan, 17–29.

Warr, J. (2012) 'Afterword', in B. Crewe and J. Bennett (eds) *The Prisoner*, Abingdon: Routledge.

Warr, J. (2014) 'Does prison size matter?', *Prison Service Journal* 211: 25–30.

Zamble, E. and Porporino, F.J. (1988) *Coping, Behavior and Adaptation in Prison Inmates*, Dordrecht: Springer-Verlag Publishers.

6 Criminal justice and working with offenders

Introduction

This chapter explores practitioner narratives and institutional cultures within the Tasmanian criminal justice field, with particular reference to key organisations that are responsible for supporting rehabilitation and reintegration. Similar to the last chapter, the central themes of culture and the social dynamics of change emerge as principal concerns. Criminal justice practitioners are quick to explain differences between perceptions of their work and what they really do in practice, emphasising how their work spans more issues and activities than is reflected in official and empirical accounts. Navigating negative change and difficult work are juxtaposed with a commonly observed desire to be at the forefront of instigating positive change and to craft work identities associated with job satisfaction and real world impact. It is these strengths, individually and institutionally, that are identified here to aid the recognition that such things are not peripheral to the work of supporting rehabilitation and reintegration, but are essential facets or ingredients in realising 'the best of what is' in the present and moving forwards.

The terms 'offender', 'prisoner', 'inmate' and 'working with offenders' are used in this chapter, reflecting their frequent use by practitioners in this field and in the literature. Terms like 'service user' are rarely used by practitioners in this particular field, in Tasmania at least, in part because of a pragmatic view that people who are the subjects of punishment and rehabilitation have little or no choice in their 'use' of these 'services'. This may be contentious in other jurisdictions, reflecting wider debates about who is the 'client' in criminal justice, especially in an era characterised by the dominance of risk and public protection agendas. There are understandable tensions in using 'offender' as a label in a book focused on supporting desistance and recovery due to its negative connotations for those to whom it is applied. A necessary preface is to question *who* is more likely become an 'offender', underscoring the disproportionate criminalisation of people living with social problems and complex needs.

The overrepresentation of social problems and complex needs in the criminal justice system

Much has already been written on the topics of the overrepresentation of people with complex needs and social problems in criminal justice systems in Australia and around the world, exposing tensions and paradoxes between what is done in the name of criminal justice and what this means in terms of social justice (for example, see Baldry *et al.*, 2009, 2013; Spivakovsky, 2013, 2014; Barak *et al.*, 2015). Critical analysts such as Stevens (2007a) and Wacquant (2009) and others have illuminated the inherent power inequalities and political motivations of dominant knowledges and discourses which uphold the criminalisation of marginalised people and groups.

Specific data from the state of Tasmanian about prisoner and offender demographics is not publicly available. However, Tasmanian data is incorporated within the national series *The Health of Australia's Prisoners* by the Australian Institute of Health and Welfare (2013a). Numerous health and social issues can be observed in the lives of those being sent to prison in Australia:

- 7 out of 10 Australian prison entrants report that they engaged in illicit drug use in the last 12 months;
- 5 out of 10 Australian prison entrants were unemployed in the 30 days prior to imprisonment;
- 43 per cent of Australian prison entrants report that they have ever received a blow to the head resulting in loss of consciousness;
- 35 per cent report that they were homeless (including living in emergency crisis accommodation) in the four weeks prior to imprisonment;
- 43 per cent of female Australian prison entrants report that they have been told by a qualified professional that they have a mental disorder (including a substance use disorder).

(*ibid.*: x–xv)

The broader research literature affirms the existence of clear trends which indicate who is disproportionately criminalised and incarcerated. These include: young people; Indigenous people and ethnic minorities; people with low or no literacy and learning disabilities; people who are former wards of the state and have been in foster care as children; people with acquired brain injuries, cognitive disabilities and mental disorders; people living in poverty; and people who have been victims of crime (Johnson and Toch, 1982; Sampson and Lauritsen, 1997; Kupers, 1999; Cunneen, 2005; Dowse *et al.*, 2011; Scraton and McCulloch, 2009; Baldry *et al.*, 2009, 2013; Spivakovsky, 2013, 2014). The plethora of issues involved in disproportionate rates of criminalisation remain fundamentally important to any reflections on rehabilitation, recovery and desistance, not only for their impact on the human beings subject to intervention, but also their impact on those responsible for doing or overseeing such interventions. Therefore, examination of systemic features and practitioner perspectives are prefaced with the recognition of the pervasive influence of these intersecting inequalities in the lives of many of the people with whom they work.

Institutional contexts

This section sets the scene by describing and contextualising the main institutions and organisations which make up the field of criminal justice in Tasmania. Particular attention is given to the state government services which employ the majority of the state's criminal justice workforce, namely Tasmania Prison Service, the Community Corrections Service, and the Correctional Primary Health Service.

Tasmania Prison Service

The Tasmanian Department of Justice Tasmania Prison Service (TPS) is the state's only prison service. There are no private prisons or privately-run corrective services for adults in the state. The TPS is responsible for the custody and supervision of adult offenders sentenced to incarceration and unsentenced 'accused persons' remanded in custody (referred to here as 'remandees') aged 18 years and older. Young people under the age of 18 who are sentenced to custody or placed on remand, as well as adult offenders with severe psychiatric disorders, are supervised in other secure facilities by the Tasmanian Department of Health and Human Services (DHHS); for example, the Ashley Youth Detention Centre operated by Youth Justice and the Wilfred Lopes Forensic Mental Health Centre which is operated by Forensic Mental Health.

The geographical location of the TPS is worthy of note because, to a certain extent, it influences local perceptions of the prison and those who live and work there. The prison is located in the relatively isolated suburb of Risdon Vale, surrounded by dense bushland and hills with only one major arterial road, the East Derwent Highway, linking the suburb of Risdon Vale and Risdon Prison with the rest of the city of Hobart. Originally conceived in the late 1950s and early 1960s as a public housing estate, the suburb of Risdon Vale continues to be known for its colourful residents and locational disadvantage, inside and outside of the prison walls. Risdon Vale is one of greater Hobart's most socioeconomically disadvantaged suburbs, with the Australian Bureau of Statistics (2013) defining this 'in terms of people's access to material and social resources, and their ability to participate in society'. Yet, an noticeable sense of community spirit among Risdon Vale residents is celebrated alongside their colourful reputation, endearingly described by some as people with 'tenacity, a little rough around the edges, infused with a no-nonsense lack of pretensions' and, more critically, by others as 'bogans' (Booth, 2008: 309). Risdon Prison (a collection of prison facilities in one location) is the most visible feature of the Risdon Vale landscape. Opened in November 1960, its construction coincided with that of the surrounding public housing estates. The original prison was quickly labelled the 'Pink Palace' (Evans, 2004) for its infamous pink reinforced concrete and laconic pastel interiors – a name which stuck for 40 years in the Tasmanian public vernacular before disappearing in the early and mid-2000s with the advent of the prison infrastructure redevelopment. The new co-located prison facilities are concrete and grey, enclosed by two imposing silver razor wire fences.

The TPS incorporates five custodial facilities across the state; however, the first three facilities listed below are separate but co-located to make up what members of the public and the media refer to as Risdon Prison:

- The Risdon Prison Complex (RPC) – men's medium and maximum security prison, including the Apsley alcohol and drug treatment unit;
- The Ron Barwick Minimum Security Prison – men's minimum security prison, including the O'Hara cottages and independent living precinct;
- The Mary Hutchinson Women's Prison – women's minimum, medium and maximum security prison, including the Mother and Baby unit;
- The Hobart Reception Prison; and
- The Launceston Reception Prison.

The latter two Reception Prison facilities differ from the others as they are smaller in prisoner population size, and co-located with or located within Tasmania Police headquarters and next to the Magistrates Court of Tasmania in the central business districts of the cities of Hobart and Launceston.

The total prison population shows some marginal fluctuations. In 2014, there were just under 450 adults in prison (prisoners and remandees), as Tasmania was the only state in Australia to see a fall in prisoner numbers, dropping 7 per cent in 12 months (Australian Bureau of Statistics (ABS), 2014). Males make up 93 per cent of the prison population; there are only approximately 30–35 female prisoners in the state. To contextualise this relative to other jurisdictions, the adult imprisonment rate in Tasmania was 112 prisoners per 100,000 adult population in 2014 (*ibid.*). This is significantly lower than the Australian national population figure (151 prisoners per 100,000 adult population), and lower than other jurisdictions such as England and Wales (148 per 100,000) and New Zealand (190 per 100,000) (Institute for Criminal Policy Research, 2015).

The TPS mission statement has changed in recent years to include an emphasis on rehabilitation, with recognition of processes of human development and community engagement as integral to supporting desistance and reintegration:

> The mission of Tasmania Prison Service (TPS) is to contribute to a safer Tasmania by ensuring the safe, secure containment of prisoners and providing them with opportunities for rehabilitation, personal development and community engagement.
>
> (Tasmanian Department of Justice, 2013: 29)

The staff of the TPS can be loosely categorised in three ways: the Prison Executive and Senior Management Team (SMT), the uniformed Correctional Officers (COs), and the non-uniformed staff who are responsible for sentence management, reintegration and therapeutic services. Within the third group, there are a number of staff teams, with different roles and responsibilities: therapeutic services (clinical psychological intervention and crisis support); programmes; needs assessment and case coordination (including sentence management and reintegration, community service activities and giving back projects); parenting and family support; prisoner education and employment; sport and recreational activities; and organisational development and training. These teams are employed in different types of job classifications (professional stream, general clerical and administrative stream) with markedly different levels of remuneration and requisite qualifications. The TPS only recently adopted the case management model in 2006, coinciding with the opening of the new Risdon Prison Complex. The non-uniformed staff offices are separate to those of the correctional officers; they are located outside of the secure correctional facilities in the renovated prison cells of the old prison hospital wing. A group of the non-uniformed prison staff have been organisationally grouped together under the title of the Integrated Offender Management (IOM) Unit, then re-named the Sentence Management, Support and Reintegration (SMSR) Unit. Some of the staff offering psychosocial interventions and programmes targeting criminogenic risk and substance misuse are grouped under the title the Intervention Programmes Unit, although their colleagues simply refer to them as 'programmes' staff. The staff are different to, but work in partnership with, the Correctional Primary Health Service staff. Some of the innovative and creative work that prison staff are involved in to support reintegration and desistance are covered in Chapter 7, in addition to the key themes discussed here.

Correctional Primary Health Service

The Correctional Primary Health Service is a part of the Tasmanian Department of Health and Human Services (DHHS), rather than the Department of Justice. It operates the prison hospital, pharmacy and health services located inside the main Risdon Prison Complex of Tasmania Prison Service, providing healthcare to prisoners and remandees within this facility and from other prison facilities. Although its work is dependent on collaboration with one another, the organisational structural and service provision boundaries between the Departments of Health and Justice in this context remain distinct. The Correctional Primary Health Service (commonly called 'Correctional Health') have been instrumental in pioneering and developing the implementation of a localised version of the Healthy Prisons Model, a biopsychosocial approach which has been developed by the World Health Organisation (Møller *et al.*, 2007). In addition to mainstream medical services, the Correctional Health staff team oversee the alcohol and other drugs detoxification and treatment services; drug overdose, suicide and self-harm responses; prison riot emergency responses involving injuries or ill-health of those involved; blood-borne virus treatment and support programmes; and general mental health care for all prisoners and remandees. They employ one Comorbidity Clinical Nurse Consultant.

In 2013, there was approximately the equivalent of 36 full-time healthcare staff in Correctional Health (Australian Government Productivity Commission, 2013).

This staff team have high caseloads, with prisoners seeking healthcare provision or treatment episodes for a recorded 1,197 'problems' (including health checks, medication, mental health, dental health, substance misuse) *in a two-week census period* (*ibid*.: 35). Correctional Health is not a health service provider for people on community-based sanctions and measures.

Community Corrections Service

The Tasmanian Department of Justice Community Corrections Service is a state-wide offender supervision service with offices across the three regions of greater Hobart (South), Launceston (North), Devonport and Burnie (North West). Outreach services are offered across rural and regional areas, including Sorrell, New Norfolk, Huonville, Swansea, St Mary's, Smithton, Ulverstone and Queenstown. The mission statement of the Community Corrections Service has a public protection emphasis: 'to work with offenders on community-based orders reduce re-offending and contribute to a safer Tasmania' (Tasmanian Department of Justice, 2013: 40). In contrast to the mission statement, the vision statement still prioritises public protection, but is more inclusive of notions and processes relevant to rehabilitation:

As a progressive organisation that has the trust and confidence of the public, Community Corrections will help protect Tasmanians by:

- Ensuring compliance and providing supervision for people on community-based orders;
- Working with offenders to facilitate change by developing pro-social behaviour;
- Working with the community to provide opportunities for reintegration.

(Tasmanian Department of Justice, 2013: 4)

The two primary functions of the Community Corrections Service are: (1) offender supervision and the management of community-based sentences; and (2) providing assessments and reports to the courts and the Parole Board of Tasmania. The types of legal orders and sentences that are supervised by the Community Corrections Service are:

- *Probation Orders* – a sentencing order imposed by a magistrate or judge, that does not exceed three years in length;
- *Parole Orders* – granted by the Parole Board of Tasmania (which is an independent body) for prisoners leaving TPS facilities;
- *Community Service Orders* – a sentencing order imposed by a magistrate or judge, involving unpaid work for the purposes of reparation in the community and/or attendance of approved rehabilitative programmes and educational courses. It may also incorporate a Monetary Penalty Community Service Order;
- *Drug Treatment Orders* – a sentencing order to divert eligible offenders into treatment and the supervision of the Court Mandated Diversion programme; and

Community Service Orders can be imposed concurrently with other types of orders. From June 2011 to June 2014, there was a 23 per cent increase in the imposition of Community Service Orders, up from 985 to 1,213 (Tasmanian Department of Justice, 2014: 58).

The total number of offenders under the supervision of the Community Corrections Service continues to rise, with 2015 estimates of approximately 2,060 offenders (Australian Government Productivity Commission, 2015). State-wide, the offender-to-operational staff ratio is 30.7, and the offender-to-other staff ratio is 151.0 (*ibid.*: 700). Community Corrections staff, including probation officers, are not uniformed staff.

Focused on illicit drug diversion, the Court Mandated Diversion (CMD) programme operates from Community Corrections, run in collaboration with the Magistrates Court of Tasmania, the DHHS Alcohol and Drug Service and community sector organisations. It is a therapeutic jurisprudential initiative for offenders with significant and lengthy histories of substance misuse that is linked to their often prolific offending behaviour. The Drug Treatment Order (DTO) is an option that is targeted towards those who would otherwise be sentenced to prison. The programme 'aims to reduce the risk of re-offending through case management and therapeutic interventions and programmes that primarily address their drug abuse, while maintaining accountability through a system of rewards and sanctions' (Tasmanian Department of Justice, 2013: 40).

Community sector organisations

In addition to the government organisations, a number of non-statutory community sector organisations offer services specifically for people in prison and under community supervision. Approximately 40–45 community sector organisations offer services to people in prison as 'external service providers'. Most of these organisations are not exclusively for people with convictions, and a significant proportion of these community sector organisations would offer alcohol and other drugs initiatives or programmes (for example, especially the medium and larger organisations such as the Salvation Army, Anglicare, and the City Mission). Because of budgetary cycles and cutbacks, there are very few residential options specifically for people leaving prison. The Community Corrections Service also makes referrals to and collaborates with community sector organisations.

Size does matter: the strengths and benefits of a small criminal justice field

One of the strengths of the Tasmanian criminal justice field is its small size. This tends to enable ease of communication and collaboration – a strength highlighted by numerous practitioners in this research. In the timeframe that the research was conducted, the Tasmanian Department of Justice and Minister for Justice and Corrections worked with the field, including people with convictions, to collaboratively develop an overarching policy framework in the form of a ten-year plan, the *Breaking the Cycle – Tasmania's Ten Year Strategic Plan for Corrections 2011–2020* (Tasmanian Department of Justice, 2011). Nearly every criminal justice practitioner participant in this research mentioned this policy with positive regard. Although the policy has been the subject of review following the change of government, *Breaking the Cycle* represents an excellent example of a cohesive and visionary policy designed with and for practitioners and service users, with sensitivity to the local context. Despite the series of leadership and infrastructure changes in Tasmania in recent years, there is a lot of support and willingness to help realise the goals of the Plan, especially as a normative amount of accountability arises from the regularity with which stakeholders see each other. These things might be more difficult in a larger jurisdiction, geographically and in terms of population relative to the number of service providers.

The benefits of having a small field are apparent in the collaboration which enables prison-parole transitions, with good lines of communication with the independent Parole Board of Tasmania.

> My current case load has me contacting them [the Parole Board] a lot, and I found them to be very helpful, very supportive, laying things down, 'this is how it works, relay that to the inmate', and I have initiated a couple of meetings with them, which has been good just to go over what we offer, so that they're clear
>
> [Frontline practitioner, community sector]

> I think in Tasmania we are a lot luckier than most. If you go to other states, they would say that in no other state in Australia would the Parole Board secretary physically meet with every person that is going on parole, before they go on parole. They don't even see them in New South Wales, they just do the Parole Board hearing on paper, because of the numbers. If you think about that, we are really lucky. Let's make the most of that and have that close communication.
>
> [Senior practitioner, Community Corrections]

Optimistic sentiments are echoed in the commitment and willingness of community sector practitioners to be actively involved in collaborative sentence planning and reintegration planning with their Department of Justice colleagues working in the prison and Community Corrections.

> If we need to sit down and have a case conference between all of us, then I easily and happily arrange that ... We're looking at the bigger post-release plan for the inmate. We want the best possible outcome, so we sit down together and discuss what each of our organisations can and are prepared to offer post-release.
>
> [Frontline practitioner]

It's such an advantage, to have that knowledge, and keep up-to-date, as much as possible with what each service is offering and doing, and as you say, that referral pathway backwards and forwards between us.

[Frontline practitioner]

Practitioner accounts, both government and community sector, in the criminal justice field are more positive in tone than those in the alcohol and other drugs field. The thematic issues arising from practitioner accounts of collaboration, particularly with regard to instigating innovative initiatives, are taken up again in Chapter 7.

Penal cultures and politics in the criminal justice field

In relation to Bourdieu's (1980) concepts and Page's (2012) description of a field outlined in Chapter 4, the Tasmanian criminal justice field is somewhat unique in that it is small in size, and enjoys the regularity of relatively stable policy and legislation which infrequently changes (and when it does, it tends to do so with moderate support of institutions and practitioners). Aside from relatively typical politics, there have been no 'shock' policy reforms in recent years preceding 2014. Thus, the formal rules and official parameters which govern 'the game' and ordering of rehabilitation work and service provision in the Tasmanian criminal justice field are relatively stable. However, irrespective of size, the field is not stable in the sense that it is constantly being changed by inter-professional and institutional dynamics, including recent industrial conflicts, which are mapped in the next section. Infrastructure has been developed at a rapid rate, which is only surpassed by the rate of change in terms of leaders and senior actors in the local field.

The field as a site of struggle: changing institutional dynamics and industrial issues

The institutional context is a dynamic one, as there have been significant amounts of change in the Tasmanian criminal justice sector in the last decade. Table 6.1 draws upon information from secondary sources and the public domain to document five key spheres of change: leadership changes; legislative, structural and policy changes; infrastructure changes; new initiatives; and key events and critical incidences in Tasmania's criminal justice sector. The content of Table 6.1 features more information about Tasmania Prison Service than the Community Corrections Service. This is partly due to the differences in the nature of service provision (closed institutions have more critical incidents). It also relates to the fact that the Community Corrections Service has had more leadership stability and its Director and Senior Management Team have consistently focused on resolving institutional issues in-house, with little or no media scrutiny.

Table 6.1 Timeline of key events in Tasmania's criminal justice sector, 2005–13

Year	Changes, Issues and Events
2005	• *Critical incident*: Two-day prison siege in men's maximum security at Risdon Prison; a correctional officer is taken hostage by 20 prisoners and facilities (including the reception, computers, files) are trashed. The prisoners give negotiators and prison management a list of 24 demands and complaints. The officer is released after the delivery of 15 pizzas (named 'siege breaker pizzas') to the rioting prisoners. • *Legislative change*: The *Community Protection (Offender Reporting) Act 2005* is legislated, establishing a 'sex offender' register for Tasmania.
2006	• *Infrastructure change*: The new $90 million prison is opened, with men's maximum and medium security facilities called the Risdon Prison Complex. The old prison facilities are renovated and re-classified as the Ron Barwick Minimum Security Prison. The co-located Mary Hutchison Women's Prison also opens. • *Infrastructure*: The Wilfred Lopes Centre for Forensic Mental Health opens as a new secure mental health unit run by the Department of Health and Human Services, separate from but co-located with Risdon Prison. • *Organisational structural and policy change*: The Integrated Offender Management Unit is established and the Case Management Model (correctional officers adopt new therapeutic responsibilities using a case management approach, working with non-uniformed case coordination staff) is implemented across Tasmania Prison Service for the first time. • *Leadership change*: There is a new Minister for Justice and Attorney-General.
2007	• *Legislative and structural change*: Two new therapeutic jurisprudence court diversion options commence in the Magistrates Court of Tasmania: • The Mental Health Diversion List (MHDL) for offenders with a mental illness: The MHDL operates without a unique legislative base, using tailored bail conditions under the existing provisions Bail Act 1994 (Tas). • The Court Mandated Diversion (CMD) Programme for offenders who engage in drug-related offending: The Sentencing Act 1997 is amended in 2007 to add the new sentencing order of a drug treatment order as the legislative base for CMD. CMD is run in partnership between the court and Community Corrections.
2008	• *Leadership change*: There is a new Attorney-General and Minister for Justice and new Minister for Corrections, with the two ministry portfolios being separate for the first time. • *Leadership change*: A new Director for Community Corrections is appointed. • *New initiative*: Reading Together Program for prisoners and their children starts at Tasmania Prison Service. • *Key event*: The final report of the independent Review of Community Corrections is released by KPMG.
2009	• *New initiative*: Community Corrections launches the Sober Driver Program, a nine-week community-based mandated psycho-educational program for adult repeat drink driving convictions. • *Critical incident*: A riot in Risdon Prison Complex medium security sees two correctional officers seriously assaulted, two fires lit, and the stand-off is ended by the Tactical Response Group. Medium security remains in lock down for two months, with prisoners locked in their cells for up to 23 hours a day.

Table 6.1 Timeline of key events in Tasmania's criminal justice sector, 2005–13 (Continued)

Year	Changes, Issues and Events
2010	• *Leadership change*: The Director of Prisons steps down and, under a hung parliament power-sharing arrangement resulting from a state parliamentary election, the new Minister for Corrections is the first Greens minister in Australia. • *Key event*: The Minister for Corrections and acting Director of Prisons go to the Industrial Commission to get an injunction to lift a two-month lock down in the men's medium security prison. They have disagreements with the prison officer's union, which attracts considerable media coverage. • *Critical incident*: High profile breach of parole (fifth breach in ten years) by a notorious 'earless' violent offender who commits a violent home invasion and assaults his victims in their home. • *Critical incident*: A violent fight in maximum security Derwent Bravo Unit sees six officers seriously injured. On the same day an inmate is taken hostage by an inmate with history of prison assaults in the Tamar Unit. • *Critical incident*: An inmate escapes his maximum security cell at the Risdon Prison Complex by tunnelling behind his toilet, highlighting a design flaw in the new prison buildings. He escapes the building, but does not successfully escape the perimeter fence. In the early hours of the morning, all maximum security male prisoners were relocated to the Ron Barwick minimum security prison. The rectification works at the Risdon Prison Complex takes two months; meanwhile the maximum security inmates are supervised by correctional officers flown in from Queensland, Victoria, New South Wales and Western Australia and the Tasmanian Tactical Response Group in the overcrowded, old minimum security prison. External community services are unable to hold professional visits or deliver services during this time of lockdown. • *Key event*: Ombudsman Tasmania releases a critical investigation report into the Risdon Prison Complex Tamar Unit and its behaviour management programme for high-risk offenders. • *New initiative*: The Pups in Prison initiative starts at Tasmania Prison Service, run by Assistance Dogs Australia. Inmates train assistance dogs every day for up to 18 months to benefit people with disabilities.
2011	• *Policy change*: The awaited ten-year plan *Breaking the Cycle: A Strategic Plan for Tasmanian Corrections 2011–2020* is launched. It is very well received by stakeholders and the media, following extensive consultations. • *Key event*: The Minister and the Director of Prisons go to the Industrial Commission after an industrial feud over the Tactical Response Group being permanently based at the prison, and changes to procedures in the maximum security Tamar Unit. Fifty-eight correctional officers are stood down without pay after refusing to undertake required duties. The officer's union publicly criticises the industrial action. The Industrial Commission finds in favour of the government, and the officers are ordered to return to work. • *Key event*: Confidential case notes about individual prisoners are leaked to *The Mercury* newspaper, which features their contents on its front page, prompting investigations by Tasmania Police. The Corrections Minister publicly accuses correctional officers of stealing case notes and reports and illegally leaking them to the media. • *Leadership change*: Two leadership changes in five months for the Minister for Justice and Attorney-General portfolios. The sitting Premier resigns and is appointed to these roles on 23 January 2011, only to resign from parliament and have the ministry portfolios resumed by a new Minister on 13 May 2011.

Table 6.1 Timeline of key events in Tasmania's criminal justice sector, 2005–13 (Continued)

Year	Changes, Issues and Events
2011	• *Key event*: A high-profile inmate successfully sues the Tasmanian government for breaches of duty of care and human rights, after years of being held indefinitely in solitary confinement in his cell for up to 23 hours a day in the Tamar Unit. He is reported to have a long history of violent attacks on prison officers and other inmates. During the court case, the government admits breaching its duty of care in this prisoner's case. • *Key event*: An edited version of *The Palmer Inquiry*, an independent inquiry into Risdon Prison Complex, is publicly released. Most of the 39 recommendations reflect moderate or serious issues in the current prison infrastructure, staffing and models. • *New initiative*: the Integrated Offender Management Unit at the prison facilitate the first prisoner art exhibition 'Artists with Conviction' with much success, in conjunction the Hobart City Council and Reclink. • *Critical incident*: An eight-hour prison siege in which inmates took two officers hostage in the maximum security Tamar Unit. Police negotiators and the Tactical Response Group resolve the situation. • *New initiative*: The Tasmania Prison Service prison community garden and food distribution network starts as a 'giving back' community service activity. It is operated in partnership with a food security charity.
2012	• *Leadership change*: The long awaited appointment of the new change manager is announced. His role is to oversee change management and reforms across Corrective Services. • *Critical incident*: Prison siege involving eight inmates in the maximum security Huon Unit using handmade weapons, taking two prison officers hostage. The Tactical Response Group resolves the incident. • *Leadership change*: A new Director of Prisons appointed, replacing the acting Director. Shortly after arriving, the new Director instigates an organisational restructure, renaming and re-arranging units and teams across Tasmania Prison Service. The Integrated Offender Management Unit of non-uniformed staff is re-named the Sentence Management, Support and Reintegration Unit. • *Infrastructure change*: The Hayes Prison Farm (minimum security, open prison), founded in 1937, is de-commissioned and closed. Remaining prisoners are re-located to facilities at Risdon Prison. • *New initiative*: Hand Made With Pride 'giving back' sewing project starts in Mary Hutchinson Women's Prison.
2013	• *Leadership change and key event*: The current Director of Prisons goes on extended leave. Three months later, it is revealed that he has had his five-year contract terminated one year in, in a confidential agreement with the state government. He lodges a complaint about senior Department of Justice staff with the Integrity Commission. A Parliamentary inquiry into his conduct and spending as Director is conducted. • *Leadership change*: A new Director of Prisons is appointed. • *Infrastructure change*: The new O'Hara independent living units are opened for minimum rated prisoners. • *Leadership change*: The current Director of Community Corrections is appointed as the new Deputy Secretary of Justice, and a new Director of Community Corrections is appointed.

Sources: Table compiled by the researcher using information from the Australian Prisons Project (2010); Evans (2004); Glaetzer (2010); Finnane (1997).

In 2014 and 2015, the TPS was affected by several deaths in custody, which was not otherwise a prominent issue in the state. There has been another change in the Minister for Corrections and Justice following a change in government after a state parliamentary election. Although they have an influence on the local field, the types and frequency of issues and events outlined in Table 6.1 are not necessarily atypical for corrective services in Western neoliberal jurisdictions.

The majority of the key events and issues presented in Table 6.1 do not directly *involve* the non-uniformed frontline practitioners responsible for service provision and supporting rehabilitation and reintegration in Tasmania. Yet they are certainly implicated and affected by these things. The series of changes affect practitioners' sense of place in the field, as well as their daily work routines. For example, during the two-month prison lockdowns in 2009, and again in 2010–11, government and non-government practitioners were denied access to the affected prison facilities, and rehabilitative services for prisoners ceased during this time. 'Snap' lockdowns could happen without warning, sometimes followed by the appearance of balaclava wearing and weapon carrying members of the Tactical Response Group (TRG).

Public discourse at the time of these conflicts and critical incidences in 2009–11 canvassed the spectrum of community attitudes about how this might affect prisoners and whether it was deserved or unfair. Yet the effect on non-uniformed prison staff was noticeably absent in media coverage of these events. The culture and atmosphere of the prison service was remarkably different, in the months following the lockdowns and the correctional officers and their union's industrial disputes with the Prison Director and Minister of Corrections.

Importantly, the culture and staff relations within the prison have been more positive and constructive from 2012–15. Considered within their overarching social context, penal politics and practices in Tasmania should not be unfairly characterised nor interpreted as scandal prone and problem-saturated. Nonetheless, the series of events described in Table 6.1 are imperative in properly contextual-ising the meaning of the data presented in the remainder of this chapter, as several of the interviews were conducted in the midst of or in the months follow-ing these events. Some practitioner comments reflect the season in which they were gathered, others do not. This, in and of itself, is reflective of the nature of criminal justice: some practitioners are strongly affected by the exigency of circumstances, deriving a perceived burden from penal culture, while others show a timeless capacity for resilience or, less commonly, indifference or ambivalence.

Sectoral similarities and differences can be observed in comparison with the last chapter. While the notable challenge for the alcohol and other drugs sector (AOD) is that AOD staff are *leaving* their jobs and the sector at significant rates, the pressing challenge for the criminal justice sector is that staff are *on leave* from their jobs at disproportionate rates. This has been acknowledged by the Tasmanian Department of Justice (2013: 30), with discussion of a workforce 'absence management strategy' as a core tenet of a Corrections Reform Program and the Change Management Program. The absence management strategy seeks to provide:

- increased awareness and proactive management of unscheduled personal leave;
- strategies for managing unplanned absences;
- greater focus on assisting staff to return to work as quickly as possible after a serious illness, minimising the staffing pressures and costs arising from unplanned absences; and
- development of a new correctional officer staffing model.

(Tasmanian Department of Justice, 2013: 30)

In Tasmania, taking a more proactive approach has arisen following several years of unscheduled staff absences and moderate rates of staff leave and worker's compensation claims in both the TPS and Community Corrections. It has reportedly cost the department millions of dollars each year, however, a total costing has not been publicly released (ABC News, 2009, 2013). In 2013, a Tasmanian Upper House Parliamentary inquiry released a final report following investigation into the determinants of employee absenteeism in Corrective Services, suggesting that there are signs 'the culture is changing' (ABC News, 2013). The effects of these issues are multi-faceted; they are experienced differently by fellow practitioners not on leave and by offenders whose service provision is affected by individual instances as well as systemic issues of staff absences. Again, patterns of staff absences through moderately high rates of sick leave and stress leave in criminal justice is not an issue that is unique to Tasmania. The prevalence of these issues and their management continue to feature in discourses about probation and prison services and, more widely about helping professionals working in health and social care, in other jurisdictions (Harris, 2015; Dudman *et al.*, 2015; Selous, 2015).

Navigating complex and difficult work

The very nature of frontline work in corrective services involves the possibility of difficult situations arising, with relative regularity. Critical incidences and complex situations can be triggered with little or no warning, requiring practitioner responses that may have lasting consequences for themselves, the offender(s) and their significant others, and the organisation (for more, see Chapter 8 'Difficult Work' in White and Graham, 2010). Issues of navigating complex and difficult work featured in various practitioners' accounts in interviews:

It is a difficult industry to work in, particularly long term, and the burnout rate is quite high.

[Senior practitioner]

Hell, working here has been a battle, and it shouldn't have been a battle.

[Frontline practitioner]

In the end, people will say 'right, I can't do this anymore. I'm burnt out, and I'm passionate about it, but I've actually burnt myself out now trying to achieve what I believed in' … but I guess everyone's going to reach that point and say, 'why am I doing this if I'm running myself in to the ground and burning out?' It's been a big cost when it reaches that point.

[Frontline practitioner]

Difficult work has a number of inter-related dimensions. It does not solely relate to direct practice in working with offenders, although the task of 'solving insoluble problems' and being confronted with those surviving but suffering (and potentially causing suffering) can take its toll (Toch, 1977, 1992). Difficult work can also involve practitioners trying to navigate through workload demands, high caseloads, working with some colleagues and managers who themselves can be difficult to work with, working in roles where their professional status and cultural capital is marginalised compared to other colleagues, and constantly grappling with divergent work-related and workplace issues (Halliday *et al.*, 2009; White and Graham, 2010). One experienced frontline practitioner was in tears as they shared their views on the complexities and barriers in their work:

I think the nature of being under-resourced and stretched and competitive is that you get so in this survival mode, and feel undervalued and stick with what your core business is, that you never get that intertwining of the specialist threads that is needed to give the strength to the intervention for people with complex needs. It is desperate, compartmentalised, and that is added to by the way services are geographically located. There are multiple layers and reasons that have stopped us moving forward … [We need more of] That sharing of professional practice wisdom – we have very limited opportunities – either because they are not coming in or we don't have an opportunity to communicate or respect each other because we're kind of fighting – they get this and we get that. That is the climate and culture that has been created from having diminished resources – survival mode.

Another practitioner spoke of 'the tyranny of the urgent' and described how complex and difficult work can become a state of perpetual busyness, affecting practitioner and organisational capacity to pursue meaningful change and to focus on advancing the aspects of work that they enjoy.

I think maybe everyone gets busy doing what they need to do at the coalface. We've all got sort of reasonably big case loads, limited staff, limited dollars, we don't often have the time to sit back and implement necessarily what we talk about what we'd like to see happen, and that's the difference … So yes, it's probably down to resources, staffing, time, and then following through, actually following through and committing to change.

[Frontline practitioner]

In addition to these things, pressures can arise from broader institutional and political dynamics which form a part of working in criminal justice. Several of the people interviewed in this research, working in the prison and community corrections, have responsibility for responding to 'ministerials' and similar requests from senior actors in the field, assisting with informing the media about positive initiatives and 'good news stories', as well as helping to avert or fix media-fuelled crises. Responding to media and political queries can range from a stimulating endeavour which is pressured but rewarding in how it acknowledges the mastery of the practitioners as some of 'the only ones' who can accurately respond in detail, through to a stressful activity affected by wider politicisation of their work, as politicians and other interested parties trade blows in the media and Parliament.

> We have to do all this additional work that people don't necessarily realise that we do. [We] do a lot of responding to ministerials and queries that come through the Minister's office and the Deputy Secretary. We have to drop everything and respond if there is a question in Parliamentary question time, and we have to respond and help out the policy people and Ministerial staff if the media have a question. A lot can happen quickly.
>
> [Practitioner]
>
> Do you subscribe to [newspaper] by any chance?[smile]
>
> [Researcher]
>
> No.
>
> [Practitioner]
>
> So you don't read that one over breakfast? [laughter]
>
> [Researcher]
>
> No, no, definitely not. [laughter]
>
> [Practitioner]

Criminal justice work and penal cultures in Tasmania, like elsewhere, are affected by the social organisation and construction of their work. In particular, prisons are hierarchical closed institutions which often have a distinct division of labour, where the work of correctional officers is differentiated from the work of non-uniformed staff focusing on therapeutic interventions and reintegration. One of the perceived inequities is that it is rarely, if ever, the staff involved in treatment and rehabilitation who are directly involved in the politicised crises and industrial conflicts such as those listed in Table 6.1, as handling this is the domain of the prison executive, government minister and the correctional officers' union. Yet staff in rehabilitative and support work roles are still affected in the intermediary time, often tasked with helping, mediating and 'cleaning up' afterwards. 'Snap lockdowns' or swift industrial action decisions for correctional officers to walk off the job or refuse to do certain tasks often means that facilities go into a caretaker style of management, only allowing essential activities and movement. The appointments and client programmes run by non-uniformed staff are cancelled during this time, for days or sometimes weeks. During these times, frontline staff may turn up to work not knowing, without having a lot of control over what their work day will entail. These issues present an interesting challenge in light of the literature that shows that the organisational commitment of employees, including prison staff, is affected by the strength or absence of proce-dural justice, fairness, trust and reciprocity (see Allen and Meyer, 1990 and Griffin and Hepburn, 2005).

The emotional geography and affective atmosphere of the prison changes in volatile circumstances. Trust and perceptions of legitimacy can be affected when access to routine rights or prisoner privileges are withdrawn at short notice because of a lockdown. Despite the nature of prison work sometimes being diffi-cult work, in this study as well as in the wider literature (see Britton, 2003), it is common for staff doing rehabilitation work in prisons to explain that their job satisfaction is derived from a few sources, but the principal reason is often given as opportunities to support rehabilitation and see real change in prisoners' lives, preparing them for reintegration and desistance post-release. For the trust and communication processes, based on interactions which are often facilitated through structured appointments and programmes, to be disrupted without warn-ing or any control may inadvertently affect the job satisfaction of some staff. This is an issue that warrants further empirical investigation.

The themes raised by research participants in this study in relation to navigating difficult work bear some similarity and congruence with those found by others in the wider literature on difficult work, job satisfaction and stress. In her book, *At Work in the Iron Cage: The Prison as Gendered Organization*, Dana Britton (2003: 166) devotes a whole chapter to 'the rest of the job', outlining the challenges and stresses that can arise from dealing with colleagues and management, and the impact on job satisfaction. She argues that 'in almost any occupation involving people work, workers discover that the primary source of stress is usually not the unruly client or rude customer, whose behaviour can be understood or rationalised as part of the job, but inflexible and illogical work rules, inept colleagues, or incompetent and unsupportive supervisors' (*ibid.*: 166). Extensive research conducted with prison staff in Israel found that 'the factors inducing the highest levels of stress are those that are not necessarily unique to working with prison inmates' (Keinan and Malach-Pines, 2007: 394). Institutional and sectoral dynamics and industrial conditions, especially issues relating to heavy workloads, vicarious trauma and emotional exhaustion, managerialism, de-skilling and depersonalisation, lack of promotion and career pathways, and industrial conflicts, are concerns for frontline staff in thinking about how they navigate difficult work (*ibid.*).

Interestingly, findings from the international literature, and in particular the Israeli study, may help to explain some of the issues and patterns observed in the Tasmanian criminal justice sector. Moderate and high rates of job-related stress – whether they derive from interpersonal, inter-professional or institutional factors – do not necessarily strongly correlate with levels of job satisfaction and workforce turnover (Blau *et al.*, 1986; Holgate and Clegg, 1991; Keinan and Malach-Pines, 2007; Garland *et al.*, 2009; Halliday *et al.*, 2009; Griffin *et al.*, 2010). In other words, even though criminal justice practitioners, especially prison staff and probation officers, have to navigate difficult work at times, this may lead them to take leave and to use self-protection and self-care strategies, but it does not necessarily lead to overall dissatisfaction with their jobs, nor the desire to quit or high rates of workforce turnover. Conversely, many of the practitioners interviewed and observed in this research demonstrate remarkable levels of professional resilience, strength and pragmatism in response to difficult work. Many of them acknowledge and, to a certain extent seem to accept, that offender supervision and working in criminal justice will always involve challenges, the roots of which are derived from a few sources.

Chapter 8 resumes this vein of discussions, theorising the professional resilience and 'job crafting' strategies employed by some criminal justice practitioners, reflecting on how and why they choose to make meaning, to navigate complexity, and to innovate and enjoy their work (instead of going on leave like some of their colleagues). The next section canvasses cognate themes and examples, illuminating the place and meaning of humour and fun among criminal justice practitioners.

Workplace humour, irony and spontaneity

In the six-year period over which this research was conducted, there have been a series of surprising and amusing circumstances transpiring while I have been on site at the prison and the Community Corrections Service. These facets of practitioners' work lives are too rarely recognised in official accounts of who they are and what they do. One of the influences of generic discourses about evidence and practice is the de-humanisation of the helping professional in the process. Strictly empiricist portrayals of rehabilitation work do not commonly communicate a capacity for good humour, or compassion, or the all-important skillset involved in keeping the peace between others (service users or staff) in challenging circumstances in the course of their work.

The beauty of being something of an 'embedded' academic also working with people in the field in different roles is that this has afforded insights and opportunities to see (and sometimes take part in) spontaneous fun and good humour among the staff. A series of anecdotal examples are provided here as illustrations, albeit with the recognition that their meaning may be quite specific to the contexts and people involved and may not translate well in terms of the personal and cultural subjectivities of humour.

Among some corrective services staff, there are relatively regular chocolate and 'caramel frenzies', or sausage roll sessions, for morning or afternoon tea. I have witnessed mock 'stages of change' assessments of unrepentant 'caramel addictions' or 'ice cream addictions' from self-confessed 'pre-contemplative' prison staff members, relishing the humorous and ironic overtones of their self-assessments and confessions of saccharine 'relapses'. Certain practitioners have a propensity to break into song, while others listen to music throughout their work day. The presence of the 'Pups on Parole' dogs at the prison, for whom the prisoners are animal foster carers and trainers, on occasion extends to moments of 'pet therapy' for staff. Some prison staff seem to have a pattern of finding reasons to appear in fancy dress attire, sometimes accompanied by comedic alter-egos and loud, hilarious performances. Spontaneous fancy 'dress ups' have been observed in the corridors of the offices, as well as in the prison facilities on the pre-text of being for the benefit and entertainment of prisoners' children and families visiting for school holidays activities as part of the Kids Days at Risdon Prison. Where this has been observed by prisoners, their responses suggest that they find it quite humourous and entertaining.

While prison staff are far from homogenous, there is a discernible sense of insider humour that can develop among some prison staff which can generally be characterised as saturated in irony, employed as a coping mechanism, and sometimes described as 'dark' or 'black humour' (Crawley and Crawley, 2008; Bennett *et al.*, 2008). Three local examples illustrate this. For a significant period of time, there was a handmade poster pinned on staff office noticeboards (not a space observable by the general public or prisoners) in staff work areas who use pro-social modelling in their work. It is a simple but deeply ironic quotation in large bold font: 'If you can't be a good example, be a horrible warning'. Secondly, there is a framed front-page newspaper headline on the wall of the office area of staff who oversee organisational training and staff development which says: '[Name of Prison]: Worst Prison in the Nation'. The third example was observed in a shared office of prison staff with helping professional roles, when I went to meet with them about this research. At the time, they each had a small whiteboard next to their desk. On that day, all of these whiteboards had the handwritten heading: 'Ten things I hate about prison', followed by their own personalised list of ten points. Another member of staff was with me during these conversations about the research and about the whiteboards. They were amused, and started to develop their own list, which attracted much mirth in response. The content of these lists was not offensive; it did not breach confidentiality or professional standards, nor was it harsh or unrealistic in its assessment of the things that affect their work within the prison. They perceived it as an ironic reminder and way of giving voice to the challenges and peculiarities that arise in the course of working in a closed institution, while emphasising they do enjoy their work.

While uniformed correctional officers are not direct participants in this research, there is anecdotal and empirical evidence that they too exhibit distinct humour and self-care strategies (Crawley and Crawley, 2008; Liebling *et al.*, 2011). In a textbook I co-authored on *Working with Offenders*, a Tasmanian correctional officer provides first-hand anecdotes of the unexpected and amusing things that can happen in prison. Some of these are initiated by prisoners, reflecting a sense of 'black humour' that is steeped in the context in which it occurs:

> It is the middle of the night and six hours into a yard jack-up (a yard jack-up is prison lingo for a riot). You are on watch at the front of the housing

accommodation block. An inmate well known to you walks out of the staff office which has been broken into. He is wearing a correctional officer's hat and
carrying a torch. He looks at you and says, 'Well, you can't really come in so I
s'pose I'll do your job for you.' He walks off and starts to conduct a cell check.
Cell checks are conducted every half hour to ensure the safety and wellbeing of
inmates during the night. So picture this: in the middle of a riot, an inmate wearing a correctional officer's hat is walking around the unit doing cell checks.

(Correctional officer in White and Graham, 2010: 20)

The sardonic satire is not solely the domain of prisoners, with examples given of
reciprocal humour between staff and prisoners in otherwise particularly challenging circumstances. In the same riot, the prisoners break into a staff office and
discover a safe, laughing and teasing the staff about finding 'treasure' in it. The
correctional officers offer a response similarly laced with a lot of laughter, enjoying telling the rioting prisoners that the safe, in fact, contains chocolate bars
(White and Graham, 2010: 20). After extensive efforts to crack the safe, one of
the prisoners drops the safe, and the door falls off. This leads the prisoners to
discover that the safe is indeed full of chocolate bars. Stories like this form a
unique part of the institutional memory, hybridising how 'critical incidences'
such as riots are remembered and represented by staff. Laughter and sardonic
banter are not among the responses which might be expected by the wider public,
and they are rarely acknowledged in official accounts of staff and institutional
responses in navigating difficult work situations.

Additionally, the Tasmanian correctional officer relays another story, this time
from Christmas Eve in the prison: 'two correctional officers dress up in fancy
dress, one as a Teletubby and the other as a big yellow dog', accompanying a
Correctional Primary Health nurse around the prison for the evening medication
round. The prisoners find the festive fancy dress very amusing, triggering banter
and jest with the correctional officers. They reach the cell of a prisoner who has
a history of mental health issues. His spontaneous response surprises the staff:
'He looks at the two [correctional officers] and is apparently unfazed. He looks
at the nurse and says, "Your new hairdo looks strange". The nurse is standing
next to a six-foot-six yellow dog and a six-foot Teletubby, and her hair looks
strange. Go figure!' (correctional officer in White and Graham, 2010: 20).

A distinctive sense of humour and irony is not delimited to the closed institution
of the prison. For example, upon my arrival for a meeting of practitioners, hosted at
a Community Corrections office, it became apparent that they and their staff had
faced particularly stressful circumstances that day which, at the time of the meeting,
had not yet been fully resolved. Well versed in the popularity of self-supplied deca-
dent afternoon teas, I had come to the meeting bearing chocolate and caramel-
themed baking, the consumption of which seemed to take on more significance
amid the humorous commentary of others that day. The phrase 'well, it's laugh or
cry' was used – a regular refrain used by practitioners across the criminal justice and
AOD fields in Tasmania. Somewhat unconventionally, we sat with a vividly multi-
coloured disco-ball party light spinning 1970s style patterns onto those present for

the two-hour duration of the meeting. The only reference to its presence was at the end of the meeting, where a quick witted senior probation officer made a quip with a sardonic smile, saying the 'party mood lighting' which 'only came out on special occasions', implying a use of black humour in linking this to the backdrop of the difficult situation. While these anecdotes may appear idiosyncratic and circumstantial, they are offered here as examples of the place and meaning of humour, irony and the spontaneity of the unconventional in criminal justice services.

Professional ideology and values at work

Just as the impetus to move towards more technical 'evidence-based' interventions and the 'What Works' agenda is not ideology free (McNeill, 2001), their implementation in practice is not either (Rudes *et al.*, 2013). Differences in cultures, staff attitudes and practices have real world effects for people with complex needs, especially those who use illicit drugs, and their access to services and supports for recovery and desistance while under the supervision of the criminal justice system (Melnick *et al.*, 2009). The dominant model and approach, as well as the ideological orientations of practitioners implementing it, affects how these needs and the priorities for their rehabilitation are seen and responded to.

One of the popular topics of conversation in interviews was for practitioners to speak of how they negotiate and make meaning of the major offender rehabilitation and assessment models and principles in their daily work. Such things are mediated by factors including professional ideology, habitus and values; education, disciplinary identification (e.g., social work) and employment histories; as well as institutional and sectoral dynamics and demands. Anecdotally, it seems that the only type of practitioners in the field that tend to be more stringent and zealous in presenting a cohesive narrative of strict observance of the model are those who have trained as clinical psychologists, which suggests a contrast in disciplinary and occupational differences. It is unsurprising that those whose expertise specialises in psychological rehabilitation tend to prefer psychological correctional models and technicist accounts of practice. The data presented in this section demonstrates how some practitioners hybridise, reconfigure and subvert rehabilitation models and principles in practice.

Both the TPS and the Community Corrections Service build their offender assessments, interventions and programmes on the foundational principles of the Risk-Need-Responsivity (RNR) Model, as their official model of practice. This includes the use of actuarial risk assessment tools such as the Level of Service Case Management Inventory (LS/CMI). However, in the TPS, not all offenders are assessed using the full LS/CMI, for reasons which have been rationalised on the grounds of cost and time constraints, meaning that narrative or clinical styles of interviews and abridged risk assessments are also conducted. In addition to this, some staff in sentence management and reintegration roles at the prison use the Good Lives Model (GLM) in supporting reintegration, including good lives case planning and assessment exercises. The same staff are involved in pioneering the application of desistance-oriented principles and practices in the prison, as part of their desire to see a systemic shift towards the use of more strengths-based approaches, where risk management is only one component among others.

Professional habitus and ideology in prison work

One of the central features of the RNR Model, and psychological rehabilitation approaches more widely, is the targeting of criminogenic risk. Interestingly, the most support expressed by prison staff for the RNR Model was in comments about the need for community sector practitioners to understand the three core principles, and tailor their service provision to fit with the RNR Model. The following comments from a prison staff member are illustrative; however, there are probation officers who share the view of their community sector colleagues needing to better understand criminogenic risk.

> In the past, we've just been reactive, having people ring up and say 'oh I've put a grant application in, I've got $50,000, can I start next Monday?' That just doesn't work for us. Now when community agencies partner with us, [we] say to them that the programme of a service that you have existing on the outside probably won't work on the inside. It's an artificial environment in prison. There's many, many more factors of which will not be negotiated, of which you have to work within. So we try to tailor the services and that's effectively applying Risk-Need-Responsivity principles to the services that come in so that we can shape them to be tailored for the inmates, encouraging them to engage with them and prioritise what is most needed at the right time and in the right measure.
>
> [Frontline practitioner]

A perceived strength of the RNR Model is its capacity to highlight priorities for professional intervention, triaging risks and needs to bring a more cohesive focus to sentence management and supporting reintegration. Another practitioner was critical in their argument that community sector practitioners fit the stereotype of the naïve 'bleeding heart' social worker, coming into a prison environment with strongly welfarist values to do 'feel good' stuff, without understanding issues of criminogenic risks and needs.

> Sadly, what happens is that it is either 'not my business' for external service providers, or 'this is only my business', or the ethos is that of 'from the heart', so they feel 'I want to help this person.' Our perspective is coming from a Risk-Needs-Responsivity Model, which is along the lines of 'Yes, but that person doesn't need help in that area. In fact, if you do that to that person too often, you are doing them a disservice'. I don't think external service providers have a very good handle on Risk-Needs-Responsivity and meeting criminogenic need. They want to come in and do personal development and feel-good stuff, because the inmates like blossoming from that, but as Professor Ogloff might say 'you'll just end up with more confident

criminals.' If our business is about making change, we need to be clear on what evidence and practice can drive that change. They don't need to have their self-esteem boosted, you are coming in and seeing them and they are saying what you want them to say because you're great company. But you could be using your time in another way.

One of the fascinating paradoxes is that there are, ostensibly, few differences in the professional values and ideologies held by the community workers and the prison practitioners making these comments. The prison practitioners instead construct their own outlook and approach as more pragmatic, as they are able to recognise and respond to issues of criminogenic risk, and work within risk-oriented systems, while still maintaining their beliefs in penal welfare values.

In the first research interview conducted in this study, a practitioner spoke of the changes that had occurred at the prison in the uses of rehabilitation models and tools. They believed that the first years of using the RNR Model were heavily dominated by concerns about 'integrity to the model' and an overly strong confidence in the robustness and effectiveness of actuarial risk assessment. This practitioner spoke of having a strong personal commitment to penal welfarist values and preferring strengths-based approaches, contrasting these as distinctly different to the values underpinning the RNR model. Some other practitioners in this study and the Tasmanian field would contest the following opinion, but it is worth highlighting as an indication that some practitioners perceive an almost irreconcilable dichotomy between the risk paradigm and risk models, including an overriding allegiance to technical integrity to the model, compared to the approaches taken within other paradigms such as desistance and strengths-based narrative models.

> Initially… things were done to inmates. It was very administrative, they had a 'you beaut' tool in the LS/CMI, and they were going to use it according to the model, without very much consideration of the use of self and what the interviewer or practitioner can bring to the exchange … It was very much 'Oh, so this is a psychometric tool, so if we just ask all of the questions, we'll get the result.' … Staff just went in there and asked these staged questions, and you could see that half way through the inmate was really bored, not engaged and just thinking 'how long is this going to take?' So it was not a pleasant experience for the interviewer or the inmate. Yes they got a result, but I have to question the validity and the reliability of the result when it comes to the dialogue that kind of wasn't happening … It was so process driven, so administrative, so done to the inmate. It was this mechanised process, and to some degree it still is, but I feel like we've now injected a kind of human quality into it that is about respect, dignity and inclusion. That's nice to see.

This perspective further highlights the need for more detailed depth of knowledge on how practitioners use rehabilitation models and tools in practice, and to extent to which this may confirm or differ from organisational and empirical accounts. In effect, this practitioner argued that using the RNR Model *without* using engagement and pro-social modelling to build rapport was unethical. They felt that there was a tendency that staff, at the time, were only adept in their knowledge of one principle – risk. This practitioner, and others like them, sought to reconfigure how the RNR Model and the LS/CMI were used in practice, with particular emphasis on the centrality of responsivity and strengths-based engagement.

The shifts in how the RNR Model is used in practice have translated into changes in language and how information and communication about offenders is framed by practitioners.

> The practitioners in our team now are about working from a problem-solving approach, and treat inmates with respect and dignity, and they really understand the value of pro-social modelling. They talk that talk now ... They used to speak in really derogatory terms. It was terrible. But that's the culture, to survive, they had picked up on the uniformed officer linguistics. So we've talked lots about the power of language and suggestion and, you know, you learn what you think when you hear yourself speak, so don't speak it. Talk strengths based. Now they will look at the issue as outside of the person, rather than pathologise them according to their problems. For me, that's the way forward ... To some degree, language and culture change is happening within uniformed ranks and that is where the greatest sphere of influence and change will happen. I see the new recruits, I hear their attitudes and them talking about their beliefs, and it's really encouraging.

Despite critiquing the past, there was a clear level of pride in influencing positive change. The deconstruction and reconfiguration of the RNR Model to be more fit for purpose within the local penal context was framed by practitioners as a good thing. The shifts in language and in how the model and tools are used give voice to different, more rehabilitation-oriented penal values.

Another practitioner offered interesting contrasts in their responses to the interview questions. Their response to initial questions of 'What do you do?' and 'What models and practices does the prison use?' were matter-of-fact in outlining their position description, roles and responsibilities, and mentioning that the prison uses the RNR Model. Yet their response to more appreciative and exploratory questions about what they enjoy and are passionate about in their work led to more vivid and passionate conversations about desistance, rehabilitation, reintegration and harm minimisation. A segment of their comments are included here to reveal how their professional ideology and values shape their sense of mission as an 'insider' hoping to support change for individuals and the institution, despite their ideological opposition to the extensive use of incarceration and the influence of risk-based penality:

> Within the broad parameters of your work, what are you passionate about? This is different to my last question of 'what do you do?' I'm interested in hearing what you really care about and enjoy, and that can take any form.
>
> [Researcher]

Reintegration [pause] and that's a really broad term. What I am passionate about is reducing reoffending and I do not believe that prisons are the best way to reduce reoffending. So to use the current jargon, in this I am talking about 'harm minimisation', and when I say that I mean reducing the negative impact that prison has on the incarcerated person. First of all, I think of that whole ethos from the medical world of 'do no harm', and then giving them the best opportunities that the inmates can possibly have to choose to make a change. If they don't want to change, they won't change. But we need to at least give them the opportunity. And if they don't want to change, let's not make them any worse than when they came in here.

[Practitioner]

This practitioner acknowledged that their values regularly resulted in questions and tensions as they navigated their ideological opposition to risk and control-oriented models and practices that, in their view, might misconstrue people's actual needs, while still having to comply with organisational expectations and standards in order to maintain integrity to their work role. This illustrates the differences and tensions that can exist between technical proficiency in specific models (e.g., the RNR Model) and professional ideology and service-orientation that is influenced different paradigms (e.g., the desistance paradigm). This practitioner expressed the view that risk management is a necessary component of harm minimisation, but that it should not be the dominant goal or ultimate value, as this would frustrate rehabilitation and reintegration.

A third practitioner expressed similar views, saying that while they understood the RNR Model, they were also passionate about supporting desistance within the process of reintegration, which they felt is inclusive of risk management but extends well beyond the realms of psychological rehabilitation. They spoke of the human agency of prisoners, as well as structural barriers and opportunities post-release. In talking about these processes, they also acknowledged that heterogeneity of practitioner perspectives and diversity of practices are a hallmark of the prison, and can help to explain the factors that are influential in divergent outcomes post-release.

That's the hidden agenda, desistance. We've always got that in the back of our minds and how we frame it up changes, but that's a common reason. Desistance, so we can provide a safer community and hopefully send these guys and girls out better than when they came in. Having said that, I don't think some prisoners do rehabilitation very well and it's a two way street, sometimes the prison doesn't do it well and sometimes the individual doesn't want to change and depending on what factors you have there and the opportunities that they have. Like if they want to say bad boys they'll stay in max and they won't get down to minimum where there's more opportunity, more scope, more services, more ability to do things as compared to hanging with your mates, getting charged, having incidents, creating a ruckus, being a hell raiser while you're still in prison to maintain a reputation and they'll be the ones who go down the driveway with a black plastic bag saying prison never helped them. So there's a range of inmates and a range of things happening in prison. It's never, ever clear cut. Prison is just not a homogenous place, and there's a whole range of things here which go towards a successful outcome, and it's trying to line those things up for even just to help one person or a group of people towards desistance and reintegration is what makes my job interesting.

The introduction of the Good Lives Model (GLM) at the prison has been welcomed by some, and questioned by others. More than one practitioner has, in conversation, suggested that they 'think it is ok' and 'has merit' but feel that it is too vague and unstructured to be the overarching practice model from which to run a prison. The GLM has attracted questions and criticisms because it uses lots of psychological terminology and conceptualisation that – similar to its RNR Model counterpart – is unfamiliar and somewhat difficult to understand in practice for those from disciplinary backgrounds other than psychology. The strengths-based and future-focused nature of the GLM seems to be well received, but Tasmanian practitioners mostly tend to see it as complementary to use in tandem with the RNR Model, rather than constituting a feasible institution-wide alternative that could replace the RNR Model.

Interestingly, differences in how models are understood and used in practice are evident between the different types of prison staff whose work supports rehabilitation. The Programmes team adopt a therapeutic focus, relying on the use of cognitive behavioural interventions, programmes and LS/CMI assessment results daily. Other practitioners come from different disciplinary and educational backgrounds, and they want this diversity to continue to be reflected in the recruitment of new staff:

> The Programmes team are pretty much like, you do the LS/CMI, you are identified for a programme, we provide some assessment, we do the programme with you, we do the write-up, and that's it. For them, the intervention is the programme ... I have always maintained that we need a broad church, rather than only having psychologists and social workers. We are interested in nurses, educators, welfare workers, and other relevant disciplines that we should be bringing in.

The 'broad church' is particularly helpful when considering the rehabilitation and reintegration of offenders with multiple complex needs, related to but extending beyond narrow risk-laden definitions of 'criminogenic needs'. From the interviews and field work, it can be suggested that staff across the spectrum of rehabilitation work roles believe that they are involved in dealing with and supporting prisoners with complex needs. Yet those in particular teams and roles with a therapeutic focus may hold the view that this is predominantly their domain, and that their colleagues in the other teams do more generalist work.

> Sentence management is about getting people together, sitting them down and saying 'Let's put the client at the centre, and discuss how our various

"outputs" impact on that person and their life. Then let's strategically plan together what we do and how we are going to interact with that person' … I think everybody respects each other pretty well. Um, the Programmes team think they are special, and doing something really wonderful [smiles]. But I am told by my contacts nationally that all Programmes people think they are special because they see themselves as actually dealing with the hard core stuff. [smiles].

Differences between actors and professional orientations notwithstanding, experienced prison practitioners employed in various roles can gain an increased sense of legitimacy and status arising from their competencies and time in the field. When new models and interventions are introduced, these are mediated by existing experienced staff who have the legitimacy amongst their peers to influence how it is translated and used in practice. One of the frontline practitioners affirmed this as a positive thing, suggesting that new employees need to learn from the practice wisdom of those who have been doing rehabilitation work long before notions of criminogenic and non-criminogenic risk came to dominate their field of work.

[I'd like to see] more opportunities for – whether it is grads or newer workers to the area who might have come from another sector – to align them around different areas with people who have been doing it for quite a while. When you watch and see, it is like it just clicks. Aha this looks like it is presenting the biggest risk, but actually it is all of these issues over here that are feeding everything … It is a very individualised response that we are trying to tailor.

In effect, this practitioner is still giving credence to the necessary professionalisation efforts to acquire the technical knowledge to be eligible to use the requisite tools and techniques, for example, training to be allowed to use the LS/CMI or Good Lives plans and mapping tools. However, they are strongly suggesting that this needs to be accompanied by processes of collegial socialisation, where a new graduate or member of staff can acquire tacit knowledge and observe experienced colleagues exercising discretion in tailoring (and, in some cases, reconfiguring or hybridising) models and processes to the individual. Combining professionalisation with professional socialisation may conserve institutional memory and the culture of longstanding attitudes and approaches in certain types of work roles and staff teams (especially those tasked with supporting rehabilitation and reintegration, compared to surveillance roles). This practitioner in particular and other experienced colleagues like them cleave to values and ideologies that can be described as 'penal welfarist'. Penal welfarism is based on the notion that 'the offender should be rehabilitated not just in the interests of his own welfare, but also more broadly, in the collective interests of society as a whole' (Robinson, 2008: 430; see also Garland, 1985). Practitioners whose perspectives are shaped by welfarism are more likely to emphasise social welfare and human rights issues as integral to a person's rehabilitation, irrespective of how they are conceptualised within current models.

Senior criminal justice practitioners who participated in this research acknowledge that this happens and have not voiced opposition to it. In fact, some of them have actively advocated the hybridisation and reconfiguration of rehabilitation models (including changing processes and tools or allowing instances where they are not required to be used with certain offenders) to make them 'more fit for purpose'.

The finding emerging from this chapter, then, is that the shift from penal welfarist 'social service professionalism' to managerialist and bureaucratic 'commercialised professionalism' (Evetts, 2012: 5) observed in criminal justice institutions in other Anglophone jurisdictions has not been as apparent in the state of Tasmania. This mirrors recent research findings by Grant (2015) and Grant and McNeill (2014) about the professional habitus, ideologies and practice orientations of Scottish criminal justice social workers (the equivalent of probation officers). Their Bourdieusian analysis shows that official and policy accounts about them and their work do not fully reflect the realities in Scotland, as distinct from England and Wales. The quality of the helping relationship, and traditional penal welfarist values, continue to be important in how practitioners evaluate their work. Resistance is one strategy employed in seasons of 'top down' imposed changes to services and the structuring of the field in an era of new public management and penal populism. There may be more bureaucracy and structured tools and processes involved in what constitutes contemporary criminal justice practices, however, the uses of these are infused with positive values and durable dispositions which pre-date such changes.

Professional habitus and ideology in probation work

Some clear synergies, as well as subtle differences, are evident in the themes that feature in community-based practitioner perspectives. The issue of criminogenic and non-criminogenic needs, and the need to hybridise models to make them 'fit for purpose' in practice, also emerged in interviews with community-based practitioners. A senior practitioner in the Community Corrections Service spoke of their support for probation officers reconfiguring the RNR Model to ensure they did not lose sight of a person's welfare.

> Look, I think one of the things for me, is that, you know, following someone's basic needs. If you haven't got your basic needs met, if your children are hungry, if you've got nowhere to live, if you can't read and write, then I think trying to focus on the bigger stuff around the bigger criminogenic needs is a total waste of time … We talk a lot about making sure the triaging of the offender is right. So if someone comes in and they haven't got high literacy skills, and they haven't got anywhere to live, and they've got lots and lots of things in their life that is happening, we need to help them get that under control, or refer them to agencies that can help them get that under control first before you sit down and go 'well I know you've got an anger management problem here, and let's address that'.
>
> [Senior practitioner]

The use of the RNR model is augmented by a pragmatic commitment to Maslow's hierarchy of needs, ensuring stability and functioning before targeting specific issues with specific interventions.

Despite uses of organisational and individual practitioner discretion, there are still subtle tensions apparent in how Community Corrections practitioners reconcile the different objectives in their work. Again, this touches on differences in professional ideology and values. Subtle ambivalence and mixed allegiances were observed in the task of 'offender management' involving a control or risk orientation to compliance, compared to a rehabilitative and desistance orientation in supervising people in the community. A typical risk orientation to compliance is evident in the following comments:

> We have got a Programmes Unit now which allows us to focus on some of that stuff. But at the end of the day, our core business is to manage the order, and to make sure people comply with that order, and they don't reoffend.

These comments contrast with the following comments, where the practitioner takes issue with others suggesting a tendency for Community Corrections to be quick to breach people and 'just' manage orders. Instead, they articulate a more moderate view on the relational dimension of managing compliance, including the use of discretion.

> We have a job to do around compliance. People just see us as 'all you do is breach people'. [There was] a question in a [name of forum] about the number of breaches of people that we do. I said 'for every breach that we do, we probably do three or four warning letters for each offender'. So if you don't turn up for your community service, we will ring you and find out, 'oh I'm sick', well OK get us a doctor's certificate, that is fine. If no you don't have one, here is a warning letter. There is another time, here is another warning letter, then another warning letter, and now we need to breach you. It is not just that we will take you back to court. So I said 'it is a really misleading statistic to say that we have taken 100 people back to court this year, when in fact we have probably dealt with 500 people who have had trouble complying with their order, but we have managed to bring them in. We have managed to work with them, because you can't expect the people that break the law and have a history of offending that, when they get on an order … It just doesn't work like that'. There is that element of us being a bit more up front about what we do and how we do it, where we don't just go 'that's it buddy, one shot and you are out'. It is actually not like that. Probation officers have a lot of discretion around what they can and can't do, in consultation with their team leader. The team leader helps them apply things consistently.
>
> [Senior practitioner]

The pragmatic cultural attitude and support for the use discretion within the implementation of the RNR Model can also be observed in the ways in which the

Community Corrections Service works at an operational and strategic level. In the international literature, some academics have described probation officers and offender supervision services as 'servants of the court' (Mawby and Worrall, 2013: 105). This still holds true in describing the legislative basis and legal expectations of probation officers in Tasmania, but it does not fully describe Community Corrections' organisational culture and institutional relationship with the Magistrates Court of Tasmania. The two institutions work collaboratively on the Court Mandated Diversion (CMD) therapeutic jurisprudential drug court initiative.

On matters of probation and offender supervision more generally, Community Corrections in Tasmania has an anecdotal reputation for being proactive in communicating with others about how they would prefer things to work. A general example relates to how the Community Corrections Service has changed its pre-sentence screening and report writing processes, because it found that the traditional assessment and pro-forma was too time consuming for, in its view, limited benefit. Senior actors in the Community Corrections Service strategically devised plans to streamline the screening and assessment process, to cut waiting times, and to target the use of staff time to assessments of cases where it is most needed. Overall, a few weeks of waiting for pre-sentence reports were cut through this proactive course of action, resulting in resources efficiencies and, importantly, more expedient decisions for people waiting on remand.

> We actually went to the magistrates and said 'what you're asking for is one option. But instead of doing that, how about we change the look of the pre-sentence report, and we shorten it so that you get what you need and we get what we need. If you want the whole Law and Peace, we can give you that still, because that is what we are required to do under the legislation. But, if you want to know whether or not this person, in our judgment, is suitable for a community-based order and they have got specific issues like sex offending or drug and alcohol issues, we can give you that and it will only take us two hours to write it rather than five hours'. They decided 'Ok well that's a bit of a no brainer'. So we have gone to that. That is our default pre-sentence report. If a magistrate wants a longer one, he or she asks for it.
>
> [Senior practitioner]

Other jurisdictions do not have probation and community corrections actors within the relative power and cultural capital to be able to ask and recommend what the judiciary should do and how the system should work.

In addition to changing the pre-sentence report templates and risk assessment processes, the Community Corrections Service has worked with researchers from the University of Tasmania to develop a new risk assessment tool, which is a reconfigured and shorter version of the LS/CMI, but which will still adhere to RNR Model principles. Within this, a desire has been expressed for the tool to be more considerate of strengths and protective factors, and to have a much greater sensitivity to criminogenic needs and responsivity issues in the areas of gender, ethnicity and culture. Again, this exemplifies a proactive ethos and pragmatic productivity that can be observed in their organisation culture – they 'get on with the job'.

In conclusion, the Community Corrections Service has experienced change across the six years in which this research has been conducted, especially in response to the rapid rise in the number of offenders under supervision in Tasmania. However, the change has largely been operational in nature, compared to the prison service which has faced more significant workforce industrial conflicts in 2009–10, several changes of Director of Prisons, and large-scale infrastructure re-development from 2006 to 2015.

Perspectives from staff in both the prison and Community Corrections about their counterparts seem to be, for the most part, positive, with participants speaking of a good working relationship between the two organisations at frontline and senior staff levels. The main critique raised by staff in both organisations is that they wished they had the time and opportunities for more (in terms of quality and quantity) communication and information sharing with one another. Institutional structural determinants are seen as inhibiting this, apart from workload constraints affecting their time. For example, several participants especially expressed their desire for an overhaul of the information technology systems to enable more information sharing between criminal justice database systems, as well as with other organisations where appropriate.

Conclusion

The essence of this chapter is exploratory in nature. Overall, the motivation to see positive change in the criminal justice field seems to be moderately high from the perspective of those in this study, yet several participants cite examples with a modest level of satisfaction where they have already been proactive in instigating positive change. Efforts to capitalise on this momentum have the potential to bolster a more positive identity for the sector, which, similar to its AOD counterpart, is otherwise tasked with undertaking difficult and 'dirty' work that can, at times, be marred by crises and negative public stereotypes.

This discussion of the field contributes new insight in seeking to understand professional habitus and how criminal justice practitioners think and make sense of their work, how they reconfigure models, principles and job tasks, and how values and ideology shape this. Themes and findings in this chapter are similar to those emerging from jurisdictions in the northern hemisphere, especially the United Kingdom, Europe and the United States, in noting the differences between official accounts and empirical accounts of practice and the diversity of what practitioners *actually do in practice* (Rudes *et al.*, 2013; Bosker *et al.*, 2013, Persson and Svensson, 2011, 2012; Robinson and Svensson 2013). In response to these emerging findings, proponents of the RNR Model (Andrews, 2011) cautiously admit that the influence of what they call 'non-programmatic factors' do affect the assessment, treatment and rehabilitation of offenders within the RNR Model. In this study, the reality that moderately significant hybridisation and reconfiguration of theoretical models and practice tools occurs as commonplace in rehabilitation work is not regarded as problematic. Practitioners tend to assert that they understand the main principles – risk, need and responsivity – and that these are helpful, but it is only through combination with their tacit knowledge, values and experiences that the model is used most ethically and effectively.

This perception is congruent with the rationale that practitioners should be involved in supporting more than one form of rehabilitation (i.e. psychological or personal), as outlined by McNeill (2012a). Simply focusing on psychological correction of criminogenic risk does not enable or produce rehabilitation and desistance. In fact, some degree of negotiation and adaptation is entirely warranted because there is no 'perfect' offender rehabilitation model:

> Even if we wished that there was a model of effective practice that could be prescribed for practitioners, there is not; precisely because offenders are heterogenous, their needs are complex and their pathways to desistance are individualised, effective practice can only really emerge from practitioners' reflective engagement and continual dialogue with those with whom they work, and with the research that should inform how they work.
>
> (McNeill, 2009b: 53)

Truly effective practice in criminal justice, then, is found in the reflexive and relational interplay between these factors, in ways that are not ignorant to diversity and context.

18   Substance abuse and offending

Pathways to recovery

David Best and Michael Savic

18.1 Introduction

In the conclusion to *Making Good*, Maruna (2001, 166) argues that "societies that do not believe that offenders can change will get offenders who do not believe that they can change". This quotation comes from the description of the sample in the Liverpool Desistance Study (LDS), in which it is clear that desistance from offending and addiction recovery are frequently the same thing. Indeed, in describing his sample of desisting and continuing offenders, Maruna observes that "almost every LDS participant … admitted to regular drug use at some point in their lives and two-thirds … said they had at some point been dependent or addicted to alcohol or drugs" (Maruna 2001, 62). This is particularly worrying where Maruna describes a concern that the US is employing a 'waste management' model of corrections in which the aim of interventions is neither to correct nor punish but rather is to incapacitate and control. Similar anxieties have been expressed in the treatment of illicit drugs, where substitute prescribing has provoked fears about the low aspirations of indefinite treatments.

Maruna (2001) also makes the point – and cites one of the Liverpool participants – that there is no shortage of services and support available while you are offending or using; however once you have started a desistance journey, there is almost no support available. This is compounded by the concern, expressed in the context of youth offenders, that while incarceration provides a space where young people generate desistance narratives, the youth justice space does not offer them the supports or resources to develop the links and skills needed to build on the foundations of imagined desistance (Soyer 2014). So young offenders can imagine a future free from crime, but they are not offered the skills or supports to make this a reality.

However, Maruna's work is not pessimistic and describes the successful self-narratives of those managing to achieve desistance (or recovery), based on the premise that desistance from crime necessitates making sense of a new identity that in turn requires a successful self-narrative of change. The successful ex-offenders "need a coherent, prosocial identity for themselves" (Maruna 2001, 7). This process may result in the evolution of a 'redemption' script or a generative story in which the person turns bad to good by giving back to their families or communities. Indeed, Maruna cites Alcoholics Anonymous (AA) as a powerful example of sustaining the desistance journey by 'giving back' and the important role of this form of growth in sustaining desistance.

This chapter will examine the recovery or desistance journey, primarily from the perspective of alcohol and drug recovery, in terms of the impact of community factors – societal beliefs and responses to recovery – on individual beliefs and experiences about what is possible in a recovery pathway or journey. This will be illustrated using two pilot projects in two Australian states: the first in the Magistrates Court in Dandenong, in south-east Melbourne, Victoria, and the second in Dooralong, an alcohol and drug rehabilitation centre on the Central Coast in New South Wales. The aim of the chapter will be to outline how communities – including professionals' attitudes – can act as facilitators or barriers to personal recovery and what impact such beliefs and attitudes have on recovery pathways and trajectories. The central aim is to outline an ecology of recovery or desistance that is based on environmental factors that create the 'ground' for the personal challenges of identity change. The chapter assumes a parallel between addiction recovery and criminal desistance that is in part predicated on the observation that, as Maruna (2001) points out, we are often talking about the same people in any case.

18.2 What is addiction recovery?

In the US, the Betty Ford Institute Consensus Group produced a definition of recovery as "a voluntarily maintained lifestyle characterised by sobriety, personal health and citizenship" (Betty Ford Institute Consensus Panel 2007, 222): the subsequent UK definition from the UK Drug Policy Commission (UKDPC) is broadly similar in both scope and composition. According to the UKDPC, recovery is "voluntarily sustained control over substance use which maximises health and well-being and participation in the rights, roles and responsibilities of society" (UK Drug Policy Commission (UKDPC) 2008, 6). In the context of mental health recovery, Deegan (1998, 11) argues that: "recovery refers to the lived experience of people as they accept and overcome the challenge of disability … they experience themselves as recovering a new sense of self and of purpose within and beyond the limits of the disability". This latter definition is important as it asserts the subjective as a key component of the recovery experience.

The US Substance Abuse and Mental Health Services Administration (SAMHSA 2012) identified four major dimensions of recovery: health (overcoming or managing one's symptoms); home (a safe place to live); purpose (meaningful daily activities); and community (social networks that provide support, friendship, love and hope). In the ten guiding principles that SAMHSA identify, four are socially or community focused: recovery is supported by peers and allies; recovery is supported through relationships and social networks; recovery is culturally-based and influenced; and recovery involves individual, family and community strengths and responsibility.

Although there have been concerns about the operationalisation of recovery, recovery rates have been estimated in a number of studies. In a review of the existing evidence, Sheedy and Whitter (2009) estimated that 58 per cent of those who have lifetime substance dependence will eventually achieve full recovery. White (2012) has reviewed overall remission rates in a review analysis of 415 scientific reports between 1868 and 2011, and has concluded that an average of 49.9 per cent of those with a lifetime substance use disorder will eventually achieve stable recovery (and this rate increases to 53.9 per cent in studies published since the year 2000). White also argues that between 5.3 and 15.3 per cent of the adult population of the US are in recovery from a substance use disorder. This suggests a high prevalence of recovery in the general population and a rate of recovery that exceeds the lay expectation.

18.3 Personal, social and community recovery capital

It does not, however, answer the question of who will recover and who will not. There is a strong argument that the transition to recovery from substance use involves identity change, echoing the view of Maruna (2001) above. The idea of identity change as central to recovery was first advanced by Biernacki (1986) who argued that, in order to achieve recovery, "addicts must fashion new identities, perspectives and social world involvements wherein the addict identity is excluded or dramatically depreciated" (Biernacki 1986, 141). Building on this theme, McIntosh and McKeganey's (2002) analysed the recovery stories of 70 ex-addicts. They concluded that, through substance misuse, the addicts' "identities have been seriously damaged by their addiction" (McIntosh and McKeganey 2002, 152) and that recovery necessitates the restoration of a spoiled identity. This restoration would appear to have a strong social quality, in which identity is embedded in social activities and social networks.

Litt and colleagues (2007; 2009) assigned individuals who completed residential detoxification from alcohol use to either standard aftercare or to a 'network support' intervention that involved developing a relationship with at least one non-drinking peer. Those who added at least one non-drinking member to their social network showed a 27 per cent increase in the likelihood of treatment success at 12 months post-treatment (defined as being without alcohol 90 per cent of the time) compared to people receiving standard after-care. This is consistent with the findings of Beattie and Longabaugh (1999) that while both general and abstinence-specific support predicted abstinence in alcoholics at three months post-treatment, only social support for abstinence goals predicted longer-term abstinence (at 15 months post-treatment).

The importance of social factors is illustrated in the concept of 'recovery capital' (Granfield and Cloud, 2001), which referred to four types of capital: personal, physical, cultural and social, to cover material possessions, personal skills and capabilities, support and friendship networks, and community resources. The concept of recovery capital offers a tantalising possibility of a metric for the quantification of recovery, but this development remains at an early stage.

Underpinning this idea is the concept of social capital described by Putnam (2000) as the supports and resources that an individual has access to and perceives themselves as able to make use of. The notion of social capital also refers to the relational quality involved; in other words, social capital is not simply a 'reserve' of resources, rather it is the embedding of the individual in social relationships and bonds that are dynamic and binding. This is particularly important for the concept of community or cultural capital, as at this level it will refer not only to what the resources available in the community are, but also to the extent that they are perceived as both accessible and desirable by the person in recovery.

The idea of cultural capital is particularly important for the concept of addiction recovery as it relates to the supports and resources available in the community. At one level, these are practical resources like houses and jobs, and other tangible resources that make a community accessible and available. It is linked to social capital in the need to have bridging to resources in the community and the accessibility and availability of supports. But cultural capital also relates to the level of community integration or disintegration that make such resources accessible and available to people. And these resources are not equivalent for everyone. Those who are excluded or stigmatised may not come to know about such resources because they may have low bridging capital. Putnam (2000) discussed two types of social capital: (1) bonding capital refers to the connections between people who belong to the same group (e.g. connections between supporters of the same sporting team); and, (2) bridging capital relates to connections between people of different groups (e.g. supporters of different sporting teams). People who are socially excluded may have a social network consisting of other socially excluded people and so their network has limited bridges to resources available in the community.

Thus, in a study of drug-using offenders assertively engaged in sports activities in the north-east of England, as a form of diversion from custody, one of the key success factors was building not only a new set of social bonds and relationships, but relationships with people who had access to community supports and resources (Landale and Best 2012). In this study, young drug-using offenders were offered a diversion programme called Second Chance that enabled them to engage in sports activities, primarily a soccer team, to build self-esteem and resilience (personal capital) as well as a sense of belonging and a positive identity (social capital). However, one of the major successes of the programme was creating new links to community resources such as housing and employment opportunities (cultural capital) that allowed the young people to translate the gains made in the programme to sustainable life improvements.

18.4 Societal attitudes and barriers to recovery

The importance of the cultural capital component of recovery capital is that it reflects the community's response to substance use and recovery and the extent to which recovery is perceived as a meaningful transition to long-term well-being.

There is considerable evidence (WHO 2001; UKDPC 2011) to show that stigma is a major problem for users of alcohol and other drugs and their families. The World Health Organisation found that illicit drug dependence is the most stigmatised health condition in the world, and alcohol dependence the fourth most (WHO 2001). In social capital terms, this stigmatisation and exclusion results in barriers to community capital and so a self-perpetuation of social exclusion. In criminology, Braithwaite (1989) has argued, in his work on reintegrative shaming, that "stigmatisation is disintegrative shaming in which no effort is made to reconcile the offender with the community" (1989, 101).

There is also evidence that individual recovery does not result in a change in perceptions of stigma or exclusion. In the US, Phillips and Shaw (2013) have shown that, relative to smoking and obesity, substance users are more stigmatised both when active users and when they are in recovery, suggesting that stigma persists even when active addiction is left behind. In this study, participants were asked about scenarios involving working beside individuals and having the individual marry into their family, with only marginal differences reported in social distance between active substance users and those in recovery. The stigmatised attitudes towards problem substance use and the public failure to differentiate between active use and recovery represents a significant barrier to effective reintegration for individuals attempting to achieve lasting recovery. As Maruna (2001, 166) has concluded "societies that do not believe that offenders can change will get offenders who do not believe that they can change". Indeed, the perception that they cannot change is reinforced to all parties by social exclusion that prevents access to the tools that would enable such changes to happen.

18.5 Visible recovery and the contagion of hope

Within the field of health geography, there is increasing interest in the concept of 'therapeutic landscapes' described as "changing places, settings, situations, locales and milieus that encompass the physical, psychological and social environments associated with treatment or healing" (Williams 1999, 2). This has been applied to recovery from alcohol and drug dependence and the importance of context in recovery. Wilton and DeVerteuil (2006) describe a cluster of alcohol and drug treatment services in San Pedro, California, as a 'recovery landscape': a foundation of spaces and activities that promote recovery. This is done through a social project that extends beyond the boundaries of the addiction services into the community through the emergence of an enduring recovery community in which a sense of fellowship is developed in the wider community.

Thus, AA programmes provide ongoing support to people in recovery in San Pedro, but there are public actions to promote recovery as well. In San Pedro, for one day a year, all of those in recovery wear red shirts and there was a public recovery rally at which around 300 people participated in a recovery celebration event. This challenges stereotypes and stigma as "programme advocates positioned themselves and their programmes in opposition to other groups who were unable to strive for norms of responsibility and productivity" (Wilton and

DeVerteuil 2006, 659). Although AA is an anonymous organisation, this does not preclude its members from engaging in visible recovery activities and the more effective AA networks have active links with formal treatment services through Hospital and Institution Committees. Thus, the therapeutic landscape of recovery will include not only the hubs of recovery but also the nodes that link them.

In one local example – in Barnsley in South Yorkshire in England – an initial training programme for workers and peers in recovery and interested community members led to the development of a voluntary Barnsley Recovery Coalition. This initially set out a recovery vision and mission for the area and then set about planning a series of activities that started with a float in the Lord Mayor's Parade, followed by a Recovery Walk and a sports fun day (Best *et al.* 2013). This is consistent with a much wider movement to recovery visibility in the UK that has been driven by 'recovery-oriented' Government drug strategies in both Scotland and England (Scottish Government 2008; HM Government 2010), promoting visible and accessible recovery groups and communities. Roth and Best (2013) outline the innovations in this approach around public events and celebrations of recovery, the emergence of grass-roots organisations and the development of community linkages. In the UK, the notion of developing 'therapeutic landscapes' is enshrined in alcohol and drug policy. However, this is based on relatively little evidence for the spread of recovery through public activity and little indication of how the 'recovery champions' outlined in the UK Drug Strategy can successfully disseminate the idea of a recovery contagion. There is also a disparate and poorly connected conceptual framework for the development of community support for recovery.

What exists is partly based on the ideas of asset-based community development (what is known as the 'ABCD' model: Kretzmann and McKnight 1993). In this model, the most important resources in a local community are its people, informal groups and formal organisations, all of which represent community (or cultural) capital. McKnight and Block (2010) have argued that building integrated and supportive communities rests on "more individual connections and more associational connections" (McKnight and Block 2010, 132), which in turn relies on identifying those who have the capacity to connect others in our communities. McKnight and Block (2010) refer to such people as community connectors, and they argue that, to make more accepting and integrated communities, "we want to make more visible people who have this connecting capacity. We also want to encourage each of us to discover the connecting possibility in our own selves" (2010, 132). This last point is crucial in that, within this model, the development of connections and communities is essentially an act of co-production between professionals and members of the community; it is not done by professionals to communities, and it is not done by community members alone – it is essentially and at heart a partnership. The remaining sections of this chapter provide basic information on the two pilot studies mentioned above (one in Dandenong, in South-East Melbourne, and the other in the Central Coast of New South Wales) that have attempted to engage in community connections activity to challenge discrimination and stigma and to create the bridges to community recovery capital for those in early recovery.

18.6 Therapeutic jurisprudence and recovery

Without support to engage in meaningful activities, or social groups that are supportive of their recovery, offenders find it difficult to achieve lasting recovery, and may relapse and re-offend. Although services and caseworkers assist offenders with referral to formal services post-release or as part of their sentencing conditions, without peer assistance people are unlikely to participate in informal community support groups, such as AA. As a consequence they may have little or no connection to the groups in the community which can provide social support, meaningful activity and a positive sense of social identity. This in turn is likely to reinforce a sense of marginalisation.

Based on a therapeutic jurisprudence model (Wexler 1999), magistrates in Dandenong (an outer suburban area of Melbourne, Victoria) engaged with Turning Point (a Victorian alcohol, drug and behavioural addiction research and treatment centre) to develop a model for continuity of care for offenders with substance use histories who were completing their sentences. The aim of the community linkage project was to identify appropriate community connectors drawn from three primary pools: substance using offenders in the community, professionals working in relevant services and other members of the community, all of whom could act as 'bridges' between offenders and community groups, such as AA, sporting clubs and other groups. This approach is underpinned by an asset-based model of community development which attempts to utilise strengths and resources that already exist in the community to achieve sustainable change. In this case, the change we are referring to includes: (1) supporting offenders' own changes in substance use and offending behaviour at the *individual* level; and (2) promoting *communities* that are welcoming and supportive of recovery as opposed to communities that stigmatise and marginalise people with substance use problems and offending histories.

Initial pilot work involved court observations and mapping community groups in the Dandenong area to examine whether we could identify offenders who might benefit from the community linkage programme, and to explore whether there were sufficient groups in the community to which offenders could be linked.

Dandenong is a suburb 30 kms south-east of Melbourne, Victoria. The Greater Dandenong area has a population of just over 135,000 and has a greater proportion of people born overseas compared to Victorian and Australian averages (Australian Bureau of Statistics, 2013). Greater Dandenong also has a higher unemployment rate and lower median income as compared to Victorian and national averages (Australian Bureau of Statistics, 2013), and has a higher crime rate than the Victorian average (Community Indicators Victoria, 2013).

Observations of public court proceedings to record substance use involvement were completed. This involved observing court proceedings from the public gallery on four different days and collecting data on the characteristics of offenders, particularly where there were clear indications of substance use problems. The court proceedings observed were a mixture of bail and bail review hearings, judicial monitoring, suspended sentence and breach of order hearings, as well as guilty plea hearings. Substance use was mentioned in just over a quarter (*n*=19, 27.9 per cent) of the 68 cases observed, with alcohol, amphetamine-type stimulants and cannabis being the most commonly mentioned substances. In most of these cases, substance use was considered to be a major underlying reason for offending. This means that around one in four cases at the Dandenong Magistrates' Court might benefit from the proposed community linkage programme.

All the individuals involved in court hearings where substance use was mentioned (except one) were male, the average age was 36 years (SD=10.4), and all had prior criminal histories. Whatever prior criminal justice responses they had received had not been a deterrent to further offending, reinforcing the need for innovative responses. Past use of substance use treatment services was mentioned in under half of the cases (*n*=8, 42.1 per cent), although 55.6 per cent of people (*n*=10) were currently engaged in some form of treatment, and in 72.2 per cent (*n*=13) of cases a recommendation for treatment was provided by the magistrate. The focus on therapeutic jurisprudence at the Dandenong Magistrates' Court was also borne out in sentencing/recommendations, where the most common outcome was a community corrections order (50 per cent) followed by bail (12.5 per cent) and deferred sentence (12.5 per cent). Imprisonment was rare in instances where substance use was involved and was limited to one case only. Family members or friends were present in only one of the 19 cases where substance use was mentioned, suggesting that this group of offenders may lack immediate social capital and might benefit from engagement in community groups.

Having identified a need for community linkage, our next task was to map community assets in the Dandenong region to understand the community groups to which offenders could potentially be linked. A number of formal health and welfare services exist in Dandenong and case managers work with people who are involved in the criminal justice system to facilitate access to these. While health and welfare services are important (and are indeed community assets) they do not always facilitate connections to broader community. Our interest was, therefore, in mapping peer-led and informal groups in the community.

We did this by searching online community directories and talking to magistrates in Dandenong. We identified 97 informal community groups in Dandenong and the diversity and scope of these is illustrated in Figure 18.1. The majority of groups identified were either sporting clubs (47.4 per cent, *n*=46) or recreation groups (33.0 per cent, *n*=32), such as fishing clubs and community bands (see Figure 18.1). Training and support groups, which were often attached to formal services, included regular group programmes on community gardening, cooking, computers, art and craft etc. and these accounted for 9.3 per cent (*n*=9) of groups. Importantly, there were also 10 (10.3 per cent) addiction recovery groups identified. These provided peer support and mutual aid for people with substance use and mental health issues, including groups like AA and SMART Recovery (a mutual aid group based on the principles of cognitive behavioural therapy).

As illustrated in Figure 18.1, recovery groups (and some training and support groups) had the specific purpose of supporting people to desist from problematic substance use and crime. Recovery groups are likely to have the most experience of, and be the most welcoming to, people who either are currently or were previously involved in the criminal justice system. These may be ideal targets for community linkage initially, and indeed there is a literature around assertive linkage to mutual aid groups (e.g. Manning *et al.* 2012), but they may not be sufficient for all individuals and across all stages of the recovery journey. As people's confidence, social networks and ability to participate in diverse group situations grow, there are a wide range of non-recovery specific groups available in Dandenong which could be accessed. Whether these groups would be welcoming of people with prior substance use issues or offending histories will require further investigation, and this will impact on the willingness and openness of the people in recovery both to be open about their recovery and to feel safe and comfortable in non-specific recovery groups. Critically we will need to explore how any barriers and stigma can be overcome.

The next steps in this project involve the identification and recruitment of community connectors whose job it will be to make this link. The connectors group will be recruited from a combination of professionals, peers in recovery and members of the local community, overseen by a coordinating committee, akin to the group in Barnsley (Best *et al.* 2013) described above.

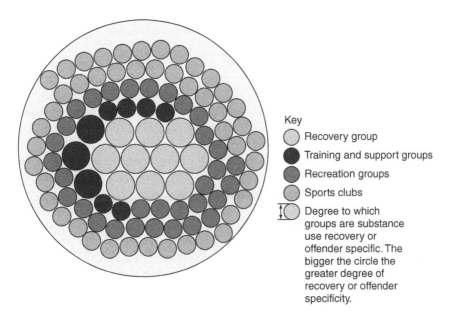

Figure 18.1 Community asset map of community groups (*n*=97) in Dandenong, Victoria.

18.6 RECOVERY COMMUNITY DEVELOPMENT

Dooralong is a 110-bedded residential rehabilitation service run by the Salvation Army in the Central Coast area of New South Wales, Australia, that offers a Therapeutic Community intervention (De Leon 2000) to substance-users with entrenched substance use history (many of whom have co-occurring offending and mental health histories). The Dooralong Transformation Centre opened not long prior to the start of the initiative and is set in a large estate of 350 acres with extensive opportunities for sport as well as a broad range of therapeutic activities.

As such, the Transformation Centre represents not only a potential hub for recovery activity, but also an asset for the community. Such a centre moves from a model of asset mobilisation to one of asset provision and so can be more appropriately referred to as a Reciprocal Community Development model, where the aim is not only to access existing connectors and resources in the community but also to ensure that the Centre, its staff and clients take on the role of providing assets to the wider community and playing an active role in engaging with and improving community life. The use of the Centre, its staff and residents as community assets is part of an attempt not only at asset development but also at building proximity and linkage between the treatment Centre and the community, and through doing this, challenging discriminatory practices and beliefs.

The pilot project at Dooralong was a partnership with the Salvation Army to identify community connectors from within the Therapeutic Community and to utilise this initial cohort to engage the wider community actively in recovery-oriented activities including those associated with challenging stigma and discrimination.

The model in Dooralong is based on four connected concepts:

- **recovery capital:** as the sum of personal, social and community resources that an individual can draw on to support them in their recovery journey;
- **assertive linkage:** although this has primarily been used in the past to link clients into AA groups, the philosophy is applied here to link in to other community resources including sports and recreation activities, education and training, peer activities and volunteering;
- **ongoing peer participation:** based on the idea that generating a growing community of peer champions increases the visibility and feasibility of recovery in the community and strengthens that community by its presence and its activities;
- **asset-based community development:** is the idea that communities have strengths and resources that are available and accessible to support recovery pathways and journeys, and tapping into those resources is essential for bridging people through transitions to their own communities.

The initial sessions recruited 15 volunteer community connectors and an asset map identified a further group of around 50 candidate community connectors or supports. This group constitutes the basis for the therapeutic landscape of recovery (Wilton and DeVerteuil 2006) but with the additional element of act-ively engaging the community as partners. The visibility of a recovery com-munity is limited if it seeks only to grow through its membership and this model is about active engagement through attraction and through the promotion of recovery as beneficial to communities, and of recovery groups and individuals as important assets in a community.

18.7 Communities and the ground for recovery

Based upon the ideas and pilot work we have discussed thus far, we imagine a therapeutic landscape of recovery to encompass several key elements as illus-trated in Figure 18.2.

This conceptualisation integrates both the formal systems that attempt to help people with substance use and offending histories and the community, in which people desist, relapse and live their lives (often in the face of considerable stigma and marginalisation). Our pilot work in Dandenong and Dooralong is predicated on the notion that recovery involves both individual and community level change. A person's individual behaviour change in treatment can be threatened when they enter corrosive community environments: environments that continue to exclude and stigmatise. However, too often the treatment and community worlds are viewed in isolation and separately. By virtue of being members of community groups and their willingness to engage with the treatment/criminal justice worlds, community connectors can act as the vital bridge between the treatment/criminal justice-worlds and the community. They facilitate access to groups in the community from which people may derive support, and a sense of belonging and ultimately wellbeing. These may be recovery groups in the first instance but as the social networks of people who have stopped using grow through participation in recovery groups,

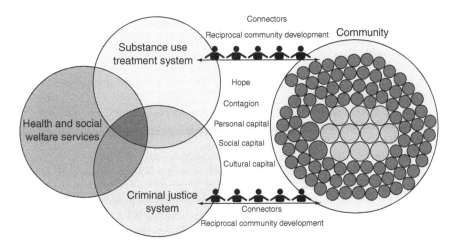

Figure 18.2 Therapeutic landscape of recovery among people with histories of substance use and offending.

opportunities for participation in other groups are also likely to grow. Importantly, however, if community connectors operate under a reciprocal community development model, they are also likely to decrease stigma and effect community level change. Together these reciprocal actions may contribute to a contagion of hope that recovery is possible and ultimately increase both the personal and social capital of the individual, and also the community's cultural capital in supporting recovery.

Acknowledgements

We would like to thank the staff at the Dandenong Magistrates' court and at the Salvation Army's Dooralong residential rehabilitation service for their support and assistance with pilot work. We would also like to thank our colleagues – Dylan Smith and Laura Abbey – who were involved in collecting data as part of the Dandenong pilot.

References

Australian Bureau of Statistics. 2013. 2011 Census Quick Stats: Greater Dandenong. Australian Bureau of Statistics. www.censusdata.abs.gov.au/census_services/getproduct/census/2011/quickstat/LGA22670.

Beattie M. and Longabaugh R. 1999. "General and alcohol-specific support following treatment". *Addictive Behaviours* 24: 593–606.

Best D., Loudon L., Powell D., Groshkova T. and White W. 2013. "Identifying and recruiting recovery champions: Exploratory action research in Barnsley, South Yorkshire". *Journal of Groups in Addiction and Recovery* 8(3): 169–184.

Biernacki P. 1986. *Pathways from heroin addiction: Recovery without treatment.* Philadelphia PA: Temple University Press.

Braithwaite J. 1989. *Crime, shame and reintegration.* New York: Cambridge University Press.

Community Indicators Victoria. 2013. *Greater Dandenong Wellbeing Report.* www.communityindicators.net.au/wellbeing_reports/greater_dandenong.

Deegan P. 1998. "Recovery: The lived experience of rehabilitation". *Psychosocial Rehabilitation Journal* 11: 11–19.

De Leon G. 2000. *The Therapeutic Community: Theory, model and method.* New York: Springer Publishing Company.

Granfield R. and Cloud W. 2001. "Social context and natural recovery: The role of social capital in overcoming drug-associated problems". *Substance Use and Misuse* 36: 1543–1570.

HM Government. 2010. *Drug Strategy 2010: Reducing demand, restricting supply, building recovery: Supporting people to live a drug-free life.* London: Her Majesty's Stationery Office.

Kretzmann J. and McKnight J. 1993. *Building communities from the inside out: A path toward finding and mobilising a community's assets.* Skokie, IL: ACTA Publications.

Landale S. and Best D. 2012. "Dynamic shifts in social networks and normative values in recovery from an offending and drug using lifestyle". In C. D. Johnston (ed.) *Social Capital: Theory, measurement and outcomes.* New York: Nova Science Publishers, 219–236.

Litt M. D., Kadden R. M., Kabela-Cormier E. and Petry N. 2007. "Changing network support for drinking: Initial findings from the Network Support Project". *Journal of Consulting and Clinical Psychology* 75(4): 542–555.

Litt M. D., Kadden R. M., Kabela-Cormier E. and Petry N. M. 2009. "Changing network support for drinking: Network Support Project 2-year follow-up". *Journal of Consulting and Clinical Psychology* 77(2): 229–242.

Manning V., Best D., Faulkner N., Titherington E., Morinan A., Keaney F., Gossop M. and Strang J. 2012. "Does active referral by a doctor or 12-step peer improve 12-step meeting attendance? Results from a pilot Randomised Control Trial". *Drug and Alcohol Dependence* 126(1): 131–137.

Maruna S. 2001. *Making Good: How ex-convicts reform and rebuild their lives.* Washington, DC: American Psychological Association.

McIntosh J. and McKeganey N. 2002. *Beating the dragon: The recovery from dependent drug use.* Harolow, UK: Pearson Education.

McKnight J. and Block P. 2010. *The abundant community: Awakening the power of families and neighbourhoods.* San Francisco: Berrett-Koehler Publishers.

Phillips L. and Shaw A. 2013. "Substance use more stigmatised than smoking and obesity". *Journal of Substance Use* 18(4): 247–253.

Putnam R. 2000. *Bowling alone: The collapse and revival of American community.* New York: Simon and Schuster.

Roth J. and Best D. 2013. *Addiction and recovery in the UK.* Abingdon, Oxon: Routledge.

Scottish Government 2008. *The road to recovery: A new approach to tackling Scotland's drug problem.* Edinburgh: Scottish Government.

Sheedy C. K. and Whitter M. 2009. *Guiding principles and elements of recovery-oriented systems of care: What do we know from the research?* HHS Publication No. (SMA) 09–4439. Rockville, MD: Center for Substance Abuse Treatment, Substance Abuse and Mental Health Services Administration.

Soyer M. 2014. "The imagination of desistance: A juxtaposition of the construction of incarceration as a turning point and the reality of recidivism". *British Journal of Criminology* 54: 91–108.

Substance Abuse and Mental Health Services Administration. 2012. http://blog.samhsa. gov/2012/03/23/definition-of-recovery-updated/.

UK Drug Policy Commission. 2008. *The UK Drug Policy Commission Recovery Consensus Group: A vision of recovery.* London: Her Majesty's Stationery Office.

UK Drug Policy Commission. 2011. *Getting serious about stigma in Scotland: The problem with stigmatising drug users.* London: Her Majesty's Stationery Office.

Wexler D. 1999. "Therapeutic Jurisprudence: An overview". Presentation at Thomas Cooley Disabilities Law Review Lay Symposium, East Lansing MI, 29 October 1999.

White W. 2012. *Recovery/remission from substance use disorders: An analysis of reported outcomes in 415 scientific reports, 1868–2011.* Philadelphia PA: Philadelphia Department of Behavioural Health and Intellectual Disability Services and the Great Lakes Addiction Technology Transfer Center.

Wilton R. and DeVerteuil G. 2006. "Spaces of sobriety/sites of power: Examining social model alcohol recovery programs as therapeutic landscapes". *Social Science and Medicine* 63: 649–661.

Williams A. 1999. "Introduction". In A. Williams (ed.) *Therapeutic landscapes: The dynamics between place and wellness.* Lanham MA: University Press of America, 1–11.

World Health Organization. 2001. *The World Health Report. Mental Health: new understanding, new hope.* Geneva: World Health Organization.

2

CONTEXTUALISING REHABILITATION

What I really need is the chance to become an acceptable, responsible, productive member of my community. A voice that can be heard. A voice that can speak for its own self. The guilt, the shame, the remorse, it's made me feel worthless. Surely my solution lies behind re-evaluated self-esteem and re-directed purpose. I'll grow when I'm ready! Just help me plant the seed, 'cos' hope is the drug that every offender needs. A new identity indentation. A source of inspiration! So show me examples of the people that succeeded, so I too can believe that I'm valued and needed.

(Duncan 2013: 13)

For me there were two significant relationships that in different ways gave me hope, determination and the courage to change. First, when I was aged 22, I met an older guy in prison who was nearing the end of a life sentence. He was previously involved in organised crime and had credibility in my eyes. During our time together he spoke about earlier beliefs, values and experiences that all conspired to result in his life sentence. More importantly, perhaps, he also spoke about the stark realities of crime and his 'wasted life' and he basically gave me a framework to examine the futility and destruction of my own offending behaviour and the effects this was having on my life and the people who cared about me. Given his past experiences, no-one else would have held so much sway over me in the same manner. Indeed, this was my first experience of a positive male role model; a convicted murderer. The second relationship came in to play when I was released from the same prison sentence and involved the social worker I had had since childhood. On reflection, her value for me wasn't necessarily in her profession, but her personality. She was a lovely, caring individual who believed firmly in the concept of change and rehabilitation, and she never lost sight of me during all those years of bedlam.

(Weaver 2013: 7)

Innate evil and mindless selfishness

We begin this chapter with quotes from two individuals who have experienced the rehabilitative endeavour of our correctional services. Although those who offend, sometimes seriously and persistently, can find ways of expressing their own journeys, it is often within the confines of academic literature, agency publicity or occasionally through the processes of the criminal justice system itself. It is much more likely that the general public will receive information about offenders from the media. On 22 February 2010, 27-year-old Jon Venables reported to his probation supervising officer that he thought his identity had been compromised. This began a series of investigations that quickly led to Venables being arrested and subsequently charged with offences relating to the downloading of pornographic images of children. On 24 February, he was recalled to prison in breach of the terms of his post-release life licence and he remained in custody until he appeared before the Central Criminal Courts on 23 July. He was sentenced to two years imprisonment for those child pornography-related offences. The case was subject to considerable scrutiny and media hysteria because as a 10-year-old boy, he had been convicted along with his co-accused, Robert Thompson, also aged 10, of the murder of 2-year-old James Bulger, abducted from a shopping centre in Merseyside by the older boys in 1993. Jon Venables and Robert Thompson were, therefore, just above the age of criminal responsibility when they killed James Bulger. They were eventually tried, convicted and sentenced in an adult Crown Court to be detained for life at Her Majesty's pleasure.

The child's body was found on a railway track, but it was the CCTV footage of the two boys holding the hand of James Bulger as they led him away from the shopping centre, along with news coverage of the subsequent baying crowds outside South Sefton Magistrates' Court that were to become iconic images and defining moments in the history of modern British criminal justice. Robert Thompson and Jon Venables became the youngest children in England and Wales to be convicted of murder in the twentieth century. The case was controversial from the outset and was complicated by legal argument in the European Court of Human Rights over the suitability of the court proceedings involving such young children in an adult court. There was also intense political debate over the appropriate length of sentence they would have to serve before being released on life licence. Following their release in 2001, both Robert Thompson and Jon Venables were provided with new identities so as to protect them from the depth of public feeling aroused by their crime. The extent to which the threat to both was real and enduring and the subsequent identity planning and security arrangements have been documented in

Sir David Omand's *Serious Further Offence* review of the Venables case, where Omand concluded that "it was the right judgement to create a complete new identity for Jon Venables given the police assessment of the level of threat" (2010: 41).

Rather than presenting the offence as aberrant or resulting from the interplay of a complex range of social, economic, biographical, cultural and psychological factors, the media portrayals of the two boys tended to pathologise them in simplistic and absolute terms. Germaine Greer observed at the time, that it seemed that almost everyone who dealt with the two children (as well as those who hadn't) was able to offer an opinion about their moral character and decided they were *innately evil*, interpreting "their every gesture whether nervous or vacant or frightened or uncomprehending as a manifestation of evil"(cited in Collett 1993: 185). The concomitant vying for professional ascendancy between so called experts was unsightly, but it was also ideological in that classifying both the crime and the perpetrators as evil "may serve to remind us that the only guarantee of safety in this increasingly dangerous society is by placing ourselves behind the thin blue line" (Collett 1993: 185).

On another level, the enduring impact of the murder of James Bulger can be seen in part as the result of a number of political contingencies fuelled by the breakdown in the post-war Butskellite consensus that had "implicitly rested on the nonpartisan character of crime and on the merit of gradual shifts towards rehabilitative policies for its control" (Downes and Morgan 1997: 128). In this respect, the murder was presented as symptomatic of a deeper moral malaise within British society; a condition that required remoralisation and condemnation through tough and uncompromising policies. For the revitalised Labour Party under the leadership of Tony Blair, "Out-toughening the Tories on law and order also included the legitimisation of simplistic, doom-laden, tabloid rhetoric that was usefully employed to convince voters that they were on the brink of a moral crisis, one which the Tories had allowed to occur and which New Labour was better equipped to address" (Green, 2008: 198). Similar crisis narratives would be invoked nearly two decades later in David Cameron's response to the riots that occurred in the summer of 2011:

> When we see children as young as 12 and 13 looting and laughing, when we see the disgusting sight of an injured young man with people pretending to help him while they are robbing him, it is clear that there are things that are badly wrong with our society. For me, the root cause of this mindless selfishness is the same thing I have spoken about for years. It is a complete lack of responsibility in parts of our society, people allowed to feel the world owes them something that their rights outweigh their responsibilities and their actions do not have consequences. Well, they do have consequences. We need to have a clearer code of standards and values that we expect people to live by and stronger penalties if they cross the line. Restoring a stronger sense of responsibility across our society in every town, in every street, in every estate is something I am determined to do.
>
> *(Quoted in New Statesman 2011)*

High profile events such as child murder or urban rioting are relatively rare but they have far-reaching consequences. This is not simply because of the extreme nature or impact of such occurrences but because they bring into question issues of public trust and confidence in the legitimacy of those institutions within society charged with protecting the public. They also challenge the role and legitimacy of professional expertise. It was perhaps inevitable, therefore, that Jon Venables' recall to prison for committing a serious further offence (SFO) would once again challenge the very notion of rehabilitation, especially for those convicted of the most serious offences, along with the efficacy of the organisations that were responsible for their supervision in the community. The media coverage surrounding Venables' recall inevitably tended to focus on some of the more salacious elements of the case. There were reports that he had had a sexual relationship with one of the residential care workers during the period of his first incarceration for the murder. Although he was a minor (13 years old) at the time, the press nevertheless hinted at his continued supposedly depraved character, thus one newspaper reported, "*Fury over Bulger killer's tryst with girl guard: 'Why was Jon Venables' sordid encounter in secure unit covered up?, asks James' mother'*" (Daily Mail, Feb 27 2011). In any other context, what happened to Venables would be viewed as institutional child sexual abuse!

Moreover, on 21 April 2011 the BBC televised a documentary entitled *What Went Wrong* which indicated a failure in the supervision and management of Venables in a provocative manner even though the Independent Serious Further Offence Review of the case led by Sir David Omand had concluded assessments made on Venables that he posed only a minor risk to the public were correct on the evidence then available and that he was appropriately managed and supervised by the Probation Service (2010). Incidents such as the recall of Venables highlight the intensely politicised nature of crime control in England and Wales rather than the real options for offender rehabilitation and the moral and philosophical bases for individual redemption within a modern democracy – as Green argues "Political culture and political economy clearly condition the ways in which crime is featured in political debates" (2008: 215). We will consider the politicisation of crime in more detail in Chapter Three but first need to analyse what delivering rehabilitation tells us about the changing nature of the state's response to crime, public protection and reducing re-offending.

So what is offender rehabilitation?

A key starting point in this task will be to discuss exactly what is meant and understood by the term *rehabilitation*. It is used in a variety of ways by those who are employed within the correctional services and it is therefore not surprising that the public are confused by the term. Does, for example, rehabilitation mean reform? These two words are often used interchangeably within official policy documents, even criminal justice statutes. For example, section 142 (1) of the Criminal Justice

Act 2003 outlines five purposes of sentencing of which the third is the *reform and rehabilitation of offenders,* (the others are punishment, crime reduction, protection of the public, and making reparation by the offender to persons affected by their offence). There is no further guidance and indeed the act does not indicate that one purpose should be more important than the other. In effect, the sentencer has the job of deciding how to apply the purposes and what the balance between them should be (see Sentencing Guidelines Council 2004: 3).

Do the public have specific expectations about the role of the state in rehabilitating individual offenders and indeed should the offender have any expectation about their own entitlement to rehabilitation? How can society best support individuals to desist from crime? Is rehabilitation different from desistance? Where and how do the rights and responsibilities of the individual and of the state play themselves out? Should probation recast itself within a framework of community justice and restorative approaches? What is success and how is it measured? Are the goals of rehabilitation absolute in the sense of individuals stopping offending, or do they reflect other relative measures relating to the level of harm and dangerousness of the offending act? Should we even consider the well-being of the offender in contrast to that of the victim? These questions are endless and the implied goals, as Raynor and Robinson suggest,

> ... reflect the different values placed on different kinds of outcome, and these values themselves often draw on further assumptions about human nature or human purposes.
>
> *(2009: 5)*

Rehabilitation was originally conceived as a means of legal requalification of individuals through the removal of the stigma of a criminal conviction (Carlen 2012, McNeill 2012). In this sense, the outcome for the individual is the regaining of their full status as a citizen and non-offender. Essentially, rehabilitation referred to the endpoint or outcome of a process that involved settling the putative debt implicit in the commission of an offence. Reform, on the other hand, has been more concerned with affecting a change in the individual in order to aid their reintegration into society with the attendant rights and responsibilities of citizenship. It has tended, historically at least, to assume a moral enterprise, backed up by help and direction (*advise, assist and befriend* in old probation parlance). Nowadays, as our reference to the current sentencing framework suggests, these terms are often used interchangeably along with more modern terms like desistance and reintegration. To complicate matters further, some definitions of rehabilitation ascribe a particular type of approach to reducing re-offending whilst others identify outcomes not just for offenders but for individual victims, communities or wider society (see Ward and Maruna 2007: Chapter 1). Finally, these terms are often not recognised by offenders who talk instead of *going straight* or *getting sorted.*

For us, the notion of rehabilitation includes both process and outcome. The process involves helping individual offenders to *go straight* by working with them to lead crime-free lives and meet their personal, family and community responsibilities. The process may be quick or drawn out over many years and will often involve setbacks. The outcome ultimately involves the restoration of the individual to their rights and obligations as full citizens whereby they no longer consider themselves or are considered an offender. This implies action by the state to both provide the resources to support the process and to acknowledge the outcomes. Our view of rehabilitation draws heavily on a burgeoning literature on desistance which moves thinking from why people commit crime to what might help them stop offending (Farrall and Calverley 2005, Maruna 2001, McNeill 2006, McNeill and Weaver 2010). A review of this literature is beyond the scope of this chapter but we wish to emphasise the following. Firstly, despite the *technicist* trends within the correctional services over the past decade or more, rehabilitation is a moral enterprise in which we should do with individuals and not to them (Burke and Collett 2008 and 2010). Secondly, techniques and structured interventions have their place and sometimes surveillance and control are necessary but often it is the expansion of and connection with personal, social and economic resources that offenders request and need. As individuals operating within a social context, the help identified and offered will be more effective if it is negotiated within a relationship that offers belief in the capacity of the individual to change and a professional commitment that it can be achieved, however difficult the circumstances. In this respect we would support Fergus McNeill's contention

> That offender management services need to think of themselves less as providers of correctional treatment (that belongs to the expert) and more as supporters of desistance processes (that belong to the desister).
>
> *(2006: 46)*

Transition, transformation or adaptability?

Notwithstanding our attempt to loosely define the rehabilitative endeavour, notions of rehabilitation can only be understood within their historical and ideological context. Nowadays, we tend to discuss rehabilitation in terms of community corrections and community-based responses to support offenders and ex-prisoners, but historically, the penitentiary, as a site of confinement, was perhaps the first practical expression of the reformative power of religious contemplation and penance through hard labour (Rotman 1990), leading to what the French philosopher Michel Foucault described as *coercive soul-transformation* (Foucault 1977). Gradually those religious ideals were supplanted by more medical and therapeutic models of rehabilitation characterised by their clinical, individualised and treatment-orientated practices (Robinson 2008). These ideas fitted well with the penal-welfare complex that emerged in the early twentieth century, with its emphasis on collective security and the provision of a safety net for the most disadvantaged through universal social benefits under the umbrella of a burgeoning welfare state. However, from the 1960s, as the power of professionals in clinical setting came under critical scrutiny, their role too was challenged both on the grounds of efficacy and morality. This resulted in the reformulation of rehabilitative practices "not as a sort of quasi-medical treatment for criminality but as the re-education of the poorly socialised" (McNeill 2012: 22).

The challenge to clinical notions of rehabilitation came from across the political spectrum and not necessarily from the usual contemporary suspects, such as the media. Rehabilitation was particularly criticised by left-wing civil libertarians because it was adjudged to interfere too much in the lives of individuals and seemed to operate unquestioningly in the interests of the state, consciously or unconsciously propagating its prevailing ideology. A fictionalised account of reha-bilitaion, Ken Kesey's novel, *One Flew Over The Cuckoo's Nest* (1962) reflected this perspective. In the field of psychiatry on both sides of the Atlantic, practitioners were questioning the ideological and medical basis of then current practice (see Szasz 1962, Szasz 1974, Boyers and Orrill 1972). Additionally, the anti-psychiatry movement itself was contested by socialist radicals such as Sedgwick who placed greater emphasis on the social context of illness and the political response to human problems (1982).

Professional knowledge and practice, ideology and socio-economic context were similar themes within the criminal justice arena. The ideological underpinning of the rehabilitative endeavour was criticised for ignoring the social context of crime and by implication presenting criminal behaviour as a *social disease* that could be treated in much the same way as a physical ailment (Bean 1976). However, the critical issues were not simply about social and economic disadvantage, but also about how far delinquent or criminal behaviour was symptomatic of individual pathology. Theoretical perspectives such as labelling theory in turn articulated the view that interventions could make matters worse by reinforcing deviant behaviour. *Due process* lawyers drew attention to the problems of injustice which stemmed from indeterminate sentencing and questioned whether unreliable predictors of future behaviour – based on the unsubstantiated claims of professional wisdom – should continue to influence sentencing. Instead, it was argued that rehabilitation should be provided within the context of a determinate sentence, the length of which should be proportionate to the seriousness of the offence (see Hudson 1997, Hudson 2003: 63). The law and order lobby, on the other hand, argued that rehabilitation was soft on crime and put the needs of the offender before those of the victim (Murray 1990). Rising crime rates during the post-war period and the absence of empirical evidence about impact of rehabilitative measures also appeared to suggest that treatment was failing to reduce criminal activity.

> Within a very short time it became common to regard the core value of the whole penal-welfare framework not just as an impossible ideal, but, much more remarkably, as an unworthy, even dangerous policy objective that was counter-productive in its effects and misguided in its objectives.
>
> *(Garland 2001: 8)*

Pat Carlen has argued that the net result of these divergent challenges was to erase "the citizen-subjects of the welfare state from the penal frame, replacing them with the risk-laden techno-entities of surveillance and security fetishism" (2012: 95). On the surface then, rehabilitation would seem to sit uneasily with the emergence of a risk-based penality (Feeley and Simon 1994) more concerned with providing a cost-effective means of managing *dangerous* individuals than reintegrating them into their communities. From this perspective rehabilitation, whatever we may want it to mean in terms of direct humanitarian work with individuals to help them turn their lives around, is in fact much more ideologically instrumental. Toward the millennium then:

> The task of the new penology is managerial, not transformative, and its discourse is characterised by an emphasis of systematic integrity and on internal evaluation based on formal rationality, rather than on external social objectives such as the elimination of crime or reintegration into the community. Consequently, it is concerned less to diagnose and treat individuals than to identify, classify and manage unruly groups sorted by dangerousness.
>
> *(Brownlee 1998: 79)*

For David Garland the replacement of the broader project of penal-welfarism with more intrusive forms of social control and surveillance can be located in the social, economic and political drivers of late modernity. Rehabilitation, with its emphasis on the collective did not resonate or was unable to respond to the increasing insecurity amongst the middle-classes and their distrust of professional penal expertise.

> The dominant voice of crime policy is no longer the expert or even the practitioner but that of the long-suffering, ill-served people – especially of "the victim" and the fearful, anxious members of the public.
>
> *(Garland 2001: 13)*

Garland's analysis of late modernity is considered in greater detail in Chapter Three but looking back on the immediate period after *The Culture of Control* was published (2001), McNeill *et al.* pick up on widespread concerns that the orthodoxy of management of risk and dangerousness, so clearly dominant in the first decade of the new millennium, has meant that "to the extent that rehabilitation endures at all, it survives only in a hollowed out managerialized form, not as an over-riding purpose but as a subordinate means" (2009: 421).

In some quarters, then, rehabilitation has become somewhat tainted, but the concept has nevertheless displayed qualities of endurance and adaptability. According to Robinson, this is because it has been able to adapt to prevailing, sometimes conflicting meta-narratives (2008). In this respect, rehabilitation, and by implication the Probation Service, has been largely successful in repositioning itself within the dominant contemporary policy and practice discourses of managerialism and risk. These developments are perhaps best encapsulated in the emergence of the *What Works* project (discussed further in Chapter Three) whose instrumentalism rested on claims that certain approaches would reduce reconviction (Canton 2012: 584). The subsequent National Offender Management Model (NOMS 2006) in which the individual's risk profile largely determines their eligibility for, intensity and type of intervention demonstrates both managerialism and risk discourses. In some senses this is not surprising given that "there is bound to be a strong motivation to seek results – such as a significant impact on offending behaviour – not least as a way of securing the future of the probation service" (Millar and Burke 2012: 318).

Rehabilitation as social utility

With the championing of *What Works* by the newly reorganised National Probation Service (NPS) in 2001, the mantra of probation increasingly became *risks, needs, and responsivity* (RNR). In essence the RNR approach was predicated on research evidence that reductions in re-offending could be achieved by closely matching the resources put into an intervention to the level of risk of re-offending posed by the individual. In short, the higher the risk the greater the resources deployed. This match of risk and needs required appropriate interventions to be delivered in a way that was responsive to the learning styles of the individual. The corollary was that a mismatch of resources particularly in relation to low risk offenders was not only wasteful but could actually increase the risk of an individual re-offending (Andrews and Bonta 2006, Underdown 1998, Ward and Maruna 2007).

The attraction of risk assessment tools was, according to Nash, that "they offered an alternative to the 'subjective' clinical interview, a method increasingly discredited in political circles. By utilising scientific method it was suggested that the assessment would be more accurate and less likely to be influenced by professionals' subjective feelings and experience" (2005: 22). Concomitantly, National Standards had also been introduced in 2001 to emphasise the timeliness of processes rather than their quality or effectiveness (Robinson *et al.* 2012) and until recently they required increasingly restricted decision-making by the worker particularly in relation to offender compliance, breach and return to custody. The increasing regimentation of probation practice and its packaging into more measureable actions and outcomes also fitted in with new ways of organising and managing the rehabilitative endeavour. As Corner contends:

> Risk-based targeting of people's needs allows commissioners, but perhaps more importantly procurement officers, to satisfy themselves that they are achieving the greatest good for the greatest number with the least resources.
>
> *(2012: 5)*

In a contemporary sense, therefore, the appeal of rehabilitation has tended to lie in its ability to protect the wider public and effectively manage risks rather than the needs and interests of those under its supervision. As such, rehabilitation has been promoted mainly in terms of its social utility. Furthermore, for the Probation Service, participation in such forums as Multi-Agency Public Protection Arrangements (MAPPA) and Multi-Agency Risk Assessment Conferences (MARAC) discussed in Chapter Six have enhanced its credentials as a partner alongside other criminal justice partners, particularly the police and prison services, where previously ideological conflict would have made such partnerships problematic, if not unthinkable (Nash 1999, Robinson *et al.* 2012).

Problems arise, however, when the social utility of the rehabilitative endeavour is questioned as fundamentally as it was in the wake of the summer riots of 2011, when the Coalition launched an attack on the correctional services for a failure to deliver higher levels of reduced re-offending. The ideological and political climate facilitated an attack not just on the concept of rehabilitation, but also on the efficacy of the state's delivery mechanisms. Although it wasn't mentioned by name, the response of Justice Secretary Ken Clarke clearly implied that the riots of 2011 were in part a reflection of Probation's failure to deliver (discussed further in Chapter Seven).

No escaping punishment: So that's what the public want?

Despite the move to making the state, in the form of the public sector, responsible for criminality, there nevertheless remains a very strong focus on individual offenders, their families, and the communities to which they are seen to belong. All too often this growing emphasis on individual responsibility has been orientated more toward apportioning blame rather than an understanding of need (Millar and Burke 2012: 321). What clearly follows from blame, though, is the apportionment of punishment, and the enduring existence of the rehabilitative endeavour can be partly explained through its adaption to the requirements for punishing offenders. As Robinson *et al.* points out, in many European jurisdictions the idea of punitive community sanctions is an anathema (2012). Indeed, implicit in the notion of probation is the avoidance of state punishment and for much of its history in this country, it was used *instead* of punishment (Canton 2012: 578). Recent attempts to promote rehabilitation's punitive credentials have been evident in attempts to rebrand community-based sanctions as *punishments in the community* providing a cheap and credible alternative to custody for less serious offenders. This has involved the *creative mixing* of multiple conditions and requirements as part of a single sanction (Bottoms *et al.* 2004). It has also been evident in the development of new *hybrid* sanctions such as the Intensive Supervision and Surveillance Programmes (ISSPs) for young offenders and the Intensive Alternative to Custody (IAC) for adults. These latter disposals have been explicitly packaged as alternatives to custody (ATC). However, in reality they do not include anything that could not have been included within a straight-forward community order, and their success seems to have depended more on the intensive management and support that was made available to the individual through supervision rather than the specific content of the order or threat of imprisonment in breach proceedings (Humberside Probation Trust 2012).

Schedule 16 of the Crime and Courts Act 2013 amends section 177 of the Criminal Justice Act 2003 by now making it a requirement that every community order must include *at least one requirement imposed for the purposes of punishment*. By prioritizing the infliction of punishment, this legislative change threatens to undermine the balance of sentencing outcomes and the underlying principles of proportionality and fairness in sentencing. The rationale for such a move appears to be based on the perennial perception of a lack of confidence in community sentences amongst the general public. This view persists despite existing research finding little evidence that the public want community sentences to be unproductively harsh (Hough and Roberts 1999, Maruna and King 2004). Indeed, adding punishment purely for the sake of general deterrence and increased public confidence has shown to have limited positive effects. Moreover, as Robinson and Ugwudike point out, equating *toughness* with *legitimacy* is extremely problematic (2012). Making community orders overly harsh and punitive in a misguided attempt to match the damaging impact of imprisonment ultimately undermines notions of legitimacy, without which compliance and desistance are jeopardised. As McNeill has noted, whilst "community punishment makes sense as a way of securing positive payback that benefits communities; it can't compete with prisons when it comes to imposing penal harm. When community punishment tries to do that, it also undermines its capacity to secure a positive contribution from reforming citizens" (2012b).

Unintended consequences: Widening the net

It has been argued that this *punitive turn* in the use of community sanctions has been largely driven by good liberal intentions to reduce the use of custody (Robinson *et al.* 2012). However, one of the unintended consequences has been the emergence of mass supervision in the community, alongside rather than diminishing the use of imprisonment (Burke and McNeill 2013: 108). The use of community sentences by the courts in England and Wales increased by 28 per cent between 1999 and 2009 (Ministry of Justice 2010a). A key driver behind this expansion has been the desire to use community sentences as a mechanism for controlling the prison population.

The *Breaking the Cycle* Green Paper estimates that the *vicious cycle* of re-offending by ex-prisoners costs the UK economy between £7–10 billion per year (Ministry of Justice 2010b). The potential role of community sentences in reducing these costs has become a key interest of contemporary penal policy, particularly in relation to using community sentences to displace shorter custodial sentences, which have higher costs per day and are typically associated with high reconviction rates. For example, a recent enquiry has calculated that diversion from custody to residential drug treatment produces a lifetime cost saving of approximately £60,000 per offender (Make Justice Work 2011). Some argue that, as well as being much less expensive than imprisonment, community sentences can produce lower re-offending rates. According to government figures, proven re-offending of those individuals receiving community orders in 2008 was 8.3 per cent lower than for those who had served prison sentences of twelve months or less, even after controlling for differences in terms of offence type, criminal record and other significant characteristics (Ministry of Justice 2012: 10). There are of course risks as well as opportunities here. It is important that the creation of intensive community punishments does not generate a net-widening effect resulting in less serious offenders being given sentences which are wasteful of limited resources and ineffective at reducing re-offending. The late Stan Cohen warned of this in his seminal work, *Visions of Social Control,* as long ago as 1985 and, notwithstanding the political and ideological consideration highlighted by Cohen, it represents a needless and ineffective waste of public resources. The evidence to date for the displacement of short-term custody by community orders remains depressing, and the prison population has continued to rise remorselessly over the recent past. The Ministry of Justice's own figures show that between 1993 and 2008 the prison population rose on average by 4 per cent annually, fuelled by increases in the number of people sent to immediate custody, increase in sentence length including the use of indeterminate sentences and increases in the numbers recalled to custody for breach of licence conditions (Ministry of Justice 2013: 6). Despite a modest fall for the first time between June 2012 and June 2013, the prison population standing at nearly 84,000 is almost twice what it was in 1992 (Ministry of Justice 2013: 8) and this against a trend of falling levels of crime since the mid-1990s.

Don't get mad, get even!

David Downes once suggested that "*the more secure we are the more insecure we feel*" (2010: 396), and attempts to allay public fears and insecurity within a highly politicised environment is itself fraught with risks. As governments become more certain about how they will deal with crime, this paradoxically heightens anxiety and fear of crime amongst the very communities they seek to protect. The impossibility of providing complete security and the inevitability of some failure means that whatever protections are provided, they will never be enough, creating profound organisational and personal consequences (see Chapter Three). The dilemma for the Probation Service is that its

> ... traditional mechanisms of protection – for want of a better expression – are to be found in the support of long-term change processes which provide relatively little security and reassurance in the short-term. Thus, although changed ex-offenders who have internalised and committed to the responsibilities of citizenship offer, a better prospect for a safer society in the long term, change programmes and services look somewhat feeble when set against the increasingly threatening offender that communities are taught to fear.
>
> *(McNeill 2009: 22)*

Of course, politicians and the political process itself find it difficult to tolerate longer-term strategies for effective rehabilitation and few if any recent Secretaries of State have shown any desire to build public confidence to support these *longer-term change processes*. Rather they exhibit knee-jerk responses to events; short-termism becomes the order of the day. One consequence is the absence of rhetoric, public policy or legislation directed toward punishment. Indeed, punitiveness has an expressive quality in the sense that it is not just the supposed instrumental benefit of punishment but its powerful emotional expressiveness that serves politicians and the political process well during times of wider pressure. It is difficult, therefore, to envisage how short-termism can ultimately strategically support a desistance-based approach to rehabilitation which by its nature requires long-term political commitment, ironically mirroring the exact same commitments to be expected from criminal justice workers and their clients!

It can also be argued that contemporary rehabilitative practices chime with the expressive nature of punishment in the sense that programmes which encourage individuals to think and behave differently and become more empathetic to their victims resonate more with neo-classical perspectives that emphasise personal responsibility. Punishment and rehabilitation both communicate, as Gwen Robinson notes,

> ... censure in response to criminal acts and seek to instil within the offender a moral compass to guide his or her future actions. Thus the 'treated' offender is presented as an individual capable of managing his or her own risks without recourse to externally imposed sanctions or controls.
>
> *(2008: 440)*

This notion of the expressive or symbolic form of punishment is in fact an instrumental means of achieving wider political and administrative goals. *Communicative* theories of punishment, on the other hand, are very different. Building on the communicative theories of the legal philosopher Antony Duff, this approach aims to give wrongdoers an opportunity to redeem themselves and ultimately to be reconciled to the community. As Ward explains:

> A significant feature of communicative theories of punishment is that crime is conceptualized as a community responsibility rather than simply an individual one. While offenders are held accountable to the community their core interests are not neglected. Relatedly, victims are not ethically required to forgive offenders but do owe them a meaningful opportunity to be reintegrated within the community once they have served their sentences. Thus, the community is obligated to actively help offenders in the process of integration by the necessary internal and external resources such as education, work training, accommodation, and access to social networks.
>
> *(2009: 118).*

In other words, rehabilitation is a two-way street and critically, findings from the desistance literature referred to earlier suggest that intervention should not be solely about the prevention of further offending but should equally be concerned with constructively addressing the harms caused by crime by encouraging offenders to make good through restorative processes and community service (in its broadest sense). As McNeill argues:

> Rehabilitation, therefore, is not just about sorting out the individual's readiness for or fitness for reintegration; it is as much about rebuilding the social relationships without which reintegration is impossible. Any would-be supporter of rehabilitation has to do more than try to sort out 'offenders'; s/he needs to mediate relationships between people trying to change and the communities in which change is impeded or impelled; s/he also has to mediate the role and limits of the state itself in the process.
>
> *(2012a: 13)*

One of the advantages of strength-based approaches, such as the *Good Lives* model (Ward and Maruna 2007) is that they provide an antidote to a preoccupation with risk-based offender management strategies. Rather than labelling offenders as criminal *others*, they are presented as having the same needs and basic human nature as the rest of us, actively searching for primary human goods in their environment which emerge from such basic needs as relationships, a sense of belonging, self-worth and the potential for creativity. In this respect, strength-based approaches shift the attention toward supporting the conditions necessary for offenders to achieve these primary human goods rather than solely focusing on their personal deficits. They provide an incentive to change by focusing on the individual's own life goals and ambitions. Commenting on this approach, Robinson argues that "correctional intervention should focus on assisting offenders to identify the functions that offending has served in their lives and to adopt ways of achieving the goods that they desire more pro-socially" (2011: 15).

However, developing the social capital of a vilified group is not easy in insecure, late-modern societies. No amount of individual support will be enough if the legal, economic and social barriers to change are not also tackled. Narrowing the scope of rehabilitation to some residual form of social utility goes against Kantian (1724–1804) conceptions of the individual as a moral being capable of choice, rather than an instrument of other people's purposes. As Malcolm Millar and Lol Burke have argued, committing criminal offences does not constitute a justification for social exclusion or for withdrawing the respect which individuals, as persons, are due.

> Forcing offenders to wear brightly-coloured jackets as a shaming form of 'punishment in the community' (Casey 2008); imposing disproportionate restrictions on individuals based on the *possibility* of further offending; or recall decisions which are of dubious legitimacy (Digard 2010) – these topics all raise moral issues; and particularly in a punitive climate, those who venture to examine them in terms of their questionable humanity in individual cases enter contentious territory.
>
> *(2012: 324)*

The domination of managerial and punitive discourses in contemporary penal policy and practices, as Canton (2012: 577) points out, has relegated the human rights of individual offenders to an issue of secondary importance and apart from some improvements in the prison system, the rights of offenders have been eroded rather than upheld (Robinson 2011: 11). Those who have argued for a system of *state-obligated rehabilitation* (Cullen and Gilbert 1982, Rotman 1990) contend that the state has a moral duty to offer rehabilitative measures in return for the individual's future compliance. However, state-obligated rehabilitation can be articulated within a wider social and economic context. Making a direct link to the work of probation and the rehabilitative endeavour, Peter Raynor expresses it in this way:

> Probation flourishes best in societies which believe that the legitimacy of government rests partly on recognising a substantial share of responsibility for the welfare of its citizens. This social contract requires that in return for expecting us to obey its laws, the State should make available, as far as it can, the resources that help and enable us to pursue satisfactory lives within the law. This is the essence of the theory of State-obligated rehabilitation.
>
> *(2012: 186)*

From this perspective a rehabilitative criminal justice strategy should form part of a social policy agenda that recognises everyone's right to have their basic needs met. The strength of these approaches, as Sam Lewis argues, is that they acknowledge that "both citizen and state have duties and that citizens are more likely to comply with the law if the demand that they do so is experienced as legitimate" (2005: 123). Legitimacy in turn cannot be achieved without professionally competent staff (see Chapter Four).

Whilst the notion of *state-obligated rehabilitation* might sound philosophically and practically aloof, the notion of long-term strategies to support the reintegration of offenders into their families and communities for the benefit of the wider communities as well as for the individual offender is not. Politicians deliver punishment because they tell us that the public want it. However, when people are engaged in the criminal justice process and particularly when they have both direct and indirect contact with offenders, all the evidence is that their desire for punishment is usually mediated and often over-ridden by the desire to see the individual supported on their travels back to citizenship. The public appear to understand the notion of *don't get mad, get even*, even if our politicians do not.

Summary: So that's what offender rehabilitation is

Justifications for rehabilitation are essentially moral arguments about what society *ought* to do in relation to offenders.

(Raynor and Robinson 2009: 5)

Of course, such moral arguments are deeply contested and the delivery of state-mandated punishment and rehabilitation happens against a complex set of expectations and political pressures. Successive administrations have their own ideological purposes and find themselves at the mercy of public opinion, which they hope to shape for their own purposes. Whilst many people experience crime at first hand and form their own opinions based on that experience, we can also see the impact of a powerful news media on public attitudes to both crime and those who commit it. The public are fed ideologically-framed and highly subjective information about both individual offenders and more general aspects of crime. This in turn chimes with wider feelings of insecurity – as Shadd Maruna *et al.* note "public punitiveness is more a symptom of free-floating anxieties and insecurities resulting from social change than a rational response to crime problems" (2004: 277).

Whilst there is much talk of punishment in the community and alternatives to custody based on arguments of effectiveness and cost, the question has to be asked whether the dominance of imprisonment is tolerated as a relatively cheap alternative to longer-term social and economic change. The cost of mass incarceration could, from one perspective be seen as a cheap price to pay for the control of particular problem populations and the maintenance of the current socio-economic order. The language of rehabilitation acts a Trojan horse for the position that punishment holds within the criminal justice system, but it could be further argued that punishment extends beyond the penal system to the ability to access a range of goods and services. This leads us to the thorny question of the role of the state in reproducing and perpetuating deprivation. As Carlen has argued:

Prime Minister Cameron was wrong when, in a speech last month, he put renewed emphasis upon punishment and rehabilitation in the community. He was wrong for several reasons, but he was fundamentally wrong because the poor, the young, the disabled and the indigent elderly and many others are already being severely punished in communities deprived of the most basic access to housing, jobs, and general welfare. In such a situation it seems obvious to me that all questions of crime and punishment have to be linked to, and most probably subsumed by, questions of social justice and inequality.

(2012: 1)

The moral arguments for the justification of the rehabilitative endeavour, the link to questions of social justice and inequality, the vested interests and the overriding political and ideological determinants of service delivery mechanisms all help to define and shape what we think rehabilitation is. It is a complex set of considerations, but at the end of all this, we remain clear that rehabilitation is about helping individuals to go straight and get sorted.

References

Andrews, D.A. and Bonta, J. (2010) *The Psychology of Criminal Conduct*, (5 ed), Newark: LexisNexis.

Bean, P. (1976) *Rehabilitation and Deviance*, Oxon: Routledge.

Bottoms, A., Rex, S. and Robinson, G. (eds) *Alternatives to Prison: Options for an Insecure Society*, Cullompton: Willan.

Boyers, R. and Orrill, R. (1972) *Laing and Anti-Psychiatry*, Harmondsworth: Penguin.

Brownlee, I. (1998) *Community Punishment: A Critical Introduction*, London: Pearson Education.

Burke, L. and Collett, S. (2008) Doing with or doing to: What now for the probation service? *Criminal Justice Matters*, 72: 9–11.

Burke, L. and Collett, S. (2010) People are not things: What New Labour has done to Probation, *Probation Journal*, 57(3): 232–249.

Burke, L. and McNeill, F. (2013) The Devil in the Detail: Community sentences, probation and the market in Dockley, A. and Loader, I. *The penal landscape: The Howard League guide to criminal justice in England and Wales*, Oxon: Routledge.

Canton, R. (2012) The point of probation: On effectiveness, human rights and the virtues of obliquity, *Criminology and Criminal Justice*, 13(5): 577–593.

Carlen, P. (2012) Against Rehabilitation; For Reparative Justice, 2012 Eve Saville lecture, Centre for Crime and Justice Studies. http://www.crimeandjustice.org.uk/resources/against-rehabilitation-reparative-justice (Accessed 14 March 2014).

Cohen, S. (1985) *Visions of Social Control: Crime, Punishment and Classification*, Polity Press: Cambridge.

Collett, S. (1993) Beyond reason and understanding: The everyday understanding of crime, *Probation Journal*, 40(4): 184–187.

Corner, J. (2014) *What is the nature of the opportunity that Transforming Rehabilitation represents?* Clinks AGM, 29 January 2014.

Cullen, F. and Gilbert, K. (1982) *Reaffirming Rehabilitation*, Cincinnati: Anderson.

Daily Mail (2011) *Fury over Bulger killer's tryst with girl guard: Why was Jon Venables' sordid encounter in secure unit covered up?, asks James' mother*, 27 February.

Downes, D. (2010) Counterblast: What went right? New Labour and Crime control, *The Howard Journal of Criminal Justice*, 49(4) 394–397.

Downes, D. and Morgan, R. (1997) *Dumping the 'Hostages to Fortune'? The Politics of Law and Order in Post-War Britain* in Maguire, M., Morgan, R. and Reiner, R. *The Oxford Handbook of Criminology*, (2nd Edition) Oxford: Oxford University Press.

Duncan, S. (2013) Judgement room: a life story, *Euro Vista*, 3(1): 11–13.

Farrall, S. and Calverley, A. (2005) *Understanding desistance from crime*, Maidenhead: Open University Press.

Feeley, M. and Simon, J. (1994) Actuarial justice: the emerging new criminal law, in Nelken, D. (ed) *The Futures of Criminology*, London: SAGE.

Foucault, M. (1977) *Discipline and Punish* [English translation], London: Allen Lane.

Garland, D. (1985) *Punishment and Welfare: A History of Penal Strategies*, Aldershot: Gower.

Garland, D. (2011) *The Culture of Control*, Oxford: Oxford University Press.

Green, D.A. (2008) Suitable vehicles: Framing blame and justice when children kill a child, *Crime, Media, Culture: An International Journal*, 4(2): 197–220.

Hough, M. and Roberts, J.V. (1999) Sentencing trends in Britain: Public knowledge and public opinion, *Punishment and Society*, 1(1): 11–26.

Hudson, B. (1987) *Justice Through Punishment: A Critique of the 'Justice' Model of Corrections*, London: Macmillan.

Hudson, B. (2003) *Understanding Justice: An Introduction to Ideas, Perspectives and Controversies in Modern Penal Theory* (2nd ed), Buckingham: Open University Press.

Humberside Probation Trust (2012) *Response to Punishment and Reform: Effective Community Sentences* (Consultation Paper CP8/2012), Humberside: Humberside Probation Trust.

Kesey, K. (1962) *One Flew Over The Cuckoo's Nest*, London: Picador.

Lewis, S. (2005) Rehabilitation: Headline or footnote in the new penal policy, *Probation Journal*, 52(2): 119–135.

Make Justice Work (2011) *Community or custody? A National Enquiry*. www.makejusticework. org.uk (Accessed 14 March 2014).

Maruna, S. (2001) *Making good: How ex-convicts reform and rebuild their lives*, Washington DC: American Psychological Association.

Maruna, S. and King, A. (2008) Selling the public on probation: Beyond the bib, *Probation Journal*, 55(4) 337–351.

Maruna, S., Matravers, A. and King, A. (2004) Disowning our shadow; a psychoanalytical approach to understanding punitive public attitudes, *Deviant Behaviour*, 25(3): 277–299.

McNeill, F. (2006) A desistance paradigm for offender management, *Criminology and Criminal Justice*, 6(1): 39–62.

McNeill, F. (2009) What Works and What's Just? *European Journal of Probation*, 1(1): 21–40.

McNeill, F. (2012a) Four forms of 'offender' rehabilitation: Towards an interdisciplinary perspective, *Legal and Criminological Psychology*, 17(1): 18–32.

McNeill, F. (2012b) *Not big, not tough, not clever, June 16*. Discovering Desistance. ESRC Knowledge Exchange. http://blogs.iriss.org.uk/discoveringdesistance/2012/06/16/not-big-not-tough-not-clever/ (Accessed 14 March 2014).

McNeill, F. and Weaver, B. (2010) *Changing lives? Desistance research and offender management*, Glasgow: Scottish Centre for Crime and Justice Research.

McNeill, F., Burns, N., Halliday, S., Hutton, N. and Tata, C. (2009) Risk, responsivity and reconfiguration: Penal adaptation and misadaption, *Punishment & Society*, 11(4): 419–442.

Millar, M. and Burke, L. (2012) Thinking Beyond 'Utility': Some Comments on Probation Practice and Training, *The Howard Journal of Criminal Justice*, 51(3): 317–330.

Ministry of Justice (2010a) *Offender Management Caseload Statistics 2009*. Ministry of Justice Statistics Bulletin, London: The Stationary Office.

Ministry of Justice (2010b) *Breaking the Cycle: Effective Punishment, Rehabilitation and Sentencing of Offenders*, London: The Stationary Office.

Ministry of Justice (2012) *Punishment and Reform: Effective Community Sentences* – Consultation Paper CP08/2012, London: Ministry of Justice.

Ministry of Justice (2013) *Prison Population Projections 2013–2019 England and Wales*, Ministry of Justice Statistical bulletin, 7 November.

Murray, C. (1990) *The Emerging British Underclass*, London: IEA Health and Welfare Unit.

Nash, M. (2005) The probation service, public protection and dangerous offenders in Winstone, J. and Pakes, F. *Community Justice: Issues for probation and criminal justice*, Cullompton: Willan.

New Statesman (2011) Cameron searches for the "root cause" of the riots, *New Statesman*, 10 August.

NOMS (2006) *The NOMS Offender Management Model 1.1*, London: Home Office.

Omand, D. (2010) *The Omand Review: Independent Serious Further Offence Review: The Case of Jon Venables*, London: Sir David Omand GCB.

Raynor (2012) Is Probation still possible? *The Howard Journal of Criminal Justice*, 2(2): 173–189.

Raynor, P. and Robinson, G. (2009) *Rehabilitation, Crime and Justice*, Basingstoke: Palgrove Macmillan.

Robinson, A. (2011) Foundations for Offender Management: Theory, Law and Policy for Contemporary Practice, Bristol: Policy Press.

Robinson, G. (2008) Late-modern rehabilitation: The evolution of a penal strategy, *Punishment & Society*, 10(4): 429–445.

Robinson, G. and Ugwudike, P. (2012) Investing in 'Toughness': Probation, Enforcement and Legitimacy, *The Howard Journal of Criminal Justice*, 51(3): 300–316.

Robinson, G., McNeill, F. and Maruna, S. (2012) Punishment in Society: The Improbable Persistence of Probation and other Community Sanctions and Measures in Simon, J. and Sparks, R. (eds) *The Sage Handbook of Punishment and Society*, London: Sage.

Rotman, E. (1990) *Beyond Punishment: A New View of the Rehabilitation of Criminal Offenders*, New York: Greenwood Press.

Sedgwick, P. (1982) *PsychoPolitics*, London: Pluto Press.

Sentencing Guidelines Council (2004) *Overarching Principles: Seriousness* – *Guideline*, London: Sentencing Guidelines Secretariat, December.

Szasz, T.S. (1972) *The Myth of Mental Illness*, London: Paladin.

Szasz, T.S. (1974) *Ideology and Insanity*, Harmondsworth: Penguin.

Underdown, A. (1998) *Strategies for Effective Offender Supervision, Report of the HMIP What Works Project*, London: Home Office.

Ward, T. (2009) Dignity and human rights in correctional practice, *European Journal of Probation*, 1(2): 110–123.

Ward, T. and Maruna, S. (2007) *Rehabilitation*, London: Routledge.

Weaver, A. and Weaver, B. (2013) Autobiography, empirical research and critical theory in desistance: A view from the inside out, *Probation Journal*, 60(3): 259–277.

8 Theorising rehabilitation work and the helping professions

Introduction: the sociology of rehabilitation work

This chapter provides theoretical reflections on the thematic accounts of the two fields emerging from Chapters 5 and 6. It considers these against the research questions, as well as the findings of others. The emerging picture is that the dynamics of rehabilitation work and service sectors, and their central actors, cannot be fully understood by re-examining the evidence and tools used, or by introducing new programmes to shift the focus of daily practices. Nor can rehabilitation workforces and cultures be fully understood where there is a blinkered focus on what is perceived to be the primary presenting issue (e.g., addiction and addiction treatment). It is more multi-faceted and oblique than that, as the capacity of practitioners to support desistance and recovery continues to be affected by wider issues than the primary focus of the professional helping relationship. Reflections are offered on why a significant number of practitioners are leaving the fields of interest, while others are going on leave? A few potential explanations are explored, with the recognition that they may apply to differing extents in their application to one field or the other, and may be experienced differently by the diverse range of actors within them.

Sociological concepts, in particular those from the sociologies of work and the professions, are used to theorise key research themes and findings. Some of these concepts have already been defined and explained in Chapter 4, and are further articulated in their application here, while others require further definition. The chapter continues to draw on the seminal work of sociologist Pierre Bourdieu, using his concepts as thinking tools. Furthermore, several decades since their original publication, Everett Hughes' (1962) notions of 'good people and dirty work' and Michael Lipsky's (1980, 2010) *Street-Level Bureaucracy* offer prescient insights which are relevant in explaining current field dynamics. This is complemented by contemporary insights from sociologists such as Julia Evetts, among others, to help identify the key drivers and impacts of 'professionalism from within' and 'professionalism from above' in the two fields. Pushes for the professionalisation of alcohol and other drugs work and criminal justice work are not ideologically or politically neutral, and carry both intended and unintended consequences.

The stigmatisation and precaritisation of rehabilitation work: dirty word, dirty work?

One of the themes apparent in this research is that some practitioners feel like their work is not valued or well understood by others. Issues of inequity, precarity and identity crisis become apparent, and these are discussed in turn throughout this chapter, with the acknowledgment that they are inter-related. The argument that some practitioners experience and perceive their work as precarious (implicating habitus and capital) speaks to the conditions and structures within which they work (the generative structures of the field). One of the potential explanations for why a significant number are leaving or going on leave is because they may feel like they are 'good people doing dirty work' (Hughes, 1962: 3), in being tasked with 'difficult work' of dealing with stigmatised 'Others' such as 'criminals' and 'drug addicts'. Issues of stigmatisation and 'dirty work' can be linked to wider post-1974 perceptions in the West that, in some circles and spheres of influence, rehabilitation has become a 'dirty word', and that it doesn't 'work' (Ward and Maruna, 2007: 1).

Under-resourcing and cutbacks amid growing caseloads is illustrative of moves towards more generic 'broker' and 'managed care' models seeking efficiencies and triage of service provision. This type of case management helps to cater for the masses within the given fiscal constraints, ensuring alcohol and other drugs services continue to achieve excellent outcomes on a shoestring budget. It may also detrimentally affect existing retention and future recruitment, by negatively impacting practitioner perceptions of their work. Seasoned practitioners who have been in the system for a long time may see their best work (working with the 'whole' person over time, building trust) as increasingly devalued or sidelined in exchange for taking on more surface level screening, assessment, referral and group facilitation, not to mention keeping up with bureaucratic demands of more paperwork, risk management and evaluation requirements (White and Graham, 2010). Paradoxically, practitioners are there to help (tasked with helping to reduce harms, risks, costs etc) and yet they are not necessarily afforded the chance to truly engage in the depth of the work of a helping professional, nor offered satisfactory levels of help and support themselves.

Precarity, inequality and the tyranny of the urgent: the precaritisation of rehabilitation work?

The generative structures of social precarity and precarious work are found in the composition and stratification of the field itself. Some practitioners feel that their work role and their field have not enjoyed the improved conditions and advances in service development and capacity building that others have. They feel the burden of inequalities in remuneration and the division of labour, relative to other more powerful, well-resourced work roles and fields. Where this concerns community sector organisations, such discussions build on the themes in Chapters 5 and 7 about issues of the structuring and procurement of rehabilitation services and work.

> Workers in the sector actually feel like they don't have a good name. It's not a good place to work; the pay's not great; the conditions aren't fantastic; you have massive caseloads and you're overworked and underpaid and under-appreciated.

> [Frontline practitioner]

Analysis of the alcohol and other drugs (AOD) field in Chapter 5 explored practitioner perspectives on issues of professional and sectoral identity crisis. Using a Bourdieusian lens, it is clear that the issues extend beyond the level of actors and their habitus. The AOD *field* is grappling with stigma, precarity and inequality; it is a site of struggle. This is encapsulated in the following quotes, the first of which has already been presented in Chapter 5:

> There's a lack of pride about what we're doing and who we are and why we're doing it and all that sort of thing. I don't think we've got a strong enough identity of being who we need to be as a sector ...

> [Senior practitioner]

Impassioned comments from one practitioner go so far as to acknowledge the reciprocal links between a lack of a cohesive identity and esteem amongst AOD practitioners and the sector's workforce, and the ways in which they are perceived and treated by those in power.

> There's a lack of pride in the ATOD sector. There is a real sense of disengagement ... I don't know how exactly to describe it, except to say it kind of feels like ATOD workers are urchins. In the Dickensian sense, they're the Oliver Twists, they're kind of outcasts and they're very separated, and nobody really knows who each other are until you get them into a room. I was in an [ATOD sectoral consultation group] recently, and one of the questions that was asked was 'would you recommend working in the ATOD sector to people that weren't in it? Would you actively recruit?' The people around my table said no they wouldn't because, first of all they don't know how to define the sector, they don't know who to send it to, or who to send them to and secondly they don't see that it's a very good sector to work in. I think that that is terribly problematic because if there isn't a sense of collegiality, if there isn't a sense of pride in their work and a sense of importance in what they're doing, then how are we going to ever convince policy makers and government heads that they're worthy of consulting with and collaborating with? If they don't see any value in themselves, how the bloody hell is everybody else going to?

The findings of this research resonate more widely with an emergent literature on the precaritisation of 'affective work' by helping professionals and volunteers in community sector and voluntary sector organisations in Western neoliberal jurisdictions. A beautifully written PhD study by Amanda Ehrenstein (2012) on 'Precarity and the crisis of social care', has explored the politics and experiences of work in women's voluntary sector organisations in the United Kingdom, amid a wider backdrop of the feminisation of helping professional and voluntary workforces and the re-structuring of the welfare state and social care. She persuasively charts how neocommunitarian neoliberalism is implicated in increasing uncertainty and the burdens of affective labour and caring work felt in this field, including '(1) the precaritisation of working conditions; (2) a loss of state support for care and community initiatives resulting in a widespread crisis of projects; (3) a reduction of the range of services and projects that were attracting state funding; and (4) a crucial role designated for affective labour political commitment and forms of apparent self-precaritisation in the organisation of work' (*ibid.*: 3–4). Her documentation of resultant issues of 'short-term, insecure, poorly remunerated' paid work supported by an increasing amount of volunteers makes it difficult for practitioners to resist precarity in social care, creating 'harmful work environments' and the intensification of inequalities between actors in the field (*ibid.*: iii).

While practitioner participants in this research are perhaps (by comparison) less pessimistic in pinpointing their narratives about their fields and work to such specific harms and problems, as they are quick to remind me in interviews that they are committed to and enjoy what they do, some of them also feel the burdens and anxieties of having to daily deal with shifts and cutbacks. Late modern hyper-flexible modes of production and the precarity of flexible work is implicated in adding pressure to helping professionals who have to work not knowing if their project or programme, or indeed their own work role, will continue to secure funding in the next competitive funding round or next electoral cycle. Furthermore, the inequalities and uneven impact of precarity may intersect along the lines of gender and age, bearing in mind that the majority of the AOD community sector workforce in Tasmania, for example, is women, and is made up of 'older' workers (see Chapter 5). An increasing number of organisations are using volunteers (ATDC, 2014), which may reflect shifts of tasks and affective labour from the paid workforce to expand to unpaid helpers.

In this research, issues of uncertainty and precarity are most overt in the narratives of the AOD community sector practitioners. However, the focus should not be unnecessarily delimited to practitioners in one sector or type of service. One of the findings of this study is that some community sector and some government staff in criminal justice also perceive that they experience inequalities and precarity, albeit perhaps different in nature to the issues faced by their counterparts in the AOD field. Some criminal justice practitioners feel like, at times when the field and their work is more politicised and volatile in the rate of change, they are doing edge-work on the margins of the mainstream penal culture, compared to the stability and hegemonic influence enjoyed by some of their better paid, more influential colleagues, especially in hierarchical organisations like prisons. There have been dynamic developments with regard to this throughout the six years in which this research was conducted, with issues among non-uniformed prison staff doing rehabilitation work being more pronounced in the early and mid-2000s, and improving in the mid-late 2000s when boundaries and caps were set on their caseloads and a level of stability in overarching processes was secured.

> For a long time, things were just this crisis driven chaos because [non-uniformed integrated offender management and reintegration workers] were being reactive all of the time, almost burning out, feeling undervalued, being treated like shit and expected to do this huge amount of work. It was insane, and I take my hat off to them for being able to stay there during that environment. Now they feel much more controlled and contained because they have been able to say 'Well, this is the limit to what we can do, this is what we can manage.'
>
> [Frontline practitioner]

One of the central features of the notion of social precarity, even as it applies to practitioners and work, is a pervasive sense of uncertainty, or reactive 'crisis driven chaos' as it is called above. Chapter 6 offers details of the scope of changes that have occurred in Tasmanian Corrective Services and the Department of Justice in the last decade. An important thematic finding of this research is that the uncertainty of precarity and inequalities in the Tasmanian criminal justice field are *encountered unevenly* by actors in the field. There are distinct institutional differences between the prison and the Community Corrections Service.

One interview participant from Community Corrections identifies acute issues of workload and facing 'the tyranny of the urgent', but probation officers are perceived as a cohort with a cohesive level of solidarity and stability. There are less apparent inequalities or differentiation between practitioners on the grounds of professional status and remuneration. This practitioner and their colleagues demonstrate a more counter-resistant stance to pressures to comply with unrealistic expectations from powerful others (e.g., the judiciary, policymakers), instead strongly emphasising the need to retain a vision of the end-goals and purposes of their work, even in the midst of the 'tyranny of the urgent':

> So it sounds like you're saying the more we reduce reoffending and promote safer communities or safer work environments, the less likely we are going to have these perpetual crises, which then cause lockdowns, which then cause disruptions to programmes or access to case coordinators or pressure on probation officers' workloads. So what you're saying is that this makes it so that you have got to have more longevity in how you see things?
>
> [Researcher]

> Yes. It does take a fair bit of metal to hold your ground, when there's a crisis and saying 'no, we're not going to do that.' [pause] As you know, we have had a huge increase in our numbers, and the spike has been very very significant. It kind of has snuck up on us a bit, but then you go back and you think 'gee we are feeling a bit pressured', then you look at the stats and realise there has been a really big increase. One of the ways we could

have dealt with that is just make sure that people comply with their order, or get in that report – ok all we are going to do is reports. Well of course in 10 years' time, the numbers will be double if we are going to do that.

[Practitioner]

This practitioner's long-term view of the issues, combined with a desire to retain their penal welfarist values and ways of working in the face of sporadic penal crises and heavy workloads contrasts with the tone of some practitioner accounts who work with offenders with complex needs.

The stratification of rehabilitation work

Issues of the precaritisation of some forms of work are rooted in the generative structures and stratification of rehabilitation work and the fields in which it occurs. Wider processes have a bearing on how this is rationalised and implemented with (or imposed on) helping professionals and workforces. The following sub-section clarifies the definition and conceptualisation of key terms such as 'professions', 'professionalisation', and 'professionalism.' These notions are contested, just as there is an undercurrent in both fields of contested professional identities and associated statuses – are all practitioners doing rehabilitation work 'helping professionals'? Or should this term only be used to denote those with specialist qualifications and expertise, privileging them as offering an advanced form knowledge-based work which differs from less skilled practitioners doing technical routinised interventions and activities?

The following sub-section and, indeed, this chapter, is less about reaching a confident conclusion in response to these questions, and more about exploring the perspectives and dynamics among actors and the fields in this study. Interestingly, those bearing the heaviest structural burdens and pressures may be the subjects of top-down professionalisation efforts that implicitly responsibilise them for improving the outcomes of their work, irrespective of working conditions and field conditions. These issues are discussed in a sub-section in the latter part of this chapter.

Helping professionals? Identity crises may reflect status anxiety

There may be a (well founded) sense of unease among some in discussions of rehabilitation work being done by 'helping professionals', with questions arising as to whether practitioners with few or no qualifications and higher education working in criminal justice and AOD should be considered as 'helping professionals.' This reflects wider doubts cast over social care and rehabilitation, as to whether it has a similar standing to other professional groups and co-located fields, including medicine, law and the judiciary.

The concept of profession is a contested one (Sciulli, 2005; c.f. Evetts, 2006; Svensson and Evetts, 2003, 2010). *Professions* are defined as 'the knowledge-based category of occupations which usually follow a period of tertiary education and vocational training and experience … they are primarily middle-class occupations sometimes characterised as the service class' (Evetts, 2003a: 397–398). The attributes that make up a profession vary because the concept itself is an ideal-type, and there are numerous taxonomies explaining the elements of a profession, which are themselves contested in knowledge or expert 'truth wars' between scholars from different traditions and expertise (Saks, 2012). Larson (1977: x) suggests a few dimensions that, together, constitute a profession:

- The *cognitive* dimension is centred on the body of knowledge and techniques which the professionals apply in their work, and on the training necessary to master such knowledge and skills.
- The *normative* dimension covers the service orientation of professionals, and their distinctive ethics, justifying the privilege of self-regulation granted them by society.
- The *evaluative* dimension implicitly compares professions to other occupations, underscoring the professions' characteristics of autonomy and prestige.

(Adapted from Larson, 1977: x)

These dimensions and attributes are neither clearly bounded nor unproblematic; they are fraught with ideology (Freidson, 1970; Larson, 1977). Professions are affected by political, economic and social mechanisms and dominant paradigms in knowledge-based work and its governance in Western neoliberal jurisdictions. As highlighted in Chapter 2, the ascendancy of the risk paradigm and the influence of the medical model and associated professional dominance is relevant to understanding professions and service work in the AOD and criminal justice sectors. Evetts (2003a: 397) argues for a different way of characterising knowledge-based occupations:

> [Alternatively we can] see professions as the structural, occupational and institutional arrangements for dealing with work associated with the uncertainty of modern lives in risk societies. Professionals are extensively engaged in dealing with risk, with risk assessment and through the use of expert knowledge, enabling customers and clients to deal with uncertainty.

These discussions have significant implications in consideration of whether there are hierarchies of knowledge and hierarchies of care associated with McNeill's (2012a) four forms of rehabilitation. Is professional status in knowledge-based work affected by their contributions to different paradigms? If so, this could help to explain why clinicians who are experts in managing risk have more professional dominance than those who may prefer to focus their work on supporting desistance and recovery, albeit with a risk management component. Furthermore, are 'helping professionals' more notionally associated with clinicians that focus on psychological rehabilitation to correct the primary presenting problem or the drugs-crime nexus, while those who focus on social rehabilitation and reintegration are differentiated as technicians doing more generalist work? Are status and capital experienced unevenly because of what type of rehabilitation work a practitioner does? These questions warrant further research and exploration.

Professionalism (another contested concept) is interpreted in two ways: professionalism as a form of moral community and a normative value system, and professionalism as ideology (Johnson, 1984; Evetts, 2003a, 2013). Practitioners do not have to be employed in occupations which are widely characterised as a profession in order for professionalism as an ideology to inform their practices (White, 1983a). In Table 8.1, Julia Evetts (2013: 788) highlights two different forms of professionalism in knowledge-based work. This conceptualisation explains relations between professions and organisations as being based around the differentiation between Durkheimian notions of respectful and egalitarian collegiality and Weberian notions of hierarchical, managerialist bureaucracy. Differences can be expected between professional norms (for example, values relating to quality of therapeutic care or probation) and organisational norms (for example, fiscal constraints, organisational efficiencies); however, the relationship is not necessarily always an antagonistic one (Bourgeault *et al.*, 2011). Professional norms may help to explain why a significant number of practitioners regularly 'go the extra mile' in supporting the desistance and recovery of service users, as differentiated from a technician (instrumental) mentality and organisational norms in doing rehabilitation work.

Professionalisation is achieved through professional training, certification and workforce development; such occupational change often involves processes of accreditation and 'credentialism' (Collins, 1979 in Evetts, 2003b). Critical questions need to be asked about the sources of power and influence in professionalisation processes, examining who is driving pushes for worker and workforce development. Professionalisation efforts carry implications for professional socialisation, including how helping professionals see themselves and make sense of their status in relation to that of others in the field (Durnescu, 2014). McClelland (1990: in Evetts, 2003a: 398) distinguishes between

Table 8.1 Forms of professionalism in knowledge-based work

Organisational Professionalism	Occupational Professionalism
• Discourse as control used increasingly by managers in work organisations. • Rational legal forms of authority. • Standardised procedures. • Hierarchical structures of authority and decision-making. • Managerialism. • Accountability and externalised forms of regulation, target-setting and performance review. • Linked to Weberian models of organisation.	• Discourse constructed within professional groups. • Collegial authority. • Discretion and occupational control of the work. • Practitioner trust by both clients and employers. • Controls operationalised by practitioners. • Professional ethics monitored by institutions and associations. • Located in Durkheim's model of occupations as moral communities.

Source: Evetts, 2013: 788.

'professionalisation from within' and 'professionalisation from above.' Professionalism *from within* affords practitioners greater autonomy and personal decision-making and professional judgment, as well as input into the requisite competencies and best practices associated with their expertise and service work. 'Professionalisation from within' fits with Durkheim's notion of occupational professionalism. Professionalisation *from above*, often taking the form of workforce development and training, and the standardisation of service work through the roll out of 'evidence-based practices', pro-formas and routinised interventions and programmes *en masse*, as has been described elsewhere in this book, may be perceived by some practitioners as forms of de-skilling and increased bureaucratisation of their work. 'Professionalisation from above' fits with Weber's notion of organisational professionalism.

Some helping professionals may perceive a lack of trust in their professional judgment and contraction of the scope of their discretion in transitioning towards a managerial form of case management and tick-a-box work practices to conform their 'service provision' to imposed expectations. These things can result in 'occupational identity crisis' (Evetts, 2003b: 23), and helps, in part at least, to make sense of the collective identity crisis and status anxiety felt by practitioners in the AOD field in Tasmania. In turn, these issues can be linked to Bourdieu's (1977) concept of *hysteresis* – which is described as 'a cultural lag or mismatch between habitus and the changing rules or regularities of the field' (McDonough and Polzer, 2012: 359). There are pressures for traditional welfarist and narrative ways of working to be overtaken by more standardised ways of working which are focused less on needs and diversity, and more on risk and efficiency. Some practitioners in this study have found themselves in the uncomfortable position of being 'in between', part of the field and yet not belonging to or having capital and status in the field to be allowed to make extensive or influential professional judgments beyond those allowed within the tools, programmes or models of practice within which they are expected to work, which may partly explain why some of them are leaving. A sense of counter-hegemonic resistance and advocacy, as explored in Chapter 7, may function, for others who are not leaving, as a source of professional resilience, enabling them to embark on job crafting which carves out a niche for them in the field. Those who innovate seem to be those whose responses to dynamic changes in the field engender a form of creative capital, bringing a differentiation and recognition of their expertise as innovative and different, perhaps partly protecting them from pressures to conform to the established orthodoxy or the new dispositions expected of them in top-down efforts to professionalise them.

A sense of status anxiety and identity crisis among helping professionals is not unique to the Tasmanian context. Halliday, Burns, Hutton, McNeill and Tata (2009) use Michael Lipsky's (1980) seminal work, *Street-Level Bureaucracy*, to reflect on inequalities between 'street-level bureaucrats' in criminal justice. Street-level bureaucrats are those who interpret and apply state policies, for example, a new policy aimed at reducing re-offending. In doing so, they 'manage their difficult jobs by developing routines of practice and psychologically simplifying their clientele and environment in ways that strongly influence the outcomes of their efforts' (Lipsky, 2010: xii). For example, conducting a pre-sentence report becomes less an exercise in assessing the whole person and their circumstances, and more of an exercise in assessing criminogenic risk factors and ensuring that the focus and tone of the pre-sentence report implicitly validates the expertise of the practitioner who wrote it in the eyes of the powerful practitioner who reads it. Penal power is used in practice for multi-faceted purposes in the hope of achieving different ends, for example, a defensible and robust pre-sentence report including recommendations aimed at reducing re-offending and legitimation of the standing and expertise of the actor as its author. In the context of Scottish courts, Halliday and colleagues (2009) analyse how criminal justice social workers (equivalent of probation officers) encounter issues of status anxiety and a desire for more professional legitimacy and credibility in the eyes of other powerful actors (e.g., the judiciary, lawyers) who might also be considered as street-level bureaucrats.

These deep-seated issues of identity and legitimacy, where they start to influence the discourses and representations of practitioners, carry particular kinds of influence. In seeking to understand rehabilitation work, a central question relates to how the identities and work of those offering professional supports are socially constructed. Professional knowledge can be distinguished in two ways: as *technical* and as *tacit* (Evetts, 2003a). In this book, technical knowledge is more akin to 'What Works' in terms of positivist notions of strictly evidence-based practice, and tacit knowledge is guided by both evidence and experience in what helps and what matters. It taps into what Bourdieusian theorists might call their 'feel for the game.' Workforce development and professionalisation efforts centring predominantly around the former tends to conceptualise practitioners as *technicians*, whereas development and professionalisation activities more focused on the latter are based on practitioners' understandings of themselves as skilled helping *professionals* with specialist expertise. Menger and Donker (2013: 286) summarise the important interplay of both in contributing to professionalism, stating that 'professional expertise consists by definition of explicit knowledge in combination with discretionary power', and arguing that documentation of explicit knowledge *alone* is a 'necessary but insufficient pre-condition for professionalism'. Instead, they argue that questions of 'What Works' need to coincide with questions of 'who works', how and why in order to more fully consider the sources of professional effectiveness.

These discussions largely tend to coalesce around the forms of capital proposed by Bourdieu (1986), which can be seen in the energy or dynamics of a given field. An actor who has *scientific capital* demonstrates a habitus (dispositions and attitudes) based on 'knowledge of a problem field' and 'mastery of techniques', claiming the 'objectivity' of evidence and science through using particular instruments and tools, combined with a 'desire for peer recognition through innovation' (Moore, 2012: 102). Here, in this study, I argue that scientific capital and the associated habitus described above is more closely aligned with 'What Works' notions of skilled technicians delivering effective interventions, with credibility resting on credentialism. An actor who has *cultural capital* demonstrates a habitus based on knowledge of 'the rules of the game' and the overarching history and cultural influences of the field, having a 'cultivated gaze', 'poise' and distinguished 'taste', combined with a 'desire for the recognition for distinction'(*ibid*.: 102). Some powerful actors and fields of work can be seen as having both scientific capital and cultural capital, for example, doctors, psychiatrists and the judiciary. Conversely, some actors and organisations or indeed, entire fields of work, may be lacking in cultural capital, and be struggling with perceptions of not possessing sufficient scientific capital, instead with helping professionals being pejoratively cast as 'bleeding heart' do-gooders who need more training in evidence-based tools to be more effective and objective. The reality is that workers are already educated and qualified, for example as shown in Tasmanian AOD workforce surveys (ATDC, 2013d, 2014), and yet conflicting perceptions persist among powerful senior actors that they need to further educated and trained to be professionalised. These issues segue into the next sub-section which considers the effects of what happens when entire groups of workers and workforces are perceived as needing 'professionalisation from above'.

Professionalisation, responsibilisation and social control of helping professionals

Professionalism 'is changing and being changed' (Evetts, 2013: 778), which has implications for how cultures and practices are changing and being changed. Drawing on the arguments of Suddaby and Viale (2011), Svensson and Åkström (2013: 558) highlight how 'professions play a central role in the development of organisations based on the idea that professional expertise, social capital, rules and standards, as well as the ability to reproduce these factors contributes to changes in organisations'. However, Svensson and Åkström (*ibid*.) place caveats on this by demonstrating that professions have less influence on organisational culture and change in sectors where professional work involves social control and regulation, for example, the punishment of offenders and the treatment of illicit drug users. Social control is managed by the State, while professionals act of agents for such organisations (*ibid*.). In turn, their work is governed and dictated to by the state, whether the state is their direct employer or indirect funder. Similarly, Fenton (2013) draws links between public anxiety about social problems and institutional ontological anxiety about the targets of social control (e.g., offenders), arguing that there are associated increases in risk-averse managerialism resulting in the social control of workers (in this case criminal justice social workers or probation officers) to try and advance a certain level of (ill-founded) actuarial certainty that workers are doing 'what works'.

The concept of *heteronomy* is relevant to these discussions, as it helps to explain the creation of bureaucratic and organisational professionalism. Johnson (1977: in White (1983c: 46)) states that 'State heteronomy arises where the authority to determine the recipients and content of practice is removed from the producer and consumer-clients … the occupation is guaranteed a clientele which is constituted by state definitions of need and the manner in which such needs may be catered for'. This is of distinct interest in adopting a critical realist strategy of analysis to consider the two fields of interest in this book, because the heteronomous ordering of an occupation is closely linked with the structural role of the institution and generative mechanisms in Western neoliberal societies (White, 1983a and b). One of the effects for practitioners working in these conditions and fields or work is that they may exert some control over their own labour, but not necessarily control *in* the labour process. These issues suggest that practitioners in knowledge-based work which involves social control and the management of social problems are unequally or disproportionately affected by pressures and priorities associated with *organisational* professionalism (as outlined in Table 8.1), rather than *occupational* professionalism. This may be used to further explain differences in the dynamics within the two fields.

Reflections on the stratification of the alcohol and other drugs field (AOD)

The collateral consequences for culture and identity that are associated with social control and organisational professional are helpful in explaining the fraught relations and power inequalities between government and community sector organisations and practitioners in the Tasmanian AOD field, as discussed in Chapter 5. It is unsurprising that local practitioners in community sector AOD services struggle with issues of legitimacy and identity in their work, and feel somewhat powerless to the established orthodoxy or *doxa* of power relations, as well as the direction of workforce and sectoral culture change. Accordingly, explanations for workforce turnover in the Tasmanian AOD community sector may be directly or indirectly associated with these issues. Issues of job stress, dissatisfaction and identity crises may be encountered by individual practitioners due to structural issues directly affecting their work (e.g., lack of recognition, remuneration and career pathways in stigmatised occupations), as well as being affected by overarching structural issues (e.g., inequity in how community sector AOD services are procured, constant changes in the field generating a sense of precarity and uncertainty, threat of cutbacks or imposed shifts in focus).

Concepts and arguments from the sociologies of work and the professions also help in analysing the tensions and divisions in perception and status between AOD clinical professionals (for example, clinical psychologists, addiction medicine specialist doctors) and those employed in non-clinical AOD work roles (for example, case managers). There is a technical division of labour based on skills and credentials, as well as a social division of labour which affects identity, status, capital and influence. Again, these divisions are mostly observed along organisational lines (government as clinical and professional, community sector as non-clinical and semi- or non-professional). However, there are some government AOD practitioners who are not clinically qualified or employed in clinical roles, just as there are community sector AOD practitioners who are clinically qualified and employed in clinical roles.

While concerted culture change and professionalisation efforts in the AOD field may have been driven, for the most part, by good intentions, they have yielded mixed results and mixed feelings. At one level, intense concentration on aligning interventions with the evidence base of 'What Works', thereby emphasising the instrumentality of practitioners (what they do and how they do it) has yielded some well documented returns in streamlining service delivery. For many, the roll-out of new and improved tools, programmes and clinical standards across the different occupations and organisational contexts that make up the AOD field represent positive steps in the right direction.

At another level, such efforts have distracted from the need to understand the context, culture and conditions in which such practices and proposed changes take place. Concentration on the tools and technologies of practice and their standardisation has surpassed and, arguably, neglected attention being given to issues that remain important to practitioners – identity, values, legitimacy and future purpose (who they are and why they do what they do). Ironically, such widespread practice standardisation and up-skilling may represent a form of 'professional marginalisation' and de-skilling, by displacing the centrality of practitioners as agents of change and imposing tools and procedures that are not sensitive enough to the multifaceted nature of the cultures, practices and practitioners that they seek to change (see McNeill *et al.*, 2010).

To further theorise the marginalisation, precarity and resistance of community sector practitioners along the lines of a Bourdieusian-style of analysis, notions of principles of division and symbolic capital are relevant. The symbolic capital and habitus of powerful government practitioners, especially clinicians, can be linked to the stability of differential stratification of the AOD field. Yet, in this research, some AOD community sector practitioners are resisting and challenging that hegemonic perspective and seemingly orthodox ordering of the professional field, asserting that their knowledge, skills and qualifications in many cases are the same (or greater) than that of their government counterparts. In light of this, they raise legitimate questions regarding the grounds upon which their authority and knowledge is regularly subjugated by those with more symbolic capital. Participants in this research are correct in highlighting the paradoxical tension in that '*if they [government AOD] could do it all themselves, they would*' but '*they can't do it without us, we do most of the work*'. These findings highlight that there are structural issues that warrant further attention, especially if meaningful change in terms of the division of labour and distribution of capital is to be realised. Instead of displacing practitioners and ignoring the influence of organisational factors, building a stronger identity and greater capacity in the AOD sector needs to start with 'changing the structures, and expected outcomes of these structures, in which people work, not just encouraging a few to use new ways of working in spite of the system' (Allsop and Stevens, 2009: 541). This would require more transparent reflection on the fact that, despite some issues of street-level bureaucracy, the frontline level of practice at the 'coalface' is not necessarily the locus of where the influential generative mechanisms and problems lie.

In light of these things, questions of status and influence in systemic advocacy and promoting cultural and structural change in this field are pertinent. One of the issues facing those who may seek to bear witness and 'speak truth to power' (see Scraton, 2002, 2007) about structural impediments and power inequalities affecting the capacity and identity of the AOD field are themselves often restricted by how their job roles are funded and governed. Nearly all AOD peak bodies, advocacy organisations, and community sector organisations in Australia are reliant on securing short-term government funding in a competitive tendering context. In 2013, the national AOD sector peak body – the Alcohol and other Drugs Council of Australia (ADCA) – unexpectedly had its funding withdrawn by the Australian federal government as a 'cost saving' strategy (Nolan, 2013). Analysts are attributing the shock axing of the 50-year national old peak body to its critical systemic advocacy for the AOD sector and its progressive public stance on harm minimisation and the decriminalisation of certain drugs (*ibid.*).

There are few other national bodies at a federal level which represent the AOD sector. Health Workforce Australia (2012) has been tasked with developing a national coordinated approach to fostering 'change, collaboration and innovation' for a more sustainable health workforce, however, it is a federal government initiative and can only operate within set parameters. These types of stakeholders will continue to be engaged for a narrow set of purposes, such as developing new competency frameworks or consultation AOD workforce minimum qualifications – that is, things which target practitioners as technicians, not the cultures, funding and structures which govern and stratify their work (Graham, 2012c). Similarly, some AOD researchers have expressed concerns about the potential for regulation and subtle forms of control in AOD research by government funding bodies, human research ethical regulators and professional gatekeepers such as professional associations and journal editorial boards (Miller *et al.*, 2006). In effect, they highlight the absence of critical examination of the realities of practice and AOD work in empirical literature, and draw links between 'he who pays the piper' and research agendas and their tunes (Graham, 2012c). In summary, these things confirm the existence and nature of issues of social control in sectors and professions tasked with doing and understanding rehabilitation and social control.

Reflections on the stratification of the criminal justice field

Inter-professional and interdisciplinary differences in standpoint in the criminal justice field are paralleled by industrial differences in employment and work role classification and remuneration. Two practitioners commented on perceived issues of professionalisation and work role status, and how these are represented in public service recruitment practices and the wider structuring of employment conditions.

> The [name of team] is made up of 'non-professionals', i.e. those roles do not even require a TAFE welfare diploma. They are employed under the General Stream, so they can just walk in to the job – we can employ people from ad-min types of processes to do that job.
>
> The team, are recruited under the Clerical and Admin award, so there is this automatic value placed on them that they are less professional, less important, than programmes. The way I see it, they are at the front end and

they do the most important piece of business, and it might be generic, but generic is equally as important as specialty. If they want to be able to retain staff, if they want to be able to move staff around within and across the organisation, pay them as professionals. Or, pay them more Clerical & Admin, because if the argument is that we can get professionals under Clerical & Admin, will stop recruiting from the other streams for professionals. Yes, they are more costly, and the pay rate does escalate at a rapid rate, the grade of it is quite steep. But look at your retention rate as well, if you are not keeping staff, why are you not keeping staff? If you're keeping shit staff, why are you keeping shit staff? … When you take a section of it out – and say 'No, we actually only want generic workers here,' for some of the staff, they will think less of those staff. There is an elitism that comes with having a degree or not having a degree. A degree is by no means a determinant of whether you are good or not! [laughter]

[Frontline practitioners]

These issues and perspectives are similar to those raised in Chapter 5 regarding the professionalisation and workforce development issues in the AOD field. In harnessing Bourdieu's (1987) and Weber's (1968) lines of analysis, the field is still a site of struggle for those with less symbolic capital and cultural capital – in this case, 'generic' case managers – compared to those with more, for example, clinical psychologists. The distinction between frontline staff employed in the General Stream or Clerical and Admin award, and those employed under professional streams and awards is the difference in attributions of professionalism afforded to the latter, and the former, by default, being seen by colleagues as working in *bureaucratised* roles (for example, processing Section 42 prisoner day leave permit applications and case planning for parole applications). The 'professional' staff may regard some non-clinical staff employed in the clerical and administrative stream as being appropriate subjects of organisational professionalisation efforts, possibly because of perceptions that they are underqualified 'technicians' doing bureaucratised and process-driven work such as non-specialist case management, and therefore having (comparatively) less scientific capital and cultural capital. By way of contrast, myself and others (Graham and White, 2015, 2016; Graham *et al.*, 2015) have heralded the innovative initiatives and collaborative work being achieved by non-uniformed staff supporting the reintegration and desistance of people leaving prison. They are helping people leaving prison realise social rehabilitation and moral rehabilitation in ways that those supporting psychological rehabilitation (as important as it is) are not. In part, this is theorised in terms of job crafting and 'intrapreneurship'.

'Job crafting', resistance and 'intrapreneurship' in criminal justice work

The discussions in this final section contrast with some of the previous discussions by highlighting how practitioners craft their work roles and innovate from the inside, departing from traditional stereotypical notions of who they are and what they do. Many of these things can be observed, in different ways, in the AOD field, but discussions here tend to focus on criminal justice, following on from the description of the creative and innovative initiatives in Tasmania outlined in Chapter 7. This section seeks to use concepts and theories to explain why such innovation and collaboration is important.

In their UK study of the cultures and identity of probation, Mawby and Worrall (2011, 2013) explore how probation officers navigate, mediate and cope with change and difficult working conditions. They build on the empirical contributions of others to explore how probation officers take pride in what others might perceive as 'dirty work' and a stigmatised workforce, how they reconcile competing demands and ideological tensions in their work, and yet remain motivated and able to survive and thrive (Mawby and Worrall, 2013). These processes and the meaning making and strategies that are incorporated within them are theorised as 'job crafting' (Wrzesniewski and Dutton, 2001; Wrzesniewski *et al.*, 2003; Rosso *et al.*, 2010; Mawby and Worrall, 2013). Job crafting takes a number of forms, but it can be defined as:

> The physical and cognitive changes individuals make in the tasks or relational boundaries of their job … changing their identity and meaning of work in the process. Job crafting is a creative and improvised process that captures how individuals locally adapt their jobs in ways that create and sustain a viable definition of the work they do and who they are at work.
>
> (Wrzesniewski and Dutton, 2001: 180)

The limited literature and knowledge from the sociology of the professions and organisational development scholarship on prisons and probation has a tendency to adopt a problem focus on issues of stress and burnout. Where strengths and strategies are considered, this is often done so in terms of 'coping strategies'. However, in this study and that of Mawby and Worrall's (2011, 2013), there is already much room for optimism, as this is something that is actively modelled by the practitioners themselves. Within a set of given parameters, they craft their job into something they enjoy, with benefits reaching more widely than themselves.

The conceptualisation of this type of creative work and co-producing collaborative innovations in justice are still emerging in criminological scholarship; however, there is a more established empirical understanding in the social innovations literature (Brayford *et al.*, 2010; Stanford Centre for Social Innovation, 2013). The concept of 'intrapreneurship' is useful in describing how certain practitioners in this research engage in creative work, start up innovative initiatives and champion change (including practice and culture change). Such efforts are for the benefit of supporting offenders but also for their own intellectual stimulation and job satisfaction. An intrapreneur is defined as 'an individual within a large organisation or institution who devises new approaches or methods, or creates new value and opportunities using entrepreneurship and innovation' (Graham and White, 2015). Entrepreneurs often do these things independently or with the support of a few, whereas intrapreneurs are changing systems and processes from the inside. To succeed at this, they are often afforded more flexibility and trust, where they are allowed to operate outside or go beyond organisational rules and routines (albeit with integrity) to pursue original and pioneering ideas and implement them with a view to achieving better outcomes (*ibid.*). In large organisations and systems which are typically bureaucratic and risk-averse, intrapreneurship involves socially competent forward-thinking and high levels of initiative and human capital to forge change and realise efficiencies and innovations that are beneficial for the different stakeholders involved (see Alpkan *et al.*, 2010; Wunderer, 2001).

There are synergies in the conceptualisation of intrapreneurship and one of the job crafting strategies observed in the UK study by Mawby and Worrall (2013: 153), which they refer to as 'responsible creativity'. In turn, this is imbued with sociological notions of 'edgework'. The value of this to practitioners is described as a way of easing pressures and tedious routine work, as well as a form of resourcefulness and 'putting professional skills to the test for the good of the offender, victims, the public and the organisation' (*ibid.*). Responsible creativity, innovation and intrapreneurship in criminal justice organisations are examples of evading, counteracting or perhaps even rebelling against bureaucratised professionalism and managerialist rationality. Garland (2001: 189) observes how managerialism can stymie innovation: 'it can limit experimentation, favour "outputs" over "outcomes", skew practice to fit performance indicators, limit the discretion of field staff, and diminish an agency's real effectiveness in order to maximise the practices that are most easily measurable.'

Innovation is a catalyst which is the realisation of long-held hopes. Hope is a central theme that continues to feature in practitioner accounts. Practitioners are quick to call attention to their belief that change is possible and there are ways of working that can produce good results, even in the midst of difficult work.

> We need to do the best, or find the best possible plan for this inmate, so how do we seek it? It's literally about making that effort to make those things happen ... Because I'm fairly passionate about what I do, I can't always wait for others to make that happen, and I'm very willing to say, 'right, I'll organise it then.' I'll get on the phone and make that appointment, I'll do it, because I'm willing to do it, and I'm passionate about it, and I want the best outcome.
>
> [Frontline practitioner]

> I think with any community worker who has been working for quite a while it's the basic talents of their craft, it is about resilience, it's about keeping going, keeping the client at the centre, not giving up, lateral thinking and finding different methods and avenues and resources to be able to get to that outcome of what's needed for the client. To simply turn up and say 'sorry we can't do that' would be totally inadequate, totally unprofessional and certainly not productive. So you need to have a can-do mindset. At times it's quite intense because there are so many factors to juggle, so many

intangibles, so many relationships to work with and you need to be able to just somehow grasp those intangibles and work with them in the context of relationship to get the outcome that's needed.

[Frontline practitioner]

I try to stay more positive and hopeful. While I think crises are terrible at the time, it is how we deal with them that is either going to be a big part of a growth process or a destructive process ... Often the discussions people are having afterwards can either go in the direction of blame and what some-one should have done, whereas I think the more important conversation is a reflective one, asking what does this mean for you? Can you see the crisis circumstances in a way that is not linked to your sense of self, so you don't tie that into the outcomes? Sometimes just after the crisis, the conversations can turn negative, but if I pull some people aside and have conversations where we think differently, that is often helpful.

[Frontline practitioner]

The capacity to 'stay positive and hopeful' is not only a coping strategy, but a source of pride and a resource for practitioners in processes of job crafting. They are able to keep a long-term view to building a different future, while retaining the values that are important to their sense of who they are in their work. Some of them seem to relish their role as an innovator from the inside, an 'intrapreneur' able to work creatively within the parameters of otherwise very structured work routines and organisations. This reflects a level of resistance by practitioners to the wider pressures of social control and responsibilisation of practitioners involved in working with the subjects of social control, in this case offenders. Without these strengths, it would be reasonable to expect that the criminal justice sector might encounter a considerably higher rate of workforce turnover.

Conclusion

The analysis in this chapter adds credence to the argument that practitioners in knowledge-based work which involves social control and the management of social problems and risks (e.g., drugs and crime) are unequally or disproportion-ately affected by pressures and priorities associated with 'professionalism from above', finding themselves subject to considerable management and monitoring of compliance. Feeling over-worked, bureaucratised and disempowered carries implications for their discretion and time available to mobilise the capital and empowerment of desisting and recovering individuals and their families. The theoretical and empirical contributions in this chapter, and more widely through-out this book, help to make sense of what is happening at the coalface, deepening understanding to reveal an emerging politics of knowledge and render more visible inequalities between professional actors in the two fields. These issues, however, cannot be taken for granted as affecting all practitioners. They are expe-rienced unevenly, and some practitioners embark on a level of creative and innovative resistance, carrying out what they believe are the core priorities of their work of supporting people against a backdrop of pressure to focus more on risk-oriented approaches.

Further efforts are warranted as a matter of urgency to better recognise and raise awareness about the various strengths of the two fields and their actors. Rehabilitation work may be difficult work, but it need not be 'dirty words' or 'dirty work'. Practitioners, organisations and the AOD community sector peak body continue to raise good ideas and potential strategies for how this might be done, in this book as well as in public documentation, for example, budget submissions and media interviews. Sectoral advocacy and actively shifting discourses and promoting awareness raising needs to be a shared endeavour – one which also implicates academia, the media, and governments. Yet it is vitally important that change in rehabilitation work and the field is motivated and co-produced by practitioners, alongside service users, that is co-produced change, not top-down strategies. A significant amount of the data from Tasmanian practitioners is imbued with resilience and hope, demonstrating how much they care about what they do and that they are good at what they do, despite the challenges. Their concerns tend to converge on issues of culture and sustainability as well as a desire to *be the change*, to be actively engaged in service and sectoral reform processes, instead of being *subject to change*, passively responsible for coping with the changing goal posts as governments stop and start funding cycles, and pilot or decommission key projects. The issues, then, of 'dirty work' do not stem from a perception among practitioners that what they do with people is 'bad' or 'unworthy'. Quite the opposite, many practitioners, as explained in Chapter 5, cite the reasons for staying in their job and their sector as being centred on the service users with whom they work. Practitioners *enjoy* supporting desistance and recovery, and believe that they bring skills and expertise to this process that transcend narrow conceptions of managing risk in knowledge-based work. What they don't enjoy is the pejorative stereotyping and pressures to change their work, as though what they do is not sufficiently valued and recognised. Wider risk-oriented policies of reducing re-offending and reducing rates and the burden of addiction may be implicated in contributing to the pressures imposed on them. It is their field of work that bears further examination as to how to shift professional and public discourses to be better recognise the realities of who they are and what they really do.

3

THREE NARRATIVES AND A FUNERAL

Community punishment in England and Wales

Gwen Robinson

Introduction

Among the jurisdictions represented in this book, it is probably fair to say that England and Wales is an extreme case in respect of the amount of recent and ongoing turbulence, both in the domain of 'community punishment' and in the surrounding penal field. It is also perhaps atypical by virtue of being a jurisdiction in which the notion of *punishment in the community* has precise – and relatively recent – origins. Today, the concept itself is hardly contested as a way of describing the field, albeit that the origins of 'probation' lie in ideas about the provision of constructive *alternatives* to punishment, and at least some practitioners in the field would seek to minimise their role in the delivery of 'punishment' (understood as something negative or painful).

This chapter begins by considering the foundations of community punishment in England and Wales, before moving on to analyse its evolution in the twentieth century. This account focuses mainly on developments since the 1980s, in the wake of a collapse in confidence in the 'rehabilitative ideal' which formerly dominated the field. It is argued that community sanctions and measures have managed to claw back legitimacy by means of their appeal to three dominant narratives, which are characterised as 'managerial', 'punitive' and 'rehabilitative'. Despite some potential for conflict between them, these narratives are largely intertwined or 'braided' (Hutchinson 2006) in policy and practice, such that both 'old' and 'new' ways of representing community punishment tend to collude in the legitimation of community punishment in the present. The chapter proceeds to consider the present state and future legitimacy of community punishment, with reference to the contemporary programme of reform which is in the process of breaking up a probation service which, for the past 100 years, has enjoyed primary responsibility for delivering punishment in the community, as well as respect across Europe.

Foundations

In England and Wales, the origins of contemporary forms of community punishment are, somewhat paradoxically, to be found in a system of probation established in the early part of the twentieth century explicitly as an *alternative* to punishment and sanctioning. In other words, probation started out as a 'measure' rather than a 'sanction', and its use was restricted to those deemed worthy or deserving of an opportunity to reform in the absence of formal punishment. In his influential study of *Punishment & Welfare* at the turn of the twentieth century, Garland (1985) argued that the establishment of probation at this time was evidence of a penal system newly alive to ideas about the possibility of offender reform, and about bringing the character and history of the individual offender into the calculus of penal thought. Garland (1985, 2001) has described the establishment of probation as one of the key elements in the development of a distinctly modern 'penal-welfare' complex, one which survived until the 1970s.

The roots of this formal system of probation, conceived of as a mode of 'reformative diversion', have been traced back to the 1820s and began in relation to juveniles, later being extended to some adult offenders (Vanstone 2004). Edward Cox, a sentencer in Portsmouth, began the practice of releasing 'suitable' offenders on recognisance, a strategy which became the basis of the Summary Jurisdiction Act of 1879. This Act permitted a conditional discharge on the giving of sureties for good behaviour or reappearance for sentence. Cox believed that this was suitable for unpractised offenders in that it offered them 'a chance of redemption under the most favourable circumstances' (Cox 1877, quoted in Radzinowicz and Hood 1990: 634). A parallel development sprang from the 'rescue' work of the Church of England Temperance Society (CETS), established in 1862 with a view to tackling the problem of drunkenness and the reformation of the intemperate (Vanstone 2004). The extension of the CETS' work with offenders led to the practice of attaching missionaries to the criminal courts – initially in London, but later elsewhere – with a view to 'saving the souls' of those habitual drunkards released to their care and oversight (McWilliams 1983). Between 1880 and 1894 the number of full-time missionaries working in the courts increased from eight to seventy (Radzinowicz and Hood 1990). The police court missionaries were pioneers in the sense that 'they developed the concept of social workers working in and for the courts; they [also] provided the rudiments of the techniques of individual concern for and a personal relationship with, offenders in the open' (Jarvis 1972: 9). By the late 1870s the CETS had extended its focus to include discharged prisoners, who were offered help with accommodation, employment and the like, as well as being invited to sign a pledge of abstinence on release (Ayscough 1923, cited in Vanstone 2004: 8).

Another influential late-nineteenth-century figure in probation's 'pre-history' was Howard Vincent, a lawyer and former Director of Criminal Investigation at Scotland Yard. In the 1880s, Vincent became the most persistent promoter of the cause to offer first offenders, both juvenile and adult, a chance of reform without recourse to the contaminating prison environment. In 1886, having visited Boston, Massachusetts where an early system of probation was in operation, Vincent introduced the Probation of First Offenders Bill. This Bill proposed that any person without previous convictions be released on probation, subject to a form of police supervision modelled on the 'ticket of leave' system (an early version of parole). In a letter to *The Times*, Vincent explained that his proposed scheme was designed 'to save hundreds from a habitual life of crime, to give back to the State many an honest citizen, and to save the pockets of the taxpayer' (26 July 1886, quoted in Vanstone 2004: 17). Although the resulting Act was a drastically amended version of Vincent's Bill, devoid of any formal supervision component, it did constitute evidence of a growing willingness to substitute consignment to a harsh prison regime with an opportunity to reform – albeit that this option was restricted to only those offenders deemed to deserve a 'second chance'.

We might summarise the 'founding narrative' of probation work in England and Wales as a reformative one – albeit fairly strictly limited to the 'deserving' and potentially 'corrigible' among the offending population, deemed worthy of a chance to avoid, or (in the case of ex-prisoners) receive help to mitigate, the moral and social damage caused by imprisonment.

Development: The twentieth century

There is a good number of published accounts of the development of what we describe in this book as 'community punishment' in England and Wales, and all tend towards periodisation, whereby separate eras or phases are identified, albeit differently labelled (McWilliams 1985, 1986, 1987; Bottoms *et al.* 2004). Thus, for example, they all describe the evolution of probation practice in the early decades of the twentieth century under the influence of the emerging discipline of psychology and the development of social casework. In this context, early ideas about the moral reformation of offenders gradually gave way to a discourse centred on diagnosis, treatment and rehabilitation, and University-based training for probation officers was introduced (Raynor and Robinson 2009). McWilliams (1986) has characterised this transition (between the late 1930s and the 1960s) in terms of a shift from the *phase of special pleading* to the *phase of diagnosis*.

Existing accounts also identify a growing crisis of confidence in rehabilitation in the 1960s and 1970s – a crisis which affected penal systems both in England and Wales and the United States – as a key turning-point in the development of probation. The so-called collapse of the rehabilitative ideal (Allen 1981) in these countries was the outcome of a three-pronged attack on rehabilitation which exposed serious weaknesses in terms of its theoretical basis, its ethical credentials and its effectiveness in terms of achieving demonstrable reductions in reoffending on the part of 'treated' individuals. In *The Culture of Control*, Garland (2001) describes the profound effects of what he terms a 'crisis of penal modernism' on those parts of the penal systems in England and Wales and the USA which had traditionally or latterly derived their legitimacy from ideas about 'normalisation', reform and rehabilitation. In England

and Wales, although it has been acknowledged that faith in rehabilitation did not collapse overnight – and, as Vanstone (2004) has argued, certainly did not evaporate among employees of the probation service – there nonetheless followed a period of uncertainty during which the probation service was extremely vulnerable to the charge that it could no longer command legitimacy (Raynor and Robinson 2009). This, then, was a period in which new justifications for existing penal structures and practices were urgently needed.

This was, however, also a period during which a growing prison population was causing concern among policymakers (Home Office 1977), and these twin problems were to provide fertile ground for the development of certain new community-based sanctions and measures in the next decade or so. The Criminal Justice Act 1967 had introduced parole for certain categories of ex-prisoner, and a further Criminal Justice Act in 1972 ushered in the community service order (requiring offenders to perform unpaid work in the community), which was intended to offer sentencers a direct alternative to custody.[1] By the end of the 1970s, academic commentators had begun to recognise the potential for probation to relegitimise itself with reference to 'systemic' concerns: specifically, by asserting the potential of probation to divert offenders from the more expensive and harmful sanction of imprisonment (Bottoms and McWilliams 1979). Thus began what, in historical accounts of probation, has generally been characterised as an era of 'pragmatism' (McWilliams 1987) or, more commonly, 'alternatives to custody'. Probation thus adopted a new, much more modest principal rationale, as 'a non-custodial penalty aiming to increase its market share and reduce imprisonment, rather than a "treatment" aiming to change people' (Raynor 1997: 27).

Contemporary narratives

Looking back at the development of community sanctions and measures over the last 25 years or so, we can see a growing consciousness of the 'systemic' role of probation and newer community sanctions and measures as a key part of an evolutionary process by which they have sought to rebuild their legitimacy. In other words, and following Robinson *et al.* (2013), a 'managerial' narrative for community sanctions and measures is an important part of the story of their adaptation and survival into the present. It is not, however, the whole story. I shall argue that we cannot fully comprehend the recent history of community sanctions and measures in the Anglo-Welsh context without also attending to two other major narrative strands which emphasise, respectively, the purported punitive and rehabilitative qualities of such interventions. Each of these three narrative strands represents one of the principal ways in which community sanctions and measures have evolved and sought legitimacy in a changing penal field.[2] I argue that the coexistence of these narratives is evidence that we have not (yet) seen the emergence of a single replacement discourse or 'meta-narrative' for community sanctions and measures in England and Wales.

237

A 'managerial' narrative

At the heart of most accounts of managerialism in the penal field has been the notion of *systemisation*; that is, the transformation of what was formerly a series of relatively independent services or agencies (courts, police, prisons, probation services etc.) into an interlinking 'system'. For Bottoms (1995), this process of systemisation has, in most jurisdictions, tended to embrace characteristics such as an emphasis on inter-agency cooperation in order to fulfil the overall goals of the system; mission statements for individual criminal justice agencies which serve those general system goals; and the creation of 'key performance indicators' for individual agencies which tend to emphasise the efficiency of internal processes rather than 'effectiveness' in relation to any overarching objective. As Garland (1996) has observed, systemisation has enabled the common adoption of a variety of devices to deal with the problem of crime in a reconfigured field characterised by an acceptance of crime as a 'normal social fact': that is, as a risk to be managed rather than a social problem to be eliminated. The key imperatives of a 'managerial' penology are thus focused on the limited goals of 'managing a permanently dangerous population while maintaining the system at a minimum cost' (Feeley and Simon 1992: 463).

In England and Wales, there have been many examples of the recasting of community sanctions and measures in ways that have emphasised their systemic legitimacy: that is, their value in serving the needs of a penal system which has been increasingly under strain. This was perhaps first evident in the adoption in the 1980s (described above) of a pragmatic rationale which emphasised the provision of credible 'alternatives to custody'. Here, the primary motivation for increasing the market share of probation and community service orders was to relieve pressure on (and the expense of) prison places (Raynor 1988). Another important example concerns the extension of post-custodial supervision of ex-prisoners subject to conditional release from custody – a population which in many jurisdictions has been escalating (Padfield *et al.* 2010). Increases in rates of imprisonment and sentence lengths have encouraged the increased use of the 'safety valve' of early release mechanisms which, in turn, have brought greater numbers of individuals under the remit of post-custodial supervision (on licence or parole) (Cavadino and Dignan 2007). For example, the Criminal Justice Act 2003 extended automatic conditional release at the half-way point of sentences of imprisonment to all prisoners serving standard determinate sentences[3] of 12 months or more and increased the length of the non-custodial element of most custodial sentences. The effect of this was an increase in the population of ex-prisoners subject to supervision (on licence) by the probation service. Between 2003 and 2013, the number of prisoners (pre- and post-release) subject to supervision by the probation service rose by 37 per cent (from just over 80,000 to over 110,000) (Ministry of Justice 2014a, Table A4.13).

These developments have been underpinned by a shifting understanding of the probation service and its employees as 'partners' working cooperatively with other parts of the system, such as police and prison services, where previously ideological conflict would have made such partnerships problematic, if not unthinkable.

In England and Wales, formal partnerships have emerged since the late 1990s between police and probation services to manage various categories of 'high risk' individuals in the community, resulting in formal Multi-Agency Public Protection Arrangements (Kemshall and Maguire 2001). More recently, police and probation services have also teamed up in new local structures called Integrated Offender Management teams, which have focused their efforts on the oversight of high-risk offenders released from custody but not necessarily subject to mandatory supervision (Wong 2013). We have also seen attempts to create a US-style 'correctional services' structure, in the guise of a National Offender Management Service (NOMS), combining prisons and probation in the pursuit of the common goal of 'public protection' (Raynor and Vanstone 2007).

Meanwhile, some of the features of the so-called new penology described by Feeley and Simon (1992) in the US context have become evident in England and Wales, most notably in the emergence and spread of new, actuarial technologies oriented to the assessment of risk and (importantly) the rationing of resources in line with those assessments (Robinson 2002). We have also seen the emergence and spread of new types of surveillant sanction oriented to what Feeley and Simon refer to as 'management in place'. The growing popularity of electronically monitored curfews and drug testing (which may be conditions of community sentences or post-custodial supervision on licence) are among the best examples of this trend towards an emphasis on the *management of risks* which offenders may pose and the deployment of new technologies to detect non-compliance with specified standards of behaviour (see Nellis 2010).

The emergence in the last decade of a discourse of 'offender management' in England and Wales is, however, perhaps the most prominent example of the sorts of trends I am describing. In 2005 the probation service implemented an 'offender management model' (OMM), developed by senior managers seconded to NOMS, which consolidated an approach towards offender supervision which had already become preoccupied with risk assessment (Robinson 2005). The OMM identified four levels or 'tiers' to which offenders were to be allocated, each implying a different focus and intensity of supervision. The tiers, labelled 'punish', 'help', 'change' and 'control', were designed to be cumulative, such that every offender would receive 'punishment', most would additionally receive 'help', fewer still would also be expected to 'change', and – reflecting their high-risk status – the final group would be primarily subject to 'control'. This illustrates very well how a fundamentally managerial approach towards offenders subject to statutory supervision in the community – that is, an approach centred on classification and differential resource allocation – has become a firmly embedded and taken-for-granted approach. It also illustrates, however, the continuing currency of other narratives for such supervision; among these, rehabilitation (implied by 'change') and, arguably at the heart of the model, in the common denominator of 'punishment', a narrative centred on making offenders feel the 'punitive weight' of the sanctions and measures to which they were subject. It is to the growing resonance of a punitive narrative for community punishment that I shall turn next.

A punitive narrative

For many advocates of community sanctions and measures, perhaps especially in European jurisdictions, the idea that these might have a deliberately punitive dimension is anathema. Traditionally, such sanctions have been associated not just with the provision of welfare, but also the avoidance of state punishment. As already noted in this chapter, the probation order established in England and Wales by the 1907 Probation of Offenders Act enjoyed the legal status of an alternative to punishment. That said, such 'alternatives' have always involved the exercise of power and control over individuals, albeit a 'softer' form of power than the prison. Drawing on Foucault's (1977) argument concerning the 'power of normalisation', Garland (1985) noted that the new regime of probation established in England and Wales in the early twentieth century represented not just a more humane response to crime, but also a more extensive and subtle network of control. Community sanctions and measures have also tended to be backed up by the possibility of other punitive sanctions in the face of non-compliance (see Raynor and Vanstone 2007; Robinson 2013).

In England and Wales in the last 25 years or so, we have seen a growing tendency to expose and enhance the 'punitive credentials' of community sanctions and measures. As I have argued elsewhere (Robinson *et al.* 2013), this has to be understood in the context of at least two developments in the Anglo-Welsh context. The first concerns the adoption of a desert-based sentencing framework in the early 1990s, a policy development which once again followed the lead of the USA and which embraced the so-called justice model (American Friends Service Committee 1971; von Hirsch 1976). Although largely driven by liberal intentions to reduce the use of custody, the introduction of desert-based sentencing necessitated thinking more consciously about penalties of all kinds in relation to their retributive content, or 'punitive weight'. Probation and community service orders thus came to be reconceptualised and calibrated along a new 'continuum of punishment', within which they were viewed as 'middle range' punishments between custody and financial penalties; that is, relatively inexpensive but nonetheless tough penalties for those guilty of less serious offences (Home Office 1990; Mair 1997). In this context, the constructive potential of such sanctions arguably became less important than their retributive qualities, which could be measured in length, intensity and intrusiveness. The 1991 Criminal Justice Act, which implemented a sentencing framework based on desert, thus inaugurated the concept of 'punishment in the community' which has had currency in England and Wales ever since (Worrall 1997).

The other key driver of the punitive narrative in England and Wales has been the politicisation of crime and criminal justice, and the increasing resort on the part of politicians and policymakers to 'populist punitiveness' or 'penal populism' (Bottoms 1995; Pratt *et al.* 2005). Much has been written in England and Wales about the increasing politicisation of 'law and order' issues (particularly since 1993[4]) and the impact of this on crime-control policy. For example, writing a decade ago, Michael Tonry described the recent history of crime control policy in this jurisdiction as 'tumultuous and schizophrenic' (2004: 1). Tonry evidenced the 'tumult' in the sheer quantity of change witnessed in the preceding decade, and the 'schizophrenia' in the 'sometimes startling contrast between the [then Labour] government's claim to engage in "evidence-based" policy-making, and its determination always and on all issues, no matter what the evidence may show, to be seen as "tough on crime"' (2004: 1). Commentators have also noted the tendency of politicians in the UK parliament to look to the USA, rather than to other parts of Europe, for policy inspiration. For example, Newburn (2007) argues that the Labour Party's rebranding as the party of law and order in the early 1990s followed the example of the US Democratic Party in the wake of the Republicans' electoral victory in 1988. At this time, the shift in Democratic penal policy was in a more punitive direction and this was premised on three core messages taken from that election: that crime had the potential to be a key issue in elections; that candidates should at all costs avoid being seen as 'soft on crime'; and that, irrespective of the substance of any policies they may endorse, candidates must appear 'tough'. It was these lessons, Newburn (2007) argues, which the Labour party took to heart in the mid-1990s and which have arguably shaped penal politics in England and Wales ever since.

Not surprisingly, much of the commentary and critique related to the politicisation of crime control in England and Wales has centred on imprisonment. Between 1993 and 2012 the prison population increased by more than 100 per cent, from 41,800 prisoners to over 86,000 (Ministry of Justice 2013a). Less attention has been paid to the impact of a 'punitive turn' in penal policy on non-custodial sanctions and measures. However, the impact has been significant. First of all, community sanctions such as probation have met with relentless criticism for being too 'soft' or too closely aligned with the needs and/or interests of those convicted of crimes, rather than those of the 'law-abiding majority' or victims of crime (Home Office 2006). One result of this, also in the mid-1990s, was that the Conservative Home Secretary Michael Howard took the decision to sever the longstanding connection between probation and the social work profession, repealing the need for probation officers to hold a social work qualification.[5] At this time, probation officers in England and Wales not only ceased to be social workers, but also saw the context for their work change, from a social work agency, to a 'law enforcement agency' (National Probation Service 2001). In this process the service lost any claim to an identity or pursuit of purposes defined outside government policy (Robinson and McNeill 2004).

Since then, we have witnessed numerous attempts to 'toughen up' both the discourse around community sanctions and measures and the experience of being subject to them. For example, we have seen the rebranding of existing sanctions in ways which have emphasised their retributive or punitive orientation. A good example here is community service, originally made available in the 1970s. In 2008 the UK Cabinet Office published a report which proposed building public confidence in what by then was being called 'unpaid work' by rebranding it as 'community payback'. The author of the report, Louise Casey, suggested that the work involved should not be something the general public would choose to do themselves (i.e. it should be unfulfilling and unpleasant) and that individuals performing it should wear high-visibility vests identifying them to members of

241

the public (Casey 2008; Maruna and King 2008). In 2013, one of the pioneers of community service in England (and until 2001 a chief probation officer) published an article in a leading British newspaper to mark the fortieth anniversary of the introduction of community service (Harding 2013). His article posed the question: 'How did a measure that required offenders to carry out socially beneficial work turn into a form of punishment?'

We have also seen the creation of a variety of new, more 'intensive' sanctions. Examples from the late 1990s include the Combination Order, which combined in one sentence probation supervision and community service. The 1990s also witnessed the introduction of technological innovations to increase the 'punitive bite' of community sanctions or to increase the restrictions placed on offenders under supervision in the community. Thus in the 1990s we saw the introduction of the curfew with electronic monitoring, the Drug Treatment and Testing Order and the Home Detention Curfew scheme for prisoners subject to early release. The Criminal Justice Act 2003 subsequently did away with the existing suite of community sentences and in their place introduced a single community sentence, the Community Order, to be made up of any combination of twelve requirements, including: supervision, unpaid work, a treatment programme, a curfew, and so on.[6] The 2003 Act also introduced a new hybrid custodial–community sentence called the Suspended Sentence Order (SSO), which enabled sentencers to suspend a period of imprisonment whilst also imposing on offenders any combination of the same twelve requirements that could be attached to a Community Order (Mair et al. 2007). More recently (2008–2011) we have seen trials of Intensive Alternatives to Custody (IAC) – combining intensive supervision with additional 'demanding requirements and interventions delivered by partner agencies' – intended to divert offenders from short-term custodial sentences (Mews and Coxon 2014: 2).

A further development connected to the 'penalisation' of community sanctions and measures has been a lowering of tolerance in respect of failures to comply (Robinson and Ugwudike 2012; Robinson 2013). According to the Ministry of Justice, harsher 'enforcement outcomes' have made a significant contribution to the rising prison population in the last decade or so. Indeed, Ministry of Justice data indicate a staggering 470 per cent increase in the numbers of offenders imprisoned for breaches of community-based sentences between 1995 and 2009, whilst in the same period the rise in the population of offenders recalled to prison while on licence was 37-fold (Ministry of Justice 2009). It is also worth noting that the traditional requirement of an offender's consent to a community order has become irrelevant in most cases[7] (Raynor 2014).

In 2013, legislation[8] was introduced requiring courts to include a 'punitive requirement' in all community sentences for adults, having already extended the maximum length of curfews and the number of hours offenders can be required to perform unpaid work. A press release announcing this development said:

> In a move to improve public confidence in community sentences, adult sentences will now have to include some form of punishment. [From

11 December] Most sentences will contain an element of formal punishment such as a fine, unpaid work, curfew or exclusion from certain areas. This could affect around 40,000 offenders per year.

(Ministry of Justice 2013b)

There is ample evidence, then, that the evolution of community sanctions and measures in England and Wales has been characterised by increasing attention to and emphasis on their punitive weight, such that the idea of punishment in the community has, since 1994, increased its purchase.

A 'rehabilitative' narrative

In the 1980s and early 1990s, following the so-called collapse of the rehabilitative ideal, several commentators argued that rehabilitation was dead and buried. Heavily influenced by the 'new penology' thesis emanating from the USA at that time, some saw the emergence of risk-based thinking in the probation service as evidence of a decisive paradigm shift, signalling the demise of 'transformative optimism' among those responsible for supervising offenders in the community. For example, Kemshall *et al.* (1997) argued that the new centrality of risk and risk assessment in the probation service indicated that the service was:

> engaged in a transition from the traditional concerns of the rehabilitative and welfare arm of criminal justice [. . .] and the language of 'need' to an agency of crime control concerned with the accurate prediction and effective management of offender risk.
>
> *(1997: 217)*

Rumours of the death of rehabilitation, however, turned out to be greatly exaggerated, as a resurgent rehabilitative ideal did in fact emerge. Starting in the late 1980s in North America, what came to be known as a 'What Works?' movement was enthusiastically taken up by a small group of British academic researchers who spread news of the revitalisation of rehabilitation via a series of conferences and workshops with both academic and practitioner participants (McGuire 1995). Ever since then, rehabilitation has crept back into penal policy: for example, being declared one of five legitimate rationales for sentencing in the Criminal Justice Act 2003 (s.42);[9] explicitly underpinning several of the conditions which may be attached to a community order or suspended sentence order; and featuring prominently in the current government's headline penal policy of a 'Rehabilitation Revolution' (Ministry of Justice 2010).

This is not, however, to say that in England and Wales we have somehow turned back time, revisiting modes of rehabilitation prominent in early mid-twentieth-century probation practice. We should not overlook the ways in which rehabilitation has been transformed and remarketed in recent years, such that, far from going against the grain of broader penal developments, it has been rendered compatible with them. As I have argued elsewhere, it is more accurate to talk of the *evolution* of rehabilitation than of its survival or revival, the latter being terms which imply a somewhat static (and inaccurate) picture (Robinson 2008). This evolutionary process has produced visions and modes of rehabilitation in the community sanctions context that have diverged from earlier incarnations in important ways, as I shall outline below.

Firstly, the 'new' rehabilitation has had to adapt to social and political contexts which have become increasingly intolerant of approaches and interventions that appear to put the needs and interests of offenders above those of (actual and potential) victims. This has meant that proponents of rehabilitation have had to de-emphasise its welfarist, humanitarian and essentially offender-centred justifications, in favour of rationales which emphasise the instrumental and more broadly 'utilitarian' value of rehabilitative sanctions. David Garland (1997: 6) was among the first to observe this realignment of rehabilitation in England and Wales when he observed that probation workers had come to 'emphasise that "rehabilitation" is necessary for the protection of the public. It is future victims who are now "rescued" by rehabilitative work, rather than the offenders themselves'. This idea that the legitimacy of contemporary rehabilitation rests on a utilitarian justification (Robinson 2008) helps to explain the spread of 'offending behaviour programmes' under the auspices of the 'What Works?' movement, the resurgence of interest and investment in the re-entry or resettlement of ex-prisoners (Farrall and Sparks 2006) and, most recently, official interest in the findings of research on desistance from offending (McNeill 2006). Thus, for example, what at first sight appears to indicate a heightened concern among policymakers with the welfare and reintegration of ex-offenders or a desire to undo the harmful consequences of imprisonment is, today, arguably more an expression of concern for the communities to which most prisoners ultimately return and resume their lives.

A related point is that rehabilitation has come to be understood less as an end in itself than as a means to other ends (Garland 1997, 2001). Specifically, rehabilitation has come to be understood as part of a toolkit of measures oriented towards the protection of the public and the management of risk. Thus, we have tended to see the repositioning of rehabilitative measures within managerial systems which have come to be dominated by the discourse of risk. In this regard, rehabilitation has not only come to be reconceived of as a means of achieving risk reduction or management, but it is also increasingly rationed in line with assessments of risk which determine the eligibility of offenders for rehabilitative interventions. Such an approach secures a space for rehabilitation among the range of legitimate responses to offending, but limits its reach and influence in new ways. I have already referred (above) to the risk-driven, differentiated approach which characterises the offender management model of probation practice which was introduced in England and Wales in 2005 (see Robinson 2005). As previously noted, this model uses the logic of risk to determine the level of resource appropriate to individual offenders. Only the third tier, 'change', contains an explicitly disciplinary or rehabilitative element, and it is targeted at those posing a medium to high risk of reoffending. This explicitly actuarial model illustrates quite clearly that contemporary rehabilitative interventions are far from inimical to managerial systems.

That said, the reframing of rehabilitation in risk-management terms and regimes has not simply entailed putting a new spin on the same old product. Importantly, the product itself has adapted as part of the evolutionary process I have described. Whilst it is probably unwise to characterise contemporary rehabilitative sanctions and measures as if they were a unified product, it is probably fair to say that, among these, the most explicitly rehabilitative are those offending behaviour programmes which emerged under the banner of the 'What Works?' movement alluded to above. Based on cognitive-behavioural principles and methods, the new offending behaviour programmes proliferated and spread throughout England and Wales in the 1990s, backed by some evidence of their effectiveness in reducing reoffending. At the same time the government convened an expert (accreditation) panel to ensure that programmes that were to receive public resources were in line with contemporary evidence about 'what works' (Raynor and Robinson 2009).

The crime reduction potential of rehabilitative programmes and interventions has then been a major selling point for their inclusion as part of community sanctions in the late twentieth century context and beyond. However, some have argued that we should not attribute the 'new' legitimacy of such interventions solely to their (putative) instrumental effectiveness. For some commentators, the dominance of cognitive-behavioural programmes in England and Wales (and elsewhere) is at least in part attributable to their expressive and communicative qualities and their resonance with advanced liberal forms of governance which emphasise personal responsibility for wrongdoing, and rely upon strategies of 'responsibilization' as the dominant response to anti-social behaviour (Garland 1996; Kendall 2004; Rose 2000). The same has been said of the contemporary resurgence of interest in restorative justice approaches in England and Wales (Dignan 2005). Both modes of intervention, it has been argued, seek to engage offenders in a 'moral discourse' which both communicates censure and seeks to instil in offenders both a measure of victim empathy and a new 'moral compass' which, it is hoped, will dissuade them from future offending (see also Duff 2001). The 'rehabilitated' offender, then, tends to be presented as an individual capable of managing his or her own risks without recourse to externally imposed sanctions or controls, and without making any claims on the state in terms of its duties to create opportunities for reform and reintegration.

Thriving – or just surviving? Analysing trends in community punishment

In this chapter I have focused on what I see as the three main narratives that have underpinned the development of community sanctions and measures in England and Wales in the last 25 years. Until now, it would appear, these narratives have more or less sustained community punishment as a legitimate endeavour – albeit one lacking the kind of 'transcendent justification' which McWilliams and Pease (1990) saw as essential to the longevity of the probation service. However, important questions remain about just how successful the adaptations I have described have been in terms of securing a bigger 'market share' for community punishment and, in particular, its impact on the use of imprisonment.

When we consider the proportion of convictions which resulted in a community sentence between 1978 and 2008, we see a gradual increase in their popularity with the courts. The market share of community sentences rose from 3.5 per cent in 1978 to 6.1 per cent in 1988 and then to 10.2 per cent in 1998, reaching a high of 14 per cent in 2008 (Ministry of Justice 2014b, Table A1.1). At first sight these statistics appear to signal good news for advocates of community sentences. However, there are two additional factors to consider. The first is that the growing popularity of community sentences has not coincided with a reducing market share for imprisonment; indeed, rates of imprisonment have increased in parallel. The second is that whilst community sentences have been used more, the use of fines has dropped considerably.[10] The overall trend, then, has been one of 'up-tariffing', such that sentencing, generally, has become harsher (Ministry of Justice 2013b).

Since 2008, the market share of community sentences has dropped steadily, from 14 per cent to 10.5 per cent in 2013 (Ministry of Justice 2014b, Table A1.1). Although it is not entirely clear why the popularity of community sentences has waned in this period, an important factor has been the introduction (in 2005) of the SSO (in 2005, under the Criminal Justice Act 2003), which offered sentencers the possibility of combining a suspended custodial sentence with a range of possible community-based requirements. This sentence has proven extremely popular with sentencers looking for an alternative to immediate custody, and the SSO has therefore displaced a potentially large number of community sentences in recent years (Mair *et al.* 2007) (see Figure 3.1).

Meanwhile, recently published statistics indicate that the total annual caseload carried by the probation service increased by 39 per cent between 2000 and 2008, reaching a high of 243,434 offenders at the end of that period (Ministry of Justice 2014c). Since then, however, the probation caseload has fallen year on year, to 219,588 at the end of 2013 (see Figure 3.2).

There are a number of important points to emphasise here. The first is that the 'probation caseload' referred to above is something of a 'mixed bag'; it includes offenders on community sentences, but also those subject to SSOs with community-based requirements, as well as offenders whose custodial sentence includes a period of statutory supervision on licence post-release. Therefore, the probation caseload includes both ex-prisoners currently under supervision in the community on licence and some prisoners who have yet to be released but who are nonetheless allocated to a probation worker to prepare for release. One of the striking facts about the probation caseload, particularly since the implementation of the Criminal Justice Act 2003,[11] is the growing proportion of offenders on probation caseloads in the latter categories; that is, those subject to suspended sentences of imprisonment or pre- or post-release supervision. This trend will

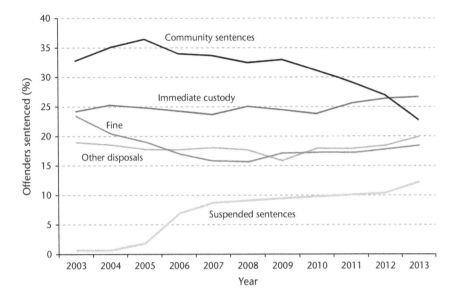

FIGURE 3.1 Sentencing outcomes for indictable offences at all courts, 2003–2013

Source: Ministry of Justice (2014b, Figure 5.2, p. 36). Available under the Open Government Licence.

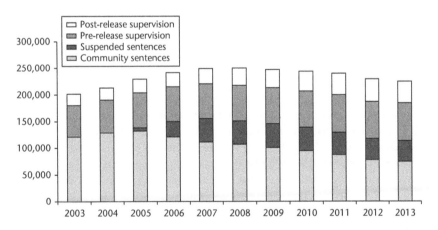

FIGURE 3.2 Number of offenders under Probation Service supervision (at end of December), 2003–2013

Source: Ministry of Justice (2014c, Figure 1.2, p. 12). Available under the Open Government Licence.

intensify when recent legislation[12] extending mandatory post-custodial supervision for sentences of less than 12 months comes into effect.

All of this means that the profile of 'community punishment' in England and Wales is changing, such that an increasing portion of it comprises quasi-custodial

provision (i.e. supervision pre- and post-release from custody, or alongside a suspended sentence of imprisonment), whilst the portion that comprises stand-alone
community sentences is reducing. It would appear, then, that attempts to rele-
gitimate community punishment have not been entirely successful, and there
are reasons to be concerned that the market share of community sentences may
continue on a downward curve in the foreseeable future, as I shall discuss below.

A new crisis of legitimacy?

At the time of writing, community punishment is subject to a widely contested
programme of reform known as 'Transforming Rehabilitation' (TR) (Ministry of
Justice 2013c; see also National Audit Office 2014; Annison *et al.* 2014). The TR
programme centres on the contracting out of the supervision of low- and medium-
risk offenders to providers from the private and not-for-profit sectors, whilst the
supervision of high-risk offenders remains in a shrunken public sector National
Probation Service (NPS). Its other major strand is the extension of mandatory post-
custodial supervision to short-term prisoners, as mentioned above. At the time of
writing, probation staff have been recently allocated to roles in either the NPS or
one of twenty-one new Community Rehabilitation Companies which are due to
be sold off towards the end of 2014.

The principal rationale offered by the Ministry of Justice for this drastic programme of reform is economic: the costs to the public purse of reoffending by known
offenders – particularly those released after short prison sentences – must be driven
down, and this is to be achieved by creating a 'market' in community punishment,
in which providers are incentivised by profit in a system of remuneration known as
'payment by results' (Hedderman 2013). Critics, however, argue that there is no evidence to support government forecasts of innovation, efficiency and effectiveness;
nor is it fair to blame the probation service – which has had no statutory responsibility
for the supervision of short-term prisoners – for this group's high reoffending rates.
Indeed, the available evidence indicates that there have been, over the past 10 years or
so, incremental reductions in reoffending by those subject to community sentences
under the supervision of public sector Probation Trusts[13] (Ministry of Justice 2014d,
Table 18a). It would therefore appear that a political ideology centred on the mar-
ketisation of public services has won through, with little to back it up besides a
purported 'lack of public confidence' in existing arrangements.[14]

In a recent newspaper headline, the Justice Secretary Chris Grayling was said to
be responsible for 'murdering the probation service' (Leftly 2014). Having already
been severed from their traditional roots in the profession of social work, probation
workers and their representatives have found themselves woefully undefended in
the struggle to maintain control over probation work. What we can tentatively say
about the TR reforms is that they will significantly widen the net of community
punishment (by introducing mandatory rehabilitative supervision to tens of thousands of short-term prisoners). We cannot, however, predict what the impact might
be on sentencing practice and more broadly the perceived legitimacy of community

sentences. How judges and magistrates will feel about passing community sentences to be managed by the new Community Rehabilitation Companies – at least some of which seem destined to fall into private ownership – remains to be seen (Allen 2013). The TR reforms are likely to normalise the idea of 'community punishment for profit' and the commodification of offenders as 'units' on a balance sheet (McCulloch and McNeill 2007; Robinson 2005). They may also drive large numbers of probation workers who, until now, have identified as public servants, out of the field. TR therefore offers a great deal of potential to deliver a new crisis of legitimacy for community punishment.

Reflections

The foregoing analysis seems to confirm much of what other analysts of the penal field and policy-making in England and Wales have sought to demonstrate – albeit that they have tended not to focus on the particular corner of the field occupied by community punishment (Lacey 2008; Cavadino and Dignan 2006; Cavadino et al. 2013; Tonry 2004). All of these accounts have drawn attention to the persistence of competing punishment narratives[15] and the chronic volatility of a penal field which has become less and less insulated from the adjacent political field. Whilst in this context ideas about evidence-based policy-making have not entirely lost their purchase, the influence of academics and others formerly recognised as 'experts' in the penal field has tended to wane in favour of lobbyists and 'think tanks' more closely aligned to the interests of particular political parties. Meanwhile, other influences have also been important and have contributed to the general volatility of the field. Economic hard times and calls for austerity across publically funded services have been one such influence. Another has been the rise of managerialism and with it the concept of 'risk' as a key organising principle in public and private domains.

As I have sought to demonstrate, the particular corner of the penal field occupied by community punishment has been deeply implicated in these various developments. Indeed, it is no exaggeration to say that, in the last 25 years, it has been in a state of almost constant flux. During this timeframe (1989–2014), the idea that we can identify distinct periods or phases in the development of community punishment has become untenable. This is not just because we cease to have a long-range view or because the pace and amount of change has intensified – although both are true (see Cavadino and Dignan 2006: Chapter 4). Rather, it is principally because the changes we can observe since the early 1990s have increasingly run in parallel, rather than in discrete, consecutive stages. Some of the time we have seen contradictions in the development of community punishments, as they have come to be pushed and pulled in a variety of directions under a range of different influences in and around the penal field. At other times, we have witnessed developments which have appeared to reflect a blending or 'braiding' (Hutchinson 2006) of different strategies and/or discourses. The picture, then, is rather complex and calls for a different approach from the traditional periodisation we see in most accounts of community punishment: one which can convey the very real variety of developments – both quantitative and qualitative – that are discernible from the perspective of the present.

I will conclude with a final observation about terminology in the English and Welsh context. I noted at the beginning of this chapter that the term 'punishment in the community' has specific origins in England and Wales in the penal policies of the early 1990s, and that the idea of 'community punishment' is therefore less controversial in this jurisdiction than it may be elsewhere in Europe. I would add, however, that 'punishment' is not, in the twenty-first century, entirely uncontentious (from the perspectives of at least some of those who work in the field); but neither is 'community'. Indeed, as it is applied to the penal field, 'community' has a somewhat vacuous character, tending to denote little more than a context outside the prison. As Bottoms (2008) has observed, recent years have seen a marked physical retreat of what we might loosely term 'probation work' from residential communities, as probation workers have increasingly based themselves in office locations, often some distance from the neighbourhoods in which their supervisees reside (see also Robinson et al. 2014; Phillips 2014). This, Bottoms argues, is a development to be regretted, for both instrumental and normative reasons. In England and Wales, then, community punishment may be very much alive in penal discourse, but is by no means an unproblematic notion.

Notes

1 The 1972 Act also empowered courts to attach supervision to certain suspended sentences.
2 The 'reparative' narrative outlined by Robinson et al. (2013) and in the introduction to this volume has played a less important role in England and Wales than it has elsewhere (e.g. in Scotland – see Chapter 10 of this volume).
3 Standard determinate sentences are custodial sentences of a fixed length (e.g. 10 weeks, 10 months, 10 years).
4 In May 1993 Michael Howard became Home Secretary and pursued a 'tough on crime' agenda, famously asserting in October 1993 in a conference speech that 'prison works'.
5 In 1997, a new 2-year training programme – the Diploma in Probation Studies – was introduced for those wishing to enter the probation service. This was revised again a decade later, but neither programme qualifies trainees to practise social work.
6 The creation of the Community Order prompted concerns that sentencers would be tempted to overload community sentences with multiple requirements, essentially setting them up to fail. However, recent statistics indicate that only about 13 per cent of Community Orders have three or more requirements, with an average of 1.6 (Ministry of Justice 2014a, Table A4.8).
7 The Crime (Sentences) Act 1997 removed the requirement for consent to a probation order.
8 Crime and Courts Act 2013.
9 These rationales are: the punishment of offenders; the reduction of crime (including its reduction by deterrence); the reform and rehabilitation of offenders; the protection of the public; and the making of reparation by offenders to persons affected by their offences.

10 In 1978 fines made up 85.8 per cent of sentences; in 2013 their use had dropped to just 67.8 per cent (Ministry of Justice 2014c, Table A1.1).
11 The Criminal Justice Act 2003 introduced the SSO and extended the length of licence periods for most prisoners.
12 Offender Rehabilitation Act 2014.
13 Electronic monitoring has been in the hands of private companies since it was introduced in the 1990s.
14 Although frequent, references in policy documents to poor public confidence in community sentences are rarely substantiated by research and, to the extent that public confidence is low, this is likely to reflect the low visibility and lack of public understanding of such sentences (Roberts and Hough 2005).
15 For example see the trio of contemporary penal strategies described by Cavadino *et al.* (2013: 6, 7). These are characterised as strategies A (highly punitive), B (managerialist) and C (human rights).

References

Allen, F. A. (1981) *The Decline of the Rehabilitative Ideal: Penal Policy and Social Purpose.* New Haven: Yale University Press.

Allen, R. (2013) 'Paying for justice: Prison and probation in an age of austerity', *British Journal of Community Justice*, 11(1): 5–18.

American Friends Service Committee (1971) *Struggle for Justice: A Report on Crime and Punishment in America.* New York: Hill and Wang.

Annison, J., Burke, L. and Senior, P. (2014) 'Transforming Rehabilitation: Another example of English "exceptionalism" or a blueprint for the rest of Europe?' *European Journal of Probation*, 6: 6–23.

Bottoms, A. E. (1995) 'The philosophy and politics of punishment and sentencing', in C. Clarkson and R. Morgan (eds) *The Politics of Sentencing Reform.* Oxford: Clarendon Press, pp. 7–49.

Bottoms, A. E. (2008) 'The community dimension of community penalties', *Howard Journal of Criminal Justice*, 47(2): 146–69.

Bottoms, A. E. and McWilliams, W. (1979) 'A non-treatment paradigm for probation practice', *British Journal of Social Work*, 9: 159–202.

Bottoms, A., Rex, S. and Robinson, G. (2004) 'How did we get here?', in A. Bottoms, S. Rex and G. Robinson (eds), *Alternatives to Prison: Options for an insecure society.* Cullompton, Devon: Willan, pp. 1–27.

Casey, L. (2008) *Engaging Communities in Fighting Crime: A Review (Casey Report).* London: Cabinet Office.

Cavadino, M. and Dignan, J. (2006) *Penal Systems: A Comparative Approach.* London: SAGE.

Cavadino, M. and Dignan, J. (2007) *The Penal System: An Introduction*, 4th edn. London: SAGE.

Cavadino, M., Dignan, J. and Mair, G. (2013) *The Penal System: An Introduction*, 5th edn. London: SAGE.

Dignan, J. (2005) *Understanding Victims and Restorative Justice.* Maidenhead: Open University Press.

Duff, A. (2001) *Punishment, Communication, and Community.* Oxford: Oxford University Press.

Farrall, S. and Sparks, R. (2006) 'Introduction', *Criminology and Criminal Justice*, 6(1): 7–17.

Feeley, M. and Simon, J. (1992) 'The new penology: notes on the emerging strategy of corrections and its implications', *Criminology*, 30: 449–74.

Foucault, M. (1977) *Discipline & Punish*. London: Allen Lane.

Garland, D. (1985) *Punishment and Welfare*. Aldershot: Gower.

Garland, D. (1996) 'The limits of the sovereign state: strategies of crime control in contemporary society', *British Journal of Criminology*, 36(4): 445–71.

Garland, D. (1997) 'Probation and the reconfiguration of crime control', in R. Burnett (ed.) *The Probation Service: Responding to Change* (Proceedings of the Probation Studies Unit First Colloquium), Oxford: University of Oxford Centre for Criminological Research, pp. 2–10.

Garland, D. (2001) *The Culture of Control*. Oxford: Oxford University Press.

Harding, J. (2013) 'Forty years of community service', *Guardian*, 8 January.

Hedderman, C. (2013) 'Payment by results: hopes, fears and evidence', *British Journal of Community Justice*, 11(2/3): 43–58.

Home Office (1977) *A Review of Criminal Justice Policy 1976*. London: HMSO.

Home Office (1990) *Crime, Justice & Protecting the Public* (Cm 965). London: HMSO.

Home Office (2006) *Rebalancing the Criminal Justice System in Favour of the Law-Abiding Majority: Cutting Crime, Reducing Re-offending and Protecting the Public*. London: Home Office.

Hutchinson, S. (2006) 'Countering catastrophic criminology: Reform, punishment and the modern liberal compromise', *Punishment and Society*, 8(4): 443–67.

Jarvis, F. (1972) *Advise, Assist and Befriend: A History of the Probation and After-Care Service*. London: NAPO.

Kemshall, H. and Maguire, M. (2001) 'Public protection, partnership and risk penality: the multi-agency risk management of sexual and dangerous offenders', *Punishment and Society*, 3(2): 237–64.

Kemshall, H., Parton, N., Walsh, M. and Waterson, J. (1997) 'Concepts of risk in relation to organizational structure and functioning within the personal social services and probation', *Social Policy and Administration*, 31: 213–32.

Kendall, K. (2004) 'Dangerous thinking: A critical history of correctional cognitive behaviouralism', in G. Mair (ed.) *What Matters in Probation*. Cullompton, Devon: Willan, pp. 53–89.

Lacey, N. (2008) *The Prisoners' Dilemma*. Cambridge: Cambridge University Press.

Leftly, M. (2014) 'Chris Grayling is accused of "murdering the probation service"', *Independent*, Sunday 17 August.

Mair, G. (1997) 'Community penalties and the probation service', in M. Maguire, R. Morgan and R. Reiner (eds) *The Oxford Handbook of Criminology* (2nd edn). Oxford: Clarendon Press, pp. 1195–232.

Mair, G., Cross, N. and Taylor, S. (2007) *The Use and Impact of the Community Order and the Suspended Sentence Order*. London: Centre for Crime and Justice Studies.

Maruna, S. and King, A. (2008) 'Selling the public on probation: beyond the bib', *Probation Journal*, 55: 337–51.

McCulloch, P. and McNeill, F. (2007) 'Consumer society, commodification and offender management', *Criminology and Criminal Justice*, 7(3): 223–42.

McGuire, J. (ed.) (1995) *What Works: Reducing Reoffending*. Chichester: Wiley.

McNeill, F. (2006) 'A desistance paradigm for offender management', *Criminology and Criminal Justice*, 6(1): 39–62.

McWilliams, W. (1983) 'The mission to the English police courts 1876–1936', *Howard Journal of Criminal Justice*, 22: 129–47.

McWilliams, W. (1985) 'The Mission transformed: Professionalism of probation between the wars', *Howard Journal of Criminal Justice*, 24: 257–74.

McWilliams, W. (1986) 'The English probation system and the diagnostic ideal', *The Howard Journal*, 25(4): 241–60.

McWilliams, W. (1987) 'Probation, pragmatism and policy', *The Howard Journal*, 26: 97–121.

McWilliams, W. and Pease, K. (1990) 'Probation practice and an end to punishment', *The Howard Journal*, 29: 14–24.

Mews, A. and Coxon, C. (2014) *Updated Analysis of the Impact of the Intensive Alternatives to Custody Pilots on Re-offending Rates* (Ministry of Justice Analytical Summary). London: Ministry of Justice.

Ministry of Justice (2009) *Story of the Prison Population 1995–2009 England and Wales*. London: Ministry of Justice.

Ministry of Justice (2010) *Breaking the Cycle: Effective Punishment, Rehabilitation and Sentencing of Offenders*. London: TSO.

Ministry of Justice (2013a) *Story of the Prison Population 1993–2012 England and Wales*. London: Ministry of Justice.

Ministry of Justice (2013b) 'Radical overhaul of sentencing continues', Press Release 2 December 2013. Available online at www.gov.uk/government/news/radical-overhaul-of-sentencing-continues (accessed 19 June 2014).

Ministry of Justice (2013c) Transforming Rehabilitation: A Strategy for Reform. (May 2013).

Ministry of Justice (2014a) Offender Management annual tables 2013. Available online at www.gov.uk/government/publications/offender-management-statistics-quarterly-october-december-2013-and-annual (accessed 23 June 2014).

Ministry of Justice (2014b) *Criminal Justice Statistics 2013*. (15 May 2014).

Ministry of Justice (2014c) *Offender Management Statistics Bulletin*. (24 April 2014).

Ministry of Justice (2014d) *Proven Reoffending Statistics Quarterly Bulletin: October 2011-September 2012, England & Wales*. London: Ministry of Justice (31 July 2014). Available online at www.gov.uk/government/collections/proven-reoffending-statistics (accessed 23 June 2014).

National Audit Office (2014) *Probation: Landscape Review*. London: National Audit Office.

National Probation Service/Home Office (2001) *A New Choreography*. London: Home Office.

Nellis, M. (2010) 'Electronic monitoring: towards integration into offender management', in F. McNeill, P. Raynor and C. Trotter (eds), *Offender Supervision: New Directions in Theory, Research and Practice*. Cullompton, Devon: Willan, pp. 509–33.

Newburn, T. (2007) '"Tough on crime": Penal policy in England & Wales', *Crime and Justice*, 36: 425–70.

Padfield, N., Van Zyl Smit, D. and Dünkel, F. (2010) *Release from Prison: European Policy and Practice*. Cullompton, Devon: Willan.

Phillips, J. (2014) 'The architecture of a probation office: A reflection of policy and an impact on practice', *Probation Journal*, 61(2): 117–31.

Pratt, J., Brown, D., Brown, M., Hallsworth, S. and Morrison, W. (eds) (2005) *The New Punitiveness: Trends, Theories, Perspectives*. Cullompton, Devon: Willan.

Radzinowicz, L. and Hood, R. (1990) *The Emergence of Penal Policy*. Oxford: Clarendon Press.

Raynor, P. (1988) *Probation as an Alternative to Custody*. Aldershot: Avebury.

Raynor, P. (1997) 'Evaluating probation: a moving target', in G. Mair (ed.) *Evaluating the Effectiveness of Community Penalties*. Aldershot: Avebury, pp. 19–33.

Raynor, P. (2014) 'Consent to probation in England & Wales: How it was abolished, and why it matters', *European Journal of Probation*, 6: 296–307.

Raynor, P. and Robinson, G. (2009) *Rehabilitation, Crime and Justice*. Basingstoke: Palgrave Macmillan.

Raynor, P. and Vanstone, M. (2007) 'Towards a correctional service', in L. Gelsthorpe and R. Morgan (eds) *Handbook of Probation*. Cullompton, Devon: Willan, pp. 59–89.

Roberts, J. and Hough, M. (2005) *Understanding Public Attitudes to Criminal Justice*. Maidenhead: Open University Press.

Robinson, G. (2002) 'Exploring risk management in the probation service: contemporary developments in England and Wales', *Punishment & Society*, 4(1): 5–25.

Robinson, G. (2005) 'What works in offender management?', *Howard Journal of Criminal Justice*, 44(3): 307–18.

Robinson, G. (2008) 'Late-modern rehabilitation: the evolution of a penal strategy', *Punishment and Society*, 10(4): 429–45.

Robinson, G. (2013) 'What counts? Community sanctions and the construction of compliance', in P. Raynor and P. Ugwudike (eds) *What Works in Offender Compliance: International Perspectives and Evidence-Based Practice*. Basingstoke: Palgrave Macmillan, pp. 26–43.

Robinson, G. and McNeill, F. (2004) 'Purposes matter: examining the 'ends' of probation practice', in G. Mair (ed.) *What Matters in Probation*. Cullompton, Devon: Willan, pp. 277–304.

Robinson, G. and Ugwudike, P. (2012) 'Investing in toughness: Probation, enforcement and legitimacy', *Howard Journal of Criminal Justice*, 51(3): 300–16.

Robinson, G., McNeill, F. and Maruna, S. (2013) 'Punishment in society: The improbable persistence of probation and other community sanctions and measures', in J. Simon and R. Sparks (eds) *Sage Handbook of Punishment and Society*. London: SAGE, pp. 321–40.

Robinson, G., Priede, C., Farrall, S., Shapland, J. and McNeill, F. (2014) 'Understanding "quality" in probation practice: Frontline perspectives in England & Wales', *Criminology and Criminal Justice*, 14(2): 123–42.

Rose, N. (2000) 'Government and control', *British Journal of Criminology* 40: 321–39.

Tonry, M. (2004) *Punishment and Politics*. Cullompton, Devon: Willan.

Vanstone, M. (2004) *Supervising Offenders in the Community*. Aldershot: Ashgate.

von Hirsch, A. (1976) *Doing Justice: The Choice of Punishments*. Report of the Committee for the Study of Incarceration. New York: Hill and Wang.

Wong, K. (2013) 'Integrated offender management: assessing the impacts and benefits – holy grail or fool's errand?', *British Journal of Community Justice*, 11(2/3): 59–81.

Worrall, A. (1997) *Punishment in the Community*. Cullompton, Devon: Willan.

Chapter 3

The Development of Penal and Correctional Policy and its Impact on Probation Practices and Culture

The New Penality

Legislation and Related Government Policy

In Garland's view, criminal justice professionals in the 1970s had their 'conceptual world turned upside down' by the increased use of custodial sentences and changes in policy (2001: 6). However, it was not until the 1990s that punishment became a prime and explicit penal objective, accompanied by the increased use of custody and changes to probation policy and practice designed to make it deliver 'punishment in the community', a 'new rehabilitation' and to assess and manage risk with a view to protecting the public.

Conservative governments from 1979 had wished to control the prison population, mainly for cost reasons and thus, for Pratt developed the principle of 'bifurcation' (2002: 166) which saw legal expression in the CJA 1982. This was intended to introduce a sentencing policy of longer custodial sentences for more serious offenders and the promotion of alternatives for those who did not pose a threat to society at large. Despite this overall objective, much of the rhetoric of this period was of the 'tough' variety. However, behind the scenes policy was somewhat different and more pragmatic, such as the quiet dropping of the 'short, sharp shock' regimes in youth Detention Centres when reconviction rates turned out to be extremely high (Cavadino and Dignan 2002: 291). In this way, the 1980s is seen as a period of paradox, when Conservative governments 'actually pursued policies of liberal reform' against a background of rising crime and the use of 'law and order' rhetoric which sought to deny any social and economic reasons for crime (Roberts et al. 2003: 44).

At the same time, the government was beginning to want to regulate the work of the probation service and direct it in other ways. The Statement of National Objectives and Priorities (SNOP, Home Office 1984) is regarded as the first attempt by government to set an agenda for the service and to begin to regulate its activities towards being increasingly concerned with efficiency and working with more serious and persistent offenders, something that continued throughout this period. Further changes followed: the Green Paper 'Punishment, Custody and the Community' (Home Office 1988) proposed that prison should be reserved for the most serious offenders and, in order to make this intention more palatable to its supporters, the purposes and aims of probation and non-custodial supervision were repackaged as 'punishment in the community'. At the same time, the Audit Commission in a report of 1989 (cited in Newburn 2003: 144) asserted that the probation service should work with more serious offenders, 'beef up' the content of supervision and thus increase the confidence of the courts in alternative to custody sentences. Whilst these views clearly reflected the lost faith in rehabilitation, they also perhaps saw the beginning of a belief that the relationship between the probation service and offenders should be one based increasingly on authority, rather than on a social work ethos of assistance.

The White Paper 'Crime, Justice and Protecting the Public' followed in 1990 (Home Office 1990). It was the basis of the CJA 1991 which stated that the service was now about punishment, management and systems, rather than any transformative agenda:

> ... the core task ... of the service ... is the strategic management and administration of punishments in the community. (Home Office 1991)

However the Act can be seen to have a range of objectives, including notions of proportionality, 'just deserts' and the limiting of the use of custody. Initially, the Act achieved one of its aims, that of the reduction in the use of custody. This was achieved mainly via the creation of sentencing bands which forced courts to legally justify the use of custody and the '1 plus 1' principle which prevented courts citing previous convictions of persistent offenders to make the current offence 'so serious' as to justify custody. Effective from October 1992, the use of custody did drop until mid 1993, when the passing of the CJA 1993 meant a reversal of these policies and the beginning of the increase in the use of custody which has continued to date (2010).

The early 1990s witnessed two events that had had a significant effect upon the popular media and the public. In 1993 the murder of the toddler Jamie Bulger, followed by the fatal shooting of a Manchester teenager were major public events and, at the same time some judges and senior police officers had spoken about 'liberal do-gooders' ruining the criminal justice system (Roberts et al. 2003: 46, Cavadino and Dignan 2002: 337). However, it is the conversion of the Labour Party to 'talking tough' that is seen as of greater importance in placing the increase in custody and continuing plans to 'toughen up' probation in context. In January 1993, Tony Blair, then Shadow Home Secretary, declared that a future Labour Government would be 'tough on crime, tough on the causes of crime'. For Roberts et al. 'penal parsimony now looked ... to be an electoral liability' (2003: 47). The main political parties now aimed to outbid each other such that:

> Populist punitiveness had now arrived in Britain, in the sense that perceived public acceptability was now a central criterion for assessing the value of a penal policy. (Roberts et al. 2003: 47)

Part of this development was a growing scepticism towards the probation service. In the mid 1990s, the Conservative government of John Major, with Michael Howard as Home Secretary saw the service as weak, failing and 'on the side of the offender' (Newburn 2003: 150). One cause of this was seen to be the service's social work base and, despite the Dews Report that reported widespread satisfaction with probation officer training (Ward and Spencer 1994) Michael Howard abolished social work training as a required qualification for probation officers. The Green Paper 'Strengthening Punishment in the Community' (Home Office 1995) and its consequent White Paper 'Protecting the Public' (Home Office 1996) stressed the importance of prison, the need for community sentences to concern themselves with punishment and the view that the courts should influence the content of such sentences, rather than it being left to the professional discretion of the probation officer. Community sentences were criticised as 'soft' and doing insufficient to emphasise the individual's responsibility for offending. In the event it was never enacted, following the 1997 General Election which brought the New Labour government to power.

With the election of the Labour government, there could be discerned differences in policy and attitude towards the service, but also some continuity. Although professional training was reinstated, it was removed from social work and was intended to provide a new generation of probation officers who could:

> ... focus on probation's top priority role of protecting the public and reducing crime through effective work with offenders. (Straw 1997)

This early period of the New Labour government is seen as somewhat contradictory in its policy and philosophy. Newburn (2003) cites Paul Boateng's introduction to the 2000 National Standards that the service is a law enforcement agency: 'It is what we are, it is what we do', but also quotes the Home Secretary, David Blunkett saying in 2001 that 'rehabilitation is the highest possible priority for those entering the criminal justice system' (Newburn 2003: 156).

Furthermore, in the view of Roberts et al. (2003), the new government saw itself as vulnerable in public opinion terms and 'cast about for fresh policy' that would be seen as tough. Examples such as on the spot fines for drunks and zero tolerance of the use of cannabis were seen to be the result of increased public concern, caused by issues as the Tony Martin case and the murder of Sarah Payne (Roberts et al. 2003: 50). Similarly, Tony makes much of the Labour government's claim to be only interested in 'evidence based' policy making and practice but he feels that this desire, whether or not it be genuine, to be overridden by their 'determination, always and on all issues, no matter what the evidence may show, to be seen as "tough on crime"' (Tonry 2004: 1).

In his view, despite spending large sums on piloting new schemes, Labour produced policies that were 'harsh and knee-jerk'. He claims that the criminal justice system was fundamentally rebuilt via the following documents and Acts of Parliament (2004: 5-6): 'The Way Ahead' (Home Office 2001); 'Making

Punishments Work' (the Halliday Report 2001); 'The Review of the Criminal Courts' (the Auld Report 2001); the White Paper 'Justice for All' (Home Office 2002); the Criminal Justice Act 2003; 'Managing Offenders, Reducing Crime – the Correctional Services Review' (Carter 2003), as well as the Criminal Justice and Court Services Act (2000), which set up the NPS.

In a similar vein Cavadino and Dignan see the Labour government as intent on introducing evidence-based policies, but with a 'subtext' of not giving the Conservative party any opportunity to accuse them of being weak on crime. This meant that policy was inevitably constrained and, at best led to policy and practice that was contradictory, resulting in an 'almost new type of "bifurcation" with government policy going in more than one direction at once' (2002: 339) in which policies such as the early release of prisoners under Home Detention Curfews can be contrasted with the absence of any questioning of the continued rise in the use of custody within this period. They see the 2001 General Election being another time of 'tough talking' on behalf of the government and something of a new departure in policy terms with the emergence of concentration on the persistent offender (2002: 340). Previous governments had subscribed to the notion of bifurcation, but the groups intended for tougher treatment were those who had committed serious offences, such as those of a sexual or particularly violent nature.

The CJA 2003 was the culmination of all these initiatives and Tonry sees some elements, such as the new community order as reasonable and based on evidence (2004: 7) but others, such as the custodial measures for 'dangerous offenders' as 'anti-civil libertarian' (2004: 21). The Act is seen as coming from a false basic premise, i.e. that the criminal justice system is either 'for' victims or 'for' offenders and that the goal of a notion of 'justice' that can be recognised by all parties did not appear to be part of the government's thinking. For the first time, the Act set in statute the purposes of sentencing (Davies et al. 2005: 296):

- The protection of the public.
- The punishment of offenders.
- The reduction of crime.
- The promotion of reparation.

It is regarded as one of the most wide-ranging and comprehensive Acts of modern times (Gibson 2004: 9), the 'most important' change concerning the role of previous convictions, which could now be treated as an aggravating factor when determining the severity of the sentence (2004: 20). In this way, the Act finally moved away from the just deserts philosophy of the CJA 1991, a move that had begun with the CJA 1993.

However, other aspects of the Act reveal a continuation of the contradictory nature of some policy and legislation throughout this period. Although 'rehabilitation' is not itself a purpose of sentencing under the Act, it is the case that the government re-asserted the importance of community sentences, creating a single generic community order which could be made up of up to 12 separate

Requirements, which were based upon an assessment of criminogenic needs, with the aim of reducing re-offending. It did not, however, question the continued use of high levels of custody.

Rhetoric from government throughout this period continued about the need for the criminal justice system to become even tougher and to be 're-balanced in favour of the victim' (and against the offender) (Napo 2006b, Travis 2006). At the same time and in another example of the government's acknowledgement of the wider social context of crime (and not just of the 'need to punish') it published the 'Reducing Offending, National Action Plan' (Home Office 2004b) and this was followed in Wales by 'Joining Together in Wales', which involved the Welsh Assembly Government (National Offender Management Service 2006a). These documents laid out a number of 'pathways' to aid the rehabilitation and resettlement of offenders, including: accommodation; education, training and employment; health (including mental health); substance misuse; finance, benefits and debt; children and families; attitudes thinking and behaviour. It looked at how such services could and should be delivered for offenders, concluding that a proper partnership approach co-ordinated by offender managers would be required.

Impact upon Probation

The changes brought about to the work of the service as a result of the developments described above were considerable. For most of its history, the probation service can be seen as an agency of modernity par excellence, in that it operated broadly within the positivist paradigm of expert diagnosis and assessment of the causes of individual offending, then seeking to reduce the likelihood of re-offending via a range of interventions. From roughly the 1920s-1930s the case work approach was pre-eminent, based in psychological approaches. Casework was seen as representing professionalism and was regarded as effective, despite the absence of effectiveness research (Raynor and Vanstone 2002: 41). The main vehicle for this, the probation order, was not a sentence of the court before the CJA 1991; previously it had been an alternative and an opportunity to reform.

These assumptions became undermined with the 'nothing works' paradigm of Martinson (Lipton et al. 1975) and the work of Brody and Folkard (Brody 1976, Folkard et al. 1976) in the 1970s. These studies purported to show that no transformative intervention had been shown to be effective in reducing re-offending. At the same time, the psychological approach was seen as being theoretically slack, ignorant of wider social context and possibly coercive, rather than humanitarian (Wootton 1959, cited in Raynor and Vanstone 2002: 42; American Friends Service Committee 1971). Although 'nothing works' was criticised and then recanted (e.g. McGuire 2001), it nevertheless had a considerable impact on official policy. The government came to see the probation order as an ineffective 'treatment for crime' and turned its attention elsewhere (Raynor and Vanstone 2002: 58). Home Office funding for research into rehabilitation virtually ceased and it became more interested in criminal justice systems and the probation service as a cheaper alternative to custody. Managerialist concepts of efficiency and effectiveness became increasingly important and outputs, rather than outcomes were to become the main indicators of success (Newburn 2003:138).

However, it is far from clear how much impact the 'nothing works' debate had on the majority of practitioners, many of whom probably continued to see their role as rehabilitative (Vanstone 2004a). Covering the period from the mid-late 1970s onwards, Vanstone describes a wide range of activity from intermediate treatment with young offenders, to family therapy, examination of social functioning, transactional analysis and task-centred casework. All these approaches, however eclectic, appeared to be based on 'scientific' theories such as behaviourism and social learning theories and relied on the probation officer as expert in the behaviour of offenders (Vanstone 2004a: 123-139). In a very different approach and as a practice-based response to 'nothing works' and concerns over other aspects of positivist intervention, Bottoms and McWilliams proposed a 'non-treatment paradigm' which recommended that probation intervention should be collaborative, regarding clients as experts in their own behaviour and should try and remove barriers to individuals living non-offending lives (Bottoms and McWilliams 1979).

There is also conflicting evidence of the depth of work carried out in this period. Vanstone cites Davies (1974) and Willis (1980); the former claiming supervision to be superficial and mainly crisis management whilst the latter describes probation officers working on 'agreed problem areas' in ways that echo the non-treatment paradigm (2004a cited:141-143). Later in the century, Boswell (1993 cited 2004a: 143) and Mair and May (1997 cited 2004a: 144) described practice in the 1980s that become primarily about the prevention of re-offending, via an examination of its causes and intervention that followed agreed supervision plans and sought to address the root causes of an individual's offending. This involved a casework approach based in 'enabling, befriending, respect and care for people and self-determination' (2004a: 143). Vanstone points out that such an approach involved working with the problems of offenders' everyday lives and for him represented a continuum of the work of the service since its inception, whether or not it was called 'treatment' (2004a: 144). In parallel, he notes the rise of group work, based on single issues such as employment, through to the social skills and problem solving 'curricula' promoted by, e.g. Priestley and McGuire (1985, cited 2004a: 149) that further developed into 'offending behaviour' programmes.

Moving into the 1990s, the CJA 1991 had a significant impact upon the probation service and influenced its policy and practice for the next decade and more. The service was intended to move 'centre stage' and provide the opportunity for the reduction in the use of custody, by delivering 'tough' community sentences. These were realised via the new National Standards, first published in 1992, with further versions in 1995, 2000, 2002, 2005 and 2007. They represented a significant reduction in the autonomy of individual probation officers, as they lay out clear guidelines around the number of contacts that were expected within the supervisory process (Harding 2000). Worrall regards them as an attempt to increase accountability, both of practitioners to management, but also of the service overall (Worrall 1997: 72). Further to this, she argues that National Standards also, due to their emphasis on breach and enforcement, affected the basic relationship between the practitioner and the individual and caused a shift in practice 'from "advise, assist and befriend" to "confront, control and monitor"' (1997: 63). Despite this, overall in the latter part of the 20th century and into the 21st probation practice may be seen as characterised by some continuity despite major organisational and policy changes (Vanstone 2004a). Vanstone cites Sandham (no date, cited 2004a: 156) listing a wide range of case work-based approaches in one probation service in the mid-1990s. Despite an eclectic approach, these provided 'tangible help' with problems about everyday survival, particularly when these were related to offending.

However, the picture is more complex than one showing a mix of traditional practices alongside the emerging use of the probation service as an administrator of punishments. The 'what works?' movement had begun to emerge from Canada in the late 1980s and early 1990s. Based in cognitive-behaviourism, claims were increasingly made that something could indeed, 'work' (see McGuire 2001). 'What works?' aimed to rehabilitate persistent offenders and saw itself as far more than an alternative to custody. In the early part of the 1990s however, its use was limited to a small number of probation services with chief probation officers who had a personal interest, until it came to be seen as central to a New Labour approach (Newburn 2003: 152-154). According to Raynor and Vanstone (2002) one major influence on the change of status of 'what works?' from a minority interest to one of central importance, was the involvement of the probation inspectorate. It commissioned a report (Underdown 1998) which found that only four from a total of 267 programmes running in local services had any credible system of evaluation. The New Labour government took up the issue and, influenced by the inspectorate, set up 'pathfinder' projects of certain cognitive-behavioural programmes, with the intention of evaluating their effectiveness in reducing re-offending (Raynor and Vanstone 2002: 94). In due course, the Home Office embraced 'what works' via the Effective Practice Initiative (Home Office 1998). These developments did meet some hostility (Gorman 2001, Mair 2000, Merrington and Stanley 2000) on the basis that these programmes were based on a pathological model, that not all individuals were suited to such programmes and that it took a 'one size fits all' approach. One interesting development was the dropping of the '?' when 'what works' was taken up by government: New Labour certainty had taken over from a more curious, enquiring approach.

However, these objections had little influence and the accredited programmes initiative represented a huge investment in transformative work and the probation service itself, but with an emphasis in keeping with developments over the previous decade. Whilst this might at first be seen as an endorsement of the probation officer 'relationship role', what has been called the 'new rehabilitation' (Vanstone 2004a) was not based on unconditional assistance, but by cognitive-behavioural programmes backed up by rigid enforcement. Furthermore, the emphasis on enforcement, breach and toughness is seen as a political and value-laden one, rather than having any evidence base; the assertion being that there is no link between tough enforcement and subsequent re-offending (Hedderman and Hough 2004: 160). At the same time, an alternative view about the role of the practitioner was being presented in the limited number of studies about individual supervision, stressing the need for a professional relationship between practitioners and their supervisees and that such an approach can be effective in terms of both compliance and re-offending (Brown 1998, Rex 1999, Trotter 1999), but at this time these had little impact upon government.

Similarly, the growth of partnership working, begun after the 1991 CJA continued to have an effect upon the way in which the service saw and defined itself. Since the 1991 CJA the service was required to spend up to 5 per cent of its overall budget (rising to 7 per cent) on services provided by the independent sector (Crow 2003: 94). Whilst initially resisted by the service as an attack upon its professionalism, this development became more accepted and viewed as the service being in a position to provide more expert services, leaving practitioners to concentrate upon offending work (e.g., Margetts 1997, Whitfield 1998, Rumgay 2000, Nellis 2002b).

Alongside all the developments and changes outlined above, the Criminal Justice and Court Services Act 2000 created the NPS and in 2004 the government announced the setting up of NOMS. These developments are considered below, but at this point, the next section will consider the rise to prominence of risk assessment and management.

The Assessment and Management of Risk

Legislation and Related Government Policy

The underlying factors behind the 'rise of risk' have been discussed in Chapter 2. More specifically, the first impact upon the service came as a result of the CJA 1991. This is seen as part of the trend evident since the 1980s of the service being moved away first from rehabilitation towards alternatives to custody and then to 'punishment in the community' (Kemshall 2003: 83). Initially the requirement for practitioners to consider issues of risk was brought in via National Standards, which inserted a new risk assessment section into pre-sentence reports. These were then to inform sentencing proposals and to influence sentencers in terms of the bifurcatory approach to offenders (see above). This development is regarded as largely driven by government, despite the 'resistance of front-line workers'. Furthermore, it is seen as a factor in ensuring staff compliance, perhaps within the wider changes that were occurring at this time (Kemshall 2003: 84-85).

Later, the New Labour government enshrined risk assessment into the work of the service with the creation of the NPS and its list of five aims, the first of which was the 'protection of the public'. This had a pre-requisite of the identification and management of offenders according to their perceived level of risk (Home Office 2001). To enable practitioners to make such assessments, the NPS created the OASys assessment system, an actuarial and clinical 'third generation' assessment tool intended to identify both risk of re-offending and harm (Home Office 2002b). Kemshall sees the risk agenda now operating at an increasingly intense level, the service embracing it in a 'pragmatic adaptation to the new penality of the New Right' (2003: 92).

In addition to assessment tools and procedures, the service was required to develop risk management procedures. Multi-Agency Public Protection Panels (MAPPPs) were also established by the Criminal Justice and Court Services Act 2000 under the Multi-Agency Public Protection Arrangements (MAPPA). These were intended to be the vehicle by which Chief Constables and Chief Officers of Probation were to exercise a duty to implement inter agency co-operation intended to both assess and manage the risks posed by violent and sexual offenders, arrangements that had been informally in place for most of the 1990s (Kemshall 2003: 93). These procedures were extended under the CJA 2003 to include a wider list of statutory partners in the MAPPA process (Gibson 2004). Finally, the coming of NOMS further reinforced the central importance of risk assessment and management, via its Offender Management Model (OMM – National Offender Management Service 2005b, National Offender Management Service 2006b). This introduced the idea of four levels, or 'tiers', which categorised offenders according to both risk dimensions and dictated the range and type of intervention that should follow. This enshrined the notion of 'resources following risk' which had become a 'buzzword' within the NPS since its inception (Home Office 2001). In brief, this meant the greater the overall mix of risk factors, the higher level of intervention an individual offender would receive, both in terms of changing behaviour and of risk management and control.

Impact upon Probation

As noted, Kemshall (2003) describes some initial practitioner resistance to the assessment of risk and it is not clear how much this became central to mainstream practice in the 1990s (Vanstone 2004a). However, given the increase in central control, it is likely that risk became more central to practice, at least in terms of pre-sentence report completion and, later, OASys assessment. However, it has been argued that probation officers had always identified 'risk' and 'dangerousness' and worked with them, but not in such formalised and pre-eminent way (e.g. Burnett et al. 2007, Faulkner 2008). Whatever the actual extent of change, practice in regards to risk has been complex. In broader terms and considering Feeley and Simon's 1992 thesis (see Chapter 2), MAPPPs are predicated on risk and actuarial techniques. However, Kemshall cites empirical research which reveals a more complex process. Although practice appeared based in the use of a sex offender assessment tool, the Structured Anchored Clinical Judgement (2003: 96) this became used, particularly by the police as a screening tool to identify those who would need to be assessed by the MAPPP. Kemshall (see also Kemshall and Maguire 2002) states that subjective and professional judgements often overrode the 'decisions' of actuarial tools, giving what she calls an 'anecdotal feel' (2003: 96). Overall, whilst Kemshall sees the rise of risk as transforming the work and character of the probation service, it did so in a manner that was neither uniform nor completely clear. She wonders how far the 'discourse of need and rehabilitation has been replaced by risk and actuarial risk management', regarding this as debatable, but ultimately sees the welfarism of the old service being superseded gradually by an 'economic rationality of crime management and a risk-driven agenda' (2003: 99).

In a similar vein, Robinson studied the role of risk in case allocation within the probation service and asserts that the notion that offenders were becoming managed as aggregates of risk as somewhat simplistic (Robinson 2002: 8) with assessments modified on the basis of practitioner judgement (2002:14). She found a tension arising from a level of acceptance of the need to manage risk and a degree of optimism about the possibilities of rehabilitation, emanating from 'what works'. However, the rehabilitation in question was not the 'old' type of unconditional assistance, but rather one of rehabilitation with an aim of reducing re-offending and hence protecting the public, all defined within a risk management agenda (2002: 18). In a study in the United States, Lynch looking at parole practitioners in California, found examples of practitioners subverting official policy, based upon their own judgements and professional preferences (Lynch 1998: 846). Whilst the official language of risk penality was to the fore and management appeared to be concerned only with performance indicators and not offenders' behaviour (1998: 849), practitioners cooperated to the point of completing paperwork and risk assessment instruments, but did this only to fulfil requirements, rather than with any sense of their importance. She concluded that practitioners made individual assessments of their cases and that these determined to 'a significant degree how they spent their time and energy' (1998: 859). Similar findings in the UK are reported by Kemshall and Maguire (2002) as mentioned above.

However, taking a rather different line, Nash and Ryan regard risk as having 'transformed' the service. Although dangerous offenders (the 'dangerous few') represent only around 1.5 per cent of the probation caseload at any one time they are seen as driving the whole policy of the government and NPS, with the attendant danger of risk inflation as a result of practitioners and managers needing to 'cover their backs' in marginal cases (2003: 164). This analysis sees the service moving to a 'tick-box' model of practice that leaves behind real interpersonal work in a highly centralised system and resulting in a reduction in local and practitioner autonomy (2003: 168).

Modernisation and the New Public Management

The emergence of NPM and later modernisation and their effect upon the wider public sector have been discussed in Chapter 2. Within the criminal justice sector, their influence has been profound and has redefined the very structure of the probation service.

Economic Efficiency and Central Control

As crime continued to increase during the 1980s the Conservative government looked to ways of controlling the very expensive use of custody, but in ways that were palatable to government and the electorate. Moreover, prison was regarded by the Home Secretary of the time, Douglas Hurd as 'an expensive way of making bad people worse' (Nash and Ryan 2003: 161), but at the same time the probation order was seen as a soft option. As a result, and following on from initial moves to control the work of the service via SNOP (Home Office 1984) discussed above, the new policy of 'punishment in the community' emerged (McLaughlin and Muncie 2000: 170). The repackaging of the probation order in this manner enabled punishment to potentially be delivered in a much cheaper manner and it was officially introduced by the CJA 1991, which stated that one of the core tasks for the service was to be 'the strategic management and administration of punishments in the community' (Home Office 2001). This in turn was intended to allow for the reduced use of imprisonment within the CJA 1991, something that had short term success until overturned by the CJA 1993, a move which saw the government of John Major abandon a policy of reducing costs via a lesser use of custody in the period leading to the 1997 general election.

New Labour and the NPS

Newburn (2003) regards the two main themes of New Labour governance from 1997 as managerialism and centralisation, although these may be seen to be contradictory to some extent, as ideal NPM models involve de-centralisation. However, New Labour desired to centralise and control the probation service as well as other agencies within the wider public sector (Clarke et al. 2000, Raine 2002) partly due to a mistrust of professional groups, which it saw as conservative and anti-modernisation (Flynn 2002a: 344-345) and thus likely to try and oppose its wider plans for the service.

The Crime and Disorder Act 1998 is seen as the first embodiment of New Labour managerialism, as it brought in consistent aims and objectives for the criminal justice system, the best use of resources, a commitment to evidence based practice and 'what works' and improved performance management, all of which was to be achieved through 'continual auditing, setting priorities and targets, monitoring, evaluation and inspection' (McLaughlin and Muncie 2000: 174). At the same time and as a precursor to the Effective Practice Initiative (see above), an influential Home Office publication anticipated the creation of the NPS. This listed weaknesses in the service in terms of a lack of effectiveness and speaks of practitioner 'inputs' and 'key tasks' for practitioners and managers, within a system of measurement of 'outputs' and the monitoring and evaluation of effectiveness (Chapman and Hough 1998).

Following on from this, the creation of the NPS in April 2001 can be seen to be employing certain aspects of the NPM, i.e. the control of professional groups and the setting of financial controls and targets. However, it is also seen to illustrate the contradiction within New Labour policy in that the creation of a centralised service within the Home Office was set against the establishment of local probation area boards with responsibility for certain aspects of policy and practice. However, overall the continuing tendency was to centralise (Nash and Ryan 2003), something identified by Martin Wargent of the Probation Boards Association, who saw, a year after the creation of the NPS that it was moving 'backwards into an over-centralised system' (Nash and Ryan 2003: 163).

Overall, the creation of the NPS saw power moving very much to the centre and the following manifestations of NPM and modernisation were proposed from the outset: performance indicators; league tables; core competencies; privatisation of non-core functions; the purchaser/provider split; partnership working. These found expression in the New Choreography which claimed that these changes to the service would have to be made 'against the grain of its past history and traditions' (Home Office 2001: 5). Flynn sees the adoption of the European Foundation for Quality Management as a further illustration of a commitment to a 'top down' approach to learning and policy within the new service (2002a: 348) whilst Nellis criticises the New Choreography as 'conceptually underdeveloped' due to it being based upon a narrow managerialist thrust (Nellis 2002a: 63). Overall, these measures were intended to change practitioner behaviour in directions approved of by government by a mixture of legislation, policy directives (e.g. National Standards) and audit (Senior et al. 2007, Raine 2002).

The National Offender Management Service

Despite the NPS being only some two years old, in 2003 the government commissioned a report to look into the overall function and management of the post-sentence elements of the criminal justice system. The 'Carter Report' – 'Managing Offenders, Reducing Crime - the Correctional Services Review' - (Carter 2003) was published in December 2003 and the government's response was made within barely a month, in January 2004. 'Reducing Crime – Changing Lives' (Home Office 2004a) announced that NOMS would be set up by 1 June 2004, with the objectives of punishing offenders and reducing re-offending. It also outlined the government's commitment to 'contestability' whereby NOMS would procure intervention services with offenders from a wide range of bodies, including from the private and voluntary sectors, through a 'planned programme of market testing' (Home Office 2004a: 34). This was seen as a way to provide more 'cost effective' intervention services (Davies et al. 2005: 10). Carter's objectives in proposing the setting up of NOMS were to 'establish a credible and effective system, which is focussed on reducing crime and maintaining public confidence, whilst remaining affordable' (Carter 2003: 13). The creation of NOMS would see an overarching body which would bring together the two 'silos' of the probation and prison services under one organisation, with one central management with the objectives of punishing offenders, reducing crime and maintaining public confidence (2003: 33). The use of the words 'offender management' for the title of new service also seemed to indicate the primacy of a managerialist agenda, rather than anything more transformative.

The probation employees' professional association and trade union, Napo was critical of the setting up of NOMS. In terms of 'evidence based practice' Napo made much of their claim that NOMS was based on political ideology and not evidence (Napo 2005) and it was criticised as little more than an additional layer of bureaucracy on top of the prison and probation services and as one not aiming to reduce the prison population (Rumgay 2005). Despite objections (e.g. Napo 2006), 'Restructuring Probation to Reduce Re-Offending' (National Offender Management Service 2005c) proposed the removal of probation boards from the NPS and replacing them with 'trusts' which in due course would compete in an open market with the voluntary and private sectors to provide services to the Regional Offender Managers (ROMS, in Wales the Director of Offender Management - DOM). It was envisaged that trusts could cease to exist in due course if they were unable to secure enough 'business' from the ROMs. These plans no longer proposed the splitting of the service into its assessment and interventions functions, as had previously been intended, but saw offender management transferring to trusts as well as interventions and similarly subject to contestability (National Offender Management Service 2005c). Legislation to introduce NOMS was introduced into parliament in November 2006. Prior to its introduction, the government sought to give assurance to probation areas that it valued the work of the service and that NOMS would not result in 'privatisation and ... the end of probation'. However, it claimed that deficiencies in the performance of the service and failures to have a positive impact on re-offending rates led the government to conclude that 'the public sector cannot do all that needs to be done on its own' (Sutcliffe 2006).

In July 2007, the Offender Management Act was finally passed creating NOMS as a legal entity. The Bill had been keenly contested through parliament, with a number of amendments made which, according to Napo prevented the NPS being 'replaced with a market' via contestability (Napo 2007b). In the end, despite contestability, the core business of the service was to be protected for three years and in a major change, the role of the ROMs was reduced to in the main commissioning the local probation area as the major provider, leaving that area to further commission services from smaller, local providers. Whilst provision for the ROM to directly commission remained, this was intended to be for certain specialist services (Straw 2007). In this way probation areas became both provider and commissioner, echoing the previous arrangements whereby areas commissioned local services under partnership arrangements. However, the Act provided for areas to become autonomous trusts, six trial trusts being set up in April 2008. On 1 April 2010, all previous probation areas became trusts, their overall number being reduced to 35.

However, this was not the end of reorganisation and following an internal review and criticism that it had been an 'expensive bureaucracy' (Travis 2007), NOMS itself was scaled down considerably, its central civil service personnel being greatly reduced. In January 2008, its functions were merged more closely with that of the prison service, under a single head, the immediate previous Director of the Prison Service, Philip Wheatley. This prompted claims by Napo that the probation service had been 'taken over' by the prison service, rather than both being more closely integrated in a smaller NOMS (McKnight 2008, Napo 2008).

Culture in Organisations and the Values, Beliefs and Attitudes of Practitioners

Early Debates

The probation service since its earliest, informal beginnings has been about a mixture and balance of care and control. The police court missionaries, emerging from the Church of England Temperance Society, began working within courts in the 1870s, interviewing individual offenders before a court appearance with a view to assessing their motivation to sign 'the Pledge' to give up alcohol, find proper accommodation and employment and to accept supervision to help achieve these goals. These activities have been characterised as 'rescuing souls' (e.g. May 1991, Whitfield 1998) but there has debate about their actual purpose. Were these developments about altruism, a religious concern to save souls or merely a way to control the drinking classes and thus shore up the status quo (Vanstone 2004a)? Throughout the last century, the values of the service and practitioners have been debated around a mix of what the purposes and practice methods of the service can and should be.

In the main, it has perhaps been generally accepted that the values of the service were based in humanitarianism, although the issues of care and control were never far beneath the surface (e.g. Raynor 1985). In more recent times, it is unlikely that practitioners' values were impervious to macro-level views about the efficacy of the transformative and rehabilitative agenda. For example, Bottoms and McWilliams (1979) had concluded, in the wake of 'nothing works' that probation's purpose should be, at least in part, the reduction of crime via appropriate help and the provision of alternatives to custody. Soon after the passing of the CJA 1991, Humphrey and Pease (1992) reported that probation officers in the late 1980s and early 1990s defined purpose and effectiveness in terms of diverting from custody. Despite this, the debate about the purpose and ethical dimension of probation supervision still included the need for rehabilitation. For example, McWilliams and Pease argued that that rehabilitation of offenders on behalf of society was a 'moral good' which prevented punishment becoming no more than state-sponsored vengeance (McWilliams and Pease 1990: 15). Citing the work of Gewirth (1978), they argued that punishment could only be morally justified as a means of returning offenders to normative behaviour. This process they saw as only being achieved through rehabilitation, rather than retributive or vengeful acts.

The Values Debate from the Mid-1990s

By 1995, probation values were seen by one commentator at least as: opposition to custody; opposition to oppression; commitment to justice for offenders; commitment to the client's right to confidentiality and openness; valuing of clients as unique and self-determining individuals; aim to ensure that victims and potential victims are protected; belief that 'purposeful professional relationships can facilitate change in clients' (Williams 1995: 12-20). Since then and increasingly with the developments described above, there has been a debate over what probation values can and ought to be and Garland has warned of the collapse of the 'solidarity project' which he saw as leading to a more divisive criminal justice system and society (Garland 1996). Nellis and others have argued that service values should be based upon the notions of restorative justice, community justice and human rights and the emphasis on public protection is seen as meaningless without an ethical dimension, as it could lead to an authoritarian service (Nellis 1999, Nellis 2002a, Nellis and Gelsthorpe 2003) which does whatever is necessary to 'protect the public', something echoed by Robinson and McNeill (2004). Nellis has also urged the service to recognise that reducing crime and the fear of crime in 'crime-blighted communities' would need to be a priority (Nellis 2005), echoing the left-realist arguments of Young and others (Young and Matthews 1992).

Writing from a different perspective Farooq, whilst seeing the change in probation practice from an unquestioning social welfare approach to one which deals more explicitly with enforcement and public protection as inevitable and correct, nevertheless argued that probation officers needed to continue to mediate between offenders and society, balancing the 'conflicting' interests of the individual, the courts, the Home Office and the wider community (Farooq 1998).

Harding argued for the probation service to align itself far more with the wider community, in order to seek the promotion of community justice as a 'transcendent justification' for its continued existence (Harding 2000: 132). He saw this as previously existing, but having been lost due to trends such as managerialism, cash limits and a certain sidelining following the undoing of the CJA 1991. In a similar vein and writing about the American experience, Clear argued for probation practitioners to work with neighbourhoods rather than individuals, to increase their ability to engage with the community and promote community and restorative justice (Clear 2005).

Robinson and McNeill report a study undertaken in 1999, which showed practitioners identifying the 'holy trinity' of public protection, rehabilitation (defined as reducing re-offending) and enforcement (2004: 286), as legitimate, if not necessarily achievable goals for the service. These were seen as important to gain credibility with the government and the public, but also to give some meaning beyond the minimal ambitions of the alternative to custody regime (2004: 287-289). Both reducing re-offending and enforcement seemed to be subsumed into an 'overarching' purpose of the protection of the public. They concluded that practitioners were tending to identify with these official aims, in part as a result of the increasing importance of the victim within the 1990s and also as a means of deflecting public criticism of the service, although they did insist that positive outcomes might be best achieved via a good working relationship and attention being paid to the social context of offending.

Taking a slightly different approach, Raynor (2004) argued that the work of the probation service could be recast as being less about preventing re-offending and more about individuals proactively seeking to 'refit themselves for participation in the community'; more about promoting desistance than prevention of recidivism (2004: 212). Furthermore, he saw the accredited programmes correctional approach as containing political hazards for the probation service if it failed to prove generally successful in terms of reducing re-offending. Arguing that the uneven results produced at that time gave succour to neo-liberal arguments that rehabilitation is a 'liberal illusion', Raynor feared that arguments that only punishment that reinforces moral accountability were likely to reduce re-offending would be strengthened and that this may result in the higher-still use of custody (2004: 214).

Napo (2006c) has asserted that much crime has its origins in social injustice and that many offenders have 'had their life opportunities curtailed by poverty, discrimination and social exclusion' (2006c: 4). Emphasising the ability of individuals to change, it set out the following values to which it is committed: respect and trust when working with perpetrators and victims; open and fair treatment for all; empowerment of individuals in order to reduce the risk of harm to themselves and others; promotion of equality and anti-discrimination; promotion of the rights of both perpetrators and victims; building on individuals' strengths as a vehicle for change (2006c: 5). Finally and writing in the aftermath of the creation of NOMS under the Offender Management Act 2007, Faulkner (2008) argued that concepts of 'offender management' and 'risk' are not new (except in their terminology and pre-eminence), with their roots in practice going back decades. He stressed that the value base of the service should be based on the recognition that the relationship between practitioners and offenders is more important than organisational structures. However, he was concerned that the notion of the relationship contained in the OMM is formalised and designed to conform to standards and hence able to be measured and controlled by management.

Values and Practice

The notion of a professional relationship has been at the core of probation work and there is some evidence that it is important in successful supervision. Trotter has shown that practitioners can affect compliance and reconviction rates by working in a 'pro-social manner' (Trotter 1999), whilst Rex argued that individual offenders can link their ability to desist from offending to the quality of the relationship they have with a supervisor, seeing it as active and participative (Rex 1999). Brown reported individuals citing the importance of their relationship with their supervisor, the quality of that relationship and 'knowing who to turn to' as key factors in success (Brown 1998) and Farrall, whilst critical of the content of much probation intervention, saw supervisors and offenders needing to promote change on the basis of an agreed set of criteria and a 'productive working relationship' (Farrall 2002: 73).

Vanstone asserted that probationers value being listened to and need the commitment of a supervisor who can 'provide the requisite challenge and support' to motivate them to change their behaviour (Vanstone 2004b: 178). Burnett and McNeill (2005) also made the argument that a relationship is basic to any notion of effectiveness, arguing that whatever the many reasons for it falling out of official favour, the systematic evaluation of its (in)effectiveness was not a factor, as they argue this has never been carried out. Emphasising a further variant in this debate, Raynor (2004) discussed the need for probation supervision to be about guidance and encouragement, not coercion, to encourage offenders to have 'less wish, need or disposition to offend' (2004: 196). He introduced a further strand to the debate, which echoes the 'non-paradigm' approach (Bottoms and McWilliams 1979) and the emerging desistance literature. This concerns the need for a 'strengths based' approach to supervision, which sees individuals as 'active participants' in their supervision (e.g. Farrall 2002: 211). This is emphasised perhaps by emerging evidence from the early years of the 2000s that cognitive-behavioural group work approaches alone had produced mixed results, at best in terms of re-offending (Raynor 2006).

Ultimately, probation practice is seen as based in *faith* that it is an effective moral good, welcomed by its recipients, but one that involves the provision of help in return for 'submission to official authority and control' (Vanstone, 2004a: 158). Compared to this is the view of the proponents of desistance (e.g. Farrall 2002, Maruna et al. 2004, McNeill 2006, Rex 1999) that probation practice should emphasise the collaborative effort between practitioner and individual offenders to identify ways in which the offender can increase social bonds and create an image of self as a non-offender, including active efforts to overcome social inequality. As mentioned, Vanstone (2004a) does mention examples of work throughout this period that may be seen as falling within this paradigm. Finally McNeill has proposed a desistance paradigm for probation practice which proposes an overall structure for practitioners to support individual movements towards desistance, rather than providing expert intervention (McNeill 2006).

Values, the NPS and NOMS

The 'New Choreography' set out the aims of the new NPS as being (Home Office 2001: iv):

- Protecting the public.
- Reducing re-offending.
- The proper punishment of offenders in the community.
- Ensuring offenders' awareness of the effects of crime on the victims of crime and the public.
- Rehabilitation of offenders.

It must be assumed that the rank ordering of these aims was quite deliberate and thus made to fit with the overall government agenda of re-aligning the service around a more explicit supervisory and punishment role within the criminal justice system. Quite clearly, whilst rehabilitation (not defined) remained an aim, it can perhaps be seen as something that might occur as a by-product of the superior aims. Later in the document, the 'vision and ethical framework' puts additional detail to these overall aims. The discourse within this section is primarily one of the need to protect the public, reduce re-offending and punish offenders and is thus consistent with the overall aims. Mention of rehabilitation is brief, although a commitment is made to (2001: 7) 'value and achieve the humane and equal treatment of offenders under its [the NPS'] supervision'.

However, some of what are listed as 'values' might be regarded as objectives (Nellis 2002a) for example a commitment to 'victim awareness and empathy', 'law enforcement', 'empiricism' and 'problem solving'. Rehabilitation is mentioned, but with little qualification and no definition (Home Office 2001: 8). Thus, although placed within a section called 'The NPS Vision and Ethical Framework', these values appear to lack any explicit ethical dimension. As mentioned, Nellis sees this 'ethical framework' as something to be resisted on the basis of the wider thrust of the document, which he sees as one on 'managerialist utopianism', which has little relationship to the reality of practice (Nellis 2002a: 77).

The potential and continued impact of NOMS upon the probation service's values and culture is difficult to assess. However, in January 2005 NOMS produced its model for case management, which appeared to include many of the elements that might be regarded as making up a 'professional relationship'. The OMM stated that NOMS would take:

> An offender-focused human services approach to work with individual offenders (National Offender Management Service 2005b: 4).

At the same time, it is argued by Burnett and McNeill (2005) that some aspects of a culture and practice linked to rehabilitation may have begun to re-emerge in the early part of the 21st century. They saw the idea of a relationship between practitioners and offenders as having been 'airbrushed' out of the discourse in the late 1990s, but argued that there were signs of a recovery (2005: 224). They cited high ranking officials within NOMS talking about the need for a 'personal relationship approach' and of the importance of 'relating to the offender' (Mann 2004, Grapes 2004, cited 2005: 225). However, Lewis has argued that any re-emergence of a rehabilitative approach is unlikely to succeed due to the main driver within the government's thinking being that of managerialism (Lewis 2005).

However, a further example of what is perhaps a slow re-emergence of the recognition of the importance of skilled interpersonal work with offenders was the work of McNeill et al. (2005) in completing a literature review for the Scottish Executive around effective supervision. They conclude that the following are vital in effecting change: good interpersonal relationships; intervention based on research, individual assessment and tailored for the individual via a therapeutic relationship. Such personal skills are at least as important as the content of any intervention. Finally, having conducted a meta analysis of studies that had evaluated the effective elements in offender supervision, Downden and Andrews (2004) concluded that these could be encapsulated in the 'core correctional practices': the effective use of authority, pro-social modelling and a genuine and effective working relationship.

At the end of the first decade of the 21st century, the emphasis placed by government and NOMS remains that of a mainly managerialist and law enforcement approach. Of course, the Labour government that had done so much to try to redirect the values and practices of the service, was removed from office in May 2010. As a result, the future involvement of government is simply unknown as are future directions for the service in terms of its culture, values and practices.

Culture and Resistance?

Given the apparent impact of changes described, the possibility of resistance to top-down imposed changes must exist. However, whilst mention is made elsewhere of resistant behaviour or attitudes (Lynch 1998, Robinson 2002, Robinson and McNeill 1999, Farrow 2004a, Kemshall and Maguire 2002), there is relatively little known in this area. One focus for resistance might be language and discourse (Scott 1990). Scott's thesis is that powerful and powerless groups behave and speak in different ways when addressing each other than when inhabiting the 'private sphere'. The 'public transcript' is used when groups interact, but this will rarely reflect their true feelings, both of whom will 'tacitly conspire' in misrepresentation (1990: 2), using the 'hidden transcript' amongst themselves to discuss and share their true feelings and attitudes. Furthermore, the public transcript will normally follow the wishes of the powerful and, provide evidence of the hegemony of dominant values, even that the powerless are willing participants in their subordination (1990: 4). Whilst the hidden transcript of the powerless can emerge into the public sphere, these are seen as 'rare and dangerous moments in power relations' (1990: 6) and most of either side's hidden transcripts will never be known to the other.

From a similar perspective Cheliotis and Lipsky discuss more 'everyday' forms of resistance (Cheliotis 2006, Lipsky 1980), the former criticises the new penality as simply moulding practitioners into conformity with risk management, either by the prevailing discourse and culture, or by power inherent in hierarchical organisations (2006: 318). Cheliotis argues that resistance is still likely to take place, despite an increasingly hierarchical division of labour within the NOMS structure, which would allow the 'breeding of a new, up-and-coming generation of blasé professionals' (2006: 319) to be promoted over the heads of an older generation of practitioners, thus reinforcing conformity. Referring to Weber's ideal typology of the 'instrumentally rational' and the 'value rational' actor (2006: 321) he rejects these as not representing reality, which is highly idiosyncratic and within which actors will always find themselves in different points on the continuum between the two ideal types. He concludes that practitioners will always have a certain amount of discretion and that what escapes the system is:

> the panoply of personal values and idiosyncratic meanings that individual decision makers bring to their decisions (Cheliotis 2006: 323).

Most resistance is seen as every day and small scale and it can be interpreted as apathy, as rarely is such behaviour manifested in overt opposition. This behaviour, which inhabits Scott's 'private sphere', enables self-preservation and the opportunity for resistance (2006: 326). These acts of agency he argues are not insignificant, but constitute instances of 'counter hegemonic ideology' (2006: 328). Lipsky's 'street level bureaucrats', of whom probation practitioners may be taken as examples, similarly have a degree of freedom which can never be completely controlled and it is in this area, where decisions are made and discretion operates, that agency may (or may not) result in acts of 'subversion'. Indeed, Lipsky argues that practitioners in such circumstances have to operate in this way; otherwise they would be paralysed and unable to act or react to crises or unexpected events.

The literature discussed in the current and preceding chapters provide the context of the book, in that they seek to link changes in government policy around the work of practitioners and the probation service to broader social changes that have had an impact on responses to crime in most western societies. The extent of that impact upon practice, attitudes, beliefs and values of practitioners is the subject of the remaining chapters of the book.

Chapter 4
Attitudes, Values and Beliefs in the Probation Service

Having discussed macro and mezzo level theories that seek to understand and explain recent changes in criminal justice policy and practice, this chapter focuses on attitudes, values and beliefs of probation practitioners and trainees and to a lesser degree, those of probation managers. By way of introduction there follows a précis of some of the broad themes identified in previous chapters. This includes views of government, NOMS and NPS, as well as the relatively limited amount of existing research about the views of practitioners and other staff.

Whilst recognising the artificiality of designating any one event or time as representing a point of change, the CJA 1991 did introduce legal changes to the status and purpose of the probation order, and the preamble to the Act stated that the service was now about punishment, the management of offenders and administration of sentences (Home Office 1991). The probation order became a sentence of the court, instead of an alternative to a sentence and probation supervision was repackaged as 'punishment in the community'. Further changes were put in place in the 1990s by successive governments, which indicated an official desire to shift the value base of the service away from the 'advising, assisting and befriending' of a client group by a social work workforce to a managing and punishing approach to groups of 'offenders' that would ensure the protection of the public via the assessment and management of risk.

Social work training as a required qualification for probation officers was abolished in 1995 and successive versions of National Standards reduced officer autonomy and increasingly emphasised the 'management' of offenders and the enforcement of probation orders. Under the New Labour government professional training was reinstated, but was removed from social work and intended to focus on protection of the public and the reduction of re-offending (Straw 1997). Otherwise there was a certain degree of apparently contradictory thought and pronouncements from ministers, the probation minister Paul Boateng stating in 2000 that the service was a law enforcement agency, whilst the Home Secretary David Blunkett referred to rehabilitation as the 'first priority' (Newburn 2003: 156).

Multiple aims were also in evidence within 'The New Choreography' (Home Office 2001) the first policy document of the NPS. The aims of the new service were to be: protecting the public; reducing re-offending; the proper punishment of offenders in the community; ensuring offenders' awareness of the effects of crime on the victims of crime and the public; rehabilitation of offenders. There is very little discussion of values within the document, but the overall message is one of the punishment and management of offenders, albeit in a 'humane and equal' manner (Home Office 2001: 7). In June 2004, the creation of NOMS was announced with initial aims of the punishment of offenders and the reduction of offending (Home Office 2004a). These later expanded to mirror those of the NPS thus: protect the public; reduce re-offending; punish offenders; rehabilitate offenders; ensure victims feel justice has been done. NOMS has also asserted the importance of the central role of the professional relationship in achieving its aims, through the OMM (National Offender Management Service 2005b, National Offender Management Service 2006b).

Regarding the attitudes of practitioners to these changes, the emphasis in the literature has been more of a theoretical debate, rather than a range of empirical explorations of actual practitioner opinion. For example, Williams (1995) argued for the retention of 'social work' values within the service and whilst acknowledging that there was no agreed list of probation values, emphasised the following: an opposition to custody and oppression; a commitment to justice for offenders, whilst protecting victims; the valuing of offenders as individuals; a belief in offenders' ability to change facilitated by a purposeful professional relationship. Elsewhere, it has been argued that service values should be based upon the notions of restorative justice, community justice and human rights (Nellis 1999, Nellis 2002a, Nellis, Gelsthorpe 2003, Robinson and McNeill 2004) whilst stress has also been placed on the quality of personal relationships with supervisees as a vehicle to promote the latter's ability to desist from crime (Raynor 2004, Rex 1999, Farrall 2002, Vanstone 2004b, Burnett and McNeill 2005, Maruna et al. 2004, McNeill 2006). The view of the probation service trade union and professional association, Napo, has been that crime has its origins in social injustice, emphasising the need for: respect and trust when working with perpetrators and victims; open and fair treatment for all; empowerment of individuals in order to reduce the risk of harm to themselves and others; promotion of equality and anti-discrimination; promotion of the rights of both perpetrators and victims; building on individuals' strengths as a vehicle for change (Napo 2006c: 5).

Empirical studies are rare, but perhaps indicate the way in which practitioners are influenced by official attempts to redefine the values and purposes of the organisation. One study in the early 1990s (Humphrey and Pease 1992) did not discuss values and attitudes directly, but reported that probation officers defined purpose and effectiveness in terms of diverting from custody, whilst later the 'holy trinity' of public protection, rehabilitation (defined as reducing re-offending) and enforcement (Robinson and McNeill 2004: 286) were identified by practitioners as legitimate goals for practice, although practice was seen as best operating based upon a good working relationship that recognised the social basis of much offending. Within this, reducing re-offending and enforcement seemed contained within a broad purpose of the protection of the public. This study concluded that practitioners were tending to identify with these official aims as a result of the increasing importance of the victim within the 1990s and as a means of deflecting public criticism of the service.

In terms of broader theories, it has been argued by, amongst others Garland (2001), Pratt (2000), Feeley and Simon (1992), and Rose (2000) that the criminal justice system has become more concerned with management and punishment of offenders, rather than reform. Therefore, the views of practitioners are analysed here with a view to throwing light on the extent to which they concur with such ideas.

Attitudes, Values and Beliefs of Practitioners, Trainees and Managers

What follows is an analysis of data obtained from semi-structured interviews and Likert statements. The following themes were identified: underpinning values and attitudes; attitudes to risk; attitudes to enforcement; attitudes to managerialism; the views of trainees; the extent to which attitudes vary across the sample depending on a range of respondent attributes. These themes came initially from pilot interviews and were used to construct Likert attitudinal statements and as the basis of the semi-structured interviews conducted with practitioners and managers. Data were drawn from interviews with practitioners and managers, two focus groups, the reading of case files and Pre-Sentence Reports (PSRs) and from Likert questionnaires completed by practitioners, middle managers and trainees.

The Underpinning Attitudes and Values of Practitioners and Trainees

No data from interviews with management grades are reported in this section as managers were not asked a specific question about underpinning attitudes and values in interview. However, managers' views have been included in sections below reporting on the Likert scale statements and any differences in their views and those of practitioners are considered in the final section.

Initially, respondents were asked: '*What role do your personal values play in your work?*'. This general, open question was posed to avoid leading questions and to allow the respondent to respond and expand as they wished. However, this question did not elicit broad responses in that very few spoke spontaneously about a range of personal values that were fundamental to the job. Many respondents replied that the question was 'difficult' and occasionally did not provide any outline value statements at all. Initial responses to the question included:

> I don't know how to answer that one. (*Female Probation Officer, 2+ years' experience*)

> Horrible, that's huge, can't answer that in 2 minutes. (*Female Probation Officer, 6+ years' experience*)

> It's a tricky one really. They do have an impact on how I would be with offenders. (*Female Probation Officer, 3+ years' experience*)

> I suppose I approach people as individuals in a set of circumstances … I don't know if that's a value or not, I'm stuck with this one, it's very difficult. (*Female Probation Officer, 3+ years' experience*)

> That's a hard one, it's difficult not to impose yours sometimes, but I've never really thought about it. (*Female Probation Service Officer, 14+ years' experience*)

> I find it hard to describe, a lot of things are from my upbringing and the person my parents brought me up to be … it's hard to pinpoint. (*Male Probation Officer, 2+ years' experience*)

The biggest category of direct responses to the question was that values (undefined) were important to individuals, but that their values had to be 'kept away' from the workplace, i.e. that their personal values should not influence their work in supervision. This was because they might adversely affect how they worked with individuals if the behaviour of those they supervised offended their own values. This imperative to keep their own values separate from the workplace was seen as necessary to avoid discriminating against the individual and was a prerequisite of acting professionally. The value being expressed was the need to address the behaviour of the individual and not to react in a judgemental manner to the behaviour in a negative way that might result in an unprofessional and/or discriminatory service being provided:

> You have to be professional and you have to separate the two, but I can't stop them creeping in. (*Female Probation Service Officer, 2+ years' experience*)

> I suppose to some extent I cut myself off because I'm here to do a job. I don't want my own feelings to actually interfere with it, although sometimes you can't help it. (*Female Probation Service Officer, 3+ years' experience*)

> That's interesting … to a certain extent you have to put them to one side. (*Female Probation Service Officer, 6+ years' experience*)

> I guess it's a lot of the time, you have to ignore your personal values, you have to go in on that professional level. (*Female Probation Service Officer, 4+ years' experience*)

This was seen as not always easy to achieve, but necessary to be controlled and used consciously. It was also necessary to accept individual offenders as people and references were made to 'disliking the behaviour, rather than the individual':

> Well I think you need to be balanced, I think you need to be aware of your own codes if you like and I think for me particularly in some areas like child protection, sex offenders or what have you … I keep hold of the fact that it's the behaviour that I dislike, that is unacceptable, not the individual. (*Female Probation Officer, 18+ years' experience*)

Despite the initial lack of 'value statements', there did emerge a number of references to what might be described as general, underpinning values and beliefs which may be seen to relate to some degree to those espoused by Williams (1995) and Napo (2006c) but less so to broader arguments put by others (e.g. Nellis 1999, Nellis 2002a). These included statements about the ability of individuals to change, although this was referred to spontaneously in only eight interviews (from the 43 conducted with practitioners). Despite this, there would appear to be a more fundamental and widespread belief in potential change. This was revealed when respondents were asked about aspects of the professional relationship between them and their supervisees and also about what they saw as the purpose of supervision and assessment.

This belief in potential change was seen as a fundamental reason why the respondents had come into the service and why they continued to work within it. Little reference was made to 'different types' of offenders and apparently respondents felt that potentially all could affect some level of change, whatever their past behaviour and offending. For some, this ability to change appears to be the result of inherent 'goodness'; the belief that individuals have committed (sometimes very serious) offences because of circumstances and poor life choices and decisions, rather than 'badness', something which it has been argued is at variance with the growing slant of government thinking (e.g. Faulkner 2008). This belief may be regarded as being towards the determinist rather than the free will end of the spectrum in terms of explaining crime:

> I couldn't do the job if I couldn't hold to the fundamental core of respect for the individual and a belief in people's ability to change. (*Female Probation Officer, 14+ years' experience*)

> … they don't want to be leading the lifestyles that they are. I don't believe people are inherently bad and they offend from choice. I think they want to change those factors. (*Male Probation Officer, 2+ years' experience*)

> People can change, we are all an open book at the outset and I think that we are products of our experience and I think and everyone's experience is different, we're not all the same and I think we need to acknowledge that. I think that generally people are good and it's generally about behaviour as a result of our experiences. (*Female Probation Officer, 18+ years' experience*)

This ability to change can be influenced by timing, intervention and choice. Most respondents referred to the general ability to change, but the following comments were also made by individuals:

> I'm a strong believer in people changing if they want to change – it's their choice, but if they are posing risks and don't want to change or look at it, that's a different thing entirely. (*Male Probation Officer, 15+ years' experience*)

> I've always believed people have the ability to change. Not everybody wants to or are ready to, but I've always had that belief people have and I guess that if I didn't I wouldn't be here and that some people need that support to take those steps. (*Female Probation Officer, 2+ years' experience*)

> But if it's about bringing people into mainstream society then the relationship is vital. You have to feel some kind of vocational …… you have to believe people can change and that this is a way to facilitate it. (*Female Probation Officer, 14+ years' experience*)

Finally, a minority of respondents made specific comments about 'helping' and 'rehabilitation'. As with other comments discussed above, these tended not to be expressed spontaneously, but after prompt questions around values and the purpose of the probation service. For example:

> I came in to help people, that's what I came in to do. Although it's not the only thing in the job, I still feel that is very much there for me and as soon as I feel I'm not doing that, I'll leave. (*Female Probation Officer, 2+ years' experience*)

> … the values that brought me in here, I wanted to help people, that's why I came into the job, I wanted to do something. (*Female Probation Officer, 2+ years' experience*)

> In the end of the day it has to be about rehabilitation, I'll use the tools I have to try and help them in a non-judgemental way and to let them know that. (*Female Probation Service Officer, 2+ years' experience*)

> Helping people in their rehabilitation … enabling them to lead a happier life. I suppose happy is not the right word, I hope I do make a difference with some people. (*Female Probation Service Officer, 15+ years' experience*)

> I came to probation, or previously social work because I obviously want to make a difference to people's lives to make things work and improve quality of life. (*Male Probation Officer, 3+ years' experience*)

Therefore views expressed did reflect to some degree notions of advising, assisting and befriending offenders for some respondents, which could result in improved social functioning and reduced levels of re-offending.

Focus Groups, Case Files and PSRs

Whilst semi-structured interviews were the primary source of data employed, others were used in order to confirm or contradict such findings. Focus group 1 had been previously interviewed as individual respondents, whilst focus group 2 had not. They were informed that an emerging theme was this issue of 'keeping values away' from the workplace to avoid discriminatory practice. Neither group contradicted this, nor offered a wider range of particular values, although group 1 responded to the statement in a way that more directly re-affirmed the idea of not allowing values to interfere with the work of supervision. Group 2 made no reference to specific values, but clearly felt that their desire to work in a flexible, humanistic way was being compromised by a management that was obsessed by targets and a managerialist approach. This was mentioned spontaneously by one respondent, who described the 'paucity of the values debate'. Group 1, when asked about service 'values' overall, also made reference to the management culture of targets, public image and accountability, rather than any interest in more values-based work. Thus these data tend to confirm that of the semi-structured interviews, as well as the lack of spontaneous broader statements around values.

Further data were collected from case files and PSRs. A total of 48 files and PSRs were examined, 24 from each of the two areas in the study. These were further divided equally between files and PSRs dating from 2000-01 and those from 2005-06, being randomly chosen as the first case commenced in a calendar month.

Examination of case records and pre-sentence reports does not provide direct personal statements about values, but it is the case that there was a clear underlying belief in the whole purpose of probation supervision being about personal change. PSR proposals referred to what might be put in place by the court in order to allow the probation service to facilitate further change. This was clearly seen as the purpose of formal contact with the service and was emphasised across a range of offence types and seriousness. This was consistent across the entire sample, which included PSRs written some years apart, from 2000-01 and 2005-06, indicating an unchanging presumption of the possibilities of change. It is also the case that case records exhibited an underlying assumption that the aim and purpose of supervision was to facilitate change in all cases, although this was acknowledged as difficult in a small minority of cases. Again, this pattern was evident across those cases from 2000-01 and 2005-06.

Summary

Whilst respondents did not spontaneously articulate a personal value system that was fundamental to their job, there were clear themes about the ability of people to change and the need to treat individual offenders professionally and fairly, whatever the nature of the offences committed, echoing the views of Williams (1995) made over a decade previously, as well as similar arguments made more recently (Napo 2006c). Finally, although a minority view, 'helping' and 'rehabilitation' were seen as fundamental to the job by respondents trained not only as social workers, but also recently via the DiPS. In terms of broader theory, there was little here to indicate that respondents emphasised the management of groups based on risk factors, or the control of individuals per se (Feeley and Simon 1992, Rose 2000).

Attitudes to Risk

The sample responding below is the same as above, with the addition of eight respondents at middle manager grade (also known as team managers, formally known as senior probation officers). Attitudes of respondents to practice developments around the risk of harm and re-offending were recorded via an attitudinal Likert scale completed prior to their personal interview. The scale was completed privately by the individual, without any involvement of the researcher.

Prior to reporting respondents' views, it is worth noting the practice and policy context within which they were operating. Emerging from the development of National Standards following the 1991 CJA, risk assessment became increasingly central to probation policy and 'official' practice, but was not accepted unequivocally by practitioners initially (Kemshall 2003: 84). At its creation in 2001, the NPS produced a list of five aims, the first of which was the 'protection of the public' and a necessary pre-requisite was the identification and management of offenders according to their perceived level of risk (Home Office 2001). To enable practitioners to make such assessments, the NPS created the OASys assessment system, an actuarial and clinical 'third generation' assessment tool intended to identify both risk of re-offending and harm (Home Office 2002b). From 2004-05, NOMS re-asserted the central importance of risk assessment and management, via its OMM (National Offender Management Service 2005b, National Offender Management Service 2006b). This introduced the idea of four levels, or 'tiers', which categorised offenders according to both risk dimensions and dictated the range and type of intervention that should follow. This enshrined the notion of 'resources following risk' which had become a 'buzzword' within the NPS since its inception (Home Office 2001). In brief, this meant the greater the overall mix of risk factors, the higher level of intervention an individual offender would receive, both in terms of changing behaviour and of risk management and control. Risk was therefore fundamental to the government's purposes for the NPS, as the basis of the protection of the public which was to be constructed on the basis of OASys assessments which would result in the allocation of individual offenders into tiers under the OMM. This in turn would dictate the level of intervention (as resources were to follow risk) and may be seen as an example, at least in outline of actuarial risk assessment and management (Feeley and Simon 1992).

The Likert statements relating to risk were as follows:

1. The assessment of an individual's risk of harm is of central importance to the work of the probation service
2. It is appropriate that 'resources follow risk'. In other words, those individuals assessed as being of higher risk of harm should receive greater involvement from the probation service
3. Resources following risk is a good thing for the probation service, although it means that individuals regarded as low risk of harm receive a poorer service
4. Too much probation time is spent on addressing risk of harm. Risk of re-offending should have more emphasis

For each statement, respondents could choose one from five possible options: 'Strongly Agree', 'Agree', 'Neither Agree nor Disagree', 'Disagree', 'Strongly Disagree'.

Table 4.1   Importance of risk assessment

Statement: The assessment of an individual's risk of harm is of central importance to the work of the probation service

	Frequency	Percent
Strongly agree	44	86.3
Agree	7	13.7
Neither Agree nor Disagree	0	0
Disagree	0	0
Strongly Disagree	0	0
Total	51	100.0

Clearly respondents have fully recognised the prominence given to risk assessment by the service, although it is not apparent whether they agreed with the statement in terms of whether or not risk assessment *should* have such pre-eminence, i.e. they may have seen the question as 'factual'. However, from responses to other Likert statements below and also to questions around risk reported on in the semi structured interviews, respondents do appear to accept risk assessment as a valid and proper task from them as practitioners and managers. This view is shared by all respondents, including those employed by the service prior to the current emphasis on assessment. This statement was the only one to result in the whole sample choosing one side of the agree/disagree 'divide'. As mentioned, the assessment of risk is very much fundamental to the official government aims for the service. Kemshall sees the risk agenda operating at an increasingly intense level, the service embracing it in a 'pragmatic adaptation to the new penality of the New Right' (Kemshall 2003: 92). Indeed, in 2007 the official aims of NOMS remained: protect the public; reduce re-offending; punish offenders; rehabilitate offenders; ensure victims feel justice has been done (National Offender Management Service 2007a).

Table 4.2   Resources should follow risk

Statement: It is appropriate that 'resources follow risk'. In other words, those individuals assessed as being of higher risk of harm should receive greater involvement from the probation service.

	Frequency	Percent
Strongly agree	16	31.4
Agree	31	60.8
Neither Agree nor Disagree	2	3.9
Disagree	2	3.9
Total	51	100.0

Further to risk assessment itself, respondents strongly endorsed the idea that those being of higher risk of harm should receive greater involvement from the service. This concept carries the implicit idea that risk of re-offending is of a reduced importance, or that it can be effectively addressed with fewer resources. As mentioned above, this statement does imply agreement with the idea of the importance of risk assessment.

Table 4.3   Level of harm and level of service

Statement: Resources following risk is a good thing for the probation service, although it means that individuals regarded as low risk of harm receive a poorer service.

	Frequency	Percent
Strongly agree	8	15.7
Agree	18	35.3
Neither Agree nor Disagree	9	17.6
Disagree	12	23.5
Strongly disagree	1	2.0
Total	48	94.1
Missing	3	5.9
Total	51	100.0

Some 51 per cent of respondents agreed/strongly agreed with this statement, in contrast to the 92 per cent who agreed/strongly agreed in Table 4.2 above (6 per cent of respondents did not complete this statement and their replies are 'missing'). It would appear that the addition of the idea of a poorer service being provided to those assessed as being of low risk of harm had an impact on respondents' thinking. In addition, just over one respondent in four disagreed/strongly disagreed with this statement. It may be the case that respondents have tended to fall into a default position of supporting the general idea of resources following risk, but that around four out of 10 have reconsidered their position when introduced to a more complex picture, particularly one which posits the possibility of a reduced, poorer service for 'lower risk' individuals. This is of note and the first example of other occasions where respondents may be reacting 'instinctively' to a 'sound bite' about a certain policy or policies central to government and the service overall and then modify their position when considering the issue in more depth.

With regards to this statement one factor is that such lower risk groups constitute the large majority of probation cases. For example, in a random selection of case files chosen for analysis, only three from 24 were assessed by the service as being 'high risk', figures that are consistent with the overall situation for England and Wales. None of the cases selected were of the highest potential risk, known as the 'critical few' (Kemshall and Wood 2007: 385), which represent only 1.5 per cent of the overall service caseload (Nash and Ryan 2003).

Table 4.4   Emphasis on risk of harm

Statement: Too much probation time is spent on addressing risk of harm. Risk of re-offending should have more emphasis

	Frequency	Percent
Strongly agree	2	3.9
Agree	12	23.5
Neither Agree nor Disagree	12	23.5
Disagree	24	47.1
Total	50	98.0
Missing	1	2.0
Total	51	100.0

This statement revealed a complexity of view, when compared to Tables 4.1 and 4.2 above and was linked to Table 4.3. Tables 4.1 and 4.2 referred to the importance of risk of harm in terms of assessment and levels of intervention. Although almost half of respondents disagreed with the statement in Table 4.4, this was considerably fewer than supported work related to risk of harm in Tables 4.1 and 4.2 and slightly over one in four respondents agreed with the idea that risk of re-offending was under-emphasised within the service. Perhaps the complexity of these concepts (and the possible ambivalence of the respondents' views) was illustrated by the one in four respondents who neither agreed nor disagreed with the statement. This would also tend to suggest that when respondents moved away from sound bite statements, their responses became more nuanced.

Case Files and PSRs

Data obtained from file reading and PSRs did relate more directly to practice, as opposed to attitudes elicited from a Likert scale and thus brought a different angle to the overall data. There were indications from the files that practitioners did tend to place more emphasis on risk of re-offending, rather than risk of harm. Of course, this did relate to the assessed level of risk of harm of the individual, but nevertheless, the data did reveal a concern with attempting to facilitate a change in the risk re-offending.

When considering the case files reviewed, in a large majority of cases, there was evidence of engagement with the individual with the aim of reducing re-offending. In such cases, there was no sense of the purpose of supervision being simply the management of risk or offenders (Feeley and Simon 1992) with the exception of one case from 2000-01. There were a minority of cases where there appeared to be little more to supervision than monitoring. However, this did not seem to be about the management of risk as such, rather it seemed to be the result, at least in part, of a perfunctory approach to the whole process. This is evident in seven cases overall from those reviewed from 2000-01. In all such cases the individual was seen as low risk of harm and re-offending and such levels of engagement may have been related to this. This pattern is repeated in the files from 2005 and thus whilst the cases have been allocated in terms of risk and tiering, there was little or no impression that the level or type of intervention was based on risk of harm levels only. Rather it was a combination of risk of harm and re-offending, as well as need that appeared to be the main drivers.

Consistently PSRs sought to explain why 'this offender committed this offence at this time' and how might the risk of re-offending be reduced in the future. Whilst risk of harm assessments were usually (but not always) made, the main purpose of the proposal was to address criminogenic needs to prevent further offending, the implication being that this would also reduce risk of harm. Invariably the court was invited to sentence on this rather than a risk of harm category and there was no sense of a sentence being imposed simply on the grounds of the latter. The only exceptions to this were the limited number of instances (three reports from the 48 reviewed) where the risk of custody was seen as high, given the serious nature of the offence. However, even in such instances, the conclusion of the report did imply that it would be important to address the risk of re-offending in due course.

Summary

A complex picture has emerged from the data in that respondents appeared to concur entirely with the importance of risk assessment and resources following risk, but that they became less unequivocal when considering the implications of more resources being used to manage higher risk of harm offenders, as this would tend to lead to a reduced service for lower risk of harm individuals who may have been of a high risk of re-offending. This tends to reflect other studies which saw practitioners initially accepting the importance of a risk category, but then changing their assessments and practice based on more personal, clinical knowledge (e.g. Robinson 2002, Lynch 1998, Kemshall and Maguire 2002). Additional data from case files and PSRs added further complexity as both tended to reveal a focus on re-offending as opposed to risk of harm. Of course, this could have been the result of the low number of such cases involving individuals with a high risk of harm.

Attitudes to Enforcement

Enforcement has become a fundamental measurement for success in the probation service, with high rates of breach for failures to comply being linked to probation area budgets (Merrington and Stanley 2007, Murphy 2004). It has been seen as a cornerstone of the previous Labour government's drive to make probation accountable to the courts and the wider public as well as making it part of punishment in the community (Home Office 2001). In recent years, breach rates have been seen to increase, the previous Justice Minister, Jack Straw noting: '95 per cent of offenders are being brought back to court for breaching their orders; in 1999 this was a mere 44 per cent' (Straw 2009: 3). The links between accountability and punishment are explicit in successive versions of National Standards describing the desire to ensure that the public can have confidence in a probation sentence being an 'effective punishment' (Merrington and Stanley 2007: 435). The OMM (National Offender Management Service 2005b, National Offender Management Service 2006b) introduced the idea of four levels, or 'tiers', which categorised offenders according to risk dimensions and dictated the range and type of intervention that should follow. All four categories are to receive 'punishment', only some are to receive 'help, change and control' (Raynor and Vanstone 2007: 80).

The Likert statements relating to enforcement were as follows:

1. More rigid enforcement is a good thing for the probation service as it increases the service's accountability.
2. More rigid enforcement is a good thing for the probation service because it means that the service is more concerned with law enforcement than enforcement that takes account of an individual's needs.
3. The reduction of individual professional discretion in respect of enforcement is a good thing because it contributes to a fairer criminal justice system.

Table 4.5   Enforcement and accountability

Statement: More rigid enforcement is a good thing for the probation service as it increases the service's accountability

	Frequency	Percent
Strongly agree	4	7.8
Agree	24	47.1
Neither Agree nor Disagree	17	33.3
Disagree	5	9.8
Strongly disagree	1	2.0
Total	51	100.0

Some 55 per cent of respondents strongly agreed/agreed with this statement, although a further one-third neither agreed nor disagreed. That said, fewer than one respondent in eight disagreed with it. However, it is of interest that only just over half of respondents identified with what is clearly a major policy for government and service management in terms of increasing the accountability of probation supervision which is itself part of making community sentences 'tougher', as outlined in the CJA 2003. These attitudes are discussed in more detail in Chapter 8 below.

Table 4.6   Law enforcement and individual needs

Statement: More rigid enforcement is a good thing for the probation service because it means that the service is more concerned with law enforcement than enforcement that takes account of an individual's needs

	Frequency	Percent
Strongly agree	1	2.0
Agree	2	3.9
Neither Agree nor Disagree	10	19.6
Disagree	30	58.8
Strongly disagree	4	7.8
Total	47	92.2
Missing	4	7.8
Total	51	100.0

The responses to this related statement would indicate that whatever respondents felt about the purposes and usefulness of enforcement, a clear majority did not agree with a policy or practice that was not linked in some way to the needs of those being supervised. In this way, whilst enforcement is clearly seen as important, it was also important that practitioner and wider service discretion was seen to operate and that the law with regards to compliance was not rigidly applied in a 'tick box' fashion. As discussed in more detail in Chapter 8, individual circumstances and differences appeared to be important and an element in the decision whether or not to enforce a community order or licence. This balance between what was previously called 'care and control' has been relevant in practice since the creation of the service (Burnett et al. 2007) and needs to be seen against the drive of government to increasingly reduce practitioner discretion in enforcement practice (Raynor and Vanstone 2007: 80).

Table 4.7   Reduction of professional discretion

Statement: The reduction of individual professional discretion in respect of enforcement is a good thing because it contributes to a fairer criminal justice system		
	Frequency	**Percent**
Strongly agree	3	5.9
Agree	13	25.5
Neither Agree nor Disagree	16	31.4
Disagree	14	27.5
Strongly disagree	4	7.8
Total	50	98.0
Missing	1	2.0
Total	51	100.0

This statement in Table 4.7 revealed ambivalence amongst respondents about whether professional discretion could result in unfair treatment for some offenders, at least in terms of enforcement. The sample was split almost equally three ways in percentage terms between agree/strongly agree, neither, or disagree/strongly disagree. This statement was related to that in Table 4.6 in that professional discretion was clearly needed if decisions about enforcement are to be linked to individual needs, as opposed to there being an administrative approach to enforcement and breach. Despite this, there was less of a rejection of this statement than for the previous one.

However, the most interesting factor was the apparent agreement of around one in three respondents that the reduction in professional discretion was a 'good thing'. Although this was qualified by the addition of a link to fairness, it is interesting that these respondents were unable to allow for the possibility of fairness being delivered via discretion and that this might compromise the fair treatment of individuals. Examining the respondents who strongly agreed or agreed with this statement, there was no pattern that emerged as all three grades were represented, as were job roles. Although it might have been expected that those involved in supervising higher risk individuals might be in agreement, there was a roughly equal split in the views of this group, with four of the seven agreeing or strongly agreeing. Of the three strongly agreeing, one was a team manager, one a probation officer in 'high risk', one a probation officer in 'low risk'. Given this diversity amongst the group, this may have been another example of the 'sound bite' reaction noted above.

Case Files and Focus Groups

Case files were an important source of data here as they brought an insight into actual practice as opposed to attitudes about practice revealed by the Likert data. In both areas and in both time periods, the majority of cases missed appointments and hence became subject to enforcement procedures, in that absences had to be designated as acceptable or unacceptable, with two unacceptable absences in any twelve month period necessitating breach proceedings. The designation of absences as acceptable or otherwise was somewhat unclear, as supervisors were supposed to seek management agreement to designate absences as acceptable if they fell outside a fairly prescriptive list, which included all sickness absences requiring medical or self-certification. Furthermore, two unacceptable absences should have always resulted in breach action without management agreement.

It is far from clear that enforcement and breach proceeding were conducted in such a manner in the sample. In both areas there was no sense of a systematic administrative approach to enforcement and breach. Many absences were accepted without evidence and there were few if any references to management grades to agree the acceptability of absences or a decision not to commence breach proceedings. There was a strong sense of clinical judgements being made about breach and enforcement based on the general attitude and level of engagement and compliance shown by the individual to date or on particular personal needs at any time. Of the 48 files read, there were 12 separate examples of individuals having two or more unacceptable absences without breach action being initiated. This is interesting in itself and suggests something of a gap between the rhetoric of the 'new, tough probation' and some practice.

The focus groups were asked to comment on the desirability of strict enforcement for accountability purposes. Both groups took a similar view, not addressing the issue directly, but making more of the importance of using professional judgement and 'creativity' in deciding whether absences should be acceptable or not. Once a second absence was unacceptable, breach was seen as inevitable.

Summary

A fairly complex picture has emerged from the data. Respondents in the Likert Scales and focus groups nor practitioners represented in the case files appeared to agree with or adhere wholeheartedly to government views on the need for strict and systematic enforcement. The key to this, in the main appears to be the crucial decision of the accepting or not of absences. These everyday decisions have a clear impact upon individual orders, but also wider policy and can be seen as examples of practitioners making important everyday decisions based on their own perceptions, values and circumstances, rather than official policy directions based in the new penality (Cheliotis 2006, Lipsky 1980).

Whilst a majority accepted stricter enforcement in terms of increasing the accountability of the service, this was replaced by a larger majority that disagreed with rigid enforcement for purely law enforcement purposes. Overall, the data suggest that whatever its importance, enforcement needs to be exercised with professional judgement, with the overall attitude, compliance and needs of individual offenders needing to be taken into consideration. Of course, there may have been a difference between (a) views about enforcement and (b) practice around enforcement. The above discussion has concentrated on views about enforcement, with the exception of the case files, which do tend to confirm respondent views.

Attitudes to Managerialism

Since the mid 1980s (Home Office 1984) successive governments have sought to increase central control over the service, finally creating the NPS in 2001. More recently the two main themes of New Labour governance between 1997 and 2010 were seen as managerialism and centralisation (Newburn 2003, Flynn 2002a, Senior et al. 2007), with one consequent policy being the setting of practice targets from the centre. An example is the setting of ambitious targets for the completion of accredited programmes. Seen as in part the result of optimism about the potential effectiveness of such programmes, these were intended to be the main component of the target set for the NPS to reduce re-offending by 5 per cent (Home Office 2000a, Home Office 2001). At the same time, what has been called 'programme fetishism' has been seen as causing a lack of concern about individual supervision and its process and content (Morgan 2003). A further factor is government pushing the need to prosecute enforcement vigorously and, via the risk, public protection and new penality agendas (Feeley and Simon 1992, Kemshall and Wood 2007) to emphasise the assessment and management of an individuals' risk, rather that engagement in transformative work, notwithstanding the promotion of accredited programmes.

The statements relating to managerialism were as follows:

1. The government and the NPD are more interested in the probation service hitting enforcement and referral targets for accredited programmes than they are in the content and quality of supervision
2. My Probation Area senior management is more interested in hitting enforcement and referral targets than it is in the content and quality of supervision
3. Individuals are often placed on accredited programmes that are not suitable because of referral targets
4. The probation service sees offenders as 'bundles of criminogenic needs' to be managed, rather than individuals with particular needs that can be addressed through supervision

For each statement, respondents could choose one from five possible options: 'Strongly Agree', 'Agree', 'Neither Agree nor Disagree', 'Disagree', 'Strongly Disagree'.

Table 4.8   Government targets for enforcement and accredited programmes

Statement: The government and the NPD are more interested in the probation service hitting enforcement and referral targets for accredited programmes than they are in the content and quality of supervision

	Frequency	Percent
Strongly agree	21	41.2
Agree	19	37.3
Neither Agree nor Disagree	5	9.8
Disagree	3	5.9
Total	48	94.1
Missing	3	5.9
Total	51	100.0

In excess of 78 per cent of respondents agreed/strongly agreed with the statement relating to this issue, with only one in around 7 actually disagreeing. This would imply a belief that government takes a managerialist approach to completion of targets and also holds individual supervision in lower regard in terms of its importance than accredited programmes. This apparent cynicism about this aspect of the government agenda is a theme that was repeated in the semi-structured interviews and is discussed in Chapters 7-9 below.

Table 4.9   Area management targets for enforcement and accredited programmes

Statement: My Probation Area senior management is more interested in hitting enforcement and referral targets for accredited programmes than it is in the content and quality of supervision

	Frequency	Percent
Strongly agree	12	23.5
Agree	24	47.1
Neither Agree nor Disagree	4	7.8
Disagree	7	13.7
Total	47	92.2
Missing	4	7.8
Total	51	100.0

It would appear that respondents in the main transferred similar views about government attitudes to accredited programmes and individual supervision to area managements, although the percentage agreeing/strongly disagreeing did drop some seven percentage points (40 to 36 individuals). Within this, however, the biggest change was between strongly agree and agree; whilst overall the two affirmative categories reduced in number, the number simply agreeing increased. The number disagreeing more than doubled, but remained at fewer than one in seven respondents. Overall, there appeared to be little difference in the attitude towards government and area managements in this regard.

Table 4.10   Unsuitable referrals to accredited programmes

Statement: Individuals are often placed on accredited programmes that are not suitable because of referral targets

	Frequency	Percent
Strongly agree	14	27.5
Agree	19	37.3
Neither Agree nor Disagree	7	13.7
Disagree	9	17.6
Strongly disagree	1	2.0
Total	50	98.0
Missing	1	2.0
Total	51	100.0

At the same time as the introduction of targets for programme completions there was developing widespread monitoring of area performance by the NPS. In turn this led in some instances to the idea that government was overly concerned about putting individuals through programmes to fulfil targets, rather than only putting suitable individuals through following practitioner assessment (e.g. Farrow 2004a, Gorman 2001) and there is evidence, for example, of first time offenders being increasingly placed on programmes intended for medium-high risk of re-offending individuals in order to fulfil targets and thus ignoring the so-called 'risk principle' (McGuire 2001, Raynor and Vanstone 2007: 73). This belief had some resonance with respondents, some 65 per cent agreeing/strongly agreeing with statement and only one respondent in five disagreeing/strongly disagreeing. Whilst this statement is clearly linked to the previous two and there remained a clear majority of two respondents in three agreeing or strongly agreeing, there is something less equivocal about the responses, with one in five disagreeing or strongly disagreeing.

Focus Groups

The focus groups were not asked questions specifically about managerialism and programme referrals, but comments did emerge about the attitude of management to these issues. Group 1 made comments that management 'only cared' about referrals to accredited programmes and other targets and were not concerned about what practitioners were doing in terms of content or quality. Moreover, they stated that in some cases individuals were placed on programmes that could be detrimental, due to the 'necessity' of hitting targets that were linked to budgets. Group 2, who had not been previously interviewed, made fewer references to these issues, but did state that management in general was now about a 'tick box' mentality not quality and that supervision by managers with practitioners about supervision content and quality did not occur. Thus these secondary data did tend to confirm the prime Likert data.

Summary

A fairly consistent picture has emerged from the data. Respondents had a consistent belief that the government and senior management of the service were following, at least in part, managerialist agenda that was about referrals to various interventions based not so much on identified offender need as on targets. This approach was implicitly rejected, the belief being that all interventions should be needs based. There was no indication that respondents thought that accredited programmes had no intrinsic value, rather that they should be used more appropriately and in a targeted manner based on identified need.

The Views of Trainees

We have so far concentrated on the views of practitioners. However, in a process parallel to the main study, the views of recently recruited trainee probation officers (TPOs) were sought around a range of similar themes (for a full discussion, see Deering 2010).

TPOs were asked a range of questions, including their reasons for becoming a trainee and views on the causes of crime. The questions were open in nature and respondents could write as much or as little as they wished. There was also a Likert scale relating to attitudes about a range of service policy and practice. A number of questions directly related to the categories put to practitioners above were asked, although these were not elicited in the same manner, nor was the wording of the questions identical. As a result, care must be taken in interpreting them in comparison to the views expressed above. As the views expressed by the two cohorts were consistent across their two year training, their responses have been aggregated.

Values, Beliefs and Attitudes

Respondents were asked 'What sort of values and beliefs do you think you need to become a Probation Officer?'. The values expressed by respondents throughout their two-year training were consistent as they were across both cohorts. In five of the six questionnaires collected, a 'belief in individuals' ability to change' was the most frequently named value, in each case being named by over 50 per cent of respondents. In the sixth set of results, the ability to change was placed second, behind a commitment to anti-discriminatory practice. As might be expected with an open question there were a wide range of responses, including the following: having a commitment to diversity and anti-discriminatory practice; treating people with respect; being non-judgemental; being empathic; having a belief that crime needs to be punished; being 'anti-crime'; having a sense of 'justice'.

In addition, TPOs were asked *'What do you think are the causes of crime?'*. Whilst not a direct question about values, it did elicit a range of views relating to personal values and their role. Consistently across the period of training and the two cohorts, the picture was one of respondents attributing crime to determinist factors such as social, economic and environmental inequalities and other structural variables. The biggest single factor was seen as the misuse of drugs and alcohol, with other personal problems also seen as important. There was overall a lack of mention of factors that emphasise personal responsibility, rational choice or 'crime as routine activity'.

It is clear that the majority of values, beliefs and attitudes listed related to the need for and importance of engaging with individuals in a meaningful and humanistic manner and the causes of crime being social and economic and, to some extent, determinist. These values and attitudes would appear to concur with the more traditional ones associated with the probation service (Williams 1995) and by arguments put forward by Napo (2006c). Overwhelmingly, the respondents believed in people's ability to change within an overall theme of rehabilitation, rather than punishment, or even management. In this regard, these views echoed those of former trainees in the Midlands and south-west of England, who in contemporary studies revealed that they had joined the service as a trainee for reasons very much connected to 'advising, assisting and befriending' offenders (Annison 2006, Annison et al. 2008).

The following data are taken from a Likert scale within the questionnaire. In each case respondents could choose one from four possible options: 'Strongly Agree', 'Agree', 'Disagree', 'Strongly Disagree'. The attitudes expressed were consistent across the period of training, so the responses for the two cohorts have been aggregated (see Table 4.11).

Attitudes to Risk

Trainees in both cohorts showed a similar unanimous view concerning the importance of risk assessment as practitioners (see Table 4.11). This was consistent across their two year training and shows that they held this view on becoming trainees and had not had to be 'trained into' the attitude. However, the same proviso as mentioned above in relation to Table 4.1 applies as the statement does not elicit whether respondents felt that this should be the case.

Table 4.11   Trainees' views on risk assessment

Statement: Risk assessment and management is a vitally important task for the probation service

First Cohort		
	Frequency	**Percent**
Strongly agree	58	65.9
Agree	28	31.8
Total	86	97.7
Missing	2	2.3
Total	88	100.0
Second Cohort		
	Frequency	**Percent**
Strongly agree	88	72.1
Agree	34	27.9
Total	122	100.0

Table 4.12   Trainees' views on enforcement

Statement: If an individual fails to keep an appointment with their probation officer, they should be immediately breached

First Cohort		
	Frequency	**Percent**
Strongly agree	2	2.3
Agree	17	19.3
Disagree	54	61.4
Strongly disagree	13	14.8
Total	86	97.7
Missing	2	2.3
Total	88	100.0
Second Cohort		
	Frequency	**Percent**
Strongly agree	1	0.8
Agree	19	15.6
Disagree	79	64.8
Strongly disagree	22	18.0
Total	121	99.2
Missing	1	0.8
Total	122	100.0

Enforcement

Whilst the statement (Table 4.12) was not the same as those put to practitioners about enforcement, there was some indication of similar beliefs underlying both sets of answers. The statement put to TPOs about immediate breach for a missed appointment may be analogous to 'rigid enforcement' in Tables 4.6 and 4.7 which was considered by practitioners. The latter were equivocal about rigid enforcement, both acknowledging its importance, but having concerns about it being applied without reference to professional discretion and the needs of individual offenders. TPOs showed a consistent opposition to rigid enforcement as operationalised by immediate breach on a missed appointment, 76 per cent of the first cohort and 83 per cent of the second either disagreeing or strongly disagreeing.

The Range of Respondents' Views

The final section in this chapter considers the extent to which the views expressed by practitioners, managers and TPOs are consistent or differ across a range of variables. In the case of practitioners and managers, the Likert scale data were analysed by comparing responses to the statements (four relating to both risk and managerialism; three relating to enforcement) by: gender, grade, qualification, race/ethnic origin, length of employment, team/unit function (i.e. supervision of high risk of harm, supervision of medium/low risk of harm and assessment) and employing probation area. As the data are nominal and ordinal, comparison between groups and significance testing uses the chi-square procedure. Due to the relatively small sample size, the chi-square tests for statistical significance are of disputed suitability (Clegg 1990) and the results, therefore must be treated with some caution.

For practitioners, the semi-structured interview data were analysed by comparing responses by: gender, grade, qualification, length of employment, team/unit function (i.e. supervision of high risk of harm, supervision of medium/low risk of harm and assessment) and employing probation area. Finally, regarding the TPOs, the responses to the open questions and the Likert statements posed in the questionnaire were analysed as a group response only, but comparisons were made between each of the three questionnaires that the cohort completed and between the two cohorts.

The most obvious theme emerging from the data was its homogeneity. Regarding the qualitative interview data, all the themes discussed above were expressed by a range of respondents across the variables and sample attributes, including gender, grade, qualification and length of time in the service. It is of interest that although not heavily represented within the sample, respondents trained as social workers did not express an obviously different range of values and beliefs to those trained more recently under the DiPS, nor indeed different to PSOs, a grade not formally qualified, but recruited directly. It is also of note that the respondents expressing most consistently and spontaneously a range of values underlying their work were TPOs. The Likert data were also homogeneous. Some 77 variables (11 statements x seven variables) were analysed and only a small minority revealed significant differences in attitude.

Significance Testing

Due to this overall homogeneity and to make the results as meaningful as possible, the data were reduced via the following three procedures:

1. Reducing the categories to 'Agree' (by merging Strongly Agree and Agree), Neither Agree Nor Disagree and 'Disagree' (by merging Strongly Disagree and Disagree).
2. Reducing the categories further by removing 'Neither Agree Nor Disagree (by treating all such replies as 'Missing').
3. By removing all management grades from the analysis and using 'Agree' and 'Disagree' categories only.

Having completed these procedures, significant differences were only found in the following instances and relate to one statement only. It will be noted that the only variable involved is now respondent grade:

Table 4.13   Referrals to accredited programmes – significance testing (1)

		Agree	Disagree
Statement: Individuals are often placed on accredited programmes that are not suitable because of referral targets			
PSO	Count	4.0	3.0
	Expected Count	5.4	1.6
PO	Count	26.0	3.0
	Expected Count	22.3	6.7
SPO	Count	3.0	4.0
	Expected Count	5.4	1.6
Total	Count	33.0	10.0

Using the chi-square test, a significant difference emerges between the POs and the other two grades (p. =.013) showing probation officers to significantly be more likely to agree with the statement. The test was repeated after removing the management responses (see Table 4.14)

Once again, a significant (although reduced) difference (p. =.038) is revealed between grades, in this instance POs and PSOs and a pattern is apparent, with POs clearly more likely to agree with the statement. These differences may be related to the idea that manager and PSO grades have more of a positive attitude towards referrals to accredited programmes due to a perceived need to hit referral and completion

Table 4.14   Referrals to accredited programmes – significance testing (2)

Statement: Individuals are often placed on accredited programmes that are not suitable because of referral targets			
		Agree	Disagree
PSO	Count	4.0	3.0
	Expected Count	5.8	1.2
PO	Count	26.0	3.0
	Expected Count	24.2	4.8
Total	Count	30.0	6.0

targets (both grades) and due to the attitude of those directly involved in the delivery of programmes as group workers (PSO grades). It may thus be reasonable to assume that these grades might have a more positive view as a result.

Conclusion

At this stage, it is worth emphasising that (and referring to the literature discussed in outline at the start of this chapter) it was not clear what views might have been expected, given the paucity of empirical studies. However, if respondents had been significantly influenced by official views and policies they might have been expected to attach great importance to risk assessment and management and enforcement.

It is apparent that overall this sample was highly homogeneous across a range of attitudes and values, both in terms of the qualitative and quantitative data. Moreover, the secondary data from focus groups, PSRs and case files, whilst not always relating directly to the issues being discussed, did not provide any contradictory data of significance. The only differences that have emerged were those apparent between trainees and practitioners as regards a range of value statements and between PO and other grades about the placing of certain individual offenders on accredited programmes for the purposes of hitting targets for participation and completion, rather than for suitability purposes. The reasons for this are discussed above but are unclear. However, it is the case that such difference largely disappeared when data from the semi-structured interviews is considered below in Chapter 8 and this may be an instance of certain grades (in this case PSOs) reacting more positively to a sound bite about referrals than they did when considering the issue more in depth.

Although there was an apparent lack of the articulation of fundamental underlying values which guide the everyday practice of individuals, a belief in an individual's ability to change was apparent, as was the need for non-discriminatory practice (Williams 1995, Napo 2006c). Furthermore, whilst there was a lack of spontaneously expressed values about the causes of offending and society's approach to crime, punishment and rehabilitation, it was nevertheless apparent that there was no support for notions of punishment or 'simple' management of offenders as overall aims for the probation service (Home Office 2001).

This issue of professional discretion was important in that one third of the sample considered it to be 'a good thing' that enforcement practice reduced professional discretion, due to the possibility that the latter might result in unfair, differential treatment of individuals. This group was from a range of grades and job roles, including four of the seven respondents who supervised higher risk individuals, but they were not identifiable as a recognisable 'type' within the overall sample. Again this could have been an example of a reaction to a sound bite.

Whilst there is some indication that respondents accept the importance of risk assessment and management and enforcement, it is the case that these views are tempered by the need to pay attention to individual offender needs. Finally, there is the issue of opposition to what is seen as a target-driven culture in which the service is required to practice in certain prescribed ways, rather than in a way more directed by individual offender need.

In summary, a number of issues emerged which are developed in later chapters:

- The extent to which practitioners are guided in their everyday practice by a fundamental set of attitudes and values.
- The reasons for the apparent homogeneity of views expressed by a sample differing in a range of attributes, such as length of service, training and gender and the impact of professional cultures in moulding the attitudes and values of individuals.
- The apparent similarity in the views of practitioners and trainees, implying that the latter do not represent a 'new breed' of employee, more obviously in agreement with shifts in government policy and intentions for the service.
- The extent to which respondents are cynical about the use of targets by government and senior management for certain areas of practice, rather than by assessed need and the significantly different views held by probation officers when compared to other grades.
- The extent to which these attitudes coincide with 'official' government and senior management views about these issues.

1 Probation – a tainted but resilient concept

Despite governmental attempts to eradicate it from criminal justice vocabulary (Worrall 2008a), the concept of 'probation' has proved remarkably resilient and has, in recent years, come to signify resistance to and subversion of the dominant penal discourse of 'offender management'. It has become an 'imaginary penality' (Carlen 2008) – an area of work where it is necessary for practitioners to act *as if* they believe in the rules about the effectiveness of 'risk-crazed governance' while knowingly using those rules in ways that will also achieve meaning.

This is not a book about the history of probation, though we set the historic scene briefly below. Those who wish to read more about the history of probation are directed to Mair and Burke's (2012) excellent and challenging work, *Redemption, Rehabilitation and Risk Management*. Nor is it a book that describes or evaluates the work of the probation service with offenders in the community. Others (Raynor and Robinson 2009; Canton 2011; Robinson 2011) have recently completed that task. This is a book about probation workers and their occupational cultures. We intend it to fit as much into the literature on the sociology of organizations as it does into criminal justice literature. It is about what motivates people to become probation workers, how they make sense of their work, how they respond to turbulent political times and media criticism, and what stories they tell about the value of their contribution to society.

While a great deal has been written about the historical, political, policy and practice changes that have shaped the role of the probation officer, very little has been written on the changes to occupational cultures and the ways in which probation workers themselves view the impact of changes to their role and very little about the relationships between probation workers and other criminal justice agencies engaged in offender management. This book aims to fill that gap by exploring the meaning of 'doing probation work' from the perspective of probation workers themselves. Based on 60 extensive interviews with a range of probation workers, the book will reach beyond criminological and policy analysis to an application of sociological and organizational theory to rich qualitative data.

The probation service reached its centenary in 2007 but the response of workers to this was muted and more akin to a wake than a celebration, despite the imaginative efforts of both NAPO, the National Association of Probation

Officers (NAPO 2007) and Senior (2008) to compile books of recollections. Mair and Burke suggest that 'a more considered response would have been to ask how it had come to this' and they liken the service to a Cinderella who 'never actually arrived at the ball' (2012: 1). They also come to the pessimistic conclusion that while community sentences probably have some sort of future in criminal justice policy, this may well not be the case for the probation service. That it still exists after 100 years is something for which we should be grateful, they say, but 'it has lost its roots, its traditions, its culture, its professionalism' (2012: 192). It is the aim of this book to challenge this view and its narrative of decline. Our research suggests that, while working in a much changed world, probation workers retain a strong sense of all these things – possibly too strong for their own good. What Mair and Burke fail to give sufficient credit for is that modern probation workers can handle the 'imaginary'. They can do what is required of them – they can be competent offender managers – while constructing identities that allow them to believe that they are still part of an 'honourable profession' (Probation Worker 3[1]).

Setting the scene

The probation service has its roots in the work of the nineteenth-century police court missionaries, first employed by the Church of England Temperance Society in 1876 to 'reclaim' offenders charged with drunkenness or drink-related offences. The Probation of Offenders Act 1907 gave magistrates' courts the right to appoint probation officers, whose job it was to 'advise, assist and befriend' offenders placed under their supervision. The Criminal Justice Act 1925 made it obligatory for every court to appoint a probation officer, and during the first half of the twentieth century the work of the service expanded to include work with juveniles and families, as well as adult offenders. Part of that work included dealing with matrimonial problems and it was through this aspect of the work that the role of Divorce Court Welfare Officer developed. By the mid-1960s, where our research starts, the service had also taken responsibility for the welfare of prisoners, both inside prison and on release. In addition to the strong interpersonal skills required for supervising offenders in the community, the distinctive professional skill that probation officers developed was that of Social Inquiry (or Enquiry) – a social work assessment of an offender in their social environment, with the specific purpose of assisting courts to make sentencing decisions (Worrall and Hoy 2005: 78).

Although there had always been a degree of tension in the role of the probation officer between caring for offenders and controlling their criminal behaviour, these two aspects of the work were viewed as part and parcel of both the psychoanalytic casework and the paternalistic common-sense advice that combined to characterize the typical probation officer of the early and mid-twentieth century. By the end of the 1960s the probation service had grown from the status of a localized mission to that of a nationwide, secular, social work service to the courts. From the 1970s onwards a number of developments had paradoxical consequences for the service and resulted in a loss of identity or, to use Harris's (1980) term, 'dissonance'. Harris argued that probation officers were experiencing three kinds of dissonance. Moral dissonance resulted from conflicting ideologies about the purpose of probation; technical dissonance resulted from discouraging empirical evidence about the effectiveness of probation in reducing criminal behaviour; and operational dissonance resulted from the tension inherent in managing the 'care and control' aspects of the daily probation task (Worrall and Hoy 2005: 79).

By the mid-1980s the service was experiencing the rise of managerialism along with many other public sector organizations (Clarke *et al.* 1994; May 1994; Mayo *et al.* 2007). The most visible effect on probation officers was their perceived loss of professional autonomy and a greater emphasis on accountability through the devising of local and area objectives and, by the end of the decade, National Standards that directed practice in all aspects of report-writing and supervision. Few disputed the need to standardize some very variable and inconsistent practice across the country and between individual officers. Professional autonomy had undoubtedly been used in the past as an excuse for poor practice, but the overriding point about National Standards was that they limited the discretion of the individual probation officer and focused on the management of supervision rather than its content. In addition to making the individual officer more accountable to management, it also made the service more accountable to government (Worrall and Hoy 2005: 84).

Despite its acceptance that probation 'is a long-established concept, well understood internationally' (Home Office 1998: para. 2.13) the new Labour government elected in 1997 expressed its determination to abolish any terminology that might be 'misunderstood' or 'associated with tolerance of crime' (para. 2.12) by seeking to rename the service and to explore the possibility of merging it with the prison service (both attempts failing but only temporarily). The compromise reached was the creation of the National Probation Service in 2001[2] and the removal of the word 'probation' from court orders.

This compromise was short-lived, however, and there were further radical changes in the governance of probation. In 2003, the Carter Review (Carter 2003) and subsequent government response (Home Office 2004a) proposed a new National Offender Management Service (NOMS) which would finally bring together the prison and probation services (from June 2004) to provide 'end-to-end management of all offenders, whether they are serving sentences in prison, the community or both' (Home Office 2004b). Carter had envisaged that the services of probation might be provided by others – independent, voluntary organizations and even by the private and commercial sector. It was argued that competition between providers would raise standards generally. The Offender Management Act 2007 therefore empowered the Secretary of State (the Minister for Justice) to commission services directly, with the clear implication that they may be commissioned from providers other than the probation service. In 2010, the Probation Areas of England and Wales were reconstituted as 35 Probation Trusts, that would both provide probation services and also themselves commission services from others. In 2011 a 'procurement competition' to run community payback included potential providers from the commercial sector as well as from Probation Trusts (Worrall and Canton 2013). The first of these contracts was awarded jointly to Serco and the London Probation Trust in July 2012 (BBC News 2012).

These changes both reflected and confirmed a major change of ethos for the probation service, which now affirmed its objectives as 'enforcement, rehabilitation and public protection' (National Probation Service 2001). This has had considerable implications for work with offenders. *Enforcement* meant ensuring that offenders met the requirements of their orders. Returning an offender to court for non-compliance with an order (known as 'breaching'), which had been seen in the past as an admission of failure by the probation officer, was now viewed as essential to the credibility of orders and an act of strength (Hedderman 2003; Hedderman and Hough 2004). *Rehabilitation* was to focus no longer on the welfare of the offender (with some ill-defined hope that this will lead in some way to reform), but on the clear objective of measurably reduced reconviction. *Public protection* was to be achieved through the sound assessment and management of risk. The level of risk became the single most important criterion in determining the amount and type of subsequent intervention. Every offender who goes to prison or is placed on a community order is subject to an assessment of their risk of reoffending and of causing serious harm. There are various methods of calculating risk but the most widely used is a computerized system called the Offender Assessment System, or OASys (Burnett, Baker and Roberts 2007; Kemshall and Wood 2007). Under the National Offender Management Model, work with offenders is now divided into four 'tiers', depending on levels of risk and dangerousness. Tier 1 offenders are to be punished; tier 2 offenders are to be punished and helped; tier 3 offenders punished, helped and changed; tier 4 offenders punished, helped, changed and controlled (NOMS 2006; Worrall and Canton 2013).

Running in parallel to the changes in practice and management were debates about the need to change training to better equip new officers to meet the requirements of the modernized service. In 1995, the government repealed the legal requirement (that had existed for approximately 25 years) for all new probation officers to hold a social work qualification. The aim was to end the control by higher education over probation training but a compromise was reached that lasted until 2010, whereby trainee probation officers were required to study for a university degree at the same time as an NVQ Level 4 award. The programme was employment-led and run by consortia of probation services and higher education. While there was little doubt that this Diploma in Probation Studies was extremely demanding there was widespread disquiet that the specificity of the roles and tasks for which trainees were equipped did not produce the flexible, reflexive and creative employees that are needed to work imaginatively with offenders (Knight 2002). Some suggested the new training contributed to the deprofessionalization of the service (Aldridge 1999a). In 2011 the introduction of the new Qualifications Framework moved even further towards a model of internal workplace training, resulting in a qualification that is intended to be available to any employer (including voluntary and private sector organizations) (Ministry of Justice 2012).

Occupational cultures

Our interest in occupational cultures was sparked during our evaluation of a number of projects involving the multi-agency supervision of prolific and priority offenders. Observation of the joint working and personal interactions between probation workers and police officers, and latterly prison officers, revealed some of the tensions and dynamics of culture clashes and crossovers between criminal justice practitioners which we have written about elsewhere (Worrall *et al.* 2003; Mawby and Worrall 2004; Mawby *et al.* 2007). During our discussions and subsequent writing about aspects of these cultural dynamics, we became convinced that the occupational cultures of probation workers was a topic worthy of further research in its own right.

At its broadest, the culture of an occupation or an organization can be described as the values shared by individuals that manifest themselves in the practices of members of that occupation or organization. Mullins (2010: 739) describes occupational culture as 'how things are done around here' and Liebling *et al.* (2011: 153) refer to common ways of thinking that affect approaches to work.

In the management and organizational behaviour literature, distinctions are made and contested between organizational, occupational and professional cultures. Schein (2010: 1–2), refers to organizational culture as applying to all kinds of government, public, private and voluntary organizations. Within these, occupational groups form subcultures, and cutting across the occupational groups there may be smaller teams that develop micro-cultures. Johnson *et al.* (2009: 320) describe occupational culture as a broader construct than professional culture, developing through 'social interaction, shared experience, common training and affiliation, mutual support, associated values and norms, and similar personal characteristics of members of a particular occupational group'. The development of cultures provides a resource which allows groups and organizations to function internally, to react and adapt to the external environment and to integrate new members into ways of working. According to Morgan (2006: 126–38) organizational culture includes: operating norms, symbols and rituals of daily routine; language used within the group; stories, legends and myths about individuals, the group, and the organization which sustain cultural values; the work atmosphere/context, including the physical environment; and shared systems of meaning that are accepted, internalized and acted upon.

Utilizing similar themes, Schein argues (2010: 23) that culture can be analysed at three different levels. The first is that of *artefacts*, and this is the level of the tangible, the visible and the obvious. The second is that of *espoused values and beliefs*, and the third level is that of *underlying assumptions*, the taken-for-granted beliefs that influence behaviours and characterize an organization.

Drawing on these concepts, our intention is to identify and explore the characteristics of the occupational cultures of probation workers where the culture of a group can be defined as:

> a pattern of shared basic assumptions learned by a group as it solved its problems of external adaptation and internal integration, which has worked well enough to be considered valid and, therefore, to be taught to new members as the correct way to perceive, think, and feel in relation to those problems.
>
> (Schein 2010: 18)

No comprehensive body of research and literature exists on the occupational cultures of criminal justice practitioners. Perhaps one of the most enduring attempts to find the common ground is Rutherford's (1993) conceptualization of the 'working credos' that underpin the daily work of criminal justice personnel. Based on interviews with senior practitioners, he developed a typology of three 'credos' – Credo One (associated with punishment and degradation), Credo Two (associated with efficiency and the smooth running of the system) and Credo Three (associated with caring and rehabilitation). He concluded that the system in the early 1990s favoured the Credo Two practitioner over the Credo Three practitioner, whose position was ambiguous and precarious. He speculated about the increasing influence of Credo One practitioners but considered that they remained more a feature of the US than the UK criminal justice system.

Despite recent re-emergent interest in the cultures of prison officers (Crewe *et al.* 2010; Tait 2011), probation officers (Burke and Davies 2011), police auxiliaries (Dolman 2008) and private security workers (Button 2007; Hucklesby 2011), only police culture has been subjected to in-depth study (for recent examples, see Skolnick 2008 and Loftus 2009, 2010). Some of the early classic studies of policing examined police culture, even if they did not explicitly seek to do so. For example, Banton (1964) and Cain (1973) explored how officers made sense of their work and Skolnick (1966: 42) developed the idea of the 'working personality' of the police officer, arguing that there existed 'distinctive cognitive tendencies in police as an occupational grouping'. Other studies have revealed racist tendencies (Holdaway 1983) and debated the difficulty of changing police culture (Chan 1997). Robert Reiner (2010) has summarized this literature and categorized the core characteristics of 'cop culture' as: mission-action-cynicism-pessimism; suspicion; isolation/solidarity; conservatism; machismo; racial prejudice and pragmatism. It is widely accepted that all organizations have cultures and that these can be resistant to change and an obstacle to progress or alternatively a source of stability and a force for good. As Reiner's core characteristics suggest, 'cop culture' has been more often regarded as a problem than an asset, evidenced through the damaging and lingering condemnation of the police investigation into Stephen Lawrence's murder in 1993 (Rowe 2007). Despite this, Foster (2003: 222) has commented on positive police culture characteristics, namely 'the sense of mission, the desire to rid the streets of "the bad guys", the dedication and long hours, the willingness, on one level, to do society's dirty work'.

It is also significant to note that researchers now recognize that police culture is not monolithic, something which carries across to the literature on prison officer culture. This literature is not large, but existing studies suggest that there are multiple cultures, yet consistent characteristics that include discretion, cynicism, suspicion, nostalgia, physical and emotional strength, male-domination, authority and solidarity (see, for example, Crawley 2005; Arnold *et al.* 2007; Liebling *et al.* 2011). As Liebling *et al.* (2011: 154–5) point out, in contrast to studies of police culture, there have been comparatively few examinations of the 'working personalities' of prison officers, possibly due to the lack of glamour in their role and their ambivalent, often stereotypically negative, media representations.

The literature on probation cultures, like that on prison officer cultures, is similarly limited in size. It is a 'largely neglected and under-researched area of academic enquiry' according to Burke and Davies (2011: 2) perhaps because, as Mair and Burke (2012) point out, probation workers have never sought the symbolic status of other criminal justice practitioners. Nevertheless, in recent years a number of welcome studies have emerged that indicate a growing interest in this area of probation research. These, together with others that inform on probation cultures without explicitly investigating them, include Nash (1999, 2004, 2008); McNeill (2001); Vanstone (2004); Treadwell (2006); Gelsthorpe (2007); Nellis (2007); Robinson and Burnett (2007); Annison *et al.* (2008); Forbes (2010); Gregory (2010); Burke and Davies (2011); Deering (2011) and Phillips (2010, 2011). Some of the themes that are prominent in these works are: the early religious and philanthropic influences, an emphasis on the individuality and creativity of probation officers and the significance of professional autonomy, 'humanistic sensibility' (Nellis 2007), and the influence of social casework and discretion. It is to this previously neglected but increasingly significant area of research that this book seeks to contribute.

Having discussed the concept of occupational cultures and referred to some of the influential literature, it is worth summarizing why occupational cultures are deserving of study. We would argue that:

- They indicate 'what really matters' and 'how things are done around here'
- They provide insight into how practitioners perceive their occupation
- They influence how work is done and how effective it will be
- They influence how new members are introduced into ways of working
- They are a resource for adapting to change and the external context
- They can be a stabilizing force for good
- They can be an obstacle to reform, change and progress
- They come to the fore during turbulent times

Probation as a tainted occupation

In seeking to characterize the occupational cultures of probation work, our starting point is the work of Ashforth and Kreiner (1999) and Ashforth *et al.* (2007)

on the concept of 'dirty work'. One of the dilemmas that emerged during our interviews was the extent to which workers felt that the social status of the probation officer had changed from that of being 'an authoritative person' (CO14) 'almost priest-like' (FPW7) to being 'a waste of time' (PW9). The cosy image of the probation officer as 'ever such a nice lady' (Todd 1964) has been transformed to someone who is doing society's dirty work and should probably be ashamed, rather than proud, of themselves, for working with the 'undeserving':

> Can't we just actually say 'well done' [to ourselves]? Is it because you're worried that a member of the press or member of parliament will walk into an office and see self-congratulation, accuse us of being complacent? Must you take away any bit of joy, just to demonstrate this public penance or incompetence?
>
> (TPO2)

Drawing on much earlier work by Hughes (1951) and Goffman (1963), Ashforth and Kreiner (1999), Kreiner *et al.* (2006) and Ashforth *et al.* (2007) have developed the concept of 'dirty work' to describe those occupations that society regards as 'necessary evils' – jobs that someone has to do but which are considered to be unpleasant, disgusting and/or morally questionable. People who undertake such work are attributed with a stigma or negative identity as 'dirty workers', who may be physically, socially or morally tainted. Workers who are physically tainted undertake work that is intrinsically dirty, such as rubbish collectors or embalmers, or they have to do their work in 'noxious' conditions, such as miners. Workers who are socially tainted have regular contact with stigmatized groups, for example prison guards and social workers, or are in a servile relationship with their employer or clients, for example domestic servants. Finally, workers who are morally tainted do work that is morally dubious, for example exotic dancers, or utilize unethical methods, for example debt collectors. While it might be argued that many occupations contain some elements of stigma, Kreiner *et al.* (2006: 622) distinguish between those where stigma is idiosyncratic (neither routine nor strong), those where stigma is compartmentalized (affecting limited aspects of the job), those where it is diluted (widespread but mild) and those where it is pervasive (where stigma is both strong and widespread). The final dimension in this schema is that of relative prestige. Using (arguably outdated) USA occupational prestige rankings, Ashforth and Kreiner (1999) and Ashforth *et al.* (2007) distinguish between high-prestige dirty work (which is perceived as requiring skill and/or specialist knowledge to a professional or semi-professional level) and low-prestige dirty work (which is not).

Within this model, it is not too difficult to identify probation workers as being socially tainted. On behalf of society, they engage regularly with stigmatized people and run the risk of being stigmatized themselves. Alongside the work of other criminal justice occupations such as police, prison guards and criminal lawyers, society reluctantly accepts the necessity for probation work:

People just want that reassurance that there's somebody doing it.

(CO4)

Most of the public don't give a toss about us, but they're quite glad to know we're around.

(CO15)

Time and again in our research, however, people told us that the public really did not know what the work was about or what it entails so the taint was, in their view, based on both limited knowledge or experience and in many cases, after initial curiosity, a reluctance to find out more:

People either don't want to have a conversation about it, they just don't wanna go there, or they say 'oh that must be depressing work – that's kind of dirty, depressing'. They don't wanna know about that, 'Let's talk about something happy'.

(CO5)

A lot of people are like 'oh what do they do?' I've found that quite a bit, that nobody really understands what probation does or ... so they start ... they're quite inquisitive about what you do and who you work with. And some people say 'oh I couldn't do that, I couldn't work with those kind of people'.

(PW14)

Some interviewees avoided saying much about their work in social situations with unfamiliar people:

I often don't say I'm a [laugh] ... I try to avoid saying I'm a probation officer ... well I remember once saying I was a plumber and then someone tried to ... then they started talking to me about fitting a [laugh] ... fitting you know, like ... I thought no, you know, so [laugh].

(PW12)

One (male) interviewee was at a party with his male partner and seemed more uncomfortable about disclosing his occupation than his sexual orientation, as his turn of phrase indicates:

There was an awkward moment ... Do I *come out* as a probation officer?

(TPO4)

One reason for the low public profile of the probation service has been its marginal media profile in the past; it has been 'a bit of a secret service' (CO12) and this has offered protection from the worst excesses of media criticism. But high-profile cases such as those of Hanson and White, Rice, and Sonnex[3] (Fitzgibbon

2011, to be discussed more fully in Chapter 5) – cases where people under probation supervision have committed murder – have changed public attitudes from benign indifference to marked negativity, as this interviewee explains with great clarity:

> I think prior to those cases, probation had a fairly good reputation amongst the public, amongst courts, amongst judges and magistrates, as an organization that was doing a good job, that was actually, you know, working positively with offenders, was very much focused about change, wasn't just about risk management, but was also about addressing needs and social work in individuals in the community. Whereas I think, you know, as the service has changed structurally and strategically, its image has shifted and it's much more of a negative perception now, I think, by the public.
>
> (FPW4)

Our argument here is that there have been significant changes in both the relative prestige and the depth of stigma dimensions within the occupation. According to the model of socially tainted 'dirty work', social workers, counsellors and police officers are considered to be relatively high in prestige, while prison guards and welfare (care) assistants are considered to be relatively low in prestige. We suggest that recent changes in their training and their organizational position (within NOMS) have caused probation workers to slip from 'high' to 'low' prestige. Additionally, while probation workers traditionally identified themselves as 'courtroom officers' (or 'servants of the court') whose experience of stigma was widespread but mild (diluted), their more recent association with prison officers has resulted in a strong and widespread (pervasive) experience of stigma.

There is nothing new about arguing that personal or occupational stigma has negative consequences, resulting in a spoiled identity (Goffman 1963). For Ashforth and Kreiner (1999), however, the research conundrum is that stigma can result in a positive identity among dirty workers:

> [T]he real issue for dirty workers, then, is not so much 'How can they do the work?' but 'How do they retain a positive self-definition in the face of social assaults on the work they do?'
>
> (Ashforth and Kreiner 1999: 418)

Ashforth *et al.*'s (2007) model of dirty work gives rise to a number of processes whereby dirty workers construct positive work identities. First, they develop ideologies that reframe, recalibrate and refocus the purpose and value of their work. They reframe by foregrounding the virtues and benefits of the work (for example, 'advise, assist and befriend' becomes 'enforcement, rehabilitation and public protection'), recalibrate by adjusting the standards that evaluate the extent of 'dirt' (for example, massaging the statistics to demonstrate reductions in reoffending) and refocusing by emphasizing the rewarding aspects of the work over the dirty ones (for example, concentrating on 'good news' stories about the offenders who have been successfully rehabilitated rather than the 'bad stories' of those who commit serious further offences). Second, dirty workers engage in social weighting tactics – not unlike Sykes and Matza's (1957) 'techniques of neutralization' – condemning those who condemn them, supporting those who support them (if any) and making selective social comparisons 'to draw more flattering inferences about themselves' (Ashforth *et al*. 2007: 150).

We use the model of 'dirty work' throughout this book to gain insight into the ways in which probation workers routinely construct and maintain a positive work identity for themselves. However, the model does not entirely capture or explain all our data. In particular, the concept of dirty work, as presented by Ashforth, Kreiner and their colleagues assumes a stable, or relatively stable, external environment and a consistent public attitude towards the work. As indicated above, our interviewees believe that public perceptions of probation work have changed. Whether this is a symptom or a cause of the turbulent political, social and economic changes in the external context of probation work is a matter of serious debate. The concept of dirty work provides us with a meso-level tool with which to analyse group attitudes and behaviour, but it does not fully account for either macro-level societal changes or micro-level individual responses. It is to these aspects of our theoretical framework that we now turn.

Turbulent times and worker responses

We have already alluded to some of the challenges faced by probation workers since the 1970s, including the onslaught of managerialism, changes in training frameworks, roles and organizational structures including a 'forced marriage' with the prison service, all contributing to a potential loss of identity and certainly an element of dissonance. The fieldwork for this research was conducted in 2010–11 and at that time a number of factors contributed to the turbulent operating conditions for probation workers.

First, following the general election of May 2010, the Conservative–Liberal Coalition Government promised (HM Government 2010: 23) to overhaul 'the system of rehabilitation to reduce reoffending and provide greater support and protection for the victims of crime'. They would do this, they claimed, through a 'rehabilitation revolution' involving paying 'independent providers to reduce reoffending'. The implied threat to the domain[4] of the probation service was reinforced in the subsequent Spending Review of October 2010 which projected budget cuts of 23 per cent for criminal justice agencies (HM Treasury 2010). On the ground, the practical consequences of this meant that as we visited probation areas to conduct our interviews, probation workers were not only unclear about the continuing place of the probation service within the criminal justice landscape, but were also awaiting announcements concerning redundancies within their offices.

Second, the training framework was changing again, with the new vocational 'Probation Qualifications Framework' replacing the Diploma in Probation Studies. The TPOs whom we interviewed in 2010 were part of the last cohort and were well aware that if they failed there was no follow-up cohorts that they could join. Third, overlaying this climate of uncertainty was a challenging political and media context in which the dominant discourses foregrounded concerns over rising prison populations, 'weak' community punishments and popular anxieties around crime and victimization (House of Commons Justice Committee 2011; Ministry of Justice 2012). These were also characterized by media interest in criminal justice failures, some of which implicated the probation service, including the previously mentioned cases of Hanson and White, Rice, and Sonnex. Such cases were constant touchstones in our interviews and during the course of the fieldwork, a fresh case emerged to question the efficacy of probation supervision, that of Jon Venables, though a case review subsequently confirmed that the level of probation supervision was appropriate.[5] In addition to negative media coverage of these cases, midway through our fieldwork, fresh media criticism of the probation service emerged after 2 September 2010, when ITV1's *Tonight* programme screened undercover footage of community punishments in three probation areas. The headlines that resulted were in the vein of 'holiday camp for offenders'.

Turbulent times have profound effects on organizations and their employees. Both, in their own ways, need to engineer responses in order that the organization meets its objectives and the employees feel that their work has a purpose and is meaningful or is at least tolerable and manageable. The specific question that arises for us from these conditions is 'How do probation workers respond and manage their identities while negotiating routine work within a difficult operating climate?' To answer this, we will draw on, and further develop, a theoretical model put forward by Hirschman.

Hirschman's (1970) 'exit, voice, and loyalty' (EVL) model has been used widely to analyse and compare employees' responses to adverse workplace conditions. As an economist Hirschman's original work examined customer and employee responses to lapses in an organization's behaviour. He posited the responses of 'exit' 'voice' and 'loyalty'. Exit includes not only employees leaving the organization (1970: 4), but also the state of thinking about leaving, that is, making a psychological exit. Voice is a response whereby employees speak up, expressing their concerns and dissatisfaction to management and others. This is not necessarily a negative response; it can be a positive attempt to improve the situation, namely a 'pro-social voice' (Van Dyne *et al*. 2003, quoted in Naus *et al*. 2007). Loyalty characterizes the employee who feels an attachment to the organization such that there is a psychological barrier to exiting and describes those employees who passively and loyally wait for better times, supporting the organization publicly and privately. A fourth component of 'neglect' has subsequently been added to applications of Hirschman's model (EVLN), evidenced through lax behaviour such as persistent lateness, absenteeism and poor performance (Farrell 1983).

More recently, the EVLN model has been further extended. Naus *et al*. (2007) added a fifth dimension of 'organizational cynicism', a response which arises in situations where employees feel that the organization has broken a psychological contract, disappointing their expectations and generating disillusionment. Employees come to believe that the organization lacks integrity and they respond in two ways. They either adopt a negative attitude toward the organization and tend to disparage it (2007: 689), affecting apathetic and alienated behaviour, or alternatively they become a more positive influence, responding as a critical but caring voice of conscience.

A sixth response of 'organizational expedience' (McLean Parks *et al.* 2010) moves us more clearly into the arena of rule-breaking, describing 'workers' behaviours that (1) are intended to fulfil organizationally prescribed or sanctioned objectives but that (2) knowingly involve breaking, bending or stretching organizational rules, directives, or organizationally sanctioned norms' (2010: 703). Arising from the subjective experiences of role overload, emotional exhaustion, tension and/or task conflict, expedient behaviour can result in increased organizational effectiveness but may also result in 'workers attempting to "make it by faking it" – acting out their roles as if they understand expectations and doing whatever it takes to look successful, while hoping results will follow' (2010: 714).

These six responses come together in a theoretical model which helps us to make sense of the data collected through our interviews with probation workers, yet they do not fully explain some aspects of the data. While the concept of 'organizational expedience' comes closest to providing an explanation of contemporary probation work, we suggest that there are some elements of the work that can only be explained in terms of 'voluntary risk-taking'. In an organization obsessed with risk assessment and risk management, we will argue that it is not inappropriate to draw upon the sociological concept of 'edgework' (in particular 'workplace edgework') to extend our understanding.

Edgework refers to activities that involve voluntary risk-taking, where there is a 'clearly observable threat to one's physical or mental well-being or one's sense of an ordered existence' (Lyng 1990: 857). It is most easily illustrated in dangerous pastimes such as sky-diving (Hardie-Bick 2011), solo rock climbing (Fawcett 2010: chapter 7) or even criminal behaviour (Ferrell *et al.* 2001), but the 'edge' can be any boundary, such as that between life and death, consciousness and unconsciousness, sanity and insanity, where the actor, potentially, can lose control. Controlling the boundary involves the deployment of a specific skill 'to maintain control over a situation that verges on complete chaos, a situation most people would regard as entirely uncontrollable' (Lyng 1990: 859). Edgework tests this skill by getting as close as possible to the edge without crossing it. It is not, therefore, gambling, recklessness or the result of a psychological predisposition to take risks (Lyng 2009: 120), and edgeworkers are unlikely to place themselves in threatening circumstances beyond *their* control.

In the analysis of our data, we have chosen to imagine that (some) probation workers engage in edgework. This is partly because 'to a considerable degree, we all engage in edgework at some time. What varies is the intensity, duration, manner and form' (Milovanovic 2005: 51–2), but more significantly because edgework is 'increasingly what institutions expect of many people' (Simon

2005: 206). By *imagining*, we are choosing to enter the world of 'imaginary penalities' where ossified official justifications continue to struggle to exclude alternative or imaginative discourses of justice (Carlen 2008: xiv). We have data that can only be made sense of in relation to a desire for autonomy and 'action'. While we might draw on Goffman's concept of action as 'knowingly taking consequential chances perceived as avoidable' (1969: 145) or Csikszentmihályi's (1975: 182) state of 'flow'[6] where enjoyment is derived from the uninterrupted internal logic of a challenging activity, neither of these concepts takes full account of the 'highly unstructured, chaotic conditions that often must be negotiated' (Lyng 2009: 111). Nor should this desire be dismissed as harking back to a 'golden age' of social work professionalism, because many probation workers have no investment in that history of probation. They are products of a service that is saturated with the concept of risk and everything they do – including their own responses to their work environment – is defined by risk assessment and risk management. If we accept Milovanovic's (2005) typologies as locating edgeworkers along an 'in-control/out-of-control' spectrum, we imagine that this data can be best understood as constituting 'workplace edgework' – firmly towards the in-control end of the spectrum but nevertheless challenging the boundaries between acceptable and unacceptable behaviour in heavily rule-governed environments (Milovanovic 2005: 57–8).

There is a structural context to edgework, which is both a form of escape from (or resistance to) the rules and routines of contemporary life (Ferrell 2005; Katz 1988) and an implicit requirement imposed by organizations that displace their collective responsibility for risk management on to individual employees through a mechanism of responsibilization (Lyng 2009: 106). Edgework is the great 'unspoken'. Paradoxically, therefore, workers are both freeing themselves from, and better integrating themselves into, modern working conditions when they pursue edgework (Lyng 2005).

Edgework is also a gendered concept. Just as Goffman concedes that 'action … seems to belong to the cult of masculinity' (1969: 156), so, traditionally, edgework relates to male-dominated activities and assumes the subjective sensations of the masculine mind and body. Increasingly women are engaging in the same activities, although their experience of the risk-taking is different, involving different emotional management (Lois 2001, 2005). Perhaps more significantly, as the definition of edgework has developed, it has increasingly embraced the experiences of women's routine lives, both at home (see Rajah, 2007 on edgework in violent intimate relationships) and, as we argue here, in the workplace. For this reason, the feminization of probation work (which we discuss in Chapter 7) does not preclude engagement with edgework.

Many probation workers spend the majority of their time in front of computers in open-plan offices, undertaking important but routine risk assessment and risk management. The rest of their time is spent interviewing offenders in the security-conscious environment of anonymous public sector offices frequently located on industrial estates or technology parks and away from the places where offenders live. The work is demanding and the consequences of making mistakes could be serious, but opportunities for action are very few. Yet probation work is as much about controlling the boundaries between order and chaos as is police work, albeit on a smaller and more specific scale, as we will seek to establish in the chapters that follow.

Methods and participants

Many of the existing criminological studies of occupational cultures have used observational methods (e.g. Skolnick 1966; Cain 1973; Punch 1979; Holdaway 1983; Young 1991; Loftus 2009). These researchers, following anthropological traditions, would no doubt argue that the most valid way to understand and interpret cultures is to observe them over a period of time. In contrast, at the outset we decided to use an interview-based design for this study. While aware of the standard criticisms of interviews as a reliable method, it was not our purpose to compare policy with practice in action or to observe the minutiae of probation work; rather we wished to examine how probation workers themselves construct, and tell the stories of, their occupational identities, values and cultures. Our aim was to investigate the stories that probation workers tell about the job they do, rather than to uncover 'truths' about how they actually behave. To achieve this, we needed to talk to current and former personnel about their working lives rather than observing them at work.

The research design was based on 60 face-to-face semi-structured interviews with current and former probation workers (Appendix A). The interview sample was constructed through our own network of contacts and, importantly, the cooperation of the Probation Chiefs Association (PCA). The former enabled the recruitment of eight former probation workers and ten trainee probation officers (through emails approved by their university lecturer). The latter endorsed our research and encouraged chief officers/CEOs to facilitate access, without at any stage trying to influence the direction or outcomes of our research. As a result 16 staff of chief officer grade agreed to be interviewed, and in two probation areas we arranged for emails to be sent to the whole workforce requesting volunteers in the sample categories to contact us direct. From these responses we undertook 26 interviews.

Geographically, we interviewed COs from across England, with the other samples taken from the south-east of England (including London) and two areas in the north of England. The sample included former and current probation workers who had: trained under different training regimes; had long and short experience of being a probation worker (from two years to over forty); had experience of different probation roles; had worked in different geographical locations, including urban and rural settings; and had worked at probation service officer, probation officer, senior probation officer or chief officer grades. The purpose of identifying a varied sample of probation workers was to examine the extent to which a range of probation workers perceived themselves to be making a unique contribution to the criminal justice system.

In terms of gender and ethnic origins, 33 (55 per cent) of our 60 interviewees were female and eight (13 per cent) identified themselves as being Indian, Black African, Black Caribbean, Irish or mixed other. Regarding age, 26 (47 per cent) were under 50 years and 34 (53 per cent) were over 50 years. Our age profile was distorted by the unexpectedly high number of COs who volunteered to be interviewed (enabling us to increase our overall sample from an original target of 50 interviews to 60). COs represent 27 per cent of our sample. We analysed their responses separately from other grades, but found no major differences to support the existence of distinct 'management' and 'operational' cultures. Indeed the similarities were marked, possibly because all the interviewed COs were career probation workers with a wealth of experience in different grades.[7] The sample's demographic profile is not greatly out of line with that of the service at the time of the fieldwork, which was approximately 68 per cent female (45 per cent of COs), 14 per cent black minority ethnic (BME) (26 per cent of support staff), and 34 per cent over 50 years (90 per cent of COs).[8]

The interviews were divided between Rob Mawby (28) and Anne Worrall (32) and all but two (due to prison rules) were recorded and transcribed. Prior to each interview, an information sheet and list of themes covered by 25 questions was sent to each participant for them to reflect on (Appendix B). During the interviews each participant talked about their working lives based on these questions. They talked about their original motivations and aspirations on joining the probation service, their knowledge of the service at the time of joining, their training experiences and career development, their views on public and media perceptions of probation work, their daily routines and relations with probationers, courts and other criminal justice practitioners, and they described crises and typical working days.

All the interviewees signed participant consent forms and we discussed carefully with them how the interview transcripts would be anonymized for archiving purposes. We then analysed the transcripts to produce thematic summaries for selected categories of probation worker. These provide the data on which we draw in the chapters that follow. We draw heavily on direct quotations throughout the book in order to convey the richness and complexity of probation work and also to evidence the arguments that we develop. We found on completing the first draft of the book that we had, without specific intent, used quotations from 59 of our 60 interviewees. We could then not resist seeking out an appropriate quotation from the final participant! Consequently, we are proud to say that everyone we interviewed has contributed to this book, not only indirectly by providing a transcript that is now archived[9] for use by future researchers, but directly by providing a range of views and illustrations, without which the book would be much the poorer.

Outline of book

In this introductory chapter the reader has been reminded briefly of the history of the probation service and the key developments that have shaped the service as it now is. This was followed by a discussion of the term 'occupational cultures' as it pertains to the criminal justice system and an introduction to the literature on police and prison officer cultures. The book's theoretical framework was then set out, focusing on the concepts of probation as a 'tainted' occupation in a context of 'turbulent times'. It has been hypothesized that probation workers respond to adverse working conditions in a number of ways, including engaging in edge-work, expedience and organizational cynicism. A description of the research on which the book is based followed and the chapter will conclude with an outline of the remainder of the book.

In Chapter 2 we explore the backgrounds and motivations alongside the significance of the changing training regimes that have taken the role of probation worker increasingly away from its religious and social work roots. Our research has established that probation workers come from a variety of backgrounds, although there are identifiable groupings that we have called 'lifers', 'second careerists' and 'offender managers'. We find many common motivations between these groups but also some important differences that both reflect and reinforce the changes within the service. In this chapter we introduce the reader to many of our interviewees and conclude by presenting pen portraits of three participants whose characteristics might be regarded as representative of the three groupings we have identified.

In Chapter 3 we attempt to answer the question, 'What do probation workers actually *do*?', by utilizing the concepts of 'time' and 'place' to structure an examination of the daily routines of probation workers and the variety of physical environments in which they work. We follow probation workers through typical and non-typical days from the past and in the present and ask how they have been transformed – for better or worse – from largely autonomous community-based workers to highly accountable desk-bound operatives.

In recent decades the probation service has been encouraged to work closely with a range of public and voluntary sector agencies. Chapter 4 examines probation's changing relationships with the courts, police and prison services. Drawing on Davidson's (1976) typology of inter-organizational relationships, we argue that, despite both structural and cultural transformations, there remain cultural continuities in each organization that create tensions, the significance of which should not be underestimated.

Our research established that probation workers feel misunderstood by family and friends, the wider public and the media. Family members are generally supportive but bemused, friends admiring or incredulous and the public contemptuous. Public perceptions and misconceptions about the work are discussed in Chapter 5 together with media representations of the work in film, fiction and television. The near-universal failure of the probation service to manage its media image, particularly in comparison with the police and especially at national level, is analysed.

Probation work is stressful, but it also offers many opportunities to work in a variety of settings that require a range of skills and provide different experiences of job satisfaction. In Chapter 6 we consider the ways in which probation workers manage – or 'craft' – their careers and the extent to which they can exercise control over their work. We examine their collective and individual coping mechanisms and the ways in which they manage their self-presentation. The perceived erosion of professional autonomy and probation workers' responses to working in turbulent times will be discussed, including organizational cynicism, expedience and workplace edgework.

Chapter 7 examines four dimensions of the cultures – or 'voices' – that have influenced the construction of the identities of probation workers over five decades. We consider the tenacity of religious influence, the declining influence of the trade union (NAPO), the service's commitment to diversity, and the 'feminization' of an organization that (unusually for a social work-based agency) was male-dominated until the early 1990s. It will be argued that this latter does not herald a return to traditional social work values but rather the emergence of a new breed of female offender manager whose influence on the organization is profound.

In our concluding chapter, we identify the characteristics of contemporary probation cultures and, using theoretically informed typologies, discuss how probation workers construct their occupational identities, values and cultures. We examine the role of nostalgia in probation cultures and we challenge the narrative of decline that pervades much writing about the probation service. We ask how such cultures contribute to, or undermine, the effectiveness of offender management and the future of probation work. We conclude that criminal justice will be much the poorer if probation work becomes fragmented and the cultures that underpin it become diluted.

Summary: the square of probation work

In this book we argue that understanding the occupational cultures of probation workers is an essential component of understanding the workings of criminal justice, specifically in England and Wales, but more generally in all those jurisdictions that take the concept of 'alternatives to custody' seriously. To assist the reader in navigating what we hope will be some complex conceptualizations, we are introducing the idea of a 'square' of probation work (Figure 1.1). This is a

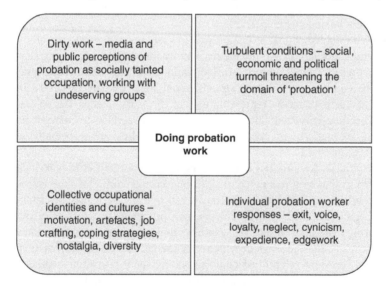

Figure 1.1 The square of probation work.

device for showing the relationships between the four key elements of our data analysis. First, we propose that probation work now ranks among the 'tainted' or 'dirty' occupations that at best attract ambivalent feelings, and at worst, public opprobrium. Second, we reiterate and restructure the well-known turbulence of the social, economic and political environment in which probation is required to function. Third, we suggest that it is possible to identify a number of characteristics that comprise collective probation cultures. Finally, we argue that, faced with these three components, individual probation workers will choose to respond in one or more ways at any given time, depending on their personal motivations and experiences.

5 Prison, community sentences and probation's contribution to sentencing

Punishment has been said to be over-determined, with an abundance of justifications and purposes (Nietzsche 1887/1998), many of which were considered in the last chapter. Yet both the *amount* and the *type* of punishment are *under-*determined, with none of several rationales pointing to a clear way in which the 'weight' of punishment is to be decided or how it is to be carried out. In the first part of this chapter, we consider trends in sentencing practice and in penal policy, which often reflect different views about what punishment might and should be, and what these developments have meant for probation. Discussion then turns to probation's contribution to sentencing through the pre-sentence reports which probation officers prepare for court.

Punishment, prison and community sentences

Although fewer than one-third of convictions for indictable offences (roughly, the more serious offences) lead to a sentence of imprisonment, prison still stands as the symbol and archetype of punishment in our society. People who are not sent to prison 'walk away' from court and non-custodial sanctions often appear as a poor substitute for the 'proper punishment' of imprisonment. Imprisonment is believed to be retributively apt, a potent deterrent and uniquely able to protect the public. For these reasons, prison comes to be seen as the standard that other sanctions must somehow try to match and with which they will be compared. Expressions like *non-custodial sentences* and *alternatives to custody* seem to concede that status to prison.

Between the mid-1960s and the early 1990s, there was a cross-party consensus that there were too many people in prison – perhaps far too many. Yet as crime and punishment became more 'politicised', politicians were anxious to avoid any imputation that they might be 'soft on crime'. The Conservative administration tried to resolve this conundrum by insisting that while punishment was fitting and proper, it did not have to take place in prison: the term *punishment in the community* began to be used (Brownlee 1998).

Table 5.1 sets out some of the legislative initiatives to reduce the prison population (discussed in Mair and Canton 2007). These initiatives have had a profound impact on the work of probation, which has had to provide almost all of these sanctions and to present them to an (often sceptical) public as realistic and

Table 5.1 Providing 'alternatives to custody'

Criminal Justice Act 1967	Suspended sentence
Criminal Justice Act 1972	Community Service Day Training Centre Hostel provision Suspended sentence supervision order Deferment of sentence Compensation
Criminal Justice Act 1982	Partial suspended sentence Tougher conditions in Probation Orders Day Centres (Schedule 11)
1988 Green Paper	Affirms punishment as the main purpose of community sanctions
Criminal Justice Act 1991	Combination Orders Curfew Orders Probation Order *as* (rather than instead of) a sentence Probation Order conditions clarified and strengthened
Crime Sentences Act 1997	s. 38 abolishes the need for the offender's consent to most community sentences
Crime and Disorder Act 1998	Drug Treatment and Testing Orders
Powers of Criminal Courts (Sentencing) Act 2000	Tougher powers on breach of community orders
Criminal Justice and Courts Services Act 2000	Orders renamed: Probation – Community Rehabilitation Order Community Service – Community Punishment Order Combination Order – Community Punishment and Rehabilitation Order Exclusion Order Drug Abstinence Order Tougher powers for courts on breach
Criminal Justice Act 2003	Generic single community order Tougher powers on breach, including a possibility of a term of imprisonment *even when the original offence was not imprisonable* (Sch. 8)

demanding punishment. Meanwhile, however, the prison population has followed its own trajectory – mostly upwards – without any apparent relationship to the increasing number of 'alternatives'.

Indeed analysis of the proportions of offenders sentenced to prison and to other penalties (Bottoms 1983) suggests that, rather than cutting into the prison population, 'alternatives' commonly take the place of other alternatives – or are imposed on offenders who might at other times been given a lesser penalty (see also Carter 2003). Between 1998 and 2008 the number of people receiving a custodial sentence increased by 2 per cent, but during the same period the number of community sentences *also increased* and was nearly one-third higher in 2009 (when the prison population was about 83,000) than in 1999 (when the prison population was 64,770) (Ministry of Justice 2010b).

Cohen (1985) argued that the relationship between prison and its supposed alternatives is more symbiotic than competitive: they work together to extend and disperse social control. While this thesis has had its critics (Bottoms 1983), it is still very difficult to point to contemporary examples of 'alternatives' leading directly to a reduction in the prison population. Even when replacing terms of imprisonment, community sentences typically displace (at best) those who would have served short terms of imprisonment and therefore tend to have no more than a modest effect on the prison population, which is influenced not only by the number of people sent there but by the length of time for which they stay (Fitzmaurice and Pease 1986).

One well-known hazard of non-custodial sanctions is their *net-widening* potential (Cohen 1985). They may deflect some offenders from custody, but draw in many more who might otherwise have been dealt with in less intrusive and cheaper ways. Over time, while probation may have worked with more serious offenders during and after periods of imprisonment, it has had to deal, on community sentences, with *less* serious offenders:

- less serious offences – an increasing proportion of those receiving community sentences are convicted of summary/less serious offences;
- less serious previous records – more first offenders, fewer have previously been in prison;
- lower assessed risk of reconviction on average (Morgan and Smith 2003; Mair and Canton 2007).

As well as involving more people in the nexus of social control, alternatives can perversely serve to increase the prison population. There is a 'recoil' effect (Bottoms 1987) whereby people sentenced to an 'alternative' come back to court and may be regarded as having failed on their last chance and deserving prison. The attempt to make community sanctions more demanding while simultaneously ensuring that they are more rigorously enforced is also likely to lead to more breach. As part of this same quest for credibility, moreover, courts are expected to impose weightier penalties for breach (Canton and Eadie 2005). A combination of these inter-related trends could tend to inflate the prison population (Tonry 2004; see also Chapter 9).

This very brief overview of community sanctions suggests a few fairly clear conclusions:

- the idea that the prison population can be reduced by providing 'alternatives' is an aspiration that has brought substantial disappointment;
- sanctions introduced as direct alternatives sometimes achieve some initial success in diverting people from terms of imprisonment, but over time go 'down tariff', widening the net to include people who had before been sentenced to other community sanctions or to financial penalties;

• the recoil effects of tough community sentences rigorously enforced could lead to increasing numbers going to prison for non-compliance.

Prison stands as a conspicuous failure, with approaching two-thirds of former prisoners reconvicted within two years of release (Hedderman 2007). Moreover, the more the number of people sent to prison, the higher this rate of reconviction is likely to rise (Hedderman 2008). Even so, in political debate it continues to hold a place as the standard which other sentences have to match. This may be because it is believed to meet three of the objectives of sentencing – punishment, deterrence, incapacitation – better than anything else, even though much of Chapter 4 attempted to show that confidence in prison's claims, even in these respects, is misplaced.

Probation has therefore had to describe its work and present its worth in the terms of a debate set by punitive priorities, to show itself as tough and prison-like. And its success in this respect, unsurprisingly, has been limited. Meanwhile, the progressive net-widening has brought onto probation caseloads offenders who not only do not need such levels of intervention, but for whom there is no evidence that probation interventions will be effective. This increase in workload dilutes probation's potential to work effectively with those who most need and might benefit from its interventions (Morgan and Smith 2003).

In the Introduction three penal policy strategies were identified. We now see these contradictory influences at work. The punitive strategy urges punishment; the management strategy recognises the costs and inefficiencies of prison; the ethical strategy is mindful too of the human cost of penal excess. This is strikingly articulated in these quotations from Secretaries of State in successive Conservative administrations.

> Prison can be an expensive way of making bad people worse.
>
> (Home Office 1990a)

> Prison works. It ensures that we are protected from murderers, muggers and rapists – and it makes many who are tempted to commit crime think twice . . . This may mean that more people will go to prison. I do not flinch from that. We shall no longer judge the success of our system of justice by a fall in our prison population.
>
> (Michael Howard, speech to Conservative party conference 6 October 1993)

> Too often prison has proved a costly and ineffectual approach that fails to turn criminals into law-abiding citizens. Indeed, in all of our experience, in our worst prisons it produces tougher criminals.
>
> (Kenneth Clarke, speech to Centre for Crime and Justice Studies, London 30 June 2010)

The Halliday report and the Criminal Justice Act 2003

A major review of sentencing was undertaken for the government by John Halliday (Home Office 2001) and many of the principles of the Criminal Justice Act 2003 are to be found in his report. Halliday was especially concerned to address perceived shortcomings in the Criminal Justice Act 1991, which was felt to be especially inadequate to deal with dangerous and with persistent offenders. Halliday also proposed a Sentencing Guidelines Council (duly established by Criminal Justice Act 2003 s. 167, though now superseded by the Sentencing Council, created in 2010). This was part of the strategy to enhance consistency in sentencing and improve its quality, using imprisonment only when necessary and rationalising the use of community sentences.

Halliday also recommended a single 'generic' community sentence, enabling the court to decide, case by case, on the requirements which would make up the sentence. This was duly enacted in Criminal Justice Act 2003 (s. 177), implemented in April 2005. The court could now impose one or more of these requirements:

1   unpaid work requirement;
2   activity requirement;
3   programme requirement;
4   prohibited activity requirement;
5   curfew requirement;
6   exclusion requirement;
7   residence requirement;
8   mental health treatment requirement;
9   drug rehabilitation requirement;
10   alcohol treatment requirement;
11   supervision requirement;
12   attendance centre requirement (under 25s).

The same set of options is available when the court imposes a Suspended Sentence Order (SSO).

There were two particular concerns about these developments, both impacting significantly upon probation. One was that courts might 'overload' sentences, including several conditions which may turn out to be too demanding (and therefore perhaps lead to breach and re-sentence) or that a court may feel that it had exhausted all its options and resort to custody when there was a further offence. A second concern was that the SSO would begin to displace the community order, with courts keen to combine rehabilitative interventions with the direct deterrent of custody, potentially accelerating reoffenders into prison.

Mair and Mills (2009), however, found that courts have not been overloading orders with large numbers of requirements: by and large, community orders are used like the separate orders that preceded them. As many as half of the requirements are rarely used. Breach rates remain high (around 40 per cent) – higher than the rate before the new orders were introduced. Mair and Mills found little evidence that either order was being used instead of short custodial sentences and half of orders made in magistrates' courts are for summary offences.

There has, however, been an increased use of the SSO, widening the net by drawing in numbers of people who might have been dealt with by a community order (or less). One reason why this was a particular worry was that breach of the SSO ought in law to lead to an immediate custodial sentence. Yet Mair and Mills (2009) found probation officers who complained that magistrates were often not responding as anticipated: warned by their supervisors that breach would lead to custody, offenders have found that often it doesn't and officers felt this detracted from the order's and their own credibility.

Probation reports for the court

Having discussed the relationship between prison and its 'alternatives' and reviewed recent developments in community sentencing, we turn next to probation's contribution to sentencing decisions through pre-sentence reports.

Preparing reports for the court is one of probation's main tasks. In 2008, probation staff prepared 216,353 reports – about three-quarters of them for the magistrates' courts (Ministry of Justice 2009d).[1] Once known as social enquiry reports, these are prepared 'with a view to assisting the court in determining the most suitable method of dealing with an offender' (Criminal Justice Act 2003 s. 158 (1) (a)).

The practice of social enquiry can be traced back to the very beginnings of probation. The earliest reports sometimes read less like an impartial exposition of information and more like a plea – typically a plea for mercy (McWilliams 1983). Later reports reflected a treatment ideology (McWilliams 1985, 1986): reports might become 'diagnostic tools' (Worrall and Hoy 2005: 100), identifying factors in the past that might illuminate the offender's present behaviour and proposing interventions accordingly. The reality fell some way short of this, with a great deal of material included without any very clear purpose, but with a vague idea that the more known about the offender the better.

> For myself I find that I welcome social enquiry reports because they make me feel cosy, inasmuch as they transform a 'case' into a human being; but, sadly, I am driven to the conclusion . . . that except in limited contexts . . . they do little to make me (or anybody else) in any sense a better sentencer.
>
> (Barbara Wootton 1978: 45)

But by the late 1980s even the aspiration had changed. With a loss of faith in the treatment model, any attempt to identify the 'causes of offending' or interventions to address them was looking forlorn. Too many reports were criticised for including 'historical' information that was merely irrelevant (Bottoms and Stelman 1988; Worrall and Hoy 2005). The Criminal Justice Act 1991 changed the name to *pre-sentence reports* (PSR), implying a more task-focused approach to the decision to be taken, rather than a general, discursive social inquiry, at a time when the Probation Service was in any case was being asked to disavow social work.

Contemporary pre-sentence reports

If reports used to be variable in structure and content, this is now tightly pre-scribed. A standard PSR will include:

1   sources of information;
2   an offence analysis;
3   offender assessment;
4   assessment of risk of harm to the public and likelihood of reoffending
5   conclusion (Probation Circular 18/2005).

Sources of information

In almost all cases, report writers interview the offender at least once, although they are expected to draw on other sources besides. The Crown Prosecution Service should enable access to depositions which give an account of the offence (from victims and witnesses) which are used to check and, as necessary, challenge the offender's own version. Victim personal statements may also be drawn upon. Where possible, factual information should be verified from other sources. In any event, the court is entitled to know the sources of information on which the report is based.

An offence analysis

Offence analysis involves a searching investigation into the circumstances of the offence, going beyond a description and looking in particular at the offender's intentions and motives – *what the offender took herself/himself to be doing and why*. In constructing this section, officers may ask:

* *How* did you come to be here/to meet this person/to do what you did? How could you avoid this in future?
* *When* did this take place? (looking not only for dates and times, but also events in the offender's life – for example, *just after I was made redundant* or *when I was in a really bad mood*).
* *Where* did this happen? (looking not only for specific places, but also answers like *on the way to my mate's house* or *just outside the pub*).
* *Who* were you with? Who suggested this? Who has been affected by this offence?
* *What* did you actually do? What did you think afterwards? What do you think you might have done differently?

•   *Why* (a common and obvious question, but to be used sparingly, because it can sound prosecutorial and often elicits defensiveness or withdrawal).

An analysis of this type not only illuminates the offence itself, but in the process normally reveals a great deal about the offender's risks and needs more generally. (For this '5WH' approach: see McGuire and Priestley 1985: 24.)

The offender's account will often be challenged, because the report author doubts (or anticipates that the court will doubt) its credibility; or because it is incompatible with information from other sources; or because it is does not fit with other things that the offender has said. There is considerable professional skill in such a challenge if it is not simply going to elicit more denial. It is hoped that through a process of exploration and negotiation author and offender progressively move towards *an agreed account of what was done* (Hudson and Bramhall 2005) – though in practice it is not always possible to agree and differences should then be recounted in the report.

This analysis has a direct bearing on judgements about culpability and therefore about seriousness. (The report is not concerned solely with the offender's welfare or even with ways of reducing their offending in future – Raynor 1980.) Whereas (arguably) the offender's legal representative's obligation is to present an account of the offence to their client's best advantage, the PSR analysis may disclose aggravating as well as mitigating factors. The best reports offer an understanding of the offence which enables the court to see an offence as an intelligible human action, however deplorable, in the context of the individual's circumstances.

Offender assessment

The offender assessment section sets out personal information relevant to an understanding of the offence and/or to the means most likely to reduce offending in the future. Previous convictions should also be considered here. Again, the report should go beyond mere description – the court has a list of criminal convictions from other sources; the PSR should *interpret* the record, relating it to the offender's personal history and explore its implications for the present decision.

This is particularly important now that the court must consider each previous conviction as an aggravating factor. An interpretation of the record contributes to a wise judgement about its relevance and the weight it should be given in sentencing. This kind of analysis is unlikely to be available to the court from any other source.

Assessment of risk of harm to the public and likelihood of reoffending

The section assessing risk of harm to the public and likelihood of reoffending draws upon the information and analysis in the preceding sections. It will cover the (properly assessed) risks of reoffending and look in particular at the risk of harm that the offender may pose to others. Since these judgements may have a decisive influence on the court's sentence, officers must be clear and explicit about how their assessments are arrived at.

This part of the report in particular alters, at least potentially, the relationship between probation and the defence. Reports have often been drawn on by the offender's legal representatives for mitigation, but there is here a possibility that the report's analysis will disclose risk factors that point to more intensive intervention or perhaps to a longer prison sentence. The assessment must therefore be rigorous, sound and well evidenced.

Conclusion

The standing of the conclusion used to be especially vexed. The report often culminated in a specific proposal, often referred to as a *recommendation*. But some sentencers objected that they did not want a 'recommendation' from a probation officer – this began to trespass upon their role – and the probation officer's opinion of what was best was just one of many considerations. Some sentencers, by contrast, welcomed a recommendation (Bottoms and Stelman 1988).

Sometimes recommendations were ignored (and sometimes openly deplored) for being 'unrealistic' – although our account of punishment (Chapter 4) reveals that the purposes of sentencing are contested, complicating the idea of what 'realistic' could mean here. Tata and colleagues (2008) also point to disparities among sentencers: a proposal that might be found unrealistic by one might be acceptable to another. Gelsthorpe and Raynor (1995) found that what courts minded most was *being told what to do* – a well-argued proposal, appropriately framed, would not be dismissed out of hand.

While the status of the conclusion might seem a rather arcane topic, it raises important questions. Report writers have sometimes been encouraged to champion the use of community penalties and to 'manage' resources. Examples include: the proposal of an 'alternative' where custody is likely; trying to persuade a court to use one community sanction rather than another; or an argument to show that probation involvement is unnecessary and that a financial penalty might suffice. Report writers have therefore constructed an argument to support a persuasive conclusion.

Sentencers, however, may see the sentencing decision as theirs and do not want to be 'persuaded'. To this extent, the dispute is one manifestation of the tensions and boundaries between the government and the judiciary over sentencing (Ashworth 2007) – a increasingly politicised debate as government tries to demonstrate its willingness and ability to reduce crime through sentencing, while the judiciary zealously defends its independence.

While research can inquire whether sentencers 'followed the recommendation', correspondence between recommendation and sentence does not necessarily mean that the court has been persuaded by the report (Hine *et al.* 1978). Perhaps report writers sometimes correctly anticipate or 'second guess' the court's decision – all the more likely now that the court normally gives an indication of the anticipated level of sentence when requesting a report.

In 2008, an immediate sentence was imposed in 88 per cent of the cases where custody was proposed; a community order was imposed in 71 per cent of the cases where it was proposed (Ministry of Justice 2009d: 12, Table 2.2). In 22 per cent of cases where a fine was proposed, the outcome was a community order – an indication, perhaps, that courts impose community sentences in many cases where probation officers feel this is unnecessary. The marked reduction in the use of the fine has been seen to lead to pressures on prison and probation caseloads (Carter 2003).

Contemporary debates about PSRs

Information or persuasion

Should reports be 'strategic documents involved in persuasive communication' or, on the other hand, just provide 'reliable, comprehensive information relevant to what the court is seeking to do' (Bottoms and McWilliams 1986: 260; Haines and Morgan 2007)? As we have seen, courts often do not want to be 'persuaded' and may well not accept probation guidance on sentencing as authoritative. Yet there have been times – especially perhaps when probation saw its principal contribution as the provision of alternatives to custody – when as a matter of policy authors tried to persuade sentencers not to send people to prison.

Authors were asked by courts to distinguish clearly between 'the facts' and their own opinions – a common-sense distinction which may be less straightforward that it appears. Bean (1976) drew on research to suggest that in some cases report writers first decide whether to present a case positively or negatively – to 'pitch' or 'denounce' – and then deploy the facts around that initial judgement. Cases are *constructed* (McConville *et al.* 1991): events and states of affairs can be characterised in many different ways and facts are looked for, interpreted and presented for particular purposes. It is not that probation officers mislead the court: just that, like others in this process, they are involved in case construction.

Much of the material in the report calls for *interpretation* – a concept that elides a tidy fact–opinion distinction. For instance, whether something is a *criminogenic need* and amenable to intervention – often the very nub of the report – is a matter for interpretation and judgement. Another example is *remorse*, often an influential consideration in mitigation (Sentencing Guidelines Council 2009) (certainly a lack of remorse is often seen as aggravating). Yet *how* the offender's attitude to the offence is to be elicited and understood is plainly a complex matter. Nor is this attitude static: the offender may have several, ambivalent and changing attitudes. For that matter, the probation officer may (often should) seek to influence the offender's feelings about their offending.

Discrimination in PSRs

Worrall and Hoy (2005: 104) draw attention to 'the image of the offender that is represented by the report' – an image which is often powerfully conveyed through nuance and tone. Things may be 'read between the lines', whether or not they were deliberately placed there. As in any other medium of communication, the message may not be received as intended (Tata *et al.* 2008). This seems particularly relevant to stereotypical racist or sexist characterisations.

Since the sentencing decision is a critical point in a criminal justice process that leads to the over-representation of black and minority ethnic groups in prison, there has been considerable attention to the way in which PSRs are written for these offenders. An inspection found that that the standard of reports for African-Caribbean offenders was not as good as for Asian and white offenders (HM Inspectorate of Probation 2000) – a finding still apparent in the follow-up inspection, although the position was improving (HM Inspectorate of Probation 2004).

Certain racial groups seem often to be represented in reports in a stereotypical manner. Hudson and Bramhall (2005) found that in discussions of *attitude towards the offence* – especially with regard to remorse – there were marked differences between reports written on Asians and white offenders. They suggest there is no 'discursive space' in which perceptions of seriousness and remorse can be explored, inhibiting the process of movement towards an agreed account (Hudson and Bramhall 2005: 730). This leads to more distancing, sceptical turns of phrase ('He tells me that . . .'; '. . . according to him') as well as sometimes suppressing aspects that are indispensable to an understanding of the offence – for example, that an offence was a response to racist harassment. While the same formal areas are covered, the lens of interpretation is quite different. Conspicuously, for the Asian offenders in their sample, there are imputations of family pressure linked to offending, which characterise the offender as over-susceptible and at the same time implicate the family and community in the offending. In this way, there is collusion with – and thereby endorsement of – stereotypes. Unsurprisingly, the presentation of weak character, strong and detrimental family influences and lack of remorse leads to assessment of higher risk and a less enthusiastic (or no) proposal for community supervision.

Hedderman and Gelsthorpe (1997) found that legal representatives sometimes deliberately conjured stereotypical accounts of women's personal circumstances to evoke the court's sympathy. They argue:

> The difficulty to be addressed is one of finding ways to challenge stereotypical pictures of men and women, without ignoring the fact that they often (but not always) do have different needs and responsibilities and these are often precisely the needs and responsibilities which fuel the stereotypes.
>
> (Gelsthorpe and Hedderman 1997: 58)

Similarly, experiences of racism are an important part of some individuals' circumstances which cannot be omitted from a report without losing key insights. Yet how such matters are dealt with calls for considerable professional skill – and for courage, both from authors and offenders. Again, discussions of sexuality and disability may be centrally relevant, but not easy to address. Probation officers must be self-aware and vigilant not only about *what* they are saying, but *how* they say it.

Fast reports

Perceived imperatives of efficiency and economy have encouraged the use of faster delivery options. Sometimes 'sentencers select the order for the offender and ask the court officer to report that he/she is a suitable candidate' (Worrall and Hoy 2005: 87). These are specific sentence reports. Fast delivery reports pose a set of specific (tick box) questions, are written quickly and may be presented orally (Bearne 2007).

While such reports are intended to be used only in the less risky and more straightforward cases, there is a marked increase in their use and a corresponding decline in the numbers of standard reports (Ministry of Justice 2009d: Chapter 2). There are at least two reasons to be troubled by these trends. First, for probation officers, the PSR has normally been a process of dialogue and negotiation, in anticipation of future work. A just sentence is the outcome of a just procedure, not merely a proportionate and fitting determination, and this requires offenders' active participation. Fast delivery options suppress this possibility. Mechanistic questioning can lead to mechanistic responses, in which offenders give the most superficial account of the offence and offer unrealistic commitments for the future – about, for example, their willingness and ability to cooperate with community penalties. Considering the earlier discussion about particular shortcomings in engaging with Asian offenders and achieving an understanding of their offence, the possible consequences of fast delivery should certainly be a matter of concern.

Second, as Whitehead (2008) shows, fast reports exclude any idea of *relational responsibility*

> which allows for different apportionment of blame between offenders and the circumstances in which they live and act . . . Lack of attention to contextual and relational aspects of culpability . . . results in injustices in that the poor and marginalised are punished more severely than others: circumstances of disadvantage which reduce legitimate choices are not constructed as reducing culpability, but as enhancing risk of reoffending.
>
> (Hudson 2005: 4–5)

To understand an offence requires an appreciation not only of motivation and immediate circumstance, but of the wider social context in which these motivations came to influence the offender, set the circumstances for the offence and circumscribed the offender's choices. Fast delivery minimises the opportunity for the probation officer to convey this to the court. This abstraction of the offender from the broad social context conceals information that is relevant to a just and wise decision. Since the offending of women in particular is often so bound up with experiences of disadvantage and oppression, such abstraction is especially likely to disadvantage them. It may be that 'justice delayed is justice denied', but justice compressed can be justice compromised, speedy justice justice spoiled.

Summary

In the first part of the chapter, we considered prison and its 'alternatives' and reviewed recent developments in community sentencing. In the second part, pre-sentence reports have been discussed. We noted that Barbara Wootton was sceptical that reports made for better sentencing, although she welcomed them as 'transforming a case into a human being'. Behind this observation, perhaps, is the aspiration that sentencing might become evidence-led and that a scientific understanding of the origins of offending might one day allow the selection of that penalty which would best fit the case. But this is forlorn if sentencing essentially involves moral decisions. Levels of retributive punishment could not, even in principle, be determined 'scientifically'; the evidence base to determine the optimal deterrent sentence does not exist (Chapter 4); and even the findings of 'what works' in rehabilitation can at best generate averages and probabilities and cannot tell us what would 'work' for this individual. But if, as we have argued, sentencing decisions rest on irreducibly moral (rather than legal or technical) considerations, transforming a case into a human being looks like an indispensable precondition for better sentencing.

Questions

- Why have 'alternatives to custody' failed to make much impact upon the size of the prison population?
- Should reports attempt to persuade the court to take a particular decision or simply convey 'the facts'?
- To what extent can (or even should) a court consider the wider social context of an offence if its duty is to assign a just punishment for the wrong that has been done?

Further reading

The evolution of community penalties is well discussed by Brownlee (1998). More recent developments are considered by Mair and Canton (2007). Solomon and Silvestri (2008) is an invaluable resource. For court reports, Bearne (2007) sets out a concise account of the legal and practice framework for PSRs. With due allowance for the many changes that have taken place since it was written, Bottoms and Stelman (1998) is still useful and interesting.

Chapter 16

Past, present and future sentences: what do we know about their effectiveness?

Carol Hedderman

Effectiveness: the historical picture

The punishment of offenders by the state may be justified philosophically in two ways: as an expression of public disapproval for what has happened (retributivism); or as a mechanism for reducing the chances of such an act being committed by the same or another offender (utilitarianism).

For a sentence to be deemed appropriate from a retributivist perspective it must be deserved in some way by the offender. As a minimum the offender should admit to being, or be proved, guilty. However, the implications of the sentence for the future behaviour of that offender, or others, are deemed to be irrelevant. In other words, retributivism looks back to the offence rather than forward to the impact of the sentence in considering the appropriate penalty.

Even in its oldest form – the biblical 'eye-for-an-eye' – retributivism may be said to include some notion of proportionality. This aspect has been made explicit by writers such as Honderich (1984) and von Hirsch (1976). Reflecting concerns that excessive levels of intervention were being justified on the grounds that they constituted helpful treatment, they argue that the magnitude of a sentence should be limited by proportionality to the crime committed ('just deserts'). It follows from this that assessing sentencing from a retributivist perspective involves measuring the degree to which the guilty are punished and proportionality is achieved, or seen to be achieved,[1] but the notion of effectiveness in terms of how sentencing affects future offending is meaningless. For this reason, the chapter focuses on the 'utilitarian' aims of sentencing.[2]

Until the middle of the eighteenth century, state systems for punishing those who transgressed criminal laws may have incorporated some notion of seeking to save an offender's soul, but from the Industrial Revolution to the early 1970s, state systems for punishing offenders in westernised democracies became increasingly concerned with transforming law-breakers into reliable members of the workforce. This was to be accomplished by reincorporating them into society after treating their offending through psychological and social interventions during a period in which their rights to liberty were suspended (Hudson 2003). Based on the work of writers such as Beccaria (1767) and Bentham (1789), the main aim of sentencing from a utilitarian perspective is a reduction in future offending. This may be achieved through deterrence of the offender or others, incapacitation or rehabilitation.

Despite the lengthy history of debates about whether sentencing should be primarily determined by retributivist or utilitarian objectives, it was only in the late 1960s and early 1970s that researchers began to systematically assess how far sentencing achieved any of its utilitarian objectives.

What can be said about effectiveness?

It is tempting to assume that one can assess the extent to which any given sentence, or intervention within a sentence, has reduced reoffending by measuring offending before and after a sentence has been imposed. But that is an impractical plan for a number of reasons. First, it assumes that nothing else has influenced the change. Second, it assumes that an offender would otherwise have maintained a steady rate of offending. Third, it is clearly not reasonable to compare the impact of a two-year period in custody with two years on a community order from the day both sentences were imposed, as the periods 'at risk' of further offending differ.[3] Fourth, as Chapter 15 documents, we cannot measure reoffending directly, but use proxies such as rearrest and reconviction or self-reported offending which all distort the underlying picture in some way.

Mair et al. (1997) even question whether it is acceptable to measure the impact of a sentence or intervention in terms of aims it was not imposed to achieve, or to measure its success in relation to only one aim when it was imposed to achieve several. In practice, even when an outcome study is accompanied by a well-conducted process evaluation (which includes asking practitioners and offenders what they think as well as collecting input and output data), researchers can only speculate on precisely how a reduction in reconviction was achieved. Generally, however, it is simply assumed that penalties which are intended to be rehabilitative and which can be shown to contain potentially rehabilitative elements such as counselling or help in finding a job, have primarily worked by fostering rehabilitation. Sentences which are intended to be severe and are imposed with the intention of deterring the offender and/or other potential offenders are assumed to have had a primarily deterrent effect. As discussed further below, given that the new sentences available under the Criminal Justice Act 2003 (CJA 2003) mix and match sentencing aims and sentencing options, the prospect of establishing a one-to-one match between a sentencing aim and behavioural outcome seems even more remote.

The lack of agreed and objective measures of incapacitation or general deterrence (Moxon 1998) also tends to limit most discussions of sentencing effectiveness. For example, while a recent review of the correctional services (Carter 2003) concluded that the increased use of custody probably made

460

a modest contribution to crime reduction during the 1990s, this conclusion relied on (unpublished) statistical modelling rather than direct observation.

Despite the considerable conceptual differences in how incapacitation and deterrence are expected to operate, the lack of adequate or agreed measures of either means that reviews tend to conclude that their effects are not distinguishable from one another (Nagin 1998; von Hirsch *et al.* 1999; Carter 2003; Bottoms 2004). Another common conclusion is that while there may be some additional incapacitative or marginal deterrence effect from increasing the use of imprisonment, increasing the actual and perceived risk of being caught is a more effective, and more cost-effective, way of securing crime reduction (von Hirsch *et al.* 1999).

In this context, it is hard to disagree with Friendship *et al.*'s (2005: 10) conclusion that: '... as an outcome measure, the value of reconviction is not in dispute because it represents the *only* readily accessible measure of reoffending' (emphasis added).

Consequently, reconviction will form the main, but not the only, measure of effectiveness in this chapter.

The effectiveness of different types of sentence

Prior to the Criminal Justice Act 2003, the main forms of community sentences for adults were discharges, fines, community rehabilitation orders (formerly probation orders), community punishment orders (formerly community service orders) and community punishment and rehabilitation orders (formerly combination orders). Most of the studies which have compared the effectiveness of different forms of sentence have focused on this range.

Of the 1.5 million offenders dealt with in England and Wales for indictable and summary offences in 2004, 70 per cent were fined, 13 per cent received a community sentence which involved some form of supervision in the community and 7 per cent were sentenced to custody. The remainder received other sentences including discharges. Limiting this breakdown to the 338,000 offenders dealt with for indictable offences, 21 per cent were fined, 33 per cent given a community sentence, 24 per cent were sentenced to custody and the remainder received other sentences (Home Office 2005a; 2005b).

It is inappropriate to compare the raw reconviction rates for different types of sentence. The courts use different sentences for different sorts of offenders – with different risks of reconviction – and, as noted above, to achieve a range of different objectives. The sorts of offenders who are typically fined are therefore expected to be *inherently* less likely to reoffend than those given intensive probation supervision. Consequently, their lower reconviction rates, in isolation, reveal nothing about the effectiveness of the two disposals in preventing further offending. An examination of trends over time in 'raw' reconviction rates can tell us something about impact, however.

Between 1993 and 2001, when the number of sentenced prisoners in England and Wales rose from 28,000 to 46,000 and the prison population as a whole rose from 44,000 to 74,000, the raw two-year reconviction rate rose from 53 per cent (Kershaw and Renshaw 1997a) to 61 per cent (Home Office 2004a;

2005c).[4] Some of the rise in reconviction rates is explained by the inclusion of additional offences into the 'Standard List' used in calculating reconviction rates (Home Office 2003). However, this is not a complete explanation. The increase in reconviction over time suggests either that the nature of the offenders received into prison had changed significantly or that prison is becoming less effective even as its use increases.

Between 1993 and 1999, reconviction rates for community penalties remained relatively stable at 56–57 per cent (Home Office 2004b). However, more recent figures (Home Office 2004a; 2005c) show a raw reconviction rate of 59 per cent for 2001. Over the same eight-year period, the Probation Service's court order caseload rose from 97,000 to 120,000 and its entire criminal supervision caseload, including those supervised on release from prison, rose from 145,000 to 207,000 (Home Office 2004a).

It is possible to conduct special analyses which allow both for differences in the types of offenders receiving different sentences and for 'pseudo-reconvictions'.[5] However, the range of information that can practically be collated on offenders centrally is limited. This means that even when such modelling is carried out, it is not clear whether differences in reconviction rates reflect differences in sentence efficacy or reflect a level of variation between offenders (e.g. in their level of drug use) which was not considered. This is most obviously true when studies compare probation orders with and without conditions (Home Office 1993; Oldfield 1997). Clearly, for all such cases the courts concluded that that probation was a more suitable sentence than any other which indicates that the offenders are broadly comparable. However, as the Home Office (1993) acknowledged, those on orders with conditions tend to be higher risk when criminal history variables are allowed for, and they are likely to have more personal problems. Such offenders will have been given conditions such as attending a drug rehabilitation centre for a reason.

A Home Office study published in 1997 showed that the two-year reconviction rates for offenders sentenced in 1993 were 60 per cent for probation, 52 per cent for community service and 61 per cent for orders which combined probation and community service (Kershaw and Renshaw 1997b). The average reconviction rate for these orders was 57 per cent. However, controlling for pseudo-reconvictions brought this down to 53 per cent which is identical to the rate for those discharged from prison in the same year (Kershaw and Renshaw 1997a).

Another study (Moxon 1998) was able to examine the effectiveness of non-custodial sentences by comparing actual reconviction rates with those expected on the basis of age, sex and criminal history for those given such disposals. Using the same data as Kershaw and Renshaw (1997b), he found the actual two-year reconviction rates of those given conditional discharges (39 per cent) or fines (43 per cent) were one percentage point lower than expected. The reconviction rates for those given community service (48 per cent) and probation (55 per cent) were respectively two and three percentage points lower than expected. However, these results were not corrected for pseudo-reconvictions and no comparison with a prison sample was included.

Two, more recent, Home Office publications have provided information on reconviction rates by sentence for adults released from prison or commencing a community sentence. In the first, Spicer and Glicksman (2004) modelled actual reconviction rates against a predicted rate for a 2001 cohort. Unlike Moxon (1998) they were able to allow for a change in the 'case mix' over time. However, once again, pseudo-reconvictions were not allowed for because the date of offence was not available. As community penalty reconviction rates include more pseudo-reconvictions than custodial rates do (Kershaw and Renshaw 1997b), this is an important limitation.

With that proviso in mind, the analysis showed an *actual* reconviction rate for those released from custody of 58.2 per cent compared to a *predicted* rate of 60.1 per cent. The difference was statistically significant at p ≤ 0.05 which means that the chances of the result happening by chance are less than one in 20. For those commencing community penalties the *actual* reconviction rate was 51.2 per cent compared with a *predicted* rate of 51.7 per cent. This difference was not statistically significant. The cautious conclusion to draw from this – bearing in mind the point about pseudo-reconvictions – is that there is currently little to choose between imprisonment and community penalties in preventing reoffending. Given this, the rise in raw reconviction rates on release from prisons is a particular source of concern as it suggests sentencers are becoming less adept at targeting sentences appropriately.

Another recent Home Office study (Cuppleditch and Evans 2005) was able to control precisely for pseudo-reconvictions in comparing reconviction rates for a sample of those released from custody or receiving a community sentence in 2002. Unlike most previous studies, which either ignore pseudo-reconvictions or make simple percentage corrections to allow for them, this study was able to actually identify pseudo reconvictions. This is because their analysis used Police National Computer (PNC) data which includes date of offence, rather than the Offenders Index which does not. The raw reconviction rate for those sentenced to community sentences (comprising community rehabilitation orders, community punishment orders, community rehabilitation and punishment orders and drug treatment and testing orders) was 53 per cent. For those released from prison the raw reconviction rate was 67 per cent. These figures do not, of course, allow for changes in the characteristics of those receiving each sentence. Nevertheless, as has been argued elsewhere (Hedderman 2006), there are good reasons to think that the increased use of imprisonment – which has led to a change in the types of offenders in prison, overcrowding and overstretched resources – has been counterproductive in terms of reducing reoffending.

One of the few random allocation studies to compare the impact of a short custodial sentence (14 days) and community service was conducted by Killias *et al.* (2000) in Switzerland. It is also unusual in that it took social factors into account and assessed outcome in terms of factors such as employment and home circumstances as well as recidivism (reconviction and rearrest). The results, based on a sample of 123 offenders, showed that those imprisoned developed antagonistic feelings towards prison and the criminal justice system. They were also more frequently arrested than those allocated to community service, although there were no outcome differences in terms of overall reconviction levels or on the social indicators.

One of the few UK studies to include information on some social factors as well as criminal history, age and sex was that conducted by May (1999). Based on a sample of more than 7,000 cases from six probation areas sentenced in 1993, this showed that social factors played a greater role in determining sentencers' choices between community penalties (community service, probation and combination orders) than criminal history. For example, males who had no social problems recorded were more likely to be sentenced to community service than other offenders. However, this did not entirely explain the better reconviction rates for this sentence. As the author concluded, the sentence itself may have had a positive effect on reconviction. Possible reasons for this are suggested by McIvor (1992) whose earlier study of community service in Scotland found that a high proportion of the offenders felt that they acquired new skills and/or a sense of satisfaction and increased self-confidence from the jobs they completed. Those who expressed the most positive views were the least likely to be reconvicted.

Overall, research studies and statistical analyses examining differences in the effectiveness of broad sentence types have usually taken variations in criminal history into account. However, as mentioned above, few studies have corrected for pseudo-reconvictions or allowed for the influence of social factors like homelessness, poor education and substance misuse. When the limits of these studies are considered alongside variations between courts, and over time, in the content and delivery of community orders and the offenders made subject to them, claims about the greater effectiveness of any particular sentence appear to be on very shaky ground. Arguably, considering the relative effectiveness of different types of community sentence will be of less relevance – and certainly harder to assess – now that the courts may impose a single 'generic' order in which the elements of previous community alternatives can be combined. The introduction of 'custody minus' option, which enables courts to combine the same wide range of community options with short spells in custody, makes comparing the effectiveness of short spells in custody with community supervision equally moot.

The effectiveness of 'new' sentences

Two major new community sentences were introduced in 1998 and 2000. The Powers of Criminal Courts (Sentencing) Act 2000 enabled courts to impose curfew orders, which require offenders to remain indoors for certain parts of the day with compliance being monitored by means of an electronic tag. The Crime and Disorder Act of 1998 empowered the courts to impose drug treatment and testing orders (DTTOs) on offenders with severe drug habits who are at risk of imprisonment.

Curfew orders
The impact of curfew orders with electronic monitoring in three pilot areas was examined by Sugg et al. (2001). The sample comprised 261 of the 375 given curfew orders in 12 months spanning 1996 and 1997 whose orders were not rescinded and who could be traced in central records. Sixty-one per cent (N = 160) of those on curfew orders were also made subject to other community sentences.

464

The expected two-year reconviction rate for those on curfew orders (based on actuarial modelling) was 67 per cent. Their actual reconviction rate was 73 per cent which suggests that they did worse than expected. However, this was similar to the reconviction rate for a comparison group of offenders on straight probation whose reconviction rates were also higher than predicted. Sugg *et al.* suggest that the most likely explanation for this is that the algorithm used to calculate an expected rate is based on national data and does not take into account local factors such as the police clear-up rate.

When the two-year reconviction results for 160 offenders on joint orders were compared with the 101 offenders on stand-alone curfew orders, the former were at a higher risk of being reconvicted (70 per cent *v* 62 per cent) and more of them were convicted (exact figures not reported).

In a recent review of what he terms 'community custody', Roberts (2004) examines the value of curfew orders and similar sentences from a number of perspectives using evidence (mainly) from the UK, North America and Australia. The review repeats the conclusions of an earlier US review (Rogers and Jolin 1989) that there is little difference between recidivism rates for electronically monitored and imprisoned offenders but also notes that curfew orders have at least two other benefits. First, while noting deficiencies in the quality and number of interview studies with offenders, Roberts reports that offenders, and their families, tended to find the experience of community custody much more restrictive than they had anticipated, but also less damaging: 'Many (but by no means all) recognise that community custody creates opportunities for them to change their lifestyle, and to preserve social relationships that would otherwise be threatened or disrupted by incarceration' (Roberts 2004: 115).

Second, Roberts presents statistical evidence to show that while the introduction of curfew orders seems to have had little impact on the decision to use custody in Britain, in a number of other countries (but especially Canada and Finland) the numbers being sent to prison reduced relatively quickly. This is not simply because the British public are less tolerant of the concept of offenders 'escaping' imprisonment, but because other jurisdictions have implemented community custody differently and presented it differently to sentencers, victims and the wider public. Roberts concludes by outlining improvements which might be made in all jurisdictions wishing to increase uptake including: locating the sanction on a scale of severity and not trying to introduce it for all forms of offending (at least initially); presenting it to the offender and the public as a form of suspended custody and ensuring that it is enforceable; distinguishing it from other forms of existing community provision; taking account of the offender's and the victim's circumstances when considering the suitability of the disposal; avoiding overloading it with conditions; allowing the sentence to be varied in line with the offender's performance and circumstances; and resourcing supervision sufficiently. Looking at this list, it is perhaps obvious why curfew orders have not been an unqualified success in England and Wales.

DTTOs
Drug treatment and testing orders are designed for offenders on the cusp of

custody. It is therefore unsurprising that the results of the pilot study (Hough *et al.* 2003; Turnbull *et al.* 2000) found that 80 per cent of the 174 offenders on whom data are available had been reconvicted within two years. This figure was eight percentage points higher than the rate of reconviction for all offenders with demographic and criminal profiles comparable to the DTTO group. This partly reflects limitations in the methods of calculating expected rates which cannot allow for key predictive factors such as dependent drug use. But equally important, the divergence could be largely attributed to the very large gap of 15 percentage points between observed and expected rates in one of the three pilot sites. The authors conclude that these results highlight the importance of implementation factors in determining the success or otherwise of an intervention.

The DTTO study also showed low completion rates: only 30 per cent of the sample finished their order successfully. There were also very marked differences in reconviction rates between those who completed orders (53 per cent reconvicted) and those whose orders were revoked (91 per cent reconvicted). McIvor's (2004) evaluation of the Scottish DTTO pilot showed a much higher completion rate (48 per cent), and a much lower overall reconviction rate (66 per cent). Meanwhile a further – and larger – reconviction study of DTTOs in England and Wales shows that at a time when probation areas were under pressure to meet DTTO commencement targets, reconviction rates rose to 90 per cent (Home Office 2004b). Taken together these findings suggest that schemes may be able to minimise reconviction rates by maximising retention rates. However, incentives to maximise the number of commencements will probably drive up reconviction rates (Hedderman and Hough 2005).

The Criminal Justice Act 2003
The Criminal Justice Act 2003 lays out the aims of sentencing as being the

- punishment of offenders;
- reduction of crime (including its reduction by deterrence);
- reform and rehabilitation of offenders;
- protection of the public; and
- making of reparation by offenders to persons affected by their offence.

Influenced by the recommendations of the Halliday Review (Home Office 2001) this list differs slightly from the traditional sentencing principles of punishment, general or individual deterrence, incapacitation and rehabilitation which have been generally understood to underlie sentencing decisions (Thomas 1979). This is an important shift for three reasons. First, it introduces a specific acknowledgement of the victim's perspective by according reparation equivalent status to other sentencing aims. Second, the legislation focuses on the impact of sentences in terms of crime reduction and public protection. Arguably these effects are more easily distinguished than incapacitation and deterrence, although identifying a direct causal link between sentencing and these aims is no more straightforward. Third, and perhaps most importantly, for the first time sentencing aims have been given statutory status. Previously sentencing aims in an individual case might be no more than the implicit or explicit aspirations of the sentencer which might or might not be shared by the offender, the victim, the supervising service or the wider public.

It is too early to assess what impact the CJA 2003 has had in practice, but the legislation alone raises concerns. The most obvious difficulty is that the different aims of sentencing are not necessarily compatible in individual cases and may even conflict with each other. Arguably, matters might have been more straightforward if the CJA 2003 had brought in a direct correspondence between a sentencing aim and a sentence (for example, community punishment and prison punish, probation reforms, compensation compensates). Instead there has been an increasing tendency to advertise all sentence types as being capable of meeting all sentencing aims. Community punishment, for example, is now expected to punish and to reform and even to provide a form of generalised reparation. But this presents sentencers with a dilemma. If community service is a bit rehabilitative and a bit punitive, should they be adding a bit of probation supervision and a bit of custody to ensure a proper measure of each? The history of the combination order shows that the temptation to overload is considerable and it is not obvious how it will be avoided as sentencers decide which of the many parts of a generic community sentence they should impose.

Although sentences might be overloaded by seeking to punish through community punishment, reform through a cognitive behavioural programme and protect through tagging, at least the decision-making process would be transparent. But given that the 'custody plus' sentence is expected to do all three, why not choose that? Perhaps of most concern is that overloading offenders with conditions may result in many offenders going to prison for failing to comply, although their original offences did not merit custody, because the CJA 2003 makes custody a much more likely outcome when an order is breached. More worrying still, the Act's potential to increase the population through increased custodial sentencing and breach seems, initially, to have been ignored. Even the highest scenario shown in the prison projections published in 2005 (de Silva *et al.* 2005) assumed that, at worst, the CJA 2003 would not affect the prison population. Otherwise it was expected to bring about a small *decrease*. The phrasing of the latest projections (de Silva *et al.* 2006) is more opaque about the effects of the CJA, but acknowledges that estimates have been revised to take into account the experience of implementing some of its provisions. Partly as a consequence, the high scenario projected for the prison population for 2010 published in 2006 is 94,020 rather than the 87,840 figure published a year earlier.

Perhaps one of the best ways of combating both sentencing and breach inflation is to provide stronger evidence about which sentencing elements are most effective at least in terms of reducing reoffending and (thereby) protecting the public and possibly even contributing to crime reduction, and also in terms of providing some reparation to victims or to society in general.

The effectiveness of interventions delivered as part of a sentence

In the mid-1960s, faced with mounting scepticism about whether prison reformed as well as punished offenders, the New York State prison service commissioned a research review to examine the rehabilitative impact of interventions in institutional and non-institutional settings. The review, conducted by Robert Martinson (1974), examined over 200 studies published over 22 years. Martinson's report supported the sceptics' perspective in that he found little evidence of interventions significantly reducing offending. Although Martinson pointed out that the result was not clear cut, because of the methodological shortcomings of some of the studies, the overall message was taken to be that 'Nothing Works'. Similar overall conclusions were reached in the UK by Brody (1976) and Folkard *et al.* (1976).

Of course, then, as now, research results were not received in a political vacuum. Raynor (2003) has suggested that one reason Martinson's caveats, and the methodological limitations of the UK studies,[6] were ignored was that 'Nothing Works' was what the US and UK governments of the day wished to hear. While a Canadian review, which was restricted to studies of a higher methodological standard, found evidence that some interventions were effective (Gendreau and Ross 1979), this was ignored in the US and the UK during the 1980s and early 1990s. The 'Nothing Works' conclusion legitimated the increasingly right-wing Conservative governments in both countries limiting public expenditure on prisons to that needed to contain and punish offenders. Public expenditure on the supervision of offenders on community sentences and post-release supervision to 'advise, assist and befriend' could no longer be justified. But probation supervision could be justified on cost grounds as an 'alternative to custody'. This shift in the purpose of probation resulted in over a decade of probation research which was almost exclusively devoted to studying how effectively it diverted offenders from custody rather than its impact on offending behaviour (Raynor 2004).[7]

A few small-scale outcome studies were conducted during this period. For example, Raynor and Vanstone (1996) found that the STOP cognitive behavioural programme was effective after one year. However, by the second year no differences were apparent in the treatment group and comparison group reconviction rates.

The resurgence of confidence that some interventions with offenders did help to reduce reoffending reflects the fact that many of those working with offenders and designing interventions for them in the UK were aware of the countervailing evidence and never lost confidence in the idea that some interventions were effective (Raynor 2003). It has also been suggested (Raynor 2004) that senior members of the Probation Inspectorate, the Home Office and the Probation Service were a receptive audience for such findings in the mid-1990s because they saw 'What Works?' as a defence against the then Home Secretary (Michael Howard) who believed that (only) 'Prison Works'.

During the late 1990s, a new role for probation was outlined in which its purpose was to reduce the reoffending of those under its supervision and to protect the public (Home Office 2001). At the very least this created a receptive context for reviews such as that by Hollin (1990) and further rigorously controlled Canadian meta-analyses (e.g. Andrews *et al.* 1990; Lipsey 1992), which showed that some interventions could be effective with some offenders in some circumstances. Taken together with the publication of McGuire's (1995) edited volume, the evidence was sufficient for both reviews of the literature and of current probation practice to be initiated by the Home Office (Vennard *et al.* 1997) and the Probation Inspectorate (Underdown 1998).

Although different authors came up with slightly different lists, the 'What Works?' literature identifies some common elements which tend to be present when interventions reduce recidivism. These are summarised in Table 16.1 (taken from Vennard *et al.* 1997). The same study found that by 1996 at least 39 of the then 54 probation areas in England and Wales reported running programmes which employed cognitive behavioural techniques, although their commitment to the full 'What Works?' agenda was questioned because of the general absence of elements such as programme integrity and adequate staff training.

In fact there were major practical difficulties to be faced in translating these findings into practice. Having been derived from meta-analyses it was rarely possible to point to a start-to-finish example of offender supervision which could be imported. Faced with a massive design and development task, the prison and probation services succumbed to the temptation of importing some stand-alone programmes. The North American 'Reasoning and Rehabilitation' programme was known to have positive effects in several other countries and a few probation areas had developed programmes to deal with special groups themselves (e.g. the Thames Valley sex offender programme). The programme

Table 16.1 Common elements identified in programmes which were successful in reducing recidivism

More intensive programmes should be targeted at high-risk offenders, those of lower risk should receive minimal intervention.	Treatment should be 'multi-modal' and designed to impart skills such as improving problem-solving through techniques including (but not limited to) those based on cognitive behavioural and social learning theories.
Interventions should focus on those factors which contribute directly to criminal behaviour, such as anti-social attitudes, drug dependency, limited cognitive skills.	Programmes which take account of risk, criminogenic need and responsiveness can work in any treatment setting, but generally work better in the community than in prison.
Teaching styles must fit offenders' learning styles. Generally this is active and participatory. Client-centred counselling is not generally successful.	Interventions should be delivered consistently over time and not allowed to drift in terms of the content or mode of delivery. This requires that those delivering the intervention are well-trained in it.

Source: Derived from Vennard *et al.* (1997).

469

designed by James Maguire, from which 'Think First' has been developed, had also been adopted in a number of probation areas (although its operation varied somewhat from one site to another). Areas were then invited to nominate other programmes which might be evaluated (Hedderman 2004).

It is also important to remember that, while 'What Works?' had become the dominant philosophy during this period, there have continued to be dissenting voices who query the evidence base (e.g. Mair 2004a), who express concerns about putting too much reliance on one approach (Bottoms *et al.* 2001) and who criticise the 'What Works' evidence base and the unthinking implementation of its principles for being blind to issues of ethnicity and gender (Shaw and Hannah-Moffat 2004).

Some senior probation practitioners, whose training emphasised sociological rather than individual theories of offending which dominated North American penology, also seemed uncomfortable with the primacy given to cognitive behavioural therapy which requires offenders to see themselves as responsible for their actions, regardless of how their social circumstances and life chances may have contributed to their offending (Mair 2004b). More frequently, however, their comments reflect reservations about putting all the Probation Service's eggs in the cognitive behavioural basket, together with concerns about the pace of change required. This view is shared by a number of psychologists, who express concerns about the way somewhat fluid psychological concepts, such as the notion of 'criminogenic' factors, and sometimes tentative findings about 'What Works?' have created a practice straightjacket which limits innovation and development. As Thomas-Peters (2006: 33) laments: 'Somewhere during the 1990s the question mark was lost from the expression "What Works?"; and with it has gone some tolerance and perspective'.

Even those who accept the broad thrust of the What Works message expressed concerns about the validity of some of the evidence base and warned against generalising too broadly from it (e.g. Vennard *et al.* 1997; Raynor and Vanstone 2002) as a careful reading of the research showed that practitioners were right to be sceptical of cognitive behavioural interventions alone securing change or that they were a panacea. For example, while noting that some studies of programmes employing such techniques showed large reductions in reoffending, Vennard *et al.* conclude:

> ... the research literature does not demonstrate that cognitive behavioural approaches, or indeed any other type of approach, routinely produce major reductions in reoffending among a mixed population of offenders ... it is not possible to identify any all-purpose methods or forms of intervention as being reliably and consistently better than standard or traditional programmes with offenders. (Vennard *et al.* 1997: 33–4)

Ignoring these reservations, the incoming Labour government focused instead on the more positive element of the same paragraph that 'Among mixed populations of offenders, programmes *might* achieve a reduction in recidivism of some 10–15 per cent ...' (p. 34, emphasis added).

Taking this optimistic estimate, and encouraged by the then Chief Inspector of Probation, Sir Graham Smith, the new Government created the Effective Practice Initiative. A highly influential Probation Inspectorate report (Underdown 1998) not only played a part in this decision, but also indicated that leaving implementation to individual areas would perpetuate inconsistent practices. This threat, together with the Government's preference for New Public Management[8] modes of working, led to the creation of the National Probation Service in 2001. At that time, the National Probation Directorate took charge of the Effective Practice Initiative, which had been driven by the Inspectorate.

A key part of the implementation of the Effective Practice Initiative involved using money from the multi-million pound Crime Reduction Programme to create a series of 'Pathfinder' projects which were intended to turn 'What Works' principles into practice. The resulting lessons would then be rolled out to other areas. Use of the term 'Pathfinder' rather than 'Pilot' is important as, while the latter acknowledges the possibility of failure, the former implies that the exercise is merely one of exemplification rather than proof. As a Cabinet Office publication (Jowell 2003: 10) warns 'By creating unrealistic expectations, they tend to make neutral evaluation more difficult'. Arguably, if trailed as pilots, the mixed results which various 'Pathfinders' have produced might have been greeted with less surprise and dismay. But, as indicated by both the nomenclature and the fact that Pathfinders were funded initially for a maximum of three years, the National Probation Service was not engaged in a neutral experiment but was under pressure to succeed and to do so very quickly. This in itself may even help to explain some negative results as compressing timescales can lead to impact assessments being adversely affected by teething problems (Jowell 2003; Hedderman 2004).

Over the last two years, a number of reports about the way Effective Practice Initiative (EPI) Pathfinders were implemented and operated have been published. Many show little sign that the lessons from previous research about managing implementation effectively (e.g. Sarno et al. 2000) had been taken into account. Indeed the level of implementation failure in some cases has been so great that reconviction studies have only been conducted in some instances. Of those an even smaller number have so far been published, although the results have been with the Home Office for more than a year,[9] raising concerns that they may never see the light of day.

This section focuses on three sets of results from the EPI: those concerning cognitive behavioural programmes which seek to alter offenders' attitudes to offending and their offending behaviour; those designed to enhance offenders' chances of obtaining employment through education, training and employment (ETE) initiatives; and restorative justice schemes which are intended to reintegrate offenders into the community as well as, as the name implies, to help victims overcome the experience of victimisation.

Cognitive-behavioural programmes

The first prison-based results looked promising, with Friendship et al. (2002) reporting an 11–14 percentage point reduction for those classified as being at

471

medium risk who were referred to two types of cognitive skills programmes. However, in both of the studies which examined accredited versions of the same programmes (Falshaw *et al.* 2003 and Cann *et al.* 2003), the comparison group appeared to outperform the treatment groups. A rare study on female offenders found similar results (Cann 2006). While the authors suggest the later results may also be a consequence of measurement failure or theory failure the most likely explanation for disappointing post-accreditation results is that some aspect of delivery was lost, with adverse consequences, as small well-implemented pilots were rolled out.

The first EPI study to report on the impact of cognitive-behavioural programmes in the community run prior to accreditation found that the treatment group had reconviction rates 22.5 percentage points higher than the comparison group (Ong *et al.* 2003). While Debidin and Lovbakke (2005) legitimately question the value of these results because the comparison group was not well matched to the treatment group, another possible explanation is that the treatment group results include those who were referred to the programme but who did not attend it. This approach accords with analytic conventions, as taking out the non-attenders is regarded as distorting the results so that only those who are most likely to change (as evidenced by their attendance patterns) are retained in the treatment group. However, it is clearly implausible that someone who does not attend a programme will be affected by it. It is also unlikely that all of those who are retained in treatment would have changed without any assistance. For this reason, the most comprehensive and recent evaluation of accredited general offending and substance abuse programmes which assessed their impact across 24 probation areas between 2000 and 2001 has reported the results as a two-way analysis (treated versus comparison group) and three-way analysis, with the treatment group divided into completers and non-completers. In the first analysis 69.9 per cent of those referred to the programmes were reconvicted after 18 months compared to 57.9 per cent of the comparison group. Splitting those referred to the programmes into those who completed and those who did not showed that only 54.5 per cent of the former were reconvicted compared to 77.6 per cent of the latter. While this is clearly not proof of effectiveness, it does highlight the need for further studies and raises questions about what the results might have looked like if some of the non-completers could have been retained.

ETE

Over half (55 per cent) of offenders subject to community sentences are unemployed at the start of their orders and three-quarters of prisoners do not have paid employment to go to on release from custody (Home Office 2004c). Unemployed offenders are significantly more likely to be reconvicted than those who are in employment (Crow *et al.* 1989; Simon and Corbett 1996; May 1999). A consistent message from the literature is that offenders are handicapped in their efforts to obtain employment by a number of major social and personal difficulties and that it is common for them to have more than one of the following problems (Fletcher *et al.* 1998; Metcalf *et al.* 2001; Lewis *et al.* 2003):

- poor literacy and numeracy skills (or 'basic skills');
- lack of, or low-level, qualifications;
- little experience of legitimate or sustained employment;
- low self-esteem, confidence and motivation to find employment;
- poor health;
- drug misuse and problem drinking;
- poverty and debt;
- homelessness/unstable housing.

It follows that any successful intervention will involve dealing with the range of an offender's problems not just one element, a point which is also supported by previous research (e.g. Gaes *et al.* 1999; Webster *et al.* 2001).

Unfortunately, the first Basic Skills and Employment Pathfinders funded under the Crime Reduction Programme were only comprehensive in their approach to ETE. Reading the evaluations report on the Basic Skills (McMahon *et al.* 2004) and Employment (Haslewood-Pocsik *et al.* 2004) Pathfinders, it also seems that those responsible for implementing both schemes did so in ignorance of the implementation problems which have undermined the effectiveness of previous schemes (e.g. Roberts *et al.* 1997; Sarno *et al.* 2000). The result was that of the 1,003 offenders assessed as probably having basic skills deficits, 155 were subject to an in-depth assessment and 20 were available for interview having completed relevant training. Twenty-two offenders completed the Employment Pathfinder of the 400 anticipated. In both cases, it was impossible to examine outcomes in terms of reconviction. This was particularly unfortunate as a previous study of two employment schemes for offenders on community supervision had given grounds for cautious optimism. Sarno *et al.* (2001) report a one-year reconviction rate of 43 per cent among 16–25 year olds who attended the London-based programme, compared to 56 per cent of those who were referred but did not attend (Sarno *et al.* 2001). Those who completed the programme were also slower to reoffend. For the reasons explained above selection effects cannot be ruled out when comparing completers and non-completers, but the results suggest that employment schemes might have some impact on recidivism, at least in the short-term.

Restorative justice

The first schemes which included elements of 'restorative justice' appear to have developed in the US in the early 1970s (Marshall 1999). By the mid-1980s, several small-scale projects were running in the UK. Then, as now, such schemes varied, in this country and elsewhere, in the ways they operated (Miers 2001; Miers *et al.* 2001). Some are an entirely pre-sentence option, others use restorative justice measures in place of a sentence or as part of a sentence. The extent of direct mediation between the victims and offenders also varies, as does whether the mediation is restricted to the victim and offender or extended to include supporters of both parties or even of the wider community.

As Crawford and Newburn (2003: 21) point out, variation in restorative justice schemes is not simply operational, but conceptual:

> ... is notoriously difficult to define ... restorative justice emerged as a critique of traditional forms of justice and, as such, is often defined in terms of what it is not rather than in terms of what it is.

Nevertheless, they are able to identify three key features which characterise a restorative justice approach. First, it recognises that a crime is more than an offence against the state and that those most affected by it should have a say in the society's response. Second, the decision-making processes must be deliberative and participatory with the aim of building consensus while restoring control to the parties most affected. Third, the ultimate aim of restorative justice should be to repair the harm done.

Given these features, it is unsurprising that most previous evaluations tended to concentrate on which forms of restorative justice achieved the highest satisfaction levels of participants. As noted above, some authors have questioned the legitimacy of assessing any intervention in relation to aims it was not explicitly intended to achieve. Arguably, reducing the likelihood of the offender repeating a similar offence is neither an essential, nor inevitable, aim of restorative justice in all cases. Nevertheless, some reconviction studies do exist, as it is reasonable to assume that if the offender is genuinely remorseful, he or she may be expected to be less likely to commit further transgressions. One of the best known was conducted in Canberra Australia (Sherman *et al.* 2000). This compared the recidivism of offenders assigned to the Canberra Reintegrative Shaming Experiments (RISE) diversionary conferences compared with others assigned to standard court processing. The overall sample size was just under 1,400. The cases involved four types of offending: drink driving by adults, shoplifting by juveniles, other property offending by juveniles and violent crimes involving offenders aged under 30. A 38 per cent decrease was reported in the one-year follow-up among the violent offenders assigned to conferences. This was not true for the other three offence groups. Detected reoffending even increased for the drink-drivers by 6 per cent. The authors recommend repeating the experiment in other venues and breaking 'violence' down into more specific categories such as assault, grievous bodily harm and robbery. However, this may be hard to operationalise successfully and ethically as the victims of at least some of these offences may be the most fearful of having direct contact with their attackers and least willing to agree to a conference.

In the first phase of the UK's Crime Reduction Programme, the Government commissioned a review of existing restorative justice schemes. Having reviewed seven schemes, Miers *et al.* (2001) concluded that, while victims' and offenders' satisfaction levels were generally high, a minority of victims expressed concerns about the offenders' motives for agreeing to participate. This was one of the few British studies of restorative justice to examine reconviction. It found that only one scheme had a significant effect on reconviction. Forty-four per cent of the 153 adult offenders who took part in direct or indirect mediation in the West Yorkshire scheme were reconvicted in contrast to 56 per cent of a comparable control group (N = 79) drawn from referrals where the scheme did not provide an intervention. These rates did not allow for differences in the profile of the two groups, but doing so was said to widen rather than narrow the reconviction gap.

A subsequent independent evaluation of three restorative justice schemes funded under the Crime Reduction Programme is due to be completed by the end of 2006. In one of the schemes (covering sites in London, Northumbria and Thames Valley) suitable cases are being randomly allocated to restorative justice or other disposals so that the differences in outcome can be rigorously assessed (Shapland *et al.* 2006).

A meta-analysis of the international literature by Bonta *et al.* (2002) found a reduction in reconviction of between 2 and 8 per cent for offenders involved in restorative justice programmes; however, the studies reviewed were methodologically flawed. None used random assignment or adequately matched control groups, leading the authors to conclude that the reconviction rates might be a consequence of siphoning those least likely to reoffend into the restorative option. Similar conclusions were reached by a more recent meta-analytic review (Latimer *et al.* 2005).

UK studies of restorative cautioning for juveniles have indicated that this has little, if any, effect on reconviction. Wilcox and Hoyle's review (2004) of the reconviction rates of 728 offenders on 34 projects who could be tracked, compared with a matched national sample weighted to allow for the fact that those on the projects were far less likely to have previous convictions (23 per cent *v* 60 per cent), found no significant difference in their 12 months reconviction rates (31 per cent *v* 33 per cent). A more recent study focused on the well-known Thames Valley scheme compared to the use of traditional cautions in two other areas also found little difference in overall reconviction rates or the frequency and seriousness of their reoffending (Wilcox *et al.* 2004).

Conclusion: making sentences and interventions more effective

Evidence about the effectiveness of different types of sentence in reducing reoffending is lamentably thin. All we can say with certainty is that the reconviction rate differences between sentence types are marginal, after taking account of demographics and criminal histories. This does not mean that reductions in reconviction rates achieved by altering sentencing practice are not worth striving for. Even if one is talking only about a percentage point shift in low single figures, this is important in both human and financial terms. As a recent government Green Paper (DfES 2005: 10) notes:

A former prisoner who re-offends costs the criminal justice system an average of £65,000 up to the point of re-imprisonment, and, after that, as much as £37,500 each year in prison ... As well as this – and often unquantifiable – are the personal costs of crime, especially the impact on victims. The families of offenders are also likely to be faced with considerable financial and personal consequences ... Each year around 125,000 children see one of their parents sent to prison.

Friendship *et al.*'s (2005) quasi-systematic review concludes that the current quasi-experimental methods which are most commonly used to examine the outcome of interventions delivered as part of a sentence are unsatisfactory. Where formal control groups are selected and compared, there are always going to be questions about the comparability of the groups. Randomised controlled trials (RCTs) are very rarely conducted into sentencing in England and Wales for ethical and practical reasons, with practitioner resistance being the most difficult obstacle to overcome (Hedderman and Hough 2005). Given the range of potential custody/community sentencing mixes which the CJA 2003 may encourage, the practicality and even the value of a sentencing RCT seems questionable.

In the medium term, the most practical research strategy for assessing the impact of entire sentences and interventions delivered as part of a sentence is probably to continue the current practice of constructing 'virtual' control groups, whereby statistical modelling techniques are used to calculate expected reconviction rates for offender groups of any given demographic and criminal profile. However, such studies should ideally control for pseudo-reconvictions and include outcome measures such as time to further offence and seriousness of subsequent offending. As date of offence is held only on the Police National Computer (PNC), the speed with which the Home Office pursues plans to merge its own (Offenders Index) reconviction database with that of the PNC will largely determine how quickly and how often this can be done.

In one of the few British random control trials of probation, Deering *et al.* (1996) allocated offenders to normal supervision or supervision with additional cognitive behavioural elements once a probation order had been imposed. There were only 60 offenders in the original pool and a third of the 30 given additional 'treatment' had to be excluded from the final analysis because they failed to complete.[10] This approach may in the longer term offer a way forward in assessing the impact of interventions delivered as part of a sentence. However, given that the completion problem it identified seems to persist and that 'going to scale' also seems to be an issue, it seems that there are more urgent problems to deal with first.

It is also worth reminding ourselves of a fundamental tenet in undertaking any research project – the nature of the question determines the nature of the methods which should be employed to address it. RCTs may be a methodologically superior way of assessing the outcome of a single intervention, but such studies, in themselves, do not tell us *why* something works. RCTs work best in laboratories where delivery is uniform and other potentially influential factors can be held constant (high internal validity), but when something works in such a falsely constrained environment it may not work in the real world (low external validity). Not only is high internal validity not achievable in the probation context, its desirability is also doubtful. It is likely that different combinations of interventions, and variations in their amounts and sequencing, may yield different outcomes according the nature of the offender and their experience of previous interventions. In seeking to simplify and control other potentially influential factors we may miss out on discovering 'what works best, for whom and in what circumstances'. This is especially true if, as it has also been suggested, the very relationship between the supervisor and offender may be a critical success factor (Partridge 2004). In this context, it would be unwise to restrict our understanding of what works to the few studies which score very highly on Friendship *et al.*'s (2005) review.

It was understandable to begin the Effective Practice Initiative with cognitive behavioural programmes, as reviews of the literature up to that point show them to be a common factor in many studies of effectiveness (see McGuire 1995 and Vennard and Hedderman 1998 for reviews). However, some of the other equally important messages contained in the literature were given less attention (Hedderman 2004). This includes recognising that as offenders commonly have more than one problem, they need more than one form of assistance; that motivational work before, and follow-up work after, attending a programme can be essential elements; that no intervention works for every one and that selection criteria should therefore be adhered to closely; that there is a balance to be struck between programme integrity and matching delivery to offenders' learning styles (responsivity); and that programmes should be delivered by well-trained and well-resourced staff.

Early reconviction results from evaluations of cognitive behavioural programmes in prison and in the community suggest that cognitive behavioural programmes have had limited impact in this country, and that this is at least partly because these other 'What Works?' principles have not been been given enough attention (Falshaw *et al.* 2003; Clarke *et al.* 2004; Hollin *et al.* 2004).

It is self-evident that for a sentence to stand a chance of being effective an offender must actually undergo it. This is not usually a problem in relation to prison as escape levels are low. However, only around half of those on probation and community service orders in three studies conducted in 1999 and 2000 attended all appointments without any unacceptable absences (Hedderman and Hearnden 2001). For some of the EPI interventions discussed above, attendance rates of 50 per cent would be a significant improvement.[11] The best answer to the question of whether differences in the reconviction results of programme completers and non-completers are real or result from selection effects is to ensure that the majority of offenders who are allocated to interventions complete them.

Ever tougher enforcement procedures are not the way to achieve higher completion rates. Ultimately this will lead to supervision being limited to those who do not need it because they are the only ones who never miss an appointment or fail to turn up for their weekend spells of custody. It is ironic that political pressure to be seen as tough on offenders has created so overzealous an enforcement system that it is undermining the very thing National Standards were originally intended to do, which is to foster compliance (Hedderman and Hough 2004). If the breach provisions in the 2003 Criminal Justice Act are fully operationalised, they are likely to undermine effective practice by further limiting what probation officers can do to encourage and insist on compliance.

The biggest challenge for both researchers and practitioners who want to know what works in reducing reoffending is to move away from examining the impact of discrete interventions to offender-focused evaluations. Although

477

programmes are important, they are only part of the 'What Works' message – they are not the message in themselves. Moreover, to be effective, all the well-established elements of 'What Works' need to be incorporated into the supervision process, not just into the programme elements.

Finally, while important, the 'What works in reducing reoffending?' question is not the only one we should be asking. As Peter Raynor (this volume; Chapter 2) notes, the heavy focus on this aspect of work with offenders has led to the 'alternative to custody' debate disappearing from the political landscape. This is so despite the evidence that the increased use of custody is neither a response to rising crime nor an antidote to it (Hedderman 2006).

I was reminded of another somewhat unfashionable reason for continuing to work with offenders by a senior member of the Prison Service recently who remarked: 'Even if research showed that education and training and resettlement work were entirely ineffective, I hope that we would still be allowed to do it, because it's the right thing to do.' I hope she is right.

Evaluations of restorative justice indicate that there are other ways in which the merits of our responses to offending can be judged. Restorative justice schemes clearly have important non-reconviction benefits. The future of such schemes looks relatively secure because of those benefits and despite the equivocal evidence of their effect on reoffending. It is equally important to consider the non-reconviction benefits of other interventions. Working with offenders to understand the consequences of their offending for themselves or others, improving their basic skills and helping them into employment may not result in all or most of them stopping offending entirely or immediately, but it may reduce the rate of their reoffending. It may also promote desistence through the maintenance of positive social relationships, creating the opportunity to make a positive contribution to society and enabling those who commit crime to become much more than simply 'ex-offenders'.

Notes

1 Examples of this sort of work include Hedderman and Gelsthorpe's (1997) examination of whether men and women convicted of the same types of offence received comparable sentences; and Hough and Roberts's (1998) discussion of how far actual sentencing severity accords with public expectations of it.

2 See Easton and Piper (2005) for a fuller discussion of both philosophical positions and a consideration of how far each has influenced current sentencing policy and legislation.

3 Even taking acts against other inmates into consideration would not resolve this problem as the prison environment clearly limits the inmate's ability to commit specific types of offence (child abuse and car theft being among the most obvious).

4 In a break with convention, the volume of Offender Management Statistics published in 2005 merely repeated the 2001 reconviction figures published in the 2004 volume rather than updating them to relate to those made subject to a community sentence or released from custody in 2002.

5 Pseudo-reconvictions are convictions which occur during the follow-up period but which result from offences committed prior to the sentence of interest. They are

excluded from reconviction studies because they are not a measure of the current sentence's effectiveness. See Chapter 15 for a detailed discussion.

6 See Chapter 15 for a discussion.

7 Bizarrely, as Raynor and Vanstone (this volume, Chapter 2) point out, the idea of 'alternatives to prison' is now itself so neglected that the term has almost entirely disappeared, at least from political debate.

8 See Clarke *et al.* (2000) for a general discussion of New Public Management, and Gelthorpe and Morgan's introduction to this volume for the way this approach has affected probation.

9 For example, those relating to Rex *et al.*'s (2004) study of community service.

10 The handling of 'drop-outs' in an analysis of this sort is of critical importance to the outcome, of course.

11 More recent figures published by NOMS on the Internet (undated) suggest that completion rates have improved but the figures are hard to interpret as no information is provided on how they are derived.

Further reading

Easton and Piper (2005) provide a highly accessible account of developments in sentencing and punishment theories, policy and practice. Sentencing effectiveness is most frequently measured by examining reconviction rates. Mair *et al.* (1997) consider how reconviction rates are calculated and the important limits this places on what differences in reconviction rates may be said to mean.

Zamble and Quinsey's book (1997) has helped to shape recent thinking about the prediction of reoffending in terms of preventive intervention, risk assessment and management, release policies and post-release supervision. Hollin and Palmer's recent work (2006) explores the theories and research underlying offending behaviour programmes, design and implementation issues and how best the impact of such programmes might be evaluated.

References

Andrews, D.A., Zinger, I., Hoge, R.D., Bonta, J., Gendreau, P. and Cullen, F.T. (1990) 'Does correctional treatment work? A clinically relevant and psychologically informed meta-analysis', *Criminology*, 28: 369–404.

Beccaria, C. (1995 [1767]) *On Crimes and Punishments and Other Writings*. Cambridge: Cambridge University Press.

Bentham, J. (1970 [1789]) *An Introduction to the Principles of Morals and Legislation*. London: Athlone Press.

Bonta, J., Wallace-Capretta, S., Rooney, J. and McAnoy, K. (2002) 'An outcome evaluation of a restorative justice alternative to incarceration', *Contemporary Justice Review*, 5: 319–38.

Bottoms, A.E. (2004) 'Empirical research relevant to sentencing frameworks', in A. Bottoms, S. Rex and G. Robinson (eds), *Alternatives to Prison: Options for an Insecure Society*. Cullompton: Willan.

Bottoms, A.E., Gelsthorpe, L. and Rex, S. (eds) (2001) *Community Penalties: Change and Challenges*. Cullompton: Willan.

Brody, S.R. (1976) *The Effectiveness of Sentencing: A Review of the Literature*, Home Office Research Study No. 35. London: HMSO.

Cann, J. (2006) *Cognitive Skills Programmes: Impact on Reducing Reconviction Among a Sample of Female Prisoners*, Findings No. 276. London: Home Office.

Cann, J., Falshaw, L., Nugent, F. and Friendship, C. (2003) *Understanding What Works: Accredited Cognitive Skills Programmes for Adult Men and Young Offenders*, Home Office Research Findings No. 226. London: Home Office.

Carter, P. (2003) *Managing Offenders, Changing Lives: A New Approach*. London: Home Office.

Clarke, A., Simonds, R. and Wydall, S. (2004) *Delivering Cognitive Skills Programmes in Prison: A Qualitative Study*, Online Report 27/04. London: Home Office.

Clarke, J., Gerwitz, S. and McLauglin, E. (eds) (2000) *New Managerialism, New Welfare?* London: Sage.

Crawford, A. and Newburn, T. (2003) *Youth Offending and Restorative Justice: Implementing Reform in Youth Justice*. Cullompton: Willan.

Crow, I., Richardson, P., Riddington, C. and Simon, F. (1989) *Unemployment, Crime and Offenders*. London: Routledge.

Cuppleditch, L. and Evans, W. (2005) *Re-offending of Adults: Results from the 2002 Cohort*, Home Office Statistical Bulletin 25/05. London: Home Office.

De Silva, N., Cowell, P. and Chow, T. (2005) *Updated and Revised Prison Population Projections, 2005–2011, England and Wales* (July), Home Office Statistical Bulletin 10/05. London: Home Office.

De Silva, N., Cowell, P. and Chow, T. (2006) *Prison Population Projection 2006–2013, England and Wales* (July), Home Office Statistical Bulletin 11/06. London: Home Office.

Debidin, M. and Lovbakke, J. (2005) 'Offending behaviour programmes in prison and probation', in G. Harper and C. Chitty (eds), *The Impact of Corrections on Re-offending: A Review of 'What Works'*, Home Office Research Study No. 291, 2nd edition. London: Home Office.

Deering, J., Thurstone, R. and Vanstone, M. (1996) 'Individual supervision: an experimental programme in Pontypridd', *Probation Journal*, 43 (2): 70–6.

DfES (2005) *Reducing Re-Offending Through Skills and Employment*, Cm 6702. London: DfES.

Easton, S. and Piper, C. (2005) *Sentencing and Punishment: The Quest for Justice*. Oxford: Oxford University Press.

Falshaw, L., Friendship, C., Travers, R. and Nugent, F. (2003) *Searching for 'What Works': An Evaluation of Cognitive Skills Programmes*, Findings No. 206. London: Home Office.

Fletcher, D., Woodhill, D. and Herrington, A. (1998) *Building Bridges into Employment and Training for Ex-Offenders*. York: Rowntree Trust.

Folkard, M. S., Smith D. D. and Smith D. E. (1976) *IMPACT Volume II: The Results of the Experiment*, Home Office Research Study No. 36. London: HMSO.

Friendship, C., Blud, L. Erikson, M. and Travers, R. (2002) *An Evaluation of Cognitive Behavioural Treatment for Prisoners*, Research Findings No. 161. London: Home Office.

Friendship, C., Street, R., Cann, J. and Harper, G. (2005) 'Introduction: the policy context and assessing the evidence', in G. Harper and C. Chitty (eds), *The Impact of Corrections on Re-offending: A Review of 'What Works'*, Home Office Research Study No. 291, 2nd edition. London: Home Office.

Gaes, G. G., Flanagan, T. J., Motiuk, L. and Stewart, L. (1999) 'Adult correctional treatment', in M. Tonry and J. Petersilia (eds), *Crime and Justice: A Review of Research*, 26: 361–426.

Gendreau, P. and Ross, R. R. (1979) 'Effective correctional treatment: bibliotherapy for cynics', *Crime and Delinquency*, 25: 463–89.

Haslewood-Pocsik, I., Merone, L. and Roberts, C. (2004) *The Evaluation of the Employment Pathfinder: Lessons from Phase I and a Survey from Phase 2*, Online Report 22/04. London: Home Office.

Hedderman, C. (2004) 'Testing times: how the policy and practice environment shaped the creation of the What Works evidence-base', *VISTA*, 8: 182–8.

Hedderman, C. (2006) 'Keeping the lid on the prison population: will it work?', in M. Hough, R. Allen and U. Padel (eds), *Reshaping Probation and Prisons: The New Offender Management Framework*. London: Polity Press.

Hedderman, C. and Gelsthorpe, L. (1997) *Understanding the Sentencing of Women*, Home Office Research Study 170. London: HMSO.

Hedderman, C. and Hearnden, I. (2001) 'To discipline or punish? Enforcement under National Standards 2000', *VISTA*, 6 (3): 215–24.

Hedderman, C. and Hough, M. (2004) 'Getting tough or being effective: what matters?', in G. Mair (ed.), *What Matters in Probation*. Cullompton: Willan.

Hedderman, C. and Hough, M. (2005) 'Diversion from prosecution at court and effective sentencing', in A.E. Perry, C. McDougall and D.P. Farrington (eds), *Reducing Crime: The Effectiveness of Criminal Justice Interventions*. Chichester: Wiley.

Hedderman, C. and Sugg, D. (1997) 'The influence of cognitive behavioural approaches: a survey of probation programmes', in *Changing Offenders' Attitudes and Behaviour: What Works?*, Home Office Research Study No. 171. London: Home Office.

Hollin, C.R. (1990) *Cognitive-Behavioral Interventions with Young Offenders*. New York: Pergamon.

Hollin, C.R. and Palmer, E.J. (2006) *Offending Behaviour Programmes: Development, Application and Controversies*. Chichester: Wiley.

Hollin, C., Palmer, E., McGuire, J., Hounsome, J., Hatcher, R., Bilby, C. and Clark, C. (2004) *Pathfinder Programmes in the Probation Service: A Retrospective Analysis*, Online Report 66/04. London: Home Office.

Home Office (1993) *Reconvictions of Those Given Probation and Community Service Orders in 1987*, Statistical Bulletin 18/93. London: Home Office.

Home Office (1995) *National Standards for the Supervision of Offenders in the Community 2000*. London: Home Office.

Home Office (2001) *Making Punishments Work: Report of a Review of the Sentencing Framework for England and Wales* (The Halliday Review). London: Home Office.

Home Office (2003) *Prison Statistics, England and Wales, 2001*, Cm 5743 London: HMSO.

Home Office (2004a) *Offender Management Caseload Statistics 2003 England and Wales*, Home Office Statistical Bulletin 15/04, London: Home Office.

Home Office (2004b) *Probation Statistics, England and Wales, 2002*. London: Home Office.

Home Office (2004c) *Reducing Reoffending: National Action Plan*. London: Home Office.

Home Office (2005a) *Sentencing Statistics 2004, England and Wales*, Home Office Statistical Bulletin 15/05. London: Home Office.

Home Office (2005b) *Criminal Statistics, England and Wales, 2004*, Home Office Statistical Bulletin 19/05. London: Home Office.

Home Office (2005c) *Offender Management Caseload Statistics 2004 England and Wales*, Home Office Statistical Bulletin 17/05. London: Home Office.

Honderich, T. (1984) *Punishment: The Supposed Justifications*. Harmondsworth: Penguin.

Hough, M. and Roberts, J. V. (1998) *Attitudes to Punishment: Findings from the British Crime Survey*, Home Office Study No. 179. London: HMSO.

Hough, M., Clancy, A., Turnbull, P.J. and McSweeney, T. (2003) *The Impact of Drug Treatment and Testing Orders on Offending: Two-Year Reconviction Results*, Findings No. 184. London: Home Office.

Hudson, B. (2003) *Understanding Justice: An Introduction to Ideas, Perspectives and Controversies in Modern Penal Theory*, 2nd edn. Maidenhead: Open University Press.

Jowell, R. (2003) *Trying It Out – The Role of 'Pilots' in Policy-making. Report of a Review of Government Pilots*. London: Cabinet Office.

Kershaw, C. and Renshaw, G. (1997a) *Reconvictions of Prisoners Discharged from Prison in 1993, England and Wales*, Statistical Bulletin 5/97. London: Home Office.

Kershaw, C. and Renshaw, G. (1997b) *Reconvictions of Those Commencing Community Penalties in 1993, England and Wales*, Statistical Bulletin 6/97. London: Home Office.

Killias, M., Aebi, M. and Ribeaud, D. (2000) 'Does community service rehabilitate better than short-term imprisonment? Results of a controlled experiment', *Howard Journal*, 39 (1): 40–57.

Langan, P. and Farrington, D. P. (1998) *Crime and Justice in the United States and in England and Wales 1981–1996*. Washington, DC: Bureau of Justice Statistics.

Latimer, J., Dowden, C. and Muise, D. (2005) 'The effectiveness of restorative justice practices: a meta-analysis', *Prison Journal*, 85 (2): 127–44.

Lewis, S., Vennard, J., Raynor, P., Vanstone, M., Raybould, S. and Rix, A. (2003) *The Resettlement of Short-term Prisoners: An Evaluation of Seven Pathfinders*. RDS Occasional Paper No. 83. London: Home Office.

Lipsey, M. W. (1992) 'The effect of treatment on juvenile delinquents: results from meta-analysis', in F. Losel, T. Bliesener and D. Bender (eds), *Psychology and Law: International Perspectives*. Berlin: de Gruyter.

Lloyd, C., Mair, G. and Hough, M. (1994) *Explaining Reconviction Rates: A Critical Analysis*, Home Office Research Study No. 136. London: Home Office.

McGuire, J. (ed.) (1995) *What Works: Reducing Reoffending*. Chichester: Wiley.

McIvor, G. (1992) *Sentenced to Serve: The Operation and Impact of Community Service by Offenders*. Aldershot: Avebury.

McIvor, G. (2004) *Reconviction Following Drug Treatment and Testing Orders*. Edinburgh: Scottish Executive.

McMahon, G., Hall, A., Hayward, G., Hudson, C. and Roberts, C. (2004) *Basic Skills Programmes in the Probation Service: An Evaluation of the Basic Skills Pathfinder*, Findings No. 203. London: Home Office.

Mair, G. (1995) 'Evaluating the impact of community penalties', *University of Chicago Law School Roundtable*, 2 (2): 455–74.

Mair, G. (2004a) 'The origins of What Works in England and Wales: a house built on sand?', in G. Mair (ed.), *What Matters in Probation*. Cullompton: Willan.

Mair, G. (2004b) 'What Works: a view from the chiefs', in G. Mair (ed.), *What Matters in Probation*. Cullompton: Willan.

Mair, G., Lloyd, C. and Hough, M. (1997) 'The limitations of reconviction rates', in G. Mair (ed.), *Evaluating the Effectiveness of Community Penalties*. Aldershot: Avebury.

Marshall, T. (1999) *Restorative Justice: An Overview*. London: Home Office.

Martinson, R. (1974) 'What works? Questions and answers about prison reform', *Public Interest*, 10: 22–54.

May, C. (1999) *Explaining Reconviction Following a Community Sentence: The Role of Social Factors*, Home Office Research Study No. 192. London: Home Office.

May, C. and Wadwell, J. (2001) *Enforcing Community Penalties: The Relationship between Enforcement and Reconviction*, Findings No. 155. London: Home Office.

Metcalf, H., Anderson, T. and Rolfe, H. (2001) *Barriers to Employment for Offenders and Ex-offenders*, Department for Work and Pensions Research Report No. 155. Leeds: CDS.

Miers, D. (2001) *An International Review of Restorative Justice*, Crime Reduction Research Series Paper 10. London: Home Office.

Miers, D., Maguire, M., Goldie, S., Sharpe, K., Hale, C., Netten, A., Uglow, S., Doolin, K., Hallam, A., Newburn, T. and Enterkin, J. (2001) *An Exploratory Evaluation of Restorative Justice Schemes*, Crime Reduction Research Series Paper 9. London: Home Office.

Moxon, D. (1998) 'The role of sentencing policy', in P. Goldblatt and C. Lewis (eds), *Reducing Reoffending: An Assessment of Research Evidence on Ways of Dealing with Offending Behaviour*, Home Office Research Study No. 187. London: Home Office.

Nagin, D. S. (1998) 'Deterrence and incapacitation', in M. Tonry (ed.), *The Handbook of Crime and Punishment*. New York: Oxford University Press.

NOMS (undated) *Performance Report on Offender Management Targets July 2005 – September 2005*. See: http://www.noms.homeoffice.gov.uk/downloads/Perf_Rep_Offender_Man_Targs%2007-2005%20-%2009-2005.pdf

Oldfield, M. (1997) 'What worked? A five-year study of probation reconvictions', *Probation Journal*, 44 (1): 2–10.

Ong, G., Roberts, C., Al-Attar, Z. and Harsent, L. (2003) *Think First: An Accredited Community-Based Cognitive Behavioural Programme in England and Wales. Findings from the Prospective Evaluation in Three Probation Areas. Report Produced for National Probation Directorate by Probation Studies Unit*. Centre for Criminological Research, University of Oxford.

Partridge, S. (2004) *Examining Case Management Models for Community Sentences*, Home Office Online Report 17/04. London: Home Office.

Raynor, P. (2003) 'Research in probation: from "Nothing Works" to "What Works"', in W.H. Chui and M. Nellis (eds), *Moving Probation Forward: Evidence, Arguments and Practice*. Harlow: Pearson Education.

Raynor, P. (2004) 'Editor's introduction', *VISTA*, 8 (3): 127–9.

Raynor, P. and Vanstone, M. (1996) 'Reasoning and rehabilitation in Britain: the results of the Straight Thinking on Probation (STOP) programme', *International Journal of Offender Therapy and Comparative Criminology*, 40 (4): 272–84.

Raynor, P. and Vanstone, M. (2002) *Understanding Community Penalties: Probation, Policy and Social Change*. Buckingham: Open University Press.

Rex, S., Gelsthorpe, L., Roberts, C. and Jordan, P. (2004) *What's Promising in Community Service: Implementation of Seven Pathfinder Projects*, Findings No. 231. London: Home Office.

Roberts, J. V. (2004) *The Virtual Prison: Community Custody and the Evolution of Imprisonment*. Cambridge: Cambridge University Press.

Roberts, K., Barton, A., Buchanan, J. and Goldson, B. (1997) *Evaluation of a Home Office Initiative to Help Offenders into Employment*. London: Home Office.

Rogers, R. and Jolin, A. (1989) 'Electronic monitoring: a review of the empirical literature', *Journal of Contemporary Criminal Justice*, 5: 141–52.

Sarno, C., Hearnden, I. and Hedderman, C. (2001) *From Offending to Employment: A Study of Two Probation Schemes in Inner London and Surrey*, Home Office Research Findings No. 135. London: Home Office Research and Statistics Directorate.

Sarno, C., Hearnden, I., Hedderman, C., Hough, M., Nee, C. and Herrington, V. (2000) *Working Their Way Out of Offending: A Study of Two Probation Employment Schemes*, Home Office Research Study No. 218. London: Home Office Research and Statistics Directorate.

Shapland, J., Atkinson, A., Atkinson, H., Chapman, B., Colledge, E., Dignan, J., Howes, M., Johnstone, J., Robinson, G. and Sorsby, A. (2006) *Restorative Justice in Practice – Findings from the Second Phase of the Evaluation of Three Schemes*, Findings No. 274. London: Home Office.

Shaw, M. and Hannah-Moffat, K. (2004) 'How cognitive skills forgot about gender and diversity', in G. Mair (ed.), *What Matters in Probation*. Cullompton: Willan.

Sherman, L., Strang, H., Woods, D. (2000) *Recidivism Patterns in the Canberra Reintegrative Shaming Experiments (RISE)*. Canberra, ACT: Australian Institute of Criminology; see: http://www.aic.gov.au/rjustice/rise/recidivism

Simon, F. and Corbett, C. (1996) *An Evaluation of Prison Work and Training*. London: Home Office.

Spicer, K. and Glicksman, A. (2004) *Adult Reconviction: Results from the 2001 Cohort*, Online Report 59/04. London: Home Office.

Sugg, D., Moore, L. and Howard, P. (2001) *Electronic Monitoring and Offending Behaviour – Reconviction Results for the Second Year of Trials of Curfew Orders*, Findings No. 141. London: Home Office.

Thomas, D.A. (1979) *Principles of Sentencing*. London: Heinemann.

Thomas-Peters, B.A. (2006) 'The modern context of psychology in corrections: influences, limitations and values of "What Works?"', in G. Towl (ed.), *Psychological Research in Prisons*. Oxford: Blackwell.

Turnbull, P. J., McSweeney, T., Webster, R., Edmunds, M. and Hough, M. (2000) *Drug Treatment and Testing Orders: Evaluation Report*, Home Office Research Study No. 212. London: HMSO.

Underdown, A. (1998) *Strategies for Effective Offender Supervision: Report of the HMIP What Works Project*. London: Home Office.

Vennard, J. and Hedderman, C. (1998) 'Effective interventions with offenders', in *Reducing Offending: An Assessment of Research Evidence on Ways of Dealing with Offending Behaviour*, Home Office Research Study No. 187. London: Home Office.

Vennard, J., Sugg, D. and Hedderman, C. (1997) *Changing Offenders' Attitudes and Behaviour: 'What Works'*, Home Office Research Study No. 171. London: Home Office.

von Hirsch, A. (1976) *Doing Justice: The Choice of Punishments*. New York: Hill & Wang.

von Hirsch, A. and Roberts, J. V. (2004) 'Legislating sentencing principles: the provisions of the Criminal Justice Act 2003 relating to sentencing purposes and the role of previous convictions', *Criminal Law Review*, August: 639–52.

von Hirsch, A., Bottoms, A., Burney, E. and Wikström, P.-O. (1999) *Criminal Deterrence and Sentence Severity: An Analysis of Recent Research*. Oxford: Hart.

Webster, R., Hedderman, C., Turnbull, P. J. and May, T. (2001) *Building Bridges to Employment for Prisoners*, Home Office Research Study No. 226. London: Home Office.

Wilcox, A. and Hoyle, C. (2004) *The National Evaluation of the Youth Justice Board's Restorative Justice Projects*. London: Youth Justice Board.

Wilcox, A., Young, R. and Hoyle, C. (2004) *An Evaluation of the Impact of Restorative Cautioning: Findings From a Reconviction Study*, Research Findings No. 255. London: Home Office.

Chapter 2

Theoretical perspectives on resettlement: what it is and how it might work

Peter Raynor

Introduction

As the previous chapter points out, when people use terms like 'resettlement' they do not always mean the same thing, and often they do not realise this, which contributes to a good deal of vagueness and confusion. This chapter is about the meanings of resettlement, and particularly about its purposes and justifications: what is it for? What is it realistically meant to achieve? The answers to these questions might seem obvious, but even a small amount of exposure to official documents and statements is enough to dispel such confidence, and studies of practice reveal different assumptions about what kind of activities and practices should be involved in resettlement. These in turn reflect different assumptions or beliefs about imprisoned offenders' needs, and about how they come to be imprisoned offenders in the first place. This chapter traces some of the changing views and concepts of resettlement which have underpinned recent and earlier policies, drawing on the author's involvement in a series of Home Office funded evaluations of resettlement services extending over the past fourteen years in collaboration with Mike Maguire, Maurice Vanstone and others (see Clancy *et al.* 2006; Lewis 2004; Lewis *et al.* 2003; Maguire and Raynor 1997, 2006; Maguire *et al.* 1996; Maguire *et al.* 2000; Raynor 2004). In addition, the chapter explores some evidence of what resettlement *can* achieve, and points to areas of convergence between the thinking behind some apparently effective resettlement work and recent studies of desistance from offending. Such work can help to throw light on what models of resettlement can be

26

regarded as realistic, in the sense that their goals might actually be achievable.

Our current concept of resettlement lacks clarity around two issues in particular. One concerns the goals of resettlement, or the state of affairs intended to result from resettlement activity. Is it, as the name rather implies, an attempt to restore people to the social environment and condition which preceded their prison sentence? The problem with this view is that it may have been an actively criminogenic environment, and even the main reason why they found themselves in prison in the first place. 'Reintegration', another currently popular term, makes little sense for those who were not integrated in the first place, and may not be the best outcome for others who were well integrated into communities or peer groups where offending was normal or accepted. If, on the other hand, the intended outcome is new social bonds and commitments which support a way of life in which offending is less likely (as suggested, among others, by Haines 1990), resettlement is not a very clear description of such a process.

The second area where there is a lack of clarity concerns the reasons for providing resettlement as a publicly funded service within the criminal justice system. Are such services provided simply because many ex-prisoners have social needs? If so, it is not clear why these welfare needs should be met by the criminal justice system rather than by other services which (at least in principle) are available to all. There is also a risk of perceived unfairness if ex-prisoners are believed to be receiving special help which is not available to people with similar needs who have not offended. (At one time it was argued by some criminal justice professionals that the development of the Welfare State would in due course make discharge grants obsolete (Home Office 1953: 11)). Or are resettlement services provided in order to meet particular needs which ex-prisoners have because they have served prison sentences? If so, are these special needs the result of damage done to prisoners by imprisonment, in which case the taxpayer is paying both to create the needs and to try to meet them, or are they a consequence of the *beneficial* impact of imprisonment, such as the need to continue and reinforce the work of rehabilitative programmes begun in prison? Or are resettlement services best understood as part of a range of work done with offenders, including those subject to community sentences, in an attempt to rehabilitate them and reduce their propensity to offend? If so, questions about the purposes and justifications of resettlement become subsumed under the broader question of why and how criminal justice systems try, or should try, to rehabilitate offenders. These are complicated

27

questions (see, for example, Raynor and Robinson 2005). In this chapter, I attempt no more than some clarification of the history of the *concept* of resettlement and its predecessors, to supplement the history of policy and practice which is reviewed in the preceding chapter. I follow this with some suggestions about how it might be understood in current circumstances in the light of evidence about what it actually achieves.

Resettlement and its predecessors – the history of an idea

What we now call 'resettlement' has had various names through the last two centuries. In the nineteenth century it was called 'Discharged Prisoners' Aid'. It was provided on a charitable basis by voluntary associations linked to local prisons (the earliest clearly traceable examples, in Gloucester, Hampshire, Shropshire and Montgomery, went back to 1800 or before (National Association of Discharged Prisoners' Aid Societies 1956)) and by publicly funded associations such as the Central Association for the Aid of Discharged Convicts, which was founded in 1910. Its first President was Winston Churchill, whose views on resettlement are discussed later in this chapter. In addition, other specialist associations were set up to assist women prisoners (the Aylesbury Association) and Borstal boys (the Borstal Association). A representative example of early charitable thinking about the plight of ex-prisoners can be found in the work of William Booth ('General' Booth of the Salvation Army) who included criminal justice issues in his social investigation of 'Darkest England' (1890):

> Absolute despair drives many a man into the ranks of the criminal class, who would never have fallen into the category of criminal convicts if adequate provision had been made for the rescue of those drifting to doom. When once he has fallen, circumstances seem to combine to keep him there ... the unfortunate who bears the prison brand is hunted from pillar to post, until he despairs of ever regaining his position, and oscillates between one prison and another for the rest of his days. (Booth 1890: 58)

Booth was particularly conscious of the difficulties encountered by many ex-prisoners in securing accommodation and employment, and in staying sober: his book gives examples of successful help, sometimes in offenders' own words. His argument is that the punishment should

28

end when prisoners are released, and further obstacles resulting from their ex-prisoner status prolong the punishment unfairly and prevent people who wish to maintain a crime-free life from doing so. He certainly does not see aid to the released prisoner as continuing the rehabilitative efforts of the prison: 'At present there seems to be but little likelihood of any real reform in the interior of our prisons. We have therefore to wait until the men come outside, in order to see what can be done' (Booth 1890: 174). However, anticipating many later authorities, he argued that successful help after release was made more likely if a relationship could be established by pre-release contact: 'We should seek access to the prisons in order to gain such acquaintance with the prisoners as would enable us the more effectually to benefit them on discharge' (Booth 1890: 175). The attitudes underpinning such relationships are clearly indicated: 'Our people ... have never learnt to regard a prisoner as a mere convict ... He is ever a human being to them ...' (Booth 1890: 174).

During the first half of the twentieth century this type of charitable and faith-based approach became more organised and began to adopt a more secular and professional guise. The separate Discharged Prisoners' Aid Societies came together as the National Association of Discharged Prisoners' Aid Societies (NADPAS) in 1936, and the associations linked to the convict prisons, the women's prison and the Borstals were merged into the Central After-Care Association in 1948. By this time the term 'after-care' was being preferred to earlier terms like 'aid' or 'relief', but the focus was still on what happened after release: the NADPAS Handbook for 1956 uses 'after-care' consistently. It also states that 'none should enter in, or remain in, this work who is not committed to the principle that every offender offers hope of reclamation' (NADPAS 1956: viii; William Booth would have agreed). However, more professional concerns about the best use of scarce resources also find their place in the Handbook, anticipating later concerns about the 'revolving door':

> In every local prison there are those serving short terms of imprisonment who are continually coming and going – some are discharged several times in one year after serving fresh sentences ... it is considered a waste of valuable time in seeing such cases ... (NADPAS 1956: 32)

In 1963 a report of the Advisory Council on the Treatment of Offenders (ACTO) proposed a major rationalisation of the provision of aftercare (Home Office 1963). Responsibilities for compulsory aftercare (provided

29

by the Central After-Care Association and often in practice by probation officers) and voluntary aftercare (provided largely by NADPAS) were to be merged, and both were to be provided by the Probation Service, to be renamed the Probation and After-Care Service. Aftercare was seen clearly in this report as a professional service ('After-care is essentially a form of social casework' – Home Office 1963: ii) and

> to be fully effective, must be integrated with the work of the penal institutions in which the offender serves his sentence, and must be conceived as a process which starts on the offender's reception into custody, is developed during his sentence, and is available for as long as necessary after his release. (Home Office 1963: 4)

Here the prison is no longer simply punishment, but is seen as doing rehabilitative 'work' in its own right, with which the aftercare must be 'integrated'. This passage also introduces the idea of a process which is continuous from the start of the sentence, anticipating the term 'throughcare', which began to replace 'aftercare' in probation officers' terminology and literature during the late 1960s.

The next few decades involved rapid development in the work of probation services, and many of the important milestones in this have been described in the previous chapter. Those which most significantly affected the concept and meaning of throughcare and aftercare included the Statement of National Objectives and Priorities (Home Office 1984), which consigned voluntary aftercare to a low-priority residual role in a service redefined as a provider of non-custodial sentences. This began a process of withdrawal by the Probation Service from the voluntary aftercare responsibilities acquired as recently as the 1960s, and incidentally fulfilled a gloomy prediction made by Radzinowicz in his dissenting note to the 1963 ACTO report. 'Throughcare' now came to mean primarily the supervision of statutory licences. A few years later this was reinforced by the 1991 Criminal Justice Act and the innovative series of Green and White Papers which preceded it (Home Office 1988, 1990a, 1990b). These developments famously redefined probation as 'punishment in the community', less severe than custodial punishment but not different in kind; in addition, they introduced the concept of the 'seamless sentence', a single punishment to be served partly in prison and partly on licence in the community, under supervision by the Probation Service. In addition to the discretionary release

30

arrangements which replaced parole for longer-sentence prisoners, all those serving sentences of at least one year but less than four years were to be subject to automatic conditional release (ACR) under supervision, normally at the halfway point. Strict new requirements relating to reporting and enforcement (Home Office 1992) emphasised the fact that this was a continuation of the sentence. Although these more punitive features were balanced by the 1991 Act's intention to bring about a significant reduction in custodial sentencing, the decarcerative elements in the Act were quickly undermined by new legislation as a crumbling Conservative administration lurched towards law and order populism. The enduring elements turned out to be the redefinition of probation service activities as punishments and the 'seamless sentence'. Interestingly, offenders subject to ACR during the first years of the new scheme clung to an earlier concept of aftercare and thought that its purpose was to help them rather than to punish them. Probation officers, however, thought that the main focus of supervision was to secure compliance with licence requirements (though they also recognised a need to address offending behaviour and offenders' problems), and probation managers stated that the primary aims of the scheme were to protect the public and to ensure compliance (Maguire *et al.* 1996). The early 1990s also saw the almost complete disappearance of voluntary aftercare for the short-term prisoners who were not included in the ACR scheme: voluntary arrangements no longer had a place in a probation service focused on coping with expanded caseloads and stricter requirements for contact and enforcement (Maguire *et al.* 2000). Although these offenders had many problems and a high risk of reconviction, they were no longer a priority.

As government policies increasingly assumed that there were strong similarities between the work of prisons and probation, with probation seen as offering lesser punishments rather than alternatives to punishment, it was a logical development to begin to think about unifying the 'correctional' services. The first major government report on this theme appeared in 1998, in the first full year of the New Labour government, with a foreword and endorsement by the then Home Secretary Jack Straw (Home Office 1998). It came to the conclusion that the two services should remain separate but should work more closely together, and that the Probation Service, locally managed until then, should become a national service for England and Wales run from the Home Office. (Those were the days when some people still believed that if you wanted something run properly, you should arrange for the Home Office to run it.) The 1998 report

31

is also important for this chapter because it marks the definitive adoption of the term 'resettlement' into official discourse:

> 'Throughcare' is the term which lies at the heart of the two services' joint work. It is unlikely to be properly understood outside of the prison and probation worlds ... We think that public and sentencer confidence would be enhanced if the focus was on the ultimate goals of 'throughcare' – high quality sentence planning and successful resettlement in the community. Our preference is for this work to be called simply 'resettlement' ... (Home Office 1998: 9)

It is not known what evidence was available that the public and sentencers did not understand 'throughcare'; however, a rather different rationale for the change is spelled out in another section of the report:

> It is important that the names, language and terminology used by the services should give accurate and accessible messages about the nature and aims of their work. Some of the terms have been criticised, for example because ... they are associated with tolerance of crime ... or they are too esoteric to be understood outside the two services (e.g. 'throughcare' which sounds more associated with the 'caring' services). (Home Office 1998: 8)

'Resettlement' was the broadly accepted term by the time the experimental 'Pathfinder' projects were funded by the Crime Reduction Programme in 1999. One of these experiments, which concerned resettlement, is discussed in the second part of this chapter. However, before moving on to the empirical side of this exploration of the meaning of resettlement, there is one more terminological shift to be taken into account. In 2003 Patrick Carter, a businessman and Downing Street advisor, was asked to undertake a further review of the operation of the criminal justice system. His report was published at the end of 2003 (Home Office 2003) and recommended the establishment of a National Offender Management Service (NOMS) combining prisons and probation, and an extension of 'contestability' within the system to allow the voluntary and private sectors to compete with the public sector to provide 'offender management' services. Within a couple of weeks the government had committed itself to implementing most of the report's recommendations, though at the time of writing we are still waiting to see exactly how.

32

As far as resettlement was concerned, the Carter Report seemed to involve another change of language: both prisons and community-based services were doing 'offender management', a term which covered everything from secure incapacitative custody to supervision in the community, and which aimed to protect the public by reducing the risk of reoffending. This was to be achieved by individualised assessment, planning and case management which could include work to address offending behaviour, or could aim to manage and reduce risk through an appropriate set of controls and restrictions, or could combine these approaches in various ways (for example, personal supervision supported by an electronically monitored curfew). Offenders' needs were not ignored: in so far as they were criminogenic, the system should try to meet them in order to reduce risk. The notion of 'end-to-end' offender management promised a more coherent and planned approach to doing this, ideally with continuity of supervision from a known person, although it was difficult to see how the proposed 'contestable' structure of services would actually deliver such a high level of continuity (Raynor and Maguire 2005). Like the 1991 Act, the Carter Report had some very positive underlying purposes: for example, to limit the prison population to 80,000; to end the use of community penalties for low-risk offenders who could be fined; and to supply the missing resettlement services to the thousands of short-sentence prisoners through a new sentence, 'Custody Plus', which was introduced by the Criminal Justice Act 2003 and would ensure that every short prison sentence was followed by a period of supervision in the community. Sadly, at the time of writing, the prison target has already been abandoned and the cost of new prisons is to be found partly from the indefinite postponement of the implementation of Custody Plus. The focus instead has been on forcing through the structural reorganisation and 'contestability', against considerable resistance from the existing services.

Through all these twists and turns of policy the official notion of what services should be provided to released prisoners and the terminology used to describe them has changed beyond recognition, and changed far more than the realities of resettlement practice. It is now time to anchor this discussion in some of these realities. The way we think about and conceptualise resettlement should reflect what it actually can and does achieve, if our thinking is to serve as a useful guide to practice rather than a source of misleading or unrealistic expectations. The largest and most detailed empirical explorations of recent mainstream resettlement practice in England and Wales have been carried out in the series of studies mentioned at the beginning

33

of this chapter, and in particular in the Resettlement Pathfinder evaluations. The next section of this chapter considers what can be learned from these studies about the nature of successful resettlement work.

What worked in the Resettlement Pathfinders

The Resettlement Pathfinders, which focused mainly on short-term prisoners, ran between 1999 and 2005 and were evaluated as part of the Crime Reduction Programme. Full accounts of the findings from these studies can be found elsewhere (Clancy *et al.* 2006; Lewis 2004; Lewis *et al.* 2003; Raynor 2004) and this summary concentrates on those aspects which are important for the purposes of this chapter. The first phase of the study, involving seven 'pathfinder' projects, was intended to improve the availability and take-up of appropriate post-release services for short-term prisoners and to help them to make a better transition back into the community. In addition, the first phase was designed to test and compare a number of different approaches to providing resettlement services. Three voluntary sector projects were to concentrate on 'welfare needs' while four probation-led projects would concentrate more on addressing offending behaviour. Although other differences between projects emerged in the course of the research, the main intended difference in approach remained and showed itself in a number of ways: for example, Offender Assessment System (OASys) assessments in the probation-led projects for male prisoners were more likely than in the voluntary sector projects to identify 'thinking' problems. The probation-led projects also attempted a considerable amount of work with individuals on problems of thinking and attitudes, and by the end of the study all four probation-led projects were using a form of group programme to address these issues.

In the three projects for male prisoners this was a cognitive-motivational programme, 'FOR – A Change', designed specifically for pre-release use with short-term prisoners (Fabiano and Porporino 2002). This programme was rather different in aims and content from the majority of accredited offending behaviour programmes. Designed for delivery in the weeks preceding release, FOR consisted of twelve group sessions and one individual session. The group sessions concentrated on developing motivation and setting goals, and included a 'marketplace' session attended by representatives of agencies likely to be of use to prisoners on the outside, in accordance with the long-

34

standing observation that the appointments most likely to be kept on release are those arranged before release (see, for example, Maguire *et al.* 2000). The rationale of the whole programme was closely based on established principles of motivational interviewing (Miller and Rollnick 1991, 2002) and was designed to be followed up through continuing contact with resettlement workers after release. The 'motivational' approach can be summed up as attempting to 'develop discrepancy', in other words promoting awareness of gaps between what prisoners want or aspire to be and their current situations or behaviour. The assumption is that prisoners will face obstacles on release, and will need motivation, resourcefulness and determination to overcome them even with the assistance of available support and services: motivated prisoners are likely to make more and better use of whatever help is available.

In analysis of the results of the seven first-phase pathfinders, it was difficult to distinguish between the results of the programme itself and of other features of the services provided in the probation-led projects, and some offenders would have been exposed to both. However, it was possible to compare some outcomes of probation-led projects with voluntary organisation-led projects, and here the results were fairly clear (see Lewis *et al.* 2003). Probation-led projects achieved significantly higher levels of continuity of contact with offenders after release, and in most cases also achieved significantly higher levels of positive change in attitudes and beliefs and in self-reported life problems as measured by repeat administration of the CRIME-PICS II questionnaire (Frude *et al.* 1994). Although the numbers (1,081 prisoners divided among the seven projects and 2,450 comparison cases) were rather small for a comparative reconviction study, later analysis showed that when other factors were controlled for, participants in two of the probation-led projects had significantly lower reconviction rates than those in the other projects. In addition, continuity of contact with project workers (especially volunteer mentors) 'through the gate' was significantly associated with lower reconviction rates (Clancy *et al.* 2006). Obviously there are likely to be selection effects involved here, since those who choose to remain in contact may be those who are already more likely to avoid reoffending, but the different rates of continuity achieved with rather similar offender populations suggest that some projects were indeed motivating offenders rather more effectively than others. The importance of continuity lies not simply in the fact that offenders are more likely to keep appointments with and take advice from somebody they know and in whom they have some confidence:

35

the challenging of discrepancy and the maintenance of motivation are also easier in the context of a relationship. Put at its simplest, we mostly find it easier to break a promise to a stranger than to let down someone we know. Some projects achieved useful levels of continuity by using professional staff; others relied on volunteer mentors, who may have more time to offer and sometimes also a more unconditional commitment to helping.

Another discussion of this study (Raynor 2004) has explored the differences between these resettlement projects in terms of underlying assumptions about offending and desistance, which constitute the 'implicit criminologies' of resettlement work. In that paper a distinction is drawn between 'opportunity deficit' models, which regard offenders as victims of circumstances who offend because of lack of access to resources, and 'offender responsibility' models (perhaps better described as 'offenders' choice' models) which highlight the role of offenders' own decisions about how to respond to the circumstances in which they find themselves. Approaches based on 'opportunity deficit' tend to concentrate on welfare needs and on facilitating access to services, on the assumption that this will lead to desistance; approaches which emphasise offenders' own choices and their response to circumstances will also pay attention to thinking and motivation. (This does not mean that offenders are somehow held responsible for circumstances and deficits which are completely beyond their control, but simply that they often also need help in developing the motivation and resourcefulness which will give them a better chance to manage their lives without offending.) In the resettlement pathfinders, the projects led by voluntary organisations appeared more likely to operate on 'opportunity deficit' assumptions, and the greater success of the probation-led projects appeared to be due, in part, to their greater focus on thinking and motivation.

Resettlement and the process of desistance

These findings are also consistent with recent research on desistance from crime which has been concerned with the roles of structure and agency in the desistance process (see, for example, Farrall and Calverley 2005; Maguire and Raynor 2006). Opportunity deficits can be considered as part of social structure, and offenders' choices as an aspect of personal agency. Research on desistance shows that agency is as important as structure: for example, Zamble and Quinsey (1997: 146–7) concluded from their large study of released male prisoners

36

in Ontario that 'factors in the social environment seem influential determinants of initial delinquency for a substantial proportion of offenders ... but habitual offending is better predicted by looking at an individual's acquired ways of reacting to common situations'. For many ex-prisoners, the latter include negative or pessimistic reactions to practical problems, which lead them to give up on attempts to avoid reoffending. Maruna's interview-based study of offenders in Liverpool added the insight that people may react differently depending upon their personal understandings or accounts of their situations and behaviour – what he calls different kinds of 'narrative', some of which support continued offending and some of which support desistance. A key element of desistance narratives was a belief that the offender had begun to take control of his or her own life: 'Whereas active offenders ... seemed to have little vision of what the future might hold, desisting interviewees had a plan and were optimistic that they could make it work' (Maruna 2000: 147). These ideas are also reminiscent of much earlier writing about resettlement, for example: 'The central object of after-care is to provide such guidance and moral support as will help the ex-prisoner to cope with his personal and peculiar difficulties, and to withstand the spirit of apathy and defeatism in which many are liable to drift back to crime' (Home Office 1953: 16).

Other findings of recent desistance research also have implications for resettlement: these are explored in more detail elsewhere (Maguire and Raynor 2006) and a summary must suffice here. One particularly important insight is that desistance is a process, not an event, and reversals and lapses are common: Burnett (2004) refers to a 'zigzag' rather than a linear process, and Maruna and Farrall (2004) refer to one involving complex progression from 'primary' to 'secondary' desistance. ('Primary' desistance is the achievement of an offence-free period; 'secondary' desistance is the adoption or consolidation of a non-offending identity and self-concept.) Different individuals may make progress at different times for different reasons, and motivation cannot be taken for granted but needs to be generated and sustained. As people change they also need new skills and capacities appropriate to their new lives, and opportunities to use them. Another way of putting this is that they need to acquire both 'human capital' (skills, personal resources, motivation) and 'social capital' (links, connections and relationships with other people, formal and informal social networks and organisations) (McNeill 2006). Both capacities and opportunities for change are needed. Also relevant here is the distinction between 'bonding' and 'bridging' social capital

37

(Putnam 2000): 'bonding' social capital links you to existing networks of relationships and resources, and tends to reinforce and stabilise current identities; 'bridging' social capital extends your contacts and opportunities and facilitates social mobility. Bonding social capital is good for 'getting by' and is described as 'a kind of sociological superglue', while bridging social capital is good for 'getting ahead' and is 'a sociological WD-40' (Putnam 2000: 23). One promotes security and stability while the other promotes change. This also suggests one possible resolution of the question raised at the beginning of this chapter about whether resettlement aims to restore ex-prisoners to the social situations which existed prior to sentence or to create new social bonds, attachments and opportunities. The answer might be that resettlement should aim to help in developing both bonding and bridging social capital as well as human capital.

All of these insights into the process of desistance have implications for 'offender management' practice, and McNeill (2006) has spelled out a number of them in his proposal for a 'desistance paradigm' for probation practice. In resettlement work, they point to a need for early individualised preparation for release; access to resources and advocacy; awareness of the importance of motivation and cognition; continuity of personal contact; empathetic support in the face of setbacks; help in acquiring relevant skills; a positive and optimistic approach; a genuine collaboration between resettlement worker and ex-prisoner, and a flexible and realistic approach to temporary lapses which does not equate them with long-term failure. It remains to be seen how far the National Offender Management Model can deliver this type of service: the impact of new structures and contestability is difficult to predict (Raynor and Maguire 2005) and the continuing preoccupation with rigid and inflexible enforcement simply recycles large numbers of ex-prisoners back into prison (Solomon 2005).

Regional plans for the reduction of reoffending are based on the 'Seven pathways' to desistance originally set out in the influential Social Exclusion Unit report on reoffending by ex-prisoners (Social Exclusion Unit 2002) and discussed in detail in the preceding chapter. The 'Pathways' are: accommodation; education, training and employment; mental and physical health; drugs and alcohol; finance, benefits and debt; children and families of offenders; and attitudes, thinking and behaviour. These pathways make the crucial point that reoffending is not just a criminal justice problem and its reduction requires collaboration between many different services and different parts of Government. The findings reviewed in this chapter also

38

suggest that for many offenders, the seventh pathway ('attitudes, thinking and behaviour') is not just another item on a list of needs, but will play a critical role in determining how effectively they use resources designed to address any of the other six.

Conclusion: resettlement as rehabilitation

It will be clear from the foregoing discussion that successful resettlement has much in common with other forms of supervision intended to rehabilitate offenders. It belongs much more plausibly in the territory of rehabilitation than in the territory of punishment: at best, it helps offenders to help themselves to stop offending. It does not look like the final part of a seamless episode of punishment: on the contrary, pursuing it in a punitive style with trigger-happy enforcement is likely to undermine any rehabilitative effect. (This is not to argue that restrictive licence conditions do not have an important part to play, particularly in relation to public protection from dangerous offenders; however, an approach which is simply or primarily restrictive is perhaps better described as risk management than resettlement. Resettlement can and often does *include* monitoring of compliance, but monitoring alone is not the same as providing a resettlement service.) As with other forms of rehabilitation, the question then arises as to why the state should provide it. Why not leave released prisoners to their own devices? There is not space in this chapter to discuss this issue in any detail, but a number of recent commentators (Carlen 1994; Cullen and Gilbert 1982; Raynor and Robinson 2005; Rotman 1990) have argued that the most satisfactory answer is that the state is obliged, as part of a social contract with its citizens, to ensure that its expectation that we should obey the laws is matched by a duty to ensure realistic opportunities to maintain a crime-free life. This view, known as 'state-obligated' rehabilitation, resembles the social contract which underlies general welfare provision: the legitimacy of the state depends in part on guaranteeing the basic conditions of life for its citizens. To expect citizens to obey the law, and to punish them for not doing so, is fair and justified only in so far as reasonable provision is made to ensure that compliance is realistically possible. Resettlement services to reduce reoffending are part of this provision, and while they may be prepared for and begun during the prison sentence, they are not part of the punitive content of the sentence.

There is again little in these ideas which is completely new. For

39

example, reference has already been made to Winston Churchill's personal interest in aftercare when he was Home Secretary in a Liberal government. His much quoted speech of 20 July 1910, in which he famously argued that 'the mood and temper of the public in regard to the treatment of crime and criminals is one of the most unfailing tests of the civilisation of any country' (Churchill 1910), also pointed to a state-obligated theory of aftercare:

> We cannot impose these serious penalties upon individuals unless we make a great effort and a new effort to rehabilitate men who have been in prison, and secure their having a chance to resume their places in the ranks of honourable industry.

He also spoke of:

> A calm and dispassionate recognition of the rights of the accused against the State, and even of convicted criminals against the State, a constant heart searching by all charged with the duty of punishment, a desire and eagerness to rehabilitate in the world of industry all those who have paid their dues in the hard coinage of punishment, tireless efforts towards the discovery of curative and regenerative processes, and an unfaltering faith that there is a treasure, if you can only find it, in the heart of every man.

How different from that later Home Secretary who was so anxious to avoid using language that might give an inappropriate impression of caring.

References

Booth, W. (1890) *In Darkest England and The Way Out*. London: International Headquarters of the Salvation Army.

Burnett, R. (2004) 'To reoffend or not to reoffend? The ambivalence of convicted property offenders', in S. Maruna and R. Immarigeon (eds), *After Crime and Punishment: Pathways to Offender Reintegration*. Cullompton: Willan, pp. 152–80.

Carlen, P. (1994) 'Crime, inequality and sentencing', in A. Duff and D. Garland (eds), *A Reader on Punishment*. Oxford: Oxford University Press, pp. 306–32.

Churchill, W. (1910) Speech to the House of Commons, 20 July. Reprinted in *Vista*, 10 (3): 155–61.

40

Clancy, A., Hudson, K., Maguire, M., Peake, R., Raynor, P., Vanstone, M. and Kynch J. (2006) *Getting Out and Staying Out: Results of the Prisoner Resettlement Pathfinders*. Bristol: Policy Press.

Cullen, F.T. and Gilbert, K.E. (1982) *Reaffirming Rehabilitation*. Cincinnati, OH: Anderson Publishing.

Fabiano, E. and Porporino, F. (2002) *Focus on Resettlement – A Change*. Canada: T3 Associates.

Farrall, S. (2004) 'Social capital and offender re-integration: making probation desistance focused', in S. Maruna and R. Immarigeon (eds), *After Crime and Punishment: Pathways to Offender Reintegration*. Cullompton: Willan, pp. 57–84.

Farrall, S. and Calverley, A. (2005) *Understanding Desistance from Crime: Theoretical Directions in Resettlement and Rehabilitation*. Milton Keynes: Open University Press.

Frude, N., Honess, T. and Maguire, M. (1994) *CRIME-PICS II Manual*. Cardiff: Michael & Associates.

Haines, K. (1990) *After-Care Services for Released Prisoners*. Cambridge: Institute of Criminology.

Home Office (1953) *Report of the Committee on Discharged Prisoners' Aid Societies*, Cmnd. 8879. London: HMSO.

Home Office (1963) *The Organisation of After-Care. Report of the Advisory Council on the Treatment of Offenders*. London: HMSO.

Home Office (1984) *Probation Service in England and Wales: Statement of National Objectives and Priorities*. London: Home Office.

Home Office (1988) *Punishment, Custody and the Community*, Cmnd 424. London: HMSO.

Home Office (1990a) *Crime, Justice and Protecting the Public*, Cmnd 965. London: HMSO.

Home Office (1990b) *Supervision and Punishment in the Community*, Cmnd 966. London: HMSO.

Home Office (1992) *National Standards for the Supervision of Offenders in the Community*. London: Home Office.

Home Office (1998) *Joining Forces to Protect the Public: Prisons–Probation*. London: Home Office.

Home Office (2003) *Managing Offenders, Reducing Crime – A New Approach: Correctional Services Review by Patrick Carter*. London: Prime Minister's Strategy Unit.

Lewis, S. (2004) 'What works in the resettlement of short-term prisoners?', *Vista*, 8 (3): 163–70.

Lewis, S., Vennard, J., Maguire, M., Raynor, P., Vanstone, M., Raybould, S. and Rix, A. (2003) *The Resettlement of Short-term Prisoners: An Evaluation of Seven Pathfinders*, RDS Occasional Paper 83. London: Home Office.

McNeill, F. (2006) 'Towards a desistance paradigm for offender management', *Criminology and Criminal Justice*, 6 (1): 39–62.

41

Maguire, M. and Raynor, P. (1997) 'The revival of throughcare: rhetoric and reality in automatic conditional release', *British Journal of Criminology*, 37 (1): 1–14.

Maguire, M. and Raynor, P. (2006) 'How the resettlement of prisoners promotes desistance from crime: or does it?', *Criminology and Criminal Justice*, 6 (1): 19–38.

Maguire, M., Perroud, B. and Raynor, P. (1996) *Automatic Conditional Release: The First Two Years*, Research Study No. 156. London: Home Office.

Maguire, M., Raynor, P., Vanstone, M. and Kynch, J. (2000) 'Voluntary after-care and the Probation Service: a case of diminishing responsibility', *Howard Journal of Criminal Justice*, 39 (3): 234–48.

Maruna, S. (2000) *Making Good*. Washington, DC: American Psychological Association.

Maruna, S. and Farrall, S. (2004) 'Desistance from crime: a theoretical reformulation', *Kölner Zeitschrift für Soziologie und Sozialpsychologie*, 43: 171–94.

Miller, W.R. and Rollnick, S. (1991) *Motivational Interviewing. Preparing People to Change Addictive Behaviours*. New York: Guildford Press.

Miller, W.R. and Rollnick, S. (2002) *Motivational Interviewing. Preparing People for Change*, 2nd edn. New York: Guildford Press.

National Association of Discharged Prisoners' Aid Societies (NADPAS) (1956) *Handbook of the National Association of Discharged Prisoners' Aid Societies*. London: NADPAS.

Putnam, R. (2000) *Bowling Alone: The Collapse and Revival of American Community*. New York: Simon & Schuster.

Raynor, P. (2004) 'Opportunity, motivation and change: some findings from research on resettlement', in R. Burnett and C. Roberts (eds), *What Works in Probation and Youth Justice*. Cullompton: Willan, pp. 217–33.

Raynor, P. and Maguire, M. (2005) 'End-to-end or end in tears? Prospects for the effectiveness of the National Offender Management Model', in M. Hough, R. Allen and U. Padel (eds), *Reshaping Probation and Prisons: The New Offender Management Framework*. Bristol: Policy Press, pp. 21–34.

Raynor, P. and Robinson, G. (2005) *Rehabilitation, Crime and Justice*. Basingstoke: Palgrave.

Rotman, E. (1990) *Beyond Punishment: A New View of the Rehabilitation of Offenders*. Westport, CT: Greenwood Press.

Social Exclusion Unit (2002) *Reducing Re-offending by Ex-Prisoners*. London: Office of the Deputy Prime Minister.

Solomon, E. (2005) 'Returning to punishment: prison recalls', *Criminal Justice Matters*, 60: 24–5.

Zamble, E. and Quinsey, V. (1997) *The Criminal Recidivism Process*. Cambridge: Cambridge University Press.

42

Chapter 34

Prisons and desistance

Fergus McNeill and Marguerite Schinkel

Introduction

Since the 'birth of the prison' (Foucault 1975), penal policymakers, administrators and practitioners have been preoccupied with the potential of the prison as an architecture and a technology for producing change in prisoners. Views about how best to design penal institutions, regimes and practices have certainly changed a great deal over the years and continue to vary in different jurisdictions; examples of different approaches include pursuing reform or rehabilitation through religious instruction and practice, or political re-education, or psychological interventions, or through the discipline and 'dignity' of labour. At other times and places, optimism about the reformative potential of imprisonment has withered or waned to the extent that even advocates of imprisonment aimed merely for 'humane containment'.

Although the development of criminology, and in particular the evolution of theory and research about rehabilitation, has been an important factor in constructing and reconstructing penal regimes (see Rotman 1990), research about how and why people come to stop offending (and stay stopped) has rarely been used either to reimagine or to critique imprisonment, despite the fact that 'desistance' research also has a relatively long history. That said, what we might term the popularization of the concept of desistance, and its emergence into criminal justice discourses and practices, is a very recent phenomenon. It is, in fact, a 21st-century phenomenon. A superficial reading of these developments would probably point to the significance of an increasing body of literature (and other materials) in which several authors have made conspicuous and consistent efforts to interpret and apply desistance theory and research for and with criminal justice policymakers and practitioners – and with those who have lived experience of punishment and rehabilitation, both in prisons and in the community. A more critical perspective might want to dig a little deeper – looking at the ways in which desistance research has been used both to resist and to support penal reform efforts of diverse and even contradictory sorts, ranging from the marketization of probation (in England and Wales), to the promotion of penal reductionism, to the reframing and/or displacement of punitive and risk discourses and practices, to the recognition and prioritization of 'user voice' in criminal justice.

Although this chapter cannot aim to provide a comprehensive and critical account of relationships between prisons and desistance, we hope that it can serve to enliven such discussion. To that end, the structure of this chapter is as follows. After a very brief account of some of the core themes in desistance research, we turn first to arguments about the implications of this evidence for penal *policy* in general, before going on to examine its implications for penal *practice*. We then move to examine more specifically the complex relationships between imprisonment and desistance, drawing primarily on the doctoral research of one of the authors (Schinkel). We go on to examine briefly two recent attempts to 'apply' desistance theory and research in redesigning the prison systems in Northern Ireland and in Scotland. In the concluding section, we consider some of the challenges and contradictions that remain for desistance research and for prison reform.

Desistance from crime

Defining desistance is far from straightforward, but most discussions begin with the idea of the cessation of offending behaviour. However, since it is impossible to know the moment at which any behaviour ceases permanently, scholars have increasingly come to conceptualize and to study desistance as a process (see, for example, Bottoms et al. 2004; Maruna 2001; Farrall 2002; Laub and Sampson 2003). More specifically, we can think of desistance as a process of human development in social context; one that involves moving *away* from offending and *into* compliance with law and social norms. Maruna and Farrall (2004) draw an important distinction between *primary* and *secondary* desistance; the former relates merely to behaviour, the latter implies a related shift in identity. They posit that shifts in identity and self-concept matter in securing longer-term, sustained changes in behaviour as opposed to mere lulls in offending. Though the importance of this distinction has been debated by some (e.g. Bottoms et al. 2004), secondary desistance and with it substantive or committed compliance to the law (see Robinson and McNeill 2008) is likely to be important for people who have been heavily involved in offending and/or heavily criminalized. 'Spoiled identities' need to be shed if change is to be secured.

We suspect it may also make sense to develop the concept of *tertiary* desistance – referring not just to shifts in behaviour or identity but to shifts in one's sense of belonging to a (moral) community. Our argument, based on developing research evidence (for example, Laub and Sampson 2003; Bottoms and Shapland 2011; Weaver 2013), is that since identity is socially constructed and negotiated, securing long-term change depends not just on how one sees oneself but also on how one is seen by others, and on how one sees one's place in society. Putting it more simply, desistance is a social and political process as much as a personal one.

In fact, the links between behaviour, identity and belonging are implicit in the main explanatory theories of desistance. These are commonly divided into ontogenic theories which stress the importance of age and maturation; sociogenic theories which stress the importance of social bond and ties; and narrative theories which stress the importance of subjective changes in identity (Maruna 2001). Recently, in an important review of desistance research, Bottoms (2014) has suggested a fourth set of explanatory factors that are situational in character (see also Farrall et al. 2014). Drawing on his expertise in socio-spatial criminology, as well as on desistance research, Bottoms points out that various aspects of our social environments and of our situated 'routine activities' also provide important influences on our behaviour, for better or worse. While our environments and activities are closely connected to our social bonds or ties (for example, bonds within intimate relationships and to families, work and faith communities), they deserve attention in their own right.

Given that desistance research itself is diverse and varied, and that there is so much debate within the field (for example, about the relative contribution of structural and subjective factors to the process), it makes little sense to talk about critical perspectives on desistance research per se. That said, some critical criminologists (e.g. Baldry 2010) have been wary both about whether desistance research might not represent another responsibilizing discourse (and therefore a discursive resource for associated oppressive practices) and about the over-generalization of theories of desistance across diverse populations. This second observation has been recognized and has begun to be addressed seriously by desistance researchers themselves (e.g. Calverley 2012; Farrall et al. 2014; Glynn 2014; Sharpe 2012; Weaver and McNeill 2010). The issue of responsibilization is more complex. While it is true that some desistance theorists have offered rational choice explanations of the process, most are highly critical of such perspectives. Even those desistance researchers who have come to stress the role of personal agency in desistance processes (e.g. Giordano et al. 2002; Maruna 2001; Farrall and Calverley 2006) tend to stress an interactionist perspective in which social structural factors continue to be seen as important.

Desistance and penal policy and practice

As well as seeking to advance explanations for or understandings of desistance, many criminologists have recently engaged with practitioners, 'ex-offenders' and others in the shared task of exploring the implications of this research for policy and practice, and in particular for how we approach the challenges of punishment and rehabilitation (McNeill 2003, 2006, 2009, 2012a; McNeill and Weaver 2007, 2010). Desistance research has particular policy salience to the extent that policy is concerned with reducing reoffending and its associated economic, human and social costs. Rather than simply observing or understanding desistance, the question becomes: 'Can we enable desistance through criminal sanctions, or do they tend to frustrate it?' In a series of publications (e.g. McNeill and Weaver 2010), recommendations for penal policies and practices have tended to centre on the following themes:

- For people who have been involved in persistent offending – and who have been persistently criminalized and penalized – desistance is a complex and difficult process, so we need to be realistic about these difficulties, and to expect and manage lapses and relapses.
- Since the process is different for different people (even if there are many common threads), interventions need to be properly individualized and tailored to the circumstances of the individual and to their subjective apprehension of resources and opportunities for positive change.
- Since desistance is relational, interventions need to work on, with and through professional and social relationships (and not just through individualized programmes). Developing social capital (meaning networks of reciprocal relationships) is crucial to supporting desistance.
- Since desistance often involves developing hope for the future, interventions need to work to nurture hope and motivation. Since hope seems to be connected to developing a sense of 'agency' (meaning the capacity to govern one's life), interventions

378

should seek to identify and mobilize personal strengths and self-determination, encouraging the acquisition of a sense of agency.

- The language of policy and practice matters; to the extent that it entrenches criminalized identities, it may frustrate desistance. We need to mind our language, as well as ensuring that we recognize and celebrate progress, so as to reinforce the development or redevelopment of positive identities.

In the recent chapter already referred to above, Bottoms (2014) suggests that we need to add to this list interventions that attend to the routine activities and social environments of offenders. In other words, we need to provide practical supports and activities that enable and sustain change.

More broadly, some desistance researchers have begun to argue that over the last 20 years our approaches to punishment and rehabilitation have become too narrowly focused on supporting personal change, not as a result of the influence of desistance research (which the trend predates), but rather because of the conjunction of narrow conceptions of evidence-based practice and the managerialization of criminal justice since the late 1980s. One of us has argued in previous papers (McNeill 2012a, 2014) that this has led to neglect of three other forms of rehabilitation – moral, social and judicial. The central argument is that no amount of personal change can secure desistance if change is not recognized and supported by the community ('social rehabilitation'), by the law and by the state ('judicial rehabilitation'). Without these forms of informal and formal recognition, legitimate opportunities (for example, for participation in the labour market or in social life) will not become available and return to offending may be made more likely. In some cases, the failure in state punishment to attend directly to the need for moral rehabilitation (the settling of debts between the offender, victim and community) may undermine social rehabilitation. Restorative justice may have something to offer here. More generally, my position is that these four forms of rehabilitation are often interdependent, and that failing to attend to all four reduces the likelihood of successful desistance.

More recently still, one of us has begun to argue that penal policy and practice needs to reconsider how it frames its goals (McNeill n.d., forthcoming). Studying and supporting desistance eventually forces us to address the complex question not of what people desist *from*, but what they desist *to*. In other words, if desistance is a process or a journey, we are eventually compelled to seek to understand and articulate its destination. The concepts of citizenship, integration and solidarity may have much to offer in addressing this question; perhaps a positively framed set of goals for criminal sanctions operationalizing these concepts (and a positive set of metrics for judging their successes) may help us move beyond an increasingly fruitless preoccupation with risk and reoffending.

'Offender management' and desistance

Initial discussions in the UK of whether and how criminal sanctions might support desistance from crime were focused on probation practice (Rex 1999; Farrall 2002; McNeill 2003, 2006). In the dissemination of these studies, most probation staff in England and Wales (and their colleagues in similar roles in other jurisdictions) were pleased to discover a body of evidence that seemed to affirm: (i) that the social context of offending and desistance matters profoundly; (ii) that offending behaviour programmes may be necessary but are not a sufficient means of supporting desistance; and (iii) that the (moral) character and quality of the relationships between supervisors and supervised are critical in supporting change.

These reactions are entirely understandable; vindication of these forms of 'practice wisdom' had been a long time coming for practitioners, many of whom felt that their professionalism had been assailed since the mid-1990s both by punitive penal policies and by a hollowed out and managerialized bastardization of 'what works' research (McNeill 2012b). Indeed, some of the associated literature has consciously and conspicuously deployed evidence from desistance studies as a resource for resisting the twin forces of punitiveness and managerialization (see, for example, McNeill 2006).

It is perhaps not surprising, then, that Probation Trusts in England and Wales have been enthusiastic readers and users of desistance research. Again, there are contextual factors at play here. The development of the National Offender Management Service's 'Offender Engagement Programme' drew on both desistance and 'what works' research to refocus development efforts on enhancing the effectiveness of one-to-one super-vision – a neglected practice (Burnett and McNeill 2005) which, after all, reaches far more people than offending behaviour programmes. The relevant national standards were also revised and significantly relaxed, so as to allow practitioners much more dis-cretion, and this seemed to generate a thirst both for new knowledge (to guide discre-tion) and for new tools and approaches. For example, the recent special edition of *Scottish Justice Matters* on desistance[1] includes a short article on one such development (see Goodwin et al. 2013). That said, the ongoing marketization and privatization of English probation now seems likely to undermine recent progress in that jurisdiction (on which see the special edition of the *British Journal of Community Justice*[2]).

The special issue of *Scottish Justice Matters* also contains a paper (McNeill et al. 2013) that summarizes the results of the ESRC-funded 'Desistance Knowledge Exchange' project.[3] That project was a UK-wide attempt to generate a dialogue between people with convictions, service users, their families and supporters, practitioners, policymakers and academics about how best to reform supervision in order to better support desis-tance. Space prohibits a full discussion of the process and its outcomes here, but the ten 'provocative propositions' that emerged were radical and wide-ranging, and extended far beyond the initial focus on practice models for supervision:

1 'There is a need for meaningful service user involvement in the design, delivery, assessment, and improvement of policies and provision across the criminal justice system; and for clear career routes for former service users that recognise and value the skills that people with convictions possess ...

2 There is a dire need to reduce the prison population, first and foremost in order to free up resources to invest in efforts more likely to support desistance ...

3 A rethink of criminal justice social work/probation is necessary to make it more "holistic" and "humanised", more focused on the service user's strengths and needs, and more flexible and open to creative work ...

4 In the future, CJSW/probation offices and officers need to become better connected with local communities with greater community involvement in all of their work ...

5 A wider circle of society should be encouraged to take responsibility for helping people stop offending ...

6   Interventions ought to focus less on risk and more readily on the positives, and what people have achieved *and can achieve* in the future ...

7   Community supervision needs to work to challenge inequality and promote fairness, equalising life chances and contributing to social justice ...

8   Redraft the Rehabilitation of Offenders Act 1974 to encourage and recognise rehabilitation much earlier, and not stand in the way of desistance in the name of "rehabilitation" ...

9   The public needs more accurate information about the lives of those in the criminal justice system and in particular on the process of leaving crime behind ...

10 Finally – but perhaps foremost in the tenor of the discussions – the criminal justice system needs to become more acquainted with hope and less transfixed with risk, pessimism and failure ...'

(McNeill et al. 2013: 4–5)

Clearly some of these proposals have some bearing on how and when we use imprisonment as a sanction and about how we organize and run prisons. We turn next to these questions.

Imprisonment and desistance

Most desistance researchers argue that prisons reflect an inherently problematic context in which to seek to support desistance. Reflecting on the four main theoretical perspectives discussed above, it is not difficult to argue, for example: (i) that the experience of imprisonment often deprives people of responsibility and may delay maturation (Liebling and Maruna 2004); (ii) that imprisonment often damages positive social ties and weakens bonds between prisoners and society; (iii) that imprisonment tends to cement spoiled identities rather than nurturing positive ones; and (iv) that the routine activities of life in prison, even if rendered 'purposeful', are detached from the desistance-supporting routines that need to be established in the community. Indeed, there is some evidence that compared with community sanctions, imprisonment in general may be somewhat criminogenic (Joliffe and Hedderman 2012). For these reasons, desistance researchers and penal reform groups have found common cause in arguing for reduced reliance on custody as a sanction (e.g. McNeill and Weaver 2007; Hough et al. 2012).

Nonetheless, as we noted at the outset, while imprisonment may have certain common features that militate against supporting desistance, ever since the inception of the penitentiary, people involved in designing and implementing prison regimes have (admittedly to varying degrees in different times and places) been attracted to the idea that institutions may, under certain circumstances, exercise some 'reformative' effect. Just as probation workers have been attracted by desistance research's counter-narrative to a narrow emphasis on psychological programmes, so contemporary prison managers and staff may have been attracted by a body of evidence that seems capable of informing how prison regimes (in the widest sense) might be more constructively reconfigured. Whereas the impact of 'what works' research (on risk assessment processes and offending behaviour programmes) has tended to be limited to the work of those in 'offender management units' (or their equivalents), the broader purview of desistance research lends it relevance across all roles and tasks. Moreover, where prisons (like probation trusts) have come to be judged increasingly on their contribution to reducing reoffending rates, it is obviously in the interests of prison managers to seek to improve processes of rehabilitation and reintegration.

Despite the problems noted at the outset of this section, some desistance studies seem to provide good news for these would-be reformers (of prisons and prisoners), suggesting that imprisonment sometimes does play a positive role in the narratives of people who have desisted. For example, Giordano et al. (2002) reported that some of their interviewees found in imprisonment the 'hook for change' that they needed to change their life around. Similarly, in Aresti et al.'s (2010) research 'defining moments' happened within the prison, where reflecting on the length of time they had to serve, and on the impact on their sense of self of the prison environment, prisoners re-evaluated their lives and their plans for the future. Indeed, the impact of having time to think in prison on the motivation to desist has figured in many descriptions of the lived experience of imprisonment (see for example, Ashkar and Kenny 2008; Barry 2006; Comfort 2008; Farrall and Calverley 2006). However, drawing on research in the USA, Comfort (2008) has suggested that ex-prisoners may be casting their prison sentence in a positive light in order to rescue some meaning from the experience, rather than having found the experience truly rehabilitative. Indeed, in the absence of any meaningful rehabilitative input, she has called this type of portrayal of imprisonment '"as if" rehabilitation'.

On the other hand, Sampson and Laub's (2005) research suggests that imprisonment might have some value in bringing about desistance by 'knifing off' prisoners from their usual lives. While this has many deleterious consequences, such as severing family ties, the loss of housing and jobs and the risk of institutionalization, it also means that, temporarily, the 'habitual offender' is not offending and is cut off from their usual identities and opportunities on the outside, which may create the space to form new ambitions and hopes. Significantly in this context, Sampson and Laub (2005) included time spent in reform schools (alongside marriage, work, military service and moving to a new place) as one of their possible 'turning points' – when their changed *circumstances* meant people came to re-evaluate their behaviour.

In recent research examining the meaning of long-term imprisonment in Scotland,[4] one of the authors found that while 'knifing off' the outside world was reflected in the prisoners' accounts, it was only a specific group of prisoners who ascribed transformative power to their prison sentence when they were interviewed just before release (Schinkel 2014). For those who had not been imprisoned before (especially when their sentence was for a first offence), imprisonment was a temporary dip in an otherwise positive life story. They fully (and realistically) expected to return to their previous positive lives after their release. Those with more serious histories of offending, but with significant resources on the outside (such as savings, family support or their own accommodation) expected these resources would help them to turn their life around. They attributed their wish to desist to having matured and become more risk-averse. By contrast, the most disadvantaged group of prisoners, those who had spent most of their adult life (and often their teenage years) in institutions and prisons, were more or less resigned to further imprisonment, and therefore did not need to explain a change in their life course. However, those who wanted to desist, but had a significant criminal record and few resources, often positioned their most recent sentence as transformative.

The aspects of imprisonment this group of prisoners credited with their transformation varied. Some felt they had made the most of the various opportunities on offer (thereby in effect transforming themselves) or benefited from time to think. Others positioned themselves as much more passive in the transformation process, instead crediting the interventions of staff, or the impact of cognitive behavioural offending behaviour programmes. Not all of their accounts therefore could be seen as descriptions of 'as if' rehabilitation.[5] On the other hand, it was clear that they imbued their imprisonment with transformative power because they had no other way to explain their future desistance. With few resources, there was nothing else to stand between them and their histories of significant offending *but* their imprisonment.

Despite, or perhaps given, the obstacles they faced upon release (having no clear prospects of suitable and stable accommodation or employment and no significant support from others), their accounts resembled 'redemption narratives' (Maruna 2001) in some ways. In order to maintain the belief that they would be able to desist in less than promising circumstances, these men ascribed 'super-agency' to their future selves (like Maruna's 'desisters') – seeing their future selves as having the power to overcome even seemingly insurmountable obstacles. In contrast, other prisoners who faced similar obstacles told more half-hearted stories about their future desistance, saying that their sentence had changed them, but later contradicting themselves and outlining the reasons why they were likely to reoffend. This might mean that those who managed to maintain coherence were more committed to their transformation through imprisonment, and therefore more likely to desist.

Sadly, however, interviews with (other) men on licence after serving long-term sentences showed that these men were unlikely to achieve what we have called 'tertiary desistance', where people have desisted in the eyes of others and are re-accepted into the community. The majority of these men described living a bleak existence. They attributed this to their isolation, to feeling under surveillance and to withdrawing from social participation – this being the only way for them to avoid further offending (see Shapland and Bottoms 2011, on diachronic self-control). They also spoke of their inability to secure a new identity and routine. The men felt most keenly the lack of employment, which their criminal records and the economic downturn had made almost impossible to secure. Their inability to move forward towards the lives they wanted (of employment, their own house and a stable relationship) meant that many of the men on licence were stuck in a kind of half-life that looked like desistance (at least in the primary sense that they were not offending), but they did not feel their lives were meaningful or that they were socially integrated. Their inability to achieve 'early goals' (Aresti 2010) meant that they lost any sense of progression and their prison-based hopes had been displaced by uncertainty about how their story would work out. For these men 'tertiary' desistance was essential to secure their happy endings (and perhaps to maintain primary and secondary desistance), but it was proving exceptionally hard to secure.

These findings go some way towards identifying what is needed from prison regimes to facilitate desistance – at least for long-term prisoners. While those with resources or minimal histories of offending will likely be able to desist despite the negative consequences of imprisonment, other groups need more support not only to develop any hope of desistance, but also to have solid ground on which to base these hopes. Crucially, interventions in the prison need to be tailored to the individual but also to reach beyond the prison gates, having positive consequences for sustaining or renewing a life outside. Ideally, obstacles upon release, such as a lack of accommodation, employment and support, need to be tackled before release. These sorts of practical help might engender greater hope in those who are less committed to a future of desistance while also making desistance more achievable for those who desire it.

Implementing desistance research in prisons

The first significant practical attempt to map out the implications of desistance research for the organization of a whole prison system was that of the recent Prisons Review Team (PRT) in Northern Ireland. The PRT was established by Minister of Justice David Ford, and was chaired by Dame Anne Owers (former chief inspector of prisons in England and Wales); it reported in 2011 after a lengthy examination of the conditions, management and oversight of prisons in Northern Ireland. One of the authors (McNeill) was a member of the review team, which also included a former chief executive of the National Offender Management Service for England and Wales, a human rights lawyer and a retired senior police officer.

As well as being influenced by desistance research, the Owers Report (2011) drew on recent work on legitimacy and criminal justice (Crawford and Hucklesby 2012), and in particular on the work of the Prisons Research Centre at the University of Cambridge on moral performance in prisons (Liebling 2004, 2011). One of the key findings of the Cambridge team, from their analysis of the results of the measuring of the quality of prison life (MQPL) survey in numerous prisons, concerns a domain of the survey that deals with 'personal development'. Since this domain concerns 'help with the development of potential', it comes closest to measuring the extent to which prisoners surveyed consider the prisons they inhabit to be sites in which progress towards desistance is possible.

The MQPL results suggest that very few prisons score well on this domain. However, in these few prisons the surveys reveal statistically significant positive correlations between personal development and the moral quality of the prison regime as measured in several other domains (listed here in order of significance):

- Help and assistance ('support and encouragement for problems, including drugs, healthcare and progression');
- Humanity ('an environment characterised by kind regard and concern for the person');
- Staff professionalism ('staff confidence and competence in the use of authority');
- Bureaucratic legitimacy ('the transparency and responsivity of the prison/prison system and its moral recognition of the individual');
- Organization and consistency ('the clarity, predictability and reliability of the prison').

(Liebling 2011)

In other words, personal development (towards desistance) seems to be more possible in some prisons than others, and specifically it seems more possible in prisons where the regimes are characterized both by the availability of practical help, and by relationships and processes that are legitimate and consistent.

Set alongside the findings of desistance research discussed above, these MQPL findings were influential in framing the recommendations in the Owers Report (2011). Some of those recommendations are specific to the Northern Irish context and its peculiar post-conflict challenges, but many have wider relevance. Chapter one of the report discusses the purposes and values of prison systems, chapter two is entitled 'Desistance: the Wider Picture', and chapter three examines the potential characteristics of 'Prisons Supporting Change'. The link between these chapters is the argument that prisons need to be places that respect human rights not merely by preventing abuse, but also by providing opportunities for human development. That said, chapter two of the Owers Report (2011) recognizes the risks of seeking to construct prisons as positive places, noting that more productive investments in services and communities outside prisons are ultimately more likely to support crime reduction. However, the report argues that unless prisons support change, they cannot benefit society or prisoners and that supporting change requires partnership with organizations, services and families outside. The authors are careful to recognize that supporting desistance is not just about personal change; as we have noted above, it is a social process and one that requires social change too.

Chapter three goes on to elaborate the seven fundamental characteristics of 'Prisons Supporting Change', arguing that such prisons require:

- *A whole prison approach*: meaning that design of the whole system, the roles of all staff and the articulation of all processes should reflect the central commitment to promoting change.
- *Fair and reasonable treatment*: recognizing that, in the light of human rights standards and of research on both moral performance (Liebling 2004) and desistance from crime, a commitment to the proper treatment of prisoners (and staff) is both morally necessary and practically required if change is to be supported.
- *Strong and meaningful relationships between staff and prisoners*: reflecting the evidence both from research that the quality and character of relationships between staff and prisoners (and prisons and families and outside services) is critical to supporting change.
- *Effective staff development, appraisal and discipline systems*: meaning that these systems need to work to develop and sustain a staff culture that promotes and supports change.
- *Prisoner motivation and achievement*: requiring prisoner progression processes to reward change efforts and not mere 'compliance'.
- *Practical help to promote a crime-free life outside*: ensuring that the right range of services and supports are available to tackle obstacles to change.
- *Supporting the development of a non-criminal identity*: suggesting the need for constructive, creative and reparative opportunities, and for a culture that recognizes and celebrates achievement.

Though there had been some prior discussion of desistance research and about the Owers review with senior managers and governors in the Scottish Prison Service (SPS), the arrival of Colin McConnell as the new chief executive in May 2012 heralded the beginning of a major and still ongoing reform effort. Significantly, McConnell brought with him the experience of having led the Northern Irish service during the Owers review.

As its title suggests, the report of the SPS Organisational Review,[6] *Unlocking Potential, Transforming Lives* (SPS 2013), reflects and elaborates many of the themes of the Owers review and in many respects goes much further, engaging seriously not just with desistance research, but also with the 'assets-based approach' popularized in the public health field by Sir Harry Burns, former chief medical officer of Scotland.

The review report runs to some 250 pages, 47 of which mention desistance. Space and time preclude any attempt here at a critical review of the way that desistance research is used in the report. In any event, as with any report, the more interesting question is whether and to what extent its recommendations will be implemented in ways that really change social and penal institutions, cultures and practices. It is much too soon to make that judgement about the SPS. The change programme will take many years. However, perhaps the most striking aspects of the report are to be found in the way that the 'vision' and 'mission' of the service are reconceived. The vision is of 'Helping to build a safer Scotland – Unlocking Potential – Transforming Lives' (SPS 2013: 5). The mission is 'Providing services that help to transform the lives of people in our care so they can fulfill their potential and become responsible citizens' (SPS 2013: 5).

The vision statement is interesting in several respects; it seems modest in recognizing that SPS can *help* build a safer Scotland, but by implication cannot do so alone; it implies a belief in the value of prisoners and in their potential; and it sets a very aspirational goal (transforming lives). The mission focuses on what the SPS will do to fulfil that aspiration. Our central observation on this statement (and a similar statement in the Scottish government's Reducing Reoffending Programme 2) is that although the focus on citizenship (rather than offending) is welcome, the emphasis remains on enabling transformation of the *individual* citizen (i.e. to fulfil his or her *responsibilities*) and less on addressing social and structural barriers to enjoying citizenship *rights*. The imbalance is most powerfully illustrated in the Scottish government's stubborn refusal to allow prisoners to vote in the recent independence referendum; for us, this was a totemic exemplar of this frustratingly asymmetric use of discourses of citizenship. That said, both the new SPS vision statement and the section of the report that deals with partnership at least suggest an appreciation of the need to work with *communities* as well as *agencies* in supporting change. In some respects, it seems too much to expect an internal prison service review to seek to argue for wider socio-structural changes – but if prison managers and practitioners really want to support desistance then perhaps this is precisely what they must do.

Conclusions: desistance and prisons

One of us (McNeill) was fortunate to have the opportunity to share and discuss a draft version of this chapter (written prior to the contribution of the second author and without reference to her work) with a reading group in a Scottish prison. The group comprised mainly people serving long prison sentences, along with some education staff, prison staff and visiting criminologists. The discussion was revealing, not just in relation to desistance theory but also in relation to the prospects of constructive reform to prison regimes.

In the former connection, the reading group members stressed differences in prison experiences and life trajectories of people who have been involved in persistent offending (but who are typically serving short sentences) and people who have been involved in serious offending, perhaps on a one-off basis (but nonetheless serving long sentences). As Schinkel's (2014) study reveals, not everyone in the latter group has a spoiled identity and not everyone requires a narrative of transformation. That said, some of those in the group (particularly those who had a longer criminal record and long-term involvement with the care and justice systems) did recognize, from their own experiences, many aspects of the desistance process described above – and it is fair to say that all members of the group recognized the relevance of desistance research for most prisoners with significant offending histories.

Unsurprisingly, however, the main focus of the discussion was not so much on desistance research itself, as on its implications for reconstructing processes of rehabilitation in prisons. Partly, the discussion centred on the prospects for significant reform of the Scottish prisons system – in line with the aspirations of the organizational review discussed above. Members of the group had different views on this. Some recognized signs of change – even in the changing discourse of the service; others were more sceptical – pointing to what they considered regressive developments, for example around delayed progression to the open estate and less support for compassionate and other forms of home leave. Many members of the group expressed concerns about the effects of risk discourses and practices on their experiences of imprisonment and rehabilitation, expressing frustration at the double bind presented by regimes that permitted progression only when it was judged that risk had reduced, but offered limited opportunities to prisoners to undertake work to reduce risk (see also Crewe 2009).

A prison staff member in the group reflected honestly on the inherent contradictions between the (new and less familiar) pressures to trust and support prisoners to change, and the (old but enduring) pressures to maintain security. As he put it, it is hard to act as a supporter of change, expressing belief in the capacity of prisoners to progress, whilst at the same time carrying out a cell search or a mandatory drug test – both of which are routine practices that communicate *dis*trust. No one in the group was in any doubt about how far the service and the staff will have to travel in order to develop not just processes and practices but also occupational and organizational cultures that are capable of supporting change.

These contradictions neatly sum up the paradoxes implied by seeking to construe prisons as 'desistance-supporting' places. Prisons can and should aim to be *capacity-building* places; indeed, their ultimate contributions to public safety and ex-prisoner reintegration cannot be secured unless they can become such places (Owers Report 2011). Liebling's (2011) research suggests that, under certain conditions, prisons can support personal development but that it is both rare and difficult for them to do so. In a sense, this is unsurprising. Prisons are inherently *incapacitating* places. Whilst the sentence of imprisonment may be intended in part to communicate to someone that they need to reflect upon and then to develop themselves, the realities of imprisonment often mitigate against such a project. To be sure, imprisonment requires adaptation – but that adaptation is typically focused on surviving the experience, not on preparing for life *after* it. As Schinkel's (2014) research (and many previous prison sociologies) make clear, these two forms of adaptation – to punishment and to life after punishment – may push and pull in opposite directions. Perhaps it is only in prison regimes that minimize the need for adaptation to life inside, that adaptation for life after punishment becomes possible.

However, if we conceive of desistance as being about processes of human growth and development (within their social contexts), then there is an even more fundamental problem with imprisonment. Imprisonment is not an act of nurture; it is an act of violence – at least insofar as it is always and everywhere underwritten by the state's claim to an entitlement to use physical force in the process of punishment. In the dishonouring of those punished – and in the insistence on their submission to processes of classification – prisons are also places of 'symbolic violence' (Bourdieu and Wacquant 1992). Imprisonment defines, categorizes and dominates its subjects (or at least it seeks to do so). It is hard to see how the power dynamics in play in these processes can be easily rendered compatible with the implications of desistance research, for example around growth, hope, agency and self-determination. Again, it seems reasonable to suggest that it is only in those prisons where these forms of violence are minimized that change can be supported.

In this context, one of the criminologist members of the reading group pointed out that there is a fundamental problem with desistance research: it implicitly accepts that crime is the problem or the phenomenon to be reduced or managed. Even if by insisting on the links between behaviour change and wider processes of social integration, desistance research has been useful in confronting penality with its own failure to support the process it often claims to support, it colludes in framing the debate in terms of reducing reoffending – and it defines the 'desister' with reference to his or her prior offending (which is, of course, an act of symbolic violence in itself). Perhaps, therefore, the more fundamental challenge is that we need to reverse the polarity of the crime–punishment nexus and start with the question of how and why we might *punish* less, or at least punish less violently. If we did that, we suspect we might find that desisting from punishment is one of the best ways of supporting desistance from crime.

Notes

1 See: scottishjusticematters.com/the-journal/december-2013-desistance-issue/ (accessed 23 July 2014).
2 See: www.cjp.org.uk/bjcj/volume-11-issue-2-3/ (accessed 23 July 2014).
3 See: blogs.iriss.org.uk/discoveringdesistance/ (accessed 24 July 2014).
4 For this study, 27 narrative interviews about their perceptions of the legitimacy and purpose of their sentence were conducted with six men at the start of their sentence, 12 men at the end of their sentences, and nine men on licence after release.
5 However, all other prisoners saw the prison as failing in its aim to rehabilitate because individual input and attention were limited; cognitive behavioural courses were often described as a cynical exercise to reassure politicians and their electorate that rehabilitation was happening.
6 For the record, I should note that I served in an advisory capacity as a member of the Review's Project Steering Group.

Bibliography

Aresti, A. (2010) *'Doing Time after Time': A hermeneutic phenomenological understanding of reformed ex-prisoners' experiences of selfchange and identity negotiation*, PhD, Birkbeck: University of London.

Aresti, A., Eatough, V. and Brooks-Gordon, B. (2010) 'Doing time after time: an interpretative phenomenological analysis of reformed ex-prisoners' experiences of self-change, identity and career opportunities', *Psychology, Crime & Law* 16(3): 169–190.

Ashkar, P.J. and Kenny, D.T. (2008) 'Views from the inside: young offenders' subjective experiences of incarceration', *International Journal of Offender Therapy and Comparative Criminology* 52(5): 584–597.

Barry, M. (2006) 'Dispensing [with?] justice: young people's views of the criminal justice system', in K. Gorman, M. Gregory, M. Hayles and N. Parton (eds) *Constructive Work with Offenders*, London: Jessica Kingsley, 177–192.

Bottoms, A. (2014) 'Desistance from crime', in Z. Ashmore and R. Shuker (eds) *Forensic Practice in the Community*, London: Routledge.

Bottoms, A. and Shapland, J. (2011) 'Steps towards desistance among male young adult recidivists', in S. Farrall, M. Hough, S. Maruna and R. Sparks (eds) *Escape Routes: Contemporary Perspectives on Life after Punishment*, London: Routledge.

Bottoms, A., Shapland, J., Costello, A., Holmes, D. and Muir, G. (2004) 'Towards desistance: theoretical underpinnings for an empirical study', *The Howard Journal* 43(4): 368–389.

Bourdieu, P. and Wacquant, L. (1992) *An Invitation to Reflexive Sociology*, Chicago, IL: The University of Chicago Press.

Burnett, R. and McNeill, F. (2005) 'The place of the officer-offender relationship in assisting offenders to desist from crime', *Probation Journal* 52(3): 221–242.

Calverley, A. (2012) *Cultures of Desistance: Rehabilitation, reintegration and ethnic minorities*, International Series on Rehabilitation and Desistance, London: Routledge.

Comfort, M. (2008) 'The best seven years I could'a done: the reconstruction of imprisonment as rehabilitation', in P. Carlen (ed.) *Imaginary Penalties*, Cullompton: Willan, 252–274.

Crawford, A. and Hucklesby, A. (eds) (2012) *Legitimacy and Compliance in Criminal Justice*, London: Routledge.

Crewe, B. (2009) *The Prisoner Society: Power, adaptation and social life in an English prison*, Oxford: Oxford University Press.

Farrall, S. (2002) *Rethinking What Works with Offenders: Probation, social context and desistance from crime*, Cullompton: Willan.

Farrall, S. and Calverley, A. (2006) *Understanding Desistance from Crime*, Maidenhead: Open University Press.

Farrall, S., Hunter, B., Sharpe, G. and Calverley, A. (2014) *Criminal Careers in Transition: The social context of desistance from crime*, Clarendon Studies in Criminology, Oxford: Oxford University Press.

Foucault, M. (1975 [English trans. 1977]) *Discipline & Punish*, London: Allen Lane.

Giordano, P.C., Cernkovich, S.A. and Rudolph, J.L. (2002) 'Gender, crime, and desistance: toward a theory of cognitive transformation', *American Journal of Sociology* 107(4): 990–1064.

Glynn, M. (2014) *Black Men, Invisibility and Crime: Towards a critical race theory of desistance*, International Series on Rehabilitation and Desistance, London: Routledge.

Goodwin, R., Tuncer, J. and Nickeas, J. (2013) 'The Wirral Desistance Project: seeing beyond the risk agenda in probation practice', *Scottish Justice Matters* (December): 7–8.

Hough, M., Farrall, S. and McNeill, F. (2012) *Intelligent Justice: Balancing the effects of community sentences and custody*, London: Howard League for Penal Reform.

Joliffe, D. and Hedderman, C. (2012) 'Investigating the impact of custody on reoffending using propensity score matching', *Crime and Delinquency* (6 December), DOI: 0011128712466007.

Laub, J. and Sampson, R. (2003) *Shared Beginnings, Divergent Lives: Delinquent boys to age seventy*, Cambridge, MA: Harvard University Press.

Liebling, A. (2011) 'Is there a role for the prison in desistance? Personal development, human flourishing and the unequal pains of imprisonment', presentation at a European Union Project Strengthening Transnational Approaches to Reducing Re-offending (STARR) Conference on 'What Works in Reducing Re-offending', Sofia, Bulgaria, 8–10 June 2011.

Liebling, A. with Arnold, H. (2004) *Prisons and their Moral Performance: A study of values, quality and prison life*, Clarendon Studies in Criminology, Oxford: Oxford University Press.

Liebling, A. and Maruna, S. (eds) (2005) *The Effects of Imprisonment*, Cullompton: Willan.

McNeill, F. (2003) 'Desistance based practice', in W.-H. Chui and M. Nellis (eds) *Moving Probation Forward: Evidence, arguments and practice*, Harlow: Pearson Education, 146–162.

McNeill, F. (2006) 'A desistance paradigm for offender management', *Criminology and Criminal Justice* 6(1): 39–62.

McNeill, F. (2009) *Towards Effective Practice in Offender Supervision*, Glasgow: Scottish Centre for Crime and Justice Research, www.sccjr.ac.uk/documents/McNeil_Towards.pdf.

McNeill, F. (2012a) 'Four forms of "offender" rehabilitation: towards an interdisciplinary perspective', *Legal and Criminological Psychology* 17(1): 18–36 (pre-publication final draft available at: www.blogs.iriss.org.uk/discoveringdesistance/useful-resources/http//blogs.iriss.org.uk/discoveringdesistance/files/2011/09/McNeill-2012-Four-forms-of-offender-rehabilitation.pdf).

McNeill, F. (2012b) 'Counterblast: a copernican correction for community sentences', *Howard Journal of Criminal Justice* 51(1): 94–99.

McNeill, F. (2014) 'Punishment as rehabilitation', in G. Bruinsma and D. Weisburd (eds) *Encyclopedia of Criminology and Criminal Justice*, DOI 10.1007/978-1-4614-5690-2, (a final draft version of this paper is available open access online at blogs.iriss.org.uk/discoveringdesistance/files/2012/06/McNeill-When-PisR.pdf): 4195–4206.

McNeill, F. (forthcoming) 'Positive criminology, positive criminal justice?', in N. Ronei and D. Segev (eds) *Positive Criminology*, London: Routledge.

McNeill, F., Farrall, S., Lightowler, C. and Maruna, S. (2013) 'Discovering desistance: reconfiguring criminal justice?', *Scottish Justice Matters* (December): 3–6.

McNeill, F. and Weaver, B. (2007) *Giving Up Crime: Directions for policy*, Edinburgh: Scottish Consortium on Crime and Criminal Justice.

McNeill, F. and Weaver, B. (2010) *Changing Lives? Desistance research and offender management*, Glasgow: Scottish Centre for Crime and Justice Research, blogs.iriss.org.uk/discoveringdesistance/files/2012/12/Changing-Lives.pdf.

Maruna, S. (2001) *Making Good*, Washington, DC: American Psychological Association.

Maruna, S. and Farrall, S. (2004) 'Desistance from crime: a theoretical reformulation', *Kvlner Zeitschrift fur Soziologie und Sozialpsychologie* 43: 171–194.

Owers Report (2011) *Review of the Northern Ireland Prison Service*, Belfast: Prison Review Team.

Priechenfried, K. (2010) 'Aftercare and transition work "through the gate"', presented at the EQUAL Conference, Budapest, ec.europa.eu/education/grundtvig/doc/conf11/wa8/priechenfried.pdf.

Rex, S. (1999) 'Desistance from offending: experiences of probation', *Howard Journal of Criminal Justice* 38(4): 366–383.

Robinson, G. and McNeill, F. (2008) 'Exploring the dynamics of compliance with community penalties', *Theoretical Criminology* 12(4): 431–449.

Rotman, E. (1990) *Beyond Punishment. A new view of the rehabilitation of criminal offenders*, New York: Greenwood Press.

Sampson, R.J. and Laub, J.H. (2005) 'A life-course view of the development of crime', *The ANNALS of the American Academy of Political and Social Science* 602(1): 12–45.

Schinkel, M. (2014) *Being Imprisoned: Punishment, adaptation and desistance*, Houndmills: Palgrave MacMillan.

Shapland, J. and Bottoms, A. (2011) 'Reflections on social values, offending and desistance among young adult recidivists', *Punishment & Society* 13(3): 256–282.

Sharpe, G. (2012) *Offending Girls: Young Women and Youth Justice*, Abingdon: Routledge.

SPS (Scottish Prison Service) (2013) *Unlocking Potential, Transforming Lives. Report of the Scottish Prison Service Organisational Review*, Edinburgh: Scottish Prison Service.

Weaver, B. (2013) *The Story of the Del: From delinquency to desistance*, PhD thesis, Glasgow: University of Strathclyde.

Weaver, B. and McNeill, F. (2010) 'Travelling hopefully: desistance research and probation practice', in J. Brayford, F. Cowe and J. Deering (eds) *What Else Works? Creative Work with Offenders*, Cullompton: Willan.

References

Probation

Note: DPOM = Canton, R. and Hancock, D. (eds) (2007) *Dictionary of Probation and Offender Management*, Cullompton: Willan.
All Internet sites accessed November 2010 unless otherwise indicated.

Aas, K. F. (2004) 'From narrative to database: technological change and penal culture', *Punishment & Society* 6 (4): 379–393.

Advisory Council on the Penal System (ACPS) (1970) *Non-Custodial and Semi-Custodial Penalties* (London: HMSO).

Akhurst, M., Brown, I. and Wessely, S. (n.d.) *Dying for Help: Offenders at Risk of Suicide*, West Yorkshire Probation Service.

Aldridge Foundation (2008) *The User Voice of the Criminal Justice System.* Available online at: http://www.aldridgefoundation.com/user_voice.

Allen, R. and Stern, V. (eds) (2007) *Justice Reinvestment: A New Approach to Crime and Justice.* Available online at: http://www.kcl.ac.uk/depsta/law/research/icps/downloads/justice-reinvestment-2007.pdf.

Andrews, D. and Bonta, J. (2010) 'Rehabilitating criminal justice policy and practice', *Psychology, Public Policy, and Law* 16 (1): 39–55.

Andrews, D., Bonta, J. and Hoge, R. (1990) 'Classification for effective rehabilitation: rediscovering psychology', *Criminal Justice and Behavior*, 17 (1): 19–52.

Annison, J. (2006) 'Style over substance: a review of the evidence base for the use of learning styles in probation', *Criminology & Criminal Justice*, 6 (2): 239–257.

Annison, J., Eadie, T. and Knight, C. (2008) 'People first: probation officer perspectives on probation work', *Probation Journal*, 55 (3): 259–271.

Ansbro, M. (2006) 'What can we learn from serious incident reports?', *Probation Journal*, 53 (1): 57–70.

Apiafi, J. (2007) 'Education: skills for life', in DPOM.

Ashcroft, A. (2007) 'Cycle of change', in DPOM.

Ashworth, A. (2007) 'Sentencing', in M. Maguire, R. Morgan and R. Reiner (eds) *The Oxford Handbook of Criminology* (4th edn), Oxford: Oxford University Press.

Ashworth, A. and Zedner, L. (2008) 'Defending the criminal law: reflections on the changing character of crime, procedure, and sanctions', *Criminal Law and Philosophy* 2: 21–51.

Bailey, R. (1995) 'Helping offenders as an element in justice' in D. Ward and M. Lacey (eds) *Probation: Working for Justice*, London: Whiting and Birch.

Bailey, R. (2007) 'Offender perception', in DPOM.

Bailey, R., Knight, C. and Williams, B. (2007) 'The probation service as part of NOMS in England and Wales: fit for purpose', in L. Gelsthorpe and R. Morgan (eds) *Handbook of Probation*, Cullompton: Willan.

Ballucci, D. (2008) 'Risk in action: the practical effects of the youth management assessment', *Social and Legal Studies*, 17 (2): 175–197.

Bandura, A. (1989) 'Social cognitive theory', in R. Vasta (ed.) *Annals of Child Development*, 6 *Six Theories of Child Development*: 1–60, Greenwich, CT: JAI.

Barry, M. (2000) 'The mentor/monitor debate in criminal justice: what works for offenders', *British Journal of Social Work*, 30: 575–595.

BBC (2004) *Homeless Face More Violent Crime* (16 December). Available online at: http://news.bbc.co.uk/1/hi/uk/4099727.stm.

BBC (2007) Fear 'stops child development' (28 October). Available online at: http://news.bbc.co.uk/1/hi/education/7062545.stm.

BBC (2009) *Probation Work in 'Chronic' State* (22 November). Available online at: http://news.bbc.co.uk/1/hi/england/london/8371175.stm.

Bauwens, A. and Snacken S. (2010) 'Modèles de guidance judiciaire: sur la voie d'un modèle intégré?, Congrès: sécurité avant tout? Chances et dangers du risk assessment dans les domaines de l'exécution des sanctions et de la probation', Paulus-Akademie, Zürich, 3–4 September 2009, 1: 93–107. Stämpfli Verlag AG Bern, Switzerland.

Bean, P. (1976) *Rehabilitation and Deviance*, London: Routledge.

Bearne, B. (2007) 'Pre-sentence report (PSR)', in DPOM.

Bennett, J. (2008) *The Social Costs of Dangerousness: Prison and the Dangerous Classes*, London: Centre for Crime and Justice Studies. Available online at: http://www.crimeand justice.org.uk/dangerousness.html.

Bhui, H. S. (1999) 'Race, racism and risk assessment', *Probation Journal*, 46 (3): 171–181.

Bhui, H. S. (2006) 'Anti-racist practice in NOMS: reconciling managerialist and professional realities', *Howard Journal* 45 (2): 171–190.

Bhui, H. S. (2007) 'Prisons', in DPOM.

Bhui, H. S. (2008) 'Foreign national prisoners', in Y. Jewkes and J. Bennett (eds) *Dictionary of Prisons and Punishment,* Cullompton: Willan.

Biestek, F. (1961) *The Casework Relationship,* London: Unwin University Books.

Bochel, D. (1976) *Probation and After-Care: Its Development in England and Wales*, Edinburgh: Scottish Academic Press.

Boeck, T. (2007) 'Social capital', in DPOM.

Bonta, J. and Andrews, D. (2007) *Risk-Need-Responsivity Model for Offender Assessment and Rehabilitation*. Available online at: http://www.publicsafety.gc.ca/res/cor/rep/risk_need_200706-eng.aspx.

Bonta, J. and Wormith, S. (2007) 'Risk and need assessment', in G. McIvor and P. Raynor (eds) *Developments in Social Work with Offenders, Research Highlights in Social Work 48*, London: Jessica Kingsley.

Bonta, J., Bourgon, G., Rugge, T., Scott, T., Yessine, A., Gutierrez, L. and Li, J. (2010) 'The strategic training initiative in community supervision: risk-need-responsivity in the real world', Public Safety Canada. Available online at: http://198.103.108.123/res/cor/rep/2010-01-rnr-eng.aspx.

Bonta, J., Hanson, K. and Law, M. (1998) 'The prediction of criminal and violent recidivism among mentally disordered offenders: a meta-analysis', *Psychological Bulletin*, 123 (2): 123–142.

Bottoms, A. (1977) 'Reflections on the renaissance of dangerousness', *Howard Journal*, 16: 70–96.

Bottoms, A. (1983) 'Neglected features of contemporary penal systems', in D. Garland and P. Young (eds) *The Power to Punish*, Aldershot: Gower.

Bottoms, A. (1987) 'Limiting prison use: experiences in England and Wales', *Howard Journal* 26: 177–202.

Bottoms, A. (1995) 'The philosophy and politics of punishment and sentencing', in C. Clarkson and R. Morgan (eds) *The Politics of Sentencing Reform*, Oxford: Oxford University Press.

Bottoms, A. (2001) 'Compliance and community penalties', in A. Bottoms, L. Gelsthorpe and S. Rex (eds) *Community Penalties: Change and Challenges*, Cullompton: Willan.

Bottoms, A. (2004) 'Empirical research relevant to sentencing frameworks', in A. Bottoms, S. Rex and G. Robinson (eds) *Alternatives to Imprisonment: Options for an Insecure Society*, Cullompton: Willan.

Bottoms, A. (2007) 'Bifurcation' in DPOM.

Bottoms, A. and McWilliams, W. (1986) 'Social enquiry reports twenty-five years after the Streatfeild Report' in P. Bean and D. Whynes (eds) *Barbara Wootton: Social Science and Public Policy – Essays in Her Honour*, London: Routledge.

Bottoms, A. and Stelman, A. (1988) *Social Inquiry Reports: A Framework for Practice Development*, Aldershot: Gower.

Bottoms, A., Shapland, J., Costello, A., Holmes, D. and Muir, G. (2004) 'Towards desistance: theoretical underpinnings for an empirical study', *Howard Journal* 43 (4): 368–389.

Boyle, J. (1977) *A Sense of Freedom*, London: Pan.

Bracken, D. (2003) 'Skills and knowledge for contemporary probation practice', *Probation Journal* 50 (2): 101–114.

Bracken, D. (2007) 'Probation in the USA and Canada', in DPOM.

Braithwaite, J. (1989) *Crime, Shame and Reintegration*, Cambridge: Cambridge University Press.

Brantingham, P. and Faust, L. (1976) 'A conceptual model of crime prevention', *Crime & Delinquency*, 22 (3): 284–296.

Bridges, A. (2007) 'Employment, training and education (ETE)', in DPOM.

Brody, S. (1976) *The Effectiveness of Sentencing: A Review of the Literature*, Home Office Research Study No. 35, London: Home Office.

Brooker, C., Syson-Nibbs, L., Barrett, P. and Fox, C. (2009) 'Community managed offenders' access to healthcare services: report of a pilot study', *Probation Journal*, 56 (1): 45–59.

Brown, M. (2000) 'Calculations of risk in contemporary penal practice', in M. Brown and J. Pratt (eds) *Dangerous Offenders: Punishment and Social Order*, London: Routledge.

Brownlee, I. (1998) *Community Punishment: A Critical Introduction*, Harlow: Longman.

Bryant, M., Coker, J., Estlea, B., Himmel, S. and Knapp, T. (1978) 'Sentenced to social work?', *Probation Journal*, 25 (4): 110–114.

Burke, L. (2005) *From Probation to National Offender Management Service: Issues of Contestability, Culture and Community Involvement*, London: NAPO.

Burke, L. (2010) 'No longer social workers: developments in probation officer training and education in England and Wales', *Revista de Asistenta Sociala* (Social Work Review), IX (3/2010): 39–48 (Romania).

Burnett, R. (2004) 'To reoffend or not to reoffend: the ambivalence of convicted property offenders', in Shadd Maruna and Russ Immarigeon (eds) *After Crime and Punishment: Pathways to offender reintegration*, Cullompton: Willan.

Burnett, R., Baker, K. and Roberts, C. (2007) 'Assessment, supervision and intervention: fundamental practice in probation', in L. Gelsthorpe and R. Morgan (eds) *Handbook of Probation*, Cullompton: Willan Publishing.

Burnett, R. and Maruna, S. (2006) 'The kindness of prisoners: strengths-based resettlement in theory and in action', *Criminology & Criminal Justice* 6 (1): 83–106.

Burnett, R. and McNeill, F. (2005) 'The place of the officer–offender relationship in assisting offenders to desist from crime', *Probation Journal*, 52 (3): 221–242.

Busfield, J. (2002) 'Psychiatric disorder and individual violence: imagined death, risk and mental health policy', in A. Buchanan (ed.) *Care of the Mentally Disordered Offender in the Community,* Oxford: Oxford University Press.

Calverley, A., Cole, B., Kaur, G. and Lewis, S. (2004) *Black and Asian Offenders on Probation*, Home Office Research Study 277, London: Home Office.

Canton, R. (1995) 'Mental disorder, justice and censure', in D. Ward and M. Lacey (eds.) *Probation: Working for Justice*, London: Whiting and Birch.

Canton, R. (1993) 'Trying to make sense of it all', *NAPO News*, London: NAPO.

Canton, R. (2005) 'Risk assessment and compliance in probation and mental health practice', in B. Littlechild and D. Fearns (eds) *Mental Disorder and Criminal Justice: Policy, Provision and Practice*, Lyme Regis: Russell House.

Canton, R. (2006) 'Penal policy transfer: a case study from Ukraine', *Howard Journal*, 45 (5): 502–520.

Canton, R. (2007) 'Probation and the tragedy of punishment', *Howard Journal*, 46 (3): 236–254.

Canton, R. (2008a) 'Working with mentally disordered offenders', in S. Green, E. Lancaster and S. Feasey (eds) *Addressing Offending Behaviour: Context, Practice, Values*, Cullompton: Willan Publishing.

Canton, R. (2008b) 'Counterblast: can audits assess good practice in the enforcement of community penalties?', *Howard Journal*, 47 (5): 529–533.

Canton, R. (2009a) 'Nonsense upon stilts? Human rights, the ethics of punishment and the values of probation', *British Journal of Community Justice*, 7 (1): 5–22.

Canton, R. (2009b) 'Taking probation abroad', *European Probation Journal* 1 (1): 66–78.

Canton, R. (2009c) 'Contemporary probation in Europe: some reflections', *EuroVista* 1 (1): 2–9.

Canton, R. (2010a) 'Not another medical model: Using metaphor and analogy to explore crime and criminal justice', *British Journal of Community Justice*, 8 (1): 40–57.

Canton, R. (2010b) 'European probation rules: what they are, why they matter', *EuroVista* 1 (2): 62–71.

Canton, R. and Eadie, T. (2004) 'Social work with young offenders', in M. Lymbery and S. Butler (eds) *Social Work Ideals and Practice Realities*, Basingstoke: Macmillan.

Canton, R. and Eadie, T. (2005) 'From enforcement to compliance: implications for supervising officers', *Vista* 9 (3): 152–158.

Canton, R. and Eadie, T. (2007) 'National Standards', in DPOM.

Canton, R. and Eadie, T. (2008) 'Accountability, legitimacy, and discretion: applying criminology in professional practice', in B. Stout, J. Yates and B. Williams (eds) *Applied Criminology*, London: Sage.

Canton, R. and Hancock, D. (eds) (2007) *Dictionary of Probation and Offender Management* (DPOM), Cullompton: Willan Publishing.

Canton, R. and Yates, J. (2008) 'Applied criminology', in B. Stout, J. Yates and B. Williams (eds) *Applied Criminology*, London: Sage.

Carlen, P. (2002) 'Women's imprisonment: Models of reform and change', *Probation Journal* 49 (2): 76–87.

Carter, P. (2003) *Managing Offenders, Reducing Crime: A New Approach,* London: Home Office.

Casey, L. (2008) *Engaging Communities in Fighting Crime*, London: Cabinet Office. Available online at: http://www.cabinetoffice.gov.uk/media/cabinetoffice/corp/assets/publications/crime/cc_full_report.pdf.

Cavadino, M. and Dignan, J. (2006a) 'Penal policy and political economy', *Criminology and Criminal Justice*, 6 (4): 435–456.

Cavadino, M. and Dignan, J. (2006b) *Penal Systems: A Comparative Approach*, London: Sage.

Cavadino, M. and Dignan, J. (2007) *The Penal System: An Introduction* (4th edn), London: Sage.

Cavadino, M., Crow, I. and Dignan, J. (1999) *Criminal Justice 2000: Strategies for a New Century*, Winchester: Waterside Press.

Chapman, T. and Hough, M. (1998) *Evidence-Based Practice*, London: Home Office.

Chapman, T. and O'Mahony, D. (2007) 'Youth and criminal justice in Northern Ireland', in G. McIvor and P. Raynor (eds) *Developments in Social Work with Offenders, Research Highlights in Social Work 48*, London: Jessica Kingsley.

Cherry, S. (2005) *Transforming Behaviour: Pro-social Modelling in Action,* Cullompton: Willan.

Cherry, S. (2007a) 'Prosocial modelling', in DPOM.

Cherry, S. (2007b) 'Solution-focused work', in DPOM.

Christie, N. (2000) *Crime Control as Industry: Towards Gulags, Western Style* (3rd edn), London: Routledge.

Christie, N. (2004) *A Suitable Amount of Crime*, London: Routledge.

Christie, N. (2010) 'Victim movements at a crossroad', *Punishment & Society*, 12 (2): 115–122.

Chui, W. H. (2003) 'What works in reducing reoffending: principles and programmes', in W. H. Chui and M. Nellis (eds) *Moving Probation Forward: Evidence, Arguments and Practice*, Harlow: Pearson Education.

CJJI (Criminal Justice Joint Inspection) (2009) *Report of a Joint Thematic Review of Victim and Witness Experiences in the Criminal Justice System*. Available online at: http://www.hmcpsi.gov.uk/index.php?id=47&docID=885.

Clark, C. (2000) *Social Work Ethics: Politics, Principles and Practice*, Basingstoke: Macmillan.

Clarke, K. (2010) 'The Government's vision for criminal justice reform', speech to the Centre for Crime and Justice Studies, London. Available online at: http://www.justice.gov.uk/sp300610a.htm.

Clear, T. (2005) 'Places not cases? Re-thinking the probation focus', *Howard Journal* 44 (2): 172–184.

Clear, T. and Karp, D. (1999) *The Community Justice Ideal: Preventing Crime and Achieving Justice*, Oxford: Westview Press.

Cohen, S. (1985) *Visions of Social Control*, Cambridge: Polity Press.

Compton, B. and Galaway, B. (1984) *Social Work Processes* (3rd edn), Chicago Ill.: Dorsey Press.

Cornish, D. and Clarke, R. (eds) (1986) *The Reasoning Criminal: Rational Choice Perspectives on Criminal Offending*, New York: Springer-Verlag. Available online at: http://www.popcenter.org/library/reading/?p=reasoning.

Corston, J. (2007), *The Corston Report: A Review Of Women With Particular Vulnerabilities In The Criminal Justice System*, London: Home Office. Available online at: http://www. homeoffice.gov.uk/documents/corston-report/.

Council of Europe (2006a) *Recommendation Rec. (2006)2 of the Committee of Ministers to member states on the European Prison Rules*, (Adopted by the Committee of Ministers 11 January 2006). Available online at: https://wcd.coe.int/ViewDoc.jsp?id=955747 (accessed November 2010).

Council of Europe (2006b) *Recommendation Rec (2006) 8 of the Committee of Ministers to member states on assistance to crime victims*. Available online at: https://wcd.coe.int/ViewDoc.jsp?id=1011109&Site=CM.

Council of Europe (2010) *Recommendation CM/Rec (2010)1 of the Committee of Ministers to Member States on the Council of Europe Probation Rules* (adopted by the Committee of Ministers 20 January 2010). Available online at: https://wcd.coe.int/ViewDoc. jsp?id=1575813&Site=CM&BackColorInternet=C3C3C3&BackColorIntranet=EDB02 1&BackColorLogged=F5D383.

Cowe, F. (2007a) 'Self-harm', in DPOM.

Cowe, F. (2007b) 'Suicide', in DPOM.

Coyle, A. (2005) *Understanding Prisons: Key Issues in Policy and Practice*, Maidenhead: Open University Press.

Craissati, J. and Sindall, O. (2009) 'Serious further offences: an exploration of risk and typologies', *Probation Journal* 56 (1): 9–27.

Crawford, A. (2007) 'Crime prevention and community safety', in M. Maguire, R. Morgan and R. Reiner (eds) *The Oxford Handbook of Criminology* (4th edn), Oxford: Oxford University Press.

Crawford, A. and Enterkin, J. (2001) 'Victim contact work in the probation service: paradigm shift or Pandora's box?', *British Journal of Criminology*, 41:707–725.

Criminal Injuries Compensation Authority (2008) *The Criminal Injuries Compensation Scheme*. Available online at: http://www.cica.gov.uk/en-gb/Can-I-apply/.

Criminal Justice Joint Inspection (2009) *Prolific and Other Priority Offenders: A Joint inspection of the PPO Programme*. Available online at: http://www.justice.gov.uk/ inspectorates/hmi-probation/docs/ppo_thematic_report_-rps.pdf.

Criminal Justice System (2006) *Code of Practice for Victims of Crime 2006*. Available online at: http://www.direct.gov.uk/prod_consum_dg/groups/dg_digitalassets/@dg/@ en/documents/digitalasset/dg_073647.pdf.

Critcher, C. (1975) 'Structures, cultures and biography', in S. Hall and T. Jefferson (eds) *Resistance through Rituals: Youth Subcultures in Post-War Britain*, London: Hutchinson.

Davies, K., Lewis, J. Byatt, J., Purvis, E. and Cole, B. (2004) *An Evaluation of the Literacy Demands of General Offending Behaviour Programmes*, Home Office Research Findings 233, London: Home Office. Available online at: http://www.homeoffice.gov. uk/rds/pdfs04/r233.pdf.

Davies, M. (1969) *Probationers in their Social Environment*, Home Office Research Study No. 2, London: Home Office.

Debidin, M. (2007) 'O-DEAT (OASys Data Evaluation And Analysis Team)', in DPOM.

Debidin, M. (ed.) (2009) *A Compendium of Research and Analysis on the Offender Assessment System (OASys) 2006–2009*, Ministry of Justice Research Series 16/09. Available online at: www.justice.gov.uk/research-analysis-offender-assessment-system. pdf.

Devlin, A. and Turney, B. (1999) *Going Straight: After Crime and Punishment*, Winchester: Waterside Press.

Dominey, J. (2002) 'Addressing victim issues in pre-sentence reports', in B. Williams (ed.) *Reparation and Victim-Focused Social Work*, London: Jessica Kingsley.

Dominey, J. (2007) 'Responsivity', in DPOM.

Dominey, J. (2010) 'Work-based distance learning for probation practice: doing the job properly', *Probation Journal* 57 (2): 153–162.

Doob, A. (1995) 'The United States Sentencing Commission Guidelines: if you don't know where you are going, you might not get there', in C. Clarkson and R. Morgan (eds) *The Politics of Sentencing Reform*, Oxford: Oxford University Press.

Dorling, D., Gordon, D., Hillyard, P., Pantazis, C., Pemberton, S. and Tombs S. (2008) *Criminal Obsessions: Why Harm Matters More Than Crime* (2nd edn), London: Centre for Crime and Justice Studies. Available online at: http://www.crimeandjustice.org.uk/harmandsocproject.html.

Dowden, C. and Andrews, D. (2004) 'The importance of staff practice in delivering effective correctional treatment: a meta-analytic review of core correctional practice', *International Journal of Offender Therapy and Comparative Criminology*, 48 (2): 203–214.

Downes, D. and Morgan, R. (1997) 'Dumping the "hostages to fortune"? The politics of law and order in post-war Britain', in M. Maguire, R. Morgan and R. Reiner (eds) *The Oxford Handbook of Criminology* (2nd edn), Oxford: Oxford University Press.

Downes, D. and Morgan, R. (2007) 'No turning back: the politics of law and order into the millennium', in M. Maguire, R. Morgan and R. Reiner (eds) *The Oxford Handbook of Criminology* (4th edn), Oxford: Oxford University Press.

Drake, D., Muncie, J. and Westmarland, L. (eds) (2010) *Criminal Justice: Local and Global*, Cullompton: Willan in association with Open University.

Drakeford, M. (2007) 'Poverty', in DPOM.

Drakeford, M. (2010) 'Devolution and youth justice in Wales', *Criminology and Criminal Justice*, 10 (2): 137–154.

Duff, A. (2007) 'Punishment as communication', in DPOM.

Duff, R. A. (2001) *Punishment, Communication and Community*, Oxford: Oxford University Press.

Dunbar, I. and Langdon, A. (1998) *Tough Justice: Sentencing and Penal Policies in the 1990s*, Oxford: Blackstone Press.

Dunkley, E. (2007) 'Approved premises', in DPOM.

Eadie, T. and Willis, A. (1989) 'National standards for discipline and breach proceedings in community service: an exercise in penal rhetoric?', *Criminal Law Review*, June: 412–419.

Eadie, T. and Winwin Sein, S. (2005) 'When the going gets tough, will the tough get going? Retaining staff during challenging times', *Vista* 10 (3): 171–179.

Easton, S. and Piper, C. (2005) *Sentencing and Punishment: The Quest for Justice,* Oxford: Oxford University Press.

Ellis, T., Hedderman, C. and Mortimer, E. (1996) *Enforcing Community Sentences,* Home Office Research Study No.158, London: Home Office.

Farrall, S. (2002) *Rethinking What Works with Offenders: Probation, Social Context and Desistance from Crime*, Cullompton: Willan.

Farrall, S. (2007) 'Desistance studies vs. cognitive-behavioural therapies: Which offers most hope for the long term?', in DPOM.

Farrall, S. and Calverley, A. (2006) *Understanding Desistance from Crime: Theoretical Directions in Resettlement and Rehabilitation*, Maidenhead: Open University Press.

Farrall, S. and Maltby, S. (2003) 'The victimisation of probationers', *Howard Journal* 42 (1): 32–54.

Farrall, S., Mawby, R. and Worrall, A. (2007) 'Prolific/persistent offenders and desistance', in L. Gelsthorpe and R. Morgan (eds) *Handbook of Probation*, Cullompton: Willan.

Farrington, D. (2007) 'Criminal careers', in DPOM.

Farrow, K. (2004) 'Still committed after all these years. Morale in the modern day probation service', *Probation Journal* 51 (3): 206–20.

Farrow, K., Kelly, G. and Wilkinson, B. (2007) *Offenders in Focus: Risk, Responsivity and Diversity*, Bristol: Policy Press.

Faulkner, D. (2002) 'Prisoners as citizens', *British Journal of Community Justice* 1 (2): 11–19.

Faulkner, D. (2006) *Crime, State and Citizen* (2nd edn), Winchester: Waterside Press.

Faulkner, D. (2007) 'Social exclusion', in DPOM.

Fawcett Society (2009) *Engendering Justice – from Policy to Practice: Final Report of the Commission on Women and the Criminal Justice System.* Available online at: http://www.fawcettsociety.org.uk/index.asp?PageID=933 .

Ferguson, K. (2007) 'Probation service officers', in DPOM.

Finkelhor, D. (1986) *A Sourcebook on Child Sexual Abuse*, New York: Sage.

Fitzmaurice, C. and Pease, K. (1986) *The Psychology of Judicial Sentencing*, Manchester: University of Manchester Press.

Fleet, F. and Annison, J. (2003) 'In support of effectiveness: facilitating participation and sustaining change', in W. H. Chui and M. Nellis (eds) *Moving Probation Forward: Evidence, Arguments and Practice*, Harlow: Pearson Longman.

Flegg, D. (1976) *Community Service: Consumer Survey 1973–1976*, Nottingham: Nottinghamshire Probation and After-Care Service.

Fletcher, H. (2007) 'Privatization', in DPOM.

Floud, J. and Young, W. (1981) *Dangerousness and Criminal Justice*, London: Heinemann.

Foucault, M. (1977) *Discipline and Punish: The Birth of the Prison*, Harmondsworth: Penguin.

Frude, N., Honess, T. and Maguire, M. (2009) CRIME-PICS II Manual. Available online at: http://www.crime-pics.co.uk/cpicsmanual.pdf.

Garland, D. (1985) *Punishment and Welfare: A History of Penal Strategies*, Aldershot: Gower.

Garland, D. (1990) *Punishment and Modern Society: A Study in Social Theory*, Oxford: Oxford University Press.

Garland, D. (2001) *The Culture of Control: Crime and Social Order in Contemporary Society*, Oxford: Oxford University Press.

Gelsthorpe, L. (2001) 'Accountability: difference and diversity in the delivery of community penalties', in A. Bottoms, L. Gelsthorpe and S. Rex (eds) *Community Penalties: Changes and Challenges*, Cullompton: Willan.

Gelsthorpe, L. (2001) 'Critical decisions and processes in the criminal courts', in E. McLaughlin and J. Muncie (eds) *Controlling Crime* (2nd edn), London: Sage in association with Open University.

Gelsthorpe, L. (2006) 'The experiences of female minority ethnic offenders: the other "other"', in S. Lewis, P. Raynor, D. Smith and A. Wardak (eds) *Race and Probation*, Cullompton: Willan.

Gelsthorpe, L. (2007) 'Dealing with diversity', in G. McIvor and P. Raynor (eds) *Developments in Social Work with Offenders, Research Highlights in Social Work 48*, London: Jessica Kingsley.

Gelsthorpe, L. (2007) 'Probation values and human rights', in L. Gelsthorpe and R. Morgan (eds) *Handbook of Probation*, Cullompton: Willan.

Gelsthorpe, L. and Hedderman, C. (eds) (1997) *Understanding the Sentencing of Women*, Home Office Research Study 170, London: Home Office.

Gelsthorpe, L. and Morris, A. (2002) 'Women's imprisonment in England and Wales: a penal paradox', *Criminal Justice* 2 (3): 277–301.

Gelsthorpe, L. and Raynor, P. (1995) 'Quality and effectiveness in probation officers' reports to sentencers', *British Journal of Criminology* 35 (2): 188–200.

Gelsthorpe, L. and Rex, S. (2004) 'Community service as reintegration: exploring the potential', in G. Mair (ed.) *What Matters in Probation*, Cullompton: Willan.

Gelsthorpe, L., Sharp, G. and Roberts, J. (2007) *Provision for Women Offenders in the Community*, London: Fawcett Society. Available online at: http://www.fawcettsociety. org.uk/documents/Provision%20for%20women%20offenders%20in%20the%20community (1).pdf.

Gerty, A. (2007) 'Victim contact', in DPOM.

Goode, A. (2007) 'Unpaid work', in DPOM.

Goode, S. (2007) 'Contestability', in DPOM.

Gorman, K. (2001) 'Cognitive behaviourism and the Holy Grail: the quest for a universal means of managing offender risk', *Probation Journal*, 48 (1): 3–9.

Grapes, T. (2007) 'Offender management', in DPOM.

Griffin, J. (2008) *On Human Rights*, Oxford: Oxford University Press.

Grounds, A. (1991) 'The mentally disordered offender in the criminal process: some research and policy questions', in K. Herbst and J. Gunn (eds) *The Mentally Disordered Offender*, Oxford: Butterworth-Heinemann.

Grounds, A. (1995) 'Risk assessment and management in clinical context', in J. Crichton (ed.) *Psychiatric Patient Violence: Risk and Relapse*, London: Duckworth.

Guardian (2010) 'Former chief inspector says Labour left 'dysfunctional' prison service in crisis', *The Guardian* (24 May). Available online at: http://www.guardian.co.uk/ society/2010/may/24/prisons-policy-labour-crisis-probation.

HM Inspectorate of Probation (2000) *Towards Race Equality: Thematic Inspection*, London: Home Office.

HM Inspectorate of Probation (2004) *Towards Race Equality: Follow-up Inspection Report*. Available online at: http://www.justice.gov.uk/inspectorates/hmi-probation/docs/ towardsraceequality04-rps.pdf.

HM Inspectorate of Probation (2010) *HM Inspectorate of Probation: A Short History*. Available online at: http://www.justice.gov.uk/inspectorates/hmi-probation/docs/ History_of_HMI_Probation-rps.pdf.

HM Prison Service (n.d.) *Statement of Purpose*. Available online at: http://www.hmprison service.gov.uk/abouttheservice/statementofpurpose/.

HMI Probation/HMI Prisons (2001) *Through the Prison Gate*, London: HMI Probation and HMI Prisons. Available online: http://www.justice.gov.uk/inspectorates/hmi-prisons/ docs/prison-gate-rps.pdf.

Hagell, A. and Newburn, T. (1994) *Persistent Young Offenders*, London: Policy Studies Institute.

Haines, K. and Morgan, R. (2007) 'Services before trial and sentence: achievement, decline and potential', in L. Gelsthorpe and R. Morgan (eds) *Handbook of Probation*, Cullompton: Willan.

Hamai, K., Villé, R., Harris, R., Hough, M. and Zvekic, U. (eds) (1995) *Probation Round the World*, London: Routledge.

Hammond, N. (2007) 'Deportation', in DPOM.

Hancock, D. (2007a) 'Accredited programmes in common use', in DPOM.

Hancock, D. (2007b) 'Carter Report', in DPOM.

Hancock, D. (2007c) 'Home visits', in DPOM.

Hancock, D. (2007d) 'Partnerships', in DPOM.

Hancock, D. (2007e) 'Prison probation teams', in DPOM.

Hancock, D. (2007f) 'Prolific and other priority offenders', in DPOM.

Hannah-Moffat, K (1999) 'Moral agent or actuarial subject: risk and Canadian women's imprisonment', *Theoretical Criminology* 3 (1): 71–94.

Hannah-Moffat, K. (2005) 'Criminogenic needs and the transformative risk subject: hybridizations of risk/need in penality', *Punishment and Society* 7 (1): 29–51.

Harding, J. (ed.) (1987) *Probation and the Community: A Practice and Policy Reader*, London: Tavistock.

Harding, J. (2003) 'Which way probation? A correctional or community justice service?', *Probation Journal*, 50 (4): 369–373.

Harding, J. (2007) 'Community justice', in DPOM.

Harper, G. and Chitty, C. (eds) (2005) *The Impact of Corrections on Re-offending: A Review of 'What Works'*, (3rd edn), Home Office Research, Development and Statistics Directorate. Available online at: http://www.homeoffice.gov.uk/rds/pdfs04/hors291.pdf.

Harris, R. (1980) 'A changing service: the case for separating "care" and "control" in probation practice', *British Journal of Social Work*, 10 (2): 163–184.

Harris, R. (1995) 'Reflections on comparative probation', in K. Hamai, R. Villé, R. Harris, M. Hough and U. Zvekic (eds) *Probation Round the World*, London: Routledge.

Haxby, D. (1978) *Probation: A Changing Service*, London: Constable.

Hearnden, I. and Millie, A. (2004) 'Does tougher enforcement lead to lower conviction?', *Probation Journal*, 51 (1): 48–59.

Hedderman, C. (2006) 'Keeping a lid on the prison population – will it work', in M. Hough, R. Allen and U. Padel (eds) *Reshaping Probation and Prisons: The New Offender Management Framework*, Bristol: Policy Press.

Hedderman, C. (2007) 'Past, present and future sentences: what do we know about their effectiveness?', in L. Gelsthorpe and R. Morgan (eds) *Handbook of Probation*, Cullompton: Willan Publishing.

Hedderman, C. (2008) 'Building on sand: why expanding the prison estate is not the way to "secure the future"', *Centre for Crime and Justice Studies Briefing Paper* No. 7. Available online at: http://www.crimeandjustice.org.uk/buildingonsand.html.

Hedderman, C. and Gelsthorpe, L. (eds) (1997) *Understanding the Sentencing of Women*, Home Office Research Study 170, London: Home Office.

Hedderman, C. and Hough, M. (2004) 'Getting tough or being effective: what matters?', in G. Mair (ed.) *What Matters in Probation,* Cullompton: Willan.

Henson, G. (2007) 'Volunteers', in DPOM.

Hine, J., McWilliams, B. and Pease, K. (1978) 'Recommendations, social information and sentencing', *Howard Journal,* 17: 91–100.

Heidensohn, F. and Gelsthorpe, L. (2007) 'Gender and crime', in M. Maguire, R. Morgan and R. Reiner (eds) *The Oxford Handbook of Criminology* (4th edn), Oxford: Oxford University Press.

Hilder, S. (2007) 'Anti-discriminatory practice', in DPOM.

Hill, R. (2007) 'National Probation Service for England and Wales', in DPOM.

Hodgett, V. (2007) 'Multi-Agency Public Protection Arrangements (MAPPAs)', in DPOM.

Holden, L. (2007) 'Offender Assessment System (OASys)', in DPOM.

Hollin, C., McGuire, J., Palmer, E., Bilby, C., Hatcher, R. and Holmes, A. (2002) *Introducing Pathfinder Programmes into the Probation Service: An Interim Report*, Home Office Research Study 247. Available online at: http://rds.homeoffice.gov.uk/rds/pdfs2/hors247.pdf.

Holt, P. (2000) *Case Management: Context for Supervision,* Leicester: De Montfort University.

Home Office (1990a) *Crime, Justice and Protecting the Public*, Cm 965, London: HMSO.

Home Office (1990b) *Partnership in Dealing with Offenders in the Community*, London: Home Office.

Home Office (1990c) *Victim's Charter: A Statement of the Rights of Victims of Crime,* London: Home Office.

Home Office (1996) *The Victim's Charter: A Statement of Service Standards for Victims of Crime.* Available online at: http://www.homeoffice.gov.uk/documents/victims-charter?view=Binary.

Home Office (1998) *Prisons – Probation Review – Final Report: Joining Forces to Protect the Public*, http://webarchive.nationalarchives.gov.uk/+/http://www.homeoffice.gov.uk/docs/pprcont.html

Home Office (1999) *National Crime Reduction Strategy*, London: Home Office

Home Office (2001) *Making Punishments Work, The Report of a review of the Sentencing Framework for England and Wales. (Halliday Report)* –http://www.homeoffice.gov.uk/documents/halliday-report-sppu/

Home Office (2002) *Justice for All*, White Paper, Presented to Parliament by the Secretary of State for the Home Department, the Lord Chancellor and the Attorney General, CM 5563. Available online at: http://www.cjsonline.gov.uk/downloads/application/pdf/CJS%20White%20Paper%20-%20Justice%20For%20All.pdf.

Home Office (2004a) *Reducing Crime, Changing Life.* Available online at: http://www.probation.homeoffice.gov.uk/files/pdf/master%2020pp%20BB.pdf

Home Office (2004b) *Reducing Re-offending: National Action Plan.* Available online at: http://www.probation.homeoffice.gov.uk/files/pdf/NOMS%20National%20Action%20Plan.pdf

Home Office and Ministry of Justice (2009) *Integrated Offender Management: Government Policy Statement*, London: Home Office.

Homes, A., Walmsley, K. and Debidin, M. (2005) *Intensive Supervision and Monitoring Schemes for Persistent Offenders: Staff and Offender Perceptions*, Home Office Development and Practice Report No. 41. Available online at: http://rds.homeoffice.gov.uk/rds/pdfs05/dpr41.pdf.

Hood, R. (1992) *Race and Sentencing*, Oxford: Oxford University Press.

Hood, R. and Shute, S. (2000) *The Parole System at Work: A Study of Risk Based Decision-making*, Home Office Research Study 202. Available online at: http://www.homeoffice.gov.uk/rds/pdfs/hors202.pdf.

Hopley, K. (2002) 'National Standards: defining the service', in D. Ward, J. Scott and M. Lacey (eds) *Probation: Working for Justice* (2nd edn), Oxford: Oxford University Press.

Hough, M. (1996) *Drugs Misuse and the Criminal Justice System: A Review of the Literature.* DPI Paper 15, London: Home Office.

Hough, M. (2007) 'Public attitudes towards probation', in DPOM.

Hough, M. and Mitchell, D. (2003) 'Drug-dependent offenders and *Justice for All*', in M. Tonry (ed.) *Confronting Crime: Crime Control Policy under New Labour,* Cullompton: Willan.

Hough, M., Allen, R. and Padel, U. (eds) (2006) *Reshaping Probation and Prisons: The New Offender Management Framework*, Bristol: Policy Press.

House of Commons Justice Committee (2009) *Cutting Crime: The Case for Justice Reinvestment*, First Report of Session 2009–10. Available online at: http://www.publications.parliament.uk/pa/cm200910/cmselect/cmjust/94/94i.pdf

Howard, P., Francis, B., Soothill, K. and Humphreys, L. (2009) *OGRS 3: The Revised Offender Group Reconviction Scale*. Available online at: http://www.justice.gov.uk/oasys-research-summary-07-09-ii.pdf.

Hoyle, C. and Zedner, L. (2007) 'Victims, victimization, and criminal justice', in M. Maguire, R. Morgan and R. Reiner (eds) *The Oxford Handbook of Criminology* (4th edn), Oxford: Oxford University Press.

Hucklesby, A. and Hagley-Dickinson, L. (2007) *Prisoner Resettlement: Policy and Practice*, Cullompton: Willan.

Hudson, B. (1996) *Understanding Justice*, Buckingham: Open University Press.

Hudson, B. (2001) 'Punishment, rights and difference: defending justice in the risk society', in K. Stenson and R. Sullivan (eds) *Crime, Risk and Justice: The Politics of Crime Control in Liberal Democracies*, Cullompton: Willan.

Hudson, B. (2005) 'Beyond punishment: rights and freedoms', *Criminal Justice Matters*, No. 60: 4–5.

Hudson, B. and Bramhall, G. (2005) 'Assessing the "other": constructions of "Asianness" in risk assessments by probation officers', *British Journal of Criminology*, 45: 721–740.

Hudson, J. (2007) 'Motivation', in DPOM.

Hull, G., Scott, P. and Smith, B. (eds) (2003) *All the Women Are White, All the Blacks Are Men: But Some Of Us Are Brave: Black Women's Studies*, New York: The Feminist Press at CUNY.

Jewkes, Y. (2007) *Handbook on Prisons*, Cullompton: Willan.

Johnstone, G. (2002) *Restorative Justice: Ideas, Values, Debates,* Cullompton: Willan.

Jones, T. and Newburn, T. (2007) *Policy Transfer and Criminal Justice: Exploring US Influence over British Crime Control Policy*, Maidenhead: Open University Press.

Karp, D. and Clear, T. (2002) (eds) *What is Community Justice: Case Studies of Restorative Justice and Community Supervision*, London: Sage.

Karstedt, S. (2002) 'Emotions and criminal justice', *Theoretical Criminology*, 6 (3) 299–317.

Karstedt, S. and Farrall, S. (2007) *Law-abiding Majority? The Everyday Crimes of the Middle Classes*, London: Centre for Crime and Justice Studies. Available online at: http://www.crimeandjustice.org.uk/opus45/Law_abiding_Majority_FINAL_VERSION.pdf

Kemshall, H. (2001) *Risk Assessment and Management of Known Sexual and Violent Offenders: A Review of Current Issues*. Available online at: http://www.homeoffice.gov.uk/rds/prgpdfs/prs140.pdf.

Kemshall, H. (2003) *Understanding Risk in Criminal Justice*, Maidenhead: Open University Press.

Kemshall, H. (2007) 'Risk assessment and risk management', in DPOM.

Kemshall, H. and Canton, R. (2002) *The Effective Management of Programme Attrition*, Leicester: De Montfort University. Available online at: http://www.dmu.ac.uk/faculties/hls/research/commcrimjustice/commcrimjus.jsp.

Kemshall, H. and Maguire, M. (2001) 'Public protection, partnership and risk penality: the multi-agency risk management of sexual and violent offenders', *Punishment and Society*, 3 (2): 237–264.

Kemshall, H. and Wood, J. (2007a) 'High-risk offenders and public protection', in L. Gelsthorpe and R. Morgan (eds) *Handbook of Probation*, Cullompton: Willan.

Kemshall, H. and Wood, J. (2007b) 'Beyond public protection: an examination of community protection and public health approaches to high-risk offenders', *Criminology and Criminal Justice*, 7 (3): 203–222.

Kemshall, H., Canton, R. and Bailey, R. (2004) 'Dimensions of difference', in A. Bottoms, S. Rex and G. Robinson (eds) *Alternatives to Imprisonment: Options for an Insecure Society*, Cullompton: Willan Publishing.

Kemshall, H., Mackenzie, G., Wood, J., Bailey, R. and Yates, J. (2005) *Strengthening Multi-Agency Public Protection Arrangements (MAPPAs)*. Available online at: http://www.homeoffice.gov.uk/rds/pdfs05/dpr45.pdf.

Kendall, K. (2004) 'Dangerous thinking: a critical history of correctional cognitive behaviouralism', in G. Mair (ed.) *What Matters in Probation*, Cullompton: Willan.

Killias, M., Aebi, M. and Ribeaud, D. (2000) 'Does community service rehabilitate better than short-term imprisonment? Results of a controlled experiment', *Howard Journal* 39 (1): 40–57.

King, M. (1981) *The Framework of Criminal Justice*, London: Croom Helm.

Knight, C. (forthcoming) 'Soft skills for hard work: using emotional literacy to work effectively with sex offenders', in J. Brayford, F. Cowe and J. Deering (eds) *Sex Offenders: Punish, Help, Change or Control?: Theory, Policy and Practice Explored*, Routledge.

Knight, C., Dominey, J. and Hudson, J. (2008) '"Diversity": contested meanings and differential consequences', in B. Stout, J. Yates and B. Williams (eds) *Applied Criminology*, London: Sage.

Knight, C. and Stout, B. (2009) 'Probation and offender manager training: An argument for an integrated approach', *Probation Journal* 56 (3): 269–283.

Knott, C. (2007) 'National Offender Management Service (NOMS)', in DPOM.

Lacey, N. (1994) 'Introduction: making sense of criminal justice', in N. Lacey (ed.) *A Reader on Criminal Justice*, Oxford: Oxford University Press.

Laming, H. (2009) 'The Protection of Children in England: A Progress Report'. Available online at: http://publications.education.gov.uk/default.aspx?PageFunction=product details&PageMode=publications&ProductId=HC+330.

Liebling, A. (2004) *Prisons and their Moral Performance: A Study of Values, Quality and Prison Life*, Oxford: Oxford University Press.

Levitt, S. and Dubner, S. (2006) *Freakonomics: A Rogue Economist Explores the Hidden Side of Everything*, London: Penguin.

Lewis, S. (2005) 'Rehabilitation: headline or footnote in the new penal policy?', *Probation Journal*, 52 (2): 119–135.

Lewis, S., Maguire, M., Raynor, P., Vanstone, M. and Vennard, J. (2007) 'What works in resettlement? Findings from seven Pathfinders for short-term prisoners in England and Wales', *Criminology and Criminal Justice* 7 (1): 33–53.

Liebling, A. (2006) 'Lessons from prison privatisation for probation', in M. Hough, R. Allen and U. Padel (eds) *Reshaping Probation and Prisons: The New Offender Management Framework*, Bristol: Policy Press.

Lipsky, M. (1980) *Street-Level Bureaucracy: Dilemmas of the Individual in Public Services*, New York: Russell Sage.

Loader, I. (2005) 'The affects of punishment: emotions, democracy and penal politics', *Criminal Justice Matters*, 60 (1): 12–13.

Loader, I. (2007) 'Has liberal criminology lost?' Eve Saville Memorial lecture, Centre for Crime and Justice Studies. Available online at: http://www.crimeandjustice.org.uk/opus253.html.

Loader, I. and Sparks, R. (2002) 'Contemporary landscapes of crime, order and control: governance, risk and globalisation', in M. Maguire, R. Morgan and R. Reiner (eds) *The Oxford Handbook of Criminology* (3rd edn), Oxford: Oxford University Press.

Lurigio, A. and Carroll, J. (1985) 'Probation officers' schemata of offenders: content, development, and impact on treatment decisions', Journal of Personality and Social Psychology 48 (5): 1112–1126.

Mackenzie, G. (2007) 'Risk of harm', in DPOM.

MacLeod, K. (2007) 'Staff supervision', in DPOM.

Macpherson, W. (1999) *The Stephen Lawrence Inquiry: Report of an Inquiry by Sir William Macpherson of Cluny advised by Tom Cook, the Right Reverend Dr John Sentamu, Dr Richard Stone, Presented to Parliament by the Secretary of State for the Home Department by Command of Her Majesty*, Cm 4262-I. Available online at: www.archive.official-documents.co.uk/document/cm42/4262/4262.htm.

Maguire, M. (2007) 'The resettlement of ex-prisoners', in L. Gelsthorpe and R. Morgan (eds) *Handbook of Probation*, Cullompton: Willan.

Maguire, M. and Raynor, P. (2006) 'How the resettlement of prisoners promotes desistance from crime: Or does it?', *Criminology and Criminal Justice*, 6 (1): 19–38.

Maguire, M., Kemshall, H., Noaks, L., Wincup, E. and Sharpe, K. (2001) *Risk Management of Sexual and Violent Offenders: The Work of Public Protection Panels*. Available online at: http://rds.homeoffice.gov.uk/rds/prgpdfs/prs139.pdf.

Mahaffey, H. (2009) 'Restorative justice at the heart of the youth community', in W. Taylor, R. Earle and R. Hester (eds) *Youth Justice Handbook: Theory, Policy and Practice*, Cullompton: Willan in association with The Open University.

Mair, G. (2001) 'Technology and the future of community penalties', in A. Bottoms, L. Gelsthorpe and S. Rex (eds), *Community Penalties: Change and Challenges*, Cullompton: Willan.

Mair, G. (2004) 'The origins of what works in England and Wales: a house built on sand?', in G. Mair (ed.) *What Matters in Probation*, Cullompton: Willan.

Mair, G. and Canton, R. (2007) 'Sentencing, community penalties and the role of the probation service', in L. Gelsthorpe and R. Morgan (eds) *Handbook of Probation*, Cullompton: Willan Publishing.

Mair, G. and May, C. (1997) *Offenders on Probation*, Home Office Research Study 167, London: Home Office.

Mair, G. and Mills, H. (2009) *The Community Order and the Suspended Sentence Order Three Years On: The Views and Experiences of Probation Officers and Offenders*, London: Centre for Crime and Justice Studies. Available online at: http://www.crimeandjustice.org.uk/publications.html.

Mair, G., Burke, L. and Taylor, S. (2006) 'The worst tax form you've ever seen? Probation officers' views about OASys', *Probation Journal* 53 (1): 7–23.

Malik, S. (2007) 'Drugs', in DPOM.

Mann, S. (2007) 'Interventions', in DPOM.

Mantle, G. (2007) 'Mediation', in DPOM.

Martin, A. (2007) 'Learning disabilities', in DPOM.

Maruna, S. (2000) *Making Good: How Ex-convicts Reform and Rebuild their Lives*, Washington: American Psychological Association.

Maruna, S. and King, A. (2004) 'Public opinion and community penalties', in A. Bottoms, S. Rex and G. Robinson (eds) *Alternatives to Imprisonment: Options for an Insecure Society*, Cullompton: Willan.

Mathiesen, T. (1990) *Prison on Trial: A Critical Assessment*, London: Sage.

Matza, D. (1964) *Delinquency and Drift*, New York: Wiley.

Mawby, R.I. (2007) 'Public sector services and the victim of crime', in S. Walklate (ed.) *Handbook of Victims and Victimology*, Cullompton: Willan.

McAra, L. and McVie, S. (2007) *Criminal Justice Transitions*, Centre for Law and Society, University of Edinburgh. Available online at: http://www.law.ed.ac.uk/file_download/ publications/3_676_criminaljusticetransitions.pdf.

McConville, M., Sanders, A. and Leng, R. (1991) *The Case for the Prosecution: Police Suspects and the Construction of Criminality*, London: Routledge.

McCulloch, C. (2004) 'Through the eyes of a missionary: probation one hundred years on', *Vista* 9 (3): 148–151.

McGuire, J. (2001) *Cognitive-Behavioural Approaches – An Introduction to Theory and Research*. Available online at: http://www.justice.gov.uk/inspectorates/hmi-probation/ docs/cogbeh1-rps.pdf.

McGuire, J. (2002) 'Multiple agencies with diverse goals', in A. Buchanan (ed.) *Care of the Mentally Disordered Offender in the Community*, Oxford: Oxford University Press.

McGuire, J. (2005) 'Is research working? Revisiting the research and effective practice agenda', in J. Winstone and F. Pakes (eds) *Community Justice: Issues for Probation and Criminal Justice*, Cullompton: Willan.

McGuire, J. (2007a) 'Programmes for Probationers', in G. McIvor and P. Raynor (eds) *Developments in Social Work with Offenders, Research Highlights in Social Work 48*, London: Jessica Kingsley.

McGuire, J. (2007b) 'Cognitive-behavioural', in DPOM.

McGuire, J. and Priestley, P. (1985) *Offending Behaviour: Skills and Stratagems for Going Straight*, London: Batsford.

McGuire, J. and Priestley, P. (1995) 'Reviewing "what works": past, present and future', in J. McGuire (ed.) *What Works: Reducing Reoffending – Guidelines from Research and Practice*, Chichester: Wiley.

McIvor, G. (1990) *Sanctions for Serious or Persistent Offenders: A Review of the Literature*, Social Work Research Centre, University of Stirling.

McIvor, G. (1992) *Sentenced to Serve*, Aldershot: Avebury.

McIvor, G. (1998) 'Jobs for the boys? Gender differences in referral to community service', *Howard Journal* 37 (3): 280–290.

McIvor, G. (2002) *What Works in Community Service?*, CJSW Briefing, Criminal Justice Social Work Development Centre for Scotland. Available online at: http://www.cjsw. ac.uk/cjsw/files/Briefing%20Paper%206_final.pdf.

McIvor, G. (2004) 'Service with a smile? Women and community "punishment"', in G. McIvor (ed.) *Women Who Offend*, Research Highlights in Social Work 44, London: Jessica Kingsley.

McIvor, G. (2007) 'Paying back: unpaid work by offenders', in G. McIvor and P. Raynor (eds) *Developments in Social Work with Offenders, Research Highlights in Social Work 48*, London: Jessica Kingsley.

McIvor, G. and McNeill, F. (2007) 'Probation in Scotland: past, present and future', in L. Gelsthorpe and R. Morgan (eds) *Handbook of Probation*, Cullompton: Willan.

McIvor, G., Murray, C. and Jamieson, J. (2004) 'Desistance from crime: is it different for women and girls?', in S. Maruna and R. Immarigeon (eds) *After Crime and Punishment: Pathways to Offender Reintegration*, Cullompton: Willan.

McNeill, F. (2003) 'Desistance-focused probation practice', in W. H. Chui and M. Nellis (eds) *Moving Probation Forward: Evidence, Arguments and Practice*, Harlow: Pearson Education.

McNeill, F. (2006) 'A desistance paradigm for offender management', *Criminology & Criminal Justice*, 6 (1): 39–62.

McNeill, F. (2009) *Towards Effective Practice in Offender Supervision*, Scottish Centre for Crime and Justice Research. Available online at: http://www.sccjr.ac.uk/pubs/Towards-Effective-Practice-in-Offender-Supervision/79.

McNeill, F. and Burnett, R. (2005) 'The place of the officer–offender relationship in assisting offenders to desist from crime', *Probation Journal*, 52 (3): 221–242.

McNeill, F. and Maruna, S. (2007) 'Giving up and giving back: desistance, generativity and social work with offenders', in G. McIvor and P. Raynor (eds) *Developments in Social Work with Offenders, Research Highlights in Social Work 48*, London: Jessica Kingsley.

McNeill, F., Batchelor, S., Burnet, R. and Knox, J. (2005) *21st Century Social Work: Reducing Re-offending: Key Practice Skills*, Glasgow: Glasgow School of Social Work. Available online at: http://www.scotland.gov.uk/Publications/2005/04/21132007/20080.

McNeill, F. and Whyte, B. (2007) *Reducing Reoffending: Social Work and Community Justice in Scotland*, Cullompton: Willan.

McWilliams, W. (1983) 'The mission to the English police courts –1876–1936', *Howard Journal* 22 (3): 129–147.

McWilliams, W. (1985) 'The mission transformed: professionalisation of probation between the wars', *Howard Journal* 24 (4): 257–274.

McWilliams, W. (1986) 'The English probation system and the diagnostic ideal', *Howard Journal* 25 (4): 41–60.

McWilliams, W. (1987) 'Probation, pragmatism and policy', *Howard Journal* 26 (2): 97–121.

McWilliams, W. (1989) 'Community service national standards: practice and sentencing', *Probation Journal* 36 (3): 121–126.

Mead, J. (2007) 'Serious further offences', in DPOM.

Merrington, S. (2006) 'Is more better? The value and potential of intensive community supervision', *Probation Journal*, 53 (4): 347–360.

Merrington, S. and Hine, J. (2001) *A Handbook for Evaluating Probation Work with Offenders*. Available online at: http://www.justice.gov.uk/inspectorates/hmi-probation/docs/whole-rps.pdf.

Merrington, S. and Stanley, S. (2007) 'Effectiveness: who counts what?', in L. Gelsthorpe and R. Morgan (eds.) *Handbook of Probation*, Cullompton: Willan.

Miller, W. and Rollnick, R. (1991) *Motivational Interviewing*, New York: Guilford Press.

Ministry of Justice (2008a) 'Offender Management Caseload Statistics 2007', London: Ministry of Justice. Available online at: http://www.justice.gov.uk/publications/prison andprobation.htm.

Ministry of Justice (2008b) *The Offender Management Guide to Working with Women Offenders*. Available online at: http://noms.justice.gov.uk/news-publications-events/publications/guidance/OM-Guide-Women (accessed August 2010).

Ministry of Justice (2009a) 'Public have their say on how criminals payback', 30 March 2009. Available online at: http://www.justice.gov.uk/news/newsrelease300309a.htm.

Ministry of Justice (2009b) *Criminal Justice Group Business Plan 2009/10: Improving the criminal justice system*. Available online at: http://www.justice.gov.uk/cjg-business-plan-09-10ii.pdf.

Ministry of Justice (2009c) *The Correctional Services Accreditation Panel Report 2008–2009*. Available online at: http://www.justice.gov.uk/publications/docs/correctional-services-report-20080-09.pdf.

Ministry of Justice (2009d) *Offender Management Caseload Statistics 2008*, London: Ministry of Justice. Available online at: http://www.justice.gov.uk/publications/prison andprobation.htm.

Ministry of Justice (2010a) *Ministry of Justice: Draft Structural Reform Plan*. Available online at: http://www.justice.gov.uk/about/docs/moj-structural-reform-plana.pdf.

Ministry of Justice (2010b) *Offender caseload management statistics 2009*. Available online at: http://www.justice.gov.uk/prisonandprobation.htm.

Ministry of Justice (2010c) *National Victims' Service*. Available online at: http://www.justice.gov.uk/news/speech270110a.htm.

Monahan, J. (2004) 'The future of violence risk management', in M. Tonry (ed.) *The Future of Imprisonment*, New York: Oxford University Press.

Moore, B. (1996) *Risk Assessment: A Practitioner's Guide to Predicting Harmful Behaviour*, London: Whiting and Birch.

Moore, L. and Blakeborough, L. (2008) *Early Findings from WAVES (Witness and Victim Experience Survey): Information and Service Provision*, Ministry of Justice Research Series 11/08. Available online at: http://www.justice.gov.uk/publications/witness-victim-experience-survey.htm.

Moore, R. (2007) *Adult Offenders' Perceptions of their Underlying Problems: Findings from the OASys Self-assessment Questionnaire*, Home Office Findings 284. Available online at: http://rds.homeoffice.gov.uk/rds/pdfs07/r284.pdf.

Moore, R., Howard, P. and Burns, M. (2006), 'The further development of OASys: realising the potential of the offender assessment system', *Prison Service Journal* 167: 36–42.

Morgan, R. (2007) 'Probation, governance and accountability', in L. Gelsthorpe and R. Morgan (eds) *Handbook of Probation*, Cullompton: Willan.

Morgan, R. and Smith, A. (2003) 'The Criminal Justice Bill 2002: the future role and workload of the National Probation Service', *British Journal of Community Justice*, 2 (2): 7–23.

Morgan, R. and Liebling, A. (2007) 'Imprisonment: an expanding scene', in M. Maguire, R. Morgan and R. Reiner (eds) *The Oxford Handbook of Criminology* (4th edn), Oxford: Oxford University Press.

Morton, S. (2009) *Can OASys Deliver Consistent Assessments of Offenders? Results from the Inter-rater Reliability Study*, Ministry of Justice Research Summary 1/09. Available online at: www.justice.gov.uk/oasys-research-summary-01-09.pdf.

Mulrenan, U. (2007) 'Supporting people', in DPOM.

Munro, M. and McNeill, F. (2010) 'Fines, community sanctions and measures in Scotland', in H. Croall, G. Mooney and M. Munro (eds) *Criminal Justice in Scotland*, Cullompton: Willan.

Murray, H. and Kluckhohn, C. (1953) *Personality in Nature, Society, and Culture*, New York: Knopf.

Napo (2009) *Literacy, Language and Speech Problems amongst Individuals on Probation or Parole*. Available online at: http://www.napo.org.uk/about/news/news.cfm/news id/40.

National Audit Office (2004) *Delivering Public Services to a Diverse Society*. Available online at: http://www.nao.org.uk/publications/0405/delivering_public_services.aspx.

National Centre for Social Research (n.d.) *Offender Management Community Cohort Study*. Available online at: http://www.natcen.ac.uk/study/offender-management-community-cohort-study-.

National Offender Management Service (NOMS) (2006) *The NOMS Offender Management Model 1.1*, London: Home Office.

National Offender Management Service (2009) *MAPPA Guidance 2009 Version 3.0*. Available online at: http://www.lbhf.gov.uk/Images/MAPPA%20Guidance%20(2009) %20Version%203%200%20_tcm21-120559.pdf.

National Probation Directorate (2003) *A Brief Introduction to Enhanced Community Punishment* (2nd edn), London: Home Office.

National Probation Service (2004) *Views of the Probation Victim Contact Scheme*, London: Home Office.

National Probation Service (2005) *Visible Unpaid Work*, Probation Circular: PC 66/2005.

National Probation Service (2007) *PC 13/2007 – Introduction of a New Skills Screening Tool: First Move – Initial Skills Checker*. Available online at: http://www.probation. homeoffice.gov.uk/files/pdf/PC13%202007.pdf.

National Probation Service (2008a) *Annual Report 2007-2008*, London: Ministry of Justice.

National Probation Service (2008b) *Snapshot of Unpaid Work 2008*. London: Ministry of Justice.

National Probation Service (n.d.) *Interventions: A Guide to Interventions in the National Probation Service*. Available online at: http://www.probation2000.com/documents/ A%20Guide%20to%20Interventions%20in%20the%20NPS.pdf.

Nelken, D. (2007) 'Comparing criminal justice', in M. Maguire, R. Morgan and R. Reiner (eds) *The Oxford Handbook of Criminology* (4th edn), Oxford: Oxford University Press.

Nellis, M (1995) 'Probation values for the 1990s', *Howard Journal*, 34 (1): 19–44.

Nellis, M. (2000) 'Creating community justice', in S. Ballintyne, K. Pease and V. McLaren (eds), *Secure Foundations: Key Issues in Crime Prevention, Crime Reduction and Community Safety*, London: Institute for Public Policy Research.

Nellis, M. (2001) 'The Diploma in Probation Studies in the Midland region: celebration and critique after the first two years', *Howard Journal* 40 (4) 377–401.

Nellis, M. (2007a) 'Humanising justice: the English probation service up to 1972', in L. Gelsthorpe and R. Morgan (eds) *Handbook of Probation*, Cullompton: Willan.

Nellis, M. (2007b) 'Probation values', in DPOM.

Nellis, M. and Gelsthorpe, L. (2003) 'Human rights and the probation values debate', in W. H. Chui and M. Nellis (eds) *Moving Probation Forward: Evidence, Arguments and Practice*, Harlow: Pearson.

Newburn, T. (2007) *Criminology*, Cullompton: Willan.

Nietzsche, F. (1887) *On the Genealogy of Morality: A Polemic*, ed. and trans. by M. Clark and A. Swenson (1998), Indianapolis: Hackett.

O'Connell, B. (2005) *Solution-focused Therapy* (2nd edn), London: Sage.

O'Donnell, I. and Edgar, K. (1998) 'Routine victimisation in prisons', *Howard Journal* 37 (3): 266–279.

Octigan, M. (2007) 'Remand services', in DPOM.

Oldfield, M. (2002) *From Welfare to Risk: Discourse, Power and Politics in the Probation Service*, Issues in Community and Criminal Justice Monograph 1, London: Napo.

Oldfield, M. (2007) 'Risk society', in DPOM.

Oldfield, M. and Grimshaw, R. (2010*) Probation Resources, Staffing and Workloads 2001–2008* (rev. edn), London: Centre for Crime and Justice Studies. Available online at: http://www.crimeandjustice.org.uk/probationspendingrevisedstructure.html.

O'Mahony, D. and Chapman, T. (2007) 'Probation, the state and community – delivering probation services in Northern Ireland', in L. Gelsthorpe and R. Morgan (eds) *Handbook of Probation*, Cullompton: Willan.

Padel, U. and Stevenson, P. (1988) *Insiders: Women's Experience of Prison*, London: Virago, 1988.

Padfield, N. and Maruna, S. (2006) 'The revolving door at the prison gate: exploring the dramatic increase in recalls to prison', *Criminology & Criminal Justice*, 6 (3): 329–352.

Parker, T. (1991) *Life after Life: Interviews with Twelve Murderers*, London: Pan.

Partridge, S. (2004) *Examining Case Management Models for Community Sentences,* Home Office Online Report 17/04. Available online at: http://rds.homeoffice.gov.uk/rds/pdfs04/rdsolr1704.pdf.

Payne, S. (2009) *Redefining Justice: Addressing the Individual Needs of Victims and Witnesses*. Available online at: www.justice.gov.uk/sara-payne-redefining-justice.pdf.

Pease, K. (1999) 'The probation career of Al Truism', *Howard Journal*, 38 (1): 2–16.

Pease, K., Billingham, S. and Earnshaw, I. (1977) *Community Service Assessed in 1976*, Home Office Research Study No. 39, London: HMSO.

Peay, J. (1982) '"Dangerousness" – ascription or description?', in P. Feldman (ed.) *Developments in the Study of Criminal Behaviour: Volume 2: Violence,* Chichester: John Wiley.

Peay, J. (1997) 'Mentally disordered offenders', in M. Maguire, R. Morgan and R. Reiner (eds) *The Oxford Handbook of Criminology* (2nd edn), Oxford: Oxford University Press.

Phillips, C. and Bowling, B. (2007) 'Ethnicities, racism, crime and criminal justice', in M. Maguire, R. Morgan and R. Reiner (eds) *The Oxford Handbook of Criminology* (4th edn), Oxford: Oxford University Press.

Philp, M. (1985) 'Michel Foucault', in Q. Skinner (ed.) *The Return of Grand Theory in the Human Sciences*, Cambridge: Cambridge University Press.

Pillay, C. (ed.) (2000) *Building the Future: The Creation of the Diploma in Probation Studies*, London: NAPO.

Priestley, P., McGuire, J., Flegg, D., Hemsley, V. and Welham, D. (1978) *Social Skills and Personal Problem Solving. A Handbook of Methods*, London, Tavistock.

Prins, H (1995) *Offenders, Deviants or Patients?* (2nd edn) London: Routledge.

Prins, H. (1999) *Will they do it again? Risk Assessment and Management in Criminal Justice and Psychiatry,* London: Routledge.

Prison Commission (1932) *The Principles of the Borstal System*, London: Home Office.

Prison Reform Trust (2005) *Private Punishment: Who Profits?* Available online at: http://www.prisonreformtrust.org.uk/Portals/0/Documents/private%20punishment%20who%20profits.pdf.

Prison Reform Trust (2009) *Bromley Briefings Prison Factfile*. Available online at: http://www.ws3.prisonreform.web.baigent.net/subsection.asp?id=685.

Probation Association (2010) *Probation Trusts in Partnerships: The New Local Performance Context*. Available online at: (http://probationassociation.co.uk/media/6141/probation%20in%20partnerships%20-%20think%20local%20update%20no.1.pdf.

Probation Board for Northern Ireland (PBNI) (2008) Corporate Plan 2008–2011. Available online at: http://www.pbni.org.uk/archive/Publications/Decision%20making/consultation%20docs/cp0811draft.pdf.

Prochaska, J. and DiClemente, C. (1992) 'In search of how people change: applications to addictive behaviors', *American Psychologist* 47 (9): 1102–1114.

Quinney, R. and Trevino, A. (2001) *The Social Reality of Crime*, New Jersey: Transaction.

Pryor, S. (2001) *The Responsible Prisoner*. Available online at: http://www.justice.gov.uk/inspectorates/hmi-prisons/docs/the-responsible-prisoner-rps.pdf.

Rack, J. (2005) *The Incidence of Hidden Disabilities in the Prison Population: Yorkshire and Humberside Research*, Egham, Surrey: Dyslexia Institute.

Radzinowicz, L. and Hood, R. (1990) *The Emergence of Penal Policy in Victorian and Edwardian England*, Oxford: Oxford University Press.

Raine, J. (2007) 'Managerialism', in DPOM.

Raine, J. and Willson, M. (1993) *Managing Criminal Justice*, London: Harvester Wheatsheaf.

Ramell, P. (2007) 'Her Majesty's Inspectorate of Probation', in DPOM.

Rawls, J. (1972) *A Theory of Justice*, New York: Oxford University Press.

Raynor, P. (1980) 'Is there any sense in social inquiry reports?', *Probation Journal* 27: 78–94.

Raynor, P. (1985) *Social Work, Justice and Control*, Oxford: Blackwell.

Raynor, P. (2004a) 'Rehabilitative and reintegrative approaches', in A. Bottoms, S. Rex and G. Robinson (eds) *Alternatives to Prison: Options for an Insecure Society*, Cullompton: Willan.

Raynor, P. (2004b) 'Opportunity, motivation and change: some findings from research on resettlement', in R. Burnett and C. Roberts (eds) *What Works in Probation and Youth Justice: Developing Evidence-based Practice*, Cullompton: Willan.

Raynor, P. (2006) 'The probation service in England and Wales: modernised or dehumanised', *Criminal Justice Matters* 65 (1): 26–27.

Raynor, P. and Maguire, M. (2006) 'End-to-end or end in tears? Prospects for the effectiveness of the National Offender Management Model', in M. Hough, R. Allen and U. Padel (eds) *Reshaping Probation and Prisons: The New Offender Management Framework*, Bristol: Policy Press.

Raynor, P. and Rex, S. (2007) 'Accreditation', in G. McIvor and P. Raynor (eds), *Developments in Social Work with Offenders*, Research Highlights in Social Work 48, London: Jessica Kingsley.

Raynor, P. and Robinson, G. (2009) *Rehabilitation, Crime and Justice*, Basingstoke: Palgrave Macmillan.

Raynor, P. and Vanstone, M. (2002) *Understanding Community Penalties: Probation, Policy and Social Change*, Buckingham: Open University Press.

Raynor, P. and Vanstone, M. (2007) 'Towards a correctional service', in L. Gelsthorpe and R. Morgan (eds) *Handbook of Probation*, Cullompton: Willan.

Raynor, P., Kinch, J., Roberts, C. and Merrington, S. (2000) *Risk and Need Assessment in Probation Services: An Evaluation,* Home Office Research Study 211, London: Home Office.

Reiman, J. (1990) *The Rich Get Richer and the Poor Get Prison: Ideology, Class and Criminal Justice* (3rd edn), New York: Macmillan.

Rex, S. (1999) 'Desistance from offending: experiences of probation', *Howard Journal*, 38 (4): 366–383.

Rex, S. (2005) *Reforming Community Penalties*, Cullompton: Willan.

Rex, S. and Gelsthorpe, L. (2002) 'The role of community service in reducing offending: evaluating Pathfinder Projects in the UK', *Howard Journal*, 41 (4): 311–325.

Rex, S. and Gelsthorpe, L. (2004) 'Using community service to encourage inclusive citizenship', in R. Burnett and C. Roberts (eds) *What Works in Probation and Youth Justice: Developing Evidence-based Practice*, Cullompton: Willan.

Rex, S., Gelsthorpe, L., Roberts, C. and Jordan, P. (2004) *Crime Reduction Programme An Evaluation of Community Service Pathfinder Projects Final Report 2002*, Home Office Occasional Paper No. 87. Available online at: http://rds.homeoffice.gov.uk/rds/pdfs2/occ87.pdf (accessed June 2010).

Rice, M. (1990) 'Challenging orthodoxies in feminist theory: a black feminist critique', in L. Gelsthorpe and Al. Morris (eds) *Feminist Perspectives in Criminology*, Milton Keynes: Open University Press.

Roberts, C. (2004) 'Offending behaviour programmes: emerging evidence and implications for practice', in R. Burnett and C. Roberts (eds) *What Works in Probation and Youth Justice: Developing Evidence-based Practice*, Cullompton: Willan.

Roberts, C. (2007) 'Assessment instruments', in DPOM.

Roberts, J. (2002) 'Women-centred: the West Mercia community-based programme for women offenders', in P. Carlen (ed.) *Women and Punishment: The Struggle for Justice*, Cullompton: Willan.

Roberts, J. (2007) 'Custody plus, intermittent custody and custody minus', in DPOM.

Robinson, A. (2004) *Domestic Violence MARACs (Multi-Agency Risk Assessment Conferences) for Very High-Risk Victims in Cardiff, Wales: A Process and Outcome Evaluation*. Available online at: http://www.cardiff.ac.uk/socsi/contactsandpeople/academicstaff/Q-S/dr-amanda-robinson-publication.html.

Robinson, A. (2009) *Independent Sexual Violence Advisors: A Process Evaluation*, Home Office Research Report 20. Available online at: http://rds.homeoffice.gov.uk/rds/pdfs09/horr20.pdf.

Robinson, A. and Tregidga, J. (2005) *Domestic Violence MARACS (Multi-Agency Risk Assessment Conferences) for Very High-Risk Victims in Cardiff, Wales: Views from the Victims*. Available online at: http://www.cardiff.ac.uk/socsi/contactsandpeople/academicstaff/Q-S/dr-amanda-robinson-publication.html.

Robinson, G. (2002) 'Exploring risk management in probation practice: contemporary developments in England and Wales', *Punishment and Society* 4 (1): 5–25.

Robinson, G. (2003a) 'Implementing OASys: lessons from research into LSI-R and ACE', *Probation Journal*, 50 (1): 30–40.

Robinson, G. (2003b) 'Risk and risk assessment', in W. H. Chui and M. Nellis (eds) *Moving Probation Forward: Evidence, Arguments and Practice*, Harlow: Pearson Longman.

Robinson, G. (2003c) 'Technicality and indeterminacy in probation practice: a case study', *British Journal of Social Work*, 33 (5): 593–610.

Robinson, G. (2005) 'What works in offender management', *Howard Journal*, 44 (3), 307–318.

Robinson, G. and Burnett, R. (2007) 'Experiencing modernization: frontline probation perspectives on the transition to a National Offender Management Service', *Probation Journal*, 54 (4): 318–337.

Robinson, G. and Crow, I. (2009) *Offender Rehabilitation*, London: Sage.

Robinson, G. and McNeill, F. (2004) 'Purposes matter: examining the "ends" of probation', in G. Mair (ed.) *What Matters in Probation*, Cullompton: Willan.

Robinson, G. and McNeill, F. (2008) 'Exploring the dynamics of compliance with community penalties', *Theoretical Criminology,* 12 (4): 431–449.

Robinson, G. and Raynor, P. (2006) 'The future of rehabilitation: what role for the probation service?', *Probation Journal* 53 (4): 334–346.

Ross, C., Polaschek, D. and Ward, T. (2008) 'The therapeutic alliance: a theoretical revision for offender rehabilitation', *Aggression and Violent Behavior* 13: 462–480.

Rotman, E. (1994) 'Beyond punishment', in R. A. Duff and D. Garland (eds) *Reader on Punishment,* Oxford: Oxford University Press.

Ruck, S. K. (ed.) (1951) *Paterson on Prisons: The Collected Papers of Sir Alexander Paterson*, London: Frederick Muller.

Rumgay, J (2003) 'Partnerships in the probation service', in W. H. Chui and M. Nellis (eds) *Moving Probation Forward: Evidence, Arguments and Practice*, Harlow: Pearson Longman.

Rumgay, J. (2004) 'Dealing with substance-misusing offenders in the community', in A. Bottoms, S. Rex and G. Robinson (eds) *Alternatives to Prison: Options for an Insecure Society*, Cullompton: Willan.

Rumgay, J. (2007) 'Partnerships in probation', in L. Gelsthorpe and R. Morgan (eds) *Handbook of Probation*, Cullompton: Willan.

Rutherford, A. (1993) *Criminal Justice and the Pursuit of Decency*, Oxford: Oxford University Press.

Sandel, M. (1998) *What Money Can't Buy: The Moral Limits of Markets*. Available online at: http://www.tannerlectures.utah.edu/lectures/documents/sandel00.pdf.

Sandel, M. (2009) *Justice: What's the Right Thing to Do?* London: Penguin.

Sandham, J. and Octigan, M. (2007) 'Motivational interviewing', in DPOM.

Scott, P. (1977) 'Assessing dangerousness in criminals', *British Journal of Psychiatry*, 131: 127–142.

Selby, P. (2007) 'Address at Westminster Abbey 11 June 2007'. Available online at: http://www.ws3.prisonreform.web.baigent.net/subsection.asp?id=916.

Sentencing Guidelines Council (2009) *Magistrates' Court Sentencing Guidelines*. Available online at: http://www.sentencingcouncil.org.uk/guidelines/guidelines-to-download. htm.

Shapland, J. (1988) 'Fiefs and peasants: accomplishing change for victims in the criminal justice system', in M. Maguire and J. Pointing (eds) *Victims of Crime: A New Deal?*, Milton Keynes: Open University Press.

Shapland, J., Atkinson, A., Atkinson, H., Dignan, J., Edwards, L., Hibbert, J., Howes, M., Johnstone, J., Robinson, G. and Sorsby, A. (2008) *Does Restorative Justice Affect Reconviction? The Fourth Report from the Evaluation of Three Schemes*, Ministry of Justice Research Series 10 /08. Available online at: http://www.justice.gov.uk/restorative-justice-report_06-08.pdf.

Sharpe, J. (1990) *Judicial Punishment in England*, London: Faber.

Shaw, M. and Hannah-Moffat, K. (2000) 'Gender, diversity and risk assessment in Canadian corrections', *Probation Journal*, 47 (3): 163–172.

Shaw, M. and Hannah-Moffat, K. (2004) 'How cognitive skills forgot about gender and diversity', in G. Mair (ed.) *What Matters in Probation*, Cullompton: Willan.

Sheffield Pathways Out of Crime Study (n.d). Available online at: http://www.scopic. ac.uk/StudiesSPooCS.html#top

Sherman, L. (2009) 'Evidence and liberty: the promise of experimental criminology', *Criminology & Criminal Justice*, 9 (1): 5–28.

Silver, E. and Miller, L. (2002) 'A cautionary note on the use of actuarial risk assessment tools for social control', *Crime and Delinquency*, 48 (1): 138–161.

Skidmore, D. (2007a) 'Conciliation', in DPOM.

Skidmore, D. (2007b) 'Drugs intervention programme', in DPOM.

Skidmore, D. (2007c) 'Offender management as seen by other agencies', in DPOM.

Skinner, B. (1973) *Beyond Freedom and Dignity*, Harmondsworth: Penguin.

Smart, C. (1976) *Women, Crime and Criminology: A Feminist Critique*, London: Routledge & Kegan Paul.

Smith, D. (1998) 'Social work with offenders: the practice of exclusion and the potential for inclusion', in M. Barry and C. Hallett (eds) *Social Exclusion and Social Work: Issues of Theory, Policy and Practice*, Lyme Regis: Russell House.

Smith, D. (2004) *The Links Between Victimization and Offending*, Centre for Law and Society, University of Edinburgh. Available online at: http://www.law.ed.ac.uk/cls/esytc/findings/digest5.pdf.

Smith, D. (2005) 'Probation and social work', *British Journal of Social Work*, 35, 621–637.

Smith, D. (2006) 'Making sense of psychoanalysis in criminological theory and probation practice', *Probation Journal* 53 (4): 361–376.

Smith, D. and Vanstone, M. (2002) 'Probation and social justice', *British Journal of Social Work*, 32 (6): 815–830.

Smith, K. (1989) *Inside Time,* London: Harrap.

Snacken, S. (2010) 'Resisting punitiveness in Europe?', *Theoretical Criminology* 14 (3): 273–292.

Snowden, A. (2007) 'Sex Offender Treatment Programmes (SOTPs)', in DPOM.

Social Exclusion Unit (2002) *Reducing Re-offending by Ex-prisoners*, Office of the Deputy Prime Minister. Available online at: www.gos.gov.uk/497296/docs/219643/431872/468960/SEU_Report.pdf.

Solomon, E. and Silvestri, A. (2008) *Community Sentences Digest* (2nd edn), London: Centre for Crime and Justice Studies. Available online at: http://www.crimeandjustice.org.uk/communitysentencesdigest2008.html.

Spalek, B. (2003) 'Victim work in the probation service: perpetuating notions of an "ideal victim"', in W. H. Chui and M. Nellis (eds) *Moving Probation Forward: Evidence, Arguments and Practice*, Harlow: Pearson Education.

Stanley, S. (2009) 'What works in 2009: progress or stagnation?', *Probation Journal* 56 (2): 153–174.

Stephens, K. and Brown, I. (2001) 'OGRS2 in practice: an elastic ruler?', *Probation Journal*, 48 (3): 179–187.

Stern, V. (1999) *Alternatives to Prison in Developing Countries*, London: International Centre for Prison Studies and Penal Reform International.

Stout, B. (2007) 'Diversity', in DPOM.

Straw, J. (2009) *Probation and Community Punishment*, speech at Probation Study School, University of Portsmouth 4 February 2009. Available online at: http://www.justice.gov.uk/news/sp040209.htm.

Stylianou, S. (2003) 'Measuring crime seriousness perceptions: what have we learned and what else do we want to know', *Journal of Criminal Justice* 31: 37–56.

Sutton, C. (2007) 'ASPIRE', in DPOM.

Sykes, G. and Matza, D. (1957) 'Techniques of neutralization: a theory of delinquency', *American Sociological Review*, 22, 664–670.

Talbot, J. (2008) *No One Knows. Prisoners' Voices: Experiences of the Criminal Justice System by Prisoners with Learning Disabilities and Difficulties*, Prison Reform Trust. Available online at: http://www.prisonreformtrust.org.uk/uploads/documents/No%20One%20Knows%20report-2.pdf.

Tata, C., Burns, N., Halliday, S., Hutton, N. and McNeill, F. (2008) 'Assisting and advising the sentencing decision process: the pursuit of "quality" in pre-sentence reports', *British Journal of Criminology* 48 (6): 835–855.

Taylor, I. (1998) 'Crime, market-liberalism and the European idea', in V. Ruggiero, N. South and I. Taylor (eds) *The New European Criminology: Crime and Social Order in Europe*, London: Routledge.

Thompson, N. (2006) *Anti-Discriminatory Practice* (4th edn), Houndmills: Palgrave Macmillan.

Tilley, N. (ed.) (2006) *Handbook of Crime Prevention and Community Safety*, Cullompton: Willan.

Tilley, N. (2009) *Crime Prevention*, Cullompton: Willan.

The Times (2009) 'Red tape is taking up 75 per cent of probation officers' time (30 October). Available online at: http://www.timesonline.co.uk/tol/news/uk/crime/article6895829.ece.

Toch, H. (1972) *Violent Men*, Harmondsworth: Penguin.

Today's *Zaman* (2009) 'Probation becomes an effective instrument for forestation'. Available online at: http://www.todayszaman.com/tz-web/detaylar.do?load=print&link=178653&yazarAd=.

Tombs, S. and Whyte, D. (2008) *A Crisis of Enforcement: The Decriminalisation of Death and Injury at Work*, London: Centre for Crime and Justice Studies. Available online at: http://www.crimeandjustice.org.uk/acrisisofenforcement.html.

Tonry, M. (1994) 'Proportionality, parsimony and interchangeability of punishments', in A. Duff and D. Garland (eds) *A Reader on Punishment*, Oxford: Oxford University Press.

Tonry, M. (1998) 'Intermediate sanctions', in M. Tonry (ed.) *The Handbook of Crime and Punishment*, New York: Oxford University Press.

Tonry, M. (2004) *Punishment and Politics: Evidence and Emulation in the Making of English Crime Control Policy*, Cullompton: Willan Publishing.

Trotter, C (1999) *Working with Involuntary Clients: A Guide to Practice*, London: Sage.

Tuddenham, R. (2000) 'Beyond defensible decision-making: towards reflexive assessment of risk and dangerousness', *Probation Journal*, 47 (3): 173–183.

Tyler, T. (2003) 'Procedural justice, legitimacy and the effective rules of law', *Crime and Justice* 30: 431–505.

Underdown, A. (1998) *Strategies for Effective Supervision: Report of the HMIP What Works Project*, London: HM Inspectorate of Probation.

van Kalmthout, A. and Derks, J. (eds) (2000) *Probation and Probation Services – A European Perspective*, Nijmegen, The Netherlands: Wolf Legal Publishers.

van Kalmthout, A. and Durnescu, I. (eds) (2008) *Probation in Europe* (2nd edn), Nijmegen: Wolf Legal Publishers.

van Zyl Smit, D. and Ashworth, A. (2004) 'Disproportionate sentences as human rights violations', *Modern Law Review*, 67 (4): 541–560.

Vanstone, M. (2000) 'Cognitive-behavioural work with offenders in the UK: a history of influential endeavour', *Howard Journal* 39 (2): 171–183.

Vanstone, M. (2004a) 'Mission control: the origins and early history of probation', *Probation Journal*, 51 (1): 34–47.

Vanstone, M. (2004b) *Supervising Offenders in the Community: A History of Probation Theory and Practice*, Aldershot: Ashgate.

Vanstone, M. (2008) 'The international origins and initial development of probation: an early example of policy transfer', *British Journal of Criminology* 48 (6): 735–755.

Vaughan, B. (2007) 'The internal narrative of desistance', *British Journal of Criminology*, 47 (3): 390–404.

von Hirsch, A. (1996) *Censure and Sanctions*, Oxford: Oxford University Press.

Victim Support (2007) *Hoodie or Goodie? The Link between Violent Victimisation and Offending in Young People*. Available online at: http://www.victimsupport.org.uk/About%20us/Publications/~/media/Files/Publications/ResearchReports/hoodie-or-goodie-report.

Walker, A. (1993) *Possessing the Secret of Joy*, London: Vintage.

Walker, H. and Beaumont, B. (1981) *Probation Work: Critical Theory and Socialist Practice*, Oxford: Blackwell.

Walker, N. (1980) *Punishment, Danger and Stigma: The Morality of Criminal Justice*, Oxford: Blackwell.

Walker, N. (1991) *Why Punish?* Oxford: Oxford University Press.

Walker, N. (ed.) (1996) *Dangerous People*, London: Blackstone.

Walker, N. (1999) *Aggravation, Mitigation and Mercy in English Criminal Justice*, London: Blackstone.

Walklate, S. (ed.) (2007) *Handbook of Victims and Victimology*, Cullompton: Willan.

Walmsley, R. (2009) World Prison Population List (8th edn), London: ICPS. Available online at: http://www.kcl.ac.uk/depsta/law/research/icps/downloads.php?searchtitle=world+prison&type=0&month=0&year=0&lang=0&author=&search=Search.

Walters, J. (2003) 'Trends and Issues in probation in Europe' – paper delivered to PACCOA Conference, Hobart, Tasmania, 1 September 2003. Available online at: http://www.paccoa.com.au/PDF%20files/John%20Walters.pdf.

Ward, T. and Brown, M. (2004) 'The good lives model and conceptual issues in offender rehabilitation', *Psychology, Crime & Law*, 10 (3): 243–257.

Ward, T. and Maruna, S. (2007) *Rehabilitation*, London: Routledge.

Wargent, M. (2002) 'The new governance of probation', *Howard Journal* 41 (2): 182–200.

Weaver, B. and McNeill, F. (2007) 'Desistance', in DPOM.

Wedge, P. (2007) 'Children and families of offenders', in DPOM.

Wham, C. (2007) 'Correctional Services Accreditation Panel', in DPOM.

Whitehead, P. (2008) 'The probation service reporting for duty', *British Journal of Community Justice*, 6 (3): 86–96.

Whitehead, P. (2010)´Social theory and probation: exploring organisational complexity within a modernising context', *Social and Public Policy Review*, 4 (2): 15–33.

Whitehead, P. and Statham, R. (2006) *The history of probation: politics, power and cultural change 1876–2005*, Crayford: Shaw and Sons.

Whitfield, D. (2001) *Introduction to the Probation Service* (2nd edn), Winchester: Waterside.

Whyte, B. (2007) 'Scottish courts and sanctions', in DPOM.

Williams, B. (ed.), *Reparation and Victim-Focused Social Work*, London: Jessica Kingsley.

Williams, B. (2007) 'Victims', in DPOM.

Williams, B. (2008) 'The changing face of probation in prisons', in J. Bennett, B. Crewe and A. Wahidin (eds) *Understanding Prison Staff*, Cullompton: Willan.

Williams, B. and Goodman, H. (2007) 'Working for and with victims of crime', in L. Gelsthorpe and R. Morgan (eds) *Handbook of Probation*, Cullompton: Willan.

Willis, A. (1977) 'Community service as an alternative to imprisonment: a cautionary view', *Probation Journal*, 24 (4): 120–125.

Woolf, Lord Justice (1991) *Prison Disturbances April 1990: Report of an Inquiry by the Rt. Hon. Lord Justice Woolf (Part I and II) and His Honour Judge Stephen Tumin (Part II)*, Cm. 1456, London: HMSO.

Wootton, B. (1978) *Crime and Penal Policy: Reflections on Fifty Years' Experience*, London: George Allen and Unwin.

Worrall, A. and Hoy, C. (2005) *Punishment in the Community: Managing offenders, making choices* (2nd edn), Cullompton: Willan.

Wright, M. (2008) *Making Good: Prisons, Punishment and Beyond* (2nd edn), Winchester: Waterside Press.

Wright, M. (2010) *Towards a Restorative Society: A Problem-solving Approach to Harm.* Available online at: http://makejusticework.org.uk/wp-content/uploads/2010/04/Martin-Wright-_-Towards-a-Restorative-Society.pdf.

Zedner, L. (2004) *Criminal Justice*, Oxford: Oxford University Press.

References

The Prison Officer

* Denotes recommended further reading.

Advisory Council on the Penal System (ACPS) (1968) *The Regime for Long-Term Prisoners in Conditions of Maximum Security*, The Radzinowicz Report. London: HMSO.

Ahmad, S. (1996) *Fairness in Prisons*. PhD thesis, University of Cambridge.

Annual Survey of Hours and Earnings (ASHE) (2005) See website: http://www.statistics.gov.uk/statbase/product.asp?vlnk=13101.

Arnold, H. (2005) 'The effects of prison work', in A. Liebling and S. Maruna (eds), *The Effects of Imprisonment*. Cullompton: Willan, pp. 391–420.

Arnold, H. (2008) 'The experience of prison officer training', in J. Bennett, B. Crewe and A. Wahidin (eds), *Understanding Prison Staff*. Cullompton: Willan, pp. 399–418.

*Arnold, H., Liebling, A. and Tait, S. (2007) 'Prison officers and prison culture', in Y. Jewkes (ed.), *Handbook on Prisons*. Cullompton: Willan, pp. 471–95.

Ayres, I. and Braithwaite, J. (1992) *Responsive Regulation – Transcending the Deregulation Debate*. Oxford: Oxford University Press.

Baldwin, R., Scott, C. and Hood, C. (1998) *A Reader on Regulation*. Oxford: Oxford University Press.

Banton, M. (1964) *The Policeman in the Community*. London: Tavistock.

Barry, A., Osborne, T. and Rose, N. (1996) *Foucault and Political Reason*. London: UCL Press.

Bauman, Z. (1989) *Modernity and the Holocaust*. Cambridge: Polity Press.

Ben-David, S. (1992) 'Staff-to-inmate relations in a total institution: a model of five modes of association', *International Journal of Offender Therapy and Comparative Criminology*, 36 (3): 209–21.

Ben-David, S. and Silfen, P. (1994) 'In quest of a lost father? Inmates' preferences of staff relation in a psychiatric prison ward', *International Journal of Offender Therapy and Comparative Criminology*, 38 (2): 131–9.

*Bennett, J., Crewe, B. and Wahidin, A. (eds) (2007) *Understanding Prison Staff*. Cullompton: Willan.

218

Biggam, F. H. and Power, K. G. (1997) 'Social support and psychological distress in a group of incarcerated young offenders', *International Journal of Offender Therapy*, 41 (3): 213–30.

Bittner, E. (1967) 'The police on skid row: a study of peacekeeping', *American Sociological Review*, 32 (5): 699–715.

Bottomley, A. K. (1994) *CRC Special Units: A General Assessment*. London: Home Office.

Bottomley, A. K., James, A., Clare, E. and Liebling, A. (1997) *An Evaluation of Wolds Remand Prison*, Research Findings No. 32. Home Office: London.

*Bottoms, A. E. (1989) 'The aims of imprisonment', in D. Garland (ed.), *Justice, Guilt, and Forgiveness in the Penal System*, Centre for Theology and Public Issues Occasional Paper No. 18. Edinburgh: University of Edinburgh, pp. 3–33.

Bottoms, A. E. (1995) 'The philosophy and politics of punishment and sentencing', in R. Morgan and C. M. V. Clarkson (eds), *The Politics of Sentencing Reform*. Oxford: Clarendon Press, pp. 17–49.

Bottoms, A. E. (1998) 'Five puzzles in von Hirsch's theory of punishment', in A. Ashworth and M. Wasik (eds), *Fundamentals of Sentencing Theory: Essays in Honour of Andrew von Hirsch*. Oxford: Clarendon Press, pp. 53–100.

Bottoms, A. E. (1999) 'Interpersonal violence and social order in prisons', in M. Tonry and J. Petersilia (eds), *'Prisons', Crime and Justice: A Review of Research*, Vol. XXVI. Chicago: University of Chicago Press, pp. 205–82.

Bottoms, A. E. (2000) 'Evaluation of a policy initiative', in A. E. Bottoms *Restorative Justice in Sociological Perspective*. Paper delivered at Restorative Justice Symposium: Cambridge, 7–8 October 2008.

Bottoms, A. E. and Light, R. (1987) *Problems of Long-Term Imprisonment*. Aldershot: Gower.

Bottoms, A. E., Hay, W. and Sparks, R. (1990) 'Situational and social approaches to the prevention of disorder in long-term prisons', *Prison Journal*, 70: 83–95.

Bryans, S. (2007) *Prison Governors: Managing Prisons in a Time of Change*. Cullompton: Willan.

Bryans, S. and Wilson, D. (2000) *The Prison Governor: Theory and Practice*. Aylesbury: Prison Service Journal.

Calvert, D. (2000) *The Role of the Prison Officers' Association*. MSt thesis, University of Cambridge.

Camp, S. D. (1994) 'Assessing the effects of organizational commitment and job satisfaction on turnover: an event history approach', *Prison Journal*, 74 (3): 279–305.

Camp, S. D. (1999) 'Do inmate survey data reflect prison conditions? Using surveys to assess prison conditions of confinement', *Prison Journal*, 79 (2): 250–68.

Carter, P. (2003) *Managing Offenders, Reducing Crime: A new approach*. http://webarchive.nationalarchives.gov.uk/+/http://www.cabinetoffice.gov.uk/strategy/downloads/files/managingoffenders.pdf

Caton, B. (2001) General Secretary of the POA, interviewed in *Prison Service Journal*, March.

Cavadino, M. and Dignan, J. (1997) *The Penal System: An Introduction*. London: Sage.

Chan, J. (1996) 'Changing police culture', *British Journal of Criminology*, 36: 109–34.

Chan, J. (1997) *Changing Police Culture: Policing in a Multicultural Society*. Cambridge: Cambridge University Press.

219

Cheek, F. E. and Miller, M. D. (1983) 'The experience of stress for corrections officers: a double-blind theory of correctional stress', *Journal of Criminal Justice*, 11: 105–20.

Cheliotis, L. K. and Liebling, A. (2006) 'Race matters in British prisons: towards a research agenda', *British Journal of Criminology*, 46: 286–317.

Christie, N. (2000) *Crime Control as Industry: Towards Gulags, Western Style*. London: Routledge.

Clare, E. and Bottomley, A. K. (2001) *An Evaluation of Close Supervision Centres*, Home Office Research Study No. 219. London: HMSO.

Cohen, S. and Taylor, I. (1972) *Psychological Survival: The Experience of Long-Term Imprisonment*. London: Penguin.

Colvin, E. (1977) *Prison Officers: A Sociological Portrait of the Uniformed Staff of an English Prison*. PhD thesis, University of Cambridge.

Cooke, D. J. (1989) 'Containing violent prisoners: an analysis of the Barlinnie Special Unit', *British Journal of Criminology*, 29 (2): 129–43.

Cooke, D. J. (1991) 'Violence in prisons: the influence of regime factors', *Howard Journal of Criminal Justice*, 30: 95–109.

Cox, T., Griffiths, A. and Thomson, L. (1997) *The Assessment and Management of Work-Related Stress in Prison Staff*. Nottingham: Centre for Organisational Health and Development.

Crawley, E. (2001) *The Social World of the English Prison Officer: A Study in Occupational Culture*. PhD thesis, Keele University.

Crawley, E. (2004) *Doing Prison Work*. Cullompton: Willan.

Crewe, B. (2006) 'Male prisoners' orientations towards female officers in an English prison', *Punishment and Society*, 8 (4): 395–421.

Crewe, B. (2009) *The Prisoner Society*. Oxford: Oxford University Press.

Crouch, B. and Alpert, G. (1982) 'Sex and occupational socialisation among prison guards: a longitudinal study', *Criminal Justice and Behavior*, 9 (2): 159–76.

Davies, W. and Burgess, P. W. (1988) 'Prison officers' experience as a predictor of risk of attack', *Medicine, Science and the Law*, 28 (2): 135–8.

Deighton, G. and Launay, G. (1993) 'The Blantyre House Experience'. Unpublished report to the Area Manager.

Department of Justice (1997) *Census of State and Federal Correctional Facilities, 1995*. Washington, DC: US Department of Justice.

Ditchfield, J. (1990) *Control in Prisons*. London: HMSO.

Ditchfield, J. (1997) 'Assaults on Staff in Male Closed Establishments: A Statistical Study'. Unpublished report, Prison Service.

Dixon, D. (1997) *Law in Policing: Legal Regulations and Policing Practices*. Oxford: Clarendon Press.

Downes, D. (1988) *Contrasts in Tolerance*. Oxford: Clarendon Press.

Drake, D. (2008) 'Staff and order in prisons', in J. Bennett, B. Crewe and A. Wahidin (eds), *Understanding Prison Staff*. Cullompton: Willan, pp. 153–67.

Driscoll, W. (1997) From Bill Driscoll: *Prison Britain III – Fresh Start*, BBC Radio 4, 5 August.

Dunbar, I. (1985) *A Sense of Direction*. London: Home Office.

Dworkin, R. (1977) *Taking Rights Seriously*. Cambridge, MA: Harvard University Press.

Elliott, C. (1999) *Locating the Energy for Change: A Practitioner's Guide to Appreciative Inquiry*. Winnipeg: International Institute for Sustainable Development.

220

*Elliott, C., Liebling, A. and Arnold, H. (2001) 'Locating the energy for change: appreciative inquiry in two local prisons', *Prison Service Journal*, 135: 3–10.

Emery, F. (1970) *Freedom and Justice within Walls: The Bristol Prison Experiment*. London: Tavistock.

Enterkin, J. (1996) *Female Prison Officers in Men's Prisons*. PhD thesis, University of Cambridge.

Evershed, S. and Fry, C. (1991) 'Parkhurst Special Unit: the first two years', in R. Walmsley (ed.), *Managing Difficult Prisoners: The Parkhurst Special Unit*. London: Home Office.

Farkas, M. A. (1999) 'Correctional officer attitudes toward inmates and working with inmates in a "get tough" era', *Journal of Criminal Justice*, 27 (6): 495–506.

Farnworth, L. (1992) 'Women doing a man's job: female prison officers working in a male prison', *Australian and New Zealand Journal of Criminology*, 25 (3): 278–96.

Federal Bureau of Prisons website: http://www.bop.gov.

Feeley, M. and Simon, J. (1992) 'The new penology', *Criminology*, 30 (4): 449–74.

Ferlie, E., Pettigrew, A., Ashburner, L. and Fitzgerald, L. (1996) *The New Public Management in Action*. Oxford: Oxford University Press.

Fleisher, M. (1989) *Warehousing Violence*. London: Sage.

Gadd, V. (in progress) 'Effective Senior Management Teams in Public Sector Prisons'. PhD thesis.

Gadd, V. and Shefer, G. with the assistance of Liebling, A., Tait, S. and McLean, C. (2007) 'Measuring the Quality of Prison Life: Staff Survey'. Unpublished report to the Prison Service – Institute of Criminology, Cambridge University.

Galligan, D. (1986) *Discretionary Powers*. Oxford: Clarendon Press.

*Garland, D. (1990) *Punishment and Modern Society*. Oxford: Clarendon Press.

Garland, D. and Sparks, R. (2000) 'Criminology, social theory and the challenge of our times', *British Journal of Criminology*, 40 (2): 189–204.

Genders, E. and Player, E. (1995) *Grendon: A Study of a Therapeutic Prison*. Oxford: Clarendon Press.

Giddens, A. (1984) *The Constitution of Society*. Cambridge: Polity Press.

Giddens, A. (1990) *The Consequences of Modernity*. Cambridge: Polity Press.

*Gilbert, M. J. (1997) 'The illusion of structure: a critique of the classical model of organisation and the discretionary power of correctional officers', *Criminal Justice Review*, 22 (1): 49–64.

Gilligan, C. (1986) *In a Different Voice: Psychological Theory and Women's Development*. Cambridge, MA: Harvard University Press.

Goffman, E. (1961) *Asylums: Essays on the Social Situation of Mental Patients and Other Inmates*. Harmondsworth: Penguin.

Goffman, E. (1968) 'On the characteristics of total institutions: staff–inmate relations', in D. Cressey (ed.), *The Prison: Studies in Institutional Organisation and Change*. New York: Holt, Rinehart & Winston.

Goodin, R. E. (1986) 'Welfare, rights, and discretion', *Oxford Journal of Legal Studies*, 6 (3): 232–61.

Grounds, A., Howes, M. and Gelsthorpe, L. (2003) 'Discretion in access to forensic psychiatric units', in L. Gelsthorpe and N. Padfield (eds), *Exercising Discretion: Decision-making in the Criminal Justice System and Beyond*. Cullompton: Willan, pp. 125–38.

221

Haney, C., Banks, C. and Zimbardo, P. (1973) 'Interpersonal dynamics in a simulated prison', *International Journal of Criminology*, 1: 69–97.

Harding, R. (1997) *Private Prisons and Public Accountability*. Buckingham: Open University Press.

Harrison, R. (1992) 'The equality of mercy', in H. Gross and R. Harrison (eds), *Jurisprudence: Cambridge Essays*. Oxford: Clarendon Press.

Hart, H. L. A. (1958) 'Dias and Hughes on Jurisprudence', *Society of Public Teachers of Law*, 4: 144–5.

Harvey, J. (2007) *Young Men in Prison: Surviving and Adapting to Life Inside*. Cullompton: Willan.

Hawkins, G. (1976) *The Prison: Policy and Practice*. Chicago: University of Chicago.

Hawkins, K. (1984) *Environment and Enforcement*. Oxford: Clarendon Press.

Hawkins, K. (1992) *The Uses of Discretion*. Oxford: Clarendon Press.

*Hay, W. and Sparks, R. (1991) 'What is a prison officer?', *Prison Service Journal*, Spring, pp. 2–7.

Hemmens, C. and Stohr, M. K. (2000) *RSAT in Idaho: A Comparison of Inmate and Staff Perceptions of the Programme*. Paper presented at the American Society of Criminology Conference, San Francisco.

Hepburn, J. R. (1985) 'The exercise of power in coercive organisations: a study of prison guards', *Criminology*, 23 (1): 145–64.

Hepburn, J. R. (1987) 'The prison control structure and its effects on work attitudes: the perceptions and attitudes of prison guards', *Journal of Criminal Justice*, 15: 49–64.

HMCIP (1987) *Report of an Inquiry by Her Majesty's Chief Inspector of Prisons for England and Wales into the Disturbances in Prison Service Establishments in England between 29 April–2 May 1986*. London: HMSO.

HMCIP (1993a) *Doing Time or Using Time*. London: Home Office.

HMCIP (1993b) *Inspection of HM Prison Blantyre House*. London: Home Office.

HMCIP (1993c) *Unannounced Inspection of HM Prison Grendon*. London: Home Office.

HMCIP (2000) *Annual Report 1998–1999*. London: Home Office.

HMP Risley (2000) *The Personal Officer*. Booklet produced by HMP Risley.

Hofling, K. C., Brotzman, E., Dalrymple, S., Graves, N. and Pierce, C. M. (1966) 'An experimental study in the nurse–physician relationship', *Journal of Nervous and Mental Disorders*, 143: 171–80.

Holloway, K. (2000) *Mental-Health Review Tribunals*. PhD thesis, University of Cambridge.

Home Office (1979) *Committee of Inquiry into the United Kingdom Prison Service*, The May Inquiry, Cmnd 7673. London: HMSO.

Home Office (1984) *Managing the Long-term Prison System: The Report of the Control Review Committee*. London: Home Office.

Home Office (1987) *Special Units for Long-Term Prisoners: Regimes, Management and Research*. London: HMSO.

Home Office (1991) *Prison Disturbances 1990*, The Woolf Report. London: HMSO.

Home Office (1994) *The Escape from Whitemoor Prison on Friday, 9th September 1994*, The Woodcock Report, Cmnd 2741. London: HMSO.

Home Office (1995) *Review of Prison Service Security in England and Wales*, The Learmont Report, Cmnd 3020. London: HMSO.

Home Office (1997) Prison Disciplinary Statistics.

Home Office (2000) *Modernising the Management of the Prison Service: An Independent Report by the Targeted Performance Initiative Working Group*, The Laming Report. London: Home Office.

222

Home Office Prison Service (1987) *Fresh Start – The New Improvements*, Bulletin 8. London: HM Prison Service.

Hood, C. (1991) 'A public management for all seasons', *Public Administration*, 69 (1): 3–19.

House of Commons (2003–4) HC Deb (2003–2004) 422, written answers, col. 1170W–1171W.

House of Commons Justice Committee (2009) *Report on the Role of the Prison Officer*. Online at: http://www.publications.parliament.uk/pa/cm200809/cmselect/cmjust/361/36102.htm.

Huckabee, R. G. (1992) 'Stress in corrections: an overview of the issues', *Journal of Criminal Justice*, 20: 479–86.

Jacobs, J. B. (1977) *Stateville: The Penitentiary in Mass Society*. Chicago: Chicago University Press.

Jacobs, J. B. (1978) 'What prison guards think: a profile of the Illinois Force', *Crime and Delinquency*, April, pp. 185–96.

Jacobs, J. B. and Crotty, N. M. (1978) *Guard Unions and the Future of Prisons*. New York: Institute of Public Employment Monograph.

James, A. L., Bottomley, A. K., Liebling, A. and Clare, E. (1997) *Privatising Prisons: Rhetoric and Reality*. London: Sage.

James, C. (2000) *Meeting Each Other's Needs: An Explanation of the Interrelationship Between Local and National Industrial Relations*. MSt thesis, University of Cambridge.

Jefferson, T. and Carlen, P. (1996) 'Masculinities, social relations, and crime', *British Journal of Criminology*, Special Edition.

Jefferson, T. and Grimshaw, R. (1984) *Controlling the Constable: Police Accountability in England and Wales*. London: Sage.

Johnson, R. (1977) 'Ameliorating prison stress: some helping roles for custodial personnel', *International Journal of Criminology and Penology*, 5: 263–73.

Johnson, R. and Price, S. (1981) 'The complete correctional officer: human service and the human environment in prison', *Criminal Justice and Behaviour*, 8: 343–73.

Joint Industrial Relations Procedural Agreement (2004) Voluntary Agreement (JIRPA).

Jones, K. and Fowles, A. J. (1984) *Ideas on Institutions: Analysing the Literature on Long-Term Care and Custody*. London: Routledge & Kegan Paul.

Jurik, N. (1985) 'Individual and organizational determinants of correctional officers' attitudes towards inmates', *Criminology*, 23: 523–39.

Kauffman, K. (1988) *Prison Officers and Their World*. Cambridge, MA: Harvard University Press.

King, R. D. and McDermott, K. (1995) *The State of Our Prisons*. Oxford: Oxford University Press.

King, R. D. and Morgan, R. (1979) *The Future of the Prison System*. Farnborough: Gower.

Klofas, J. (1986) 'Discretion among correctional officers: the influence of urbanization, age and race', *International Journal of Offender Therapy and Comparative Criminology*, 30: 11–124.

Klofas, J. and Toch, H. (1982) 'Alienation and desire for job enrichment among correction officers', *Federal Probation*, 46 (1): 35–47.

Kriminalforsorgens Uddannelsescenter (1994) *Indstilling Om Konfliktforebyggelse Og-Losning*. Copenhagen: Kriminalforsorgens Uddannelsescenter.

223

Laming, Lord (2000) *Modernising the Management of the Prison Service*. London: Home Office.

Lasky, G. L., Gordon, B. C. and Srebalus, D. J. (1986) 'Occupational stressors among federal correctional officers working in different security levels', *Criminal Justice and Behaviour*, 13 (3): 317–27.

Lewis, D. (1997) *Hidden Agendas*. London: Hamish Hamilton.

Liebling, A. (1992) *Suicides in Prison*. London: Routledge.

Liebling, A. (1995) 'Vulnerability and prison suicide', *British Journal of Criminology*, 35 (2): 173–87.

Liebling, A. (1999) 'Doing prison research: breaking the silence?', *Theoretical Criminology*, 3 (2): 147–73.

*Liebling, A. (2000) 'Prison officers, policing, and the use of discretion', *Theoretical Criminology*, 4 (3): 333–57.

Liebling, A. (2008a) 'Why prison staff culture matters', in J. M. Byrne, D. Hummer and F. S. Taxman (eds), *The Culture of Prison Violence*. New York: Pearson, pp. 105–22.

Liebling, A. (2008b) 'Incentives and earned privileges revisited: fairness, discretion, and the quality of prison life', *Journal of Scandinavian Studies in Criminology and Crime Prevention*, 9: 25–41.

Liebling, A. (ed.) (in progress) *Prison Officers, Relationships and Prison Culture*.

Liebling, A. and Krarup, H. (1993) *Suicide Attempts and Self-Injury in Male Prisons*. London: Home Office Research and Planning Unit.

Liebling, A. and Price, D. (1999) *An Exploration of Staff–Prisoner Relationships at HMP Whitemoor*, Prison Service Research Report No. 6. London: Prison Service.

Liebling, A. and Sparks, R. (2000) Interview with Martin Narey.

Liebling, A. and Tait, S. (2006) 'Improving staff–prisoner relationships', in G. E. Dear (ed.), *Preventing Suicide and Other Self-Harm in Prison*. London: Palgrave-Macmillan, pp. 103–17.

Liebling, A., Tait, S., Stiles, A., Durie, L. and Harvey, J.; assisted by Rose, G. (2005) *An Evaluation of the Safer Locals Programme*, Report submitted to the Home Office, pp. 215.

*Liebling, A., assisted by Arnold, H. (2004) *Prisons and Their Moral Performance: A Study of Values, Quality and Prison Life*. Oxford: Oxford University Press.

Liebling, A., Elliott, C. and Arnold, H. (2001) 'Transforming the prison: romantic optimism or appreciative realism?', *Criminal Justice*, 1 (2): 161–80.

Liebling, A., Price, D. and Elliott, C. (1999) 'Appreciative inquiry and relationships in prison', *Punishment and Society*, 1 (1): 71–98.

Liebling, A., Muir, G., Rose, G. and Bottoms, A. (1997) *An Evaluation of Incentives and Earned Privileges: Final Report to the Prison Service*. Cambridge: Institute of Criminology.

Livingstone, S. and Owen, T. (1998) *Prison Law*. Oxford: Oxford University Press.

Lombardo, L. (1981) *Guards Imprisoned: Correctional Officers at Work*. New York: Elsevier.

Long, N., Shouksmith, G., Voges, K. E. and Roache, S. (1986) 'Stress in prison staff: an occupational study', *Criminology*, 24 (2): 331–45.

Loucks, N. (2000) *Prison Rules: A Working Guide*. London: Prison Reform Trust.

Lucas, J. R. (1980) *On Justice*. Oxford: Clarendon Press.

Lygo, R. (1991) *The Management of the Prison Service*. London: Home Office.

McAllister, D., Bottomley, A. K. and Liebling, A. (1992) *From Custody to Community: Throughcare for Young Offenders*. Aldershot: Avebury.

224

McDermott, K. and King, R. (1988) 'Mind games – where the action is in prisons', *British Journal of Criminology*, 28: 357–77.

McDermott, K. and King, R. (1989) 'A Fresh Start: the enhancement of prison regimes', *Howard Journal*, 28 (3): 161–76.

McKenzie, I. K. and Gallagher, G. P. (1989) *Behind the Uniform: Policing in Britain and America*. New York: St. Martin's Press.

McLean, C. and Liebling, A. (2008) 'Prison staff in the public and private sector', in J. Bennett, B. Crewe and A. Wahidin (eds), *Understanding Prison Staff*. Cullompton: Willan, pp. 92–114.

Maguire, M., Vagg, J. and Morgan, R. (1985) *Accountability and Prisons: Opening Up a Closed World*. London: Tavistock.

Mandaraka-Sheppard, A. (1986) *The Dynamics of Aggression in Women's Prisons in England*. Aldershot: Gower.

Marquart, J. W. (1986) 'Prison guards and the use of physical coercion as a mechanism of prisoner control', *Criminology*, 24 (2): 347–66.

Marsh, A., Dobbs, J. and Monk, J. (1985) *Staff Attitudes in the Prison Service*. London: Office of Population Censuses and Surveys.

Martin, J. P. (1991) 'Parkhurst Special Unit: some aspects of management', in R. Walmsley (ed.), *Managing Difficult Prisoners: The Parkhurst Special Unit*. London: Home Office.

Milgram, S. (1974) *Obedience to Authority*. London: Tavistock.

Morgan, R. (1997) 'Imprisonment since World War II', in M. Maguire, R. Morgan and R. Reiner (eds), *The Oxford Handbook of Criminology*. Oxford: Oxford University Press.

Morris, T. and Morris, P. (1963) *Pentonville*. London: Routledge & Kegan Paul.

Muir, W. K. (1977) *Police: Streetcorner Politicians*. Chicago: Chicago University Press.

National Offender Management Service (NOMS) (2008) Foreword by Jack Straw to the Agency Framework Document: http://webarchive.nationalarchives (full document available at: http://www.justice.gov.uk/news/announcement170708a.htm).

Needs, A. (1993) *Hull Special Unit: A Descriptive Report Covering the Third and Fourth Years of Operation*. Unpublished report submitted to the Home Office.

Office for National Statistics (1990) *New Earnings Survey 1990*. London: Office for National Statistics.

Office for National Statistics (1996–9) *New Earnings Survey 1996, 1997, 1998, 1999*. London: Office for National Statistics.

Office for National Statistics (2005) *Annual Survey of Hours and Earnings 2005*. London: Office for National Statistics.

Padfield, N. and Liebling, A., with Arnold, H. (2001) *An Exploration of Decision-Making at Discretionary Lifer Panels*, Home Office Research Study No. 213. London: Home Office.

Personnel Directorate (1997) *Equal Opportunities in the Prison Service*. London: Prison Service.

Pilling, J. (1992) 'Back to Basics: Relationships in the Prison Service', Eve Saville Memorial Lecture, ISTD; reprinted in Revd A. R. Duce (ed.), *Relationships in Prison* (transcript of a Conference held 18–25 April 1993 at Bishop Grossteste College, Lincoln). Lincoln: Bishop of Lincoln.

225

Pogrebin, M. and Poole, E. (1997) 'The sexualised work environment: a look at women jail officers', *Prison Journal*, 77 (1): 41–57.

Pollitt, C. (1993) *Managerialism and the Public Services*. Oxford: Blackwell Business.

Pratt, J. (2000) 'The return of the wheelbarrow men; or the arrival of postmodern penality?', *British Journal of Criminology*, 40 (1): 127–45.

Price, D. and Liebling, A. (1998) 'Staff–Prisoner Relationships: A Review of the Literature'. Unpublished manuscript submitted to the Prison Service.

Prison Governors' Association (2001) *The Key* (magazine of the PGA), January.

Prison Officers' Association (POA) (1963) 'Memorandum on the role of the modern prison officer', *Prison Officers' Magazine*, November, pp. 1–3.

Prison Service (1990) *Report on the Work of the Prison Service 1989–1990*. London: HMSO.

Prison Service (1994) *Prison Service Briefing 74 – Staff Survey*. London: Prison Service.

Prison Service (1997) *Prison Service Review*. London: Prison Service.

Prison Service (2000a) 'Prison Service Staff Survey'. Unpublished report.

Prison Service (2000b) *Prison Service Business Plan 2000–2001*. London: Prison Service.

Prison Service (2000c) *Prison Service Annual Report 1999–2000*. London: Prison Service.

Prison Service (2006) *Prison Service Annual Report 2005–2006*. London: Prison Service.

Prison Service Pay Review Body (2001) see online at: http://www.ome.uk.com/Prison_Service_Pay_Review_Body.aspx

Prison Service Pay Review Body (2005) *Privately Managed Custodial Services*. Liverpool: MCG Consulting.

Prison Service Pay Review Body (2006) *Fifth Report on England and Wales*. Norwich: HMSO.

Prisons Ombudsman (2000) *Annual Report*. London: Home Office.

Punch, M. (1983) 'Officers and men: occupational culture, inter-rank antagonism and the investigation of corruption', in M. Punch (ed.), *Control in the Police Organisation*. Cambridge MA: MIT Press.

Quinn, P. M. (1985) 'Prison management and prison discipline: a case study of change', in M. Maguire, J. Vagg and R. Morgan (eds), *Accountability and Prisons: Opening Up a Closed World*. London: Tavistock.

Quinn, P. M. (1995) 'Reflexivity run riot: the survival of the prison catch-all', *Howard Journal*, 34 (4): 354–62.

Rasmussen, K. and Levander, S. (1996) 'Individual rather than situational characteristics predict violence in a maximum security hospital', *Journal of Interpersonal Violence*, 11 (3): 376–90.

Reiner, R. (1992) 'Police research in the United Kingdom: a critical review', in N. Morris and M. Tonry (eds), *Modern Policing*, Chicago: Chicago University Press.

Reiner, R. (1997) 'Policing and the police', in M. Maguire, R. Morgan and R. Reiner (eds), *The Oxford Handbook of Criminology*. Oxford: Oxford University Press, pp. 997–1050.

Relationships Foundation (1995) *Relational Prison Audits: Methodology and Results of a Pilot Audit – Greenock Prison, November/December 1994*. Cambridge: Relationships Foundation.

Rorty, R. (1989) *Contingency, Irony and Solidarity*. Cambridge: Cambridge University Press.

Rose, N. and Miller, P. (1992) 'Political power beyond the state: problematics of government', *British Journal of Sociology*, 43: 173–205.

Rowan, J. R. (1996) 'Who is safer in maximum security prisons?', *Corrections Today: Journal of the American Correctional Association (ACA)*, 58, April.

Rutherford, A. (1993) *Criminal Justice and the Pursuit of Decency*. Winchester: Waterside Press.

Rynne, J. (2007) Personal communication.

Saylor, W. G. (1984) *Surveying Prison Environments*. Washington, DC: Federal Bureau of Prisons.

Saylor, W. G. and Wright, K. N. (1992) 'Status, longevity, and perceptions of the work environment among federal prison employees', *Journal of Offender Rehabilitation*, 17 (3/4): 133–60.

Scott, A. (1999) 'The Role of the Probation Service in a Local Prison'. MSt thesis, Cambridge University.

Shapira, R. and Navon, D. (1985) 'Staff–inmate co-operation in Israeli prisons: towards a non-functionalist theory of total institutions', *International Review of Modern Sociology*, 15: 131–46.

Shefer, G. and Liebling, A. (2008) 'Prison privatisation: in search of a business-like atmosphere?', *Criminology and Criminal Justice*, 8 (3): 261–78.

Sim, J. (1994) 'Tougher than the rest? Men in prison', in T. Newburn and E. Stanko (eds), *Just Boys Doing Business: Men, Masculinities and Crime*. London: Routledge, pp. 100–17.

Skolnick, J. H. (1966) *Justice Without Trial*. New York: Wiley.

Smith, A. (1759, reissued 2006) *The Theory of Moral Sentiments*, Dover Philosophical Classics Series.

Smith, D. (1986) 'The framework of law and policing practice', in J. Benyon and C. Bourne (eds), *The Police: Powers, Procedures, and Proprieties*. Oxford: Pergamon.

*Sparks, R., Bottoms, A. E. and Hay, W. (1996) *Prisons and the Problem of Order*. Oxford: Clarendon Press.

Stern, V. (1987) *Bricks of Shame*. London: Penguin.

Stern, V. (1993) *Bricks of Shame*, 2nd edn. London: Penguin.

Stohr, M. K., Lovrich, N. P. and Wilson, G. L. (1994) 'Staff stress in contemporary jails: assessing problem severity and the payoff of progressive personnel practices', *Journal of Criminal Justice*, 22 (4): 313–27.

Stohr, M. K., Lovrish, N. P. and Wood, M. J. (1996) 'Service versus security concerns in contemporary jails: testing gender differences in training topic assessments', *Journal of Criminal Justice*, 24 (5): 437–48.

Straw, J. (2008) Foreword to the National Offender Management Service Agency Framework Document 2008 – see NOMS (2008) online at: http://webarchive.nationalarchives.

*Sykes, G. (1958) *The Society of Captives*. Princeton, NJ: Princeton University Press.

Sykes, G. and Brent, E. (1983) *Policing: A Social Behaviourist Perspective*. New Brunswick, NJ: Rutgers University Press.

Tait, S. (2008a) 'Prison officers and gender', in J. Bennett, B. Crewe and A. Wahidin (eds), *Understanding Prison Staff*. Cullompton: Willan.

227

*Tait, S. (2008b) 'Care and the prison officer: beyond "turnkeys" and "carebears"', *Prison Service Journal*, 180: 3–11.

Tait, S. (2008c) *Prison Officer Care for Prisoners in One Men's and One Women's Prison*. PhD thesis, Institute of Criminology, University of Cambridge.

Tait, S., Gadd, V., Shefer, G., Liebling, A. and McLean, C. (in progress) 'Measuring Staff Quality of Life: Implications for Research on Prison Culture'.

Taylor, I. (1999) *Crime in Context: A Critical Criminology of Market Societies*. Oxford: Polity Press.

Thomas, J. E. (1972) *The English Prison Officer since 1850*. London: Routledge & Kegan Paul.

Thornton, D., Curran, L., Grayson, D. and Holloway, V. (1984) *Tougher Regimes in Detention Centres: Report of an Evaluation of the Young Offender Psychology Unit*. London: HMSO.

Toch, H. and Klofas, J. (1982) 'Alienation and desire for job enrichment among correction officers', *Federal Probation*, 46 (1): 35–47.

Triplett, R., Mullings, J. L. and Scarborough, K. E. (1996) 'Work-related stress and coping among correctional officers: implications from organisational literature', *Journal of Criminal Justice*, 24 (4): 291–308.

Twining, W. and Miers, D. (1991) *How to Do Things With Rules*. London: Butterworths.

Tyler, T. R. (1990) *Why People Obey the Law*. London: Yale University Press.

Waddington, P. A. J. (1999) 'Police (canteen) sub-culture: an appreciation', *British Journal of Criminology*, 39 (2): 287–309.

Wheatley, P. (2010) Personal communication.

White, S. and Howard, L. (1994) *Survey of Prison Service Staff 1994*. London: Home Office.

White, S., Howard, L. and Walmsley, R. (1991) *The National Prison Survey 1991: Main Findings*. London: HMSO.

Whitehead, J. T., Linquist, C. and Klofas, J. (1987) 'Correctional officer professional orientation: a replication of the Klofas-Toch Measure', *Criminal Justice and Behavior*, 14 (4): 468–86.

Willett, T. (1983) 'Prison guards in private', *Canadian Journal of Criminology*, 25 (1): 1–18.

Williams, M. (1999) Personal communication.

Williams, M. and Longley, D. (1987) 'Identifying control problem prisoners in long-term dispersal prisons', in A. E. Bottoms and R. Light (eds), *Problems of Long-Term Imprisonment*. Aldershot: Gower.

Williams, T. A. (1983) 'Custody and conflict: an organisational study of prison officers' roles and attitudes', *Australian and New Zealand Journal of Criminology*, 16: 44–55.

Williams, T. A. and Soutar, G. N. (1984) 'Levels of custody and attitude differences among prison officers: a comparative study', *Australian and New Zealand Journal of Criminology*, 17: 87–94.

Wilson, P. (2000) 'Experiences of Staff Working in Close Supervision Centres'. Unpublished MSt thesis, Cambridge University.

Woodbridge, J. (1999) *Review of Comparative Costs and Performance of Privately and Publicly Operated Prisons 1996–97*. London: Prison Service.

Wright, K. N. and Saylor, W. G. (1991) 'Male and female employees' perceptions of prison work: is there a difference?', *Justice Quarterly*, 8 (4): 505–24.

228

Wright, K.N., Saylor, W. G., Gilman, E. and Camp, S. (1997) 'Job control and occupational outcomes among prison workers', *Justice Quarterly*, 14 (3): 525–46.

Zimbardo, P. (2007) *The Lucifer Effect: How Good People Turn Evil*. London: Random House Group/Rider & Co.

229

428

References

Rehabilitation Work

ABC News (2009) 'Cost Blow Out in Prison Overtime', 24 June 2009, http://www.abc.net.au/news/2009-06-24/cost-blow-out-in-prison-overtime/1330518 (Accessed 14 January 2014).

ABC News (2013) 'Upper House Inquiry Finds "Absurd" Prison Overtime Costs Blow the Budget', 13 November 2013, http://www.abc.net.au/news/2013-11-13/prison-overtime-costs-found-to-have-been-absurd/5087692 (Accessed 14 January 2014).

Aho-Mustonen, K., Miettinen, R., Koivisto, H., Timonen, T., and Raty, H. (2008) 'Group Psychoeducation for Forensic and Dangerous Non-forensic Long-term Patients with Schizophrenia: A Pilot Study'. *European Journal of Psychiatry* 22(2): 84–92.

Albertson, K. (2015) 'Creativity, Self-Exploration and Change: Creative Arts-based Activities Contribution to Desistance Narratives'. *The Howard Journal of Criminal Justice* 54(3): 277–291.

Alcohol and Drug Services (ADS) (2014) 'Services' Tasmanian Department of Health and Human Services Alcohol and Drug Service, http://www.dhhs.tas.gov.au/mentalhealth/alcohol_and_drug/services (Accessed 1 February 2014).

Alcohol, Tobacco and other Drugs Council of Tasmania (ATDC) (2011) *Alcohol, Tobacco and Other Drugs Community Sector Organisations Workforce Development Survey 2010.* Hobart: Alcohol, Tobacco and Other Drugs Council of Tasmania.

ATDC (2013a) *2012 Workforce Survey Fact Sheet #1: Community Sector Organisations.* Hobart: Alcohol, Tobacco and Other Drugs Council of Tasmania.

ATDC (2013b) *2012 Workforce Survey Fact Sheet #2: Community Sector ATOD Staff* Hobart: Alcohol, Tobacco and Other Drugs Council of Tasmania.

ATDC (2013c) *2012 Workforce Survey Fact Sheet #3: Workplace Practices.* Hobart: Alcohol, Tobacco and Other Drugs Council of Tasmania.

ATDC (2013d) *2012 Workforce Survey Fact Sheet #4: Professional Development and Training.* Hobart: Alcohol, Tobacco and Other Drugs Council of Tasmania.

ATDC (2013e) *2012 Workforce Survey Fact Sheet #5: Recruitment and Retention.* Hobart: Alcohol, Tobacco and Other Drugs Council of Tasmania.

ATDC (2013f) *2012 Workforce Survey Fact Sheet #6: External Challenges.* Hobart: Alcohol, Tobacco and Other Drugs Council of Tasmania.

ATDC (2013g) *Budget Priorities Statement 2013–2014.* Available online at http://www.atdc.org.au/about-us/atdc-position-papers/ (Accessed 1 May 2013).

ATDC (2014) *Findings from the 2014 ATDC Workforce Survey.* Hobart: Alcohol, Tobacco and Other Drugs Council of Tasmania.

Allen, D. (2004) 'Ethnomethodological Insights into Insider-Outsider Relationships in Nursing Ethnographies of Healthcare Settings'. *Nursing Inquiry* 11(1): 14–24.

Allen, N., and Meyer, J. (1990) 'The Measurement and Antecedents of Affective, Continuance and Normative Commitment to the Organisation'. *Journal of Occupational Psychology* 63: 1–18.

Allsop, S., and Stevens, C. (2009) 'Evidence-based Practice or Imperfect Seduction? Developing Capacity to Respond Effectively to Drug-related Problems'. *Drug and Alcohol Review* 28: 541–549.

Alpkan, L., Bulut, C., Gunday, G., Ulusoy, G., and Kilic, K. (2010) 'Organizational Support for Intrapreneurship and its Interaction with Human Capital to Enhance Innovative Performance'. *Management Decision* 48(5): 732–755.

Altrows, I. (2002) 'Rational Emotive and Cognitive Behaviour Therapy with Adult Male Offenders'. *Journal of Rational Emotive and Cognitive Behaviour Therapy* 20(4): 201–222.

American Psychiatric Association (2013) *The Diagnostic and Statistical Manual of Mental Disorders (DSM 5)* (5th ed.). Washington, D.C: American Psychiatric Publishing.

Andrews, D. (2011) 'The Impact of Nonprogrammatic Factors on Criminal Justice Interventions'. *Legal and Criminological Psychology* 16(1): 1–23.

Andrews, D., and Bonta, J. (1994) *The Psychology of Criminal Conduct*. New Jersey: Lexis Nexis.

Andrews, D., and Bonta, J. (1995) *The Level of Service Inventory–Revised*. Toronto, Canada: Multi-Health Systems.

Andrews, D., and Bonta, J. (2010a) *The Psychology of Criminal Conduct* (5th ed.). New Jersey: LexisNexis.

Andrews, D., and Bonta, J. (2010b) 'Rehabilitating Criminal Justice Policy and Practice'. *Psychology, Public Policy and Law* 16(1): 39–55.

Andrews, D., Bonta, J., and Wormith, S. (2011) 'The Risk-Need-Responsivity (RNR) Model: Does Adding the Good Lives Model Contribute to Effective Crime Prevention?'. *Criminal Justice and Behavior* 38: 735–755.

Andrews, D., and Dowden, C. (2005) 'Managing Correctional Treatment for Reduced Recidivism: A Meta-Analytic Review of Programme Integrity'. *Legal and Criminological Psychology* 10: 173–187.

Anthony, W. (1993) 'Recovery from Mental Illness: The Guiding Vision of the Mental Health Service System in the 1990s'. *Innovations and Research in Clinical Services, Community Support and Rehabilitation* 2: 17–24.

Antoncic, B., and Hisrich, R. (2001) 'Intrapreneurship: Construct Refinement and Cross-Cultural Validation'. *Journal of Business Venturing* 16: 496–527.

Antoncic, B., and Hisrich, R. (2003) 'Clarifying the Intrapreneurship Concept'. *Journal of Small Business and Enterprise Development* 10(1): 7–24.

Ashford, G., and Patkar, S. (2001) *The Positive Path: Using Appreciative Inquiry in Rural Indian Communities*. Winnipeg: International Institute for Sustainable Development.

Australian Bureau of Statistics (ABS) (2008) *National Survey of Health and Wellbeing 2007: Summary of Results*. Canberra: Australian Bureau of Statistics.

Australian Bureau of Statistics (ABS) (2012) *State and Territory Statistical Indicators 2012*. Canberra: Australian Bureau of Statistics.

Australian Bureau of Statistics (ABS) (2013) 'New Data from the 2011 Census Reveals Tasmania's Most Advantaged and Disadvantaged Areas'. Media Release, 28 March 2013.

Australian Bureau of Statistics (ABS) (2014) 'Tasmania', in *Prisoners in Australia, 2014* http://www.abs.gov.au/ausstats/abs@.nsf/Lookup/by%20Subject/4517.0~2014~Main%20 Features~Tasmania~10020 (Accessed 11 October 2015).

Australian Bureau of Statistics (2015) General Social Survey: Summary Results: Australia, 2014. Available online: http://www.abs.gov.au/ausstats/abs@.nsf/mf/4159.0 (Accessed 1 September 2015).

Australian Government Productivity Commission (2013) *Report on Government Services 2013*. Canberra: Steering Committee for the Review of Government Service Provision, Australian Government.

Australian Government Productivity Commission (2015) *Report on Government Services 2015*. Canberra: Steering Committee for the Review of Government Service Provision, Australian Government.

Australian Institute of Health and Welfare (AIHW) (2005) *National Comorbidity Initiative: A Review of Data Collections relating to People with Coexisting Substance Use and Mental Health Disorders*. Canberra: Australian Institute of Health and Welfare.

AIHW (2007) *Homeless SAAP Clients with Mental Health and Substance Use Problems 2004–05*. Canberra: Australian Government.

AIHW (2012) *Alcohol and Other Drug Treatment Services in Australia 2010–2011: Report on the National Minimum Data Set (Drug Treatment Series no. 18)*. Canberra: Australian Institute of Health and Welfare.

AIHW (2013a) *The Health of Australia's Prisoners*. Canberra: The Australian Government Department of Health and Ageing.

AIHW (2013b) *National Minimum Data Set: Alcohol and Other Drug Treatment Services in Australia*. Canberra: Australian Government Department of Health and Ageing.

Australian Prisons Project (2010) *Tasmania: Key Moments in Prison Culture 1970–Present*. Sydney: Australian Prisons Project, University of New South Wales.

Baker, A., and Lee, N. (2003) 'A Review of Psychosocial Interventions for Amphetamine Use'. *Drug and Alcohol Review* 22: 323–335.

Baldry, E. (2010) 'Women in Transition from Prison To ...'. *Current Issues in Criminal Justice* 22(2): 253–267.

Baldry, E., Clarence, M., Douse, L., and Trollor, J. (2013) 'Reducing Vulnerability to Harm in Adults with Cognitive Disabilities in the Australian Criminal Justice System'. *Journal of Policy and Practice in Intellectual Disabilities* 10(3): 222–229.

Baldry, E., Dowse, L., Snoyman, P., Clarence, M., and Webster, I. (2009) 'A Critical Perspective on Mental Health Disorders and Cognitive Disability in the Criminal Justice System', in Cunneen, C., and Salter, M. (eds) *Proceedings of the Second Australia and New Zealand Critical Criminology Conference, 19–20 June 2008, Sydney*. Sydney: Sydney Institute of Criminology.

Barak, G., Leighton, P., and Cotton, A. (2015) *Class, Race, Gender and Crime: The Social Realities of Justice in America* (4th ed.). Lanham, MA: Roman and Littlefield.

Barber, C. (2008) *Comfortably Numb: How Psychiatry is Medicating a Nation*. New York: Pantheon Books.

Barnett, G., and Wood, J. (2008) 'Agency, Relatedness, Inner Peace and Problem Solving in Sexual Offending: How Sexual Offenders Prioritize and Operationalize Their Good Lives Conceptions'. *Sexual Abuse* 20(4): 444–465.

Barry, M. (2009) 'Promoting Desistance Among Young People', in Taylor, W., Earle, R., and Hester, R. (eds.) *Youth Justice Handbook: Theory, Policy and Practice*. Cullompton: Willan Publishing.

Barry, M. (2013) 'Desistance by Design: Offenders' Reflections on Criminal Justice Theory, Policy and Practice'. *European Journal of Probation* 5(2): 47–65.

Bartkowiak-Théron, I., and Travers, M. (eds.) (2013) *The 6th Annual Australian and New Zealand Critical Criminology Conference Proceedings 2012.* Hobart: University of Tasmania.

Bassuk, E., Bucknew, J., Perloff, J., and Bassuk, S. (1998) 'Prevalence of Mental Health and Substance Use Disorders among Homeless and Low Income Housed Mothers'. *American Journal of Psychiatry* 155(1): 1561–1564.

Bauman, Z. (2000) 'Social Issues of Law and Order'. *British Journal of Criminology* 40(2): 205–221.

Bean, P. (2008) *Drugs and Crime* (3rd ed.). Cullompton: Willan Publishing.

Bean, P. (2014) *Drugs and Crime* (4th ed.). London: Routledge.

Beck, A., Rush, A., Shaw, B., and Emery, G. (eds.) (1979) *Cognitive Therapy of Depression.* New York: The Guilford Press.

Beck, U. (1992) *Risk Society: Towards a New Modernity.* London: SAGE.

Becker, H. (1967) 'Whose Side are We On?'. *Social Problems* 14(3): 234–247.

Bellinger, A., and Elliott, T. (2011) 'What are You Looking At? The Potential of Appreciative Inquiry as a Research Approach in Social Work'. *British Journal of Social Work* 41: 708–725.

Benda, B. (2005) 'Gender Differences in Life-Course Theory of Recidivism: A Survival Analysis'. *International Journal of Offender Therapy and Comparative Criminology* 49(3): 325–342.

Bennett, J., Crewe, B., and Wahidin, A. (eds.) (2008) *Understanding Prison Staff.* Cullompton: Willan Publishing.

Bergland, M., Thelander, S., and Jonsson, E. (2003) *Treating Alcohol and Drug Abuse: An Evidence-Based Review.* Weinheim: Wiley.

Best, D., Gow, J., Knox, T., Taylor, A., Groshkova, T., and White, W. (2012) 'Mapping the Recovery Stories of Drinkers and Drug Users in Glasgow: Quality of Life and its Associations with Measures of Recovery Capital'. *Drug and Alcohol Review* 31(3): 334–341.

Best, D., McKitterick, T., Beswick, T., and Savic, M. (2015) 'Recovery Capital and Social Networks among People in Treatment and Among Those in Recovery in York, England'. *Alcoholism Treatment Quarterly* 33(3): 270–282.

Best, D., Rome, A., Hanning, K., White, W., Gossop, M., Taylor, A., and Perkins, A. (2010) *Research for Recovery: A Review of the Drugs Evidence Base.* Edinburgh: Scottish Government Social Research.

Bhaskar, R. (1978) *A Realist Theory of Science.* Brighton: Harvester Press.

Bhaskar, R. (1997) 'On the Ontological Status of Ideas'. *Journal for the Theory of Social Behaviour* 27(2/3): 139–147.

Bhaskar, R. (2008) *A Realist Theory of Science.* London: Routledge.

Bhaskar, R. (2010) *Reclaiming Reality: A Critical Introduction to Contemporary Philosophy.* London: Routledge.

Bhaskar, R., and Danermark, B. (2006) 'Metatheory, Interdisciplinarity and Disability Research: A Critical Realist Perspective'. *Scandinavian Journal of Disability Research* 8(4): 278–297.

Bilby, C., Caulfield, L., and Ridley, L. (n.d.) *Re-Imagining Futures: Exploring Arts Interventions and the Process of Desistance.* London: Arts Alliance, CLINKS.

Birgden, A. (2002) 'Therapeutic Jurisprudence and "Good Lives": A Rehabilitation Framework for Corrections'. *Australian Psychologist* 37(3): 180–186.

Birgden, A. (2004) 'Therapeutic Jurisprudence and Responsivity: Finding the Will and the Way in Offender Rehabilitation'. *Psychology, Crime and Law* 10(3): 283–295.

Blau, J., Light, S., and Chamlin, M. (1986) 'Individual and Contextual Effects on Stress and Job Satisfaction: A Study of Prison Staff'. *Work and Occupations* 13(1): 131–156.

Blumstein, A., and Nakamura, K. (2012) 'Paying a Price, Long After the Crime'. *New York Times*, 9 January 2012.

Boeck, T. Fleming, J., and Kemshall, H. (2006) 'The Context of Risk Decisions: Does Social Capital Make a Difference?'. *Forum: Qualitative Social Research* 7(1): 1.

Bonta, J., and Andrews, D. (2003) 'A Commentary on Ward and Stewart's Model of Human Needs'. *Psychology, Crime and Law* 9(3): 215–218.

Bonta, J., and Andrews, D. (2010) 'Viewing Offender Assessment and Rehabilitation through the Lens of the Risk-Need-Responsivity Model', in McNeill, F., Raynor, P., and Trotter, C. (eds.) (2010) *Offender Supervision: New Directions in Theory, Research and Practice*. Cullompton: Willan Publishing.

Booth, K. (2008) 'Risdonvale: Place, Memory, and Suburban Experience'. *Ethics, Place and Environment: A Journal of Philosophy and Geography* 11(3): 299–311.

Booth, K. (2010) 'Place Matters: Finding Deep Ecology Within Towns and Cities'. Unpublished PhD Thesis, University of Tasmania: Hobart.

Borg, M., and Kristiansen, K. (2004) 'Recovery-Oriented Professionals: Helping Relationships in Mental Health Services'. *Journal of Mental Health* 13(5): 493–505.

Bosker, J., Witteman, C., and Hermanns, J. (2013) 'Agreement about Intervention Plans by Probation Officers'. *Criminal Justice and Behavior* 40(5): 569–581.

Bottoms, A. (2001) 'Compliance with Community Penalties', in Bottoms, A., Gelsthorpe, L., and Rex, S. (eds.) *Community Penalties: Change and Challenges*. Cullompton: Willan Publishing.

Bottoms, A. (2008) 'The Community Dimension of Community Penalties'. *The Howard Journal of Criminal Justice* 47(2): 146–169.

Bottoms, A., and McWilliams, W. (1979) 'A Non-Treatment Paradigm for Probation Practice'. *British Journal of Social Work* 9(2): 159–202.

Bourdieu, P. (1962) 'Les relations entre les sexes dans la société paysanne'' *Les Temps Modernes* 195: 307–331.

Bourdieu, P. (1968) 'Structuralism and Theory of Sociological Knowledge'. *Social Research* 35(4): 681–706.

Bourdieu, P. (1977) *Outline of a Theory of Practice* Cambridge: Cambridge University Press.

Bourdieu, P. (1979/1984) *Distinction: A Social Critique of the Judgment of Taste*. Cambridge: Harvard University Press.

Bourdieu, P. (1980) *The Logic of Practice* (trans.). Cambridge: Polity Press.

Bourdieu, P. (1986) 'Forms of Capital' (pages 241–258) in Richardson, J. (ed.) *Handbook of Theory and Research for the Sociology of Education*. New York: Greenwood.

Bourdieu, P. (1987) 'The Force of Law: Toward a Sociology of the Juridicial Field'. *The Hastings Law Journal* 38: 814–853.

Bourdieu, P. (1989) 'Social Space and Symbolic Power'. *Sociological Theory* 7(1): 14–25.

Bourdieu, P. (1990) *The Logic of Practice* Stanford: Stanford University Press.

Bourdieu, P., and Wacquant, L. (1992) *An Invitation to Reflexive Sociology*. Cambridge: Polity Press.

Bourgeault, I., Hirschkorn, K., and Sainsaulieu, I. (2011) 'Relations Between Professions and Organisations'. *Professions and Professionalism* 1(1): 67–86.

Bourgon, G., and Gutierrez, L. (2012) 'The General Responsivity Principle in Community Supervision: The Importance of Probation Officers Using Cognitive Intervention Techniques and Its Influence on Recidivism'. *Journal of Crime and Justice* 35(2): 149–166.

Bovaird, T. (2007) 'Beyond Engagement and Participation: User and Community Coproduction of Public Services'. *Public Administration Review* 67(5): 846–860.

Bracken, D., Deane, L., and Morrissette, L. (2009) 'Desistance and Social Marginalisation: The Case of Canadian Aboriginal Offenders'. *Theoretical Criminology* 13(1): 61–78.

Braslow, J. (2013) 'The Manufacture of Recovery'. *The Annual Review of Clinical Psychology* 9: 781–809.

Brayford, J., Cowe, F., and Deering, J. (eds.) (2010) *What Else Works? Creative Work with Offenders*. Cullompton: Willan Publishing.

Britton, D. (2003) *At Work in the Iron Cage: The Prison as Gendered Organization*. New York: New York University.

Brown, M., and Ross, S. (2010) 'Mentoring, Social Capital and Desistance: A Study of Women Released from Prison'. *The Australian and New Zealand Journal of Criminology* 43(1): 31–50.

Brown, R., and Lewinsohn, P. (1984) 'A Psychoeducational Approach to the Treatment of Depression: Comparison of Group, Individual and Minimal Contact Procedures'. *Journal of Consulting and Clinical Psychology* 52(5): 774–783.

Browne, B. (1999) 'IMAGINE Chicago: A Chicago Case Study of Intergenerational Appreciative Inquiry', http://appreciativeinquiry.case.edu/intro/bestcasesDetail.cfm?coid=42 (Accessed 10 September 2013).

Buckingham, H. (2009) 'Competition and Contracts in the Voluntary Sector: Exploring the Implications for Homelessness Service Providers in Southampton'. *Policy and Politics* 37(2): 235–254.

Burnett, R. (2007) 'The Personal Touch in Ex-Offender Reintegration'. Paper presented to the Deakin University 3rd Annual *Reintegration Puzzle* Conference 'Fitting the Pieces Together', Sydney, 7–8 May 2007.

Burnett, R., and Maruna, S. (2004) 'So "Prison Works" Does It? The Criminal Careers of 130 Men Released from Prison Under Home Secretary, Michael Howard'. *The Howard Journal of Criminal Justice* 43(4): 390–404.

Calverley, A. (2013) *Cultures of Desistance: Rehabilitation, Reintegration and Ethnic Minorities*. London: Routledge.

Cameron, H., and Telfer, J. (2004) 'Cognitive-Behavioural Group Work: Its Application to Specific Offender Groups'. *Howard Journal of Criminal Justice* 43(1): 47–64.

Canton, R. (2011) *Probation: Working with Offenders*. London: Routledge.

Canton, R., and Hancock, D. (eds.) (2007) *Dictionary of Probation and Offender Management*. Cullompton: Willan Publishing.

Carroll, K., Ball, S., Nich, C., Martino, S., Frankforter, T., Farentinos, C., Kunkel, L., Mikulich-Gilbertson, S., Morgenstern, J., Obert, J., Polcin, D., Snead, N., and Woody, G. (2006) 'Motivational Interviewing to Improve Treatment Engagement and Outcome in Individuals Seeking Treatment for Substance Abuse: A Multi-Site Effectiveness Study'. *Drug and Alcohol Dependence* 81(3): 301–312.

Carlton, B., and Baldry, E. (2013) 'Therapeutic Correctional Spaces, Transcarceral Interventions: Post-Release Support Structures and Realities Experienced by Women in Victoria, Australia', in Carlton, B., and Segrave, M. (eds.) *Women Exiting Prison: Critical Essays on Gender, Post-Release Support and Survival*. London: Routledge.

Carter, B., Bradley, S., Richardson, R., Sanders, R., and Sutton, C. (2006) 'Appreciating What Works: Discovering and Dreaming Alongside People Developing Resilient Services for Young People Requiring Mental Health Services'. *Issues in Mental Health Nursing* 27: 575–594.

Case, S., and Haines, K. (2009) *Understanding Youth Offending: Risk Factor Research, Policy and Practice*. Cullompton: Willan Publishing.

Chapman, S. (2013) *Over Our Dead Bodies: Port Arthur and Australia's Fight for Gun Control*. Sydney: Sydney University Press.

Chapman, S., Alpers, P., Agho, K., and Jones, M. (2006) 'Australia's 1996 Gun Law Reforms: Faster Falls in Firearm Deaths, Firearm Suicides, and a Decade Without Mass Shootings'. *Injury Prevention* 12: 365–372.

Cheliotis, L. (ed.) (2012) *The Arts of Imprisonment: Control, Resistance and Empowerment*. Surrey: Ashgate Publishing.

Cheliotis, L. (2014) 'Decorative Justice: Deconstructing the Relationship between the Arts and Imprisonment'. *International Journal for Crime, Justice and Social Democracy* 3(1): 16–34.

Cherney, A., and Sutton, A. (2007) 'Crime Prevention in Australia: Beyond "What Works?"'. *The Australian and New Zealand Journal of Criminology* 40(1): 65–81.

Cherry, S. (2005) *Transforming Behaviour: Pro-Social Modelling in Practice*. Cullompton: Willan Publishing.

Cherry, S. (2007) 'Pro-Social Modelling', in Canton, R., and Hancock, D. (eds.) *Dictionary of Probation and Offender Management*, Cullompton: Willan Publishing.

Clark, M. (2005) 'Motivational Interviewing for Probation Staff: Increasing the Readiness to Change', *Federal Probation* 69(2): 22–28.

Clarke, G. (1979) 'In Defense of Deinstitutionalization', *Health and Society* 57(4): 461–479.

Coffey, A., and Atkinson, P. (1996) *Making Sense of Qualitative Data*, London: SAGE Publications.

Coghlan, A., Preskill, H., and Catsambas, T. (2003) 'An Overview of Appreciative Inquiry in Evaluation', in Preskill, H., and Coghlan, A. (eds.) *Using Appreciative Inquiry in Evaluation*. Hoboken: John Wiley and Sons.

Cohen, S. (1985) *Visions of Social Control*. Cambridge: Polity Press.

Cohen, S. (1996) 'Crime and Politics: Spot the Difference'. *The British Journal of Sociology* 47(1): 1–21.

Cole, K., and Vaughan, F. (2005) 'The Feasibility of Using Cognitive Behaviour Therapy for Depression Associated with Parkinson's Disease: A Literature Review'. *Parkinsonism and Related Disorders* 11(5): 269–276.

Colom, F., Vieta, E., Sanchez-Moreno, J., Palomin-Ontiniano, R., Reinares, M., Goikolea, J., Bennabarre, A., and Martinez-Aran, A. (2009) 'Group Psychoeducation for Stablised Bipolar Disorders: 5 Year Outcome of a Randomised Clinical Trial'. *British Journal of Psychiatry* 194: 260–265.

Connell, R., Fawcett, B., and Meagher, G. (2009) 'Neoliberalism, New Public Management and the Human Service Professions'. *Journal of Sociology* 45(4): 331–338.

Cooley, C.H. (1902) *Human Nature and the Social Order*. New York: Scribner's.

Cooper, A. (2005) *Stretching the Model of 'Coalitions of the Willing' (Working Paper #1)*. Waterloo: The Centre for International Governance Innovation.

Cooper, D. (ed.) (2011) *Developing Services in Mental Health-Substance Use*. Oxon: Radcliffe Publishing.

Cooper, T., and White, R. (1994) 'Models of Youth Work Intervention', in White, R. (ed.) (2009) *Concepts and Methods of Youth Work*. Hobart: Australian Clearinghouse for Youth Studies.

Cooperrider, D., and Whitney, D. (2000) 'A Positive Revolution in Change: Appreciative Inquiry,' in Cooperrider, D., Sorenson, P., Whitney, D., and Yaeger, T. (eds.) *Appreciative Inquiry*. Champaign, IL: Stipes Publishing.

Copeland, J., Swift, W., Roffman, R., and Stephens, R. (2001) 'A Randomized Control Trial of Brief Cognitive-Behavioral Interventions for Cannabis Use Disorder'. *Journal of Substance Abuse Treatment* 21(2): 55–64.

Cosgrove, F., and Francis, P. (2011) 'Ethnographic Research in the Context of Policing' in Davies, P., Francis, P., and Jupp, V. (eds.) *Doing Criminological Research* (2nd ed.). London: SAGE Publications.

Coulson, S. (2007) 'Person-Centred Planning as Co-Production', in Hunter, S., and Ritchie, P. (eds.) *Co-Production and Personalisation in Social Care: Changing Relationships in the Provision of Social Care (Research Highlights 49)*. London: Jessica Kingsley Publishers.

Crawford, A., and Hucklesby, A. (eds.) (2013) *Legitimacy and Compliance in Criminal Justice*. London: Routledge.

Crawley, E., and Crawley, P. (2008) 'Understanding Prison Officers: Culture, Cohesion and Conflicts', in Bennett, J., Crewe, B., and Wahidin, A. (eds.) *Understanding Prison Staff*. Cullompton: Willan Publishing.

Craze, L., and Mendoza, J. (2011) *Building Capacity in Non-Government Alcohol and Drug Services – The Queensland Experience – A Tough but Perfect Confluence*. Brisbane: Queensland Network of Alcohol and Drug Agencies (QNADA).

Crossley, M., and Crossley, N. (2001) '"Patient" Voices, Social Movements and the Habitus: How Psychiatric Survivors "Speak Out"'. *Social Sciences and Medicine* 52: 1477–1489.

Croton, G. (2011) 'An Australian Rural Service System's Journey Towards Systemic Mental Health-Substance Use Capability', in Cooper, D. (ed.) *Developing Services in Mental Health-Substance Use*. Oxon: Radcliffe Publishing.

Cullen, F. (2005) 'The Twelve People Who Saved Rehabilitation: How the Science of Criminology Made a Difference'. *Criminology* 43(1): 1–42.

Cullen, F. (2012) 'Taking Rehabilitation Seriously: Creativity, Science and the Challenge of Offender Change'. *Punishment and Society* 14(1): 94–114.

Cullen, F., and Gendreau, P. (2000) 'Assessing Correctional Rehabilitation: Policy, Practice and Contexts'. *Criminal Justice* 3: 109–175.

Cullen, F., and Gilbert, K. (2013) *Reaffirming Rehabilitation* (2nd ed.). Waltham, MA: Anderson Publishing.

Cunneen, C. (2005) 'Racism, Discrimination and the Over-representation of Indigenous People in the Criminal Justice System'. *Current Issues in Criminal Justice* 17(3): 329–346.

Cunneen, C., Baldry, E., Brown, D., Brown, M., Schwartz, M., and Steel, A. (2013) *Penal Culture and Hyperincarceration: The Revival of the Prison*. Surrey: Ashgate Publishing.

Cursley, J., and Maruna, S. (2015) *A Narrative-Based Evaluation of 'Changing Tunes' Music-Based Prisoner Reintegration Interventions – Full Report* England. Available online: http://www.artsevidence.org.uk/media/uploads/final-report-cursley-and-maruna-changing-tunes.pdf (Accessed 5 October 2015).

Danermark, B., Ekström, M., Jacobsen, L., and Karlsson, J. (2002) *Explaining Society: Critical Realism in the Social Sciences*. London: Routledge.

Davison, G., Neale, J., and Kring, A. (2004) *Abnormal Psychology* (9th ed.). Hoboken, NJ: John Wiley and Sons.

Day, A., Casey, S., Ward, T., Howells, K., and Vess, J. (2010) *Transitions to Better Lives: Offender Readiness and Rehabilitation*. Cullompton: Willan Publishing.

Deegan, G. (2003) 'Discovering Recovery'. *Psychiatric Rehabilitation Journal* 26(4): 368–376.

Degenhardt, L., Randall, D., Hall, W., Law, M., Butler, T., and Burns, L. (2009) 'Mortality Among Clients of a State-Wide Opioid Pharmacotherapy Program Over 20 Years: Risk Factors and Lives Saved'. *Drug and Alcohol Dependence* 105(2): 9–15.

Delany, P., Fletcher, B., and Shields, J., (2003) 'Reorganizing Care for the Substance Using Offender – The Case for Collaboration'. *Federal Probation* 67(2): 64–67.

De Leon, G. (1996) 'Integrative Recovery: A Stage Paradigm'. *Substance Abuse* 17(1): 51–63.

Department of Health and Human Services (2014) 'Alcohol and Drug Services in Tasmania: Our Aim' http://www.dhhs.tas.gov.au/mentalhealth/alcohol_and_drug (Accessed 1 December 2014).

Department of Health and Human Services (n.d.) 'Tobacco Control', http://www.dhhs.tas.gov.au/publichealth/tobacco_control (Accessed 26 April 2013).

Department of Treasury and Finance (2015) *Population*. The State Government of Tasmania: Hobart. Available at: https://www.treasury.tas.gov.au/domino/dtf/dtf.nsf/LookupFiles/Population.pdf/$file/Population.pdf (Accessed 1 November 2015).

Dickens, C. (1859, 2003) *A Tale of Two Cities* (Reprint). London: Penguin Classics.

Digard, L., and Liebling, A. (2012) 'Harmony Behind Bars: Evaluating the Therapeutic Potential of a Prison-based Music Programme', in Cheliotis, L. (ed.) *The Arts of Imprisonment: Control, Resistance and Empowerment*. Surrey: Ashgate Publishing.

Dolan, K., Rouen, D., and Kimber, J. (2004) 'An Overview of the Use of Urine, Hair, Sweat and Saliva to Detect Drug Use'. *Drug and Alcohol Review* 23(2): 213–218.

Dorrepaal, E., Thomaes, K., Smit, J., van Balkom, A., van Dyck, R., Veltman, D., and Draijer, N. (2010) 'Stabilizing Group Treatment for Complex Posttraumatic Stress Disorder Related to Childhood Abuse Based on Psycho-Education and Cognitive Behavioural Therapy: A Pilot Study'. *Child Abuse and Neglect* 34: 284–288.

Douglas, B., and McDonald, D. (2012) *The Prohibition of Illicit Drugs is Killing and Criminalising Our Children and We are Letting it Happen (Report of a High Level Australia 21 Roundtable)*. Weston, ACT: Australia 21.

Dowden, C., and Andrews, D. (2000) 'Effective Correctional Treatment and Violent Reoffending: A Meta-Analysis'. *Canadian Journal of Criminology* 42: 449–467.

Dowse, L., Clarence, M., Baldry, E., Trofimovs, J., and James, S. (2011) *People with Mental Disorders and Cognitive Disabilities in the Criminal Justice System: The Impact of Acquired Brain Injury (Report)*. Sydney: Brain Injury Association of NSW and Brain Injury Australia.

Drake, R., Mueser, K., Clark, R., and Wallach, M. (1996) 'The Course Treatment and Outcome of Substance Disorder in Persons with Severe Mental Illness'. *Journal of Orthopsychiatry* 66(1): 42–51.

Dryden, W., and Neenan, M. (2004) *Rational Emotive Behavioural Counselling in Action* (3rd ed.). London: SAGE Publications.

Dudman, J., Isaac, A., and Johnson, S. (2015) 'Revealed: How the Stress of Working Public Services is Taking Its Toll on Staff'. *The Guardian*, 10 June 2015.

Duncan, B., Miller, S., and Sparks, J. (2004) *The Heroic Client: A Revolutionary Way to Improve Effectiveness Through Client Directed, Outcome Informed Therapy* (revised ed.). San Francisco: John Wiley and Sons.

Duraisingam, V. (2005) 'Retention' in Skinner, N., Roche, A., O'Connor, J., Pollard, Y., and Todd, C. (eds.) *Workforce Development TIPS (Theory Into Practice Strategies): A Resource Kit for the Alcohol and Other Drugs Field*. Adelaide: National Centre for Education and Training on Addiction (NCETA), Flinders University.

Duraisingam, V., Pidd, K., and Roche, A.M. (2009) 'The Impact of Work Stress and Job Satisfaction on Turnover Intentions: A Study of Australian Specialist Alcohol and Other Drugs Workers'. *Drugs: Education, Prevention and Policy* 16(3): 217–231.

Duraisingam, V., Pidd, K., Roche, A.M. and O'Connor, J. (2006) *Stress, Satisfaction and Retention among Alcohol and Other Drug Workers in Australia.* Adelaide: National Centre for Education and Training on Addiction (NCETA), Flinders University.

Durnescu, I. (2014) 'Probation Skills Between Education and Professional Socialisation'. *European Journal of Criminology* 11(4): 429–444.

Durnescu, I., and McNeill, F. (eds.) (2013) *Understanding Penal Practice.* London: Routledge.

Eby, L., Burk, H., and Maher, C. (2010) 'How Serious of a Problem is Staff Turnover in Substance Abuse Treatment? A Longitudinal Study of Actual Turnover'. *Journal of Substance Abuse Treatment* 39: 264–271.

Edgar, K., Aresti, A., and Cornish, N. (2012) *Out for Good: Taking Responsibility for Resettlement.* London: Prison Reform Trust.

Egan, G. (2010) *The Skilled Helper: A Problem Management and Opportunity Development Approach to Helping* (9th ed.). Belmont, CA: Brooks/Cole, Cengage Learning.

Ehrenstein, A. (2012) *Precarity and the Crisis of Social Care: Everyday Politics and Experiences of Work in Women's Voluntary Organisations.* Cardiff: PhD thesis, Cardiff University.

Elliott, C. (1999) *Locating the Energy for Change: An Introduction to Appreciative Inquiry.* Winnipeg: International Institute for Sustainable Development.

Ellis, A. (1980) 'Rational-Emotive Therapy and Cognitive Behavioural Therapy: Similarities and Differences'. *Cognitive Therapy and Research* 4(4): 325–340.

Ellis, J., and Gregory, T. (2011) *Demonstrating the Value of the Arts in Criminal Justice.* London: CLINKS.

Emmons, K., and Rollnick, S. (2001) 'Motivational Interviewing in Healthcare Settings: Opportunities and Limitations'. *American Journal of Preventive Medicine* 20(1): 68–74.

Evans, C. (2004) *A 'Pink Palace'? Risdon Prison, 1960–2004* Hobart: Tasmanian Department of Justice.

Evetts, J. (2003a) 'The Sociological Analysis of Professionalism: Occupational Change in a Modern World'. *International Sociology* 18(2): 395–415.

Evetts, J. (2003b) 'The Construction of Professionalism in New and Existing Occupational Contexts: Promoting and Facilitating Occupational Change'. *The International Journal of Sociology and Social Policy* 23(4–5): 22–34.

Evetts, J. (2006) 'Short Note: The Sociology of Professional Groups – New Directions'. *Current Sociology* 54(1): 133–143.

Evetts, J. (2011) 'Sociological Analysis of Professionalism: Past, Present and Future'. *Comparative Sociology* 10: 1–37.

Evetts, J. (2012) 'Similarities in Contexts and Theorising: Professionalism and Inequality'. *Professions and Professionalism* 2(2): 322–337.

Evetts, J. (2013) 'Professionalism: Value and Ideology'. *Current Sociology* 61(5–6): 778–796.

Fabio, A., Tu, L., Loeber, R., and Cohen, J. (2011) 'Neighborhood Socioeconomic Disadvantage and the Shape of the Age-Crime Curve'. *American Journal of Public Health* 101(S1): S325–S332.

Farrall, S. (2002) *Rethinking What Works with Offenders.* Cullompton: Willan Publishing.

Farrall, S. (2007) 'Desistance Studies vs. Cognitive Behavioural Therapies: Which Offers Most Hope for the Long Term?', in Canton, R., and Hancock, D. (eds.) *Dictionary of Probation and Offender Management.* Cullompton: Willan Publishing.

Farrall, S., and Calverley, A. (2006) *Understanding Desistance from Crime: Theoretical Directions in Resettlement and Rehabilitation.* Berkshire: Open University Press.

Farrall, S., Godfrey, B., and Cox, D. (2009) 'The Role of Historically Embedded Structures in Processes of Criminal Reform: A Structural Criminology of Desistance'. *Theoretical Criminology* 13(1): 79–104.

Farrall, S., Hough, M., Maruna, S., and Sparks, R., (eds.) (2011) *Escape Routes: Contemporary Perspectives on Life After Punishment*. London: Routledge.

Farrall, S., Lightowler, C., McNeill, F., and Maruna, S. (2013) 'Discovering Desistance: Provocative Propositions for Reconfiguring Criminal Justice', http://blogs.iriss.org.uk/discoveringdesistance/files/2013/08/DesKE-Propositions.pdf (Accessed 15 January 2014).

Farrington, D. (1986) 'Age and Crime'. *Crime and Justice* 7: 189–250.

Farrington, D. (2000) 'Explaining and Preventing Crime: The Globalization of Knowledge – The American Society of Criminology 1999 Presidential Address'. *Criminology* 38(1): 1–24.

Farrington, D. (2007) 'Advancing Knowledge about Desistance'. *Journal of Contemporary Criminal Justice* 23(1): 125–134.

Feeley, M., and Simon, J. (1992) 'The New Penology: Notes on the Emerging Strategy of Corrections and its Implications'. *Criminology* 30(4): 449–474.

Fenton, J. (2013) 'Risk Aversion and Anxiety in Scottish Criminal Justice Social Work: Can Desistance and Human Rights Agendas have an Impact?'. *The Howard Journal of Criminal Justice* 52(2): 77–90.

Fine, G. (1993) 'Ten Lies of Ethnography: Moral Dilemmas of Field Research'. *Journal of Contemporary Ethnography* 22(3): 267–294.

Finnane, M. (1997) *Punishment in Australian Society*. South Melbourne: Oxford University Press.

Fischer, B., Rehm, J., Kim, G., and Kirst, M. (2005) 'Eyes Wide Shut? A Conceptual and Empirical Critique of Methadone Maintenance Treatment'. *European Addiction Research* 11(1): 1–14.

Fleetwood, S. (2004) 'The Ontology of Organisation and Management Studies', in Ackroyd, S., and Fleetwood, S. (eds.) *Realist Applications in Organisation and Management Studies*. London: Routledge.

Fortune, C., Ward, T., and Willis, G. (2012) 'The Rehabilitation of Offenders: Reducing Risk and Promoting Better Lives'. *Psychiatry, Psychology and Law* 19(5): 646–661.

Foucault, M. (1965) *Madness and Civilization: A History of Insanity in the Age of Reason*. New York: Random House.

Foucault, M. (1977) *Discipline and Punish: The Birth of the Prison*. New York: Vintage Books.

Foucault, M. (1978) 'About the Concept of the "Dangerous Individual" in 19th Century Legal Psychiatry.' *International Journal of Law and Psychiatry* 1(1): 1–18.

Foucault, M. (1980) *Power/Knowledge: Selected Interviews and Other Writings 1972–1977*. Brighton: Harvester Wheatsheaf.

Foucault, M. (1982) 'The Subject and Power'. *Critical Inquiry* 8(4): 777–795.

Fox, A., Fox, C., and Marsh, C. (2012) 'Could Personalisation Reduce Re-offending?'. *Criminal Justice Matters* 90(1): 30–31.

Freedman, R., and Moran, A. (1984) 'Wanderers in a Promised Land: The Chronically Mentally Ill and Deinstitutionalisation' *Medical Care* 22(12): Supplement 1–68.

Freiberg, A. (2001) 'Affective versus Effective Justice: Instrumentalism and Emotionalism in Criminal Justice'. *Punishment and Society* 3: 265–278.

Freidson, E. (1970) *Professional Dominance: The Social Structure of Medical Care*. New Brunswick: Transaction Publishers.

Freidson, E. (1994) *Professionalism Reborn: Theory, Prophecy and Policy*. Cambridge: Polity.

Frese, F., Stanley, J., Kress, K., and Vogel-Scibilia, S. (2001) 'Integrating Evidence-Based Practices and the Recovery Model'. *Psychiatric Services* 52(11): 1462–1468.

Frisher, M., and Beckett, H. (2006) 'Drug Use Desistance'. *Criminology and Criminal Justice* 6(1): 127–145.

Fry, C., and Bruno, R. (2002) 'Recent Trends in Benzodiazepine Use by Injecting Drug Users in Victoria and Tasmania'. *Drug and Alcohol Review* 21: 363–367.

Fry, C., Smith, B., Bruno, R., O'Keefe, B., and Miller, P. (2007) *Benzodiazepine and Pharmaceutical Opioid Misuse and their Relationship to Crime: An Examination of Illicit Prescription Drug Markets in Melbourne, Hobart and Darwin*. Hobart: National Drug Law Enforcement Research Fund, Commonwealth of Australia.

Galea, S., Nandi, A., and Vlahov, D. (2004) 'The Social Epidemiology of Substance Use'. *Epidemiologic Reviews* 26: 36–54.

Garfinkel, H. (1967) *Studies in Ethnomethodology*. Englewood Cliffs: Prentice Hall.

Garland, B., McCarty, W., and Zhao, R. (2009) 'Job Satisfaction and Organisational Commitment in Prisons: An Examination of Psychological Staff, Teachers and Unit Management Staff'. *Criminal Justice and Behavior* 36(2): 163–183.

Garland, D. (1985) *Punishment and Welfare: A History of Penal Strategies*. Aldershot: Gower.

Garland, D. (1990) *Punishment and Modern Society: A Study in Social Theory*. Oxford: Oxford University Press.

Garland, D. (2001) *The Culture of Control: Crime and Social Order in Contemporary Society*. Chicago: University of Chicago Press.

Garland, D. (2006) 'Concepts of Culture in the Sociology of Punishment'. *Theoretical Criminology* 10(4): 419–447.

Garner, B., Hunter, B., Modisette, K., Ihnes, P., and Godley, S. (2012) 'Treatment Staff Turnover in Organizations Implementing Evidence-Based Practices: Turnover Rates and Their Association with Client Outcomes'. *Journal of Substance Abuse Treatment* 42: 134–142.

Gendreau, P., Smith, P., and Theriault, Y. (2009) 'Chaos Theory and Correctional Treatment: Commonsense, Correctional Quackery and the Law of the Fartcatchers'. *Journal of Contemporary Criminal Justice* 25(4): 384–396.

Giddens, A. (1991) *The Consequences of Modernity*. Cambridge: Polity.

Giordano, P., Cernkovich, S., and Holland, D. (2003) 'Changes in Friendship Relations Over the Lifecourse: Implications for Desistance from Crime'. *Criminology* 41(2): 293–328.

Giordano, P., Cernkovich, S., and Rudolph, J. (2002) 'Gender, Crime and Desistance: Toward a Theory of Cognitive Transformation'. *The American Journal of Sociology* 107: 990–1064.

Glaetzer, S. (2010) 'Earless Crim Terrorises Family After Fifth Parole Release in Ten Years'. *The Mercury*, 3 February 2010.

Glick, I., Burti, L., Okonogi, K., and Sacks, M. (1994) 'Effectiveness in Psychiatric Care III: Psychoeducation and Outcome for Patients with Major Affective Disorder and their Families'. *The British Journal of Psychiatry* 164: 104–106.

Goddard, T. (2012) 'Post-Welfarist Risk Managers? Risk, Crime Prevention and the Responsibilisation of Community-Based Organizations'. *Theoretical Criminology* 16(3): 347–363.

Goffman, E. (1961) *Asylums: Essays on the Social Situation of Mental Patients and Other Inmates*. New York: First Anchor Books.

Gorman, K. (2001) 'Cognitive Behaviourism and the Holy Grail: The Quest for a Universal Means of Managing Offender Risk'. *Probation Journal* 48: 3–9.

Gottfredson, M., and Hirschi, T. (1986) 'The True Value of Lambda would Appear to be Zero: An Essay on Career Criminals, Criminal Careers, Selective Incapacitation, Cohort Studies, and Related Topics'. *Criminology* 24(2): 213–234.

Gough, D. (2012) 'Risk and Rehabilitation: A Fusion of Concepts?', in Pycroft, A., and Clift, S. (eds.) *Risk and Rehabilitation: Management and Treatment of Substance Misuse and Mental Health Problems in the Criminal Justice System*. Bristol: The Policy Press.

Graham, H. (2007) 'A Foot in the (Revolving) Door? A Preliminary Evaluation of Tasmania's Mental Health Diversion List'. Masters of Criminology and Corrections Thesis, Hobart: School of Sociology and Social Work, University of Tasmania.

Graham, H. (2010a) 'Coalitions of the Willing: Working Together Towards Recovery-Oriented Systems of Care'. Paper presentation at the Alcohol, Tobacco and Other Drugs Council *Reducing Harm across the Lifespan Conference*, 18–20 October 2010, Wrest Point Convention Centre, Hobart.

Graham, H. (2010b) 'Coalitions of the Willing: Exploring the Dynamics of Interdisciplinary Collaboration and Integrated Care in Offender Management'. Paper presentation at the *Australia and New Zealand Society of Criminology Conference*, 28–30 September 2010, Alice Springs Convention Centre, Northern Territory.

Graham, H. (2010c) 'International Innovation in Offender Reintegration'. Paper presentation at the *Reintegration Puzzle Conference*, 23–25 June 2010, Hobart, hosted by the Centre for Offender Reintegration, Deakin University.

Graham, H. (2011) 'A Marriage of (In)Convenience? Navigating the Research Relationship between Ethical Regulators and Criminologists Researching Vulnerable Populations, in Bartels, L., and Richards, K. (eds.) (2011) *Qualitative Criminology: Stories from the Field*. Sydney: Federation Press.

Graham, H. (2012a) 'The Path Forward: Policing, Diversion and Desistance', in Bartkowiak-Théron, I., and Asquith, N. (eds.) (2012) *Policing Vulnerability*. Canberra: Federation Press.

Graham, H. (2012b) 'Promising Practices and Candid Reflections from the Coalface of the Tasmanian ATOD and Justice Sectors'. Presentation at the Alcohol, Tobacco and Other Drugs Council *Challenging Conversations: Creating an Inclusive System Conference*, 15–16 May 2012, Hotel Grand Chancellor, Hobart.

Graham, H. (2012c) 'Subject to Change: Identity, Culture and Change in the Alcohol and Other Drugs Sector in Tasmania'. Paper presentation at the 6th Annual Australian and New Zealand Critical Criminology Conference *Changing the Way We Think About Change: Shifting Boundaries, Changing Lives Conference*, 12–13 July 2012, hosted at the University of Tasmania, Hobart.

Graham, H. (2012d) 'A Tale of Two Sectors: Sharing Insights from an Academic Apprenticeship'. Presentation to the Criminology, Law and Policing Research Group Postgraduate Showcase to Industry Partners, 21 September 2012, at the University of Tasmania, Hobart.

Graham, H. (2012e) 'Critical Reflections on Risk, Desistance and Responsibility'. Paper presentation at The Australian Sociological Association Crime and Governance Group's *Symposium on Punishment*, 24 September 2012, hosted at Deakin University City Campus, Melbourne.

Graham, H. (2013a) 'Appreciative Inquiry', in Walter, M. (ed.) *Social Research Methods* (3rd ed.). South Melbourne: Oxford University Press.

Graham, H. (2013b) 'Subject to Change: Identity, Culture and Change in the Alcohol and Other Drugs Sector in Tasmania', in Bartkowiak-Théron, I., and Travers, M. (eds.)

(2013) *The 6th Annual Australian and New Zealand Critical Criminology Conference Proceedings 2012*. University of Tasmania, Hobart.

Graham, H. (2013c) '"Pracademia", Co-Production and Innovation: Growing Learning and Research Cultures in the Tasmanian Alcohol and Other Drugs Field'. Invited opening address as the 2013 Drug and Alcohol Research Symposium, hosted by the Alcohol, Tobacco and other Drugs Council of Tasmania (ATDC) at the University of Tasmania, Hobart.

Graham, H. (2015a) 'On Knowing and Being Known: Trust and Legitimacy in Co-Producing Desistance'. Blog on the Co-Producing Desistance blog, 8 May 2015, http://www.coproducingdesistance.org.uk/on-knowing-and-being-known-trust-and-legitimacy-in-co-producing-desistance-by-hannah-graham/ (Accessed 25 January 2016).

Graham, H. (2015b) 'Reproducing Co-Production and Upscaling Innovation: The Growth of Forums Supporting Desistance'. Blog on the Co-Producing Desistance blog, 22 May 2015, http://www.coproducingdesistance.org.uk/reproducing-co-production-and-upscaling-innovation-the-growth-of-forums-supporting-desistance-by-hannah-graham/ (Accessed 25 January 2016).

Graham, H., and Chapman, P. (2006) *Hepatitis C in Prisons and Implications for the Community* (Unpublished Masters Field Research Project Report). Hobart: School of Sociology and Social Work, University of Tasmania.

Graham, H., Graham, S., and Burton, P. (forthcoming) 'Prison Community Gardens: Sustaining the Growth of a Greening Justice Initiative' Unpublished draft article.

Graham, H., Graham, S., and Field, J. (2015) 'Returning Citizens: A Quiet Revolution in Prisoner Reintegration'. *Scottish Justice Matters* 3(1): 32–33.

Graham, H., and McNeill, F. (forthcoming) 'Desistência: Prevendo Futuros' (Desistance: Envisioning Futures), in França, L., and Carlen, P. (eds.) *Criminologias Alternativas* (Portugese language ed.). Brasília: iEA Academia.

Graham, H., and White, R. (2014) 'Innovative Justice – According to Whom?', in Lumsden, K., and Winter, A. (eds.) *Reflexivity in Criminology: Experiences with the Powerful and Powerless*. Basingstoke: Palgrave Macmillan.

Graham, H., and White, R. (2015) *Innovative Justice*. London: Routledge.

Graham, H., and White, R. (2016) 'The Ethics of Innovation in Criminal Justice', in Jacobs, J., and Jackson, J. (eds.) *The Routledge Handbook of Criminal Justice Ethics*. London: Routledge.

Grant, S. (2015) 'Constructing the Durable Penal Agent: Tracing the Development of Habitus within English Probation Officers and Scottish Criminal Justice Social Workers'. *British Journal of Criminology* (Advanced online access 27 July 2015).

Grant, S., and Humphries, M. (2006) 'Critical Evaluation of Appreciative Inquiry: Bridging an Apparent Paradox'. *Action Research* 4(4): 401–418.

Grant, S., and McNeill, F. (2014) 'What Matters in Practice? Understanding 'Quality' in the Routine Supervision of Offenders in Scotland'. *British Journal of Social Work* (Advanced online access 26 May 2014): 1–18.

Griffin, M., and Hepburn, J. (2005) 'Side-Bets and Reciprocity as Determinants of Organizational Commitment Among Correctional Officers'. *Journal of Criminal Justice* 33: 611–625.

Griffin, M., Hogan, N., Lambert, E., Tucker-Gail, K., and Baker, D. (2010) 'Job Involvement, Job Stress, Job Satisfaction, and Organisational Commitment and the Burnout of Correctional Staff'. *Criminal Justice and Behavior* 37(2): 239–255.

Haines, F., and Sutton, A. (2000) 'Criminology as Religion? Profane Thoughts About Sacred Values'. *British Journal of Criminology* 40: 146–162.

Hall, K., and Iqbal, F. (2010) *The Problem with Cognitive Behavioural Therapy*. London: Karnac Books.

Hall, W., Prichard, J., Kirkbride, P., Bruno, R., Thai, P., Gartner, C., Lai, F., Ort, C., and Meuller, J. (2012) 'An Analysis of Ethical Issues in Using Wastewater Analysis to Monitor Illicit Drug Use'. *Addiction* 107(10): 1767–1773.

Halliday, S., Burns, N., Hutton, N., McNeill, F., and Tata, C. (2009) 'Street Level Bureaucracy, Interprofessional Relations, and Coping Mechanisms: A Study of Criminal Justice Social Workers in the Sentencing Process'. *Law and Policy* 31(4): 405–428.

Halsey, M., and Harris, V. (2011) 'Prisoner Futures: Sensing the Signs of Generativity'. *Australian and New Zealand Journal of Criminology* 44(1): 74–93.

Hammersley, R. (2008) *Drugs and Crime*. Cambridge: Polity Press.

Hammond, S. (1998) *The Thin Book of Appreciative Inquiry* (2nd ed.). Bend: Thin Book Publishing Company.

Hannah-Moffat, K. (1999) 'Moral Agent or Actuarial Subject: Risk and Canadian Women's Imprisonment'. *Theoretical Criminology* 3(1): 71–94.

Hannah-Moffat, K. (2000) 'Prisons that Empower'. *British Journal of Criminology* 40(3): 510–531.

Hannah-Moffat, K. (2004) 'Gendering Risk at What Cost: Negotiations of Gender and Risk in Canadian Women's Prisons'. *Feminism and Psychology* 14(2): 243–249.

Hannah-Moffat, K. (2005) 'Criminogenic Needs and the Transformative Risk Subject: Hybridizations of Risk/Need in Penality'. *Punishment and Society* 7: 29–51.

Hannah-Moffat, K. (2009) 'Gridlock or Mutability: Reconsidering "Gender" and Risk Assessment'. *Criminology and Public Policy* 8(1): 209–219.

Harper, D., and Speed, E. (2012) 'Uncovering Recovery: The Resistable Rise of Recovery and Resilience'. *Studies in Social Justice* 6(1): 9–25.

Harper, R., and Hardy, S. (2000) 'An Evaluation of Motivational Interviewing as a Method of Intervention with Clients in a Probation Setting'. *British Journal of Social Work* 30: 393–400.

Harris, L. (2015) 'Prison Sickies: Rise in Jail Escapes Blamed on Alarming Staff Shortages'. *The Daily Telegraph*, 17 October 2015.

Hawkings, C., and Gilburt, H. (2004) *Dual Diagnosis Toolkit: Mental Health and Substance Misuse: A Practical Guide for Professionals and Practitioners*. London: Turning Point (UK) and Rethink.

Health Workforce Australia (2012) http://www.hwa.gov.au/ (Accessed 30 August 2012).

Healy, K. (2009) 'A Case of Mistaken Identity: The Social Welfare Professions and New Public Management'. *Journal of Sociology* 45(4): 401–418.

Heath, B. (2010) 'The Partnership Approach to Drug Misuse', in Pycroft, A., and Gough, D. (eds.) *Multi-Agency Working in Criminal Justice: Control and Care in Contemporary Correctional Practice*. Bristol: The Policy Press.

Hemminger, P. (2005) 'Damming the Flow of Drugs into Drinking Water'. *Environmental Health Perspectives* 113(10): A678–A681.

Henle, M. (2006) 'The Influence of Gestalt Psychology in America'. *Annals of the New York Academy of Sciences* 291(1): 3–12.

Henry-Edwards, S. (2009) 'Getting SMART: Enabling Offenders in the NSW Department of Corrective Services to Understand SMART Recovery'. Paper presented at the Australian Institute of Criminology conference, *Making a Difference: Responding to Need in Developing, Implementing and Evaluating Correctional Programmes*, Melbourne, 5–6 March 2009.

Hirschi, T., and Gottfredson, M. (1983) 'Age and the Explanation of Crime'. *American Journal of Sociology* 89: 552–584.

Hodges, C., Paterson, S., Taikato, M., McGarrol, S., Crome, I., and Baldacchino, A. (2006) *Comorbid Mental Health and Substance Misuse in Scotland*. Edinburgh: Scottish Executive.

Holgate, A., and Clegg, I. (1991) 'The Path to Probation Officer Burnout: New Dogs, Old Tricks'. *Journal of Criminal Justice* 19(4): 325–327.

Holt, M., Treloar, C., McMillan, K., Schultz, L., Schultz, M., and Bath, N. (2007) *Barriers and Incentives to Treatment for Illicit Drug Users with Mental Health Comorbidities and Complex Vulnerabilities (Monograph no. 61)*. Canberra: Australian Government Department of Health and Ageing.

Hope, T. (2009) 'The Illusion of Control: A Response to Professor Sherman'. *Criminology and Criminal Justice* 9(1): 125–134.

Hopkins, B., and Breen, M. (2007) *Clusters*. Sheffield: ACPI.

Horvath, A., and Velten, E. (2000) 'SMART Recovery®: Addiction Recovery Support from a Cognitive Behavioural Perspective'. *Journal of Rational Emotive and Cognitive-Behavior Therapy* 18(3): 181–191.

Hough, M. (2007) 'How Do We Find Out What Works?'. *Criminal Justice Matters* 69(1): 30–31.

Hough, M. (2010) 'Gold Standard or Fools Gold? The Pursuit of Certainty in Experimental Criminology'. *Criminology and Criminal Justice* 10(1): 11–22.

Houston, S. (2001) 'Beyond Social Constructionism: Critical Realism and Social Work'. *British Journal of Social Work* 31(6): 845–861.

Hubband, N., McMurran, M., Evans, C., and Duggan, C. (2007) 'Social Problem-Solving Plus Psychoeducation for Adults with Personality Disorder: Pragmatic Randomised Control Trial'. *British Journal of Psychiatry* 190: 307–313.

Hudson, B. (2003) *Justice in the Risk Society: Challenging and Re-Affirming 'Justice' in Late Modernity*. London: SAGE Publications.

Hudson, J. (2007) 'Motivation', in Canton, R., and Hancock, D. (eds.) *Dictionary of Probation and Offender Management*. Cullompton: Willan Publishing.

Hughes, E. (1962) 'Good People and Dirty Work'. *Social Problems* 10(1): 3–11.

Hulse, G., and Tait, R. (2002) 'Six Month Outcomes Associated with a Brief Alcohol Intervention for Adult In-Patients with Psychiatric Disorders'. *Drug and Alcohol Review* 21: 105–112.

Hulse, G., and Tait, R. (2003) 'Five Year Outcomes of a Brief Alcohol Intervention for Adult In-patients with Psychiatric Disorders'. *Addiction* 98: 1061–1068.

Hunter, S., and Ritchie, P. (2007a) 'Introduction: With, Not To: Models of Co-Production in Social Welfare', in Hunter, S., and Ritchie, P. (eds.) *Co-Production and Personalisation in Social Care: Changing Relationships in the Provision of Social Care (Research Highlights 49)*. London: Jessica Kingsley Publishers.

Hunter, S., and Ritchie, P. (eds.) (2007b) *Co-Production and Personalisation in Social Care: Changing Relationships in the Provision of Social Care (Research Highlights 49)*. London: Jessica Kingsley Publishers.

Hutchinson, S. (2006) 'Countering Catastrophic Criminology: Reform, Punishment and the Modern Liberal Compromise'. *Punishment and Society* 8(4): 443–467.

Institute for Criminal Policy Research (2015) 'World Prison Brief – Prison Population Rate', http://www.prisonstudies.org/highest-to-lowest/prison_population_rate?field_region_taxonomy_tid=All (Accessed 11 October 2015).

Jardine, C. (2013) 'Putting the Pieces Together: Prisoners, Family and Desistance'. *Scottish Justice Matters* 1(2): 15–16.

Jeffery, D., Ley, A., McLaren, S., and Siegfried N. (2007) 'Psychosocial treatment programmes for people with both severe mental illness and substance misuse'. *Cochrane Database of Systematic Reviews* 2: 1–35.

Jiggens, J. (2005) 'The Cost of Drug Prohibition in Australia'. Paper presented to the *Social Change in the 21st Century Conference*, 28 October 2005, Centre for Social Change Research at the Queensland University of Technology, Brisbane.

Johnson, T. (1984) 'Professionalism: Occupation or Ideology', in Goodlad, S. (ed.) *Education for the Professions*. London: Open University Press.

Johnson, R., and Toch, H. (eds.) (1982) *Pains of Imprisonment*. Thousand Oaks, CA: SAGE.

Kaplan, L. (2008) *The Role of Recovery Support Services in Recovery-Oriented Systems of Care*. Rockville, MD: US Department of Health and Human Services Substance Abuse and Mental Health Services Administration.

Katz, R. (2000) 'Explaining Girls' and Women's Crime and Desistance in the Context of their Victimisation Experiences: A Developmental Test of Revised Strain Theory and the Life Course Perspective'. *Violence Against Women* 6(6): 633–660.

Kavanagh, D., Mueser, K., and Baker, A. (2003) 'Management of Comorbidity', in Teeson, M., and Proudfoot, H. (eds.) (2003) *Comorbid Mental Disorders and Substance Use Disorders: Epidemiology, Prevention and Treatment*. Canberra: Australian Government Department of Health and Ageing.

Kawa, S., and Giordano, J. (2012) 'A Brief Historicity of the *Diagnostic and Statistical Manual of Mental Disorders*: Issues and Implications for the Future of Psychiatric Canon and Practice'. *Philosophy, Ethics and Humanities in Medicine* 7: 1–9.

Kazemian, L. (2007) 'Desistance from Crime: Theoretical, Empirical, Methodological and Policy Considerations'. *Journal of Contemporary Criminal Justice* 23(1): 5–27.

Kazemian, L., and Maruna, S. (2009) 'Desistance From Crime', in Krohn, M., Lizotte, A., and Hall, G. (eds.) *Handbook on Crime and Deviance*. New York: Springer.

Kazi, M. (1999) 'Paradigmatic Influences in Practice Research: A Critical Assessment', in Potocky-Tripodi, M., and Tripodi, T. (eds.) *New Directions for Social Work Practice Research*. Washington DC: NASW Press.

Kazi, M. (2000) 'Contemporary Perspectives in the Evaluation of Practice'. *British Journal of Social Work* 30: 755–768.

Kazi, M. (2003) *Realist Evaluation in Practice: Health and Social Work*. London: SAGE Publications.

Kazi, M., Pagkos, B., and Milch, H. (2011) 'Realist Evaluation in Wraparound: A New Approach in Social Work Evidence-Based Practice'. *Research in Social Work Practice* 21(1): 57–64.

Keinan, G., and Malach-Pines, A. (2007) 'Stress and Burnout Among Prison Personnel: Sources, Outcomes and Intervention Strategies'. *Criminal Justice and Behavior* 34(3): 380–398.

Kelly, J. (1818) *A Complete Collection of Scottish Proverbs Explained*. London: Rodwell and Martin.

Kemshall, H. (2002) 'Effective Practice in Probation: An Example of "Advanced Liberal" Responsibilisation?'. *The Howard Journal of Criminal Justice* 41(1): 41–58.

Kemshall, H. (2003) *Understanding Risk in Criminal Justice*. Berkshire: Open University Press/McGraw-Hill.

Kemshall, H. (2006) 'Crime and Risk', in Taylor-Gooby, P., and Zinn, J. (eds.) *Risk in Social Science*. Oxford: Oxford University Press.

Kemshall, H. (2011) 'Crime and Risk: Contested Territory for Risk Theorising'. *International Journal of Law, Crime and Justice* 39: 218–229.

King, R., Massoglia, M., and MacMillan, R. (2007) 'The Context of Marriage and Crime: Gender, the Propensity to Marry, and Offending in Early Adulthood'. *Criminology* 45(1): 33–65.

King, S. (2013a) *Desistance Transitions and the Impact of Probation*. London: Routledge.

King, S. (2013b) 'Early Desistance Narratives: A Qualitative Analysis of Probationers' Transitions Towards Desistance'. *Punishment and Society* 15(2): 147–165.

Kistenmacher, B., and Weiss, R. (2008) 'Motivational Interviewing as a Mechanism for Change in Men who Batter'. *Violence and Victims* 23(5): 558–570.

Konrad, E. (1996) 'A Multidimensional Framework for Conceptualising Human Services Integrated Initiatives', in Marquart, J., and Konrad, E. (eds.) *Evaluating Initiatives to Integrate Human Services*. San Francisco: Jossey-Bass.

Konrad, N. (2002) 'Prisons as the New Asylums'. *Current Opinion in Psychiatry* 15(6): 583–587.

Kopec, A. (1995) 'Rational Emotive Behaviour Therapy in a Forensic Setting: Practical Issues'. *Journal of Rational Emotive and Cognitive Behaviour Therapy* 13(4): 243–253.

Kreager, D., Matsueda, R., and Erosheva, E. (2010) 'Motherhood and Criminal Desistance in Disadvantaged Neighbourhoods'. *Criminology* 48(1): 221–258.

Kristiansen, K. (2007) 'Recovery in Psychosis: Moments and Levels of Collaboration', in Hunter, S., and Ritchie, P. (eds.) *Co-Production and Personalisation in Social Care: Changing Relationships in the Provision of Social Care (Research Highlights 49)*. London: Jessica Kingsley Publishers.

Kupers, T. (1999) *Prison Madness: The Mental Health Crisis Behind Bars and What We Must Do About It*. San Francisco: Josey-Bass Publishers.

Lamb, H. (1981) 'What Did We Really Expect from Deinstitutionalisation?'. *Hospital and Community Psychiatry* 32(2): 105–109.

Landenberger, N., and Lipsey, M. (2005) 'The Positive Effects of Cognitive-Behavioral Programs for Offenders: A Meta-Analysis of Factors Associated with Effective Treatment'. *Journal of Experimental Criminology* 1: 451–476.

Langeland, W., and Van den brink, W. (2004) 'Child Sexual Abuse and Substance Use Disorders: Role of Psychiatric Comorbidity'. *The British Journal of Psychiatry* 185: 353.

Larson, M. (1977) *The Rise of Professionalism: A Sociological Analysis*. Berkeley: University of California Press.

Latessa, E., Cullen, F., and Gendreau, P. (2002) 'Beyond Correctional Quackery – Professionalism and the Possibility of Effective Treatment'. *Federal Probation* 66(2): 43–49.

Laub, J., and Sampson, R. (2001) 'Understanding Desistance from Crime'. *Crime and Justice* 28: 1–69.

Lazarus, A. (1979) 'A Critique of Rational Emotive Therapy', in Ellis, A., and Whiteley, J. (eds.) *Theoretical and Empirical Foundations of Rational-Emotive Therapy*. California: Brooks/Cole.

Leafe, K. (2015) 'Practice Note: Building Recovery, Reducing Crime'. *Practice: The New Zealand Corrections Journal* 3(1): 30–32.

Leahy, R. (2003) *Cognitive Therapy Techniques: A Practitioner's Guide*. New York: Guilford Press.

LeBel, T. (2007) 'An Examination of the Impact of Formerly Incarcerated Persons Helping Others'. *Journal of Offender Rehabilitation* 46(1): 1–24.

LeBel, T., Burnett, R., Maruna, S., and Bushway, S. (2008) 'The "Chicken and Egg" of Subjective and Social Factors in Desistance from Crime'. *European Journal of Criminology* 5(2): 131–159.

Lee, N., and Jenner, L. (2010) 'Development of the *PsyCheck* Screening Tool: An Instrument for Detecting Common Mental Health Conditions Among Substance Use Treatment Clients'. *Mental Health and Substance Use* 3(1): 56–65.

Lee, N., Jenner, L., Baker, A., Ritter, A., Hides, L., Norman, J., Kay-Lambkin, F., Hall, K., Dann, F., and Cameron, J. (2011) 'Screening and Intervention for Mental Health Problems in Alcohol and Other Drugs Settings: Can Training Change Practitioner Behaviour?'. *Drugs: Education, Prevention and Policy* 18(2): 157–160.

Lerman, P. (1980) 'Trends and Issues in the Deinstitutionalization of Youths in Trouble'. *Crime and Delinquency* 26(3): 281–298.

Leverentz, A. (2006) 'The Love of a Good Man? Romantic Relationships as a Source of Support or Hindrance for Female Ex-Offenders'. *Journal of Research in Crime and Delinquency* 43(4): 459–488.

Leverentz, A. (2014) *The Ex-Prisoners' Dilemma: How Women Negotiate Competing Narratives of Re-Entry and Desistance*. New York: Rutgers University Press.

Lewis, C.S. (1949) 'The Humanitarian Theory of Punishment'. *The Twentieth Century: An Australian Quarterly Review* 3(3): 5–12.

Lewis, S. (2016) *Therapeutic Correctional Relationships: Theory, Research and Practice*. London: Routledge.

Li, E., Feifel, C., and Strohm, M. (2000) 'Locus of Control and Spirituality in Alcoholics Anonymous and SMART Recovery members'. *Addictive Behaviors* 25(4): 633–640.

Liamputtong, P., and Ezzy, D. (2005) *Qualitative Research Methods* (2nd ed.). South Melbourne: Oxford University Press.

Liau, A., Shively, R., Horn, M., Laundau, J., Barriga, A., and Gibbs, J. (2004) 'Effects of Psychoeducation for Offenders in a Community Correctional Facility'. *Journal of Community Psychology* 32(5): 543–558.

Liebling, A. (2006) 'Lessons from Prison Privatisation for Probation', in Hough, M., Allen, R., and Padel, U. (eds.) *Reshaping Probation and Prisons: The New Offender Management Framework*. Bristol: The Policy Press.

Liebling, A. (2009) 'Research as Reform?'. *Criminal Justice Matters* 77(1): 18–19.

Liebling, A. (2010) 'Identifying, Measuring and Establishing the Significance of Prison Moral Climates'. 'What Works in Reducing Re-Offending?' *European Union Project Strengthening Transnational Approaches to Reducing Re-Offending (STARR) Conference*, 30 April 2010, Downing College, Cambridge.

Liebling, A. (2011) 'Being a Criminologist: Investigation as a Lifestyle and Living', in Bosworth, M., and Hoyle, C. (eds.) *What is Criminology?*. Oxford: Oxford University Press.

Liebling, A., and Arnold, H. (2004) *Prisons and Their Moral Performance: A Study of Values, Quality and Prison Life*. Oxford: Oxford University Press.

Liebling, A., Arnold, H., and Straub, C. (2015) 'Prisons Research Beyond the Conventional: Dialogue, "Creating Miracles" and Staying Sane in a Maximum Security Prison', in Drake, D., Earle, R., and Sloane, J. (eds.) *The Palgrave Handbook of Prison Ethnography*. Basingstoke: Palgrave Macmillan.

Liebling, A., and Crewe, B. (2013) 'Staff-Prisoner Relationships, Moral Performance and Privatisation', in Durnescu, I., and McNeill, F. (eds.) *Understanding Penal Practice*. London: Routledge.

Liebling, A., Hulley, S., and Crewe, B. (2012) 'Conceptualising and Measuring the Quality of Prison Life', in Gadd, D., Karstedt, S., and Messner, S. (eds.) *The SAGE Handbook of Criminological Methods*, London: SAGE Publications.

Liebling, A., and Price, D. (2001) *The Prison Officer*, London: Waterside Press.

Liebling, A., Price, D., and Elliot, C. (1999) 'Appreciative Inquiry and Relationships in Prison', *Punishment and Society* 1(1): 71–98.

Liebling, A., Price, D., and Shefer, G. (2011) *The Prison Officer* (2nd ed.). Cullompton: Willan Publishing.

Liebrich, J. (1993) *Straight to the Point: Angles on Giving Up Crime*. Otago, NZ: University of Otago Press.

Liem, M., and Richardson, N. (2014) 'The Role of Transformation Narratives in Desistance among Released Lifers'. *Criminal Justice and Behavior* 41(6): 692–712.

Lipsky, M. (1980) *Street-Level Bureaucracy: Dilemmas of the Individual in Public Services*. New York: Russell Sage Foundation.

Lipsky, M. (2010) *Street-Level Bureaucracy: Dilemmas of the Individual in Public Services* (30th Anniversary expanded ed.). New York: Russell Sage Foundation.

London School of Economics Expert Group on the Economics of Drug Policy (2014) *Ending the War on Drugs: Report of the LSE Expert Group on the Economics of Drug Policy*. London: London School of Economics.

Lösel, F. (2012) 'Toward a Third Phase of "What Works" in Offender Rehabilitation', in Loeber, R., and Welsh, B. (eds.) *The Future of Criminology*. Oxford: Oxford University Press.

MacDonald, R. (2006) 'Social Exclusion, Youth Transitions and Criminal Careers: Five Critical Reflections on "Risk"'. *Australian and New Zealand Journal of Criminology* 39(3): 371–383.

MacKenzie, D. (2000) 'Evidence-Based Corrections: Identifying What Works.' *Crime and Delinquency* 46(4): 457–471.

Mahoney, M. (1974) *Cognition and Behavior Modification*. Cambridge: Ballinger.

Mahoney, M. (1979) 'A Critical Analysis of Rational-Emotive Theory and Practice', in Ellis, A., and Whiteley, J. (eds.) *Theoretical and Empirical Foundations of Rational-Emotive Therapy*, California: Brooks/Cole.

Maidment, M. (2002) 'Toward a "Woman-Centred" Approach to Community-Based Corrections'. *Women and Criminal Justice* 13(4): 47–68.

Mair, G. (2004) *What Matters in Probation*. Cullompton: Willan Publishing.

Mairs, A., and Tolland, H. (2013) 'Women Offenders, Mentoring and Desistance'. *Scottish Justice Matters* 1(2): 17–18.

Maletzsky, B., and Steinhauser, C. (2002) 'A 25 Year Followup of Cognitive Behavioural Therapy with 7,275 Sexual Offenders'. *Behavior Modification* 26(2): 123–147.

Marsh, B. (2011) 'Narrating Desistance: Identity Change and the 12 Step Script'. *Irish Probation Journal* 8: 49–68.

Martel, J., Brassard, R., and Jaccoud, M. (2011) 'When Two Worlds Collide: Aboriginal Risk Management in Canadian Corrections'. *British Journal of Criminology* 51(2): 235–255.

Martinson, R. (1974) 'What Works? Questions and Answers About Prison Reform'. *The Public Interest* 35: 22–54.

Martinson, R. (1979) 'New Findings, New Views: A Note of Caution Regarding Sentencing Reform'. *Hofstra Law Review* 7: 242–258.

Maruna, S. (2001) *Making Good: How Ex-Convicts Reform and Rebuild Their Lives* Washington D.C.: American Psychological Association.

Maruna, S. (2004a) 'Desistance from Crime and Explanatory Style: A New Direction in the Psychology of Reform'. *Journal of Contemporary Criminal Justice* 20(2): 184–200.

Maruna, S. (2004b) 'Is Rationalisation Good for the Soul? Resisting "Responsibilisation" in Corrections and the Courts', in Arrigo, B. (ed.) *Psychological Jurisprudence: Critical Explorations in Law, Crime and Society*. Albany: State University of New York Press.

Maruna, S. (2010) 'Mixed Method Research in Criminology: Why Not Go Both Ways?', in Piquero, A., and Weisburd, D. (eds.) *Handbook of Quantitative Criminology*. New York: Springer.

Maruna, S. (2011) 'Why Do They Hate Us? Making Peace Between Prisoners and Psychology'. *International Journal of Offender Therapy and Comparative Criminology* 55(5): 671–675.

Maruna, S. (2012a) 'Elements of Successful Desistance Signalling'. *Criminology and Public Policy* 11(1): 73–86.

Maruna, S. (2012b) 'Desistance Signals'. Discovering Desistance Blog and Knowledge Exchange, http://blogs.iriss.org.uk/discoveringdesistance/2012/02/08/desistance-signals/ (Accessed 1 March 2012).

Maruna, S., and Barber, C. (2011) 'Why Can't Criminology Be More Like Medical Research? Be Careful What You Wish For', in Bosworth, M., and Hoyle, C. (eds.) *What is Criminology?*. Oxford: Oxford University Press.

Maruna, S., and Farrall, S. (2004a) 'Desistance Focused Criminal Justice Policy Research: Introduction to a Special Issue on Desistance from Crime and Public Policy'. *Howard Journal of Criminal Justice* 43: 358–367.

Maruna, S., and Farrall, S. (2004b) 'Desistance from Crime: A Theoretical Reformulation'. *Kölner Zeitschrift für Soziologie und Sozialpsychologie* 43: 171–194.

Maruna, S., and Immarigeon, R. (eds.) (2004) *After Crime and Punishment: Pathways to Offender Reintegration*. Cullompton: Willan Publishing.

Maruna, S., Immarigeon, R., and LeBel, T. (2004) 'Ex-Offender Reintegration: Theory and Practice', in Maruna, S., and Immarigeon, R. (eds.) *After Crime and Punishment: Pathways to Offender Reintegration*. Cullompton: Willan Publishing.

Maruna, S., LeBel, T., and Lanier, C. (2004) 'Generativity Behind Bars: Some "Redemptive Truth" about Prison Society', in de St. Aubin, E., McAdams, D., and Kim, T. (eds.) *The Generative Society: Caring for Future Generations* Washington DC: American Psychological Association.

Maruna, S., and LeBel, T. (2010) 'The Desistance Paradigm in Correctional Practice: From Programmes to Lives', in McNeill, F., Raynor, P., and Trotter, C. (eds.) *Offender Supervision: New Directions in Theory, Research and Practice*. Cullompton: Willan Publishing.

Maruna, S., and Toch, H. (2005) 'The Impact of Imprisonment on the Desistance Process', in Travis, J., and Vishner, C. (eds.) *Prisoner Reentry and Crime in America*. Cambridge: Cambridge University Press.

Massoglia, M., and Uggen, C., (2010) 'Settling Down and Aging Out: Toward an Interactionist Theory of Desistance and the Transition to Adulthood'. *American Journal of Sociology* 116(2): 543–582.

Maume M., Ousey, G., and Beaver K. (2005) 'Cutting the Grass: A Re-examination of the Link between Marital Attachment and Delinquent Peers and Desistance from Marijuana Use'. *Journal of Quantitative Criminology* 21: 27–53.

Mawby, R., and Worrall, A. (2011) *Probation Workers and Their Occupational Cultures (Research Report)*. Leicester and Keele: Department of Criminology, University of Leicester and Keele University.

Mawby, R., and Worrall, A. (2013) *Doing Probation Work: Identity in a Criminal Justice Occupation*. London: Routledge.

Maxwell, J. (2012) *A Realist Approach for Qualitative Research*. London: SAGE Publications.

McCambridge, J., and Strang, J. (2004) 'The Efficacy of Single Session Motivational Interviewing in Reducing Drug Consumption and Perceptions of Drug Related Risk and Harm Among Young People: Results from a Multi-Site Cluster Randomized Trial'. *Addiction* 99(1): 39–52.

McClintock, C. (1998) *Healthy Communities: Concepts and Collaboration Tools (Research Findings)*. New York: Policy Perspectives.

McCulloch, T. (2005) 'Probation, Social Context and Desistance: Re-Tracing the Relationship'. *Probation Journal* 52(1): 8–22.

McCulloch, T. (2013) 'Re-Analysing the Compliance Dynamic: Toward a Co-Productive Strategy and Practice', in Ugwudike, P., and Raynor, P. (eds.) *What Works in Offender Compliance: International Perspectives and Evidence Based Practice*. Basingstoke: Palgrave Macmillan.

McDermott, S. (2012) *Moving Forward: Empowering Women to Desist from Offending (Research Paper 2012/02)*. London: The Griffin Society.

McDonough, P., and Polzer, J. (2012) 'Habitus, Hysteresis and Organisational Change in the Public Sector'. *Canadian Journal of Sociology* 37(4): 357–379.

McGuire, J. (2007) 'Cognitive Behavioural', in Canton, R., and Hancock, D. (eds.) *Dictionary of Probation and Offender Management*. Cullompton: Willan Publishing.

McIvor, G. (2009) 'Therapeutic Jurisprudence and Procedural Justice in Scottish Drug Courts'. *Criminology and Criminal Justice* 9(1): 29–49.

McIvor, G. (2015) 'Offending and Desistance amongst Young Women', in Kruttschnitt, C., and Bijleveld, C. (eds.) *Lives of Incarcerated Women: An International Perspective*. London: Routledge.

McIvor, G., Murray, C., and Jamieson, J. (2004) 'Desistance From Crime: Is It Different for Women and Girls', in Maruna, S., and Immarigeon, R. (eds.) *After Crime and Punishment: Pathways to Offender Reintegration*. Cullompton: Willan Publishing.

McKnight, J. (1987) 'Regenerating Community'. *Social Policy* (Winter) 17: 54–58.

McKnight, J. (1995) *The Careless Society: Community and Its Counterfeits*. New York: Basic Books.

McKnight, J. (1997) 'A 21st Century Map for Healthy Communities and Families'. *Families in Society: The Journal of Contemporary Social Services* 78(2): 117–127.

McKnight, J. (1999) 'Two Tools for Wellbeing: Health Systems and Communities'. *Journal of Perinatology* 19(6): 12–15.

McKnight, J. (2003) *Regenerating Community: The Recovery of Space for Citizens (The IPR Distinguished Public Policy Lecture Series)*. Evanston: Institute for Policy Research, Northwestern University.

McLaughlin, E. (2011) 'Critical Criminology: The Renewal of Theory, Politics and Practice', in Bosworth, M., and Hoyle, C. (eds.) *What is Criminology?*. Oxford: Oxford University Press.

McLaughlin, E., Muncie, J., and Hughes, G. (2001) 'The Permanent Revolution: New Labour, New Public Management and the Modernization of Criminal Justice'. *Criminal Justice* 1(3): 301–318.

McMahon, T. (2013) 'A Social Approach to the Process of Rehabilitation'. *British Journal of Community Justice* 11(2–3): 159–163.

McMurran, M. (2004) 'Assessing and Changing Motivation to Offend', in Cox, W., and Klinger, E. (eds.) *Handbook of Motivational Counselling: Concepts, Approaches and Assessments*. Chichester: John Wiley.

McMurran, M. (2009) 'Motivational Interviewing with Offenders: A Systematic Review'. *Legal and Criminological Psychology* 14: 83–100.

McMurran, M., and Wilmington, R. (2007) 'A Delphi Survey of the Views of Adult Male Patients with Personality Disorders on Psychoeducation and Social Problem-Solving Therapy'. *Criminal Behaviour and Mental Health* 17: 293–299.

McNeill, F. (2000) 'Making Criminology Work: Theory and Practice in Local Context'. *Probation Journal* 47(2): 108–118.

McNeill, F. (2001) 'Developing Effectiveness: Frontline Perspectives'. *Social Work Education* 20(6): 671–687.

McNeill, F. (2004) 'Desistance, Rehabilitation and Correctionalism'. *Howard Journal of Criminal Justice* 43: 420–436.

McNeill, F. (2006) 'A Desistance Paradigm for Offender Management' *Criminology and Criminal Justice* 6(1): 39–62.

McNeill, F. (2009a) 'What Works and What's Just?'. *European Journal of Probation* 1(1): 21–40.

McNeill, F. (2009b) *Towards Effective Practice in Offender Supervision (Report)*. Glasgow: Scottish Centre for Crime and Justice Research.

McNeill, F. (2012a) 'Four Forms of 'Offender' Rehabilitation: Towards an Interdisciplinary Perspective'. *Legal and Criminological Psychology* 17(1): 18–36.

McNeill, F. (2012b) '"Ex-Offenders" or "Re-Citz"?'. Discovering Desistance Blog and Knowledge Exchange, http://blogs.iriss.org.uk/discoveringdesistance/2012/06/29/ex-offenders-or-re-citz/ (Accessed 30 June 2012).

McNeill, F. (2012c) 'What Matters? Thinking Differently … And Talking'. Discovering Desistance Blog and Knowledge Exchange, http://blogs.iriss.org.uk/discoveringdesistance/2012/01/31/what-matters-thinking-differently-and-talking/ (Accessed 7 July 2012).

McNeill, F. (2013a) 'Moving On: Desistance and Rehabilitation'. *Scottish Justice Matters* 1(2): 2.

McNeill, F. (2013b) 'Changing Lives, Changing Work: Social Work and Criminal Justice', in Durnescu, I., and McNeill, F. (eds.) *Understanding Penal Practice*. Basingstoke: Palgrave Macmillan.

McNeill, F. (2014) 'Desistance, Rehabilitation and (Prisoner?) Learning' (25 April 2014), http://blogs.iriss.org.uk/discoveringdesistance/2014/04/25/desistance-rehabilitation-and-prisoner-learning/ (Accessed 1 May 2014).

McNeill, F. (2016) 'Desistance and Criminal Justice in Scotland', in Croall, H., Mooney, G., and Munro, M. (eds) *Crime, Justice and Society in Scotland*. London: Routledge.

McNeill, F., Batchelor, S., Burnett, R., and Knox, J. (2005) *21st Century Social Work – Reducing Re-Offending: Key Practice Skills*. Edinburgh: Scottish Executive.

McNeill, F., and Beyens, K. (eds.) (2013) *Offender Supervision in Europe*. Basingstoke: Palgrave Macmillan.

McNeill, F., Burnett, R., and McCulloch, T. (2010) *Culture, Change and Community Justice (Report No.02/2010)*. Glasgow: Scottish Centre for Crime and Justice Research.

McNeill, F., Burns, N., Halliday, S., Hutton, N., and Tata, C. (2009) 'Risk, Responsibility and Reconfiguration'. *Punishment and Society* 11(4): 419–442.

McNeill, F., and Farrall, S. (2013) 'A Moral in the Story? Virtues, Values and Desistance from Crime', in Cowburn, M., Duggan, M., Robinson, A., and Senior, P. (eds.) *Values in Criminology and Community Justice*. Bristol: Policy Press.

McNeill, F., Farrall, S., Lightowler, C., and Maruna, S. (2012a) *How and Why People Stop Offending: Discovering Desistance (IRISS Insight #15)*. Glasgow: Institute for Research and Innovation in Social Services.

McNeill F., Farrall, S., Lightowler, C., and Maruna, S. (2012b) 'Re-Examining Evidence-Based Practice in Community Corrections: Beyond "A Confined View" of What Works'. *Justice Research and Policy*, 14(1), 35–60.

McNeill, F., Farrall, S., Lightowler, C., and Maruna, S. (2013) 'Discovering Desistance: Reconfiguring Criminal Justice?'. *Scottish Justice Matters* 1(2): 3–6.

McNeill, F., and Robinson, G., (2013) 'Liquid Legitimacy and Community Sanctions', in Crawford, A., and Hucklesby, A. (eds.) *Legitimacy and Compliance in Criminal Justice*. London: Routledge.

Meadows, G., Singh, B., and Grigg, M. (2007) 'Looking Forward', in G. Meadows, B. Singh, and M. Grigg (eds.) (2007) *Mental Health in Australia: Collaborative Community Practice* (2nd ed.). South Melbourne: Oxford University Press.

Mechanic, D., and Rocheford, D. (1990) 'Deinstitutionalization: An Appraisal of Reform'. *Annual Review of Sociology* 16: 301–327.

Meisler, A. (1999) 'Group Treatments for People with PTSD and Comorbid Alcohol Abuse', in Young, B., and Blake, D. (eds.) *Group Treatments for Post-Traumatic Stress Disorder*. Philadelphia: Brunner/Mazzel.

Melnick, G., Ulaszek, W., Lin, H., and Wexler, H. (2009) 'When Goals Diverge: Staff Consensus and the Organizational Climate'. *Drug and Alcohol Dependence* 103(1): 17–22.

Menger, A., and Donker, A. (2013) 'Sources of Professional Effectiveness', in Durnescu, I., and McNeill, F. (eds.) *Understanding Penal Change*. London: Routledge.

Merrington, S., and Stanley, S. (2000) 'Doubts About the What Works Initiative'. *Probation Journal* 47: 272–275.

Miller, P., Moore, D., and Strang, J. (2006) 'The Regulation of Research by Funding Bodies: An Emerging Ethical Issue for the Alcohol and Other Drug Sector?'. *International Journal of Drug Policy* 17(1): 12–16.

Miller, W., and Rollnick, S. (2002) *Motivational Interviewing*. New York: Guildford Press.

Mills, K., Deady, M., Proudfoot, H., Sannibale, C., Teeson, M., Mattick, R., and Burns, L. (2009) *Guidelines on the Management of Co-Occurring Alcohol and Other Drug and Mental Health Conditions*. Canberra: Australian Government Department of Health and Ageing.

Ministerial Council on Drug Strategy (2011) *National Drug Strategy 2010–2015: A Framework for Action on Alcohol, Tobacco and Other Drugs*. Canberra: Commonwealth Department of Health and Ageing.

Møller, L., Stöver, H., Jürgens, R., Gatherer, A., and Nikogosian, H. (eds.) (2007) *Health in Prisons: A WHO Guide to the Essentials in Prison Health*. Copenhagen: World Health Organisation.

Moore, R. (2012) 'Capital' in Grenfell, M. (ed.) *Pierre Bourdieu: Key Concepts* (2nd ed.). Durham: Acumen Publishing.

Morash, M. (2009) 'A Great Debate Over Using the Level of Service Inventory – Revised (LSI-R) with Women Offenders'. *Criminology and Public Policy* 8(1): 173–182.

Morley, S., Eccleston, C., Williams, A. (1999) 'Systematic Review and Meta-Analysis of Randomized Control Trials of Cognitive Behaviour Therapy and Behaviour Therapy for Chronic Pain in Adults, Excluding Headache'. *Pain* 80: 1–13.

Murphy, A. (2002) *The Political Writings of William Penn*. Indianapolis: Liberty Fund Press.

Murphy, J., and Datel, (1976) 'A Cost-Benefit Analysis of Community versus Institutional Living'. *Psychiatric Services* 27(3): 165.

Musser, P., Semiatin, J., Taft, C., and Murphy, C. (2008) 'Motivational Interviewing as a Pre-Group Intervention for Partner-Violent Men'. *Violence and Victims* 23(5): 539–557.

Najavits, L., Weiss, R., and Liese, B. (1996) 'Group Cognitive Behavioural Therapy for Women with PTSD and Substance Use Disorder'. *Journal of Substance Abuse Treatment* 13(1): 13–22.

Najavits, L., Weiss, R., Shaw, S., and Muenz, L. (1998) '"Seeking Safety": Outcome of a New Cognitive-Behavioural Psychotherapy for Women with Posttraumatic Stress Disorder and Substance Dependence'. *Journal of Traumatic Stress* 11(3): 437–456.

National Drug and Alcohol Research Centre (2014) 'Comorbidity Guidelines', http://ndarc.med.unsw.edu.au/resource/comorbidity-guidelines-full-document (Accessed 30 January 2014).

Nellis, M. (2012) 'Prose and Cons: Autobiographical Writing by British Prisoners', in Cheliotis, L. (ed.) *The Arts of Imprisonment: Control, Resistance and Empowerment*. Surrey: Ashgate Publishing.

New South Wales Department of Health (2007) *Mental Health Reference Resource for Drug and Alcohol Workers*. North Sydney: NSW Department of Health.

Neyroud, P. (2011a) 'More Police, Less Prison, Less Crime? From Peel to Popper – The Case for More Scientific Policing'. *Criminology and Public Policy* 10(1): 77–83.

Neyroud, P. (2011b) 'Offender Desistance Policing and Operation Turning Point in West Midlands', http://cambridgecriminologyphd.blogspot.com.au/2011/10/offender-desistance-policing-and.html (Accessed 9 January 2012).

Neyroud, P., and Slothower, M. (2014) 'Wielding the Sword of Damocles: The Challenges and Opportunities in Reforming Police Out-Of-Court Disposals in England and Wales', in Wasik, M., and Santatzoglou, S. (eds.) *The Management of Change in Criminal Justice: Who Knows Best?*. Basingstoke: Palgrave Macmillan.

Nicholas, R., Adams, V., Roche, A., White, M., and Batams, S. (2013) *A Literature Review to Support the Development of Australia's Alcohol and Other Drugs Workforce Development Strategy*. Adelaide: National Centre for Education and Training on Addiction and Flinders University.

Noaks, L., and Wincup, E. (2004) *Criminological Research: Understanding Qualitative Methods*. London: SAGE.

Nolan, T. (2013) 'Alcohol and Other Drugs Council of Australia Placed in Voluntary Administration after Coalition Cuts Funding' ABC News http://www.abc.net.au/news/2013-11-27/alcohol-and-other-drugs-council-adca-administration-funding-cut/5119744 (Accessed 26 January 2014).

Ogloff, J., and Davis, M. (2004) 'Advances in Offender Assessment and Rehabilitation: Contributions of the Risk-Need-Responsivity Approach'. *Psychology, Crime and Law* 10(3): 229–242.

Ogloff, J., Lemphers, A., and Dwyer, C. (2004) 'Dual Diagnosis in an Australian Forensic Psychiatric Hospital: Prevalence and Implications for Services'. *Behavioural Sciences and the Law* 22: 543–562.

O'Connor, T., and Bogue, B. (2010) 'Collaborating with the Community, Faith Volunteers and Faith Traditions: Building Social Capacity and Making Meaning to Support

Desistance', in McNeill, F., Raynor, P., and Trotter, C. (eds.) *Offender Supervision: Directions in Theory, Research and Practice.* Cullompton: Willan Publishing.

O'Malley, P. (1992) 'Risk, Power and Crime Prevention'. *Economy and Society* 21: 252–275.

O'Malley, P. (1999) *The Risk Society: Implications for Justice and Beyond.* Victoria: Department of Justice.

Opsal, T. (2012) '"Livin' on the Straights": Identity, Desistance and Work among Women Post-Incarceration'. *Sociological Inquiry* 82(3): 378–403.

Ouimette, P., Finney, J., and Moos, R. (1997) 'Twelve-Step and Cognitive Behavioral Treatment for Substance Abuse: A Comparison of Treatment Effectiveness'. *Journal of Consulting and Clinical Psychology* 65(2): 230–240.

Page, J. (2012) 'Punishment and the Penal Field', in Simon, J., and Sparks, R. (eds.) *The SAGE Handbook of Punishment and Society.* London: SAGE Publications.

Page, J. (2013) 'The Shape of Re-Entry: Probation and the Penal Field in Minnesota'. COST Offender Supervision in Europe blog post, 2 April 2013, http://www. offendersupervision.eu/blog-post/the-shape-of-re-entry-probation-and-the-penal-field-in-minnesota (Accessed 1 November 2015).

Paternoster, R., and Bushway, S. (2009) 'Desistance and the "Feared Self": Towards an Identity Theory of Criminal Desistance'. *The Journal of Criminal Law and Criminology* 99(4): 1103–1156.

Patenaude, A. (2004) 'No Promises, but I'm Willing to Listen and Tell What I Hear: Conducting Qualitative Research Among Prison Inmates and Staff'. *The Prison Journal* 84(4): 698–918.

Patomäki, H., and Wight, C. (2000) 'After Postpositivism? The Promises of Critical Realism'. *International Studies Quarterly* 44(2): 213–237.

Pawson, R. (2006) *Evidence-Based Policy: A Realist Perspective.* London: SAGE Publications.

Pawson, R., and Tilley, N. (1997) *Realistic Evaluation.* London: SAGE Publications.

Payne, J., and Gaffney, A. (2012) 'How Much Crime is Drug or Alcohol Related? Self-Reported Attributions of Police Detainees'. *Trends and Issues in Crime and Criminal Justice No. 439.* Canberra: Australian Institute of Criminology.

Peacock, A., de Graaff, B., and Bruno, R. (2015) *Tasmanian Drug Trends 2014: Findings from the Illicit Drug Reporting System (IDRS).* Sydney: National Drug and Alcohol Research Centre, University of New South Wales.

Pearson, F., Lipton, D., Cleland, C., and Yee, D. (2002) 'The Effects of Behavioural/ Cognitive Behavioural Programs on Recidivism'. *Crime and Delinquency* 48(3): 476–496.

Peele, H. (2006) 'Appreciative Inquiry and Creative Problem Solving in Cross-Functional Teams'. *The Journal of Applied Behavioural Science* 42(4): 447–467.

Pennacchia, J. (2013) *Exploring the Relationships Between Evidence and Innovation in the Context of Scotland's Social Services.* Glasgow: Institute for Research and Innovation in Social Services (IRISS).

Persson, A., and Svensson, K. (2011) 'Signs of Resistance? Swedish Probation Officers' Attitudes Towards Risk Assessments'. *European Journal of Probation* 3(3): 95–107.

Persson, A., and Svensson, K. (2012) 'Shades of Professionalism: Risk Assessment in Pre-Sentence Reports in Sweden'. *European Journal of Criminology* 9(2): 176–190.

Phillips, L., and Ilcan, S. (2004) 'Capacity Building: The Neoliberal Governance of Development'. *Canadian Journal of Development Studies* 25(3): 393–409.

Polaschek, D. (2012) 'An Appraisal of the Risk-Need-Responsivity (RNR) Model of Offender Rehabilitation and its Application in Correctional Treatment'. *Legal and Criminological Psychology* 17: 1–17.

Pollack, S. (2012) 'An Imprisoning Gaze: Practices of Gendered, Racialised and Epistemic Violence'. *International Review of Victimology* 19(1): 103–114.

Pomati, F. (2007) 'Pharmaceuticals in Drinking Water: Is the Cure Worse than the Disease?'. *Environmental Science and Technology* 41(24): 8204.

Pomeroy, E., Kiam, R., and Green, D. (2000) 'Reducing Depression, Anxiety and Trauma of Male Inmates: an HIV/AIDS Psychoeducational Group Intervention'. *Social Work Research* 24(3): 156–167.

Porporino, F. (2010) 'Bringing Sense and Sensitivity to Corrections: From Programmes to 'Fix' Offenders to Services to Support Desistance', in Brayford, J., Cowe, F., and Deering, J. (eds.) *What Else Works? Creative Work with Offenders*. Cullompton: Willan Publishing.

Porporino, F., Fabiano, E., and Robinson, D. (1991) *Focusing on Successful Reintegration: Cognitive Skills Training for Offenders*. Ontario: Correctional Service of Canada.

Postma, W. (1998) 'Capacity Building: The Making of a Curry'. *Development in Practice* 8(1): 54–63.

Pratt, J. (2002) *Punishment and Civilisation*. London: SAGE.

Pratt, J. (2007) *Penal Populism*. London: Routledge.

Priday, E. (2006) 'New Directions in Juvenile Justice: Risk and Cognitive Behaviourism'. *Current Issues in Criminal Justice* 17(3): 343–359.

Priebe, S., Badesconyi, A., Fioritti, A., Hansson, L., Kilian, R., Torres-Gonzales, F., Turner, T., and Wiersma, D. (2005) 'Reinstitutionalisation in Mental Health Care: Comparison of Data on Service Provision from Six European Countries'. *British Medical Journal* 330: 123–126.

Prochaska, J., and DiClemente, C. (1983) 'Stages and Processes of Self-Change of Smoking: Towards an Integrative Model of Change'. *Journal of Consulting and Clinical Psychology* 51(3): 390–395.

Public Health Information Development Unit (2013) *A Social Health Atlas of Australia 2011* (online, updated). The University of Adelaide, at http://www.publichealth.gov.au/interactive_mapping/aust_multiple_2010_synthetic_predictions/tas/atlas.html (Accessed 14 January 2013).

Purvis, M., Ward, T., and Willis, G. (2011) 'The Good Lives Model in Practice: Offence Pathways and Case Management'. *European Journal of Probation* 3(2): 4–28.

Pycroft, A., and Clift, S. (eds.) (2012) *Risk and Rehabilitation: Management and Treatment of Substance Misuse and Mental Health Problems in the Criminal Justice System*. Bristol: The Policy Press.

Pycroft, A., and Gough, D. (eds.) (2010) *Multi-Agency Working in Criminal Justice: Control and Care in Contemporary Correctional Practice*. Bristol: The Policy Press.

Quirion, B. (2003) 'From Rehabilitation to Risk Management: The Goals of Methadone Programmes in Canada'. *International Journal of Drug Policy* 14(3): 247–255.

Raymond, E., and Hall, C. (2008) 'The Potential for Appreciative Inquiry in Tourism Research'. *Current Issues in Tourism* 11(3): 281–292.

Raynor, P., and Vanstone, M. (1994) 'Probation Practice, Effectiveness and the Non-Treatment Paradigm'. *British Journal of Social Work* 24(4): 387–404.

Rees, A., (2010) 'Dual Diagnosis: Issues and Implications for Criminal Justice Partnerships', in Pycroft, A., and Gough, D. (eds.) *Multi-Agency Working in Criminal Justice: Control and Care in Contemporary Correctional Practice*, Bristol: The Policy Press.

Richer, M., Richie, J., and Marchionni, C. (2009) "'If we can't do more, let's do it differently!": Using Appreciative Inquiry to Promote Innovative Ideas for Better Work Environments', *Journal of Nursing Management* 17: 947–955.

Ritter, A., and Lancaster, K. (2013) 'Illicit Drugs, Policing and the Evidence-Based Policy Paradigm', *Evidence and Policy: A Journal of Research, Debate and Practice* 9(4): 457–472.

Roberts, L. (2002) 'Ethics and Mental Illness Research', *Psychiatric Clinics of North America* 25: 525–545.

Robinson, G. (1999) 'Risk Management and Rehabilitation in the Probation Service: Collision and Collusion'. *The Howard Journal of Criminal Justice* 38(4): 421–433.

Robinson, G. (2002) 'Exploring Risk Management in Probation Practice: Contemporary Developments in England and Wales'. *Punishment and Society* 4(1): 5–25.

Robinson, G. (2008) 'Late-Modern Rehabilitation: The Evolution of a Penal Strategy'. *Theoretical Criminology* 10(4): 429–445.

Robinson, G., and Crow, I. (2009) *Offender Rehabilitation: Theory, Research and Practice*. London: SAGE.

Robinson, G., and McNeill, F. (2004) 'Purposes Matter: Examining the "Ends" of Probation Practice', in Mair, G. (ed.) *What Matters in Probation*. Cullompton: Willan Publishing.

Robinson, G., and McNeill, F. (2010) 'The Dynamics of Compliance with Offender Supervision', in McNeill, F., Raynor, P., and Trotter, C. (eds.) *Offender Supervision: New Directions in Theory, Research and Practice*, Cullompton: Willan Publishing.

Robinson, G., McNeill, F., and Maruna, S. (2013) 'Punishment *in* Society: The Improbable Persistence of Probation and other Community Sanctions and Measures', in Simon, J. and Sparks, R. (eds.) *The SAGE Handbook of Punishment and Society*. London: SAGE.

Robinson, G., Priede, C., Farrall, S., Shapland, J., and McNeill, F. (2012) 'Doing "Strengths-Based" Research: Appreciative Inquiry in a Probation Setting'. *Criminology and Criminal Justice* 13(1): 3–20.

Robinson, G., Priede, C., Farrall, S., Shapland, J., and McNeill, F. (2013) 'Understanding "Quality" in Probation Practice: Frontline Perspectives in England and Wales'. *Criminology and Criminal Justice* 14(2): 123–142.

Robinson, G., and Svensson, K. (2013) 'Practising Offender Supervision', in McNeill, F., and Beyens, K. (eds.) *Offender Supervision in Europe*. Basingstoke: Palgrave Macmillan.

Roche, A. (2009) 'New Horizons in AOD Workforce Development'. *Drugs: Education, Prevention and Policy* 16(3): 193–304.

Roche, A. (2013) 'Looking to the Future: The Challenges Ahead'. *Of Substance: The National Alcohol, Tobacco and Other Drugs Magazine* 11(1): 17.

Roche, A., and Pidd, K. (2010) *Alcohol and Other Drugs Workforce Development Issues and Imperatives: Setting the Scene* Adelaide: National Centre for Education and Training on Addiction (NCETA), Flinders University.

Roche, A., Pidd, K., and Freeman, T. (2009) 'Achieving Professional Practice Change: From Training to Workforce Development' *Drug and Alcohol Review* 28(5): 550–557.

Rodermond, E., Kruttschnitt, C., Slotboom, A., and Bijleveld, C. (2015) 'Female Desistance: A Review of the Literature'. *European Journal of Criminology* (Advanced online access 11 August 2015).

Rogler, L. (1997) 'Making Sense of Historical Changes in the Diagnostic and Statistical Manual of Mental Disorders: Five Propositions'. *Journal of Health and Social Behavior* 38(1): 9–20.

Rose, N. (1996) 'The Death of the Social? Re-Configuring the Territory of Government'. *Economy and Society* 25(3): 327–356.

Rose, N. (2000) 'Government and Control'. *British Journal of Criminology* 40: 321–339.

Rosso, B., Dekas, K., and Wrzesniewski, A. (2010) 'On the Meaning of Work: A Theoretical Integration and Review'. *Research in Organisational Behaviour* 30: 91–127.

Roth, J., and Best, D. (eds.) (2013) *Addiction and Recovery in the UK*. London: Routledge.

Roy, A., and Buchanan, J. (2015) 'The Paradoxes of Recovery Policy: Exploring the Impact of Austerity and Responsibilisation for the Citizenship Claims of People with Drug Problems'. *Social Policy Administration* (Advanced online access 4 May 2015).

Russell, E., and Carlton, B. (2013) 'Pathways, Race and Gender Responsive Reform: Through an Abolitionist Lens'. *Theoretical Criminology* 17(4): 474–492.

Rubin, L. (2004) 'Merchandising Madness: Pills, Promises and Better Living Through Chemistry'. *The Journal of Popular Culture* 38(2): 369–383.

Rudes, D., Viglione, J., and Taxman, F. (2013) 'Professional Ideologies in United States Probation and Parole', in Durnescu, I., and McNeill, F. (eds.) *Understanding Penal Practice*. London: Routledge.

Rumgay, J. (2004) 'Scripts for Safer Survival: Pathways Out of Female Crime'. *The Howard Journal of Criminal Justice* 43(4): 405–419.

Saks, M. (2012) 'Defining a Profession: The Role of Knowledge and Expertise'. *Professions and Professionalism* 2(1): 1–10.

Saldaña, J. (2009) *The SAGE Coding Manual for Qualitative Researchers*. London: SAGE Publications.

Sampson, R. (2010) 'Gold Standard Myths: Observations on the Experimental Turn in Quantitative Criminology'. *Journal of Quantitative Criminology* 26: 489–500.

Sampson, R., and Laub, J. (2003) 'Lifecourse Desisters? Trajectories of Crime among Delinquent Boys Followed to Age 70'. *Criminology* 41(3): 555–592.

Sampson, R., and Lauritsen, J. (1997) 'Racial and Ethnic Disparities in Crime and Criminal Justice in the United States'. *Crime and Justice* 21: 311–374.

Sandham, J., and Octigan, M. (2007) 'Motivational Interviewing', in Canton, R., and Hancock, D. (eds.) *Dictionary of Probation and Offender Management*. London: Willan Publishing.

Sarre, R. (2001) 'Beyond 'What Works'? A 25-Year Jubilee Retrospective of Robert Martinson's Famous Article'. *Australian and New Zealand Journal of Criminology* 34(1): 38–46.

Sciulli, D. (2005) 'Continental Sociology of Professions Today: Conceptual Contributions'. *Current Sociology* 53(6): 915–942.

Schroeder, R., Giordano, P., and Cerncovich, S. (2007) 'Drug Use and Desistance Processes'. *Criminology* 45(1): 191–222.

Scott, D. (2013) 'Prison Research: Appreciative or Critical Inquiry?'. *Criminal Justice Matters* 95(1): 30–31.

Scottish Government (2008) *The Road to Recovery: A New Approach to Tackling Scotland's Drug Problem*. Edinburgh: Scottish Government.

Scraton, P. (2002) 'Defining 'Power' and Challenging 'Knowledge': Critical Analysis as Resistance in the UK', in Carrington, K., and Hogg, R. (eds.) *Critical Criminology: Issues, Debates, Challenges*. Cullompton: Willan Publishing.

Scraton, P. (2007) *Power, Conflict and Criminalisation*. London: Routledge.

Scraton, P. (2014) 'Bearing Witness to the 'Pain of Others': Researching Power, Violence and Resistance in a Women's Prison'. Plenary Keynote at the 8th Annual Australian and New Zealand Critical Criminology Conference, 4– 5 December 2014 at Monash University, Melbourne.

Scraton, P., and McCulloch, J. (eds.) (2009) *The Violence of Incarceration*. London: Routledge.

Seddon, T. (2006) 'Drugs, Crime and Social Exclusion: Social Context and Social Theory in British Drugs-Crime Research'. *British Journal of Criminology* 46: 680–703.

Selous, A. (2015) 'Ministry of Justice National Probation Service for England and Wales Sick Leave', http://www.parliament.uk/business/publications/written-questions-answers-statements/written-question/Commons/2015-06-15/2536/ (Accessed 30 October 2015).

Shammas, V., and Sandberg, S. (2015) 'Habitus, Capital, and Conflict: Bringing Bourdieusian Field Theory to Criminology'. *Criminology and Criminal Justice* (Advanced online access September 2015): 1–19.

Sharpe, G. (2015) 'Precarious Identities: 'Young' Motherhood, Desistance and Stigma' *Criminology and Criminal Justice* (Advanced online access 18 August 2015): 1–16.

Shaw, M., and Hannah-Moffat, K. (2000) 'Gender, Diversity and Risk Assessment in Canadian Corrections'. *Probation Journal* 47(3): 163–172.

Shaw, M., and Hannah-Moffat, K. (2004) 'How Cognitive Skills Forgot About Gender and Diversity', in Mair, G. (ed.) *What Matters in Probation*. London: Willan Publishing.

Sheehan, R., McIvor, G., and Trotter, C. (eds.) (2011) *Working with Women Offenders in the Community*. London: Willan Publishing.

Sherman, L. (2011a) 'Offender Desistance Policing (ODP): Less Prison and More Evidence in Rehabilitating Offenders', in Bliesener, T., Beelmann, A., and Stemmler, M. (eds.) *Anti-Social Behaviour and Crime: Contributions of Developmental and Evaluation Research to Prevention and Intervention*. Cambridge, MA: Hoegrefe.

Sherman, L. (2011b) 'Criminology as Invention', in Bosworth, M., and Hoyle, C. (eds.) *What is Criminology?*. Oxford: Oxford University Press.

Sherman, L., Gottfredson, D., MacKenzie, D., Eck, J., Reuter, P., and Bushway, S. (1998) *Preventing Crime: What Works, What Doesn't, What's Promising*. Washington DC: National Institute of Justice.

Sherman, L., and Neyroud, P. (2012) *Offender-Desistance Policing and the Sword of Damocles* London: Civitas: Institute for the Study of Civil Society. Online at: http://www.civitas.org.uk/pdf/TheSwordofDamoclesApril12.pdf (Accessed 1 October 2015).

Shover, N., and Thompson, C. (1992) 'Age Differential Expectations and Crime Desistance'. *Criminology* 30(1): 89–104.

Silverman, D. (2005) *Doing Qualitative Research* (2nd ed.). London: SAGE Publications.

Skinner, C. (2010) 'Clients or Offenders? The Case for Clarity of Purpose in Multi-Agency Working', in Pycroft, A., and Gough, D. (eds.) *Multi-Agency Working in Criminal Justice: Control and Care in Contemporary Correctional Practice*. Bristol: The Policy Press.

Skinner, N., Roche, A., Freeman, T., and McKinnon, A. (2009) 'Health Professionals' Attitudes Towards AOD-related Work: Moving the Traditional Focus from Education and Training to Organizational Culture'. *Drugs: Education, Prevention and Policy* 16(3): 232–249.

Smedslund, G., Berg, R., Hammerstrøm, K., Steiro, A., Leik
nes, K., Dahl, H., and Karlsen, K. (2011) 'Motivational Interviewing for Substance Abuse'. *Cochrane Database of Systematic Reviews* 5: 1–112.

Smith, P., Cullen, F., and Latessa, E. (2009) 'Can 14,737 women be wrong? A Meta-Analysis of the LSI-R and Recidivism for Female Offenders'. *Criminology & Public Policy* 8(1): 183–208.

Sommers, I., Baskin, D., and Fagan, J. (1994) 'Getting Out of the Life: Crime Desistance by Female Street Offenders'. *Deviant Behavior* 15(2): 125–149.

Spivakovsky, C. (2013) *Racialized Correctional Governance: The Mutual Constructions of Race and Criminal Justice*. Burlington, VT: Ashgate.

Spivakovsky, C. (2014) 'From Punishment to Protection: Containing and Controlling the Lives of People with Disabilities in Human Rights'. *Punishment and Society* 16(5): 560–577.

Spooner, C., and Dadich, A. (2009) *Non-Government Organisations in the Alcohol and Other Drugs Sector: Issues and Options for Sustainability (ANCD Research Paper 17)*. Canberra: Australian National Council on Drugs.

Spooner, C., and Dadich, A. (2010) 'Issues for Sustainability of Non-Government Organisations in the Alcohol and Other Drugs Sector'. *Drug and Alcohol Review* 29: 47–52.

Srivastva, S., and Cooperrider, D. (eds.) (1990) *Appreciative Management and Leadership: The Power of Positive Thought and Action in Organisations*. San Francisco: Jossey-Bass.

Stanford Centre for Social Innovation (2013) 'Social Innovation', http://csi.gsb.stanford.edu/social-innovation (Accessed 25 January 2016).

Stelovich, S. (1979) 'From the Hospital to the Prison: A Step Forward in Deinstitutionalization?'. *Hospital and Community Psychiatry* 39(9): 618–620.

Stevens, A. (2007) '"When Two Dark Figures Collide": Evidence and Discourse on Drug-Related Crime'. *Critical Social Policy* 27(1): 77–99.

Stevens, A. (2012a) '"I am the Person Now I was Always Meant to Be": Identity Reconstruction and Narrative Reframing in Therapeutic Community Prisons'. *Criminology and Criminal Justice* 12(5): 527–547.

Stevens, A. (2012b) *Offender Rehabilitation and Therapeutic Communities: Enabling Change the TC Way*. London: Routledge.

Stone, R. (2015) 'Desistance and Identity Repair: Redemption Narratives and Resistance to Stigma'. *British Journal of Criminology* (Advanced online access 12 August 2015).

Stump, E., Beamish, P., and Stellenberger, R. (1999) 'Self Concept Changes in Sex Offenders following Prison Psycho-educational Treatment'. *Journal of Offender Rehabilitation* 29(1/2): 101–111.

Substance Abuse and Mental Health Services Administration (SAMHSA) (2009) *Guiding Principles and Elements of Recovery-Oriented Systems of Care: What Do We Know From the Research?*. Rockville, MD: US Department of Health and Human Services, SAMHSA.

SAMHSA (2012) *SAMHSA's Working Definition of Recovery – 10 Guiding Principles of Recovery*. Rockville, MD: US Department of Health and Human Services, SAMHSA.

SAMHSA (2013) 'Co-Occurring Disorders', http://www.samhsa.gov/co-occurring/ (Accessed 1 December 2013).

Suddaby, R., and Viale, T. (2011) 'Professionals and Field Level Change: Institutional Work and the Professional Project'. *Current Sociology* 59: 423–442.

Svensson, K., and Åkström, K. (2013) 'The Field of Social Regulation: How the State Creates a Profession'. *Professions and Professionalism* 3(2): 557–573.

Svensson, L., and Evetts, J. (eds.) (2003) *Conceptual and Comparative Studies of Continental and Anglo-American Professions*. Göteborg: Göteborg University.

Svensson, L., and Evetts, J. (eds.) (2010) *Sociology of Professions: Continental and Anglo-Saxon Traditions*. Göteborg: Daidalos.

Swartz, J., and Lurigio, A. (1999) 'Psychiatric Illness and Comorbidity amongst Adult Male Jail Detainees in Drug Treatment'. *Psychiatric Services* 50: 1628–1630.

Szasz, T. (2007) *Coercion as Cure: A Critical History of Psychiatry*. New Brunswick: Transaction Publishers.

Talbott, J. (1979) 'Deinstitutionalization: Avoiding the Disasters of the Past'. *Hospital and Community Psychiatry* 30(9): 621–624.

Tasmanian Department of Justice (2011) *Breaking the Cycle – A Strategic Plan for Tasmanian Corrections 2011–2020.* Hobart: Tasmanian Department of Justice. Available online at http://www.justice.tas.gov.au/__data/assets/pdf_file/0005/168881/Breaking_the_Cycle_strategic_plan.pdf (Accessed 1 February 2014).

Tasmanian Department of Justice (2013) *Department of Justice Annual Report 2012–2013.* Hobart: Tasmanian Department of Justice.

Tasmanian Department of Justice (2014) *Department of Justice Annual Report 2013–2014.* Hobart: Tasmanian Department of Justice.

Tasmanian Department of Police and Emergency Management (2011) *Annual Report 2010–2011.* Hobart: State Government of Tasmania.

Tasmanian Department of Premier and Cabinet (2011) *Cost of Living Indicators for Tasmania: Final Report.* Hobart: Social Inclusion Unit, Department of Premier and Cabinet, State Government of Tasmania.

Taylor, K., and Blanchette, K. (2009) 'The Women are Not Wrong: It is the Approach that is Debatable'. *Criminology and Public Policy* 8(1): 221–229.

Terdiman, R. (1987) 'Translator's Introduction to "The Force of Law: Toward a Sociology of the Juridicial Field" by Pierre Bourdieu'. *The Hastings Law Journal* 38: 805–813.

Thompson, M., and Petrovic, M. (2009) 'Gendered Transitions: Within-Person Changes in Employment, Family and Illicit Drug Use'. *Journal of Research in Crime and Delinquency* 46(3): 377–408.

Thompson, M., and Uggen, C. (2012) 'Dealers, Thieves, and the Common Determinants of Drug and Non-Drug Illegal Earnings'. *Criminology* 50(4): 1057–1087.

Thompson, N., Stradling, S., Murphy, M. and O'Neill, P. (1996) 'Stress and Organisational Culture'. *British Journal of Social Work* 26: 647–665.

Tierney, D., and McCabe, M. (2002) 'Motivation for Behavior Change Among Sex Offenders: A Review of the Literature'. *Clinical Psychology Review* 22: 113–129.

Toch, H. (1977) *Living in Prison: The Ecology of Survival.* New York: Free Press.

Toch, H. (1992) *Mosaics of Despair: Human Breakdowns in Prison.* Washington DC: American Psychological Association.

Toohey, J. (2012) *'Sobering Thoughts': An Examination of Tasmania's Sober Driver Program (Field Research Report).* Hobart: School of Social Sciences, University of Tasmania.

Tonry, M. (2011) 'Making Peace, Not a Desert: Penal Reform Should be About Values Not Justice Reinvestment'. *Criminology and Public Policy* 10(3): 637–649.

Toomey, T., and Kluin, M., (2007) *Mental Health and Substance Abuse: Working with Aboriginal Communities for Improved in Mid Western NSW.* Orange, NSW: Centre for Rural and Remote Mental Health.

Tournier, R. (1979) 'Alcoholics Anonymous as Treatment and Ideology'. *Journal of Studies on Alcohol and Drugs* 40(3): 230–239.

Townsend, M. (2004) 'Stay Calm Everyone, There's Prozac in the Drinking Water'. *The Guardian*, 8 August 2004. Available online at http://www.theguardian.com/society/2004/aug/08/health.mentalhealth (Accessed 20 November 2013).

Travers, M. (2013) 'Qualitative Interviewing Methods', in Walter, M. (ed.) *Social Research Methods* (3rd ed.). South Melbourne: Oxford University Press.

Trotter, C. (1999) *Working with Involuntary Clients.* London: SAGE Publications.

Trotter, C. (2009) 'Pro-Social Modelling'. *European Journal of Probation* 1(2): 142–152.

Turning Point Alcohol and Drug Centre (2012) 'PsyCheck', http://www.psycheck.org.au/ (Accessed 10 December 2012).

Tyler, T. (ed.) (2007) *Legitimacy and Criminal Justice: International Perspectives*. New York: Russell Sage Foundation.

Uggen, C. (2000) 'Work as a Turning Point in the Lifecourse of Criminals: A Duration Model of Age, Employment and Recidivism'. *American Sociological Review* 65(4): 529–546.

Uggen, C. (2012) 'Stale Records'. Christopher Uggen's Blog, 13 January 2012, http://chrisuggen.blogspot.com.au/2012/01/stale-records.html (Accessed 30 January 2013).

Uggen, C., and Kruttschnitt, C. (1998) 'Crime in the Breaking: Gender Differences in Desistance'. *Law and Society Review* 32(2): 339–366.

Uggen, C., Manza, J., and Behrens, A. (2004) 'Less than the Average Citizen: Stigma, Role Transition and the Civic Reintegration of Convicted Felons', in Maruna, S., and Immarigeon, R. (eds.) *After Crime and Punishment: Pathways to Offender Reintegration*. Cullompton: Willan Publishing.

Uggen, C., Manza, J., and Thompson, M. (2006) 'Citizenship, Democracy and the Civic Reintegration of Criminal Offenders'. *The Annals of the American Academy of Political and Social Science* 605: 281–310.

Uggen, C., and Piliavin, I. (1998) 'Asymmetrical Causation and Criminal Desistance'. *Journal of Criminal Law and Criminology* 88(4): 1399–1422.

Uggen, C., and Thompson, M. (2003) 'The Socio-Economic Determinants of Ill-Gotten Gains: Within-Person Changes in Drug Use and Illegal Earnings'. *American Journal of Sociology* 100: 146–185.

Ugwudike, P. (2010) 'Compliance with Community Penalties: The Importance of Interactional Dynamics', in McNeill, F., Raynor, P., and Trotter, C. (eds.) *Offender Supervision: New Directions in Theory, Research and Practice*. Cullompton: Willan Publishing.

van der Haar, D., and Hosking, D. (2004) 'Evaluating Appreciative Inquiry: A Relational Constructivist Perspective'. *Human Relations* 57(8): 1017–1036.

van Ginneken, E. (2014) 'Making Sense of Imprisonment: Narratives of Post-Traumatic Growth among Female Prisoners'. *International Journal of Offender Therapy and Comparative Criminology* (Advanced online access 2 September 2015): 1–20.

Veldhuis, T. (2012) *Designing Rehabilitation and Reintegration Programmes for Violent and Extremist Offenders: A Realist Approach*. The Hague: International Centre for Counterterrorism – The Hague.

Victorian Government Department of Health (2011a) *Recovery-Oriented Practice Literature Review*. State of Victoria: Melbourne.

Victorian Government Department of Health (2011b) *Framework for Recovery-Oriented Practice*. Melbourne: State of Victoria.

Von Drehle, D. (2010) 'Why Crime Went Away: The Murder Rate in America is at an all-time low. Will Recession Reverse that?'. *TIME Magazine*, 22 February 2010.

Wacquant, L. (2004) 'Following Pierre Bourdieu into the Field'. *Ethnography* 5(4): 397–414.

Wacquant, L. (2009) *Punishing the Poor: The Neoliberal Government of Social Insecurity*. Durham: Duke University Press.

Walgrave, L. (2008) *Restorative Justice, Self Interest and Responsible Citizenship*. Cullompton: Willan Publishing.

Walter, M. (2010a) 'The Nature of Social Science Research', in Walter, M. (ed.) *Social Research Methods* (2nd ed.). South Melbourne: Oxford University Press.

Walter, M. (2010b) 'Participatory Action Research', in Walter, M. (ed.) *Social Research Methods* (2nd ed.). South Melbourne: Oxford University Press.

Walter, M. (ed.) (2013) *Social Research Methods* (3rd ed.). South Melbourne: Oxford University Press.

Walters, S., Clark, M., Gingerich, R., and Meltzer, M. (2007) *Motivating Offenders to Change: A Guide for Probation and Parole* Washington DC: National Institute of Corrections.

Ward, T. (2012) 'Moral Strangers or Fellow Travellers? Contemporary Perspectives on Offender Rehabilitation'. *Legal and Criminological Psychology* 17: 37–40.

Ward, T., and Brown, M. (2003) 'The Risk-Need Model of Offender Rehabilitation: A Critical Analysis', in Ward, T., Laws, D., and Hudson, S. (eds.) *Sexual Deviance: Issues and Controversies*. Thousand Oaks, CA: SAGE.

Ward, T., and Fortune, C. (2013) 'The Good Lives Model: Aligning Risk Reduction with Promoting Offenders' Personal Goals'. *European Journal of Probation* 5(2): 29–46.

Ward, T., and Maruna, S. (2007) *Rehabilitation: Beyond the Risk Paradigm*. London: Routledge.

Ward, T., Melser, J., and Yates, P. (2007) 'Reconstructing the Risk-Need-Responsivity Model: A Theoretical Elaboration and Evaluation'. *Aggression and Violent Behaviour* 12: 208–228.

Ward, T., and Stewart, C. (2003) 'Criminogenic Needs and Human Needs: A Theoretical Model'. *Psychology, Crime and Law* 9(2): 125–143.

Ward, T., Yates, P., and Willis, G. (2012) 'The Good Lives Model and the Risk-Need-Responsivity Model: A Critical Response to Andrews, Bonta and Wormith'. *Criminal Justice and Behavior* 39(1): 94–110.

Warr, M. (1998) 'Life-Course Transitions and Desistance from Crime'. *Criminology* 36: 183–216.

Weaver, A. (2013) 'This is Who I Am'. *EuroVista Probation and Community Justice* 3(1): 4.

Weaver, B. (2009) 'Communicative Punishment as a Penal Approach to Supporting Desistance'. *Theoretical Criminology* 13(1): 9–29.

Weaver, B. (2011) 'Co-Producing Community Justice: The Transformative Potential of Personalisation for Penal Sanctions'. *British Journal of Social Work* 41(6): 1038–1057.

Weaver, B. (2012) 'The Relational Context of Desistance: Some Implications and Opportunities for Social Policy'. *Social Policy and Administration* 46(4): 395–412.

Weaver, B. (2013a) 'Co-Producing Desistance: Who Works to Support Desistance?', in Durnescu, I., and McNeill, F. (eds.) *Understanding Penal Practice*. Basingstoke: Palgrave Macmillan.

Weaver, B. (2013b) 'The Importance of Social Relations in Personal Change'. *Scottish Justice Matters* 1(2): 12–14.

Weaver, B. (2014) 'Control or Change? Developing Dialogues between Desistance Research and Public Protection Practices'. *Probation Journal* 61(1): 8–26.

Weaver, B. (2015) *Offending and Desistance: The Importance of Social Relations*. London: Routledge.

Weaver, B., and McCulloch, T. (2012) *Co-Producing Criminal Justice (Report)*. Glasgow: Scottish Government Social Research.

Weaver, B., and McNeill, F. (2008) *Giving Up Crime: Directions for Policy*. Glasgow: Scottish Centre for Crime and Justice Research.

Weaver, B., and McNeill, F. (2010) 'Travelling Hopefully: Desistance Research and Probation Practice', in Brayford, J., Cowe, F., and Deering, F. (eds.) *What Else Works? Creative Work with Offenders*. Cullompton: Willan Publishing.

Weaver, B., and McNeill, F. (2015) 'Lifelines: Desistance, Social Relations and Reciprocity'. *Criminal Justice and Behavior* 42(1): 95–107.

Weaver, B., and Nicholson, D. (2012) 'Co-Producing Change: Resettlement as a Mutual Enterprise'. *Prison Service Journal* 204: 9–16.

Weber, M. (1968) *Economy and Society*. Totowa, NJ: Bedminster.

Welch, M. (1997) 'The War on Drugs and Correctional Warehousing: Alternative Strategies for the Drugs Crisis' *Journal of Offender Rehabilitation* 25(1/2): 43–60.

West, R. (2005) 'Time for a Change: Putting the Transtheoretical (Stages of Change) Model to Rest'. *Addiction* 100: 1036–1039.

White, R. (1983a) 'Teacher Militancy, Ideology and Politics'. *The Australian and New Zealand Journal of Sociology* 19(2): 253–271.

White, R. (1983b) *Teachers as State Workers and the Politics of Professionalism*. Doctor of Philosophy Thesis. Canberra: Australian National University.

White, R. (1983c) 'On Teachers and Proletarianisation'. *Discourse: Studies in the Cultural Politics of Education* 3(2): 45–57.

White, R., and Graham, H. (2010) *Working with Offenders: A Guide to Concepts and Practices*. Cullompton: Willan Publishing.

White, R., and Graham, H. (2015) 'Greening Justice: Examining the Interfaces of Criminal, Social and Ecological Justice'. *British Journal of Criminology* (Advanced online release 3 February 2015).

White, R., Haines, F., and Asquith, N. (2010) *Crime and Criminology* (5th ed.). South Melbourne: Oxford University Press.

White, R., Haines, F., & Asquith, N. (2012) *Crime & Criminology* (5th ed.). Oxford University Press: South Melbourne.

White, W. (2001) 'A Lost Vision: Addiction Counselling as Community Organization'. *Alcoholism Treatment Quarterly* 19(4): 1–32.

White, W. (2005) 'Recovery: Its History and Renaissance as an Organising Construct Concerning Alcohol and Other Drug Problems'. *Alcoholism Treatment Quarterly* 23(1): 3–15.

White, W. (2007) 'Addiction Recovery: Its Definition and Conceptual Boundaries'. *Journal of Substance Abuse Treatment* 33(3): 229–241.

White, W. (2008a) 'Recovery: Old Wine, Flavour of the Month or New Organising Paradigm?'. *Substance Use and Misuse* 43(12–13): 1987–2000.

White, W. (2008b) *Recovery Management and Recovery-Oriented Systems of Care: Scientific Rationale and Promising Practices*. Rockville, MD: Centre for Substance Abuse Treatment, Substance Abuse and Mental Health Services Administration.

White, W. (2010) 'Non-Clinical Addiction Recovery Support Services: History, Rationale, Models, Potentials, and Pitfalls'. *Alcoholism Treatment Quarterly* 28(3): 256–272.

White, W., Kurtz, E., and Sanders, M. (2006) *Recovery Management*. Rockville, MD: Centre for Substance Abuse Treatment, Substance Abuse and Mental Health Services Administration.

Whyte, B. (2007) 'Restoring "Stakeholder" Involvement in Justice', in Hunter, S., and Ritchie, P. (eds.) *Co-Production and Personalisation in Social Care: Changing Relationships in the Provision of Social Care (Research Highlights 49)*. London: Jessica Kingsley Publishers.

Williams, I. (2009) 'Offender Health and Social Care: A Review of the Evidence on Inter-Agency Collaboration'. *Health and Social Care in the Community* 17(6): 573–580.

Wilson, M. (2012) 'Art Therapy in Addictions Treatment: Creativity and Shame Reduction' in Malchiodi, C. (ed.) *Handbook of Art Therapy* (2nd ed.). New York: Guilford Press.

Wilson, D., Bouffard, L., and MacKenzie, D. (2005) 'A Quantitative Review of Structured, Group Oriented Cognitive Behavioural Programs for Offenders'. *Criminal Justice and Behavior* 32(2): 172–204.

Woods, R. (2008) 'A Tale of Two Psyches', in Allsop, S. (ed.) *Drug Use and Mental Health: Effective Responses to Co-Occurring Drug and Mental Health Problems*. Melbourne: IP Communications.

World Health Organisation (1994) *Lexicon of Alcohol and Drugs Terms*. Geneva: World Health Organisation. Available online at: http://apps.who.int/iris/bitstream/10665/39461/1/9241544686_eng.pdf (Accessed 1 September 2015).

Wormith, J., Althouse, R., Simpson, M., Reitzel, L., Fagan, T., and Morgan, R. (2007) 'The Rehabilitation and Reintegration of Offenders: The Current Landscape and Some Future Directions for Correctional Psychology'. *Criminal Justice and Behavior* 34(7): 879–892.

Wormith, J., Gendreau, P., and Bonta, J. (2012) 'Deferring to Clarity, Parsimony and Evidence in Reply to Ward, Yates and Willis'. *Criminal Justice and Behavior* 39(1): 111–120.

Wright, A. (2010) 'Strange Bedfellows? Reaffirming Rehabilitation and Prison Privatisation'. *Journal of Offender Rehabilitation* 49(1): 74–90.

Wrzesniewski, A., and Dutton, J. (2001) 'Crafting a Job: Revisioning Employees as Active Crafters of Their Work'. *The Academy of Management Review* 26(2): 179–201.

Wrzesniewski, A., Dutton, J., and Debebe, G. (2003) 'Interpersonal Sensemaking and the Meaning of Work'. *Research in Organisational Behaviour* 25: 93–135.

Wunderer, R. (2001) 'Employeers as "Co-Intrapreneurs" – A Transformation Concept'. *Leadership and Organization Development Journal* 22(5): 193–211.

Yates, R. (2011) 'Therapeutic Communities: Can-Do Attitudes for Must-Have Recovery'. *Journal of Groups in Addiction and Recovery* 6(1–2): 101–116.

Yates, R., and Malloch, M. (eds.) (2010) *Tackling Addiction: Pathways to Recovery*. London: Jessica Kingsley Publishers.

Young, J. (2011) *The Criminological Imagination*. Cambridge: Polity Press.

Young, L., Sigafoos, J., Suttie, J., Ashman, A., and Grevell, P. (1998) 'Deinstitutionalisation of Persons with Intellectual Disabilities: A Review of Australian Studies'. *Journal of Intellectual and Developmental Disability* 23(2): 155–170.

Zedner, L. (2006) 'Neither Safe Nor Sound? The Perils and Possibilities of Risk'. *Canadian Journal of Criminology and Criminal Justice* 48(3): 423–434.

Zedner, L. (2007) 'Pre-Crime and Post-Criminology?'. *Theoretical Criminology* 11(2): 261–281.

Zehr, H. (2005) *Changing Lenses: A New Focus for Crime and Justice* (3rd ed.). Scottsdale: Herald Press.

Bibliography
Probation Practice
and the New Penology

American Friends Service Committee 1971, *The Struggle for Justice*. New York: Hill and Wang.

Andrews, D. and Bonta, J. 2010, Rehabilitating Criminal Justice Policy and Practice. *Psychology, Public Policy and Law*, 16(1), 39-55.

Annison, J., Eadie, T. and Knight, C. 2008, People First: Probation Officer Perspectives on Probation Work. *Probation Journal*, 55(3), 259-271.

Annison, J. 2006, *Career Trajectories of Graduate Trainee Probation Officers*. Plymouth: University of Plymouth.

Ashworth, A. 2000, *Sentencing and Criminal Justice*, 3rd Edition. London: Butterworths.

Beaumont, B. 1999, Assessing Risk in Work with Offenders in *Risk Assessment in Social Care and Social Work*, edited by P. Parsloe. London: Jessica Kingsley.

Bernfeld, G., Farrington, D. and Leschied, A. 2001, *Offender Rehabilitation in Practice*. Chichester: Wiley.

Bottoms, A. 2001, Compliance and Community Penalties in *Community Penalties: Changes and Challenges*, edited by A. Bottoms, L. Gelsthorpe and S. Rex. Cullompton: Willan.

Bottoms, A. 1995, The Philosophy and Politics of Punishment and Sentencing in *The Politics of Sentencing Reform*, edited by C. Clarkson and R. Morgan. Oxford: Clarendon Press.

Bottoms, A. and McWilliams, W. 1979, A Non-Treatment Paradigm for Probation Practice. *British Journal of Social Work*, 9, 159-202.

Bourdieu, P. 1990, *The Logic of Practice*. Cambridge: Polity Press.

Bourdieu, P. 1977, *Outline of a Theory of Practice*. Cambridge: Cambridge University Press.

Brody, S. 1976, *The Effectiveness of Sentencing*. London: HMSO.

Brown, I. 1998, Successful Probation Practice in *Proceedings of the Probation Studies Unit Second Colloquium*, edited by A. Gibbs. Oxford: Oxford Centre for Criminological Research.

Burnett, R., Baker, K. and Roberts, C. 2007, Assessment, Supervision and Intervention: Fundamental Practice in Probation in *Handbook of Probation*, edited by L. Gelsthorpe and R. Morgan. Cullompton: Willan.

Burnett, R. and McNeill, F. 2005, The Place of the Officer-Offender Relationship in Assisting Offenders to Desist from Crime. *Probation Journal*, (52)3, 221-242.

Carter, P. 2003, *Managing Offenders, Reducing Crime: the Correctional Services Review*. London: Home Office Strategy Unit.

Causer, G. and Exworthy, M. 1999, Professionals as Managers Across the Public Sector in *Professionals and the New Managerialism in the Public Sector*, edited by M. Exworthy and S. Halford. Buckingham: Open University Press.

Cavadino, M. and Dignan, J. 2002, *The Penal System – an Introduction*, 3rd Edition. London: Sage.

Chapman, T. and Hough, M. 1998, *Evidence Based Practice: A Guide to Effective Practice*. London: HMIP.

Cheliotis, L. 2006, How Iron is the Iron Cage of New Penology? The Role of Human Agency in the Implementation of Criminal Justice Policy. *Punishment and Society*, 8(3), 313-340.

Clarke, K. 30 June 2010, 2010-last update, *Revolving door of crime and reoffending to stop says Clarke*. Available: http://www.justice.gov.uk/news/newsrelease300610a.htm [28 July 2010].

Clarke, J., Gewirtz, S. and McLaughlin, E. 2000, Reinventing the Welfare State in *New Managerialism, New Welfare?*, edited by J. Clarke, S. Gewirtz and E. McLaughlin. London: Sage.

Clear, T. 2005, Places not Cases? Re-thinking the Probation Focus. *Howard Journal*, 44(2), 172-184.

Clegg, F. 1990, *Simple Statistics*. Cambridge: Cambridge University Press.

Cohen, S. 1985, *Visions of Social Control*. Cambridge: Polity Press.

Crow, I. 2003, *The Treatment and Rehabilitation of Offenders*. London: Sage.

Davies, M., Croall, H. and Tyrer, J. 2005, *Criminal Justice: An Introduction to the Criminal Justice System in England and Wales*, 3rd Edition. Harlow: Pearson.

Davies, M., Croall, H. and Tyrer, M. 1998, *Criminal Justice. An Introduction to the Criminal Justice System in England and Wales*, 2nd Edition. Harlow: Longman.

Deering, J. 2010, Attitudes and Beliefs of Trainee Probation Officers – a New Breed? *Probation Journal*, 57(1), 9-26.

Digard, L. 2010, When Legitimacy is Denied: Offender Perceptions of the Prison Recall System. *Probation Journal*, 57(1), 43-62.

Doherty, T. and Horne, T. 2002, *Managing Public Services: Implementing Changes*. London: Routledge.

Downden, C. and Andrews, D. 2004, The Importance of Staff Practice in Delivering Effective Correctional Treatment: a Meta Analysis. *International Journal of Offender Therapy and Comparative Criminology*, 48, 203-214.

Downs, G. 1986, *The Search for Government Efficiency: From Hubris to Helplessness*. New York: Random House.

Egan, G. 2002, *The Skilled Helper*, 7th Edition. Pacific Grove: Brooks Cole.

Evans, D., Hearn, M., Uhlemann, M. and Ivey, A. 1998, *Essential Interviewing: a Programmed Approach to Effective Communication*, 5th Edition. London: Brooks Cole.

Exworthy, M. and Halford, S. 1999, Professionals and Managers in a Changing Public Sector – Conflict, Compromise and Collaboration? in *Professionals and the New Managerialism in the Public Sector*, edited by M. Exworthy and S. Halford. Buckingham: Open University Press.

Farooq, M. 1998, Probation, Power and Change. *Vista*, 3(3), 208-220.

Farrall, S. 2002, *Rethinking What Works with Offenders*. Cullompton: Willan.

Farrington, D. 1996, Criminological Psychology: Individual and Family Factors in the Explanation and Prevention of Offending in *Working with Offenders: Psychological Practice in Offender Rehabilitation*, edited by C. Hollin. Chichester: Wiley.

Farrow, K. 2004a, Still Committed after all These Years? Morale in the Modern-Day Probation Service. *Probation Journal*, 51(3), 206-220.

Farrow, K. 2004b, Sustaining Staff Commitment during Organisational Change. *Vista*, 9(2), 80-89.

Faulkner, D. 2008, The New Shape of Probation in England and Wales: Values and Opportunities in a Changing Context. *Probation Journal*, 55(1), 71-83.

Feeley, M. and Simon, J. 1992, The New Penology: Notes on the Emerging Strategy for Corrections. *Criminology*, 30(4), 449-475.

Fitzgibbon, D. 2008, Fit for Purpose? OASys Assessments and Parole Decisions. *Probation Journal*, 55(1), 55-69.

Flynn, N. 2002a, Organisation and Management: a Changing Agenda in *Probation: Working for Justice*, edited by D. Ward, J. Scott and M. Lacey, 2nd Edition. Oxford: Oxford University Press.

Flynn, N. 2002b, *Public Sector Management*, 4th Edition. Harlow: Pearson.

Folkard, M., Smith, D.E. and Smith, D.D. 1976, *IMPACT: Intensive Matched Probation and After-Care Treatment*. London: HMSO.

Foster, J. 2003, Police Cultures in *Handbook of Policing*, edited by T. Newburn. Cullompton: Willan.

Foucault, M. 1977, *Discipline and Punish: The Birth of the Prison*. London: Allen Lane.

Frauley, J. 2005, Representing Theory and Theorising in Criminal Justice Studies: Practising Theory Considered. *Critical Criminology*, 13, 245-265.

Garland, D. 2001a, *The Culture of Control*. Oxford: Oxford University Press.

Garland, D. 2001b, *Mass Imprisonment: Social Causes and Consequences*. London: Sage.

Garland, D. 1996, The Limits of the Sovereign State. *British Journal of Criminology*, 36(4), 445-471.

Gibson, B. 2004, *Criminal Justice Act 2003*. Winchester: Waterside.

Giddens, A. 1998, Risk Society: the Context of British Politics in *The Politics of Risk Society*, edited by J. Franklin. Cambridge: Polity Press.

Goodsell, C. 1993, Reinventing Government or Rediscovering it? *Public Administration Review*, 53, January-February, 85-86.

Gorman, K. 2001, Cognitive-Behaviourism and the Holy Grail, *Probation Journal*, 48(1), 3-9.

Hampson, N. 1968, *The Enlightenment*. Harmondsworth: Penguin.

Hannah-Moffat, K. 2005, Criminogenic Needs and the Transformative Risk Subject: Hybridizations of Risk/Need Penality. *Punishment and Society*, 7(1), 29-51.

Harding, J. 2000, A Community Justice Dimension to Effective Probation Practice. *Howard Journal of Criminal Justice*, 39(2), 132-149.

Hedderman, C. and Hough, M. 2004, Getting Tough or Being Effective: What Matters? in *What Matters in Probation*, edited by G. Mair. Cullompton: Willan.

Hennesey, J. 1998, Reinventing Government: Does Leadership make a Difference? *Public Administration Review*, 58, November-December, 522-532.

Home Office 2006a, *The Offender Assessment System: an Evaluation of the Second Pilot*. London: Home Office.

Home Office 2006b, *Statistical Bulletin: Offender Management Case Management Statistics 2005*. London: RDS NOMS.

Home Office 2005, *National Standards for the Supervision of Offenders in the Community*. London: Home Office.

Home Office 2004a, *Reducing Crime: Changing Lives*. London: Home Office.

Home Office 2004b, *Reducing Re-Offending: National Action Plan*. London: Home Office.

Home Office 2002a, *National Probation Service Briefing: Introduction to OASys*. London: Home Office.

Home Office 2002b, *Offender Assessment System: OASys*, 2nd Edition. London: Home Office.

Home Office 2001, *A New Choreography: An Integrated Strategy for the National Probation Service for England and Wales*. London: Home Office.

Home Office 2000a, *The Accredited Programmes Initiative. Home Office Probation Circular 60/2000*. London: Home Office.

Home Office 2000b, *National Standards for the Supervision of Offenders in the Community*. London: Home Office.

Home Office 1998, *Effective Practice Initiative: Probation Circular 35/98*. London: Home Office.

Home Office 1996, *Protecting the Public*. London: Home Office.

Home Office 1995, *Strengthening Punishment in the Community*. London: Home Office.

Home Office 1992, *National Standards for the Supervision of Offenders in the Community*. London: Home Office.

Home Office 1991, *The Criminal Justice Act 1991*. London: Home Office

Home Office 1990, *Crime, Justice and Protecting the Public*. London: Home Office.

Home Office 1988, *Punishment, Custody and the Community*. London: Home Office.

Home Office 1984, *Statement of National Objectives and Priorities*. London: Home Office.

Hudson, B. 2003, *Understanding Justice*. Buckingham: Open University Press.

Hudson, B. 2002, Punishment and Control in *The Oxford Handbook of Criminology*, edited by M. Maguire, R. Morgan and R. Reiner, 3rd Edition. Oxford: Oxford University Press.

Hughes, G. and Gilling, D. 2004, Mission Impossible? The Habitus of the Community Safety Manager and the New Expertise in the Local Partnership Governance of Crime and Safety. *Criminal Justice*, 4(2), 129-149.

Humphrey, C. and Pease, K. 1992, Effectiveness Measurement in Probation – a View from the Troops. *Howard Journal of Criminal Justice*, 31(1), 31-52.

Jones, T. and Newburn, T. 2007, *Policy Transfer and Criminal Justice. Exploring US Influence over British Crime Control Policy.* Buckingham: Open University Press.

Kazi, M. and Wilson, J. 1996, Applying Single-Case Evaluation in Social Work. *British Journal of Social Work*, 26, 699-717.

Kemshall, H. 2003, *Understanding Risk in Criminal Justice.* Buckingham: Open University Press.

Kemshall, H. and Maguire, M. 2002, Public Protection, Partnership and Risk Penality: The Multi-Agency Risk Management of Sexual and Violent Offenders in *Criminal Justice, Mental Health and the Politics of Risk*, edited by N. Gray, J. Laing and L. Noaks, London: Cavendish.

Kemshall, H. and Wood, J. 2007, High Risk Offenders and Public Protection in *Handbook of Probation*, edited by L. Gelsthorpe and R. Morgan. Cullompton: Willan.

Lewis, S. 2005, Rehabilitation: Headline or Footnote in the New Penal Policy? *Probation Journal*, 522, 119-135.

Light, P. 1994, Partial Quality Management. *Government Executive*, 26, April, 65-66.

Lipsky, M. 1980, *Street-Level Bureaucracy: Dilemmas of the Individual in Public Services*. New York: Russell Sage Foundation.

Lipton, D., Martinson, R. and Wilks, J. 1975, *The Effectiveness of Correctional Treatment*. New York: Praeger.

Loader, I. and Sparks, R. 2002, Contemporary Landscapes of Crime, Order and Control. Governance, Risk and Globalisation in *Oxford Handbook of Criminologyi*, edited by M. Maguire, R. Morgan and R. Reiner, 3rd Edition. Oxford: Oxford University Press.

Lynch, M. 1998, Waste Managers? The New Penology, Crime Fighting and Parole Agent Identity. *Law and Society Review*, 32(4), 839-869.

Maguire, M. and Raynor, P. 2010. Putting the OM into NOMS: Problems and Possibilities for Offender Management in *What Else Works? Creative Work with Offenders*, edited by J. Brayford, F. Cowe and J. Deering. Cullompton: Willan.

Maguire, M. 2008, *Supervision Discussion – Personal Notes*.

Maguire, M. 2002, Crime Statistics: the 'Data Explosion' and Its Implications in *The Oxford Handbook of Criminology*, edited by M. Maguire, R. Morgan and R. Reiner, 3rd Edition. Oxford: Oxford University Press.

Mair, G. 2000, Credible Accreditation. *Probation Journal*, 47(4), 268-271.

Mair, G. and Canton, R. 2007, Sentencing, Community Penalties and the Role of the Probation Service in *Handbook of Probation*, edited by L. Gelsthorpe and R. Morgan. Cullompton: Willan.

Margetts, T. 1997, The Future of Partnership Work within the Probation Service. *Probation Journal*, 44(4).

Marsh, K., Fox, C. and Sarmah, R. 2009, Is Custody an Effective Sentencing Option for the UK? Evidence from a Meta-Analysis. *Probation Journal*, 56(2), 129-151.

Maruna, S., Immarigeon, R. and LeBel, T. 2004, Ex-Offender Reintegration: Theory and Practice in *After Crime and Punishment: Pathways to Offender Reintegration*, edited by S. Maruna and R. Immarigeon. Cullompton: Willan.

Matthews, J. 2009, People First: Probation Officers' Perspectives on Probation Work: a Practitioner's Response. *Probation Journal*, 56(1), 61-67.

May, C. and Wadwell, J. 2001, *Enforcing Community Penalties: the Relationship between Enforcement and Reconviction*. London: Home Office.

May, T. 1991, *Probation: Politics, Policy and Practice*. Buckingham: Open University Press.

McAra, L. 2005, Modelling Penal Transformation. *Punishment and Society*, 7(3), 277-302.

McGuire, J. 2001, What Works in Correctional Intervention? Evidence and Practical Implications in *Offender Rehabilitation in Practice: Implementing and Evaluating Effective Programs*, edited by G. Bernfeld, D. Farrington and A. Leschied, Chichester: Wiley.

McIvor, G. and McNeill, F. 2007, *Promoting Desistence: Supervision Skills and Beyond*, First Conference of the Collaboration of Researchers for the Effective Development of Offender Supervision (CREDOS). University of Monash, Prato, Italy, 13 September 2007.

McKnight, J. 2008, 22 May 2008-last update, *Has Probation Been Taken Over by the Prison Service?* [Homepage of Napo], [Online]. Available: www.napo2.org.uk/napolog/archives/2008/05/has_probation_b.html [2 June 2008].

McLaughlin, E. and Muncie, J. 2000, The Criminal Justice System: New Labour's New Partnerships in *New Managerialism, New Welfare?*, edited by J. Clarke, S. Gewirtz and E. McLaughlin. London: Sage.

McNeill, F., Burns, N., Halliday, S., Hutton, N. and Tata, C. 2009, Risk, Responsibility and Reconfiguration. Penal Adaptation and Misadaptation. *Punishment and Society*, 11(4), 419-442.

McNeill, F. 2006, A Desistance Paradigm for Offender Management. *Criminology and Criminal Justice*, 6(1), 39-62.

McNeill, F., Batchelor, S., Burnett, R. and Knox, J. 2005, *21st Century Social Work. Reducing Re-Offending: Key Practice Skills*. Edinburgh: Scottish Executive.

McSweeney, T. and Hough, M. 2006, Supporting Offenders with Multiple Needs. Lessons for the 'Mixed Economy' Model of Service Provision. *Criminology and Criminal Justice*, 6(1), 107-125.

McWilliams, W. and Pease, K. 1990, Probation Practice and an End to Punishment. *Howard Journal of Criminal Justice*, 29(1), 14-24.

Merrington, S. and Stanley, S. 2007, Effectiveness: Who Counts What? in *Handbook of Probation*, edited by L. Gelsthorpe and R. Morgan. Cullompton: Willan.

Merrington, S. and Stanley, S. 2000, Doubts about the What Works Initiative. *Probation Journal*, 47(4), 272-275.

Mehta, A. 2008, Fit for Purpose? OASys Assessments and Parole Decisions: A Practitioner's View. *Probation Journal*, 55(2), 189-194.

Miller, W. and Rollnick, S. 2002, *Motivational Interviewing: Preparing People for Change*, 2nd Edition. London: Guilford Press.

Milner, J. and O'Byrne, P. 2002, *Assessment in Social Work*. 2nd Edition, Basingstoke; Palgrave.

Ministry of Justice 2008, *Community Sentencing – Reducing Re-Offending, Changing Lives*. London: Ministry of Justice.

Ministry of Justice 2007a, *Human Resources Workforce Profile Report*. London: Ministry of Justice.

Ministry of Justice 2007b, *National Standards for the Supervision of Offenders in the Community*. London: Ministry of Justice.

Minogue, M., Polidano, C. and Hulme, D. 1998, *Beyond the New Public Management: Changing Ideas and Practices in Governance*. Cheltenham: Edward Elgar.

Moe, R. and Gilmore, R. 1995, Rediscovering Principles of Public Administration: The Neglected Foundation of Public Law. *Public Administration Review*, 55, March, 135-163.

Morgan, R. 2003, *'Foreword' in Her Majesty's Inspectorate of Probation Annual Report 2002/03*. London: Home Office.

Mullins, L. 1999, *Management and Organisational Behaviour* 5th Edition. London: Pitman.

Murphy, S. 2004, *National Probation Service: Performance Report 12*. London: National Probation Service.

Naisbitt, J. 1985, *Reinventing the Corporation: Transforming your Job and Your Company for the New Information Society*. New York: Warner Books.

Napo 2010a, *Extensive Cuts: the Threat to Probation and Cafcass. Napo News* (219). London: Napo.

Napo 2010b, *Cuts Conspirators: Probation Faces Privatisation Threats and Administrative Chaos. Napo News* (222). London: Napo.

Napo 2008, *Justice: Re-organised Again. Napo News* (197). London: Napo.

Napo 2007a, *Changing Lives: An Oral History of Probation.* London: Napo.

Napo 2007b, *Offender Management Bill Reaches Statute Book. Napo News* (192). London: Napo.

Napo 2006, *Restructuring Probation - What Works? Napo's Response to the Home Office Consultation Paper 'Restructuring Probation to Reduce Re-Offending'.* London: Napo.

Napo 2006a, 25 October 2006-last update, *Fourfold Increase in Recalls to Prison.* Available: www.napo.org.uk [28 March 2007].

Napo 2006b, *NOMS Legislation Pulled! Napo News* (176). London: Napo.

Napo 2006c, *Probation Values: Commitment to Best Practice*. London: Napo.

Napo 2005, *NOMS - the Vision*. London: Napo.

Napo, 2003, *OASys and PSR Questionnaire - Summary*. *Napo News* (152) London: Napo.

Nash, M. and Ryan, M. 2003, Modernising and Joining-up Government: The Case of the Prison and Probation Services. *Contemporary Politics*, 9(2), 157-169.

National Offender Management Service 2008, 30 May 2008-last update, *Prison Population and Accommodation Briefing for 30th May 2008*. Available: http://www.hmprisonservice.gov.uk/assets/documents/10003A8330052008_web_report.doc [2 June 2008].

National Offender Management Service 2007a, *Our Aims*. Available: http://www.noms.homeoffice.gov.uk/ [19 November 2007].

National Offender Management Service 2007b, *Probation Circular 10/2007: Inform, Consult, Engage – an Offender Engagement Good Practice Guide*. London: NOMS.

National Offender Management Service 2006a, *Joining Together in Wales*. London: NOMS.

National Offender Management Service 2006b, *The NOMS Offender Management Model*. 2nd Edition, London: NOMS.

National Offender Management Service 2005a, *Home Secretary's Speech to the Prison Reform Trust, 19 September 2005*. London: NOMS.

National Offender Management Service 2005b, *The NOMS Offender Management Model*. London: NOMS.

National Offender Management Service 2005c, *Restructuring Probation to Reduce Re-Offending*. London: NOMS.

National Probation Service 2005, *Careers in Probation*. London: National Probation Service.

National Probation Service 2004a, *Bold Steps: The National Probation Service Business Plan 2004-05*. London: National Probation Service.

National Probation Service 2004b, *Careers in the National Probation Service*. London: National Probation Service.

National Probation Service 2004c, *Revised Targeting Strategy*. London: National Probation Service.

Nellis, M. 2005, *The Future of the Probation Ideal*. Presentation to Napo AGM 15 October 2005, Llandudno.

Nellis, M. 2002a, Community Justice, Time and the New National Probation Service. *Howard Journal*, 41(1), 59-86.

Nellis, M. 2002b, Probation, Partnerships and Civil Society in *Probation: Working for Justice*, edited by D. Ward, J. Scott and M. Lacey, 2nd Edition. Oxford: Oxford University Press.

Nellis, M. 1999, Towards the Field of Corrections: Modernising the Probation Service in the late 1990s. *Social Policy*, 33(3), 302-323.

Nellis, M. and Gelsthorpe, L. 2003, Human Rights and the Probation Values Debate in *Moving Probation Forward*, edited by W. Chui and M. Nellis. Harlow: Pearson.

Newburn, T. 2003, *Crime and Criminal Justice Policy* 2nd Edition. Harlow: Longman.

O'Malley, P. 2000, Risk Societies and the Government of Crime in *Dangerous Offenders*, edited by M. Brown and J. Pratt, London: Routledge.

Osborne, D. and Gaebler, T. 1992, *Reinventing Government: How the Entrepreneurial Spirit is Transforming the Public Sector*. Reading: Addison-Wesley.

Osborne, D. and Plastrik, P. 1997, *Banishing Bureaucracy: Five Strategies for Reinventing Government*. Reading: Addison-Wesley.

Parole Board 2009, *Annual Report and Accounts 2008-09*. London: The Stationery Office, London.

Parole Board 2008, *Annual Report and Accounts 2007-08*. London: The Stationery Office, London.

Parole Board 2001, *Annual Report and Accounts 2000-01*. London: The Stationery Office, London.

Partridge, S. 2004, *Examining Case Management Models for Community Sentences*. London: Home Office.

Pawson, R. and Tilley, N. 1997, *Realistic Evaluation*. London: Sage.

Porporino, F. 2010, Bringing Sense and Sensitivity to Corrections in *What Else Works? Creative Work with Offenders*, edited by J. Brayford, F. Cowe and J. Deering. Cullompton: Willan.

Pratt, J., Brown, D., Brown, M., Hallsworth, S. and Morrison, W. 2005. *The New Punitiveness: Trends, Theories, Perspectives*. Cullompton: Willan.

Pratt, J. 2002, *Punishment and Civilisation*. London: Sage.

Prochaska, J. 1994, *Systems of Psychotherapy: a Transtheoretical Analysis*. Pacific Grove: Brooks Cole.

Raine, J. 2002, Modernisation and Criminal Justice in *Probation: Working for Justice*, edited by D. Ward, J. Scott and M. Lacey, 2nd Edition. Oxford: Oxford University Press.

Rainey, H. and Steinbauer, P. 1999, Galloping Elephants: Developing Elements of a Theory of Effective Government Organisations. *Journal of Public Administration Research and Theory*, 9, January, 1-32.

Ranson, S. and Stewart, J. 1994, *Management for the Public Domain. Enabling the Learning Society*. Basingstoke: Macmillan.

Raynor, P. 2008, Community Penalties and Home Office Research: On the Way Back to 'Nothing Works'?. *Criminology and Criminal Justice*, 8(1),73-87.

Raynor, P. 2006, *The 'What Works' Experiment in England and Wales: Achievements and Lessons to be Learned*, Lecture to the University of Wales, Newport. Gregynog, Powys, June 2006.

Raynor, P. 2004, Rehabilitative and Reintegrative Approaches in *Alternatives to Prison: Options for an Insecure Society*, edited by A. Bottoms, S. Rex and G. Robinson. Cullompton: Willan.

Raynor, P. 1985, *Social Work, Justice and Control*. Oxford: Blackwells.

Raynor, P. and Maguire, M. 2010, Putting the OM into NOMS: Problems and Possibilities for Offender Management in *What Else Works? Creative Work with Offenders*, edited by J. Brayford, F. Cowe and J. Deering. Cullompton: Willan.

Raynor, P. and Maguire, M. 2006, End-to-End or End in Tears? Prospects for the Effectiveness of the National Offender Management Model in *Reshaping Probation and Prisons: the New Offender Management Framework*, edited by M. Hough, R. Allen and U. Padel. Bristol: Policy Press.

Raynor, P. and Vanstone, M. 2007, Towards a Correctional Service in *Handbook of Probation*, edited by L. Gelsthorpe and R. Morgan. Cullompton: Willan.

Raynor, P. and Vanstone, M. 2002, *Understanding Community Penalties: Probation, Policy and Social Change*. Buckingham: Open University Press.

Raynor, P. and Vanstone, M. 1994, *Straight Thinking on Probation: Third Interim Evaluation Report*. Bridgend: Mid Glamorgan Probation Service.

RDS NOMS 2006, *Offender Management Caseload Statistics 2005*. London: Home Office.

Reiner, R. 2000, *The Politics of the Police*, 3rd Edition. Oxford: Oxford University Press.

Rex, S. 1999, Desistence from Offending: Experiences of Probation. *Howard Journal of Criminal Justice*, 38(4), 366-383.

Roberts, J., Stalans, L., Indermaur, D. and Hough, M. 2003, *Penal Populism and Public Opinion*. Oxford: Oxford University Press.

Robinson, G. 2005, What Works in Offender Management?. *Howard Journal of Criminal Justice*, 44(3), 307-318.

Robinson, G. 2003, Risk and Risk Assessment in *Moving Probation Forward*, edited by W. Chui and M. Nellis. Harlow: Pearson.

Robinson, G. 2002, Exploring Risk Management in Probation Practice. Contemporary Developments in England and Wales. *Punishment and Society*, 4(1), 5-25.

Robinson, G. and Burnett, R. 2007, Experiencing Modernisation: Frontline Probation Perspectives on the Transition to a National Offender Management Service. *Probation Journal*, 54(4), 318-337.

Robinson, G. and McNeill, F. 2007, *Effective Individual Supervision: Taking Compliance Seriously*, First Conference of the Collaboration of Researchers for the Development of Effective Offender Supervision (CREDOS), University of Monash, Prato, Italy, 13 September 2007.

Robinson, G. and McNeill, F. 2004, Purposes Matter: Examining the 'Ends' of Probation in *What Matters in Probation*, edited by G. Mair. Cullompton: Willan.

Rose, N. 2000, Government and Control. *British Journal of Criminology*, 36(4), 321-339.

Rumgay, J. 2005, Counterblast: NOMS Bombs? *Howard Journal*, 44(2), 206-208.

Rumgay, J. 2000, *The Addicted Offender: Developments in British Policy and Practice*. Basingstoke: Palgrave

Russell, G. and Waste, R. 1998, The Limits of Reinventing Government. *American Review of Public Administration*, 28, December, 325-346.

Schein, E. 1992, *Organizational Culture and Leadership*, 2nd Edition. San Francisco: Jossey-Bass.

Schein, E. 1985, *Organizational Culture and Leadership*. San Francisco: Jossey-Bass.

Scott, J. 1990, *Domination and the Arts of Resistance: Hidden Transcripts*. London: Yale University Press.

Senior, P., Crowther-Dowey, C. and Long, M. 2007, *Understanding Modernisation in Criminal Justice*. Buckingham: Open University Press.

Simon, J. 2007, *Governing Through Crime*. Oxford: Oxford University Press.

Smale, G. 2000, *Social Work and Social Problems: Working Towards Social Inclusion and Social Change*. London: Macmillan.

Straw, J. 6 February 2009, 2009-last update, *Speech to Trainee Probation Officers, Probation Study School, University of Portsmouth, 4th February 2009*. Available: www.justice.gov.uk/news/speeches-2009 [6 February 2009, 2009].

Straw, J. 2007, *Letter to Neil Gerrard, M.P.*. London: Ministry of Justice.

Straw, J. 1997, *Commons Written Reply*, Hansard. London: Houses of Parliament.

Sutcliffe, G. 2006, *Letter to Chiefs and Chairs of Probation Boards in England and Wales*. London: Home Office

T3 Associates 2000, *Reasoning and Rehabilitation Revised: A Handbook for Teaching Cognitive Skills*. Ottawa: T3 Associates.

Taxman, F. and Ainsworth, S. 2009, Correctional Milieu: the Key to Quality Outcomes. *Victims and Offenders*, 4, 334-340.

Tonry, M. 2004, *Punishment and Politics: Evidence and Emulation in the Making of English Crime and Control Policy*. Cullompton: Willan.

Tonry, M. 2003, *Confronting Crime. Crime Control Policy under New Labour*. Cullompton: Willan.

Travis, A. 2007, *'Disaster Area' Prison and Probation Agency to be Scrapped in Weeks*. *The Guardian*, London.

Travis, A. 2006, *Government Acts to Stem Probation Crisis. The Guardian*, London.

Trotter, C. 1999, *Working with Involuntary Clients*. London: Sage.

Underdown, A. 1998, *Strategies for Effective Offender Supervision*. London: Home Office.

Vanstone, M. 2004a, *Supervising Offenders in the Community: a History of Probation Theory and Practice*. Aldershot: Ashgate.

Vanstone, M. 2004b, What Works and the Learning Organisation. *Vista*, 8(3), 177-181.

Vanstone, M. 1994, *A Moral Good Examined: A Survey of Work Undertaken within the Framework of the Standard Probation Order in Mid Glamorgan*. Bridgend: Mid Glamorgan Probation Service.

Ward, D. and Spencer, J. 1994, The Future of Probation Qualifying Training. *Probation Journal*, 41(2), 95-98.

Wells, O. 2005, *Napo Probation Directory 2005*. Kent: Shaw and Sons.

Whitfield, D. 1998, *Introduction to the Probation Service*. Winchester: Waterside.

Wilcox, A. 2003, Evidence-Based Youth Justice? Some Valuable Lessons from an Evaluation for the Youth Justice Board. *Youth Justice*, 3(1), 9-33.

Williams, B. 1995, *Probation Values*. London: Venture Press.

Willie, C. 2007, *Equality of Opportunity for Racial Minorities in the UK Civil Service: the Impact of Organisational Culture*, unpublished PhD, Cardiff University, Cardiff.

Worrall, A. 1997, *Punishment in the Community: the Future of Criminal Justice*. London: Longman.

Young, J. and Matthews, R. (eds) 1992, *Re-Thinking Criminology: the Realist Debate*. London: Sage.

Zedner, L. 2006, Managing the Market for Crime Control. *Criminology and Criminal Justice*, 6(3), 267-288.

References

Doing Probation Work

Aldridge, M. (1999a) 'Probation officer training, promotional culture and the public sphere', *Public Administration*, 77, 1: 73–90.

Aldridge, M. (1999b) 'Poor relations: state social work and the press in the UK', in B. Franklin (ed.) *Social Policy, the Media and Misrepresentation*, London: Routledge, 89–103.

Allard, T.J., Wortley, R.K. and Stewart, A.L. (2003) 'Role conflict in community corrections', *Psychology, Crime and Law*, 9, 3: 279–89.

Allen, J., Livingstone, S. and Reiner, R. (1998) 'True Lies: changing images of crime in British postwar cinema', *European Journal of Communication*, 13, 1: 53–75.

Annison, J. (2007) 'A gendered review of change within the probation service', *Howard Journal of Criminal Justice*, 46, 2: 145–61.

—— (2009) 'Delving into *Probation Journal*: portrayals of women probation officers and women offenders', *Probation Journal*, 56, 4: 435–50.

Annison, J., Eadie, T. and Knight, C. (2008) 'People first: probation officer perspectives on probation work', *Probation Journal*, 55, 3: 259–72.

Armitage, S. (1989) *Zoom!* Newcastle upon Tyne: Bloodaxe Books.

Armitage, S. (1998/2009) *All Points North*, Harmondsworth: Penguin.

Arnold, H., Liebling, A. and Tait, S. (2007) 'Prison officers and prison culture', in Y. Jewkes (ed.) *Handbook on Prisons*, Cullompton: Willan Publishing, 471–95.

Ashforth, B.E. and Kreiner, G.E. (1999) '"How can you do it?" Dirty work and the challenge of constructing a positive identity', *Academy of Management Journal*, 24, 3: 413–34.

Ashforth, B.E., Kreiner, G.E., Clark, M.A. and Fugate, M. (2007) 'Normalizing dirty work: managerial tactics for countering occupational taint', *Academy of Management Journal*, 50, 1: 149–74.

Audit Commission (1998) *A Fruitful Partnership – Effective Partnership Working*, London: Home Office.

Bailey, R. and Brake, M. (eds) (1975) *Radical Social Work*, London: Arnold.

Banton, M. (1964) *The Policeman in the Community*, London: Tavistock.

BBC News (13/7/2012) 'London probation contract won by private firm', available at www.bbc.co.uk/news/uk, accessed 13 July 2012.

Behan, B. (1958) *Borstal Boy*, London: Hutchinson.

Bennett, J. (2008) 'Reel life after prison: repression and reform in films about release from prison', *Probation Journal*, 55, 4: 353–68.

Berry, G., Briggs P., Erol, R. and van Staden, L. (2011) *The Effectiveness of Partnership Working in a Crime and Disorder Context: A Rapid Evidence Assessment*, London: Home Office Research Report 52.

Birkbeck, J. (1982) 'I believe in you', *Probation Journal*, 29, 3: 83–6.

Blauner, P. (1991) *Slow Motion Riot*, London: Penguin Books.

Bonnett, A. (2010) *Left in the Past: Radicalism and the Politics of Nostalgia*, London: Continuum.

Brake, M. and Bailey, R. (eds) (1980) *Radical Social Work and Practice*, London: Arnold.

Brogden, M. (1991) *On the Mersey Beat: Policing Liverpool between the Wars*, Oxford: Oxford University Press.

Bullock, K. (2011) 'The construction and interpretation of risk management technologies in contemporary probation practice', *British Journal of Criminology*, 51, 1: 120–35.

Burke, L. and Davies, K. (2011) 'Introducing the special edition on occupational culture and skills in probation practice', *European Journal of Probation*, 3, 3: 1–14.

Burnett, R. and Stevens, A. (2007) 'Not of much significance (yet): NOMS from the perspective of prison staff', *Prison Service Journal*, 172: 3–11.

Burnett, R., Baker, K. and Roberts, C. (2007) 'Assessment, supervision and intervention: fundamental practice in probation', in L. Gelsthorpe and R. Morgan (eds) *Handbook of Probation*, Cullompton: Willan Publishing, 210–47.

Button, M. (2007) *Security Officers and Policing: Powers, Culture and Control in the Governance of Private Space*, Aldershot: Ashgate.

Cain, M. (1973) *Society and the Policeman's Role*, London: Routledge.

Caless, B. (2011) *Policing at the Top: The Roles, Values and Attitudes of Chief Police Officers*, Bristol: Policy Press.

Canton, R. (2011) *Probation: Working with Offenders*, Abingdon: Routledge.

Carlen, P. (1975/2010) 'Magistrates' courts: a game theoretic analysis', *Sociological Review*, 23, 2: 347–79, reprinted in P. Carlen, *A Criminological Imagination,* Farnham, Ashgate, 11–44.

—— (2008) 'Imaginary penalities and risk-crazed governance' in P. Carlen (ed.) *Imaginary Penalities*, Cullompton: Willan Publishing, 1–25.

Carter, P. (2003) *Managing Offenders, Reducing Crime: A New Approach*, London: Home Office.

Cartmell, M. and Green, N. (2011) 'Under arrest: police budgets', *PRWeek*, 17 November 2011, available at www.prweek.com/uk/features/1104418/under-arrest-police-budgets/, accessed 8 August 2012.

Casey, L. (2008) *Engaging Communities in Fighting Crime*, London: Cabinet Office.

Chan, J. (1997) *Changing Police Culture: Policing in a Multicultural Society*, Cambridge: Cambridge University Press.

Cherry, S. and Cheston, L. (2006) 'Towards a model regime for approved premises', *Probation Journal*, 53, 3: 248–64.

Clarke, D.R. (2010) *The Parole Officer*, Mustang, OK: Tate Publishing.

Clarke, J., Cochrane, A. and McLaughlin, E. (eds) (1994) *Managing Social Policy*, Sage: London.

Clear, T.R. (2005) 'Places not cases? Re-thinking the probation focus', *Howard Journal of Criminal Justice*, 44, 2: 172–84.

Collins, S. (2008) 'Statutory social workers: stress, job satisfaction, coping, social support and individual differences', *British Journal of Social Work*, 38: 1173–93.

Collins, S., Coffey, M. and Cowe, F. (2009) 'Stress, support and well-being as perceived by probation trainees', *Probation Journal*, 56, 3: 238–56.

Corbett, R. (1998) 'Probation blue: the promise (and perils) of probation–police partnerships', *Correctional Management Quarterly*, 2: 31–9.

Corcoran, M. and Fox, C. (2012) 'A seamless partnership? Developing mixed economy interventions in a non-custodial project for women', *Criminology and Criminal Justice*.

Crawley, E. (2005) *Doing Prison Work*, Cullompton: Willan Publishing.

Crawley, E. and Crawley, P. (2008) 'Understanding prison officers: culture, cohesion and conflict', in J. Bennett, B. Crewe and A. Wahidin (eds) *Understanding Prison Staff*, Cullompton: Willan Publishing, 134–52.

Crewe, B., Liebling, A. and Hulley, S. (2010) 'Staff culture, use of authority and prisoner quality of life in public and private sector prisons', *Australian and New Zealand Journal of Criminology*, 44, 1: 94–115.

Csikszentmihályi, M. (1975) *Beyond Boredom and Anxiety: The Experience of Play in Work and Games*, London: Jossey-Bass Limited.

Dale, H. (2007) 'Lesbians and gay men in probation', in R. Canton and D. Hancock (eds) *Dictionary of Probation and Offender Management*, Cullompton: Willan Publishing, 154.

Davidson, S. (1976) 'Planning and coordination of social services in multi-organisational contexts', *Social Services Review*, 50: 117–37.

Davies, K. (2009) 'Time and the probation practitioner', *British Journal of Community Justice*, 17, 3: 46–60.

Davis, F. (1979) *Yearning for Yesterday: A Sociology of Nostalgia*, New York: Free Press.

Deering, J. (2010) 'Attitudes and beliefs of trainee probation officers: a new breed?', *Probation Journal*, 57, 1: 9–26.

—— (2011) *Probation Practice and the New Penology: Practitioner Reflections*, Aldershot: Ashgate.

Dews, V. and Watts, J. (1994) *Review of Probation Officer Recruitment and Qualifying Training*, London: Home Office.

Dolman, F. (2008) *Community Support Officers, their Occupational Culture and the Development of Reassurance Policing*, European Society of Criminology Conference paper. Edinburgh University.

Donzelot, J. (1979) *The Policing of Families*, London: Hutchinson.

Dugdall, R. (2010) *The Woman Before Me*, London: Legend Press Ltd.

—— (2011) *The Sacrificial Man*, London: Legend Press Ltd.

Dunkley, E. (2007) 'Approved premises', in R. Canton and D. Hancock (eds) *Dictionary of Probation and Offender Management*, Cullompton: Willan Publishing, 12–13.

Durnescu, I. (2012) 'What matters most in probation supervision: staff characteristics, staff skills or programme?', *Criminology and Criminal Justice*, 12, 2: 193–216.

Eadie, T. (2000) 'From befriending to punishing: changing boundaries in the probation service' in N. Malin (ed.) *Professionalism, Boundaries and the Workplace*, London: Routledge, 161–77.

Ely, R.J. and Meyerson, D.E. (2000) *Theories of Gender in Organizations: A New Approach to Organizational Analysis and Change*, Working Paper No. 8, Boston, MA: Center for Gender in Organizations.

Emery, F.E. and Trist, E.L. (1965) 'The causal texture of organizational environments', *Human Relations*, 18: 21–32.

Evetts, J. (2012) *Professionalism in Turbulent Times: Changes, Challenges and Opportunities*, Paper presented at Propel International Conference, Stirling, available at www.propel.stir.ac.uk/conference2012/speakers.php, accessed 6 July 2012.

Farrell, D. (1983) 'Exit, voice, loyalty, and neglect as responses to job dissatisfaction: a multidimensional scaling study', *Academy of Management Journal*, 26, 4: 596–607.

Fawcett, R. (2010) *Rock Athlete*, Sheffield: Vertebrate Publishing.

Ferguson, E. (2012) 'Rewind TV: *Public Enemies*', *Observer*, 8 January. http://www.guardian.co.uk/tv-and-radio/2012/jan/08/sherlock-public-enemies-tv-review, accessed 11 October 2012 .

Ferrell, J. (2005) 'The only possible adventure: edgework and anarchy', in S. Lyng (ed.) *Edgework: The Sociology of Risk-Taking*, London: Routledge, 75–88.

Ferrell, J., Milovanovic, D. and Lyng, S. (2001) 'Edgework, media practices, and the elongation of meaning', *Theoretical Criminology*, 5, 2: 177–202.

Fieldhouse, P. and Williams, T. (1986) 'Shared working in prison', *Probation Journal*, 33, 4: 143–47.

Filkin, E. (2011) *The Ethical Issues arising from the Relationship between Police and Media. Advice to the Commissioner of Police of the Metropolis and his Management Board*, London: MPS.

Fitzgibbon, W. (2011) *Probation and Social Work on Trial: Violent Offenders and Child Abusers*, Basingstoke: Palgrave Macmillan.

Fletcher, H. (2012) 'TV drama *Public Enemies* reflects the reality of probation officers', *Guardian*, 3 January 2012.

Forbes, D. (2010) 'Probation in transition: a study of the experiences of newly qualified probation officers', *Journal of Social Work Practice*, 24, 1: 75–88.

Foster, J. (2003) 'Police cultures', in T. Newburn (ed.) *Handbook of Policing*, Cullompton: Willan Publishing, 196–227.

Fournier, V. (2000) 'Boundary work and the (un)making of the professions', in N. Malin (ed.) *Professionalism, Boundaries and the Workplace*, London: Routledge, 67–86.

Freidson, E. (2001) *Professionalism: The Third Logic*, Cambridge: Polity Press.

Garland, J. and Bilby, C. (2011) '"What next, dwarves?" Images of police culture in *Life on Mars*', *Crime Media Culture*, 7, 2: 115–32.

Gelsthorpe, L. (2007) 'Probation values and human rights', in L. Gelsthorpe and R. Morgan (eds) *Handbook of Probation*, Cullompton: Willan Publishing, 485–517.

Gieryn, T. (2002) 'What buildings do', *Theory and Society*, 31, 1: 35–74.

Glanfield, P. (1985) 'Withdrawal from prisons policy', *Probation Journal* 32, 2: 66.

Goffman, E. (1963) *Stigma: Notes on the Management of Spoiled Identity*, Englewood Cliffs, NJ: Prentice-Hall.

—— (1969) *Where the Action Is*, London: Penguin Press.

Goodman, A.H. (2012) *Rehabilitating and Resettling Offenders in the Community*, London: John Wiley and Sons Ltd.

Gregory, M. (2010) 'Reflection and resistance: probation practice and the ethic of care', *British Journal of Social Work*, 40, 7: 2274–90.

Haines, K. and Morgan, R. (2007) 'Services before trial and sentence: achievement, decline and potential', in L. Gelsthorpe and R. Morgan (eds) *Handbook of Probation*, Cullompton: Willan Publishing, 182–209.

Hallsworth, S. (2005) 'The feminization of the corporation, the masculinization of the state', *Social Justice*, 32, 1: 32–40.

Hardie-Bick, J. (2011) 'Skydiving and the metaphorical edge', in D. Hobbs (ed.) *Ethnography in Context, Vol. 3*, London: Sage.

Harris, R. (1980) 'A changing service: the case for separating care and control in probation practice', *British Journal of Social Work*, 10, 2: 163–84.

Harvey, J. (1987) *Hard Cases*, London: Ravette.

Haxby, D. (1978) *Probation: A Changing Service*, London: Constable.

Hedderman, C. (2003) 'Enforcing supervision and encouraging compliance', in W.H.

Chui and M. Nellis (eds) *Moving Probation Forward: Evidence, Arguments and Practice*, Harlow: Pearson Longman, 181–94.

Hedderman, C. and Hough, M. (2004) 'Getting tough or being effective: what matters?', in G. Mair (ed.) *What Matters in Probation*, Cullompton: Willan Publishing, 146–69.

Heer, G. (2007) 'Asian employees in the probation service', *Probation Journal*, 54, 3: 281–85.

Heer, G. and Atherton, S. (2008) '(In)visible barriers: The experience of Asian employees in the probation service', *Howard Journal of Criminal Justice*, 47, 1: 1–17.

Heidensohn, F. (1992) *Women in Control? The Role of Women in Law Enforcement*, Oxford: Clarendon Press.

Hilder, S. (2007) 'Anti-discriminatory practice', in R. Canton and D. Hancock (eds) *Dictionary of Probation and Offender Management*, Cullompton: Willan Publishing, 10–11.

Hirschman, A.O. (1970) *Exit, Voice and Loyalty: Responses to Decline in Firms, Organizations and States*, Cambridge, MA: Harvard University Press.

HM Government (2010) *The Coalition: Our Programme for Government*, London: Cabinet Office.

HM Treasury (2010) *Spending Review 2010*, London: The Stationery Office.

HMIC (2011) *Without Fear or Favour: A Review of Police Relationships*, London: HMIC.

Hochschild, A. (1983) *The Managed Heart: Commercialization of Human Feelings*, Berkeley, CA: University of California Press.

Holdaway, S. (1983) *Inside the British Police*, Oxford: Basil Blackwell.

Home Office (1998) *Joining Forces to Protect the Public*, London: Home Office.

—— (2004a) *Reducing Crime, Changing Lives*, London: Home Office.

—— (2004b) *Reducing Crime, Changing Lives* (press release 5/2004), London: Home Office.

House of Commons Justice Committee (2011) *The Role of the Probation Service*, London: The Stationery Office.

Hucklesby, A. (2011) 'The working life of electronic monitoring officers', *Criminology and Criminal Justice*, 11, 1: 59–76.

Hughes, E.C. (1951) 'Work and the self', in J.H Rohrer and M. Sherif (eds) *Social Psychology at the Crossroads*, New York: Harper and Brothers, 313–23.

Hughes, J.A., Sharrock, W.W. and Martin, P.J. (2003) *Understanding Classical Sociology: Marx, Weber, Durkheim*, 2nd edn, London: Sage.

Innes, M. (2004) 'Signal crimes and signal disorders: notes on deviance as communicative action', *British Journal of Sociology*, 55: 335–55.

Jepson, N. and Elliott, K. (1985) *Shared Working Between Prison and Probation Officers*, London: Home Office.

Jewkes, Y. (2006) 'Creating a stir? Prisons, popular media and the power to reform', in P. Mason, (ed.) *Captured by the Media*, Cullompton: Willan, 137–53.

—— (2008) 'Offending media: the social construction of offenders, victims and the Probation Service', in S. Green, E. Lancaster and S. Feasey (eds) *Addressing Offender Behaviour: Context, Practice and Values*, Cullompton: Willan, 58–72.

—— (2010) *Media and Crime*, 2nd edn, London: Sage.

Johnson, P. and Ingram, B. (2007) 'Windows of opportunity for unpaid work?', *Probation Journal*, 54, 1: 62–9.

Johnson, S.D., Chye Koh, H. and Killough, L.N. (2009) 'Organizational and occupational culture and the perception of managerial accounting terms: an exploratory study using perceptual mapping techniques', *Contemporary Management Research*, 5, 4: 317–42.

Katz, J. (1988) *Seductions of Crime: The Moral and Sensual Attractions of Doing Evil*, New York: Basic Books.

Kay, S. (1993) 'Judgements of worth', *Probation Journal*, 40, 2: 60–5.

Kemshall, H. and Maguire, M. (2001) 'Public protection, partnership and risk penality: the multi-agency risk management of sexual and violent offenders', *Punishment and Society*, 3, 2: 237–64.

Kemshall, H. and Wood, J. (2007) 'High risk offenders and public protection', in L. Gelsthorpe and R. Morgan (eds) *Handbook of Probation*, Cullompton: Willan Publishing, 381–97.

Kerfoot, D. (2002) 'Managing the "professional" man', in M. Dent and S. Whitehead (eds) *Managing Professional Identities: Knowledge, Performativity and the 'new' Professional*, London: Routledge, 81–95.

Kirton, G. (2012) *Women in NAPO: Survey of Women Members*, London: Queen Mary University.

Knight, C. (2002) 'Training for a modern service', in D. Ward, J. Scott and M. Lacey (eds) *Probation: Working for justice*, 2nd edn, Oxford: Oxford University Press, 276–96.

Kreiner, G.E., Ashforth, B.E. and Sluss, D.M. (2006) 'Identity dynamics in occupational dirty work: integrating social identity and system justification perspectives', *Organization Science*, 17, 5: 619–36.

Lacey, M. and Read, G. (1985) 'Probation working in prison', *Probation Journal* 32, 2: 61–5.

Leech, M. (1991) 'Recommended for release', *Probation Journal*, 38, 1: 10–14.

Le Mesurier, L. (1935) *A Handbook of Probation*, London: NAPO.

Leishman, F. and Mason, P. (2003) *Policing and the Media: Facts Fictions and Factions*, Cullompton: Willan Publishing.

Leonard, E. (1992/2007) *Maximum Bob*, London: Phoenix.

Liebling, A., Price, D. and Shefer, G. (2011) *The Prison Officer*, 2nd edn, Cullompton: Willan Publishing.

Lindblom, C.E. and Woodhouse, E.J. (1993) *The Policy Making Process*, 3rd edn, Englewood Cliffs, NJ: Prentice Hall.

Lipsky, M. (1980) *Street-level Bureaucracy: Dilemmas of the Individual in Public Services*, New York: Russell Sage Foundation.

Loader, I. (1997) 'Policing and the social: questions of symbolic power', *British Journal of Sociology*, 48, 1: 1–18.

—— (2006) 'Fall of the platonic guardians: liberalism, criminology and political responses to crime in England and Wales', *British Journal of Criminology*, 46, 3: 561–86.

Loftus, B. (2009) *Police Culture in a Changing World*, Oxford: Oxford University Press.

—— (2010) 'Police occupational culture: classic themes, altered times', *Policing and Society*, 20, 1: 1–20.

Lois, J. (2001) 'Peaks and valleys: the gendered emotional culture of edgework', *Gender and Society*, 15, 3: 381–406.

—— (2005) 'Gender and emotion management in the stages of edgework', in S. Lyng (ed.) *Edgework: The Sociology of Risk-Taking*, London: Routledge, 117–52.

Lyng, S. (1990) 'Edgework: a social psychological analysis of voluntary risk taking', *The American Journal of Sociology*, 95, 4: 851–86.

—— (2005) 'Sociology at the edge: social theory and voluntary risk taking', in S. Lyng (ed.) *Edgework: The Sociology of Risk-Taking*, London: Routledge, 17–49.

—— (2009) 'Edgework, risk, and uncertainty', in J.O. Zinn (ed.) *Social Theories of Risk and Uncertainty: An Introduction*, Oxford: Blackwell Publishing Ltd, 106–37.

McFarlane, M. (1993) 'Women and promotion', *Probation Journal*, 40, 2: 66–7.

McGarry, R. and Walklate, S. (2011) 'The soldier as victim: peering through the looking glass', *British Journal of Criminology*, 51, 6: 900–17.

McLean Parks, J.M., Ma, L. and Gallagher, D.G. (2010) 'Elasticity in the "rules" of the game: exploring organizational expedience', *Human Relations*, 63, 5: 701–30.

McNeill, F. (2001) 'Developing effectiveness: frontline perspectives', *Social Work Education*, 20, 6: 671–87.

McWilliams, W. (1981) 'The probation officer at court: from friend to acquaintance', *The Howard Journal of Criminal Justice*, 20, 2: 97–116.

Maguire, M. (2007) 'The resettlement of ex-prisoners', in L. Gelsthorpe and R. Morgan (eds) *Handbook of Probation*, Cullompton: Willan Publishing, 398–424.

Mahood, L. (1995) *Policing Gender, Class and Family Britain 1850–1940*, London: UCL Press.

Mair, G. (2004) 'What works: a view from the chiefs', in G. Mair (ed.) *What Matters in Probation*, Cullompton: Willan Publishing, 255–77.

Mair, G. and Burke, L. (2012) *Redemption, Rehabilitation and Risk Management: A History of Probation*, Abingdon: Routledge.

Mair, G., Burke, L. and Taylor, S. (2006) '"The worst tax form you've ever seen?" Probation officers' views about OASys', *Probation Journal*, 53, 1: 7–23.

Manning, P.K. (1997) *Police Work: The Social Organization of Policing*, 2nd edn, Prospect Heights, IL: Waveland Press.

Mason, J. (1988) 'As good as you could hope for', *Probation Journal*, 35, 1: 37.

Mason, P. (ed.) (2006) *Captured by the Media*, Cullompton: Willan.

Mathiesen, T. (1965) *Defences of the Weak: A Sociological Study of a Norwegian Correctional Institution*, London: International Library of Criminology.

Mawby, R.C. (2002) *Policing Images: Policing, Communication and Legitimacy*, Cullompton: Willan.

—— (2003) 'Completing the "half-formed picture"? Media images of policing', in P. Mason (ed.) *Criminal Visions*, Cullompton: Willan Publishing, 214–237.

—— (2007) *Police Service Corporate Communications: A Survey of forces in England, Wales and Scotland*, Birmingham: University of Central England.

—— (2008) 'Built-in, not bolted-on', *Public Service Review: Home Affairs*, 17: 149–50.

—— (2010a) 'Chibnall revisited: crime reporters, the police and "law-and-order news"', *British Journal of Criminology*, 50, 6: 1060–76.

—— (2010b) 'Police corporate communications, crime reporting, and the shaping of policing news', *Policing and Society*, 20, 1: 124–39.

—— (2012) 'Crisis? What crisis? Some research-based reflections on police-press relations', *Policing: A Journal of Policy and Practice*, 6, 4: 272–80.

Mawby, R.C. and Worrall, A. (2004) 'Polibation revisited: policing, probation and prolific offender projects', *International Journal of Police Science and Management*, 6, 2: 63–73.

—— (2011) '"They were very threatening about do-gooding bastards": probation's changing relationships with the police and prison services in England and Wales', *European Journal of Probation*, 3, 3: 78–94.

Mawby, R.C., Crawley, P. and Wright, A. (2007) 'Beyond polibation and towards prisipolibation? Joint agency offender management in the context of the Street Crime Initiative', *International Journal of Police Science and Management*, 9, 2: 122–34.

May, T. (1994) 'Transformative power: a study in a human service organization', *The Sociological Review*, 618–38.

Mayo, M., Hoggett, P. and Miller, C. (2007) 'Navigating the contradictions of public service modernization: the case of community engagement professionals', *Policy and Politics*, 35, 4: 667–81.

Milovanovic, D. (2005) 'Edgework: a subjective and structural model of negotiating boundaries', in S. Lyng (ed.) *Edgework: The Sociology of Risk-Taking*, London: Routledge, 51–72.

Ministry of Justice (2011) *Statistics on Race and the Criminal Justice System 2010*, London: Ministry of Justice.

—— (2012) *Punishment and Reform: Effective Probation Services*, Consultation Paper CP7/2012, London: Ministry of Justice.

Morgan, G. (2006) *Images of Organization*, London: Sage.

Morgan, J. (1991) *Safer Communities: The Local Delivery of Crime Prevention through the Partnership Approach, Report of the Home Office Standing Conference on Crime Prevention*, London: Home Office.

Morran, D. (2008) 'Firing up and burning out: the personal and professional impact of working in domestic violence offender programmes', *Probation Journal*, 55, 2: 139–52.

Morris, A. (1987) *Women, Crime and Criminal Justice*, Oxford: Blackwell.

Mott, J.R. (1992) *Probation, Prison and Parole: A True Story of the Work of a Probation Officer*, Lewes: Temple House Books.

Mullins, L. (2010) *Management and Organisational Behaviour*, 9th edn, London: Prentice Hall.

Murphy, D. and Lutze, F. (2009) 'Police-probation partnerships: professional identity and the sharing of coercive power', *Journal of Criminal Justice*, 37: 65–76.

NAPO (2007) *Changing Lives: An Oral History of Probation*, London: NAPO.

—— (2008) *Ex-armed Forces Personnel and the Criminal Justice System*, briefing paper, available at www.napo.org.uk/publications/Briefings.cfm, accessed 6 June 2012.

—— (2009) *Armed Forces and the Criminal Justice System*, briefing paper, available at www.napo.org.uk/publications/Briefings.cfm, accessed 6 June 2012.

—— (2012) *Newsletter: Centenary Souvenir Issue*, May, London: NAPO.

Nash, M. (1999) 'Enter the "polibation officer"', *International Journal of Police Science and Management*, 1, 4: 360–8.

—— (2004) 'A reply to Mawby and Worrall', *International Journal of Police Science and Management*, 6, 2: 74–6.

—— (2008) 'Exit the polibation officer? Decoupling police and probation', *International Journal of the Sociology of Law*, 10, 3: 302–12.

Nash, M. and Walker, L. (2009) 'Mappa – is closer collaboration really the key to effectiveness?', *Policing: A Journal of Policy and Practice*, 3, 2: 172–80.

National Audit Office (2001) *Joining Up to Improve Public Services*, London: HMSO.

National Probation Service (2001) *A New Choreography: An Integrated Strategy for the National Probation Service for England and Wales – Strategic Framework 2001–2004*, London: Home Office.

—— (2003) *The Heart of the Dance*, London: Home Office.

Naus, F., van Iterson, A. and Roe, R. (2007) 'Organizational cynicism: extending the exit, voice, loyalty, and neglect model of employees' responses to adverse conditions in the workplace', *Human Relations*, 60, 5: 683–718.

Nellis, M. (2007) 'Humanising justice: the English probation service up to 1972', in L.

Gelsthorpe and R. Morgan (eds) *Handbook of Probation*, Cullompton: Willan Publishing, 25–58.

—— (2008) '*Hard Cases*: a probation TV drama series', in P. Senior (ed.) *Moments in Probation*, Crayford: Shaw and Sons, 213–14.

—— (2010) 'Images of British probation officers in film, television drama and novels', unpublished paper.

NOMS (2006) *The NOMS Offender Management Model*, London: NOMS.

Oakley, A. (2011) *A Critical Woman: Barbara Wotton, Social Science and Public Policy in the Twentieth Century*, London: Bloomsbury Academic.

Omand, D. (2010) *Independent Serious Further Offence Review: The Case of Jon Venables*, www.justice.gov.uk/downloads/publications/corporate-reports/MoJ/2010/omand-review-web.pdf, accessed 23 June 2012.

Othen, M.J. (1975) 'Prison welfare – time to think again?', *Probation Journal*, 22, 4: 98–103.

Parker, T. (1963) *The Unknown Citizen*, London: Hutchinson.

Parkinson, G. (1988) 'It's not bad!', *Probation Journal*, 35, 1: 36.

Parsloe, P. (1967) *The Work of the Probation and After-Care Officer*, London: Routledge and Kegan Paul.

Pearson, G. (1983) *Hooligan: A History of Respectable Fears*, London: Macmillan.

Pease, K. (1992) 'Preface', in R. Statham and P. Whitehead (eds) *Managing the Probation Service: Issues for the 1990s*, Harlow: Longman, x–xi.

Peelo, M. (2006) 'Framing homicide narratives in newspapers: mediated witness and the construction of virtual victimhood', *Crime Media Culture: An International Journal*, 2, 2: 159–75.

Petrillo, M. (2007) 'Power struggle: issues for female probation officers in the supervision of high risk offenders', *Probation Journal*, 54, 4: 394–406.

Phillips, C. (2005) 'Facing inwards and outwards? Institutional racism, race equality and the role of Black and Asian professional associations', *Criminal Justice*, 5, 4: 357–77.

Phillips, C. and Bowling, B. (2012) 'Ethnicities, racism, crime, and criminal justice', in M. Maguire, R. Morgan and R. Reiner (eds) *The Oxford Handbook of Criminology*, 5th edn, Oxford: Oxford University Press, 370–97.

Phillips, J. (2010) 'The social construction of probation in England and Wales and the United States of America: implications for the transferability of probation practice', *British Journal of Community Justice*, 18, 1: 5–18.

—— (2011) 'Target, audit and risk assessment cultures in the probation service', *European Journal of Probation*, 3, 3: 108–22.

Poxton, R. (2004) 'What makes effective partnerships between health and social care?', in Glasby, J. and Peck, E. (2004) *Care Trusts: partnership working in action*, Abingdon: Radcliffe Medical Press, 11–22.

Pratt, M. (1975) 'Stress and opportunity in the role of the prison welfare officer', *British Journal of Social Work* 5, 4: 379–96.

Priestley, P. (1972) 'The prison welfare officer: a case of role strain', *British Journal of Sociology*, 23, 2: 221–35.

Punch, M. (1979) *Policing the Inner City: A Study of Amsterdam's Warmoesstraat*, London: Macmillan.

Rajah, V. (2007) 'Resistance as edgework in violent intimate relationships of drug-involved women', *British Journal of Criminology*, 47, 2: 196–215.

Raynor, P. and Robinson, G. (2009) *Rehabilitation, Crime and Justice*, Basingstoke: Palgrave Macmillan.

Reeves, C. (2011) 'The changing role of probation hostels: voices from the inside', *British Journal of Community Justice*, 9, 3: 51–64.

Reiner, R. (1991) *Chief Constables: Bobbies, Bosses or Bureaucrats?*, Oxford: Oxford University Press.

—— (1994) 'The dialectics of Dixon: the changing image of the TV cop', in M. Stephens and S. Becker (eds) *Police Force Police Service*, London: Macmillan, 11–32.

—— (2010) *The Politics of the Police*, 4th edn, Oxford: Oxford University Press.

Robinson, A. (2011) *Foundations for Offender Management: Theory, Law and Policy for Contemporary Practice*, Bristol: The Policy Press.

Robinson, G. and Burnett, R. (2007) 'Experiencing modernization: frontline probation perspectives on the transition to a NOMS', *Probation Journal*, 54, 4: 318–37.

Ross-Smith, A. and Huppatz, K. (2010) 'Management, women and gender capital', *Gender, Work and Organization*, 17, 5: 547–66.

Rowe, M. (ed.) (2007) *Policing Beyond Macpherson: Issues in Policing, Race and Society*, Cullompton: Willan.

Rumgay, J. (2003) 'Partnerships in the probation service', in W.H. Chui and M. Nellis (eds) *Moving Probation Forward*, Harlow: Pearson Education, 195–213.

Rutherford, A. (1993) *Criminal Justice and the Pursuit of Decency*, Winchester: Waterside Press.

Saunders, D. and Vanstone, M. (2010) 'Rehabilitation as presented in British film: shining a light on desistance from crime', *The Howard Journal*, 49, 4: 375–93.

Savage, M. and Williams, K. (eds) (2008) *Remembering Elites*, Oxford: Blackwell.

Schein, E. (2010) *Organizational Culture and Leadership*, 4th edn, San Francisco, CA: Jossey-Bass.

Senior, P. (2008) *Moments in Probation*, Crayford: Shaw and Sons.

Silvestri, M. (2007) '"Doing" police leadership: enter the "new smart macho"', *Policing and Society*, 17, 1: 38–58.

Simon, J. (2005) 'Edgework and insurance in risk societies: some notes on Victorian lawyers and mountaineers', in S. Lyng (ed.) *Edgework: The Sociology of Risk-Taking*, London: Routledge, 203–26.

Simpson, R. and Lewis, P. (2007) *Voice, Visibility and the Gendering of Organizations*, Basingstoke: Palgrave Macmillan.

Simpson, R., Slutskaya, N., Lewis, P. and Hopfl, H. (eds) (2012) *Dirty Work: Concepts and Identities*, Basingstoke: Palgrave Macmillan.

Singh, G. (2007) 'National Association of Asian Probation Staff', in R. Canton and D. Hancock (eds) *Dictionary of Probation and Offender Management*, Cullompton: Willan Publishing, 173–75.

Skeggs, B. (1997) *Formations of Class and Gender: Becoming Respectable*, London: Sage.

Skolnick, J. (1966) *Justice Without Trial*, New York: Wiley.

—— (2008) 'Enduring issues of police culture and demographics', *Policing and Society*, 18, 1: 35–45.

Smith, P. (2012) '*Public Enemies*, BBC One, review', *The Telegraph*, 4 January. www.telegraph.co.uk/culture/tvandradio/8990454/Public-Enemies-BBC-One-review.html, accessed 11 October 2012.

Stanton, A. (1985) 'Why probation isn't working in prison', *Probation Journal*, 32, 3: 107–8.

Statham, D. (1978) *Radicals in Social Work*, London: Routledge.

Stone, N. (1986) 'In discussion with the POA', *Probation Journal*, 33, 3: 81–6.

Strangleman, T. (2012) 'Work identity in crisis? Rethinking the problem of attachment and loss at work', *Sociology*, 46, 3: 411–25.

Sykes, G. and Matza, D. (1957) 'Techniques of neutralization', *American Sociological Review*, 22: 664–70.

Tait, S. (2011) 'A typology of prison officer approaches to care', *European Journal of Criminology*, 8, 6: 440–54.

Thomas, T. (1994) *The Police and Social Workers*, 2nd edn, Aldershot: Ashgate.

Thompson, N. (2006) *Anti-Discriminatory Practice*, 4th edn, Houndsmill: Palgrave Macmillan.

Thurston, P. (2002) 'Just practice in probation hostels', in D. Ward, J. Scott and M. Lacey (eds) *Probation: Working for Justice*, Oxford: Oxford University Press, 207–19.

Todd, M. (1964) *Ever Such a Nice Lady*, London: Victor Gollancz Ltd.

Towl, G. and Crighton, D. (2008) 'Psychologists in prison', in J. Bennett, B. Crewe and A. Wahidin (eds) *Understanding Prison Staff*, Cullompton: Willan Publishing, 316–29.

Treadwell, J. (2006) 'Some personal reflections on probation training', *The Howard Journal*, 45, 1: 1–13.

—— (2010) 'More than casualties of war? Ex-military personnel in the criminal justice system', *The Howard Journal*, 49, 2: 73–7.

Turney, B. (2002) *I'm Still Standing*, Winchester: Waterside Press.

Van Dyne, L., Ang, S. and Botero, I.C. (2003) 'Concetualizing employee silence and employee voice as multidimensional constructs', *Journal of Management Studies*, 40, 6, 1359–92.

Vanstone, M. (2004) *Supervising Offenders in the Community: A History of Probation Theory and Practice*, Aldershot: Ashgate.

Waddington, P.A.J. (1999) 'Police (canteen) sub-culture: an appreciation', *British Journal of Criminology*, 39, 2: 287–309.

Waldron, V. (2009) 'Emotional tyranny at work: suppressing the moral emotions', in P. Lutgen-Sandvik and B.D. Sypher (eds) *Destructive Organizational Communication*, London: Routledge, 9–26.

Walmsley, R. (2012) *World Female Imprisonment List*, 2nd edn, London: International Centre for Prison Studies.

Walker, H. and Beaumont, B. (1981) *Probation Work: Critical Theory and Socialist Practice*, Oxford: Blackwell.

Watson, K. (2012) '*Public Enemies* had a promising start but ultimately lost its edge', *The Metro*, 4 December. http://www.metro.co.uk/tv/reviews/886299-public-enemies-had-a-promising-start-but-ultimately-lost-its-edge#ixzz1sxAU1yw8, accessed 11 October 2012.

Weatheritt, M. (1986) *Innovations in Policing*, London: Croom Helm.

Weinberger, B. (1995) *The Best Police in the World: An Oral History of English Policing from the 1930s to the 1960s*, Aldershot: Scholar Press.

White, I. (1984) 'Residential work: the Cinderella of the probation service?', *Probation Journal*, 31, 2: 59–60.

Whitehead, P. and Statham, R. (2006) *The History of Probation: Politics, Power and Cultural Change 1876–2005*, Crayford: Shaw and Sons.

Wigley, J. (1992) *Out of Bounds: Story of Malcolm Worsley, Prisoner to Probation Officer*, Godalming: Highland Books.

Williams, B. (1991) 'Probation contact with long term prisoners', *Probation Journal* 38, 1: 4–9.

—— (2008) 'The changing face of probation in prisons', in J. Bennett, B. Crewe and A. Wahidin (eds) *Understanding Prison Staff*, Cullompton: Willan Publishing, 279–97.

Williams, R. (1973) *The Country and the City*, Oxford: Oxford University Press.

Wilson, D. and O'Sullivan, S. (2004) *Images of Incarceration: Representations of Prison in Film and Television Drama*, Winchester: Waterside Press.

—— (2005) 'Re-theorizing the penal reform functions of the prison film', *Theoretical Criminology*, 9, 4: 471–91.

Wincup, E. (2002) *Residential Work with Offenders: Reflexive Accounts of Practice*, Aldershot: Ashgate.

Worrall, A. (1995) 'Equal opportunity or equal disillusion? The probation service and anti-discriminatory practice', in B. Williams (ed.) *Probation Values*, Birmingham: Venture Press, 29–46.

—— (1997) *Punishment in the Community: The Future of Criminal Justice*, Harlow: Addison Wesley Longman.

—— (2008a) 'The "seemingness" of the "seamless management" of offenders', in P. Carlen (ed.) *Imaginary Penalities*, Cullompton: Willan Publishing, 113–34.

—— (2008b) 'Gender and probation in the second world war: reflections on a changing occupational culture', *Criminology and Criminal Justice*, 8, 3: 317–33.

Worrall, A. and Canton, R. (2013) 'Community sentences and offender management', in C. Hale, K. Hayward, A. Wahidin and E. Wincup (eds) *Criminology*, 3rd edn, Oxford: Oxford University Press.

Worrall, A. and Gelsthorpe, L. (2009) 'What works with women offenders: the past 30 years', *Probation Journal*, 56, 4: 329–45.

Worrall, A. and Hoy, C. (2005) *Punishment in the Community: Managing Offenders, Making Choices*, Cullompton: Willan Publishing.

Worrall, A., Mawby, R.C., Heath, G. and Hope, T. (2003) *Intensive Supervision and Monitoring Projects*, Home Office Online Report 42/03, London: Home Office.

Wrzesniewski, A. and Dutton, J. (2001) 'Crafting a job: revisioning employees as active crafters of their work', *Academy of Management Review*, 26, 2: 179–201.

Young, M. (1991) *An Inside Job: Policing and Police Culture in Britain*, Oxford: Clarendon Press.